Principles of
Microeconomics

NINTH EDITION

JOHN E. SAYRE

Professor Emeritus
Capilano University

ALAN J. MORRIS

Associate Alumnus
Capilano University

Mc
Graw
Hill
Education

PRINCIPLES OF MICROECONOMICS
Ninth Edition

Statistics Canada information is used with the permission of Statistics Canada. Users are forbidden to copy the data and redisseminate them, in an original or modified form, for commercial purposes, without permission from Statistics Canada. Information on the availability of the wide range of data from Statistics Canada can be obtained from Statistics Canada's Regional Offices, its World Wide Web site at www.statcan.gc.ca, and its toll-free access number 1-800-263-1136.

The Internet addresses listed in the text were accurate at the time of publication. The inclusion of a Web site does not indicate an endorsement by the authors or McGraw-Hill Ryerson, and McGraw-Hill Ryerson does not guarantee the accuracy of the information presented at these sites.

ISBN-13: 978-1-25-946090-6
ISBN-10: 1-25-946090-8

1 2 3 4 5 6 7 8 9 10 TCP 22 21 20 19 18

Printed and bound in Canada.

Care has been taken to trace ownership of copyright material contained in this text; however, the publisher will welcome any information that enables them to rectify any reference or credit for subsequent editions.

PORTFOLIO DIRECTOR, BUSINESS AND ECONOMICS, INTERNATIONAL: Nicole Meehan
PORTFOLIO MANAGER: Kevin O'Hearn
DIRECTOR, PORTFOLIO MARKETING: Joy Armitage Taylor
CONTENT DEVELOPER: Melissa Hudson
SENIOR PORTFOLIO ASSOCIATE: Stephanie Giles
SUPERVISING EDITOR: Jessica Barnoski
PHOTO/PERMISSIONS EDITOR: Alison Lloyd Baker
COPY EDITOR: Rodney Rawlings
PLANT PRODUCTION COORDINATOR: Sarah Strynatka
MANUFACTURING PRODUCTION COORDINATOR: Emily Hickey
COVER DESIGN: Michelle Losier
COVER IMAGE: Yin Yang/Getty Images
INTERIOR DESIGN: Michelle Losier
COMPOSITION: Aptara®, Inc.
PRINTER: Transcontinental Printing Group

To my first granddaughter:

Addy

(JES)

———————— A N D ————————

To the ones I love:

Brian, Trevor, and in memory of Jean

(AJM)

ABOUT THE AUTHORS

John E. Sayre earned a BSBA at the University of Denver and an MA from Boston University. He began teaching principles of economics while in the Peace Corps in Malawi. He came to Vancouver to do PhD studies at Simon Fraser University and ended up teaching at Capilano University for the next thirty-nine years. John was honoured with the designation of Professor Emeritus by Capilano University in June of 2014. Now retired from Capilano, John is an avid golfer who also enjoys walking with his dog, and listening to New Age and classical music.

Alan J. Morris, though loath to admit it, first worked as an accountant in England, where he became an Associate of the Chartered Institute of Secretaries and obtained his first degree in 1971 in Manchester, U.K. He subsequently obtained his Master's degree at Simon Fraser University, B.C., in 1973. He worked on his doctorate at Leicester University, U.K., and returned to work in business in Vancouver, B.C., until his appointment at Capilano University in 1988. Now retired, he currently lives in North Vancouver and is an avid devotee of classical music, birding, soccer, and beer. To his knowledge, he has never been an advisor to the Canadian government.

BRIEF CONTENTS

	PREFACE		xii
	ECONOMICS TOOLKIT		xxii
CHAPTER	**1**	The Economic Problem	1
CHAPTER	**2**	Demand and Supply: An Introduction	37
CHAPTER	**3**	Demand and Supply: An Elaboration	84
CHAPTER	**4**	Elasticity	121
CHAPTER	**5**	Consumer Choice	161
CHAPTER	**6**	A Firm's Production Decisions and Costs in the Short Run	205
CHAPTER	**7**	Costs in the Long Run	239
CHAPTER	**8**	Perfect Competition	264
CHAPTER	**9**	An Evaluation of Competitive Markets	304
CHAPTER 10		Monopoly	338
CHAPTER 11		Imperfect Competition	375
CHAPTER 12		The Factors of Production	414
CHAPTER 13		International Trade	454
	STATISTICAL INFORMATION APPENDIX		AP-1
	GLOSSARY		GL-1
	INDEX		IN-1

CONTENTS

PREFACE		xii
ECONOMICS TOOLKIT		xxii

CHAPTER 1 — The Economic Problem — **1**

1.1	The Relevance of Economics	2
	Controversy One	*3*
	Controversy Two	*3*
	Controversy Three	*3*
	Controversy Four	*4*
1.2	What Is Economics?	4
1.3	Efficiency and Allocation	8
	The Importance of Efficiency	*12*
1.4	The Power of Trade	13
1.5	The Three Fundamental Questions	14
	What to Produce?	*14*
	How to Produce?	*15*
	For Whom?	*15*
1.6	Four Types of Economies: The Four Cs	16
	Co-operative Economies	*16*
	Command Economies	*17*
	Customary Economies	*18*
	Competitive Economies	*18*
	Mixed Economies	*18*
1.7	Production Possibilities	19
	The Law of Increasing Costs	*21*
	Shifts in the Production Possibilities Curve:	
	The Causes of Economic Growth	*23*
	Study Guide	28

CHAPTER 2 — Demand and Supply: An Introduction — **37**

2.1	Demand	38
	Individual Demand	*38*
	Why Is the Demand Curve Downward Sloping?	*40*
	Market Demand	*42*
2.2	Supply	44
	Individual Supply	*44*
	Market Supply	*46*
2.3	The Market	48
2.4	Market Equilibrium	49

2.5	Change in Demand	52
	Determinants of a Change in Demand	*54*
	The Effects of an Increase in Demand	*56*
	The Effects of a Decrease in Demand	*57*
2.6	Change in Supply	59
	Determinants of a Change in Supply	*60*
	The Effects of an Increase in Supply	*62*
2.7	Final Words	65
	Study Guide	68
	APPENDIX TO CHAPTER 2: THE ALGEBRA OF DEMAND AND SUPPLY	79

CHAPTER 3		Demand and Supply: An Elaboration	84
	3.1	Markets Matter	85
	3.2	Simultaneous Changes in Demand and Supply	87
	3.3	How Well Do Markets Work?	92
	3.4	Price Ceilings	94
	3.5	Price Floors	98
		The Minimum Wage	*100*
	3.6	Production Quotas	104
	3.7	Taxes and Subsidies	105
		Taxes	*105*
		Subsidies	*108*
		Study Guide	111

CHAPTER 4		Elasticity	121
	4.1	Price Elasticity of Demand	122
		Determinants of Price Elasticity	*123*
	4.2	Measuring Price Elasticity	126
		Elasticity in Action	*129*
	4.3	Price Elasticity Graphically	130
		Elasticity and Total Revenue, Graphically	*134*
	4.4	Applications of Price Elasticity	135
		Who Pays Sales Taxes?	*135*
		Why Do Governments Impose "Sin Taxes"?	*137*
		Why Might a War on Drugs Increase Crime Rates?	*138*
		When Is a Good Harvest Bad for Farmers?	*139*
	4.5	Other Elasticity Measures	141
		Ticket Scalping	*143*
		Income Elasticity	*145*
		Cross-Elasticity of Demand	*147*
		Study Guide	150

CHAPTER 5		Consumer Choice	161
	5.1	The Law of Diminishing Marginal Utility	162
	5.2	Optimal Purchasing Rule	165

5.3	Applications of Marginal Utility Theory	172
	Why Our Favourite Things Are Not Always Our Favourites	*172*
	What Determines Your Priority Spending?	*172*
	Don't Some Things Improve with Age?	*172*
	Shouldn't Incomes Be More Equally Distributed?	*172*
5.4	Marginal Utility and Demand	174
5.5	Consumer Surplus	177
5.6	Price Discrimination	180
	Study Guide	185
	APPENDIX TO CHAPTER 5: INDIFFERENCE CURVE ANALYSIS	197

CHAPTER 6 A Firm's Production Decisions and Costs in the Short Run   **205**

6.1	The Role of the Firm	206
6.2	Explicit and Implicit Costs	207
6.3	Theory of Production	210
	Total, Average, and Marginal Product	*210*
6.4	Marginal and Variable Costs	216
6.5	Total Costs and Average Total Costs	219
6.6	How Can a Firm Cut Costs?	224
	Study Guide	228

CHAPTER 7 Costs in the Long Run   **239**

7.1	The Short and the Long Run	240
7.2	Constant Returns to Scale	241
7.3	Economies of Scale	244
7.4	Diseconomies of Scale	246
7.5	What Is the Right Size of Firm?	248
7.6	Changes in Short- and Long-Run Costs	251
7.7	Can a Market Be Too Small?	252
	Does Size Matter Anymore?	*254*
	Study Guide	256

CHAPTER 8 Perfect Competition   **264**

8.1	Characteristics of Different Markets	265
8.2	Perfect Competition and the Market System	267
	Features of Perfect Competition	*267*
	Examples of Perfectly Competitive Markets	*267*
8.3	The Competitve Industry and Firm	271
	Total, Average, and Marginal Revenues	*271*
	Price, Profit, and Output Under Perfect Competition	*273*
	The Marginal Approach to Profitability	*276*
8.4	Break-Even Price and Shutdown Price	278
8.5	The Firm's Supply Curve	283

8.6   The Industry Demand and Supply   287
Long-Run Effects of an Increase in Demand   287
Long-Run Effects of a Decrease in Demand   289

8.7   Long-Run Supply of the Industry   291
Study Guide   294

CHAPTER 9   An Evaluation of Competitive Markets   304

9.1   How Competitve Markets Adjust to Long-Run Changes   305
Technological Improvement and Perfect Competition   306
The Effect of Perfect Competition on the Size of the Firm   306

9.2   The Benefits of Perfect Competition   308
Productive and Allocative Efficiency   309
Other Benefits of Competitive Markets   310

9.3   Market Failures   313
Income and Wealth Inequalities   313
Instability of Competitive Markets   316
The Forces of Uncompetition   316
Provision of Public and Quasi-Public Goods   317
Externalities   319

9.4   Dealing with External Costs   322
Legislative Controls to Limit Pollution   322
Taxation to Limit Pollution   322
Cap and Trade   324

9.5   Integrating External Benefits   325
The Provision of Quasi-Public Goods   325
Providing Subsidies   325
Study Guide   329

CHAPTER 10   Monopoly   338

10.1   What Monopolies Are and How They Come into Existence   339
Total, Average, and Marginal Revenues   340

10.2   Profit-Maximizing Output for the Monopolist   345

10.3   What Is So Bad About Monopoly?   349
Price Discrimination   349

10.4   Monopoly and Perfect Competition Contrasted   353

10.5   In Defence of Monopoly   357

10.6   Controlling the Monopolist   359
Taxing the Monopolist   360
Government Price Setting   361
Nationalization   362
Study Guide   364

CHAPTER 11   Imperfect Competition   375

11.1   Production Differentiation   376

**11.2   The Difference Between the Two Types
of Imperfect Competition**   379

11.3 Monopolistic Competition   381
The Short-Run and Long-Run Equilibrium for the
  Monopolistically Competitive Firm   *381*
Appraisal of Monopolistic Competition   *384*
Explaining the Franchise Phenomenon   *386*
Blocked Entry as a Result of Government Policy   *387*

11.4 Oligopoly   387

11.5 The Temptation to Collude   389
Collusive Oligopoly   *393*

11.6 Noncollusive Oligopoly   398
Price Leadership   *398*
The Kinked Demand Curve   *399*
An Appraisal of Oligopoly   *400*
Are Firms Profit Maximizers?   *401*

Study Guide   404

CHAPTER 12   The Factors of Production   414

12.1 The Competitive Labour Market   415
The Demand for Labour   *415*
The Supply of Labour   *418*
Market Equilibrium   *419*
Changes in the Supply of Labour   *420*
Changes in the Demand for Labour   *421*
Productivity and the Real Wage   *422*

12.2 Imperfect Labour Markets   425
The Case of Monopsony   *425*
The Effects of Trade Unions and Professional Associations   *427*
Explanations of Wage Differentials   *430*

12.3 The Concept of Economic Rent   433
Economic Rent and Professional Athletes   *434*

12.4 The Natural Resource Market   437
Common Property Resources   *439*

12.5 The Capital Goods Market   441

12.6 The Entrepreneurial Market   443

Study Guide   445

CHAPTER 13   International Trade   454

13.1 Specialization and Trade   455
Current Trends in World Trade   *456*
Specialization   *456*
Factor Endowment   *458*
Theory of Absolute Advantage   *460*

13.2 Theory of Comparative Advantage   462

13.3 Terms of Trade   466
Terms of Trade and Gains from Trade, Graphically   *468*
The Benefits of Free Trade   *470*
Some Important Qualifications   *471*

13.4 The Effect of Free Trade 474

13.5 Trade Restrictions and Protectionism 477

The Imposition of Import Quotas 477

The Imposition of Tariffs 479

Other Trade Restrictions 480

Protectionism 481

Study Guide 484

STATISTICAL INFORMATION APPENDIX AP-1

GLOSSARY GL-1

INDEX IN-1

PREFACE

TO THE STUDENTS

So, you may well ask, why take a course in economics? For many of you, the obvious answer to this question is, "Because it is a requirement for the program or educational goal that I have chosen." Fair enough. But there are other reasons. It is a simple truth that if you want to understand the world around you, you have to understand some basic economics. Much of what goes on in the world today is driven by economic considerations, and those who know nothing of economics often simply cannot understand why things are the way they are. In this age of globalization, we are all citizens of the world and we need to function effectively in the midst of the enormous changes that are sweeping across almost every aspect of the social/political/economic landscape. You can either be part of this, and all the opportunities that come with it, or not be part of it because you cannot make sense of it.

It is quite possible that you feel a little apprehensive because you have heard economics is difficult. Though there may be a grain of truth in this, we are convinced that almost any student can succeed in economics if he or she makes the effort.

Here are some tips on the general approach to this course that you might find helpful. First, read the **Economics Toolkit** that appears at the beginning of the book. The section "The Canadian Reality" offers basic information on Canada and its economic picture. "Graphing Reality" gives a quick lesson on graphs, which are an essential part of economics. These two sections will give you a solid foundation on which to build your knowledge of economics.

Second, before each lecture, quickly look over the chapter that will be covered. (In this lookover, you do not need to worry about the glossary boxes, the Added Dimension boxes, the Test Your Understanding questions, or the integrated Study Guide.) Third, take notes as much as you can during the lecture, because the process of forcing yourself to express ideas *in your own words* is a crucial stage in the learning process. Fourth, reread the chapter, again taking notes and using your own words (do not just copy everything word for word). While doing this, refer to your classroom notes and try to integrate them into your reading notes. When you finish, you will be ready to take on the Study Guide.

Painful as it might be to hear, we want to say loud and clear that you should do *all* the questions and problems in the Study Guide. You may be slow at first, but you will be surprised at how much faster you become in later chapters. This is a natural aspect of the learning process. It might be helpful for you to form a study group with one or two other students and meet once or twice a week to do the questions. You may be amazed to find that explaining an answer to a fellow student is one of the most effective learning techniques.

If you ever come across a question you simply cannot understand, it is a sure sign that you need to approach your instructor (or teaching assistant) for help. Do not get discouraged when this happens; it will probably happen more at the beginning of your learning process than later on in the term.

We are convinced that if you follow this process consistently, beginning in the very *first* week of class, you will succeed in the course—and most likely do well. All it takes is effort, time management, and consistent organization.

Finally, an enormous part of becoming educated is gaining self-confidence and a sense of accomplishment. An A in a "tough" economics course can be a great boost. We wish you all the best.

TO THE INSTRUCTORS

GENERAL PHILOSOPHY Over the years, we have become increasingly convinced that most economics textbooks are written to impress other economists rather than to enlighten beginning students. Such books tend to be encyclopedic in scope and intimidating in appearance. Small wonder, then, that students often emerge from an economics course feeling that the discipline really is daunting and unapproachable. We agree that the study of economics is challenging, but our experience is that students can also see it as intriguing and enjoyable if the right approach is taken. It starts with a really good textbook that is concise without sacrificing either clarity or accepted standards of rigour.

In preparing this book, we attempted to stay focused on four guiding principles. The first was to create a well-written text: to write as clearly as possible, to avoid unnecessary jargon, to speak directly to the student, and to avoid unnecessary abstraction and repetition.

Of equal importance was our second principle, a focused emphasis on student learning. Many years of teaching the principles courses have convinced us that students *learn* economics by *doing* it. To this end, Test Your Understanding questions are scattered throughout each chapter. This encourages students to apply what they have just read and gives them continuous feedback on their comprehension of the material being presented. Further, we feel that we offer the most comprehensive and carefully crafted Study Guide on the market, which has evolved over the years as a result of continued use in our own classes. In addition, all the chapter sections end with a Section Summary.

Our third principle has been to avoid making an encyclopedic text. It seems that in an effort to please everyone, authors sometimes include bits and pieces of almost everything. The result is that students are often overwhelmed and find it difficult to distinguish the more important from the less important.

The fourth principle was to avoid problems of continuity that can occur when different groups of authors prepare separate parts of a total package. Accordingly, we are the sole authors of the text, the instructor's manual, and the integrated Study Guide. We have also carefully supervised the development of all supplementary materials. We have tried to ensure that as much care and attention went into the ancillary materials as into the main textbook.

Few things are more satisfying than witnessing a student's zest for learning. We hope that this textbook adds a little to this process.

NINTH EDITION CHANGES

There are eight additions or changes in each of the thirteen chapters. First, we have added a new feature, In a Nutshell, a half-page visual (humorous and/or thoughtful) that seeks to convey an important idea found within the chapter. Second, we have added a new feature at the beginning of each Study Guide section entitled What's the Big Idea?, in which we try to present the thrust of the chapter very simply and straightforwardly. Our third addition is a feature called It's News to Me, which consists of a short news item relating to material in the chapter along with two or more multiple-choice questions on the article.

Fourth, the end-of-chapter summaries are gone, replaced by Section Summaries throughout each chapter. Fifth, we have updated all data to the latest available (2016 or 2017). Sixth, we have moved the position of the Comprehensive Problem to the beginning of the Study Problems and provided answers and explanations alongside the question. Seventh, we are pleased to be able to present the Study Guide sections in single columns, which makes them easier to read. Finally, the Study Tips section has been removed from the Study Guide and made available to students on the McGraw-Hill online resource.

- In **Chapter 1**, we have reduced the number of Controversies in Section 1.1 from six to four and tried to give them a more topical slant. We reduced the size of the example of a student's choice of activities and more clearly brought out the point that opportunity cost involves lost benefits. A brief section on the five ways goods and services can be allocated was added. We divided Section 1.5 into two separate sections: The Three Fundamental Questions and Four Types of Economies: The Four Cs (giving both ancient and modern examples of each type). A Great Economists box on Karl Marx was included, as was a new Added Dimension (AD) box, "Just What Is an Economist?" Finally, we have added one more problem to Problems for Further Study.

- In **Chapter 2**, we have changed the name of one of the determinants of supply from "business taxes" to "government taxes and subsidies." Glossary items for the terms "taxes" and "subsidies" were added. In the initial introduction to demand we now include a brief mention of all the other factors—in addition to price—that would also affect quantities demanded. We provided a new AD box, "Just What Is a Product?" We added two new graphical Study Problems that require students to shift curves.

- We have changed **Chapter 3** quite extensively by old deleting Section 3.5, Some Elaborations, as being of only minor significance to most instructors (and students). In addition, we added a new Section 3.6 on quotas and moved some of the material from the discussion of price floors to this new section. We also wrote a new Section 3.7 on taxes and subsidies and moved some of the material from Chapter 4, Section 4.4, on taxes to this new section. In addition, we added three new Test Your Understanding questions, four new Connect Study Problems and two new Problems for Further Study. Finally, we added an AD box on temporary foreign workers and moved the material from the AD box on the minimum wage into the text and rewrote that section.

- In **Chapter 4**, we rewrote Section 4.1 entirely, reducing its size and using simpler numerical examples. We also rewrote and moved Section 4.3 on the determinant of price elasticity into Section 4.1. In addition, we wrote a new Section 4.2 showing how to calculate price elasticity using the same numerical examples from Section 4.1. Finally, we moved Section 4.2 on graphing elasticity to Section 4.3 so that it now comes after the calculation of elasticity, and eliminated the example of the effect of a sales tax since this is now done in Chapter 3.

- In **Chapter 5**, we expanded the explanation of the optimal purchasing rule. We also wrote a new section that extended the conclusion to the numerical example in Section 5.2 and added two graphs to illustrate. We also added an AD box on economic behaviorism.

- In **Chapter 6**, we converted the introductory material into a new Section 1 in which we more clearly define the term "firm" and give examples of five different types of business organizations. As well, in Section 6.5 we more explicitly note that technological change will also shift the short-run curves. We also added an AD box on zero marginal costs and wrote a new Comprehensive Problem.

- In **Chapter 7**, we expanded Section 7.1 and explained in more detail the distinction between the long and the short run and also why a firm might have difficulty relocating. We re-wrote the Section on changes in short- and long-run costs and added a graph showing the effects of a decrease in input prices or technological improvement. We also re-drew Figure 7.4 so that it clearly shows that the LAS is a curve that envelopes the short-run curves. Finally, we shifted Section 7.5 so that it now comes after the section determining on the right size of firm, as it had somewhat interrupted the narrative flow.

- In **Chapter 8**, we expanded the introduction and tightened up Section 2 by eliminating some of the less-important material. We moved the material on average costs from the end of Section 3 into Section 4 and revised Section 4 so that it now illustrates, in order, the break-even price, a profitable firm and shutdown price with a graph for each. We reduced the contents of the AD boxes on competition and the Internet and on perfect competition and the market system.

- In **Chapter 9**, we added calculations to the section on producer and consumer surplus to help clarify the ideas and added a new AD box on day care in Canada. We also revised and updated the AD boxes on the rich and the poor and on Canada's record on greenhouse gas emissions. In Section 9.4 we added information regarding Canada's carbon tax. We added a Great Economists box for Richard Lipsey and new questions on consumer and producer surpluses in Test Yourself, Connect Study Problems, and Problems for Further Study.

- In **Chapter 10**, Section 10.1, we changed our example from that of a brewer to that of an ink refill company so as to deal in single, discrete units rather millions. We replaced old Figure 10.9 so that it now depicts the same firm and the same cost increase in both graphs. We also added an AD box on monopolists that are little known to the public.

- In **Chapter 11**, Section 11.3, we more clearly explained the two factors that determine the elasticity of demand for the monopolistically competitive producer. We also replaced Figure 11.3 with two graphs so that the contrast between monopolistic and perfect competition is clearer. We defined and more fully explained the term *franchise* and added a table showing the world's biggest franchises. In addition, we rewrote and tightened up parts of Section 11.5 and, in doing so, eliminated Table 11.2. Finally, we updated the AD boxes on oil prices and on the world's largest economic entities.

- In **Chapter 12**, we moved and rewrote the portions on the long-run supply, demand, and productivity from Section 12.2 to Section 12.1 and in doing so made Section 12.1 a self-contained section,

"The Competitive Labour Market." We moved "The Case for Monopsony" from Section 12.1 to Section 12.2, the latter of which is now titled "Imperfect Labour Markets." We revised Figure 12.13 so that it more accurately reflects the short- and the long-run supply of oil. We also repositioned Figure 12.4 to be adjacent to Figure 12.3 and more clearly show the link between the two. In addition, we revised the AD boxes on David Ricardo and hockey prices and on the Luddites and the fear of machines, and added a Great Economists box for Schumpeter.

- In **Chapter 13**, we expanded the discussion of the various types of factor endowments and the discussion of trade protection. We revised the AD boxes on Canada as the "Great Trader" and on NAFTA, and added a new box, "Trade, Politics, and the Future." Study Problem 4 was simplified, and we added a new Test Your Understanding question and a new Study Problem question.

TEXTBOOK FEATURES

As an initial review, and an ongoing resource, the book opens with the **Economics Toolkit**. The first section, The Canadian Reality, offers basic information on Canada and its economy. The second section, Graphing Reality, provides the student with a primer on how to interpret and create tables and graphs. We have provided a number of features to help the student come to grips with the subject matter.

Learning Objectives, listed at the beginning of each chapter, form a learning framework throughout the text, with each objective repeated in the margin at the appropriate place in the body of the chapter. Each chapter opens with a vignette that provides context and an overview.

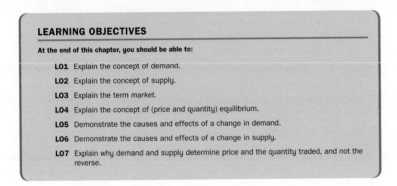

LEARNING OBJECTIVES

At the end of this chapter, you should be able to:

LO1 Explain the concept of demand.

LO2 Explain the concept of supply.

LO3 Explain the term *market*.

LO4 Explain the concept of (price and quantity) equilibrium.

LO5 Demonstrate the causes and effects of a change in demand.

LO6 Demonstrate the causes and effects of a change in supply.

LO7 Explain why demand and supply determine price and the quantity traded, and not the reverse.

Glossary terms, given in bold type in the main text, indicate the first use of any term that is part of the language of economics. The Glossary itself appears at the end of the book.

Test Your Understanding question boxes appear at important points throughout the body of each chapter. They give students immediate feedback on how well they understand the more abstract concept(s) discussed. In doing this, we have tried to establish what we believe to be a minimum standard of comprehension all students should strive for. Students can check their own progress by comparing their answers with those in the Student Answer Key, which is available on the McGraw-Hill online resource.

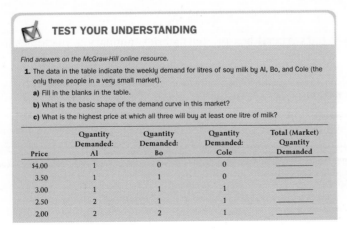

TEST YOUR UNDERSTANDING

Find answers on the McGraw-Hill online resource.

1. The data in the table indicate the weekly demand for litres of soy milk by Al, Bo, and Cole (the only three people in a very small market).

a) Fill in the blanks in the table.

b) What is the basic shape of the demand curve in this market?

c) What is the highest price at which all three will buy at least one litre of milk?

Price	Quantity Demanded: Al	Quantity Demanded: Bo	Quantity Demanded: Cole	Total (Market) Quantity Demanded
$4.00	1	0	0	_____
3.50	1	1	0	_____
3.00	1	1	1	_____
2.50	2	1	1	_____
2.00	2	2	1	_____

Added Dimension boxes identify material that is either general information or supplementary material that we hope adds a little colour to students' reading.

 ADDED DIMENSION

Just What Is an Economist?

When a person says "I am an economist" he/she might actually be doing one of a variety of jobs. Broadly speaking these work types fall into four categories.

You are familiar with the first type: *academic economists* who are found teaching in educational institutions. In addition to their teaching duties, these economists also engage in research activities and sometimes are seconded to governments and other organizations for specific projects or advisory duties.

The second type might be called *financial economists*. These work in the many wealth-management firms and often engaged directly with members of the general public to help them plan their retirement or establish a safe, steady flow of income from the money they have acquired through their work or from an inheritance. These economists might also be employed at banks engaging in similar

Great Economists boxes include short biographies of some of the major economists, past and present, so that students can have an insight into the lives of the creators of the ideas that are the cornerstones of our discipline.

 GREAT ECONOMISTS: JOHN STUART MILL

John Stuart Mill (1806–73) is considered the last great economist of the classical school. His *Principles of Political Economy*, first published in England in 1848, was the leading textbook in economics for 40 years. Raised by a strict disciplinarian father (James), John Stuart began to learn Greek at the age of three, authored a history of Roman government by 11, and studied calculus at 12—but did not take up economics until age 13. Not surprisingly, this unusual childhood later led to a mental crisis. Mill credited his decision to put his analytical pursuits on hold and take up an appreciation of poetry as the primary reason for his recovery. He was a true humanitarian, who held a great faith in human progress, had a love of liberty, and was an advocate of extended rights for women.

A **Question of Relevance** boxes relate the material of the chapter to the lifetime experience of the reader.

A QUESTION OF RELEVANCE ...

Jon and Ashok are both avid soccer fans and play for local teams. They both like old movies and chess and use Twitter. They are both seventeen years of age, neither has a steady girlfriend, and both are vegetarians. The other thing they have in common is that their fathers are in banking. Jon's father is the executive vice-president of customer relations for the Royal Bank of Canada in Toronto. Ashok's father is a night janitor at a branch of the Bank of India in the dock area of Bombay. All of these points are relevant in forming a mental picture of a person, but you will probably agree that a person's economic circumstances have an enormous impact. In truth, economics is one of the most relevant subjects you will study.

Each chapter's **What's Ahead** box presents a brief summary of the topics to be covered in the chapter.

 WHAT'S AHEAD ...

In this first chapter, we introduce you to the study of economics and hope to arouse your curiosity about this fascinating discipline. First, we present four controversial statements to illustrate how relevant economics really is. Next, we discuss the nature of the discipline. From this, we derive a formal definition of economics. Then, we examine what efficiency means and why it is so important. The next step is to look at three of the fundamental questions that all societies face and see how four different types of economies address them. Following that, we introduce the production possibilities model, which enables us to illustrate many of these concepts. Finally, we discuss seven important macroeconomic goals and briefly look at the policy tools used to achieve them.

Each **Section Summary** presents a brief review of the main topics of each section.

SECTION SUMMARY

a) Demand is the price–quantity relationship of a product that consumers are willing and able to buy per period of time.

b) The demand curve is downward sloping because of
  - the substitution effect
  - income effect

c) Products can be related as
  - complements
  - substitutes

d) Market demand is the conceptual summation of each individual's demand within a given market.

The **It's News to Me** feature consists of a short news item relating to material in the chapter along with two or more multiple-choice questions on the article.

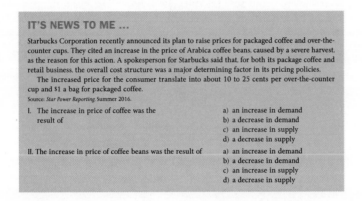

IT'S NEWS TO ME …

Starbucks Corporation recently announced its plan to raise prices for packaged coffee and over-the-counter cups. They cited an increase in the price of Arabica coffee beans, caused by a severe harvest, as the reason for this action. A spokesperson for Starbucks said that, for both its package coffee and retail business, the overall cost structure was a major determining factor in its pricing policies.

The increased price for the consumer translate into about 10 to 25 cents per over-the-counter cup and $1 a bag for packaged coffee.

Source: *Star Power Reporting,* Summer 2016.

I. The increase in price of coffee was the result of
  a) an increase in demand
  b) a decrease in demand
  c) an increase in supply
  d) a decrease in supply

II. The increase in price of coffee beans was the result of
  a) an increase in demand
  b) a decrease in demand
  c) an increase in supply
  d) a decrease in supply

The **In a Nutshell** feature is a half-page visual (humorous and/or thoughtful) that seeks to convey an important idea found within the chapter.

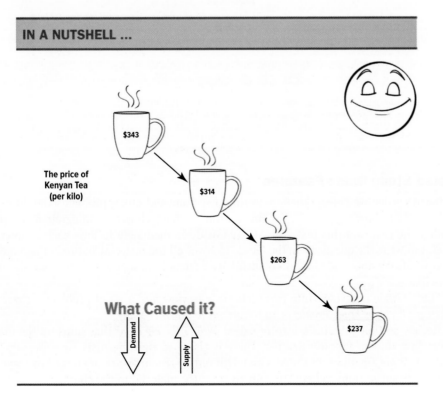

IN A NUTSHELL …

The price of Kenyan Tea (per kilo)

$343

$314

$263

$237

What Caused it?

Demand

Supply

Highlighted concepts are important ideas pulled out and presented in a separate box—signalling to students that this material is particularly relevant and crucial to their understanding.

> An increase in price will lead to an increase in the quantity supplied and is illustrated as a movement up the supply curve.

> A decrease in price will cause a decrease in the quantity supplied and is illustrated as a movement down the supply curve.

Simple, clear, and uncomplicated **visuals** are found throughout the text, supported by captions that thoroughly explain the concepts.

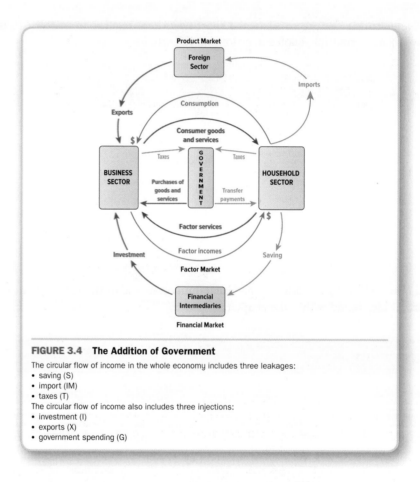

FIGURE 3.4   The Addition of Government

The circular flow of income in the whole economy includes three leakages:
- saving (S)
- import (IM)
- taxes (T)

The circular flow of income also includes three injections:
- investment (I)
- exports (X)
- government spending (G)

Integrated Study Guide Features

As mentioned earlier, we believe that answering questions and doing problems should be an *active part of the students' learning process*. For this reason, we have chosen to integrate a complete study guide within the covers of this text. The **Study Guide** immediately follows each chapter. We have been careful to write the questions in the Guide to cover all the material, but only the material found in the text itself. We hope the Guide's colourful, user-friendly design will encourage significant student participation.

The Study Guide is divided into two sections: a Review and a set of problems. These include a *Comprehensive Problem, Study Problems,* and *Problems for Further Study.*

The Review section contains a feature called *What's the Big Idea?* that sums up the main idea of the chapter in a student-friendly manner. There is also a section that lists *New Glossary Terms and Key Equations. Study Tips* (now on the McGraw-Hill online resource) are organized by learning objective and provide suggestions to help students manage the material in the chapter.

Study Guide

Review

WHAT'S THE BIG IDEA?

The production possibilities model is a good way to look at some of the important aspects of economics. Although it is used mostly to describe what happens in an economy, it is equally useful in adding insights to business or everyday life.

Imagine yourself as the CEO of production facility that has a maximum capacity to produce either 1000 trucks or 20/00 SUVs per week and you have decided to produce one-half each kind of vehicle—500 trucks and 1000 SUVs. Things are humming along fine for a while, but this begins to change. You notice that while you continue to sell all of the 1000 SUVs the demand for trucks must have increased, as your orders for more trucks begin to exceed the output of 500 per week. Since

NEW GLOSSARY TERMS

allocative efficiency	land	productive efficiency
capital	law of increasing costs	profit
consumer goods and services	macroeconomics	rent
enterprise	microeconomics	resources
factors of production	normative statements	scientific method
inputs	opportunity cost	technology
interest	positive statements	wages
labour	production possibilities curve	

The **Comprehensive Problem** addresses several key chapter learning objectives and is complete with answers and explanations.

Comprehensive Problem

(LO 2, 4, 5) Assume that there is only one movie theatre and only one video streaming outlet in a small mining town in northern Manitoba. The weekly demand, by all the townspeople, for movies and streamed video rentals is given in Table 4.9.

TABLE 4.9

Prices of Movies	Quantity of Movies Demanded	Total Revenue	Prices of Videos	Quantity of Streamed Videos Demanded	Total Revenue
$3	450	____	$2.00	950	____
4	400	____	2.50	900	____
5	350	____	3.00	825	____
6	300	____	3.50	750	____
7	250	____	4.00	650	____
8	200	____	4.50	550	____
9	150	____	5.00	425	____

The **Study Problems** have been grouped into three learning levels: basic, intermediate, and advanced. Students can judge their progress by working through these problems, and checking their answers against those in the Student Answer Key available on the McGraw-Hill online resource.

Study Problems

Find answers on the McGraw-Hill online resource.

Basic (Problems 1–5)

1. **(LO 1)** Given Jan's total utility from consuming packets of potato chips in Table 5.13, calculate her marginal utility for each unit.

TABLE 5.13

Quantity	Total Utility	Marginal Utility
1	60	____
2	110	____
3	140	____
4	155	____
5	167	____
6	177	____
7	186	____
8	192	____
9	195	____
10	196	____

Finally, there is a set of **Problems for Further Study** (with answers for instructors found on the McGraw-Hill online resource).

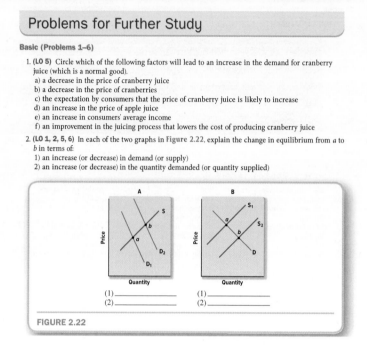

Problems for Further Study

Basic (Problems 1–6)

1. **(LO 5)** Circle which of the following factors will lead to an increase in the demand for cranberry juice (which is a normal good).
    a) a decrease in the price of cranberry juice
    b) a decrease in the price of cranberries
    c) the expectation by consumers that the price of cranberry juice is likely to increase
    d) an increase in the price of apple juice
    e) an increase in consumers' average income
    f) an improvement in the juicing process that lowers the cost of producing cranberry juice

2. **(LO 1, 2, 5, 6)** In each of the two graphs in Figure 2.22, explain the change in equilibrium from *a* to *b* in terms of:
    1) an increase (or decrease) in demand (or supply)
    2) an increase (or decrease) in the quantity demanded (or quantity supplied)

(1) _____   (1) _____
(2) _____   (2) _____

FIGURE 2.22

SUPERIOR LEARNING SOLUTIONS AND SUPPORT

The McGraw-Hill Education team is ready to help you assess and integrate any of our products, technology, and services into your course for optimal teaching and learning performance. Whether it's helping your students improve their grades or putting your entire course online, the McGraw-Hill Education team is here to help you do it. Contact your Learning Solutions Consultant today to learn how to maximize all of McGraw-Hill Education's resources!

For more information, please visit us online: http://www.mheducation.ca/he/solutions.

ACKNOWLEDGMENTS

We begin with acknowledgment to our colleagues, past and present, in the Economics Department of Capilano University—Nigel Amon, Ken Moak, Mahak Yaseri, C.S. Lum, Chieko Tanimura, and Camlon Chau—for their encouragement and vigilance in spotting errors and omissions in earlier editions. Numerous colleagues in other departments also gave us encouragement, and sometimes praise, which is greatly appreciated. We would also like to thank our many students, past and present, for their helpful comments (and occasional criticism).

Most particularly, we wish to acknowledge the continued help and support of Kevin O'Hearn, our Senior Product Manager. Kevin immediately took an active interest in the book, and his desire to make it better is always apparent.

We are pleased to mention the high degree of professionalism displayed by Melissa Hudson, our Product Developer. Working with her involved many pleasant encounters. In addition we acknowledge the work of Jessica Barnoski, our Supervising Editor.

Rodney Rawlings' editing and proofing provided excellent professional skills, which are greatly appreciated.

In the end, of course, any errors or confusion that remain are our responsibility.

Finally, we wish to acknowledge the continued love and support of our families and those close to us.

The Complete Course Solution

We listened to educators from around the world, learned about their challenges, and created a whole new way to deliver a course.

Connect2 is a collaborative teaching and learning platform that includes an instructionally designed complete course framework of learning materials that is flexible and open for instructors to easily personalize, add their own content, or integrate with other tools and platforms.

- Save time and resources building and managing a course.
- Gain confidence knowing that each course framework is pedagogically sound.
- Help students master course content.
- Make smarter decisions by using real-time data to guide course design, content changes, and remediation.

MANAGE — Dynamic Curriculum Builder

Quickly and easily launch a complete course framework developed by instructional design experts. Each Connect2 course is a flexible foundation for instructors to build upon by adding their own content or drawing upon the wide repository of additional resources.

- Easily customize Connect2 by personalizing the course scope and sequence.
- Get access to a wide range of McGraw-Hill Education content within one powerful teaching and learning platform.
- Receive expert support and guidance on how best to utilize content to achieve a variety of teaching goals.

MASTER — Student Experience

Improve student performance with instructional alignment and leverage Connect2's carefully curated learning resources. Deliver required reading through Connect2's award-winning adaptive learning system.

- Teach at a higher level in class by helping students retain core concepts.
- Tailor in-class instruction based on student progress and engagement.
- Help focus students on the content they don't know so they can prioritize their study time.

MEASURE — Advanced Analytics

Collect, analyze and act upon class and individual student performance data. Make real-time course updates and teaching decisions backed by data.

- Visually explore class and student performance data.
- Easily identify key relationships between assignments and student performance.
- Maximize in-class time by using data to focus on areas where students need the most help.

Course Map

The flexible and customizable course map provides instructors full control over the pre-designed courses within Connect2. Instructors can easily add, delete, or rearrange content to adjust the course scope and sequence to their personal preferences.

Implementation Guide

Each Connect2 course includes a detailed implementation guide that provides guidance on what the course can do and how best to utilize course content based on individual teaching approaches.

Instructor Resources

A comprehensive collection of instructor resources are available within Connect2. Instructor Support and Seminar Materials provide additional exercises and activities to use for in-class discussion and teamwork.

For more information, please visit www.mheconnect2.com

ECONOMICS TOOLKIT

Some students take economics because it is a requirement for a program they have chosen or degree they are working toward. Some are interested in a career in business, and taking economics seems like a natural choice. Some even take it because they think that they might like it. Whatever your reasons for taking economics, we are glad you did and hope you will not be disappointed. Economics is a challenging discipline to learn, but it is also one of the most rewarding courses you will ever take. The logic and analysis used in economics is very powerful, and successfully working your way through the principles of economics over the next term will do for your mind what a serious jogging program will do for your body. Bon voyage!

THE CANADIAN REALITY

The Land

Canada is a huge country—in fact, the second-largest country on this planet. It contains 7 percent of the world's land mass. It stretches 5600 kilometres from the Atlantic to the Pacific Ocean and encompasses six time zones. Ontario alone, which is the second-largest province (after Quebec), is larger than Pakistan, Turkey, Chile, France, or the United Kingdom. Canada's ten provinces range in size from tiny Prince Edward Island to Quebec, which is nearly 240 times as large. In addition, its three territories—the Northwest Territories, Yukon, and Nunavut—demand that we describe this country's reach as being from sea to sea *to sea*.

Within Canada, there are at least six major mountain ranges: the Torngats, Appalachians, and Laurentians in the east, and the Mackenzie, Rocky, and Coast ranges in the west. Any one of these rivals the European Alps in size and grandeur. In addition, Canada has vast quantities of fresh water—9 percent of the world's total—in tens of thousands of lakes and numerous rivers, of which the St. Lawrence and the Mackenzie are the largest.

Canada is richly endowed with natural resources, including gas, oil, gold, silver, copper, iron, nickel, potash, uranium, zinc, fish, timber, and, as mentioned above, water—lots of fresh water. The conclusion is inescapable: Canada is a big, beautiful, and rich country.

The People

The word *Canada* comes from a Huron-Iroquois word meaning *village*. In a sense this is very appropriate, because, big as the nation is geographically, it is small in terms of population. Its over 35 million people make up only 0.5 percent of the world's population. In fact, there are more people in California or in greater Tokyo than there are in the whole of Canada. Interestingly, Canada's annual population growth rate, at 1 percent, is the highest among G8 countries, primarily because of Canada's high rate of immigration. Thirty-eight percent of Canadians live in the province of Ontario and 24 percent in Quebec. On the other hand, Prince Edward Island has a population of only 140 000, less than that of the cities of Sherbrooke, in Quebec, or North Vancouver, in British Columbia.

Despite the popular images of small Maritime fishing villages, lonely Prairie grain farmers, or remote B.C. loggers, Canada is, in fact, an urban nation. Over 80 percent of Canadians live in what Statistics Canada calls "urban" areas. There are six Canadian metropolitan areas with populations of over 1 million: Toronto, with 5.6 million; Montreal, with 3.8 million; Vancouver, with 2.3 million; Calgary and Edmonton, each with 1.2 million; and Ottawa–Gatineau, with 1.2 million. It is also true that the vast majority of the nearly 36 million Canadians live in a narrow band stretching along the border with the United States, which, incidentally, is the longest unguarded border in the world.

Approximately half of the Canadian population is active in the labour force. The labour-force participation rate in 2015 was 71 percent for males and 61 percent for females.

Multiculturalism

Within this vast, thinly populated country there is a truly diverse, multicultural mix of people. This reality was officially recognized in 1988 when Parliament passed the *Multiculturalism Act.*

There are two official languages in Canada, yet 18 percent of Canadians speak a language other than English or French. In fact, at least 60 languages are spoken in this country. In each year of the 2000s, more than 200 000 new immigrants arrived in Canada. Over 18 percent of the entire population are first-generation Canadians. In both Toronto and Vancouver, over half the students in the public school system are from non-English-speaking homes. There are over 100 minority language publications in Toronto, and Vancouver has three daily Chinese-language newspapers.

Canada's First Nations people number 1.1 million (3.8 percent of the total population), and a quarter of them live in Ontario.

Government

Canada is a constitutional monarchy with a democratic parliament made up of the House of Commons, with 308 elected members, and the Senate, with 105 appointed members. In addition to Parliament, the other two decision-making divisions of the federal government are the Cabinet, composed of the prime minister and 25 (or so) ministers and their departments, and the judiciary, which includes the Supreme Court as well as the federal and tax courts.

Just as there are two official languages in this country, Canada has two systems of civil law—one uncodified and based on common law in English Canada, and the other a codified civil law in Quebec. Canada's current constitution, the first part of which is the *Canadian Charter of Rights and Freedoms,* came into being in 1982, a full 115 years after Confederation created the country in 1867.

The fact that Canada is a confederation means the federal government shares responsibilities with the provinces. For example, while the federal government has jurisdiction in national defence, international trade, immigration, banking, criminal law, fisheries, transportation, and communications, the provinces have responsibility for education, property rights, health, and natural resources. Inevitably, issues arise from time to time that do not fit neatly into any one of these categories, with the result that federal–provincial disputes are a continuous part of the Canadian reality.

Canada the Good

Most Canadians are well aware that they live in a good country. But perhaps many do not realize just how good. The average family after-tax income is currently over $74 000, which puts the Canadian living standard among the highest in the world.

The United Nations maintains a Human Development Index that considers factors in addition to average income levels, including lifespans and years of schooling. In 2014, this index ranked Canada as the number nine nation in the world in which to live. One reason for this high ranking is that Canadian governments spend over 10 percent of the country's gross domestic product (GDP) on health care.

More than 70 percent of Canadians own their homes, well over 90 percent are literate, and over 80 percent of all Canadians have access to the Internet. All three of these statistics are among the highest in the world.

Canada the Odd

Canada is a good country in which to live; however, it does have its oddities. In 1965—98 years after Confederation—it was decided that Canada really should have a national flag. A parliamentary selection committee was set up to choose one, and received no less than two thousand designs. The flag debate was acrimonious, to say the least, although today most Canadians seem quite comfortable with the Maple Leaf. The English-language lyrics of Canada's national anthem, "O Canada," were formally approved only in 1975. Canada adopted the metric system of measurement in the 1970s. But the imperial system is still in wide use; for example, Statistics Canada still reports the breadth of this country in miles, we sell sizes of wood in inches (such as 2 × 4s), and football fields are 110 yards long.

In this bilingual country, it is odd to note that there are more Manitobans who speak Cree than British Columbians who speak French. In this affluent country of ours, it is also interesting to note that 4 percent of Canadian homes are heated exclusively by burning wood. Canada's official animal is—the beaver.

On a more serious note, it is a sad fact that the trade of many goods, and even some services, between any one province and the United States is freer than trade between provinces. There is an interesting history concerning trade patterns in North America. At the time of Confederation, trade patterns on this continent were mostly north–south. The Maritimes traded with the New England states, Quebec with New York, Ontario with the Great Lakes states to its south, and the West Coast with California. Canada's first prime minister, John A. Macdonald, was also elected as its third. During his second administration, he implemented his party's National Policy, which resulted in (1) the building of a railway to the west coast, which encouraged British Columbia to join Canada; (2) an offer of free land to new immigrants on the prairies in order to settle this area; and (3) the forcing of trade patterns into an east–west mode by erection of a tariff wall against American imports. British Columbia did join Confederation; people were enticed to settle in Manitoba, Saskatchewan, and Alberta; and the pattern of trade did become more east–west.

So was the National Policy a success? Some would argue yes, pointing out that it built a nation and that Canada as we know it might not exist today without it. Others are not so sure, and would argue that it set back Canada's development by encouraging and protecting new, less efficient industries through the creation of a branch-plant economy. This occurred because American firms that had previously exported to Canada simply jumped over the tariff walls and established Canadian branch plants. Some believe that the National Policy also promoted Canadian regionalism and aggravated relations between regions because both the West and the Maritimes felt that most of its economic benefits favoured central Canada.

In any case, as a result of the North American Free Trade Agreement (NAFTA) of 1992, trade with the United States (and Mexico) is now mostly without tariffs and north–south trade patterns are re-emerging. Historically, Canadian policy has come full circle. However, the trade barriers between provinces, which were built piece by piece over a century, remain.

The Economy

Canada is among the ten largest economies in the world, despite its small population. In 2015, Canada's GDP was $1983 billion. This figure can be broken down as illustrated in Table T.1.

TABLE T.1

Category	Amount ($billions)	% of GDP
Personal expenditures	1140	57.5
Investment spending	389	19.6
Government spending	500	25.2
Exports	547	31.5
Less imports	583	33.8
Net exports	<46>	<2.3>
Total GDP	1983	

Source: Adapted by the authors from the Statistics Canada CANSIM database, http://cansim2.statcan.ca, Table 380-0064, July 5, 2016.

The provincial breakdown of the 2015 GDP figure of $1983 billion is shown in Table T.2.

TABLE T.2

Province	Population (millions)	GDP ($billions)	GDP per Capita ($thousands)
Newfoundland (and Labrador)	0.53	30.1	56.8
Prince Edward Island	0.15	6.2	41.3
Nova Scotia	0.94	40.2	42.8
New Brunswick	0.75	33.1	44.1
Quebec	8.26	381.0	46.1
Ontario	13.80	763.3	55.3
Manitoba	1.30	65.9	50.7
Saskatchewan	1.13	79.4	70.3
Alberta	4.18	326.4	78.1
British Columbia	4.69	250.0	53.3
Yukon	0.04	2.7	72.5
Northwest Territories (pre-Nunavut)	0.04	4.8	109.1
Nunavut	0.04	2.5	67.0

Source: Adapted by the authors from the Statistics Canada CANSIM database, http://cansim2.statcan.ca, Tables 384-0038 and 051-0001, May 11, 2017.

This table illustrates the wide disparity in GDP per capita between provinces, from a low of $41 300 per person in Prince Edward Island to a high of $78 100 in Alberta.

In most years the economy grows and the GDP figure rises. To accurately compare growth in GDP, however, we need to use a common set of prices so that a simple rise in prices is not confused with an actual increase in the output of goods and services. Using *real* GDP figures, which correct for inflation, accomplishes this. Table T.3 looks at some recent real GDP figures, using 2007 prices.

TABLE T.3

Year	Real GDP ($billions)	Increase/Decrease ($billions)	% Increase
2011	1640	+47	+3.0
2012	1669	+29	+1.8
2013	1706	+37	+2.2
2014	1748	+42	+2.5
2015	1767	+19	+1.1

Source: Adapted by the authors from the Statistics Canada CANSIM database, http://cansim2.statcan.ca, Table 380-0064, July 5, 2016.

Next, let us look at a breakdown of Canada's GDP by industry in Table T.4, presented in order of importance.

TABLE T.4

Industry	Percentage of GDP
Real estate	12.9
Trade (wholesale and retail)	11.1
Manufacturing	10.6
Professional and technical	8.7
Mining/oil	8.1
Construction	7.2
Finance and insurance	7.0
Health	6.8
Public administration	6.5
Education	5.2
Transportation	4.3
Information and cultural	3.1
Utilities	2.3
Accomodation and food	2.1
Other services	2.0
Agriculture, fishing, and forestry	1.6
Arts and entertainment	0.7

Source: Adapted from the Statistics Canada CANSIM database, http://cansim2.statcan.ca, Table 379-0031, July 5, 2016.

This information is helpful in many ways. For example, it is certainly time to put to rest the idea that Canada is a resource-based economy and that Canadians are simply "hewers of wood and drawers of water," as many of us were taught in school. In fact, agriculture/fishing/forestry and mining/oil make up less than 10 percent of our economy's GDP. Only 4 percent of working Canadians are employed in primary industries, down dramatically from 13 percent a quarter of a century ago.

In contrast, one can marshal the argument that Canada is quite a sophisticated and technologically advanced economy. For example, it is not generally recognized that Canada was the world's third nation to go into space, with the *Alouette I* satellite in 1962. Canadian industries pioneered long-distance pipeline technology, and Canada is a world leader in several areas of aviation, including turboprop, turbofan, and firefighting aircraft, not to mention the well-known Canadarm used on space shuttles. Canada is also a world leader in commercial submarine technology, and routinely maintains one of the world's longest and most efficient railway systems.

One can also point to many outstanding Canadian companies that are truly world leaders in technology and performance, including Bombardier in transportation equipment, Ballard Power in fuel cell technology, SNC Lavalin in aluminum plant design, Rio Tinto in mining, Trizec Hahn in real estate development, and Magna International in automobile parts manufacturing.

Exports: The Engine That Drives the Economy

Exports are a fundamental part of the Canadian economy. Over 30 percent of its GDP is exported, which makes Canada one of the world's greatest trading nations. Exports to the United States alone directly support over 1.5 million Canadian jobs, and a $1 billion increase in exports translates into 11 000 new jobs. Again, contrary to historical wisdom, only 25 percent of Canadian exports are resources—the figure was 40 percent a quarter of a century ago.

Table T.5 breaks down the $625 billion worth of goods and services Canada exported in 2015 into nine categories in order of size.

TABLE T.5

Export Category	Percentage of Total Exports
Industrial goods	18.0
Services	16.0
Automotive products	14.0
Machinery and equipment	13.7
Energy products	13.4
Consumer goods	11.2
Forestry products	6.4
Agricultural and fishing products	5.1
Others	2.3

Source: Adapted from the Statistics Canada CANSIM database, http://cansim2.statcan.ca, Tables 228-0059, July 5, 2016.

A Mixed Economy

At the start of the twenty-first century, the market system dominates most of the world's economies, and Canada is no exception. Yet government also plays a big role in our economy. For example, in 2009 the three levels of government collected $586 billion in tax revenue, which represented over 38 percent of Canada's 2009 GDP. Table T.6 shows the sources and the uses of this revenue.

TABLE T.6

Government Revenues	% of Total	Government Expenditures	% of Total
Personal income taxes	32.3	Social services	25.6
Consumption taxes	18.3	Health	20.5
Property taxes	9.4	Education	16.1
Investment income	9.2	Protection of persons and property	8.5
Sales of goods and services	9.2	Debt charges	7.6
Corporate incomes taxes	8.5	Environment	6.3
Social security premiums	6.0	Transportation	5.4
Other taxes	5.3	Government services	3.8

Source: Adapted by the authors from the Statistics Canada CANSIM database, http://cansim2.statcan.ca, Table 385-0001, January 12, 2011.

The largest single source of the government's tax revenue, 32 percent, was personal income taxes. Consumption taxes include, most significantly, the GST (goods and services tax) and the PST (provincial sales tax) as well as gasoline, alcohol, and tobacco taxes, customs taxes, and gaming income. These indirect (consumption) taxes accounted for 18 percent of total revenue. Thus, we can see that the majority of the government's tax revenue comes from individual Canadians in the form of direct income taxes or consumption taxes.

And how does government spend these billions of dollars of tax revenue? The right column of Table T.6 shows us.

Here, we see that government's largest single category of spending, 26 percent, was on social service payments to individuals. The lion's share of this expenditure (approximately two-thirds) was social services (pensions, unemployment benefits, and welfare) payments. Thus, we see that a large percentage of spending by government is an attempt to direct income to poorer Canadians. Since all Canadians pay for most of these expenditures, we can see that government is actively involved in *transferring* income from higher-income to lower-income families and individuals. This income distribution role is seen by many Canadians as an important function of government.

On the other hand, some Canadians take the view that government has gone too far in its interventionist role and yearn for less governmental involvement in the economy. They often point to the United States as an example of an economy in which welfare, unemployment, and pension payments to individuals and direct government aid to poor regions of the country are lower. The difference in the general approach of the two governments may well lie in historical differences in the attitudes of Canadians and Americans toward government. Over the years, Canadians, by and large, have trusted governments to act in their best interests and have been more tolerant of government attempts at income redistribution. Americans, on the other hand, have a history of being suspicious of big government and have repeatedly rejected attempts to expand its role. The recent controversy in the United States over attempts to implement a national health care (Obamacare) policy is an example. Another is the Canadian government's direct aid to cultural endeavours, including the funding of national television and radio networks, while no such efforts exist in the United States.

The next two largest categories of spending are on two essentials, health and education. In 2009, the Canadian government allocated 21 and 16 percent of spending in these two areas. The fourth category, protection of persons and property, includes expenditures on the military, police, fire departments, court system, and prisons. Interest on the national debt was the fifth-biggest item of spending at just under 8 percent. The amount spent in this area has steadily declined in the last few years as Canada has started to get government budget deficits under control. (As recently as 1998, servicing the national debt amounted to as much as 30 percent of total spending.) The other categories include a host of such items as culture (the Canada Council), housing, foreign affairs, immigration, labour, and research.

This completes our brief look at the Canadian economic reality. We hope that it has helped fill in some gaps in your knowledge of the country. We are confident that you will come to know your country much better after a thorough grounding in the principles of economics, for, in a very real sense, economics is about understanding and improving on what we already know.

GRAPHING REALITY

Let's face it, a lot of students hate graphs. For them a picture is not worth a thousand words. It may even be true that they seem to understand some economic concepts just fine until the instructor draws a graph on the board. All of a sudden, they lose confidence and start to question what they previously thought they knew. For these students, graphs are not the solution but the problem. This section is designed to help those students overcome this difficulty. For those other, more fortunate students who can handle graphs and know that they are used to illustrate concepts, a quick reading of this section will reinforce their understanding.

It is probably true that if an idea can be expressed clearly and precisely with words, then graphs become an unnecessary luxury. The trouble is that, from time to time, economists find themselves at a loss for words and see no way of getting a certain point across except with the use of a graph. On the other hand, by themselves graphs cannot explain everything; they need to be accompanied by a verbal explanation. In other words, they are not a substitute for words but a complement. The words accompanied by a picture can often give us a much richer understanding of economic concepts and happenings.

Graphing a Single Variable

The graphing of a single variable is reasonably straightforward. Often, economists want to concentrate on a single economic variable, such as Canada's exports, or consumers' incomes, or the production of wine in Canada. In some cases, they want to look at the composition of that variable, say different categories of exports. In other cases, they are interested in seeing how one variable changed over a period of time, such as total exports for each of the years 2005 through 2009. In the first instance, we would be looking at a cross-section; in the second instance, we are looking at a time series.

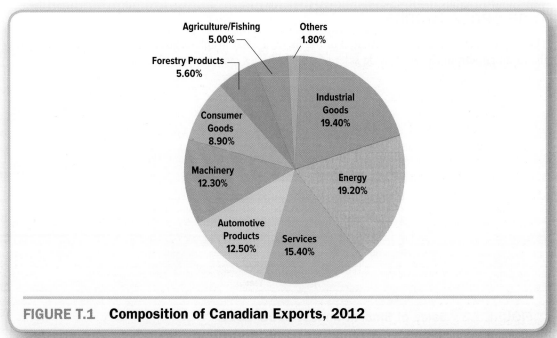

FIGURE T.1 **Composition of Canadian Exports, 2012**

Source: Adapted from the Statistics Canada CANSIM database, http://cansim2.statcan.ca, Tables 228-0059, January 9, 2014.

Cross-Sectional Graphs

One popular way of showing cross-sectional data is in the form of a pie chart. **Figure** T.1, for instance, shows the composition of Canada's exports for 2012 in terms of the type of goods or services that Canada sells abroad. (This is the same data as presented in **Table** T.5. Which presentation format—table or graph—do you prefer? Which do you find easier to read and understand?) The size of each slice indicates the relative size of each category of exports. But the picture by itself is not 'always enough. We have added the percentage of total exports that each type represents. Note, however, that there are no dollar amounts for the categories.

Alternatively, the same information could be presented in the form of a bar graph, as in **Figure** T.2. Unlike the pie chart, the bar graph allows us to more easily compare the relative sizes of each category since they are now placed side by side.

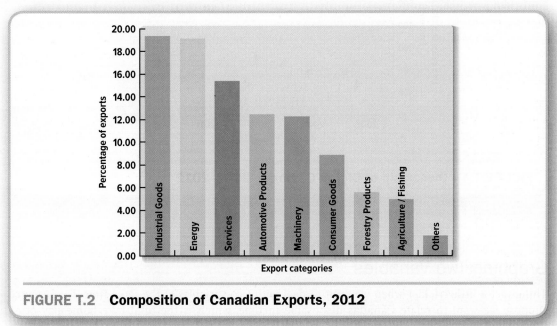

FIGURE T.2 **Composition of Canadian Exports, 2012**

Source: Adapted from the Statistics Canada CANSIM database, http://cansim2.statcan.ca, Tables 228-0059, January 11, 2011.

Time-Series Graphs

Time-series data can also be presented in the form of a bar graph. **Figure T.3** is a bar graph showing the rapid growth in the worldwide sales of smart phones over the past five years.

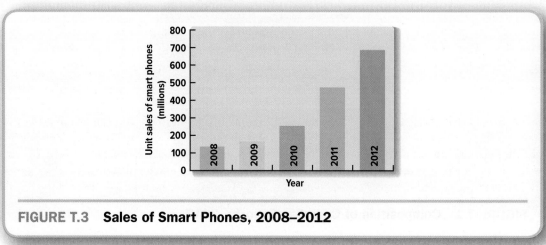

FIGURE T.3   Sales of Smart Phones, 2008–2012

Source: Adapted from Gartner.com, retrieved January 10, 2014.

The same information can be presented in a line graph, as is done in **Figure T.4**. Note that in both cases, the years (time) are shown on the horizontal axis; early years are on the left and later years on the right. This is because graphs are always read from left to right.

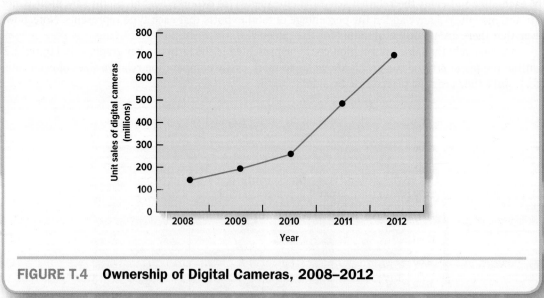

FIGURE T.4   Ownership of Digital Cameras, 2008–2012

Source: Adapted from Gartner.com, retrieved January 10, 2014.

Graphing Two Variables

Things get a little trickier when we want to deal with two variables at the same time. For instance, suppose we want to relate Canada's disposable income, which is the total take-home pay of all Canadians, and the amount spent on consumer goods (these numbers are in billions and are hypothetical). One obvious way to do this is with a table, as is done in **Table T.7**.

TABLE T.7

Year	Disposable Income	Spending on Consumer Goods
1	$100	$ 80
2	120	98
3	150	125
4	160	134
5	200	170

A time-series graph, using the same data, is presented in **Figure T.5**. You can see that the two lines in the figure seem to be closely related, and that is useful information. To more clearly bring out the relationship, we could plot them against each other. But if you look again at **Table T.7**, you will see that there are really three different variables involved: the time (five years), the values of disposable income, and the values of spending. However, it is very difficult to plot three variables, all three against each other, on a two-dimensional sheet of paper.

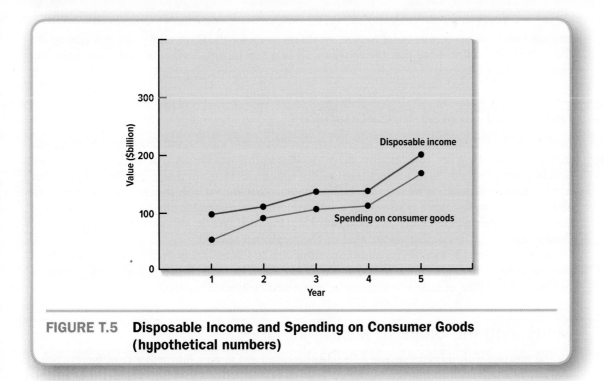

FIGURE T.5   Disposable Income and Spending on Consumer Goods (hypothetical numbers)

Instead, in **Figure T.6**, we will put disposable income on the horizontal axis (also called the *x-axis*) and consumer spending on the vertical axis (also called the *y-axis*) and indicate time with written notation. There is a rule about which variable goes on which axis, but we will leave that for later in this book.

Next, we need to decide on a scale for each of the two axes. There is no particular rule about doing this, but just a little experience will enable you to develop good judgment about selecting these values. We have chosen to give each square on the axes the value of $20. This can be seen in **Figure T.6**.

We started plotting our line using year 1 data. In that year, disposable income was $100 and consumer spending was $80. Starting at the origin (where the vertical and horizontal axes meet), which has an assigned value of zero, we move five squares to the right. Now, from this income of $100, we move up vertically four squares, arriving at a value of $80 for consumer spending. This is our first plot (or point). We do the same for year 2. First, we find a value of $120 on the horizontal (disposable income) axis and a value of $98 (just less than five squares) on the vertical axis. The place where these

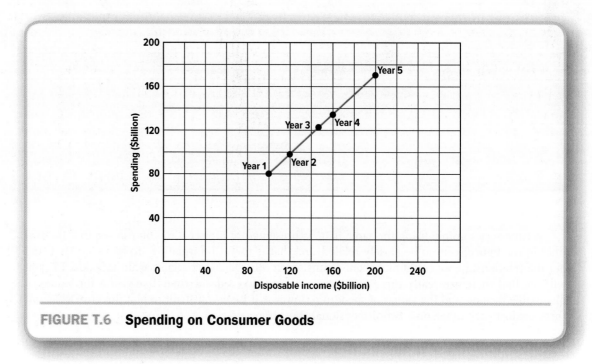

FIGURE T.6   Spending on Consumer Goods

two meet gives us our second point to plot. We do the same for the three next years, and join up the five points with a line. Note that the relationship between income levels and consumer spending plots as a straight line.

Direct and Inverse Relationships

Next, if you look back at **Table T.7**, you will see that disposable income and consumer spending rise together over time. When two variables move together in this way, we say that there is a *direct* relationship between them. Such a direct relationship appears as an upward-sloping line. On the other hand, when two variables move in opposite directions so that one variable increases as the other variable decreases, we say there is an *inverse* relationship between them. In that case, plotting the two variables together would result in a downward-sloping line. (When we say "upward-sloping" and "downward-sloping," remember we are reading the graphs left to right.)

One last point: the income–consumer spending line in **Figure T.6** is straight. This is not always the case. Some data might plot as a straight line, and other data might be nonlinear when plotted (as in **Figure T.5**). Either, of course, could still be downward or upward sloping.

Measuring the Slope of a Straight Line

As you proceed with this course, you will find that you need to go a bit further than merely being able to plot a curve. (In economics, by the way, all lines are described as curves whether they are linear or nonlinear.) You will also need to know just how steep or how shallow the line is that you have plotted. In other words, you will need to measure the slope of the curve. What the slope shows, in effect, is how much one variable changes in relation to the other variable as we move along a curve. In graphic terms, this means measuring the change in the variable shown on the vertical axis (known as the *rise*), divided by the change in the variable shown on the horizontal axis (known as the *run*). The rise and the run are illustrated, using our disposable income/consumer-spending example, in **Figure T.7**.

Note that as we move from point *a* to point *b*, consumer spending increases by 80 (from 80 to 160). This is the amount of the rise. Looking along the horizontal axis, we see that disposable income increases by 100 (from 100 to 200). This is the amount of the run. In general, we can say

$$\text{Slope} = \frac{\text{rise}}{\text{run}} = \frac{\text{change in the value on the vertical axis}}{\text{change in the value on the horizontal axis}}$$

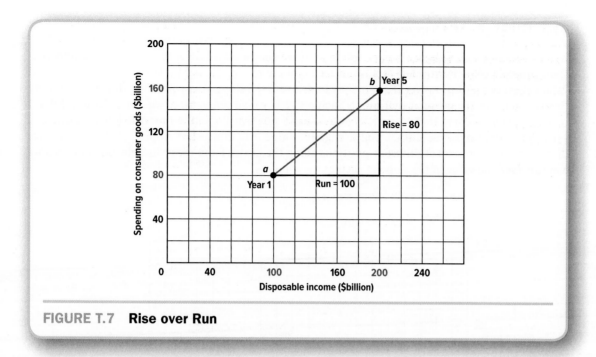

FIGURE T.7   Rise over Run

Specifically, the slope of our line is therefore equal to

$$\frac{+80}{+100} = +0.8$$

Figure T.8 shows four other curves, two upward sloping and two downward sloping, with an indication for each as to how to calculate the various slopes. In each case, we measure the slope by moving from point *a* to point *b*.

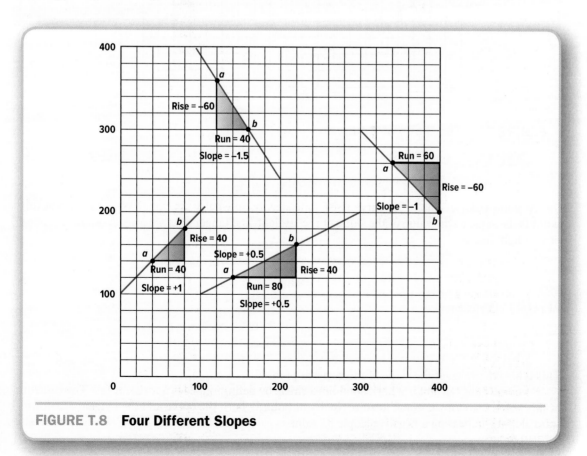

FIGURE T.8   Four Different Slopes

The Slopes of Curves

If a line is straight, it does not matter where on it we choose to measure the slope; the slope is constant throughout its length. But this is not true of a curve. The slope of a curve will have different values at every point. However, it is possible to measure the slope at any point by drawing a straight line that touches the curve at that point. Such a line is called a *tangent to the curve*. **Figure T.9**, for instance, shows a curve that, at various points, has a positive slope (the upward-sloping portion), a zero slope (the top of the curve), and a negative slope (the downward-sloping portion). We have drawn in three tangents at different positions along the curve. From these straight-line tangents we can calculate the value of the slope at each of these points.

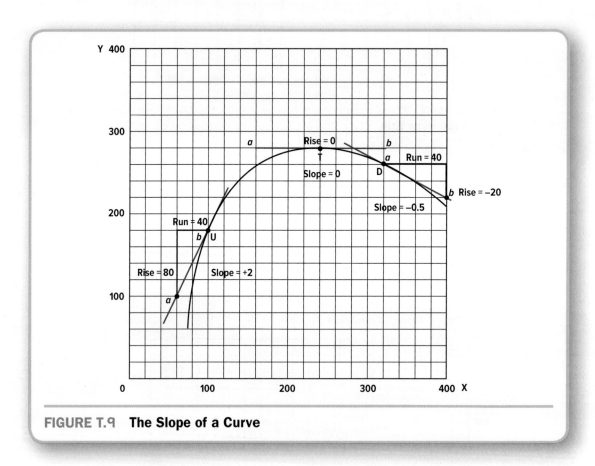

FIGURE T.9   The Slope of a Curve

At point U, for example, the curve rises quite steeply. So what is its slope? Well, its slope at this point is the same as the value of the slope of the straight-line tangent. As we already know the slope of a straight line is

$$\frac{\text{Rise}}{\text{Run}}$$

At point U, this is equal to

$$\frac{+80}{+40} = +2$$

This is also the value of the slope of the curve at point U.

At point T, the tangent is a horizontal line, which, by definition, does not rise or fall. The rise/run at this point, therefore, is equal to zero. Finally, at point D, both the curve and the tangent are downward sloping, indicating a negative slope. Its value is calculated, as before, as rise/run, which equals −20/40 or −0.5.

Equations for a Straight Line

In economics, graphs are a very important and useful way to present information. Thus, you will find the pages of most economics books liberally sprinkled with them. But there are other, equally useful ways of presenting the same data. One of these is an algebraic equation. You will often find it very useful to be able to translate a graph into algebra. In this short section, we will show you how to do this. To keep things simple, we will restrict our attention to straight-line graphs.

In order to find the equation for any straight line, you need only two pieces of information: the slope of the line and the value of the Y-intercept. You already know how to calculate the value of the slope. The value of the Y-intercept is simply the value at which the line crosses the vertical axis. In general, the algebraic expression for a straight line is given as

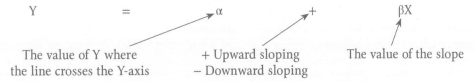

$$Y \qquad = \qquad \alpha \qquad + \qquad \beta X$$

The value of Y where   + Upward sloping   The value of the slope
the line crosses the Y-axis   − Downward sloping

For instance, in **Figure T.10**, line 1 has a slope of +1 (the line is upward sloping and therefore has a positive slope and rises by 10 units for every run of 10 units). The line crosses the y-axis at a value of 50. The equation for line 1, therefore, is

$$Y = 50 + (1)X$$

Armed with this equation, we could figure out the value of Y for any value of X. For example, when X (along the horizontal axis) has a value of 40, Y must be equal to

$$Y = 50 + 40 = 90$$

You can verify this in **Figure T.10**. In addition, we can work out values of X and Y that are not shown on the graph. For example, when X equals 200, Y equals 50 + 200 = 250.

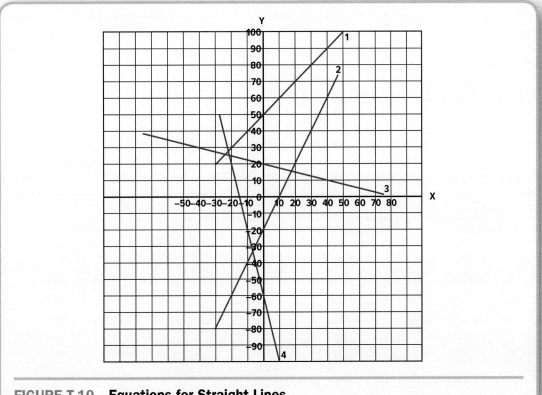

FIGURE T.10   **Equations for Straight Lines**

Let us work out the equations for the other lines shown in **Figure T.10**. Line 2 is also upward sloping, but it is steeper than line 1 and has a slope of +2 (it rises by 20 for every run of 10).

Its intercept, however, is in the negative area of the y-axis and crosses at the value of −20. The equation for line 2, then, is

$$Y = -20 + 2X$$

Again, you can check that this is correct by putting in a value for X, finding the corresponding value of Y, and looking on the graph to see if it is correct. For instance, when X has a value of 40, the equation tells us that

$$Y = -20 + 2(40) = 60$$

You can confirm in **Figure T.10** that this is indeed the case.

In contrast, line 3 has a negative slope of 0.25 and a Y-intercept at 20. Its equation, therefore, is

$$Y = 20 - 0.25X$$

Finally, line 4 has the equation

$$Y = -60 - 4X$$

Finding the Intersection Between Two Curves

A good deal of economics is concerned with investigating two variables that are related to a common factor. As we shall see in Chapter 2, the quantities of a product that consumers want to buy and the amount that producers wish to sell (demand and supply) are both related to the price of that product. Similarly, the number of employees who are willing to work and the number of people employers are willing to hire are both related to the wage offered. You will therefore often need to be able to graph two sets of data and find where they coincide.

Let us illustrate with a non-economics example. Suppose one early morning Jo is sitting at the bottom of a 2500 metre mountain, and Ed is sitting at the top. Assuming they start off at the same time (say 8 a.m.) with Jo climbing up at a rate of 400 metres per hour and Ed climbing down at 600 metres per hour, let us see if we can work out where on the mountain and at what time they will meet.

First, we need to transfer this data into a table showing where each individual climber will be at what time. This information is shown in **Table T.8**.

TABLE T.8

JO'S ASCENT		ED'S DESCENT	
Elapsed Time	**Elevation (metres)**	**Elapsed Time**	**Elevation (metres)**
0 (8 a.m.)	0	0 (8 a.m.)	2500
1 (9 a.m.)	400	1 (9 a.m.)	1900
2 (10 a.m.)	800	2 (10 a.m.)	1300
3 (11 a.m.)	1200	3 (11 a.m.)	700
4 (12 noon)	1600	4 (12 noon)	100
5 (1 p.m.)	2000	4:10 (12:10 p.m.)	0
6 (2 p.m.)	2400		
6:15 (2:15 p.m.)	2500		

We can also show their ascent and descent graphically. In **Figure T.11**, we will use the vertical axis to show the elevation and the horizontal axis to show the time elapsed. According to the graph, it seems that they will meet after exactly 2½ hours, that is, at 10:30 a.m. at an elevation of 1000 metres.

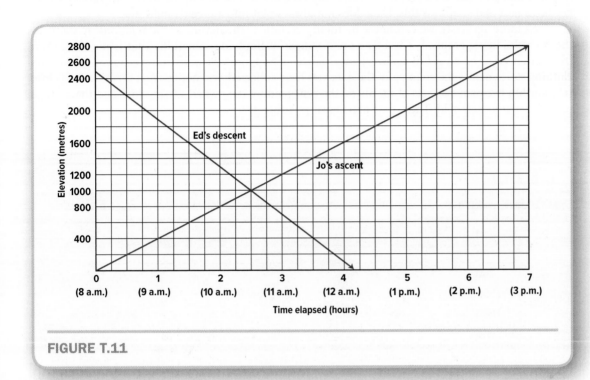

FIGURE T.11

We can confirm this result if we translate these data into an algebraic expression. Let us look at Jo's ascent. Her elevation depends on how fast she climbs and how long she climbs. We know she starts at the bottom of the mountain (elevation zero) and climbs at a rate of 400 metres per hour. If we let the elevation equal Y and the time elapsed equal X, then her ascent can be shown as

Jo's elevation: $Y = 0 + 400X$

In contrast, Ed starts at an elevation of 2500 metres and his elevation falls as he climbs down. His descent can therefore be shown as

Ed's elevation: $Y = 2500 - 600X$

To find out when and where they will meet is to recognize that whatever this point is, it occurs on the mountain at the same point for the two of them. In other words, Jo and Ed's elevation will be the same. Algebraically, we make the two equations equal and solve. Thus

$$400X = 2500 - 600X$$
$$1000X = 2500$$
$$X = 2.5$$

So they will meet after 2.5 hours (2 hours and 30 minutes), or at 10:30 a.m. To find out where they will meet, simply replace X with 2.5 in Jo's and/or Ed's elevation equation.

Jo: $400(2.5) = 1000$ (metres)

Ed: $2400 - 600(2.5) = 1000$

Graphs and Logic

Now let us look at some potential problems in illustrating data with graphs. For example, the relationship between income and consumer spending in Table T.7 is hypothetical, since we created it so that it would plot well on a graph. However, any real-world relationship between two variables may not be as neat and simple as this. Data does not always plot into a nice straight line.

Even more seriously, we can never be totally certain of the nature of the relationship between the variables being graphed. There is a great danger of implying something that is not there. You therefore need to be on guard against logical fallacies. Suppose you were doing a survey of women's clothing stores across the country. In the data you have collected, you notice what seems to be a close relationship between two sets of numbers: the rent paid by the owners of the store and the average price of wool jackets sold. These data are shown in Table T.9.

TABLE T.9

Monthly Rent (per 100 m²)	Average Jacket Price
$1500	$ 80
1600	90
1700	100
1800	110
1900	120
2000	130

The higher the monthly rent, the higher the price of jackets charged in that store. It seems clear, therefore, that the higher rent is the cause of the higher price, and the higher price is the effect of the higher rent. After all, the store owner must recoup these higher rent costs by charging her customers a higher price. If you think this, then you are guilty of the logical fallacy of *reverse causality*. As you will learn in economics, although rent and product prices are indeed related, the causality is in fact the other way around. This is because stores in certain areas can charge higher product prices because of their trendy location, and landlords charge those stores higher rents for the same reason—it is a desirable location. Higher prices, therefore, are the cause and high rents the effect. This is not obvious and illustrates how using raw economic data without sound economic theory can lead to serious error.

A second logical fallacy is that of the *omitted variable*, which can also lead to confusion over cause and effect. Table T.10 highlights this error. Here, we see hypothetical data on rates of alcoholism and the annual income levels of individuals.

TABLE T.10

Average Income Levels ($)	Alcoholism (per thousand of population)
5 000	40
15 000	35
25 000	30
35 000	25
45 000	20
55 000	15

There certainly seems to be a very close relationship between these two variables. Presented in this form, without any commentary, one is left to wonder if low income causes alcoholism or alcoholism is the cause of low income. Perhaps some people with low incomes drink in order to try to escape the effects of poverty. Or perhaps it implies that people who drink to excess have great difficulty in finding or keeping a good job. In truth, it is possible that neither of these views is true. Simply because two sets of data seem closely related does not necessarily mean that one is the cause of the other. In fact, it may well be that both are caused by an omitted variable. In the above example, it is possible, for instance, that both high alcoholism and low income levels are the result of low educational attainment.

A third fallacy can occur when people see a cause-and-effect relationship that does not really exist. This is known as the fallacy of *post hoc, ergo propter hoc*, which literally means "after this, therefore because of this." That is to say, it is a fallacy to believe that, just because one thing follows another, one is the result of the other. For example, just because my favourite soccer team always loses whenever I go to see them, that does not mean I am the cause of their losing!

There is a final fallacy you should guard against, a fallacy, unfortunately, that even the best economists commit from time to time. This is the *fallacy of composition*, which is the belief that because something is true for a part, it is true for the whole. You may have noticed, for instance, that fights occasionally break out in hockey games. These fights often occur in the corners of the rink, which makes them difficult to see. The best way for individuals to get a better view is by standing, and, of course, when everybody stands, then most people cannot see. Thus, what is true for a single fan—standing up to see better—is not true for the whole crowd. Similarly, a teacher who suggests that in order to get good grades students should sit at the front of the class is guilty of the same kind of logical fallacy!

We hope that this little primer on Canada and on graphing has been helpful. It is now time to move on to the study of economics.

Study Guide

Problems for Further Study

Indicate whether the following statements are true or false:

1. **T or F**   Canada is the world's largest country in area and has 1 percent of the world's population.

2. **T or F**   Ontario has the largest provincial economy and the largest provincial population, and it is Canada's largest province in area.

3. **T or F**   Over 50 percent of Canada's exports are resources.

4. **T or F**   The largest single source of government tax revenue is personal income taxes.

5. **T or F**   Spending on social services is the largest category of spending by (all) governments in Canada.

6. **T or F**   Three popular types of graphs are pie charts, bar graphs, and line graphs.

7. **T or F**   Since disposable income and consumer spending both rise together over time, there is a direct relationship between the two.

8. **T or F**   The slope of a straight line is measured by dividing the run by the rise.

9. **T or F**   If the equation Y = 5 + 2X were plotted, the slope of the line would be equal to 1/2.

10. **T or F**   The logical fallacy *post hoc, ergo propter hoc* means "after this, therefore because of this."

Simple Calculations

11. Table T.11 shows the dollar value of commercial sea fishing in Canada for 2002.
    a) From these data, construct a bar chart.
    b) Construct a pie chart showing the percentage of the total that each species represents.

TABLE T.11

	$millions
Groundfish (including cod, halibut, etc.)	288
Pelagic fish (including salmon and herring)	185
Lobster	594
Crab	505
Shrimp	294
Other shellfish	254
Total value	2,120

12. Complete the following schedules, and plot the following equations:
    a) Y = −200 + 2X

Y	X
	0
	100
	200
	300
	400

b) Y = 500 − 4X

Y	X
	0
	100
	200
	300
	400

13. Given the lines shown in **Figure T.12**, complete the following tables, and calculate the equations for the lines:

a)

Y	X
	0
	20
	40
	60
	80
	100

b)

Y	X
	0
	20
	40
	60
	80
	100

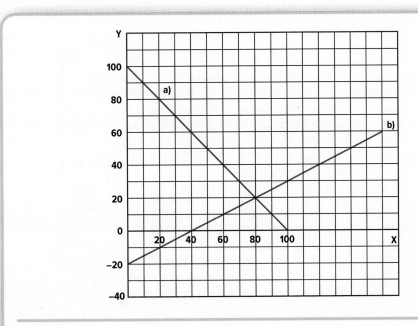

FIGURE T.12

14. The data in **Table T.12** show the results of market research done on the latest Guns 'n' Butter album. The numbers indicate the total quantity of albums that fans would purchase at the various prices.

TABLE T.12	
Price per CD	**Quantity (hundreds of thousands)**
$20	20
19	30
18	40
17	50
16	60
15	70
14	80

a) Graph the table with the price on the vertical (y) axis and the quantity on the horizontal (x) axis.
b) What is the slope of the line?
c) What is the value of the Y-intercept?
d) What is the equation for this line?

15. What are the values of the slopes of the four lines shown in **Figure T.13**?

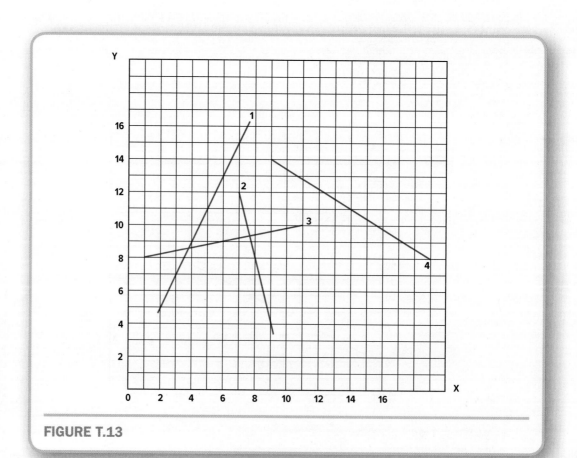

FIGURE T.13

16. What are the equations that correspond to the four lines shown in **Figure T.14**?

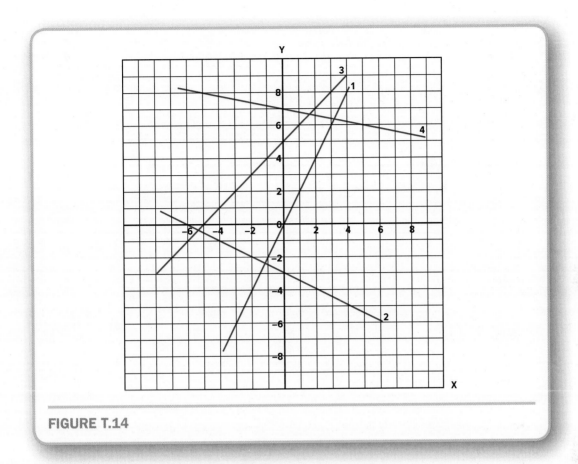

FIGURE T.14

17. Graph the following equations on a single graph, using the same scale for each axis, with the horizontal axis to 120 and the vertical axis to 200, both in squares of 10.
    a) Y = ½X
    b) Y = 40 + X
    c) Y = 160 − ½X
    d) Y = −10 + 2X

CHAPTER 1
The Economic Problem

LEARNING OBJECTIVES

At the end of this chapter, you should be able to:

LO1 Describe why economics is a very relevant discipline by demonstrating that many of the controversies in our society have a distinct economic flavour.

LO2 Define economics and then make a distinction between microeconomics and macroeconomics.

LO3 Demonstrate that because scarcity, choice, and opportunity cost are at the heart of economics, efficiency—both productive and allocative—provides a major cornerstone.

LO4 Explain why greater trade results in more productive economies.

LO5 Explain the three fundamental questions that all societies must address.

LO6 Explain the four different ways that economic societies can be organized.

LO7 Use the production possibilities model to illustrate choice and opportunity cost, as well as efficiency and unemployment.

WHAT'S AHEAD...

In this first chapter, we introduce you to the study of economics and hope to arouse your curiosity about this fascinating discipline. First, we present four controversial statements to illustrate how relevant economics really is. Next, we discuss the nature of the discipline. From this, we derive a formal definition of economics. Then, we examine what efficiency means and why it is so important. The next step is to look at three of the fundamental questions that all societies face and see how four different types of economies address them. Following that, we introduce the production possibilities model, which enables us to illustrate many of these concepts. Finally, we discuss seven important macroeconomic goals and briefly look at the policy tools used to achieve them.

A QUESTION OF RELEVANCE ...

Jon and Ashok are both avid soccer fans and play for local teams. They both like old movies and chess and use Twitter. They are both seventeen years of age, neither has a steady girlfriend, and both are vegetarians. The other thing they have in common is that their fathers are in banking. Jon's father is the executive vice-president of customer relations for the Royal Bank of Canada in Toronto. Ashok's father is a night janitor at a branch of the Bank of India in the dock area of Bombay. All of these points are relevant in forming a mental picture of a person, but you will probably agree that a person's economic circumstances have an enormous impact. In truth, economics is one of the most relevant subjects you will study.

W hat might you expect from a course in economics? Well, it will probably not help you balance your chequebook and may not be directly helpful in your choice of the right stocks or bonds to buy. But the study of economics will give you a broad understanding of how a modern market economy operates and what relationships are important within it. If you see yourself as a budding businessperson, the study of economics can offer general insights that will be helpful; however, you will not find specific tools or instructions here. Economics is an academic discipline, not a self-help or how-to course.

The common perception that economics is about money is only partly true. Economists do study money, but their goal is to better understand how it works and the effects of different central-bank money policies rather than how to make it. The study of economics may or may not help you function better in the world, but it will certainly help you to better understand how the world functions.

1.1   The Relevance of Economics

> **LO1** Describe why economics is a very relevant discipline by demonstrating that many of the controversies in our society have a distinct economic flavour.

Both of your authors believe that an introductory course in economics will be one of the most important and useful courses that you will take in your college/university career. Unfortunately, economics has acquired a reputation for being both dull and overly theoretical. Nothing could be further from the truth. In fact, economics is at the centre of many vital controversies that engage us all. One of the most effective ways to demonstrate this is to look at four important issues that are provoking public opinion and creating debate within the discipline.

Controversy One

- Economic growth is something that we should applaud and always strive to achieve.

PRO: In real terms—that is, after removing the effects of inflation—the economic well-being of the average Canadian has more than doubled in the last two generations. This has meant a huge improvement in people's lives and has come about not because the world has become fairer but because of economic growth. As a result of this growth, the individual choices available to Canadians—ranging from education and career choices to lifestyle choices—have increased significantly. In addition, economic growth contributes a great deal to social and political stability simply because finding ways to divide up a growing pie is much easier than trying to divide one that is shrinking, or even one that is stable. Over just the last few generations, economic growth has accompanied a falling birth rate, which has meant lower population growth rates. This provides welcome relief from threats to the environment.

CON: There is no question that economic growth has the benefits mentioned above but to embrace growth for growth's sake ignores the reality that there are substantial costs associated with growth as well. The threat of global warming is a classic example. If the pattern of growth we have been experiencing continues in the next couple of decades this threat will intensify—perhaps with catastrophic results. We need to shift our attitudes about economic growth by recognizing that it is the *type of growth* that really counts. If consumers become more conscious about the environmental effects of their purchases (electric cars, solar-powered houses, etc.); if large corporations accept the idea that more environmentally sound investment spending is worth the additional price tag; and if governments provide a judicious mix of incentives and tax policies that encourage more output but lower carbon emissions—then we could make a step toward embracing continued growth while addressing the more negative spinoffs of a serious problem that is clearly on humankind's horizon.

Controversy Two

- Government should use its policy tools—Employment Insurance, welfare coverage, and pension plans—to channel more income from the rich to the poor and encourage firms to pay a living wage to their employees.

PRO: There is too much poverty in this country, and the gap between the rich and poor is growing. In Canada, the average after-tax income disparity has increased dramatically in the last twenty years. While it is true that during this period those in both the lowest and the middle income quintile experienced a percentage rise in average income, those in the highest quintile saw their incomes rise by much higher percentage. Consequently, the difference between the top and the bottom income group increased by over 40 percent. This is a significant rise in income disparity, and a first move to reversing this trend would be an increase in government benefits and in pressure put on firms to pay a living wage.

CON: The solution to the problem of poverty is not to pay higher taxes for more unemployment coverage, welfare, and public pensions nor is it to impel firms to pay what some consider is a "living wage." Higher taxes, and higher wages, are a disincentive to the job creators who work hard and are willing to take on the risks of expanding more investment in the private economy. In contrast, polices that stimulate more growth will ultimately benefit all Canadians. This means lower, not higher, taxes. The ultimate answer to the issue of poverty is to grow the economy and enlarge the size of the income pie.

Controversy Three

- The time has come to introduce road pricing in congested Canadian cities to reduce traffic during peak "rush hours."

PRO: Economists know that people respond to financial incentives, and charging drivers for using highways and bridges (more during rush hours and less for off-peak times) will spread out road usage and thereby reduce congestion. This would also raise needed revenue for more road construction—highways and bridge are very expensive to build—and save lives through reduced accident rates.

CON: Our system of unrestricted and free road usage has worked for generations, and road pricing would simply be another government tax grab and an unfair burden on Canadian drivers. It would also mean that those with low income would pay proportionately more of their incomes for road fees than those with high-incomes. This is true for both drivers and non-drivers, since the bulk of all our purchases are transported by road.

Controversy Four

- Globalization only benefits large multinational corporations, not ordinary people.

PRO: Globalization leads to large corporations moving jobs from rich countries to poor countries. This creates a race to the bottom among the poor countries that are willing to maintain weak environmental- and labour-standards regulations to appease the corporations and thus attract new foreign investment. While this lowers the cost of production for the corporation, it comes at the expense of the people whose middle-level (and relatively well paid) jobs have been displaced.

CON: Globalization means increased world trade, and economic theory clearly demonstrates that more trade means more benefits to those who trade. In fact, UN statistics demonstrate that, within the last twenty years, a billion people in the world have been pulled up out of "abject poverty" (less than $1 a day income) into higher-income categories. Much of this is the direct result of the increased trade associated with globalization.

We could have examined many other controversies in addition to the four above. For example: Should we introduce private-market elements into our public health care system? Is a carbon-trading system better that a carbon tax to fight climate change? Are economic incentives better than government regulations for addressing environmental issues? But the point is made: Our complex society with its diverse interests and political views is rife with controversy.

We have put these four sample debates up front not because economists have the right answers to any of them but to demonstrate that almost any issue that faces us today as a society—and thus also as individuals—has an economic dimension. In short, economics is one of the most relevant courses you will ever take.

1.2   What Is Economics?

> **LO2**   Define economics and then make a distinction between microeconomics and macroeconomics.

From our discussion of controversies, are we to conclude that any person's position on these issues is just a matter of opinion? No, we do not believe that. Economics, as you will discover, provides a unique way of approaching various controversies, helping us reach reasoned positions on these and other vital issues. You will, we hope, discover the importance of economic theories in doing this.

We all ask questions to make sense of our existence. The answers to What? When? and Where? are reasonably straightforward, because they involve questions of fact. But the most important question of all, and often the most difficult to answer, Why?, always involves cause and effect and addresses the relationship between facts. Few believe that things occur randomly in our world; we recognize that actions are related. A road is covered in ice and a car crashes; a person smokes heavily for forty years and dies of lung cancer; an army of beetles bores into a tree trunk and the tree falls. Explaining why these things happen is a matter of uncovering the links between phenomena. That is what theory is all about: explaining *why* things happen.

But in order to begin an explanation, we first need to know *what* happened. Theory is *not* just a matter of opinion; it is built on the solid foundation of facts, or what are termed **positive statements**. Positive statements are assertions about the world that can be verified using empirical data.

"Sidney Crosby scored thirty goals last year" and "The unemployment rate in Canada is presently 6.2 percent" are both positive statements, because their truth can be verified by finding the appropriate data. But "Sidney Crosby should score more goals" or "The unemployment rate in Canada is far too high" are both what are termed **normative statements** because they are based on a person's beliefs or value systems and, as such, cannot be verified by appealing to facts. Note also that positive statements may not always be easily or readily verified. For instance, the statement "It will rain tomorrow" is a positive statement despite the fact that it cannot be verified until tomorrow.

Economic theory uses what we call the **scientific method** to find a relationship between positive statements. Consider the statement *If the price of apples decreases then people will buy more apples*. In order to build a theory about apple prices and apple purchases, we need to set up a simple *hypothesis*. For example, the lower the price of a product, the greater the quantity that will be bought. But along with the hypothesis, we need to define the terms involved. What types of apples are we talking about—Granny Smiths, Galas, or all types? And what price are we considering? Wholesale? Retail? Vancouver prices? Ottawa prices? Besides this, we need to spell out the assumptions (conditions) under which the hypothesis is true: People will buy more apples when the price falls, *as long as peoples' incomes do not fall* or *as long as the prices of other fruits remain the same*, and so on. The hypothesis is now ready for testing by gathering actual data and then accepting, rejecting, or possibly modifying the relationship under consideration.

The scientific method implies, among other things, that the results the theory predicts should be valid regardless of who does the testing and that different people should be able to repeat the tests and obtain the same results.

However, some say there is no way economics can ever be considered a true science, even though the discipline does use the scientific method. In some senses, this is true. Economics can never approach the pure sciences in terms of universality. It can never predict how every (or even one particular) consumer will react to a drop in the price of apples. But it can predict how the average consumer will react; that is, it deals in *generalities*. It is also true that the time lag between the cause and the effect is often far longer in the social sciences than it is in the pure sciences, which makes theorizing a lot more difficult. But to criticize economics because it is too abstract and unrealistic is not really fair. In fact, it might be suggested that the more realistic economic theory becomes, the less valuable it is. No

The scientific method can be used to explain the apple market.

Kentoh/Dreamstime.com

one expects a map to be "realistic"; if it were, every tree, house, and road would have to be drawn to scale, and the scale would have to be 1:1! So, while a map can capture a great deal of reality, trying to make it even more realistic can also make it less useful.

You may have heard jokes about economists, such as, "What do you get when you put five economists in the same room? Answer: Six opinions." Economists do often disagree with one another, as is easily seen in the popular media. This is a natural by-product of a discipline that is part science and part art. An important reason for such disagreement is that, like everyone else, economists have particular sets of values accumulated over a lifetime, and these values vary, sometimes radically, from person to person. Nonetheless, if each of us uses the scientific method in developing our arguments, lively debate can be fruitful despite the different value systems with which we started.

It is also true, however, that there is wide agreement among economists on many questions—which is remarkable given that they ask a wide variety of questions many of which are not asked in other disciplines. For example, why do firms produce some goods internally and buy others in the market? Why do nations sometimes both export and import similar goods? Why does society provide some things to children without charge (education) but not other things (food)?

Trying to understand economic theory can be challenging and certainly does not come easily, but the rewards, in terms of a better understanding of the world we live in, are great. Economics is the study of ideas, and in a very real way this is the most important thing you can study. One of the most famous of twentieth-century economists, John Maynard Keynes, said: "The ideas of economists, both when they are right and when they are wrong, are more powerful than is commonly understood. . . . But soon or late, it is ideas, not vested interests, which are dangerous for good or evil."[1]

There are any number of definitions of economics but most agree that it is about how best to use the resources we have available. For instance:

> Economics studies the ways that humans and societies organize themselves to make choices about the use of scarce resources, which are used to produce the goods and services necessary to satisfy human wants and needs.

This gives us the essence of the discipline. We need, then, to understand how societies attempt to satisfy seemingly unlimited human wants in the face of limited resources. As we shall see in the next section, it means that we humans are faced with some very difficult choices.

 ADDED DIMENSION

Just What Is an Economist?

When a person says "I am an economist" he/she might actually be doing one of a variety of jobs. Broadly speaking these work types fall into four categories.

You are familiar with the first type: *academic economists* who are found teaching in educational institutions. In addition to their teaching duties, these economists also engage in research activities and sometimes are seconded to governments and other organizations for specific projects or advisory duties.

The second type might be called *financial economists*. These work in the many wealth-management firms and often engaged directly with members of the general public to help them plan their retirement or establish a safe, steady flow of income from the money they have acquired through their work or from an inheritance. These economists might also be employed at banks engaging in similar work.

Next, we have what might be called *corporate economists* who, as the name implies, are employed by large corporations (banks would be included here as well) and are engaged in relevant research, and sometimes branch out into broad management roles of many types, such as vice-president of domestic operations.

Finally, we have what might be called *governmental or organizational economists*. These work directly for provincial or federal governments in virtually every ministry collecting and analyzing data and are often engaged in research. Others work for any one of over 500 non-governmental organizations such as the World Bank, the International Monetary Fund, Oxfam, or the World Wide Fund for Nature.

If you are still wondering what you might major in, you might well consider economics. This is a major that closes no doors (for example, many students of law majored in economics as undergraduates) and will likely sharpen your ability to think logically and engage in the process of sound decision making—in work as well as in life.

Finally, we need to make the distinction between macroeconomics and microeconomics. **Macroeconomics** is the study of how the major components of the economy—such as consumer spending, investment spending, government policies, and exports—interact. It includes most of the topics a beginning student would expect to find in an economics course: unemployment, inflation, interest rates, taxation and spending policies of governments, and national income determination.

Microeconomics studies the outcomes of decisions made by individual people and firms, and includes such topics as supply and demand, the study of the costs of production, and the nature of market structures—competitive or monopolistic. This distinction can be described metaphorically as a comparison between the use of the wide-angle lens and the telephoto lens of a camera. In the first

---

[1] John Maynard Keynes, *The General Theory of Employment, Interest and Money* (1936).

instance (macroeconomics) we see the big picture. In the second instance (microeconomics) a very small part of that big picture appears in much more detail. Most colleges and universities offer a separate course for each of these fields of study.

The following table will help you understand the distinction between macro- and microeconomics.

Topic	Micro View	Macro View
Prices	Of particular products, such as gasoline or real estate	Of a composite of all prices, such as the Consumer Price Index, and the inflation associated with prices rising
Production	Of particular firms, such as Ford or Apple, or industries such as wheat or oil	Of the whole economy, such as Canada's gross domestic product and its influence on economic growth
Incomes	Wages by profession or factor incomes such as the amount going to wages and profits	Total (national) income, regardless of the source, and how this relates to the economic well-being of the population
Employment	By firm, industry, or occupation	Overall national employment (and unemployment)
Taxes	As they affect individual take-home pay or the profits of a particular firm	As they affect total consumption spending and government revenue

 TEST YOUR UNDERSTANDING

Find answers on the McGraw-Hill online resource.

1. Identify each of the following statements as either positive (P) or normative (N).

  a) The federal government's budget this year is the largest in history.

  b) The national debt is at a manageable level and therefore is nothing to worry about.

  c) The price of gasoline is higher than it needs to be.

  d) Rising Canadian exports are creating many new jobs in the country.

2. Identify which of the following topics would likely appear in a microeconomics course (Mi) and which in a macroeconomics course (Ma).

  a) The price of iPods

  b) Unemployment rates

  c) The presence of monopolies

  d) The rate of economic growth

SECTION SUMMARY

a) Economics is a social science that uses the *scientific method* in order to construct theories which explain the world about us. In doing so, it attempts to explain the relationship between events looking at actual data. It needs to be careful to distinguish between facts (positive statements) and personal beliefs (normative statements).

b) The discipline of economics is subdivided into microeconomics, which studies the decisions made by people and firms, and macroeconomics, which studies the results of those decisions, how the major components of the whole economy interact, and how well an economy achieves economic goals such as full employment and economic growth.

1.3   Efficiency and Allocation

> **LO3** Demonstrate that because scarcity, choice, and opportunity cost are at the heart of economics, efficiency—both productive and allocative—provides a major cornerstone.

Economists put a great deal of emphasis on scarcity and the need to economize. Individual households face income limitations and therefore must allocate income among alternative uses. Most individuals also face a scarcity of time and must somehow decide where to spend time and where to conserve it. In the same sense, an economy as a whole has limited resources and must allocate those resources among competing uses.

Thus, economists see **resources** (or **factors of production** or **inputs**) as *scarce* in the sense that no economy has sufficient resources to be able to produce all the goods and services everyone wants. Even though there may be some people who say they have all they want, there are millions of people who possess a seemingly endless list of wants, with millions more like them waiting to be born. Since the economy cannot produce all that everyone wants, the resources available for production are scarce.

And exactly what constitutes a resource? Well, of the myriad different resources that are or have been used to produce goods and services, economists are generally agreed that there are, in fact, four categories: labour, capital, land, and enterprise. **Labour** refers to a broad spectrum of human effort, ranging from the work of a skilled physician to that of a construction worker. **Capital** is made up of the tools, equipment, factories, and buildings used in the production process, and is not to be confused with financial capital, such as money, stocks, or bonds. **Land** is defined as any natural resource, such as fertile soil, forests, fishing grounds, or minerals in the ground. Finally, **enterprise** (some economists prefer the term *entrepreneurship*) is that very special human talent that is able to apply abstract ideas in a practical way. Entrepreneurs are innovators who invent new products or devise new forms of organization and are willing to take the risks to see such projects through to successful completion.

In a market economy, incomes are earned through the payment of wages, interest, rent, and profits to the private owners of the factors of production: labour, capital, land, and enterprise. The general term **wages** includes all forms of payment to the various kinds of labour services such as salaries, stock bonuses, gratuities, commissions, and various employee benefits. **Interest** means payments to the factor of real capital. **Rent** is the income received for the use of the factor of land, such as royalty payments for a stand of timber. Finally, **profit** is the return on entrepreneurial effort.

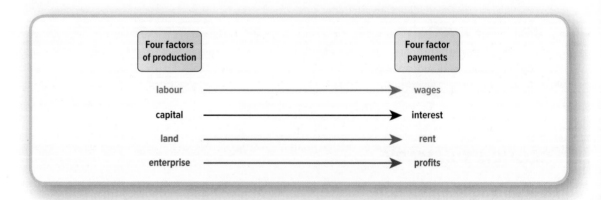

Now, the way these four factors of production are combined is what economists mean by a **technology**. A technology does not necessarily imply the use of things like machines or computers; it simply means a method of production. However, whatever technology we use to produce goods and services, the fact remains that we are simply not capable of producing everything people want.

Therefore, some kind of mechanism must be put in place for choosing what will be produced and, by implication, what will not be. This is why economics is sometimes called the *science of choice*.

In short:

> In the face of people's unlimited wants and society's limited productive resources, choice becomes a necessity. Because of these choices, the decision to produce one thing means that some other thing will not be produced.

This last point is so fundamental that economists have coined a special term to identify it: **opportunity cost**. For instance, suppose that government is considering the purchase of new military aircraft with a price tag of $5 billion. In the conventional sense, that is their cost. However, economists would argue that it is more revealing to measure the cost of the helicopters in terms of, say, ten hospitals that will not be built because a budget constraint does not allow the purchase of both. Opportunity costs can thus be defined as what must be given up as a result of making a particular choice: in this case, the hospitals are given up for the aircraft.

Let us continue to look at the concept of opportunity cost by shifting to a microeconomic context. Suppose it is lunchtime on Saturday and you have just returned home from your morning job at a local convenience store. You have the whole afternoon ahead of you and are wondering what best to do. One alternative would be to have a nice sleep on the sofa. You deserve it. Alternatively, you might hang out with friends at the mall. But then, you are going to see them all at tomorrow's game. Perhaps a nice bike ride? After all, it's a pleasant afternoon and you could do with some good exercise. But at the back of your mind you realize you need to study because two exams are coming up next week. What to do? Since you obviously can't do everything, you have to make a choice, and it really comes down to either studying or cycling. And what are the costs of each?

Well, economists look at costs in terms of benefits forgone. If you were to study for the rest of the afternoon, you will be sacrificing the benefits of cycling—better health, feeling good, and being fitter. And what if you were to go cycling instead? Well, this would mean that the benefit of a better grade in the upcoming exams is compromised. Notice that we have not viewed the costs in this situation in terms of money, which is the normal way, because many sacrifices in life do not involve money. But they are costly, nevertheless.

Recognizing that there are opportunity costs involved in making any decision forces us to rethink our idea of what we mean by "free." Simply because money does not change hands does not mean that a product is free. For the individual, the constraint is either a limited amount of time, as we just saw, or a limited amount of income. For example, you might think of the cost of going to two movies on the weekend as the sacrifice of a haircut. If you want to think of both these choices (two movies or one haircut) as each costing about $20, that is fine. But thinking of the one as costing the other is often more effective. In general, your income will not allow you to have everything you may want, and so you are forced to make choices about what you buy. And the cost of these choices can be measured in terms of what must be given up as a result of making the choice.

A classic example of this trade-off in economics is sacrificing consumer goods to produce more capital goods. As we shall see later in the chapter, nations that wish to grow more quickly can achieve this if they produce more factories, tools, and equipment—more capital goods—that are used to make other goods. But, of course, an increase in capital goods production necessarily means a reduction in the output of **consumer goods and services**, which are defined as products used to satisfy human wants and needs. Note that only consumers buy consumer goods and only firms (or governments) buy capital goods.

Our next example of opportunity cost is one that faces many students who have to choose between taking more courses at college or university and continuing to work in a part-time job. If a student is presently taking three courses and working twenty hours a week, and feels that this is a full-time load, then taking five courses next semester may well mean giving up the job. Thus, the opportunity cost of the two extra courses is the income sacrificed as a result of no longer working at

IN A NUTSHELL …

It's Saturday night and Alex has $12 left in his entertainment budget. Which to choose … ?

The concept of opportunity cost reminds Alex that **you can't have both**.

the part-time job. We should also point out that there must be some benefit to be gained from the alternative you do choose. For instance, returning to our example above, if you chose the two movies, the benefit from that choice, in your view, exceeds (or at least equals) the opportunity cost of the haircut.

A society faces a similar set of choices, imposed not by limited income but by a constraint on the quantity and quality of the available factors of production.

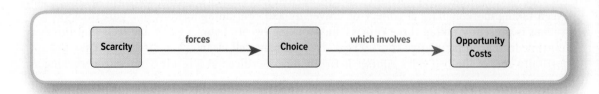

TEST YOUR UNDERSTANDING

3. Below is a list of economic goods. Decide whether each is a consumer good (C), a capital good (K), or possibly both (B), depending on the context in which it is used.

   a) a jackhammer

   b) a carton of cigarettes

   c) an office building

   d) a toothbrush

   e) a hammer

   f) a farm tractor

4. Below is a list of resources. Indicate whether the resource in question is labour (L), capital (K), land (N), or enterprise (E):

   a) a bar-code scanner in a supermarket

   b) fresh drinking water

   c) copper deposits in a mine

   d) the work of a systems analyst

   e) the first application of e-technology to an economics textbook

   f) an office building

IT'S NEWS TO ME ...

The U.S. federal government has been subsidizing public school breakfast programmes in various designated poverty-area school districts for a long time. In a recent year over $3.3 billion flowed through this effort reaching 16 million schoolchildren in 89,000 schools. Children from households designated as "in poverty" received these meals free of charge.

Canada does not have such a federal programme but some provinces and a few large cities do have a limited version of free school-breakfasts in some schools.

Recently, we see an example of the private sector stepping up in this effort when the *Vancouver Sun* newspaper sponsored an "Adopt-a-School Breakfast Club" at the local Douglas Road Elementary School in Burnaby. The SFU Beedie School of Business then agreed to do a follow-up study of this experiment and reports a "significant positive impact on student performance and a reduction in the incidence of late attendance."

Source: *Star Power Reporting.* Summer 2016.

I. Is there such a thing as a "free meal"?
   a) Yes, if the money comes from private donors.
   b) Yes, if the money is provided by the government.
   c) Yes, if it is just a transfer of resources from one sector to another.
   d) No, if it involves the use of resources which have alternative uses.

II. In economics, what does "free" mean?
   a) It does not involve a cost to taxpayers.
   b) It does not involve a cost for consumers.
   c) It does not lead to the reduction of depletable resources.
   d) It does not require a payment by anyone.

III. How would an economist measure the cost of these school meals?
   a) The dollar costs of the labour and materials involved in their production
   b) The value of other activities that the funds could have been spent on
   c) The total cost to taxpayers or the corporate donors of providing for these meals
   d) The costs that parents would otherwise have incurred in providing these meals

The Importance of Efficiency

Perhaps not surprisingly, economists, like any other group of people, do not agree on the most important economic goals that an economy should pursue. Nor are they necessarily in agreement on the best methods to achieve those goals. However, they are generally in agreement on the importance of *efficiency*. In fact, this term crops up with great regularity in economic literature. As a result, it is important to have some initial understanding of what the term means and why economists attach so much importance to it.

One of the simplest ways of expressing efficiency is to suggest that it implies getting the most for the least. For example, a technology that requires the use of 10 units of inputs in order to produce an output of 100 units of goods and services would be preferable to one that uses 20 units of inputs to produce those same 100 units of output. Similarly, the same technology that uses 10 inputs to produce 100 units of output would be considered inferior to another technology that uses those same inputs but could produce an output of 150 units. In other words, economists define **productive efficiency** in terms of the ratio of outputs produced to inputs used. Those technologies that produce at a lower ratio will result in lower costs of production.

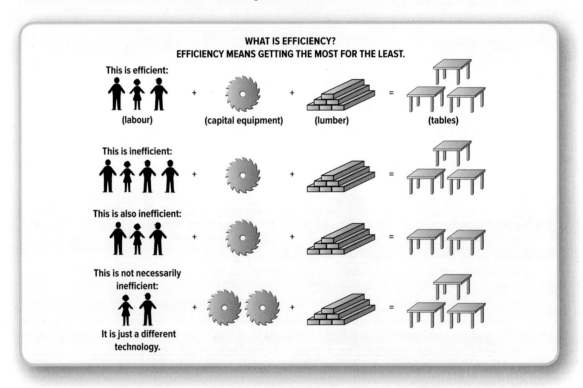

When you hear the term *productivity* used in the popular press it is usually referring to productive efficiency and is often measured in terms of the amount of output per hour of labour (or machine) input. If we want to be careful in our use of resources, it is of great importance that every one of us tries to be efficient. However, productive efficiency does not take us far enough. It is all right to produce things at low cost, but it is of little use if people are simply not interested in buying them. For instance, what would be the point of producing big-screen TVs at $50 each if they could only play programs in black and white? In other words, it is just as important to be efficient in what we produce as in how we produce it. Societies therefore need to ensure that the right type of products are produced, those that match the demands of the public. This is what economists mean by **allocative efficiency**.

Allocative efficiency puts the emphasis on the production of the right type of products. However, since all of us have different tastes, the right products for you might not be the right ones for someone else. So it is important that products be allocated efficiently among people. In *Filthy Lucre*, Joseph Heath gives an amusing example illustrating this idea. Imagine you have been given the task of allocating candies to a group of children at a birthday party. Trying to be fair, you count out the different types of candies so that each child gets an equal number of each. But you discover that some of the kids are not too happy. One is most upset because he has been given peanut brittle, and the poor boy is allergic to peanuts! One girl positively detests raisins. Some kids hate dark chocolate, others milk chocolate. You can see that without increasing the overall quantity of candies, you could increase the general happiness of these children just by redistributing the candies. The kids might easily handle this allocation themselves by trading, something that children tend to do quite naturally.

So what is the best method of allocating goods and resources? How do we decide who gets what? In general, there are five different ways:

1. *First come, first served.* This is the time-honoured way of distributing things in high demand. It means that products are given according to the order in which people apply whether that's done by lining up, by phoning in, or by registering on a website.
2. *Lottery.* Everyone is entered into a draw and has an equal chance of obtaining the product.
3. *Sellers' preference.* This means that the seller of the product makes the decision on who gets what and what criteria will be used.
4. *Government decree.* Here, the ruling authority decides on the allocation.
5. *The market.* This is where the forces of demand and supply determine how much each buyer obtains. To a large extent, this is based upon how much people are willing to pay and how much they can afford. It is this method of allocation that gets the most attention from economists and our next chapter will try to explain in some detail.

SECTION SUMMARY

a) Scarcity forces choice (for society, government, and the individual), and choice involves an opportunity cost which is the sacrificed benefit of the next best alternative.

b) Efficiency implies that economies make the best use of their resources and technology. There are two major types of efficiency: productive efficiency and allocative efficiency, and both are important.

c) There are five different allocative methods: first come, first served; lottery; sellers' preference; government decree; and the market.

1.4 The Power of Trade

LO4 Explain why greater trade results in more productive economies.

In the last quarter-century we have been witnessing something very significant: economies that put an emphasis on the market system and international trade—Canada, South Korea, and China, for example—continued to enjoy economic growth and a rising standard of living for their citizens, while economies that rely more on centrally controlled systems and self-sufficiency—the former USSR or today's Cuba and North Korea, for example—faltered.

Adam Smith, the father of economics, gave us a simple but elegant idea that goes a long way toward explaining why, throughout history, some economies have prospered, while others have not. This is the recognition that *voluntary trade* always benefits both parties to the trade. If two peasants voluntarily trade a sack of rice for two bags of carrots, then we can assume that they both must feel that they have benefited, as otherwise they would not have done it. If you buy a slice of pizza and a pop for lunch for $3.50, then we must assume that you feel you have gained by giving up the money and receiving the lunch—otherwise, why did you do it? Likewise, the owner of the business that sold you the lunch must feel that she gained, or she would not have been willing to offer the lunch for sale. There is a gain to both parties engaged in voluntary trade.

It follows that *the more trade there is, the greater are the overall benefits that accrue to those engaged in the trade.* It comes as a surprise to many people that the same principle that applies to individuals in this regard also applies to nations. We can demonstrate that this is true by using the concept of opportunity costs to construct a simple example of two hypothetical countries—Athens and Sparta—each of which produces only two goods: bread (a consumer good) and plows (a capital good).

Suppose that the maximum quantities that can be produced of each product are (in thousands of units):

Athens	20 bread	or	10 plows
Sparta	10 bread	or	20 plows

If each country is self-sufficient (no trade between them) and each devotes half its resources to producing the two products, the output in each country would be:

| **Athens** | 10 bread | and | 5 plows |
| **Sparta** | 5 bread | and | 10 plows |

Clearly, the combined output of the two economies is 15 units of bread and 15 plows. It is also clear that Athens is far better at producing bread and Sparta is much better at producing plows. Thus, if the two countries could overcome their sense of rivalry, and if Athens concentrated on producing bread and Sparta on producing plows, then the total combined production of the two countries would be:

| **Athens** | 20 bread | (no plows) |
| **Sparta** | 20 plows | (no bread) |

With specialization, the two countries can produce a combined total that is five more of each product (20 units of bread and 20 plows) than when each was self-sufficient. This illustrates why specialization is so important—countries enjoy more output when they do what they do best (produce only the products with the lowest opportunity cost) rather than trying to produce both products. For Athens, the opportunity cost of producing plows is a large sacrifice in bread production, while in Sparta the opportunity cost of producing bread is a large sacrifice in plow production. However, when they both specialize in what they do best, big benefits can be gained. But to reap the benefits of specialization, trade becomes imperative—unless, of course, the countries are happy just consuming one product (which is most unlikely). In our example, if Athens were to trade 10 bread for 10 plows from Sparta, both countries would finish up with 10 units of bread and 10 plows—an improvement for both.

Returning to our original point about market economies versus planned economies, we know that specialization and trade are maximized when markets are used extensively. This simple illustration helps us understand that every economy faces important choices about what to produce. Let us expand on this point by turning to the three fundamental economic questions faced by every economy.

SECTION SUMMARY

Greater specialization and trade can make economies more productive.

1.5   The Three Fundamental Questions

LO5 Explain the three fundamental questions that all societies must address.

A broad perspective on the discipline of economics can be obtained by focusing on the three fundamental questions of economics: *What? How?* and *For whom?* That is, economics is about what and how much gets produced, how it is produced, and who gets it.

What to Produce?

As we have just seen, underlying the question of *what* should be produced is the reality of scarcity. Any society has only a fixed amount of resources at its disposal. Therefore, it must have a system in place to make an endless number of decisions about production, from big decisions such as whether the government should buy more military aircraft or build more hospitals down to more mundane ones such as how many brands of breakfast cereal should be produced.

If we decide to produce hospitals, should we produce ten without research facilities for the study of genetics or eight without and one with such facilities? Should society exploit natural resources faster to create more jobs and more tax revenue, or slower to conserve these resources for the future? Should our resources be directed toward more preschool day-care facilities so that parents are not so tied to the home? Or should those same resources be directed toward increasing the number of graduate students studying science and technology so that the Canadian economy can win the competitive international race in the twenty-first century?

Let us once again emphasize that no economist would claim to have the *right* answer to any of these questions. That is no more the role of an economist than it is of any other member of society. What the economist can do, however, is identify and measure both the benefits and the costs of any one answer—of any one choice.

How to Produce?

Let us move on to the second fundamental economic question that every society must somehow answer: *What is the most appropriate technology to employ?* We could reword this question by asking *how* we should produce what we choose to produce.

For example, there are many ways to produce ten kilometres of highway. At one extreme, a labour-intensive method of production could be used involving rock crushed with hammers, roadbed carved from the landscape with shovels, and material moved in wheelbarrows. The capital equipment used in this method is minimal. The labour used is enormous, and the time it will take is considerable. At the other extreme, a capital-intensive method could be used involving large earthmoving and tarmac-laying machines, surveying equipment, and relatively little—but more highly skilled—labour. In between these two extremes is a large variety of capital–labour mixes that could also produce the new highway.

The answer to the question of how best to build the highway involves, among other things, knowing the costs of the

Capital-intensive technologies using heavy equipment are the most appropriate methods in many countries because they are relatively cheap.

Steve Allen/Getty Images

various resources that might be used. Remember that technology means the way the various factors of production are combined to obtain output. The most appropriate technology for a society to use (the best way to combine resources) depends, in general, on the opportunity costs of these resources. Thus, in the example above, the best way to build a highway depends on the opportunity costs of labour and of capital as well as the productivity of each factor.

For Whom?

Now, let's move to the third fundamental economic question that every society must somehow answer: *For whom?* Here, we are asking how the total output of a society should be shared among its citizens. In the end, we are really asking how the total income in a society should be distributed. Should it involve an equal share for all, or should it, perhaps, be based on people's needs? Alternatively, should it be based on the contribution of each member of society? If so, how should this contribution be measured—in numbers of hours, in skill level, or in some combination of the two? Further, how should we define what constitutes an important skill and which ones are less important?

Wrapped up in all this is the question of the ownership of resources and whether it is better for certain resources (such as land and capital) be owned by society as a whole or by private individuals. In short, the *for whom* question cannot be adequately addressed unless we look at society's attitude toward the private ownership of resources and the question of who has the power to make crucial decisions.

You can see that in addressing the *for whom* question, other questions about the fairness of income distribution, the role of incentives, and the ownership of resources all come into play. John Stuart Mill pointed out, nearly 150 years ago, that once an economy's goods are produced and the initial market distribution of income has occurred, society can intervene in any fashion it wishes in order to redistribute such income; that is, there are no laws of distribution other than the ones that society wants to impose. Whether this observation by Mill gives enough consideration to the incentive for productive effort remains an open question to this day.

GREAT ECONOMISTS: JOHN STUART MILL

John Stuart Mill (1806–73) is considered the last great economist of the classical school. His *Principles of Political Economy*, first published in England in 1848, was the leading textbook in economics for 40 years. Raised by a strict disciplinarian father (James), John Stuart began to learn Greek at the age of three, authored a history of Roman government by 11, and studied calculus at 12—but did not take up economics until age 13. Not surprisingly, this unusual childhood later led to a mental crisis. Mill credited his decision to put his analytical pursuits on hold and take up an appreciation of poetry as the primary reason for his recovery. He was a true humanitarian, who held a great faith in human progress, had a love of liberty, and was an advocate of extended rights for women.

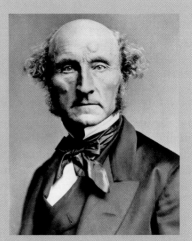

Pictorial Press Ltd/Alamy Stock Photo

How these three fundamental questions actually get answered depends, to a large extent, on the way that different societies organize themselves. Let us now look at the four types of economic organization.

SECTION SUMMARY

The three fundamental questions that all societies must somehow answer are:

- What is the right combination of consumer goods to produce, and what is the right balance between consumer goods and capital goods?
- How should these various goods be produced?
- Who is to receive what share of these goods once they are produced?

1.6   Four Types of Economies: The Four Cs

> **LO6**   Explain the four different ways that economic societies can be organized.

Societies have, throughout history, developed systems to coordinate their economies in order to answer the fundamental questions of what to produce, how, and for whom. Each of the numerous possible systems has used some blend of the four Cs: cooperation, command, custom, and competition. Whatever blend was used, it was a reflection of who owns and who controls the important resources of that economy.

Co-operative Economies

In the foraging societies of prehistory, the few tools, weapons, and cooking items the people possessed were commonly owned, belonging to the band as a whole and not to any one individual. Since these bands were nomadic, they did not preserve or store food, because carrying it around was difficult and seemed unnecessary. They lived very much a day-to-day existence. This meant that these societies did not produce a surplus above subsistence that could be used to support non-producers. Consequently, since all were producers of the necessaries of life, they had no armies, no leaders, no priests, and no ruling hierarchy. The result was a society where decision making was democratic and egalitarian. In short, the members of foraging bands relied primarily on *cooperation* with one another in order to survive the dual threats of starvation and predators.

It is difficult, if not impossible, to find an example of a country in the modern age in which the economic decisions are made cooperatively by all the citizens. However, we can find many examples of small, self-contained communes in which there is an emphasis on common ownership and consensus decision making. Included would be the kibbutzim of Israel or religious communities such as the Hutterites in the Canadian Prairies or (historically) the Doukhobors of British Columbia. Even the internal decision-making process in today's large corporations, one that stresses the use of team play and group consensus, is a form of cooperative behaviour. This same point can be made in reference to most family units within our society. Further, what, if not cooperation, would one call the fact that nearly half of all adults in our society engage (at some point in their lives) in voluntary unpaid activities such as coaching soccer or helping out at a local hospital or community centre?

Command Economies

There are many examples of command economies in the ancient world. In the empires of ancient Egypt and Rome, we see that the most important resource was slaves, and whoever owned slaves was, almost by definition, rich and powerful. An elite group headed by a pharaoh or emperor made decisions and dictates that were ruthlessly enforced. The fundamental questions of what to produce, how to produce, and who reap the rewards of production were answered by this elite, whose decisions were unopposed.

To find examples of command economies in the modern world, we need look no further than the brutal totalitarian regimes of the twentieth century: fascism in Italy, Nazism in Germany, and communism in the Soviet Union. In all three examples the state, which was totally controlled by the very few, had significant influences on the *what, how,* and *for whom* questions and also controlled many aspects of routine life.

Communism, as seen in the twentieth century, owes a great deal to the writings of Karl Marx, who was outraged at the cruel injustices of early capitalism. He felt that what he termed the "internal contradictions of capitalism" would eventually lead to its self-destruction. What he meant by this is that while production, as a result of the industrial revolution, was becoming increasingly "socialized" in that it needed a great deal of planning and coordination in order to mass-produce products, the ownership was still based upon the private ownership of resources. Marx argued that this "dichotomy" would eventually lead to its collapse. While this, of course, never happened, many subsequent critics of capitalism (the market system) were concerned at what they considered to be the chaotic and unpredictable nature of the system. In the twentieth century a number of countries, including France and Sweden (and in an extreme form the USSR), all introduced state planning into their economies to prevent then from suffering oversupply, bottlenecks, and shortages so that state investment behaviour could be modified in a timely fashion to reduce the incidence of market disequilibrium.

 GREAT ECONOMISTS: KARL MARX

Karl Marx (1818–1883) was a social philosopher and founder of scientific socialism. He is the author of the *Manifesto of the Communist Party* and of the seminal work *Das Kapital* (1869).

He was born in Trier, Prussia (Germany) to a Jewish family who converted to Protestantism. After studying in Germany, he spent most of his adult life in England.

His very name has called forth huge doses of vitriol, disgust, and hatred, and in almost equal measure he has been admired, revered, and worshipped; but what is undeniable is that he is difficult to ignore and has proven to be one of the most influential figures in history. The number of people who hate Marx without actually having read him is probably equal to those who venerate him also without bothering to do much reading.

© Ingram Publishing

Customary Economies

In the age of feudalism in Europe, which filled the vacuum left by the fall of the Roman Empire, we see power centred on the ownership of land. The landowners—royalty, the aristocracy, and the Church—were very powerful, and everyone else knew his or her place within this rigidly hierarchical system. It was the age of *custom* (or *tradition*), which dictated who performed which task—sons followed the work of their fathers and daughters followed the roles of their mothers—and traditional technology was superior to new ways of doing things, since it had been tried and tested and could therefore be trusted. Above all, custom required that serfs turn over a portion of their produce to the feudal lords.

Even very traditional societies can have a small role for the market.

Marion Bull/GetStock.com

In the modern age, custom is very much alive in a number of Islamic republics such as Iran, where traditional values, enforced by religion, dominate most aspects of people's lives. But we also see that custom has a part to play in our own society. For instance, movie theatres provide expensive washrooms free of charge while charging exorbitant prices for popcorn and soft drinks, rather than providing free drinks and charging a fee to enter the washrooms. A much more significant example is the custom in our market economy of allowing people to pass wealth on to their children in the form of inheritance, so that the income of the future generation is often based less on what they contribute to the economy and more on who their parents were.

Competitive Economies

The Industrial Revolution effectively brought feudalism to an end and ushered in the machine age. It is here that capital, in the form of factories, machines, and railroads, became the economy's most important resource, and the industrial capitalists became very rich and powerful, while the ordinary people, the land-less, capital-less working class, were left with nothing but their labour to sell. This marks the birth of the market system with its emphasis on *competition* as the coordinating mechanism and the private ownership of resources as a main characteristic. Many people are surprised to learn how modern an invention this form of economic organization really is. What today we call the *market economy* did not begin to emerge until approximately 250 years ago, although, of course, specific *markets* have existed for thousands of years.

Competition is the primary feature of today's capitalistic, or market, economies. Here, the forces of demand and supply determine most of what is produced, as well as what technology is used and how much people earn. In a pure market economy, government plays no role whatsoever. This means, for instance, that corporations would be totally unregulated, schools and hospitals would all charge fees, and those unable to work would simply receive no income and no support from government at all.

Mixed Economies

In today's world, there are probably no examples of countries using only a single one of the Four Cs. Instead, all modern economies use a combination of all four, with competition and command being the dominant ones. Perhaps this is due to the rise in the importance of knowledge as the most important resource in today's fast-changing world; it is difficult to monopolize ownership of this particular resource. At the same time, today we see only a single example of a purely command economy: North Korea. Even "communist" China and Cuba have opened up their economies to some private ownership and enterprise.

This blend of competition and command includes the large role played by governments through the provision of, for example, health care and education, leaving the private sector to provide the majority of consumer goods for personal use. The role of government in our economy represents the command function in the sense that the taxes needed to finance government activities are not voluntary, and in the same sense, the various laws governing human conduct and behaviour must be adhered to. This recognition of the roles of both market and government in our society is what we mean by the term *mixed economy*. On the one hand, few of us would wish to live in a pure market economy where, for example, young children from dysfunctional families with no income would be left to starve, and where there was no standardization of weights and measures and no "rules of the game" concerning the way business is conducted—think of meat inspection by government as an example. On the other hand, few of us would want to live in a society where every decision about our lives was made by government. Some blend of the market, and the efficiencies achieved from its use, combined with the order and fairness imposed by government, does seem to be the way to go. However, exactly what constitutes the right amount of government intervention imposed upon the market is, of course, an issue of endless debate.

You have no doubt heard the terms *capitalism* and *socialism* used in the media and in conversation. Just what do these terms mean to an economist? Basically, they distinguish different degrees in the competition–command mix used by society to organize its economic affairs and answer the three fundamental questions. In socialist Sweden, for example, the state (government) plays a much larger role in the economy than it does in the capitalist United States. While Sweden does not have central planning, as found in the former Soviet Union, and does have private property, it also has high taxes and high levels of social spending. Eighty percent of the work force is unionized; everyone receives a generous number of paid vacation days per year and generous sick leave benefits at nearly full pay. Sweden has a wide-ranging unemployment insurance plan, which also includes mandatory retraining for those laid off from their jobs. The Danish government mandates an investment fund requiring that corporations give a percentage of their profits to the central bank, which would then release these funds back to the companies in times of recession, with stipulations on how they were to be spent. By contrast, the United States has almost none of this and relies on a policy of *laissez-faire*, which minimizes the role of government and emphasizes the role of the market in the economy. Canada, France, and the United Kingdom lie somewhere in the middle of these examples.

SECTION SUMMARY

There are four fundamental ways to organize society:

- Cooperation (foraging societies)
- Command (totalitarian states)
- Custom (traditional, religious societies)
- Competition (market economies)

1.7   Production Possibilities

LO7   Use the production possibilities model to illustrate choice and opportunity cost, as well as efficiency and unemployment.

Economists often use economic models when trying to explain the world in which we live. Let us explain what we mean by a *model* and look at one example. Imagine walking into the sales office of a condominium project under construction. Part of the sales presentation is a model of the entire project sitting on a table. You would have no trouble recognizing the model as an abstraction, a representation of what the building will eventually look like. This is true despite the fact that many of the details such as the elevators, interior walls, and appliances are absent from the model.

So, too, in making their models, do economists abstract from reality only the features that are relevant, ignoring extraneous material. Clearly, economists cannot construct a physical model of the economic world. Instead, the level of abstraction is greater because the model is all on paper and often in the form of numbers, equations, and graphs. But for all that, the aim is not to make the simple and straightforward seem unnecessarily complicated. Just the opposite: the goal is to make the complexities of reality as clear and simple as possible.

Let us now construct a very basic model of a country's production possibilities. This allows us to return to a point that we made earlier: every economy is faced with the constraint of limited resources. Imagine a society that produces only two products—cars and wheat. Let us then figure out what this economy is capable of producing if it works at maximum potential. This would mean that the society is making use of all of its resources: the labour force is fully employed, and all of its factories, machines, and farms are fully operational. But it means more than this. It also means that the society is making use of the best technology and, as a result, overall efficiency is being achieved. Given all of this, and since it can produce either cars or wheat, the exact output of each depends on how much of its resources it devotes to the production of cars or how much to wheat. Table 1.1 shows six possible output combinations, as well as the percentage of the economy's resources used in producing each combination. There may well be hundreds of possible combinations, but six is enough to make our model effective. In the table they are labelled A through F.

TABLE 1.1
Production of Cars and Tonnes of Wheat (millions of units)

	CARS		WHEAT	
Possible Output Combination	% of Resources Used	Output	% of Resources Used	Output
A	0	0	100	100
B	20	50	80	95
C	40	90	60	85
D	60	120	40	65
E	80	140	20	40
F	100	150	0	0

The finite resources available to this economy allow it to produce up to a maximum of 100 tonnes of wheat per year if 100 percent of its resources are used in wheat production. Note that this can be done only if no cars are produced (combination A). At the other extreme, a maximum of 150 cars per year can be produced if all available resources are used in car production. This, of course, would mean that no wheat is produced (combination F). There are many other possible combinations in between these two extremes, and Table 1.1 identifies four (B, C, D, and E).

Since we want to focus on what is produced (the outputs) rather than on what resources are used to produce them (the inputs), we can present Table 1.1 in the form of a production possibilities table, as is shown in Table 1.2:

TABLE 1.2
Production Possibilities for Cars and Wheat

	A	B	C	D	E	F
Cars	0	50	90	120	140	150
Wheat	100	95	85	65	40	0

Further, we can take the data from Table 1.2 and use it to graph what is called a **production possibilities curve**, which is a visual representation of the various outputs that can be produced. What appears in **Figure 1.1** is simply another way of presenting the data in Table 1.2.

Now, recall that:

> The three assumptions that lie behind the production possibilities curve are full employment, the use of the best technology, and productive efficiency.

On the one hand, if any one of these three assumptions does not hold, then the economy will be operating somewhere inside the production possibilities curve, as illustrated by point *u*, which is 90 cars and 65 tonnes of wheat. On the other hand, point *x* represents an output of 120 cars and 95 tonnes of wheat, which, given this economy's current resources and technology, is unattainable.

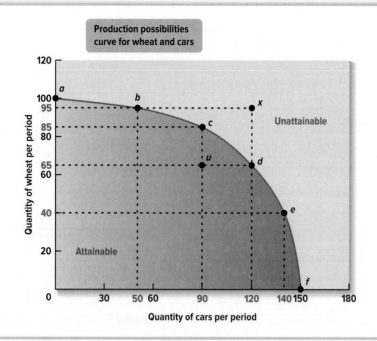

FIGURE 1.1   Production Possibilities Curve I

This society's limited resources allow for the production of a maximum of 100 tonnes of wheat if no cars are produced, as represented by point a. Moving down the curve from point a, we find other combinations of fewer tonnes of wheat and more cars until we reach point f, where 150 cars and no wheat are produced. Point u indicates either the underemployment of resources, inefficiency in resource use, or the use of inappropriate technology. Point x is unattainable.

The Law of Increasing Costs

Next, let us consider the actual shape of the curve. Why is it bowed out this way? We need to understand the implication of this particular shape. **Figure** 1.2 will help.

Assume that our hypothetical economy is currently producing 95 tonnes of wheat and 50 cars, as illustrated by point *b* on the production possibilities curve. Then, assume that production decisions are made to reallocate 20 percent of the productive resources (labour, machines, materials) from wheat production to car production. This new output is illustrated by point *c*. Note that the opportunity cost of producing the additional 40 cars is *not* the additional 20 percent of resources that must be allocated to their production *but* the decreased output of wheat that these resources could have produced. That is to say, the additional 40 cars could only be obtained by reducing the output of wheat from 95 tonnes to 85 tonnes. Thus, 40 more cars cost 10 tonnes of wheat. This can be restated as *1 more car costs 0.25 tonnes of wheat* (10 divided by 40). This seems clear enough, but we are not done.

Next, assume that society, still at point *c*, decides to produce even more cars, as illustrated by moving to point *d* (120 cars and 65 tonnes of wheat). This time, an additional 20 percent of the resources produces only 30 more cars (90 to 120) at a cost of 20 units of wheat (85 to 65). This can be restated as *0.67 tonnes of wheat for every additional car*. This is considerably more than the previous cost of 0.25 units of wheat per car. Another shift of 20 percent of resources would move the economy from point *d* to *e*, which adds only 20 more cars at a cost of 25 tonnes of wheat. Now each additional car costs 1.25 (20 divided by 25) units of wheat. **Table** 1.3 summarizes all the figures above.

We have just identified what economists call the **law of increasing costs**. This law states that as the economy's total production of any single item increases, the per-unit cost of producing additional units of that item will rise. Note that this law is developed in the context of a whole economy and, as we will see in later chapters, need not apply to the situation of an individual firm.

As the total production of cars increases, the rising per-unit cost of cars gives the production possibilities curve its bowed-out shape.

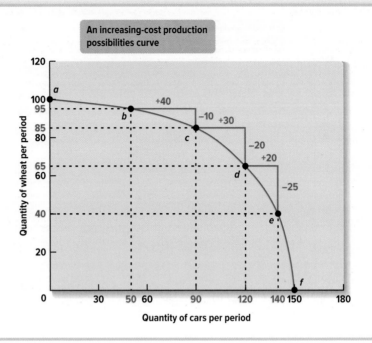

An increasing-cost production possibilities curve

FIGURE 1.2   Production Possibilities Curve II

At point *b*, 95 tonnes of wheat and 50 cars are being produced. If this society decided that it wanted 40 more cars (point *c*), then 10 tonnes of wheat would have to be sacrificed. Thus, 1 more car would cost 0.25 tonnes of wheat. Moving from point *c* to *d* would increase car production by 30 (90 to 120) at a sacrifice of 20 tonnes of wheat (from 85 to 65). In this instance, 1 more car costs 0.67 tonnes of wheat. Moving from point *d* to *e* would increase car production by only 20 (from 120 to 140), while wheat production would drop by 25 (from 65 to 40). Thus, the cost of 1 more car rises to 1.25 tonnes of wheat.

TABLE 1.3
Opportunity Cost per Car

Graphical Movement	Gain in Cars	Opportunity Costs in Wheat	Opportunity Cost per Car
a to *b*	50	5	0.10
b to *c*	40	10	0.25
c to *d*	30	20	0.67
d to *e*	20	25	1.25
e to *f*	10	40	4.00

But why does the per-unit cost of cars increase—what is the reason behind the law of increasing costs? The answer is that not all resources are equally suitable for the production of different products. Our hypothetical society has a fixed amount of resources that are used to produce different combinations of both wheat and cars. However, some of these resources would be better suited to producing cars, whereas others would be better suited to producing wheat. An increase in the production of cars requires that some of the resources currently producing wheat would need to be reallocated to the production of cars. It is only reasonable to assume that the resources that are reallocated first are the ones that are relatively well suited to the production of cars and are perhaps not so well suited to farming. (Perhaps some of the farm workers are immigrants with manufacturing experience, or maybe some of them are allergic to the dust present in the harvesting of wheat.) After all this has taken place, if even *more* cars are to be produced, the only resources left to reallocate will be ones that are not very well suited for the production of cars. Therefore a larger quantity of less well suited resources will have to be reallocated to obtain the desired increase in car production. This will increase the per-unit cost of cars, because a larger sacrifice of wheat production will be required.

TEST YOUR UNDERSTANDING

5. Given the accompanying figure:

    a) If society produces 1000 units of butter, what is the maximum number of guns it can produce?

    b) Suppose that society produces the combination shown as point *b* on the production possibilities curve. What is the cost of 1000 additional units of butter?

    c) Would the opportunity cost of 1000 additional units of butter be greater, the same, or smaller as society moves from point *c* to *d*, compared with a move from point *b* to *c*?

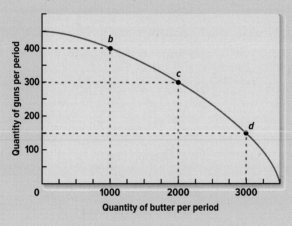

Shifts in the Production Possibilities Curve: The Causes of Economic Growth

A production possibilities curve is like a snapshot of an economy: it shows in one quick diagram what our hypothetical economy is capable of producing at a particular moment. But economies change from year to year—usually, although not always, for the better. The sources of economic growth have been debated for centuries, but our simple model is able to explain some of the important aspects of growth. **Figure 1.3**, for instance, illustrates three ways growth can be shown diagrammatically. In **Figure 1.3A** we see that maximum car production has increased; the PP (production possibilities) curve has shifted out along the horizontal axis. Previously, the maximum amount of cars the country could produce was 150 but this has now increased to 180. In **Figure 1.3B** we see a shift up the vertical axis showing that the maximum production of wheat has increased from 100 tonnes to 120 tonnes. Then in **Figure 1.3C** we see a shift out in the curve indicating that the output of both products increases.

We have to be careful about how we interpret these shifts. Remember that a production possibilities curve shows us what an economy is *capable* of producing; it does not show us what it is *actually* producing. The rightward shift from PP1 to PP2, then, does *not* say that this is economy is now producing more goods and services. It simply shows that it is capable of producing more products; in other words, its potential has now improved. And what could have brought about this change? The conditions under which we constructed the curve provide a clue.

We have assumed that the economy is operating at maximum efficiency: that is to say, it is fully employing its resources and using the best technology. An improvement in either the quantity or quality of resources, or a change in technology, will therefore shift the curve in one of the three ways just illustrated. An increase in quantity of resources could mean things such as increased population, the discovery of new oil fields, or perhaps improved infrastructure. An increase in quality of resources could be the result of a better educated work force, smarter machines, or perhaps whole new ways of organizing production (remember the legendary story of the importance of assembly line production introduced by Henry Ford).

Looking back at **Figure 1.3A** we see what might have been better machines in car production, while in **Figure 1.3B** it might have been better fertilizers used in the production of wheat, and in **Figure 1.3C** perhaps it was the computer revolution that improved the production possibilities of both products.

Now let us use **Figure 1.4** to explain a phenomenon that students often find, at first, hard to believe. Start with the economy operating efficiently on the production possibilities curve PP1 at point *a*.

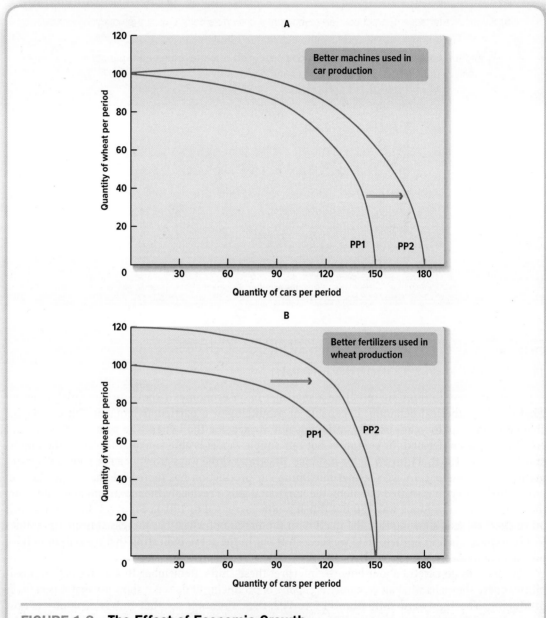

FIGURE 1.3   **The Effect of Economic Growth**

In graph A, the production possibilities curve has shifted from PP1 to PP2, which shows that this economy is now capable of producing more cars but not more wheat. In B, the shift from PP1 to PP2 shows that the economy is now capable of producing more wheat but not more cars. In C we note that more of both goods can be produced.

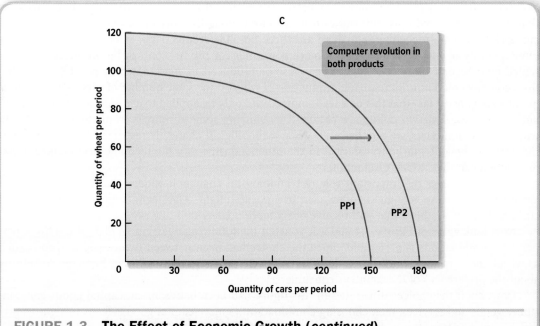

FIGURE 1.3 **The Effect of Economic Growth (*continued*)**

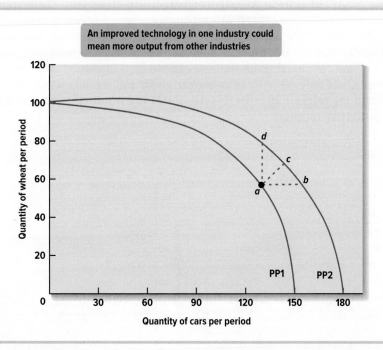

FIGURE 1.4 **The Effect of Technological Change on the Production Possibilities Curve**

Start at point *a*, which is a point of efficient production on PP1. An improvement in technology in the car industry shifts the production possibilities curve to PP2. This creates three possible results. First, the same quantity of wheat and more cars can now be produced, as represented by point *b*. Alternatively, more wheat as well as cars could be produced, as represented by point *c*. Point *d* represents the third possible result, which is more wheat along with the same quantity of cars, despite the fact that the technological change was in the consumer goods and services industry.

Now let us assume that a new technology becomes available that has application *only* in car production. This is illustrated by a shift outward in the curve along the horizontal axis as seen in the new curve PP2. Next we recognize that there are three possible results. First, as one would expect, the same quantity of wheat production but more consumer car production can be produced as represented by *b*. Second, more of *both* goods can also be produced, as represented by point *c*. And third, this economy could now increase the production of wheat if the same number of cars were produced (point *d*) *despite* the fact that this new technology could only be applied to car production. As pointed out above, these last two points are obtained by shifting some resources from car production to wheat production. Thus, we see that even when technological change is restricted to one particular industry, the benefit can be transferred to the other industry as well—technological change in car production can raise wheat production.

This emphasizes the important role of technological change. It widens the choices (that word again!) available to society and is often seen in a positive light. Alas, technological change also has costs, and this is a subject that will receive our attention later.

Now, look again at **Figure** 1.4 and ask yourself the following question: Which of the three new possible combinations is preferable? Since the choice had been between two consumer goods, such as wheat and cars, we cannot give a definitive answer to this question without knowing something about the preferences of the country's consumers.

However, if the choices illustrated in this figure had been between, say, capital goods and consumer goods and services, then choosing combination *d*—more capital goods—leads to significantly different effects from those of choosing combination *b*.

This difference is illustrated in **Figure** 1.5, in which we show two different economies. Let us assume that Atlantis puts greater emphasis on the production of capital goods than does Mu (which chose point *b*). This can be seen by comparing point a_1 (40 units of capital goods) with point b_1 (20 units of capital goods). This emphasis on capital goods production also means a lower production of consumer goods (30 units in Atlantis compared with 50 in Mu). The emphasis on capital goods production in Atlantis means that it will experience more economic growth in the future. This faster growth is illustrated by the production possibilities curve shifting, over time, more to the right in the case of Atlantis than in Mu. After the increase in production possibilities, Atlantis can continue producing 40 units of capital goods but now can produce 70 units of consumer goods (a_2). Mu, by contrast, can produce only 60 units of consumer goods and services while maintaining capital goods production at the original 20 units (b_2). All of this is a result of a different emphasis on the output choices by the two economies.

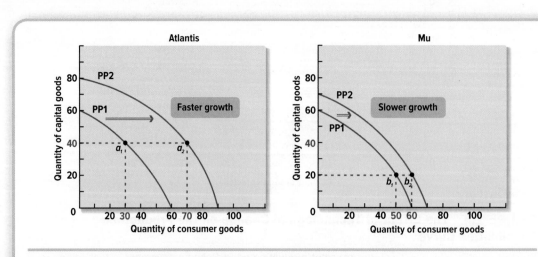

FIGURE 1.5   Different Growth Rates for Two Economies

We begin with Atlantis and Mu the same size, as indicated by identical PP1 curves. However, since Atlantis chooses to emphasize the production of capital goods (point a_1), while Mu emphasizes the production of consumer goods and services (point b_1), Atlantis will grow faster. The result of this faster growth is that, over time, PP2 shifts out farther in the case of Atlantis than it does in the case of Mu.

A sage of some bygone age once said, "There is no such thing as a free lunch." We can now make some sense out of this idea. Producing more of anything—a lunch, for example, which involves the use of scarce resources—necessarily means producing less of something else. The lunch might be provided free to the people who eat it, but from the point of view of society as a whole, it took scarce resources to produce it, and therefore the lunch is *not* free.

 TEST YOUR UNDERSTANDING

6. Assume that the economy of Finhorn faces the following production possibilities:

QUANTITIES PER YEAR				
	A	B	C	D
Grain	0	25	40	50
Tools	12	8	4	0

a) Draw a production possibilities curve (PP1). Label the horizontal axis Tools and the vertical axis Grain. Now assume the development of a new technology that can be used only in the tool industry, and that it increases tool output by 50 percent.

b) Draw a new production possibilities curve (PP2) that reflects this new technology.

c) If Finhorn produced 12 units of tools per year, how many units of grain could be produced after the introduction of the new technology?

SECTION SUMMARY

The production possibilities model is an abstraction and simplification that helps illustrate

- the necessity of choice in deciding what to produce (movement along the PP curve)
- the opportunity cost involved in making a choice (movement along the PP curve)
- inefficient production and the consequences of unemployed resources (inside the PP curve)
- economic growth (outward shift in the PP curve)

Study Guide

Review

WHAT'S THE BIG IDEA?

The production possibilities model is a good way to look at some of the important aspects of economics. Although it is used mostly to describe what happens in an economy, it is equally useful in adding insights to business or everyday life.

Imagine yourself as the CEO of production facility that has a maximum capacity to produce either 1000 trucks or 20/00 SUVs per week and you have decided to produce one-half each kind of vehicle—500 trucks and 1000 SUVs. Things are humming along fine for a while, but this begins to change. You notice that while you continue to sell all of the 1000 SUVs the demand for trucks must have increased, as your orders for more trucks begin to exceed the output of 500 per week. Since your *resources are scarce* (the plant is running at capacity) this apparent increase in the demand for trucks forces you to make a *choice*—sit tight and disappoint some of your potential truck customers or shift some production from SUVs to trucks. At this point, the visualization of the production possibilities curve pops into your head—SUVs on the vertical axis, trucks on the horizontal axis. More trucks carries an opportunity cost of fewer SUVs as you move along the downward-sloping curve. While this cost is currently 1 truck for 2 SUVs, you also remember that the *law of increasing cost* will mean that this cost will escalate, since the capital and labour resources used in production are not equally good at producing both trucks and SUVs—that is, the PP curve gets steeper as more trucks are produced.

Is there another way out of this "satisfy customer demand but absorb higher production costs" dilemma? Yes. You could expand you plant capacity (graphically, shift the PP curve out to the right) so that you could produce more trucks and keep production of SUVs at its current level. But this takes time and money and is thus a risk—one that may well pay off in the long run if truck demand reminds high, but still a risk.

Then you remember, way back in your Econ 101 course, the instructor saying, "Welcome to the real world of economics."

NEW GLOSSARY TERMS

allocative efficiency	land	productive efficiency
capital	law of increasing costs	profit
consumer goods and services	macroeconomics	rent
enterprise	microeconomics	resources
factors of production	normative statements	scientific method
inputs	opportunity cost	technology
interest	positive statements	wages
labour	production possibilities curve	

Comprehensive Problem

Questions

(LO 7) Table 1.4 contains the production possibilities data for capital goods and consumer goods in the economy of New Harmony.

TABLE 1.4

	A	B	C	D	E
Capital goods	0	8	14	18	20
Consumer goods	30	27	21	12	0

a) Use the grid in **Figure 1.6** to draw the production possibilities curve for New Harmony, and label it PP1. Label each of the five output combinations with the letters *a* through *e*.

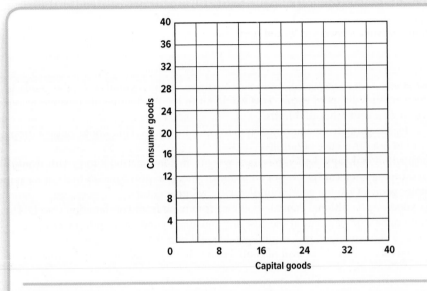

FIGURE 1.6

b) Assume that the people of New Harmony have decided to produce 12 units of consumer goods. How many units of capital goods could be produced?
c) Assume that the people of New Harmony have decided to produce 11 units of capital goods. Approximately how many units of consumer goods could be produced?

Answers

a) See the following figure:

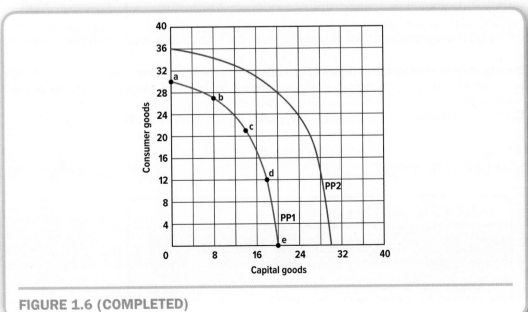

FIGURE 1.6 (COMPLETED)

b) 18 units of capital goods. This is combination D in **Table 1.4**.
c) 24 units of consumer goods. This is halfway between combinations B and C. Halfway between 21 and 27 consumer goods is 24 units.

Questions

d) What is the total cost of the first 14 capital goods produced?
e) Assuming the economy is producing combination C, what is the total cost of 6 additional consumer goods?
f) Assuming the economy is producing combination B, what is the approximate per-unit cost of an additional capital good?
g) Assuming the economy is producing combination C, what is the approximate per-unit cost of an additional capital good?
h) What law is illustrated in your answers to (f) and (g)?

Answers

d) 9 units of consumer goods. This means going from combination A, which entails 0 capital goods, to combination C, which entails 14 capital goods. This would mean the production of consumer goods would drop from 30 to 21, a difference of 9 units.
e) 6 capital goods. This means going from combination C to combination B. This would cause a drop in capital goods from 14 to 8, a difference of 6 units.
f) 1 consumer good. An additional capital good means moving from combination B to C. This would mean an additional 6 capital goods at the cost of 6 consumer goods, a drop from 27 to 21. If 6 capital goods cost 6 consumer goods, 1 capital good would cost 1 consumer good.
g) 2¼ (2.25) consumer goods. An additional capital good means moving from combination C to D. This would mean an additional 4 capital goods at the cost of 9 consumer goods, a drop from 21 to 12. If 4 capital goods costs 9 consumer goods, 1 capital good would cost 9/4 consumer goods.
h) The Law of Increasing Costs: The cost per unit of capital goods increases as we try to produce more capital goods.

Questions

i) Fill in **Table 1.5** assuming that, 10 years later, the output potential of capital goods has increased by 50 percent while the output potential for consumer goods has risen by 6 units for each combination A through D in **Table 1.5**.

TABLE 1.5

	V	W	X	Y	Z
Capital goods	—	—	—	—	—
Consumer goods and services	—	—	—	—	—

j) Using the data from this table, draw PP2 on **Figure 1.6**.
k) As a result of the economic growth, can New Harmony now produce 24 capital goods and 26 consumer goods?
l) What are three possible reasons that would explain the shift from PP1 to PP2?

Answers

i) See Table 1.5 (Completed).

TABLE 1.5 (COMPLETED)

	V	W	X	Y	Z
Capital goods	0	12	21	27	30
Consumer goods	36	33	27	18	0

j) See **Figure** 1.6 (Completed) above.

k) No, it would be impossible to produce this combination.

l) Improved technology; an increase in its resources (such as a larger capital stock); or an improvement in its resources (such as a better-trained labour force or increased efficiency).

Study Problems

Find answers on the McGraw-Hill online resource.

Basic (Problems 1–3)

1. **(LO 7)** Answer the questions below based on **Figure** 1.7, which is for the country of Quantz.

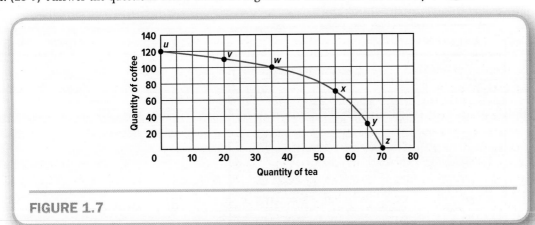

FIGURE 1.7

How much tea is gained and what is the cost in coffee?

a) In moving from u to v _____ tea is gained at the cost of _____.

b) In moving from w to x _____ tea is gained at the cost of _____.

c) In moving from y to z _____ tea is gained at the cost of _____.

2. **(LO 7)** Table 1.6 shows the production possibilities for the country of Emilon.

TABLE 1.6

	A	B	C	D	E
Rice	0	50	90	120	140
Beef	50	45	35	20	0

Complete the following (approximate) possibilities for Emilon:

a) 130 rice and _____ beef

b) _____ rice and 40 beef

Which of the following possibilities is Emilon capable of producing?

c) 100 rice and 40 beef _____

d) 70 rice and 35 beef _____

3. **(LO 7)** Table 1.7 shows the production possibilities for the country of Emilon.

TABLE 1.7

	A	B	C	D	E
Rice	0	50	90	120	140
Beef	50	45	35	20	0

a) What is the total cost of producing 90 rice?
   Answer: _____ (rice/beef)
b) What is the total cost of going from possibility C to possibility D?
   Answer: _____ (rice/beef)
c) What is the approximate per-unit cost of going from possibility C to possibility D?
   Answer: _____ (rice/beef)
d) What is the total cost of going from possibility D to possibility C?
   Answer: _____ (rice/beef)

Intermediate (Problems 4–7)

4. **(LO 7)** Utopia produces only two products: cheese and wine. The production levels are shown in Table 1.8.

TABLE 1.8

CHEESE		WINE	
% Inputs	Output	% Inputs	Output
0	0	0	0
20	30	20	40
40	50	40	70
60	65	60	95
80	75	80	105
100	80	100	110

a) From these data, calculate Utopia's production possibilities to complete Table 1.9.

TABLE 1.9

	A	B	C	D	E	F
Cheese	0	___	___	___	___	___
Wine	___	___	___	___	___	0

b) Can Utopia produce 65 cheese and 95 wine?
   Answer: _____
c) If Utopia is at D, what is the total cost of 10 more cheese?
   Answer: _____
d) If Utopia is at D, what is the total cost of 25 more wine?
   Answer: _____

5. **(LO 7)** Table 1.10 shows Lanark's production possibilities:

TABLE 1.10

	A	B	C	D	E	F
Wheat	0	20	35	45	50	52
Cars	21	20	18	14	8	0

a) If Lanark is producing 16 cars, approximately how much wheat can it produce?
   Answer: _____
b) If Lanark is currently producing combination C, what is the cost of 10 more wheat?
   Answer: _____
c) If Lanark is currently producing combination D, what is the approximate unit cost of an
   additional car?
   Answer: _____

6. **(LO 7)** Shangri-La produces only two goods: bats and balls. Each worker comes with a fixed quantity
   of material and capital, and the economy's labour force is fixed at 50 workers. Table 1.11 indicates
   the amounts of bats and balls that can be produced daily with various quantities of labour.

TABLE 1.11

Number of Workers	Daily Production of Balls	Number of Workers	Daily Production of Bats
0	0	0	0
10	150	10	20
20	250	20	36
30	325	30	46
40	375	40	52
50	400	50	55

a) Complete the production possibilities in Table 1.12.

TABLE 1.12

	A	B	C	D	E	F
Balls	0	___	___	___	___	___
Bats	___	___	___	___	___	0
Bats 2	___	___	___	___	___	0

b) What is the opportunity cost of increasing the output of bats from 46 to 52 units per day?
   _____
c) Suppose that a central planning office dictates an output of 250 balls and 61 bats per day. Is this
   output combination possible? _____
d) Now, assume that a new technology is introduced in the production of bats so that each worker
   can produce half a bat more per day. Complete the Bats 2 row in Table 1.12.
e) Can the planning office's goal of 250 balls and 61 bats now be met? _____

7. **(LO 6)** The data below show the total production (in millions) of the only two goods produced in
   Kitchener and Waterloo, two small planets in deep space:

   Kitchener: 16 kiwis or 12 trucks; Waterloo: 8 kiwis or 14 trucks
   a) What is the opportunity cost of a kiwi in Kitchener? _____
   b) What is the opportunity cost of a kiwi in Waterloo? _____
   c) What is the opportunity cost of a truck in Kitchener? _____
   d) What is the opportunity cost of a truck in Waterloo? _____
   e) If, before trade, each planet was devoting half its resources to producing each product, what is the
      total amount produced by both? _____
   f) If the two planets were to specialize in producing the product they do best, what would be the
      total amount they could produce? _____
   g) What are the total gains as a result of specialization? _____

Advanced (Problems 8–10)

8. **(LO 7)** The data in Table 1.13 are for the small country of Xanadu. Assume that the economy is originally producing combination C, but technological change occurs that enables it to produce 60 percent more units of capital goods (for outputs B through F).

TABLE 1.13						
	A	**B**	**C**	**D**	**E**	**F**
Capital goods	0	25	40	50	55	58
Capital goods 2	___	___	___	___	___	___
Consumer goods	50	40	30	20	10	0

a) Complete the Capital goods 2 row in Table 1.13.

b) If the economy wants to continue with the same quantity of consumer goods, how many more capital goods can it now have as a result of the technological improvement? _____

c) If the economy wants to continue with the same quantity of capital goods, how many more consumer goods can it now have as a result of the technological improvement? _____

d) Before the technological change, what was the opportunity cost of the first 40 consumer goods? _____

e) After the technological change, what was the opportunity cost of the first 40 consumer goods? _____

9. **(LO 7)** Jennifer is planning how to spend a particularly rainy Sunday, and the choice is between watching video movies (each lasting two hours) or studying her economics textbook. She has 10 hours available to her. If she decides to study, she could read the following number of pages at the rate as shown in Table 1.14.

TABLE 1.14	
Hours	**Pages**
2	80
4	130
6	160
8	175
10	180

a) From this information, complete the production possibilities in Table 1.15.

TABLE 1.15						
	A	**B**	**C**	**D**	**E**	**F**
Movies watched	0	___	___	___	___	___
Pages studied	___	___	___	___	___	0

b) From Table 1.15, draw Jennifer's production possibilities curve between movies watched and pages studied on the grid in Figure 1.8.

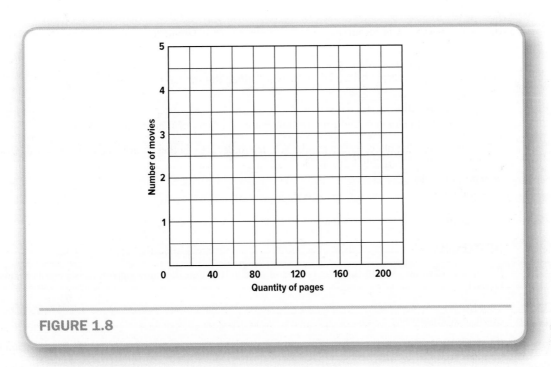

FIGURE 1.8

c) What is the opportunity cost of watching 2 movies? _____

d) Could Jennifer watch 3 movies and study 150 pages of her textbook? _____

e) If Jennifer has already watched 4 movies, what is the opportunity cost of watching the fifth movie? _____

10. **(LO 5)** Below are the data for the maximum production of the only two products for the countries of Oz and Zas.

    Oz: 40 food units OR 20 equipment units

    Zas: 20 food units OR 30 equipment units

a) If each country is self-sufficient, with no trade between them, and each uses one-half of its resources to produce each of the two products, what is the output in each country?

    Oz: _____ food units and _____ equipment units _____

    Zas: _____ food units and _____ equipment units _____

b) What is the total production of each product?

    _____ food units and _____ equipment units

c) If, instead, each country specializes and produces only the product that it can produce best, what will be the output in each country?

    Oz: _____ food units and _____ equipment units _____

    Zas: _____ food units and _____ equipment units _____

d) Now what is the total production of each product?

    _____ food units and _____ equipment units

e) What is the term economists use to explain your answers when comparing answers (b) and (d)? It is the _____.

Problems for Further Study

Basic (Problems 1–5)

1. **(LO 3)** Identify each of the following statements as positive or normative:

a) Canada is the best country in the world to live in. _____

b) Canada's national income has risen for the last five years. _____

c) If the world price of wheat rises, Canada will export less wheat. _____

d) Unemployment is a more serious problem than inflation. _____

2. **(LO 4)** Below is a list of resources. Indicate whether each is labour (L), capital (K), land (N), or enterprise (E).
   a) an irrigation ditch in Manitoba _____
   b) the work done by Jim Plum, a labourer who helped dig the irrigation ditch _____
   c) a lake _____
   d) the air we breathe _____
   e) the efforts of the founder and primary innovator of a successful new software company _____

3. **(LO 4)** Below is a list of economic goods. You are to decide whether each is a consumer good (C), a capital good (K), or possibly both (B), depending on the context in which it is used.
   a) a pair of socks _____
   b) a golf course _____
   c) a Big Mac hamburger _____
   d) a wheelbarrow _____

4. **(LO 3)** Explain why the discipline of economics is sometimes called the *science of choice*.

5. **(LO 6)** Identify and explain the four factors of production and the names given to payments received by each.

Intermediate (Problems 6–8)

6. **(LO 3, 6)** Write down a normative statement that relates to economics. Next, change your statement to make it a positive one.

7. **(LO 7)** Illustrate economic growth using a production possibilities curve (remember to label the axes). What are two possible causes of economic growth?

8. **(LO 7)** Suppose the country of Catalona produces leather shirts and leather moccasins, and the production of each requires the same amount of leather and the same tools. Workers in Catalona are equally capable of producing either product. Draw a production possibilities curve for Catalona, and comment on its shape.

Advanced (Problems 9–12)

9. **(LO 3)** Explain the analogy between the use of theory and the use of a map.

10. **(LO 6)** To what extent is the organization of a family based on the four Cs? Give examples of how each of the four Cs is used to assign household chores to its members. What blend of the four Cs do you think is preferable, and why?

11. **(LO 4)** Kant Skatte is a professional player in the National Hockey League. Because he loved the game so much, Kant dropped out of high school and worked very hard to develop his physical strength and overcome his limitations. Eventually, he made it to the NHL. What data are needed to estimate Kant's annual opportunity costs, in dollars, of continuing to play in the NHL?

12. **(LO 7)** Assume that an economy can produce either 300 tonnes of coffee and no rubber or 100 tonnes of rubber and no coffee. You may further assume that this 3:1 coffee/rubber ratio is constant. Draw a production possibilities curve for this economy with coffee on the vertical axis. Next, indicate with the letters *a* and *b* an increase in rubber production. Finally, illustrate with a triangle the cost of this additional rubber.

CHAPTER 2
Demand and Supply: An Introduction

LEARNING OBJECTIVES

At the end of this chapter, you should be able to:

LO1 Explain the concept of demand.

LO2 Explain the concept of supply.

LO3 Explain the term *market*.

LO4 Explain the concept of (price and quantity) equilibrium.

LO5 Demonstrate the causes and effects of a change in demand.

LO6 Demonstrate the causes and effects of a change in supply.

LO7 Explain why demand and supply determine price and the quantity traded, and not the reverse.

WHAT'S AHEAD ...

This chapter introduces you to the fundamental economic ideas of demand and supply. First, we distinguish between individual and market demands, and look at the various reasons that the demand for products changes from time to time. We then examine things from the producer's point of view and explain what determines the amounts that they put on the market. Next, we describe how markets are able to reconcile the wishes of the two groups and introduce the concept of equilibrium. Finally, we look at how the market price and the quantity traded adjust to changes in demand or supply.

A QUESTION OF RELEVANCE ...

Have you ever wondered why the prices of some products, such as computers or HDTVs, tend to fall over time, while the prices of other products, such as cars or auto insurance, tend to rise? Or perhaps you wonder how the price of a house can fluctuate tens of thousands of dollars from year to year. Why does a poor orange harvest in Florida cause the price of apple juice made in Ontario to rise? And why do sales of fax machines continue to fall despite their lower prices? This chapter will give you insights into questions such as these.

If the average person were to think about the subject matter of economics, it is unlikely that she would immediately think of choice or opportunity costs, which were principal topics of Chapter 1. More likely, she would think in terms of money or interest rates and almost certainly demand and supply. Most people realize, without studying the topic, that demand and supply are central to economics. In our own ways, and as a result of our experiences in life, most of us feel that we know quite a lot about the subject. After all, who knows more about the reaction of consumers to changes in the market than consumers themselves? However, as we will see shortly, the way economists define and use the terms *demand* and *supply* differs from the everyday usage. To make matters worse, there does not seem to be a consensus among non-economists about the meaning of either of these two words: there is a range of meanings. This is often the case with language, but it does lead to a great deal of confusion, which can be illustrated in the following exchange between two observers of the consumer electronic goods market:

Justine: "Have you noticed that the price of HDTVs has dropped quite a bit recently?"

Eric: "Well, yes, but that is just supply and demand."

Justine: Are you saying that the supply has gone up?"

Eric: "Sure, must have."

Justine: "But why would supply go up if the price is going down?"

Eric: "Well, I don't know—maybe it is because demand has gone up, as well."

There is much confusion here. While Eric's belief that the price has fallen because supply went up is probably correct in this context, we see that price will also fall if demand decreases. Justine's second question about why supply would go up if the price goes down reveals a common confusion over cause and effect. And Eric's final response is confused because he is not aware that demand and supply factors are separate and not interrelated.

We hope to soon clarify all of this type of confusion. It is probably clear to you already that economists are very fussy about defining and using economic terms correctly, and this is particularly true in a discussion about demand and supply. As we shall see in this chapter, demand does not simply mean *what people want to buy*, and supply is not just *the amount being produced*.

Another source of confusion in the above discussion is a misunderstanding of cause and effect. Is the change in TV prices the effect of changing demand, or is it the cause? This chapter will clear up some of the confusion and give us a basis upon which to analyze and clarify some real, practical problems. First, let us take a look at the concept of demand.

2.1 Demand

LO1 Explain the concept of demand.

Individual Demand

There are several dimensions to **demand**. First, economists use the word in the sense of wanting something, not in the sense of commanding or ordering. However, this "want" also involves the ability to buy. In other words, demand refers to both the *desire* and the *ability* to purchase a good or service.

This means that although I may well have a desire for a new top-of-the-line BMW, I unfortunately do not have the ability to buy one at current prices and therefore my quantity demanded is zero. Similarly, I might have the income to buy only expensive, upmarket wines but no desire to do so.

Second, there are many factors which might affect an individual's demand for a product. Certainly, how much you and I have to pay for the product is an important factor. But there are many others too. For instance, how much a person earns certainly affects their ability to purchase. (Surprise, rich people buy more than poor people!) As well, if you are going to buy a used Honda, for example, you will probably want to check out the prices of other comparable cars before you make a deal. Similarly, you might hold off buying altogether if you hear that the car company is going to have a sale next month. So in addition to the price of the product, people are obviously affected by how much they earn, the price of comparable products and their expectations of the future. We will look at each of these factors and others later in the chapter. For now, we will concentrate on what many consider to be the most important factor when deciding whether to purchase: the price of the product.

When we look at the concept of demand then, we are investigating the relationship between the price of the product and the quantities people are willing and able to purchase assuming all these other factors remain the same. The Latin phrase for this perspective is *ceteris paribus*. Literally the phrase means "other things being equal"; however, it is usually interpreted by economists to mean "other things remaining the same." Demand is the relationship between the price of a product and the quantities demanded, *other things remaining the same.*

Third, demand is a hypothetical construct that expresses this desire and ability to purchase, not at a single price, but over a *range of* hypothetical prices. Finally, demand is also a flow concept in that it measures quantities over a period of time. In summary, demand

- involves both the desire and the ability of consumers to purchase
- assumes that other things are held constant
- refers to a range of prices
- measures quantities over time

All of these aspects of demand are captured in **Table 2.1**, which shows the **demand schedule** for energy bars for Tomiko, who is an energy bar enthusiast and buys her bars by the case once a month.

TABLE 2.1
Individual Demand

Price per Case	Quantity Demanded (number of cases per month)
$18	6
19	5
20	4
21	3
22	2

Once again, what we mean by demand is the entire relationship between the various prices and the quantities that people are willing and able to purchase. This relationship can be laid out in the form of a demand schedule. The above schedule shows the amounts per month that Tomiko is willing and able to purchase at the various prices shown. Note that there is an inverse relationship between price and quantity. This simply means that at higher prices, Tomiko would not be willing to buy as much as at lower prices. In other words:

The higher the price, the lower will be the quantity demanded, and the lower the price, the higher will be the quantity demanded.

Another, less obvious statement of this law of demand is to say that in order to induce Tomiko to buy a greater quantity of energy bars, the price must be lower. Tomiko's demand schedule is graphed in **Figure 2.1**.

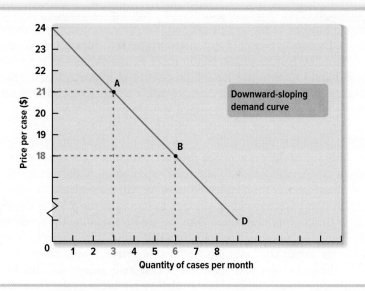

FIGURE 2.1   Individual Demand Curve

At a price of $18 per case, Tomiko is willing and able to buy 6 cases per month (point B). At a higher price, $21 per case, the amount she is willing and able to buy falls to 3 cases (point A). The higher the price, then, the lower is the quantity demanded. (Note that the vertical axis contains a "broken" portion. In general, an axis is often broken in this manner whenever the information about, say, low prices, is unavailable or unimportant.)

In **Figure 2.1**, at a price of $21 per case, the quantity demanded by Tomiko is 3 cases per month, while at a lower price of $18 per case, she would be willing to buy 6 cases. The demand is therefore plotted as a downward-sloping curve by connecting these two price/quantity coordinates and then extending a straight line. (To economists, curves include straight lines!) Once again, note that when we say *demand*, *demand schedule*, or *demand curve*, we are referring to a whole array of different prices and quantities.

It is very important for you to note that since the price of any product is part of what we call the "demand" for that product, a change in the price cannot change the demand. It can, however, affect the amounts we are willing to purchase, and we express this by saying that:

> A change in the price of a product results in a **change in the quantity demanded** for that product.

In other words, point A in **Figure 2.1** represents a price of $21 and a quantity demanded of 3 cases. Point B shows another possible combination: at a price of $18, the quantity demanded is 6 cases. The *quantity demanded*, then, is a single point on the demand curve, whereas the *demand* is the entire collection of points.

This is illustrated in **Figure 2.2**. Graphically, as we move the demand curve from $19 to $18, the quantity demanded increases from 5 to 6 cases; as we move up from $21 to $22, the quantity demanded decreases from 3 to 2 cases.

Why Is the Demand Curve Downward Sloping?

People tend to buy more at lower prices than at higher prices. Most of us can confirm from experience that a lower price will induce us to buy more of a product or to buy something that we would or could not purchase before. Witness the big crowds attracted to

A SALE sign is often all it takes to attract consumers.

PhotoLink/Getty Images

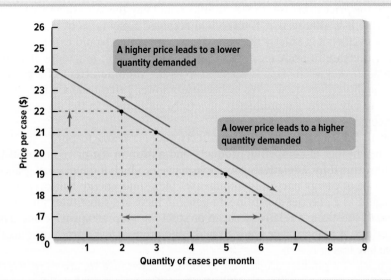

FIGURE 2.2   Changes in the Quantity Demanded

Whenever the price changes, there is a movement along the demand curve. A decrease in the price from $19 to $18 leads to an increase in the quantity demanded from 5 to 6. An increase in the price from, say $21 to $22, causes a decrease in the quantity demanded from 3 to 2. Neither the demand nor the demand curve changes, however.

 ADDED DIMENSION

Just What Is a Product?

Economist speak a great deal about the supply of, and demand for "products" such as cars, computers, cell phones, and houses. This is done so that we are able to focus on the *concept* of demand—people want to buy these things—and supply—firms want to make a profit providing these things. This process is what the current chapter is all about.

But you do need to realize that "car" is also a bit of an abstraction. It might mean a current-model Honda Civic, Ford Fiesta, or Chevy Cruze, costing around $20 000; or an Audi A3 or Hyundai Genesis with a price tag around twice as much.

A "car" might also mean a meticulously reconstructed 1957 Chevy Impala with vintage licence plates that some enthusiast spent countless hours and $100 000 working on.

Economics is full of abstractions, but that is the only way we can develop and construct concepts that help us better understand the world in which we live. So how do we chose to define "a product" in this text? A product is simply any item offered for sale. It can be a service or an item. It can be physical or in virtual or cyber form.

nothing more than a sign saying "SALE." In addition, most microeconomic research done over the years tends to confirm this law of demand, and theories of consumer behaviour (such as the marginal utility theory, which we will study in Chapter 5) lend additional support to the idea. But is it that simple? Let us explore the question of why people tend to buy more at lower prices.

Remember that our demand for products is a combination of our desire to purchase and our ability to purchase. A lower price affects both of these. The lower the price of a product, the more income a person has left to purchase additional products. Assume, for instance, that the price of energy bars in Table 2.1 was $20 and Tomiko was buying 4 cases per month for a total expenditure of

$80 per month. If the price decreases to $18, Tomiko could buy the same quantity for an outlay of $72, saving a total of $8. It is almost as if Tomiko had received a pay raise of $8. In fact, in terms of its effect on Tomiko's wallet, it is exactly the same. Or, as economists would express it, her **real income** has increased. A decrease in price means that people can afford to buy more of a product (or more of other products) if they wish. This is referred to as the **income effect** of a price change, and it affects people's *ability* to purchase. This is because a lower price means a higher real income, so people will tend to buy more of a product. (Conversely, an increase in the price effectively reduces a person's real income.)

In addition to this, a price change also affects people's *desire* to purchase. We are naturally driven to buy the cheaper of competing products, and a drop in the price of one of them increases our desire to substitute it for a relatively more expensive product. If the price of granola bars were to drop (or if the price of energy bars were to increase), then some energy-bar lovers might well switch to what they regard as a cheaper substitute. In general, there are substitutes for most products, and people will tend to substitute a relatively cheap product for a more expensive one. This is called the **substitution effect**. A higher price tends to make the product less attractive to us than its substitutes, and so we buy less of it.

When the price of a product drops, we buy more of it because we are *more able* (the income effect) and because we are *more willing* (the substitution effect). Conversely, a price increase means we are less able and less willing to buy the product, and therefore we buy less.

The close relationship that exists between price and the quantity demanded is so pervasive that it is often referred to as the *law of demand*.

Market Demand

Up to this point, we have focused on individual demand. Now, we want to move to **market demand** (or total demand). Conceptually, this is easy enough to do. By summing every individual's demand for a product, we are able to obtain the market demand. **Table 2.2** provides a simple example.

TABLE 2.2
Deriving the Market Demand

	NUMBER OF CASES PER MONTH				
Price per Case	Tomiko's Quantity Demanded	Meridith's Quantity Demanded	Abdi's Quantity Demanded	Jan's Quantity Demanded	Market Quantity Demanded
$18	6	3	4	9	22
19	5	2	4	7	18
20	4	2	4	6	16
21	3	0	3	3	9
22	2	0	3	1	6

Let us say we know not only Tomiko's demand but also the demands of three of her friends in a small, four-person economy. The market demand, then, is the horizontal summation of individual demands, so to find the quantities demanded at $18, we add the quantities demanded by each individual: 6 + 3 + 4 + 9 = 22. The same would be done for each price level. This particular market demand is graphed in **Figure 2.3**. Note that this demand curve, which is the summation of the specific numbers of the four people in **Table 2.2**, is not a straight line. Yet it is still downward sloping and so conforms to the law of demand. (For the most part, we will work with straight-line demand curves, although there is no reason to assume that all real-life demand curves plot as straight lines.)

Note that, as with the individual demand curve, the market demand curve also slopes downward. This is because people buy more as the price drops—and more people buy. In our example, Meridith is not willing to buy any energy bars at a price of $22. Only if the price is $20 or lower will all four people buy energy bars.

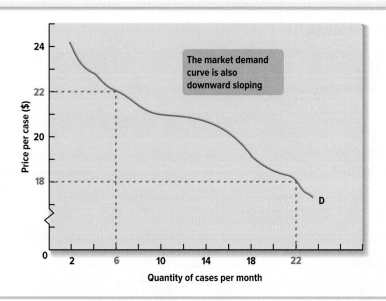

FIGURE 2.3   **The Market Demand Curve**

At a price of $18, the total or market quantity demanded equals 22 cases. As with individual demand, when the price increases to $22, the quantity demanded will drop, in this case to 6. This is because at a higher price each individual buys less, and there are fewer people who can afford or are willing to buy any at all. (Meridith has dropped out of the market.)

Finally, before we look at the supply side of the market, note again that our demand schedule tells us only what people *might* buy; it tells us nothing about what they are actually buying. To know this, we need to know the actual price. And to find out what the price of energy bars should be, we need to know ... yes, the supply.

 TEST YOUR UNDERSTANDING

Find answers on the McGraw-Hill online resource.

1. The data in the table indicate the weekly demand for litres of soy milk by Al, Bo, and Cole (the only three people in a very small market).

a) Fill in the blanks in the table.

b) What is the basic shape of the demand curve in this market?

c) What is the highest price at which all three will buy at least one litre of milk?

Price	Quantity Demanded: Al	Quantity Demanded: Bo	Quantity Demanded: Cole	Total (Market) Quantity Demanded
$4.00	1	0	0	_____
3.50	1	1	0	_____
3.00	1	1	1	_____
2.50	2	1	1	_____
2.00	2	2	1	_____

SECTION SUMMARY

a) Demand is the price–quantity relationship of a product that consumers are willing and able to buy per period of time.

b) The demand curve is downward sloping because of
  - the substitution effect
  - income effect

c) Products can be related as
  - complements
  - substitutes

d) Market demand is the conceptual summation of each individual's demand within a given market.

2.2   Supply

LO2   Explain the concept of supply.

Individual Supply

In many ways, the formulation of supply is very similar to that of demand. Both measure hypothetical quantities at various prices, and both are flow concepts. However, we now need to look at things through the eyes of the producer rather than the eyes of the consumer. We will assume for the time being that the prime motive for the producer is to maximize profits, although we will examine this assumption in more detail in a later chapter. For now, we can certainly agree with Adam Smith who, in *The Wealth of Nations*, noted that few producers are in business to please consumers. Neither, of course, do consumers buy products to please producers. Both are motivated by self-interest.

The term **supply** refers to the quantities that suppliers are *willing* and *able* to make available to the market at various prices. **Table 2.3** shows a hypothetical **supply schedule** for Flic, the owner of an energy bar manufacturing firm.

TABLE 2.3
The Supply Schedule for Flic, the Energy Bar Manufacturer

Price per Case	Quantity Supplied (number of cases per month)
$18	2
19	3
20	4
21	5
22	6

Note that there is a *direct* relationship between price and the quantity supplied, which means that a higher price will induce Flic to produce more. Remember that Flic's reason for being in business is to make as much profit as possible. How much would Flic, hypothetically, be prepared to supply if the energy bars could be sold at $18 per case? Knowing what her costs are likely to be, she figures that she could make the most profit if she produces two cases. At a higher price, there is a likelihood of greater profits, and therefore she is willing to produce more. Also, as we shall see in Chapter 6, when firms produce more, the cost per unit tends to rise. Therefore, a producer needs the incentive of a higher price *in order to* increase production. For the time being, however, we can rely on the proposition that a higher price means higher profits and therefore will lead to higher quantities produced. This is illustrated in **Figure 2.4**.

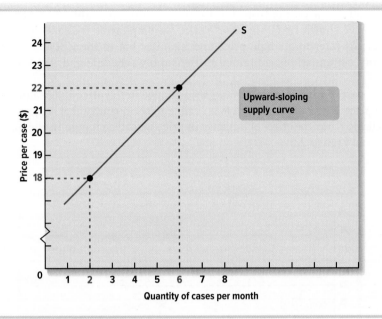

FIGURE 2.4 **Individual Supply Curve**

At a low price of $18, the most profitable output for Flic is 2 cases. If the price increased, she would be willing and able to produce more, since she would be able to make greater profits. At $22, for instance, the quantity she would produce increases to 6 cases.

 ## GREAT ECONOMISTS: ADAM SMITH

Adam Smith (1723–90) is generally regarded as the founding father of economics. In his brilliant work *The Wealth of Nations*, Smith posed so many interesting questions and provided such illuminating answers that later economists often felt that they were merely picking at the scraps he left behind. Smith was born and brought up in Scotland and educated in Glasgow and Oxford. He held the Chair of Moral Philosophy at Glasgow College for many years. He was a lifelong bachelor and had a kind but absent-minded disposition.

Smith was the first scholar to analyze the business of "getting and spending" in a detailed and systematic manner. In doing this, he gave useful social dignity to the professions of business and trading. Besides introducing the important idea of the *invisible hand*, which was his way of describing the coordinating mechanism of capitalism, he examined the division of labour, the role of government, the function of money, the advantages and disadvantages of free trade, what constitutes good and bad taxation, and a host of other ideas. For Smith, economic life was not merely a peripheral adventure for people but their central motivating force.

Library of Congress Prints and Photographs Division

Joining the individual points from the supply schedule in **Table** 2.3 gives us the upward-sloping supply curve shown in **Figure** 2.4. Again, we emphasize the fact that, like *demand*, the term *supply* does not refer to a single price and quantity but to the whole array of hypothetical price and quantity combinations contained in the supply schedule and illustrated by the supply curve.

Since price is part of what we mean by *supply*, a change in the price level cannot change the supply. A change in price does, of course, lead to a change in the quantity that a producer is willing and able to make available. Thus, the effect of a change in price we call a **change in the quantity supplied**. This is illustrated in **Figure** 2.5.

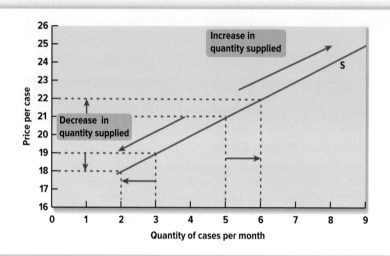

FIGURE 2.5   Changes in the Quantity Supplied

A price change will lead to a movement along the supply curve. An increase in the price from, say, $21 to $22 will cause an increase in the quantity supplied from 5 to 6. A decrease in the price from $19 to $18 will lead to a decrease in the quantity supplied from 3 to 2. The supply curve itself, however, does not change.

To summarize:

An increase in price will lead to an increase in the quantity supplied and is illustrated as a movement up the supply curve.

A decrease in price will cause a decrease in the quantity supplied and is illustrated as a movement down the supply curve.

Market Supply

As we did with the market demand, we can derive the **market supply** of a product by summing the supply of every individual supplier. A word of caution, however. We must make the assumption that producers are all producing a similar product and that consumers have no preference as to which supplier or product they use. Given this, it is possible to add together the individual supplies to derive the market supply. In our example, suppose that the manufacturer Flic is competing with three other manufacturers of similar size and with similar costs. The market supply of energy bars in this market would be as shown in **Table** 2.4.

TABLE 2.4
Deriving the Market Supply

	NUMBER OF CASES PER MONTH		
Price per Case	Flic Quantity Supplied	Quantity Supplied of Other Manufacturers	Market Quantity Supplied
$18	2	6	8
19	3	9	12
20	4	12	16
21	5	15	20
22	6	18	24

The total quantities supplied by the three other manufacturers are equal to the quantities that Flic would supply at each price, multiplied by three. The fourth column, market supply, is the addition of every energy bar manufacturer's supply—the second column plus the third column.

The market supply is illustrated in **Figure** 2.6.

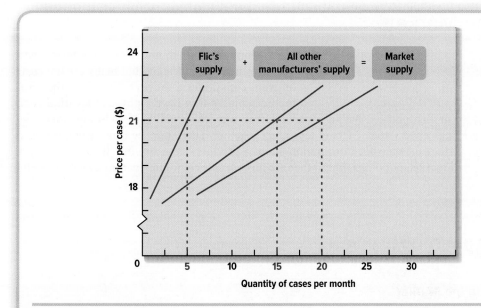

FIGURE 2.6   The Market Supply

The market supply is the horizontal summation of each individual producer's supply curve. For instance, at a price of $21, Flic would supply 5 cases; the other manufacturers combined would supply 15 cases. The market quantity supplied, therefore, is the total quantity supplied of 20 cases. In short, to derive the market supply curve, we add the totals of each supplier at each price level.

The *market* supply curve is upward sloping primarily for the same reason the *individual* supply curve is upward sloping: because higher prices imply higher profits and will therefore induce a greater quantity supplied. But there is an additional reason. In our example, we assumed, for simplicity's sake, that the suppliers are of similar size and have similar costs. In reality, that is unlikely; costs and size probably differ, so a price that generates a profit for one firm may mean a loss for another.

In summary, a higher price, which deters consumers from buying more, is an incentive for suppliers to produce more. Conversely, a lower price induces consumers to buy more but is a reason for suppliers to cut back their output.

The motives of consumers and producers are very different: consumers wish to obtain the lowest price possible, and producers want to sell at the highest. How can their wishes converge? How is trade possible at all in these circumstances? Certainly, it is not possible for *all* prospective consumers and suppliers to be satisfied. But it is almost always possible for *some* of these people to be satisfied. Of course, this will require that they be able, in some sense, to meet and get together. A market enables them to do just that.

SECTION SUMMARY

a) Supply is the price–quantity relationship of a product that producers are willing and able to sell per period of time.

b) The supply curve is upward sloping because higher prices imply higher profits and therefore increased production.

c) Market supply is the conceptual summation of each firm's supply within a given market.

2.3   The Market

LO3   Explain the term *market*.

Most people are able to understand the terms *market price* and *market demand*, but many are not clear on what constitutes a **market**. Certainly, the term includes places that have a physical location such as a local produce or fish market. But in broader terms, a market really refers to any exchange mechanism that brings buyers and sellers of a product together. There may be times when we need to inspect or get further on-the-spot information about a product before we buy it, and this is the purpose of the retail market. But other times, when we possess sufficient information about a product

 ADDED DIMENSION

Reinventing the Market

The modern market system first emerged and began to spread about 250 years ago, as commerce moved out of the village markets of Europe into the age of factory-centred manufacturing, which was later combined with widespread systems of wholesaling and retailing. However, this transformation also introduced a less predictable chain of supply and demand. While the seller in the village market was in direct contact with the buyer, the evolution of mass markets and mass production techniques gave rise to vast gulfs in time and space between buyer and seller. Producers became much less sure of what the demand for their product was, and buyers were never sure there wasn't a better deal somewhere else. In response to this, sellers used the blunt tool of a fixed price list and adjusted output in response to fluctuations in demand, while buyers just did the best they could. The invention of the Internet is also reinventing commerce; as the seller's market horizon expands, buyers have more information, real-time sales become routine, and the need to stockpile inventory diminishes. In short, supply-chain bottlenecks are being eradicated. What is emerging is far *more efficient markets* and the rise of dynamic pricing based on constantly fluctuating demand and supply.

or a producer, it is not necessary to actually see either of them before we purchase. This applies, for instance, if you wish to buy stocks and bonds or make a purchase on the Internet. Increasingly, in these days of higher costs of personal service and greater availability of electronic communication, markets are becoming both wider and more accessible. The market for commodities such as copper, gold, and rubber, for instance, is both worldwide and anonymous in that the buyers and sellers seldom meet in person.

By a market, then, we mean any relatively open environment in which buyers and sellers can communicate and that operates without preference. So when we speak of the market price, we mean the price available to *all* buyers and sellers of a product. By market demand we mean the total quantities demanded, and market supply we mean the quantity made available by all suppliers at each possible price.

Later, you will encounter several different types of markets, some of which work very well and others that work poorly if at all. The analysis in this chapter assumes that the market we are looking at is very (economists call it "perfectly") competitive. We will devote all of Chapter 8 to examining this type of market in more detail. For now, we need to mention that a perfectly competitive market is, among other things, one in which there are many small producers, each selling an identical product. With this caution in mind, let us see how such a market works.

SECTION SUMMARY

A market is a mechanism that brings buyers and sellers together.

2.4   Market Equilibrium

LO4   Explain the concept of (price and quantity) equilibrium.

We now examine the point at which the wishes of buyers and sellers coincide by combining the market demand and supply for energy bars in Table 2.5.

TABLE 2.5
Market Supply and Demand

	NUMBER OF CASES PER MONTH		
Price per Case	Market Quantity Demanded	Market Quantity Supplied	Surplus (+)/ Shortage (−)
$18	22	8	−14
19	18	12	−6
20	16	16	0
21	9	20	+11
22	6	24	+18

You can see from this table that there is only one price, $20, at which the wishes of consumers and producers coincide. Only if the price is $20 will the quantity demanded and the quantity supplied be equal. This price level is referred to as the **equilibrium price**. Equilibrium, in general, means that there is balance between opposing forces; here, those opposing forces are demand and supply. The word *equilibrium* also implies a condition of stability. If this stability is disturbed, there will be a tendency to automatically find a new equilibrium.

To understand this point, refer to Table 2.5 and note that if the price were, say, $18, then the amount being demanded, 22, would exceed the amount being supplied, which is 8. At this price, there is an excess demand, or more simply, a shortage of energy bars, to the tune of 14 cases. This amount is shown in the last column and marked with a minus sign. In this situation, there would be a lot of unhappy energy-bar eaters. Faced with the prospect of going without their bars, many of them will be prepared to pay a higher price and will therefore bid the price up. As the price of energy bars starts to rise, the reaction of consumers and producers will differ. Some energy-bar eaters will not be able to afford the higher prices, so the quantity demanded will drop. On the supply side, producers will be delighted with the higher price and will start to produce more—and the quantity supplied will increase. Both these tendencies will combine to reduce the shortage as the price goes up. Eventually, when the price has reached the equilibrium price of $20, the shortage will have disappeared and the price will no longer increase. Part of the law of demand suggests, then, that:

Shortages cause prices to rise.

This is illustrated in **Figure 2.7**.

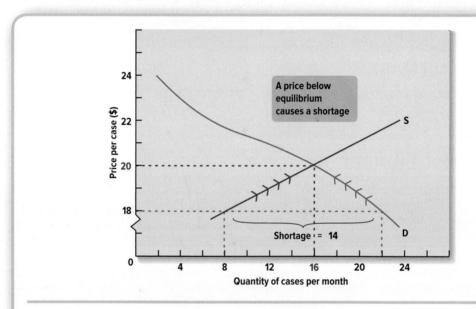

FIGURE 2.7   How the Market Reacts to a Shortage

At a price of $18, the quantity supplied of 8 is far below the quantity demanded of 22. The horizontal distance between the two shows the amount of the shortage, which is 14. As a result of the shortage, price bidding between consumers will force up the price. As the price increases, the quantity demanded will drop, but the quantity supplied will rise until these two are equal at a quantity of 16.

Now, again using Table 2.5, let us see what will happen if the price happens to be above equilibrium, at $22 a case. At this price, the quantity demanded is 6 cases, and the quantity supplied is 24 cases. There is insufficient demand from the producers' point of view, or more simply, there is a surplus (or excess supply) of 18 cases. This is shown in the last column of Table 2.5 as +18. This is not a stable situation because firms cannot continue producing a product that they cannot sell. They will be forced to lower the price in an attempt to sell more. As the price starts to drop, two things happen concurrently. Consumers will be happy to consume more, or to use economic terms, there will be an increase in the quantity demanded.

In **Figure 2.8**, note that as the price falls the quantity demanded increases, and this increase is depicted as a movement down the demand curve. At the same time, faced with a falling price, producers will be forced to cut back production—decreasing the quantity supplied. In the same figure, this is shown as a movement along (down) the supply curve. The net result of this will be the eventual elimination of the surplus as the price moves toward equilibrium. In other words:

Surpluses cause prices to fall.

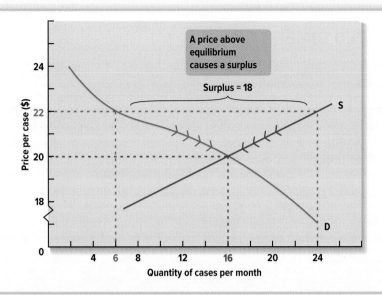

FIGURE 2.8 How the Market Reacts to a Surplus

A price above equilibrium will produce a surplus. At $22, the quantity supplied of 24 exceeds the quantity demanded of 6. The horizontal distance of 18 represents the amount of the surplus. The surplus will result in producers dropping the price in an attempt to increase sales. As the price drops, the quantity demanded increases, while the quantity supplied falls. The equilibrium quantity is 16.

Only if the price is $20 will there be no surplus or shortage, and the quantity produced will be equal to the quantity demanded. This is the equilibrium price. The quantity prevailing at the equilibrium price is known as the **equilibrium quantity**, in this case 16 cases. This equilibrium quantity is the quantity both demanded and supplied (since they are equal).

 TEST YOUR UNDERSTANDING

2. What effect does a surplus have on the price of a product? What about a shortage?

3. The following table shows the demand and supply of eggs (in hundreds of thousands per day).

   a) What are the equilibrium price and the equilibrium quantity?

   b) Complete the surplus/shortage column. Using this column, explain why your answer to question (a) must be correct.

   c) What would be the surplus/shortage at a price of $2.50? What would happen to the price and the quantity traded?

   d) What would be the surplus/shortage at a price of $4? What would happen to the price and the quantity traded?

Price	Quantity Demanded	Quantity Supplied	Surplus/ Shortage
$2.00	60	30	_____
2.50	56	36	_____
3.00	52	42	_____
3.50	48	48	_____
4.00	44	54	_____

ADDED DIMENSION

Sales Always Equal Purchases

It is important not to confuse the terms *demand* and *supply* with *purchases* and *sales*. As we have seen in this chapter, the quantity demanded and the quantity supplied are not always equal. However, purchases and sales, since they are two sides of the same transaction, must always be equal. The accompanying graph explains the differences in the terms.

The equilibrium price is $12, and at this price, the quantity demanded and supplied are equal at 40 units—this is the amount traded and is the same thing as the amount sold and purchased. However, if the price happened to be above equilibrium—$16—then the quantity demanded is denoted by *a* (30 units) and the quantity supplied by *b* (60 units). Clearly, the two quantities are not equal. But how much is bought and sold at this price? The answer is quantity *a*. It really does not matter how much is being produced, since at this price quantity *a* is the maximum amount that consumers are willing to buy. The difference *ab* represents the amount unsold, or a surplus of 30.

But what is the effect of a price that is below equilibrium? Suppose the price is $8, where the quantity supplied of 20 units (*c*) is less than the quantity demanded of 50 units (*d*)? This time, how much is being bought and sold? The answer must be quantity *c*. It does not matter how much of this product consumers want to buy if producers are only making quantity *c* available. In general, the amount bought and sold is always equal to the smaller of the quantity demanded or the quantity supplied.

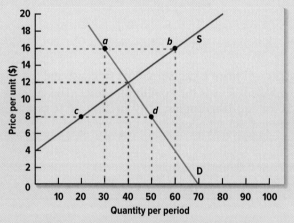

SECTION SUMMARY

a) Shortages cause prices to rise; surpluses cause prices to fall.

b) Market equilibrium occurs when the quantity demanded and the quantity supplied are equal at a particular price.

2.5   Change in Demand

LO5 Demonstrate the causes and effects of a change in demand.

Recall from the definition of demand that the concept refers to the *relationship* between various prices and quantities. In other words, both price and quantity make up what is known as demand. Thus, a change in price cannot cause a change in demand but does cause a change in the quantity demanded. That said, we must now ask: What are the other determinants, besides price, that influence how much of any particular product consumers will buy? Or once equilibrium price and quantity have been established, what might disturb that equilibrium? One general answer to this question is a **change in demand**. Table 2.6 shows such a change in the demand for energy bars.

TABLE 2.6		
An Increase in Demand		
	NUMBER OF CASES PER MONTH	
Price per Case of Energy Bars	**Quantity Demanded 1**	**Quantity Demanded 2**
$18	16	22
19	15	21
20	14	20
21	13	19
22	12	18

Here, we will introduce new figures for demand in order to revert to straight-line demand curves. Let us say that D_1 is the demand for energy bars that existed last month and D_2 is the demand this month. Demand has increased by 6 cases per month at each price, so whatever the price, consumers are willing and able to consume an additional 6 cases. Thus, there has been an increase in demand. Figure 2.9 graphically illustrates an increase in demand.

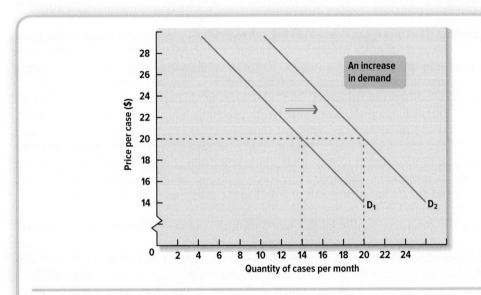

FIGURE 2.9   An Increase in Demand

At each price, the quantities demanded have increased. In this example, the increase is by a constant amount of 6, thus producing a parallel shift in the demand curve. For example, at $20 the quantity demanded has increased from 14 to 20.

An increase in demand, then, means an increase in the quantities demanded *at each price,* that is, a total increase in the demand schedule, which is illustrated by a rightward shift in the demand curve. Similarly, a decrease in demand means a reduction in the quantities demanded at each price—a decrease in the demand schedule—and this is illustrated by a leftward shift in the demand curve.

Determinants of a Change in Demand

Now that we know what an increase in demand looks like, we need to look at the factors that could bring about such a change. Some of these determinants of demand affect people's willingness to purchase, others affect their ability to purchase, and still others affect both.

The first factor that affects our willingness to purchase a product is our own *preference*. An increase in demand as shown in Table 2.6 could simply have been caused by a change in consumer preferences: consumers now prefer more energy bars.

But many things could affect our preferences. Tastes change over time and are influenced by the weather, advertising, articles and reports in books and magazines, opinions of friends, special events, and much more. Specific examples would include decreased demand for steak as the summer barbecue season passes, increased demand for a book after it wins a prestigious literary award, or increased demand for hotel rooms in the host city of the Olympics.

The second factor affecting the demand for a product is the *income* of consumers. This affects their ability to consume. Generally speaking, you would expect that an increase in income leads most people to increase their purchases of most products and that a decrease in income generally causes a drop in demand—that is, there is a direct relationship between income and demand. This is true for most products that we buy. These products are called **normal products** and they include items such as sushi, soft drinks, cars, and movies.

But it is certainly not true for all people and all products. For instance, as the incomes of most people increase, these consumers tend to buy less of such things as low-quality meats, boxes of macaroni and cheese, cheap toilet paper, and so on. Instead, they start to substitute higher-quality and higher-priced articles that they could not previously afford. When income is low, we buy lower-quality staple products that economists call **inferior products**. There is an inverse relationship between income and the demand for inferior products: as income levels go up, the demand goes down. It also means that as incomes fall, demand for these inferior products will rise. In our energy bars example from Table 2.6, the increase in market demand could have been caused by an increase in incomes because energy bars are normal products.

A third important determinant of demand is the *price of related products*. A change in the price of related products will affect people's willingness and ability to purchase a particular good. Products are related if a change in the price of one causes a change in the demand for the other. For instance, if the price of Pepsi were to increase, a number of Pepsi drinkers might well switch over to Coke.

There are, in fact, two ways in which products may be related. They may be related as substitutes, or they may be related as complements. **Substitute products** (also known as *competitive products*) are those that are so similar in the eyes of most consumers that price is the main distinguishing feature. Pepsi and Coke, therefore, are substitute products because an increase in the price of one will cause an increase in the demand for the other. The relationship between the price of a product and the demand for its substitute is therefore a direct one. It also means that if the price of a product falls, then the demand for its substitute will also fall, since many consumers are now buying a cheaper product.

Complementary products tend to be purchased together, and their demands are interrelated. Skis and ski boots are complementary products, as are cars and gasoline or beer and pretzels. If the price of one product increases, causing a decrease in the quantity demanded, then people will also purchase less of the complement. If the price of greens fees were to increase so that people were buying fewer rounds of golf, then we would also expect a decrease in the demand for complementary products such as golf balls and golf tees.

There is, in this case, an inverse relationship between the price of a product and the demand for its complement: an increase in price of one product leads to a decline in the demand for the complementary product. Similarly, a decrease in the price of a product will lead to an increase in the demand for a complement.

A fourth determinant of demand is consumers' *expectations of the future*. There are many ways that our feelings about the future influence our present behaviour. Future expected prices and incomes can affect our present demand for a product, as can the prospect of a shortage. If consumers think that the price of their favourite beverage is likely to increase in the near future, they may well stock up, just in case. The present demand for the product will therefore increase. Conversely, expected future price declines cause people to hold off their current purchases while awaiting the hoped-for lower prices.

An anticipated pay increase may cause some people to spend more immediately as they adjust to their expected higher standard of living. People who fear a layoff or some other loss of income may cut down spending in advance of the fateful date. Finally, the possibility of future shortages, such as those caused by an impending strike, may cause a frantic rush to the stores by anxious customers trying to stock up in advance.

These four determinants of demand—preferences, income, prices of related products, and future expectations—affect individual demand to varying degrees. If we shift our attention to market demand, these four factors still apply. In addition, a few other factors need to be mentioned. The *size of the market population* will affect the demand for all products. An increase in the size of the population, for example, leads to an increase in the demand for everything from houses and cars to sports equipment and credit cards. In addition, a *change in the distribution of incomes* leads to an increase in the demand for some products and a decrease in the demand for others. For example, if the percentage of total income earned by those over 65 years of age rises, while the percentage going to those under the age of 24 falls, then we would expect to see an increase in the demand for holiday cruises and a decrease in the demand for entry into popular night clubs.

Increasingly busy lifestyles and more demands in the workplace have increased the sales of energy bars in Canada.

McGraw-Hill Education Mark Dierker Photographer

The same will also be true for the *age composition of the population.* An aging population increases the demand for products that largely appeal to older people (Bruce Springsteen albums) and decrease the demand for those that appeal only to the young (Justin Bieber recordings).

Note that one factor is *not* included on this list of determinants of demand: supply. Economists are scrupulous in their attempts to separate the forces of demand and supply. Remember that the demand formulation is a hypothetical construct based on the quantities that consumers are willing and able to purchase at various prices. There is an implied assumption that the consumer will be able to obtain these quantities, otherwise the demand schedule itself would not be relevant. In other words, when specifying demand, we assume that the supply will be available, just as when formulating supply, we make the assumption that there will be sufficient demand.

In summary, the determinants of demand are as follows:

- consumer preferences
- consumer incomes
- prices of related goods
- expectations of future prices, incomes, or availability
- population size, or income and age distribution

 TEST YOUR UNDERSTANDING

4. The accompanying table shows the initial weekly demand (D$_1$) and the new demand (D$_2$) for packets of pretzels (a bar snack).

To explain the change in demand from D$_1$ to D$_2$, what might have happened to the price of a complementary product such as beer? Alternatively, what might have happened to the price of a substitute product such as nuts?

Price	Quantity Demanded (D$_1$)	Quantity Demanded (D$_2$)
$2.00	10 000	11 000
3.00	9 600	10 600
4.00	9 200	10 200

The Effects of an Increase in Demand

We have just seen that the demand for any product is affected by many different factors. A change in any of these factors will cause a change in demand, which, as we shall see, leads to a change in price and production levels. Let us first consider the effects of an *increase* in the demand for a product. Any one of the following could cause such an increase in the market demand:

- a change in preferences toward the product
- an increase in incomes if the product is a normal product or a decrease in incomes if the product is an inferior product
- an increase in the price of a substitute product
- a decrease in the price of a complementary product
- the expectation that future prices or incomes will be higher or that there will be a future shortage of the product
- an increase in the population or a change in its income or age distribution

Any of these changes could cause people to buy more of a product, regardless of its price. As an example, let us combine supply and demand data in Table 2.7.

TABLE 2.7
The Effects of an Increase in Demand on the Market

	NUMBER OF CASES PER MONTH		
Price per Case	Quantity Supplied	Quantity Demanded 1	Quantity Demanded 2
$18	10	16	22
19	12	15	21
20	14	14	20
21	16	13	19
22	18	12	18

You can see that at the old demand (Demand 1) and supply, the equilibrium price was $20 and the quantity traded was 14 cases. Assume now that the demand for energy bars increases (Demand 2). Since consumers do not usually signal their intentions to producers in advance, producers are not aware that the demand has changed until they have evidence. The evidence will probably take the form of unsatisfied customers. At a price of $20 a case, the producers in total have produced 14 cases. At this price, the new quantity demanded is 20 cases. There is a **shortage** of 6 cases, and some customers will go home disappointed because there are not enough energy bars, at a price of $20, to satisfy all customers. Will these manufacturers now increase production to satisfy the higher demand? The surprising answer is no—at least, not at the present price. Manufacturers are not in the business of satisfying customers, they are in the business of making profits. As Adam Smith wrote over 200 years ago:

> It is not from the benevolence of the butcher, the brewer, or the baker that we expect our dinner but from regard to their own self-interest.[1]

You may say that unless firms are responsive to the demands of customers, they will soon go out of business. And you are right. But a firm that is *solely* responsive to its customers will go out of business even faster. Look again at the supply schedule in Table 2.7. At a price of $20, the manufacturers are prepared to produce 14 cases. They are not prepared to produce 20 cases, the amount that consumers now want. Why is that? It may be because they can make more profits from producing 14 cases than from producing 20 cases; otherwise, they would have produced 20 in the first place. In fact, it may well be that if they produced 20 cases at the current price of $20, they would end up

---

[1] Adam Smith, *The Wealth of Nations* (Edwin Cannan edition, 1877), pp. 26–27.

incurring a loss. Does this mean that the shortage of energy bars will persist? No. As we saw earlier, *shortages drive prices up* until the shortage disappears and the new quantity demanded is equal to the quantity supplied. This will occur at a price of $22, where the quantity demanded and the quantity supplied are equal at the equilibrium quantity of 18. This adjustment process can be seen in **Figure 2.10**.

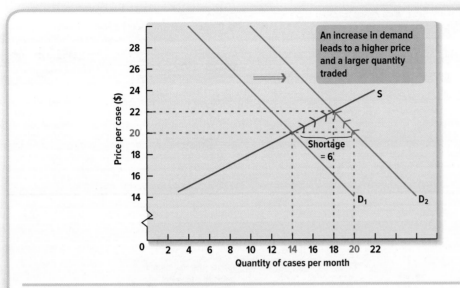

FIGURE 2.10 Adjustment to an Increase in Demand

The increase in demand from D₁ to D₂ creates an immediate shortage of 6. This will cause an increase in the price of energy bars. The increase affects both producers, who will now increase the quantity supplied, and consumers, who will reduce the quantity demanded. Eventually, the price will reach a new equilibrium at $22, where the equilibrium quantity is 18 and there is no longer a shortage.

You can see in the graph that at the old price of $20, the new quantity demanded exceeds the quantity supplied. This shortage causes the price to rise. As it does so, the quantity of energy bars that producers make also rises; that is, there will be an increase *in the quantity supplied*. Producers will produce more, not because there is a shortage but because the shortage causes a rise in price. Note also that the increase in price causes some customers to reduce their purchases of energy bars that is, there is a decrease *in the quantity demanded*. The price of these bars will continue to increase as long as there is a shortage and will stop as soon as the shortage disappears. This occurs when the price has increased to $22. At the new equilibrium price, the quantity demanded will again equal the quantity supplied but at a higher quantity traded of 18 cases.

An increase in demand causes an increase in both price and the quantity traded.

The Effects of a Decrease in Demand

Now, let us see what happens when there is a decrease in demand. Remember that a decrease in demand cannot be caused by an increase in price but is caused by a change in any of the nonprice determinants, including

- a decrease in preferences for the product
- a decrease in incomes if the product is a normal product, or an increase in incomes if the product is an inferior product
- a decrease in the price of a substitute product
- an increase in the price of a complementary product
- the expectation that future prices or incomes will be lower
- a decrease in the population or a change in its income or age distribution

A decrease in demand is shown in Table 2.8 and illustrated in Figure 2.11.

TABLE 2.8
The Effects on the Market of a Decrease in Demand

	NUMBER OF CASES PER MONTH		
Price per Case	Quantity Supplied	Quantity Demanded 1	Quantity Demanded 3
$18	10	16	10
19	12	15	9
20	14	14	8
21	16	13	7
22	18	12	6

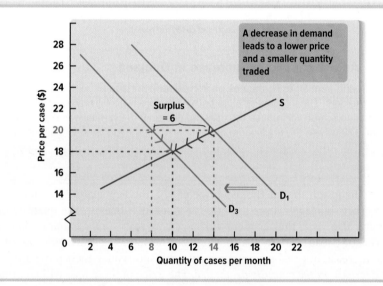

FIGURE 2.11   Adjustment to a Decrease in Demand

The drop in demand from D_1 to D_3 will cause an immediate surplus of 6, since the quantity supplied remains at 14 but the quantity demanded drops to 8. This surplus will cause the price to fall, and as it does, the quantity demanded will increase while the quantity supplied will fall. This process will continue until the surplus is eliminated. This occurs at a new equilibrium price of $18 and an equilibrium quantity of 10.

The initial equilibrium price is $20, and the quantity traded is 14. Assume that the demand now decreases to Demand 3 in the table and D3 in Figure 2.11. At a price of $14, producers will continue to produce 14 cases, yet consumers now wish to purchase only 8 cases. A **surplus** is immediately created in the market. The growth of unsold inventories and more intensive competition between suppliers will eventually push down the price. Note in Figure 2.11 that as the price decreases, the quantity supplied also starts to decrease, and the quantity demanded begins to increase. Both these factors will cause the surplus to disappear. The price will eventually drop to a new equilibrium of $18, where the quantity demanded and the quantity supplied are equal at 10 cases. In short:

A decrease in demand will cause both price and the quantity traded to fall.

TEST YOUR UNDERSTANDING

5. What effect will the following changes have on (i) the demand for, (ii) the price of, and (iii) the quantity traded of commercially brewed beer?

a) a new medical report affirming the beneficial health effects of drinking beer (in moderation, of course)

b) a big decrease in the price of home-brewing kits

c) a rapid increase in population

d) talk of a strike by brewery workers

e) a possible future recession

SECTION SUMMARY

a) All products are either normal products or inferior products. With normal products, demand *increases* when incomes increase; with inferior products demand *decreases* when incomes increase.

b) Market demand changes if there is a change in

- consumers' preferences
- consumers' incomes
- the price of related products
- expectations of future prices, incomes, or availability
- the size of the market, or income and age distribution

c) An increase in demand will cause a shortage and cause both price and the quantity traded to rise.

d) A decrease in demand will cause a surplus and cause both price and the quantity traded to fall.

2.6   Change in Supply

> **LO6**   Demonstrate the causes and effects of a change in supply.

Let us reiterate what we mean by supply: it is the relationship between the price of the product and the quantities producers are willing and able to supply. Price is *part* of what economists call supply. In other words, supply does not mean a single quantity. We now need to address what could cause a **change in supply**. What factors will cause producers to offer a different quantity on the market, even though the price has not changed—what will cause a change in supply? We begin with **Table 2.9**, where an increase in supply is illustrated. For reasons we will soon investigate, suppliers are now willing to supply an extra 6 cases of energy bars at every possible price. This is illustrated in **Figure 2.12**.

TABLE 2.9
An Increase in Supply

	NUMBER OF CASES PER MONTH	
Price per Case of Energy Bars	Quantity Supplied 1	Quantity Supplied 2
$18	10	16
19	12	18
20	14	20
21	16	22
22	18	24

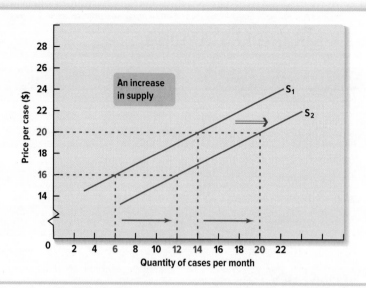

FIGURE 2.12   **An Increase in Supply**

At each price, the quantities supplied have now increased; that is, the supply curve has shifted right, from S_1 to S_2. For example, at a price of $20, the original quantity of 14 has now increased to 20. Similarly, at a price of $16, the quantity supplied has increased from 6 to 12. In this example, the quantities supplied have increased by 6 units at every price level, thus causing a parallel shift in the supply curve.

An increase in supply causes the whole supply curve to shift right. (Do not be tempted to describe it as a downward shift, because then you would be saying that as the supply goes up, the supply curve goes down, which could make things very confusing! It would be better to talk about a rightward shift.) This means that at each and every price, producers are now willing to produce more.

Determinants of a Change in Supply

What could have happened in the manufacturers' world to make them wish to produce more, even though the price is unchanged? Since we are assuming that the prime motivation for the supplier is profit, then something must have happened to make the manufacture of energy bars more profitable, which is inducing a higher supply. Profit is the difference between revenue and cost, and since the price (and therefore revenue) is unchanged, then something must have affected the cost of producing energy bars.

First, we will look at the *price of resources*. For energy-bar makers, this includes the price of wheat, granola honey, and other ingredients, as well as the cost of baking ovens, and so on. If any of these should drop in price, then the cost for the makers will fall, and profits will rise. Under these circumstances, since they are now making a bigger profit on each case of energy bars, they will be very willing to produce more. A fall in the price of resources will lead to an increase in supply. Conversely, an increase in the price of resources will cause a decrease in supply.

Another way of looking at the increase in supply, as shown in **Figure 2.12**, is to say that rather than firms being willing to produce more at a given price, they are willing to accept lower prices to produce any given quantity. For instance, previously, in order to induce the manufacturers to supply a total of 20 cases per week, the price needed to be $17. Now that the costs of production have dropped, these same manufacturers are able to make the same profits by producing the 20 cases at a lower price of $14: the manufacturers are now willing to produce the same quantities as before at lower prices. Again, this would produce a rightward shift in the supply curve.

It is often suggested that the availability of resources is a major determinant of the supply of a product. A poor grape harvest—grapes being the key input in the making of wine—will obviously have an impact on the supply of wine. However, it is not really the difficulty in obtaining grapes that causes a decrease in the wine supply, since most things can be obtained *at a price*. But there's the rub. A poor grape harvest will cause the price of grapes to increase, and this increase will reduce the profitability and production of wine producers.

A second major determinant of supply is *government taxes and subsidies*. The major type of taxes imposed on suppliers are sales taxes such as the GST (general sales tax) and, in some provinces, the HST (harmonized sales tax). In addition, there are **excise taxes** which are special sales taxes imposed on products like alcohol, cigarettes, and gasoline. For suppliers, these taxes are similar to the other costs of doing business, and an increase in them will lead to a decrease in the firm's profits and thus cause a decrease in supply. A reduction in these taxes, on the other hand, will encourage firms to increase supply. In contrast, a **subsidy** is the reverse of a tax and is a payment made by the government to suppliers. The

A poor grape harvest is likely to cause the price of grapes to rise.

sonsam/Shutterstock

Canadian government, for instance, provides subsidies to the farmers of certain types of agricultural products and other specific products like solar panels. A subsidy will encourage greater production and therefore an increase in supply. A reduction or elimination of a subsidy will decrease supply.

A third determinant of supply is the *technology* used in production. An improvement in technology means nothing more than an improvement in the method of production. This will enable a firm to produce more with the same quantity of resources (or to produce the same output with fewer resources). An improvement in technology will not affect the actual price of the resources, but because more can now be done with less, it will lead to a fall in the per-unit cost of production. This means that an improvement in technology will lead to an increase in supply.

The price of related products also affects supply, just as it affected demand. But we must be careful, since we are looking at things from a producer's point of view and not a consumer's. What a producer regards as related will usually differ from what a consumer regards as related. A fourth determinant of supply, then, is the *price of substitutes in production*. To a wheat farmer, the price of other grains such as rye and barley will be of great interest because the production of all grain crops are related in terms of production methods and equipment. A significant increase in the price of rye may well tempt the wheat farmer to grow rye in the future instead of wheat. In other words, an increase in the price of one product will cause a drop in the supply of products that are substitutes in production. A decrease will have the opposite effect.

A fifth determinant of supply is the *future expectations of producers*. This is also analogous to the demand side of the market, but with a difference. While consumers eagerly look forward to a drop in the price of products, producers view the same prospect with great anxiety. Producers who feel that the market is going to be depressed in the future and that prices are likely to be lower may be inclined to change production now, before the anticipated collapse. Lower expected future prices therefore tend to increase the present supply of a product. Anticipating higher prices has the opposite effect; producers hold off selling all of their present production hoping to make greater profits from the future higher prices, assuming the product is something like oil, which is not perishable.

Finally, market supply will also be affected by the *number of suppliers*. An increase in the number of suppliers will cause an increase in market supply, whereas a decrease in the number of suppliers will reduce overall market supply.

Again, note that one thing omitted from this list of supply determinants is any mention of demand. At the risk of repetition, firms are not in business to satisfy demand but to make profits. Increased demand for a product does not mean that producers will immediately increase production to satisfy the higher demand. However, the higher demand will cause the price to increase, and this increase induces firms to supply more. But this is an increase in the quantity supplied and *does not* imply an increase in supply—the supply curve remains unchanged.

In summary, the determinants of market supply are

- prices of resources
- business taxes
- technology
- prices of substitutes in production
- future expectations of suppliers
- number of suppliers

The Effects of an Increase in Supply

We have just discussed six different factors that might affect the supply of a product. Let us be more specific and look at what can cause an *increase* in supply:

- a decrease in the price of resources
- a decrease in business taxes (or increase in subsidies)
- an improvement in technology
- a decrease in the price of a productively related product
- the expectation of a decline in the future price of the product
- an increase in the number of suppliers

Let us see the effects of an increase in supply using the original demand for energy bars and the increase in supply in **Table 2.10**.

TABLE 2.10

The Effect of an Increase in Supply on the Market

	NUMBER OF CASES PER MONTH		
Price per Case of Energy Bars	Quantity Demanded 1	Quantity Supplied 1	Quantity Supplied 2
$18	16	10	16
19	15	12	18
20	14	14	20
21	13	16	22
22	12	18	24

At the original demand (Quantity Demanded 1) and supply (Quantity Supplied 1), the equilibrium price was $20 per case, and the quantity traded was 14 cases. Assume that the supply now increases to Quantity Supplied 2. At the present price of $20, there will be an immediate surplus of 6 cases.

Before we look at the implications of this surplus, we ought to address a couple of possible qualms that some students might have. The first is this: Won't customers take up this excess of energy bars? It is easy to see that at this price, consumers have already given their response. They want to buy 14 cases, not 20 cases, or any other number. In other words, consumers are buying energy bars to satisfy their own tastes, not to satisfy the manufacturers. A second question is this: Why would producers produce 20 cases, knowing that the demand at this price is only 14 cases? The answer is that they do not know. Producers know the circumstances in their own companies and know that, until now, they have been able to sell everything they have produced. With the prospect of higher profits coming from, say, a decrease in costs, a manufacturer wants to produce more. If all producers do the same, there will be a surplus of energy bars. **Figure 2.13** shows what happens as a result of this surplus.

Faced with a surplus of energy bars, market price will be forced down. As price falls, the quantity demanded increases and the quantity supplied falls. Production increased initially but is now dropping slightly because of the resulting drop in price. The price will continue to drop until it reaches $18. **Table 2.10** shows that at this price the quantity demanded and the quantity supplied are now equal at 16 cases. The effect of the increase in supply, then, is a lower price and a higher quantity traded.

We leave it to you to verify that a decrease in supply will cause a shortage that will eventually raise the price of the product. (The factors that cause such a decrease in supply are exactly the same as those mentioned above that cause an increase—except they move in the opposite direction.) The net result will be a higher price but a lower quantity traded.

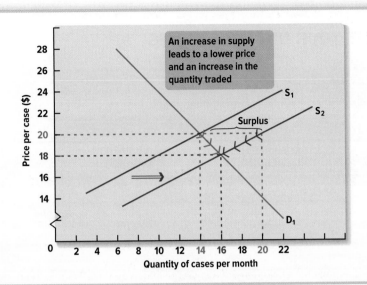

FIGURE 2.13   **Adjustment to an Increase in Supply**

The increase in the supply has the immediate effect of causing a surplus because the demand has remained unchanged. In this figure, at a price of $20, the quantity supplied has increased from 14 to 20, causing a surplus of 6. This will cause the price to drop, and as it does, the quantity demanded increases and the quantity supplied decreases until a new equilibrium is reached at a new equilibrium price of $18 and quantity of 16.

IN A NUTSHELL ...

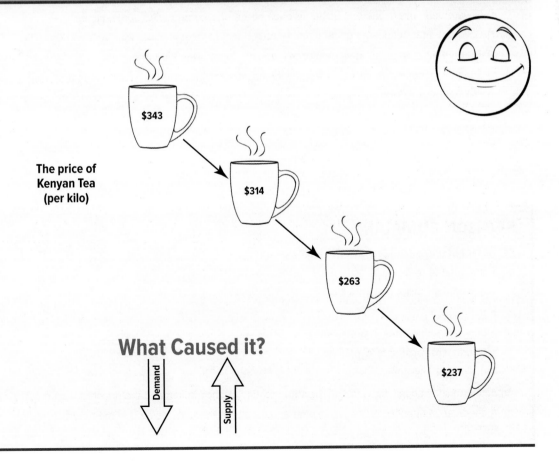

TEST YOUR UNDERSTANDING

6. Suppose that the demand and the supply for strawberries in Corona are as follows (the quantities are in thousands of kilos per week):

| | | QUANTITY | |
Price	Quantity Demanded	Quantity Supplied 1	Quantity Supplied 2
$4.00	140	60	_____
4.50	120	80	_____
5.00	100	100	_____
5.50	80	120	_____

a) What are the present equilibrium price and equilibrium quantity? Graph the demand and supply curves, labelling them D_1 and S_1, and indicate equilibrium.

b) Suppose that the supply of strawberries were to increase by 50 percent. Show the new quantities in the Quantity Supplied 2 column. What will be the new equilibrium price and quantity? Draw in S_2 on your graph, and indicate the new equilibrium.

7. What effect will the following changes have on the supply, price, and quantity traded of wine?

a) A poor harvest in the grape industry results in a big decrease in the supply of grapes.

b) The number of wineries increases.

c) The sales tax on wine increases.

d) The introduction of a new fermentation method reduces the time needed for the wine to ferment.

e) Government introduces a subsidy for each bottle of wine produced domestically.

f) Government introduces a quota limiting the amount of foreign-made wine entering Canada.

g) There is a big increase in wages for the workers in the wine industry.

h) A big increase occurs in the prices of wine coolers (an industry that is similar in technology to the wine industry).

SECTION SUMMARY

a) Market supply changes if there is a change in

- the price of resources
- government taxes and subsidies
- technology
- prices of substitutes in production
- future expectations of suppliers
- the number of suppliers

b) An increase in supply causes a surplus and results in price falling and the quantity traded rising.

c) A decrease in supply causes a shortage and results in the price rising and the quantity traded falling.

2.7   Final Words

LO7   Explain why demand and supply determine price and the quantity traded, and not the reverse.

To complete this introduction to demand and supply, let us use the following chart as a summary:

↑ Demand	→	shortage	→	↑ P	and	↑ Q traded
↓ Supply	→	shortage	→	↑ P	and	↓ Q traded
↓ Demand	→	surplus	→	↓ P	and	↓ Q traded
↑ Supply	→	surplus	→	↓ P	and	↑ Q traded

Note that when demand changes, both price and the quantity traded move in the same direction; when supply changes, the quantity traded moves in the same direction, but price moves in the opposite direction.

From this table, you should confirm in your own mind that it is the supply of and demand for a product that determine its price and not price that determines supply and demand. A change in any of the factors that affect demand or supply will therefore lead to a change in price. The price of a product *cannot* change *unless* there is a change in either demand or supply. It follows therefore that you cannot really analyze any problem that starts: "What happens if the price increases (decreases)...?" The reason for this, as the above chart makes clear, is that an increase in the price of a product might be caused by either increasing demand or decreasing supply. But in the case of an increase in demand, the quantity traded also increases, whereas in the case of a decrease in supply, the quantity traded falls. In the first case, we are talking about an expanding industry; in the second, we are looking at a contracting industry.

Finally, make sure you understand clearly the distinction between changes in the quantities demanded and supplied and changes in demand and supply as illustrated in **Figure 2.14**.

   ADDED DIMENSION

The Famous Scissors Analogy

Since the time of Adam Smith, economists have emphasized the importance of understanding the role of price determination. Toward the end of the nineteenth century, there were two schools of thought about what determined price. The first was made up of those who believed that the cost of production was the main determinant—the supply-side view. The second was made up of those, including the famous economist Alfred Marshall, who believed that consumer demand was the main determinant—the demand-side view.

Marshall, writing at the end of that century, was the first to present a lucid synthesis of the two views and suggest that neither demand nor supply alone can provide the answer to the determination of price. His famous analogy of the scissors states, "We might as reasonably dispute whether it is the upper or the under blade of scissors that cuts a piece of paper as whether value [price] is governed by utility or cost of production. It is true that when one blade is held still, and the cutting is effected by moving the other, we may say with careless brevity that the cutting is done by the second; but the statement is not strictly accurate and is to be excused only so long as it claims to be merely a popular and not a strictly scientific account of what happens."[2]

---

[2] Alfred Marshall, *Principles of Economics*, 8th edition, Macmillan (1920). Reproduced with permission of Palgrave Macmillan.

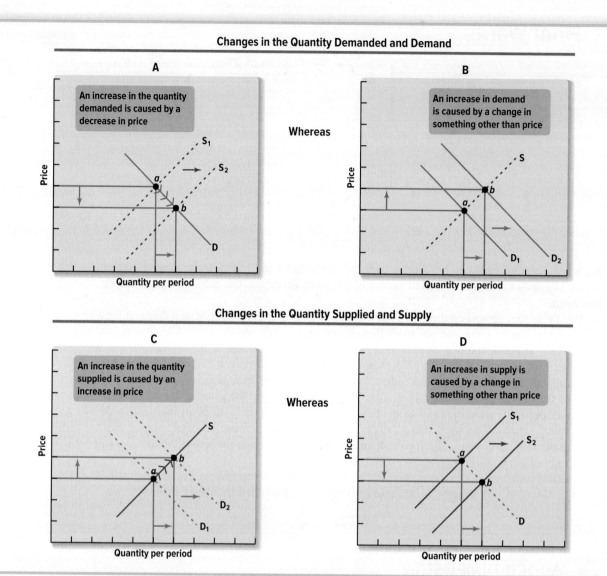

FIGURE 2.14   Distinction Between Changes in the Quantities Demanded and Supplied and Changes in Demand and Supply

Now, let us look back at the discussion that started this chapter and see if we can make sense of it. Justine made an observation about the price of HDTVs falling, and Eric responded rather flippantly, "But that is just supply and demand." We now know that price can fall because either supply increased or demand decreased. Justine asked if Eric thought that the price fall was due to an increase in supply and Eric said, "Sure." Then came the really hard question: Why would supply go up if price was falling? Eric once again responded that this was just supply and demand. Of course, we now know that Eric should have said that the supply had gone up—perhaps because of increased technology—and that increased supply caused the price to fall. That is, changes in supply cause changes in price, not the other way around.

All of this is summarized in **Figure 2.14**. In graph A, we see a movement from point *a* to *b*, which is an increase in the quantity demanded resulting from the fall in price caused by an increase in supply (S_1 to S_2). Graph B shows an increase in demand, which causes an increase in price and in the quantity supplied (*a* to *b*). Graph C shows an increase in the quantity supplied (*a* to *b*), which follows an increase in price caused by an increase in demand (D_1 to D_2). Finally, in graph D, we see an increase in supply (S_1 to S_2) resulting in a fall in price and an increase in the quantity demanded (*a* to *b*). This allows us to conclude that:

> An increase in the quantity demanded results when an increase in supply pushes price down (A). An increase in demand increases price, and thus the quantity supplied increases (B).

> An increase in the quantity supplied results when an increase in demand pushes price up (C). An increase in supply decreases the price and thus the quantity demanded increases (D).

You now know what an important and versatile tool supply-and-demand analysis can be—but, like all tools, you must handle it properly and clean it after every use!

 TEST YOUR UNDERSTANDING

8. The following are changes that occur in different markets. Explain what will happen to either demand or supply and to the equilibrium price and quantity traded.

a) an increase in income on the market for an *inferior product*

b) a decrease in the price of steel on the *automobile industry*

c) a government subsidy given to operators of *day-care centres*

d) a government subsidy given to parents who want their children to attend *day-care centres*

e) a medical report suggesting that *wine* is very fattening

f) a big decrease in the amount of Middle East oil exports on the *refined-oil market*

g) an increase in the popularity of *antique furniture*

h) an increase in the price of coffee on the *tea market*

IT'S NEWS TO ME ...

Starbucks Corporation recently announced its plan to raise prices for packaged coffee and over-the-counter cups. They cited an increase in the price of Arabica coffee beans, caused by a severe harvest, as the reason for this action. A spokesperson for Starbucks said that, for both its package coffee and retail business, the overall cost structure was a major determining factor in its pricing policies.

The increased price for the consumer translate into about 10 to 25 cents per over-the-counter cup and $1 a bag for packaged coffee.

Source: *Star Power Reporting*. Summer 2016.

I. The increase in price of coffee was the result of
    a) an increase in demand
    b) a decrease in demand
    c) an increase in supply
    d) a decrease in supply

II. The increase in price of coffee beans was the result of
    a) an increase in demand
    b) a decrease in demand
    c) an increase in supply
    d) a decrease in supply

SECTION SUMMARY

The demand for and supply of a product determine the price; price does not determine demand and supply.

Study Guide

Review

WHAT'S THE BIG IDEA?

One of the important things to remember from this chapter is that the terms "demand" and "supply" do not refer to specific quantities. For instance, you cannot say that the demand for iPhones increased from 10 million units to 12 million units or that the supply of apples has fallen by 20 percent this year. As confusing as it might seem at first, you have to remember that economics defines them a little differently from everyday language. Both demand and supply refer to whole lists of prices and corresponding quantities. Think of these two concepts as tables of numbers, or better still, as lines on a graph. If you are able to do this, you will find that demand and supply analysis is a really powerful tool in understanding the world around us. The other important thing to remember is that the price of a product does not determine demand and supply. It's the other way around: demand and supply determines the price of most products.

Now suppose that you are thinking of starting up your own small company offering lawn cutting and garden services to households in your neighbourhood. One of the reasons for this is that it seems like easy money! You've figured out that many of the other companies now charge $50 a cut for the average lawn whereas only two years ago the price was $35. But before you start investing your money and energy, it will pay you to find out why the price has increased. In general, this can only be caused by an increase in the demand or a decrease in supply. If it is because of a higher demand, find out why. More homes have been built, perhaps? Or more lawns laid? Higher income people moving into the area? Or perhaps, people in the neighbourhood getting older? Or could the cause be that the supply has dropped? Perhaps other firms have had difficulty hiring workers and have to increase wages significantly? Or have a number of firms gone out of business because of conditions in that industry?

So whenever you hear of prices going up or down, try to work out whether it is demand or supply that has changed. If it is demand, think of the 5 factors that might cause this; if it is supply, remember there are 6 major causes.

NEW GLOSSARY TERMS

ceteris paribus
change in demand
change in supply
change in the quantity
   demanded
change in the quantity
   supplied
complementary products
demand

demand schedule
equilibrium price
equilibrium quantity
excise taxes
income effect
inferior products
market
market demand
market supply

normal products
real income
shortage
subsidy
substitute products
substitution effect
supply
supply schedule
surplus

Comprehensive Problem

Questions

(LO 1, 2, 4, 5, 6) Table 2.11 shows the market for wool in the economy of Odessa (the quantities are in tonnes per year).

TABLE 2.11

Price ($)	100	200	300	400	500	600	700
Quantity Demanded	130	110	90	70	50	30	10
Quantity Demanded 2	—	—	—	—	—	—	—
Quantity Supplied	10	20	30	40	50	60	70
Quantity Supplied 2	—	—	—	—	—	—	—

a) Plot the demand and supply curves on **Figure 2.15**, and label them D_1 and S_1. Mark the equilibrium as e_1 on the graph.

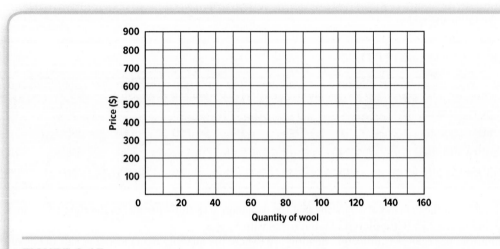

FIGURE 2.15

b) What are the values of equilibrium price and quantity?
c) If the price of wool were $600, would there be a surplus or shortage? How much? Indicate the amount of the surplus or shortage on the graph.

Answers

a) See the following figure:

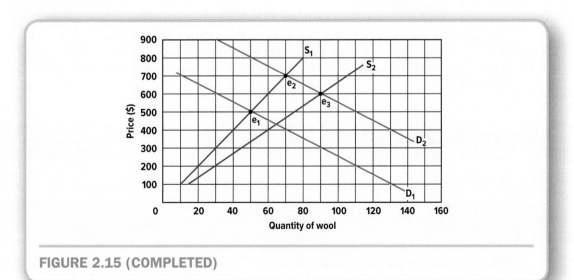

FIGURE 2.15 (COMPLETED)

The plotting of the curves is straightforward. For the demand curve, plotting just the first point (price $100 and quantity demanded 130) and the last point (price $700, quantity demanded 10) is sufficient. Similarly with the supply curve.

b) Equilibrium price: $500; equilibrium quantity: 50.

c) Surplus of 30. A price of $600 is above the equilibrium price of $500. Any price above equilibrium will produce a surplus because the quantity supplied will exceed the quantity demanded. The amount of the shortage is the distance between the curves. In this case it is 3 squares or 30 units.

Questions

d) Suppose that the demand were to increase by 60. Show the new Quantity Demanded 2 in Table 2.11.

e) Draw and label the new demand curve as D_2. Mark the new equilibrium as e_2 on the graph.

f) What are the new values of equilibrium price and quantity?

Answers

d) See the following table:

TABLE 2.11 (COMPLETED)							
Price ($)	100	200	300	400	500	600	700
Quantity Demanded	130	110	90	70	50	30	10
Quantity Demanded 2	190	170	150	130	110	90	70
Quantity Supplied	10	20	30	40	50	60	70
Quantity Supplied 2	15	30	45	60	75	90	105

e) An increase in the demand of 60 means that the demand curve shifts parallel to the right by 6 squares to D_2 in Figure 2.15 (Completed). D_2 intersects with S_1, at e_2.

f) Equilibrium price: $700; equilibrium quantity: 70 (where the quantity demanded 2 equals the quantity supplied).

Questions

g) Following the change in (d), suppose that the supply were to increase by 50 percent. Show the new Quantity Supplied 2 in Table 2.11.

h) Draw and label the new supply curve as S_2. Mark the new equilibrium as e_3.

i) What are the new values of equilibrium price and quantity?

Answers

g) See Table 2.11 (Completed):

h) An increase in supply of 50 percent means that the supply curve shifts right to reflect a quantity that is 50 percent higher at each price level (for example, at price $300 it is now 45 rather than 30). This is plotted above as S_2 in Figure 2.15 (Completed). The intersection with the D_2 curve is marked as e_3.

i) Equilibrium price: $600; and equilibrium quantity: 90 (where the quantity demanded 2 equals the quantity supplied 2).

Study Problems

Find answers on the McGraw-Hill online resource.

Basic (Problems 1–5)

1. (LO 4)
   a) Given the data in Table 2.12, draw the demand curve in Figure 2.16.
   b) What is the equilibrium price and quantity?
      Price: _____ Quantity: _____

TABLE 2.12

Price	Quantity Demanded
1	80
2	70
3	60
4	50
5	40
6	30

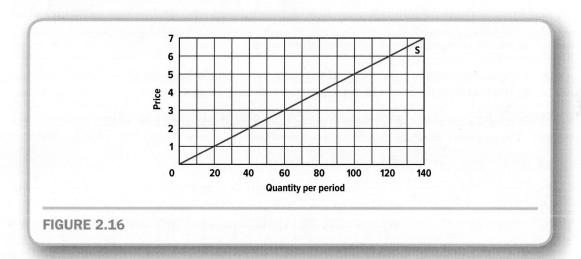

FIGURE 2.16

2. **(LO 3)** Figure 2.17 shows the market for large bags of potato chips.

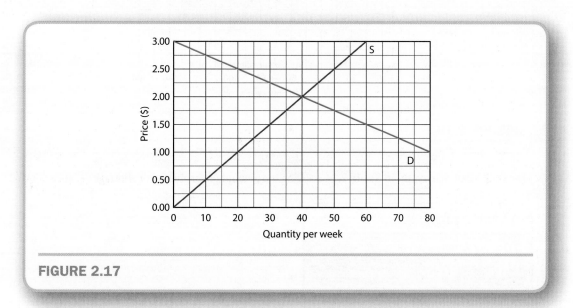

FIGURE 2.17

a) What is the equilibrium price and quantity?
 Price: _____ Quantity: _____
b) If the price is $2.25, is there a surplus or shortage of potato chips?
 Surplus/shortage _____ of _____ units
c) If the price is $1.50, is there a surplus or a shortage of potato chips?
 Surplus/shortage _____ of _____ units

3. **(LO 4, 5, 6)** Table 2.13 shows the market demand and supply for Fuji apples in Peterborough.

TABLE 2.13

Price	Quantity Demanded	Quantity Supplied 1	Quantity Supplied 2
0	180	90	_____
2	170	110	_____
4	160	130	_____
6	150	150	_____
8	140	170	_____
10	130	190	_____

a) What is the equilibrium price and quantity traded?
   Price: _____ Quantity: _____
b) Suppose that supply increases by 30. Complete the column in Table 2.13.
c) What would be the price and quantity traded at the new equilibrium?
   Price: _____ Quantity: _____
d) After the increase in supply, what would be the surplus/shortage at a price of $8?
   Surplus/shortage of _____

4. **(LO 3)** Figure 2.18 shows the market for halibut fillets.

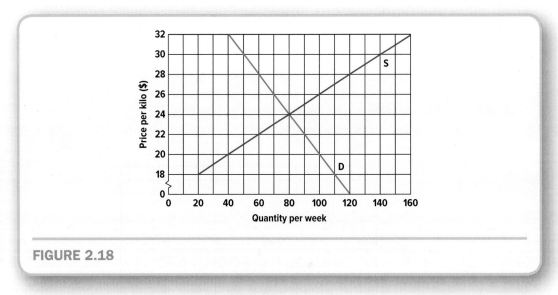

FIGURE 2.18

For the halibut market, fill in Table 2.14 showing the amount of surplus (+) or shortage (−) at each price.

TABLE 2.14

Price per Kilo $	+/−
18	_____
20	_____
22	_____
24	_____
26	_____
28	_____
30	_____

5. **(LO 5)** Figure 2.19 shows the market for pizzas.

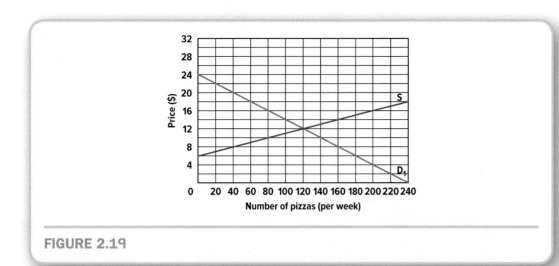

FIGURE 2.19

a) Suppose that the demand for pizzas were to increase by 60 pizzas per day. Show the new demand, labelled D_2, _____ in Figure 2.19.
b) If the price stays at the old equilibrium, there would be a _____ (surplus/shortage) of _____ pizzas.
c) What would be the new equilibrium price and quantity?
   Equilibrium price: $_____
   Equilibrium quantity: _____

Intermediate (Problems 6–8)

6. **(LO 4, 5, 6)** Table 2.15 shows the demand for new townhouses for 2011, 2012, and 2013.

TABLE 2.15

Price $	2011 Quantity Demanded	2012 Quantity Demanded	2013 Quantity Demanded
320 000	5 200	5 500	5 300
340 000	5 100	5 400	5 200
360 000	5 000	5 300	5 100
380 000	4 900	5 200	5 000
400 000	4 800	5 100	4 900
420 000	4 700	5 000	4 800
440 000	4 600	4 900	4 700

a) When the price in 2011 changed from $400 000 to $420 000, what happened in the market for townhouses?
   Answer: There was a(n) (increase/decrease) of _____ in the (demand/quantity demanded) _____ .

b) What happened between 2011 and 2012?
   Answer: There was a(n) (increase/decrease) of _____ in the (demand/quantity demanded) _____ .

c) What happened between 2012 and 2013?
    Answer: There was a(n) (increase/decrease) of _____ in the (demand/quantity demanded) _____.

d) When the price in 2013 changed from $400 000 to $380 000, what happened in the market for townhouses?
    Answer: There was a(n) (increase/decrease) of _____ in the (demand/quantity demanded) _____.

7. **(LO 4, 5, 6)** Table 2.16 shows the demand and supply for the World Cup Final game in the Maracana Stadium in Rio.

TABLE 2.16

Price $ per Ticket	Quantity Demanded 1	Quantity Supplied	Quantity Demanded 2
150	119 000	79 000	_____
200	109 000	79 000	_____
250	99 000	79 000	_____
300	89 000	79 000	_____
350	79 000	79 000	_____
400	69 000	79 000	_____
450	59 000	79 000	_____

a) If the organizers wish to ensure a sellout for the final game, what is the highest price per ticket they should charge?
    Price of: _____

b) What would happen if the organizers decided to charge a price of $200 per ticket?
    Answer: There would be a (surplus/shortage) _____ of _____ tickets.

c) Suppose that the demand for each game in the qualifying rounds is 20 000 less than for the final game. Show the new demand in Table 2.16.

d) If the organizers wish to ensure a sellout for each game, what is the highest price per ticket they can charge for a qualifying round game?
    Price of: _____

8. **(LO 5)** Figure 2.20 shows the market for soya beans:

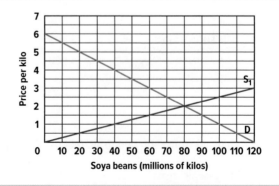

FIGURE 2.20

a) Suppose that due to a bad harvest the supply of soya beans is reduced by 50 percent. (The quantities at every price are one-half of what they are at present.) Draw the new supply curve, labelled S_2.

b) As a result of the drop in supply, what are the new equilibrium price and quantity?
Equilibrium price: $_____
Equilibrium quantity: _____

Advanced (Problems 9–12)

9. **(LO 1, 4)** In Kirin, at a market price of $1 per kilo, there is a shortage of 60 kilos of avocados. For each 50-cent increase in the price, the quantity demanded drops by 5 kilos while the quantity supplied increases by 10 kilos.
   a) Complete Table 2.17.

TABLE 2.17

Price	1.00	__	__	__	__	__	__	__	__
Quantity Supplied	100	__	__	__	__	__	__	__	__
Quantity Demanded	__	__	__	__	__	__	__	__	__
Surplus/ Shortage	-60	__	__	__	__	__	__	__	__

b) What will be the equilibrium price?
Price: _____

c) What will be the surplus/shortage at a price of $4.50?
Surplus/shortage of kilos: _____

10. **(LO 4)** Figure 2.21 shows the market for the new Guns and Butter album, *Live at Saskatoon.*

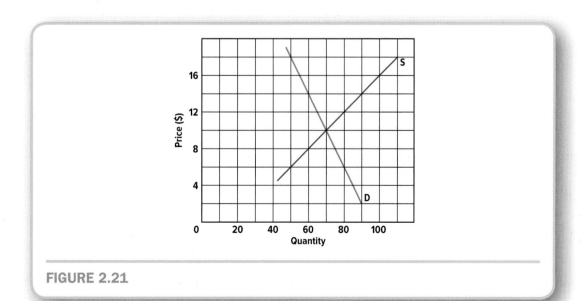

FIGURE 2.21

a) Suppose that the album producers put it on sale for $8 each. How much will be the surplus or shortage? How many will be sold?
Surplus/shortage of: _____
Quantity sold: _____

b) What is the maximum price at which the quantity actually sold in (a) could have been sold?
Maximum price: _____

c) If the album producers had actually put the album on the market at the price mentioned in (b), what would have been the resulting surplus/shortage?
Surplus/shortage of: _____

11. **(LO 4)** **Figure 2.21** shows the market for the new Guns and Butter album, *Live at Saskatoon*.

a) Suppose that the album producers put it on sale for $14 each. How much will be the surplus or shortage? How many will be sold?
Surplus/shortage of: _____
Quantity sold: _____

b) What is the minimum price that suppliers would accept in order to produce the quantity actually sold in (a)? _____
Minimum price: _____

c) If the album producers had actually put the album on the market at the price mentioned in (b), what would have been the resulting surplus/shortage?
Surplus/shortage of: _____

12. **(LO 4, 5, 6)** Table 2.18 shows the market for probiotic yogurt in Canada.

	1	2	3	4	5	6
	Price per Carton	Quantity Demanded (1)	Quantity Supplied (1)	Quantity Demanded (2)	Quantity Demanded (3)	Quantity Supplied (2)
	2.00	120	60	_____	_____	_____
	2.25	115	70	_____	_____	_____
	2.50	110	80	_____	_____	_____
	2.75	105	90	_____	_____	_____
	3.00	100	100	_____	_____	_____
	3.25	95	110	_____	_____	_____
	3.50	90	120	_____	_____	_____

TABLE 2.18

a) Suppose the price of a complementary product were to increase in price causing the demand to change by 30. Show the new demand in column 4 in Table 2.18.

b) What will be the new equilibrium price and quantity?
Price: _____ Quantity: _____

c) Suppose that *instead* the average income were to increase (and probiotic yogurt is a normal product), causing the demand to change by 15. Show the new demand in column 5 in Table 2.18.

d) What will be the new equilibrium price and quantity?
Price: _____ Quantity: _____

e) Suppose that *instead* the price of factors of production were to decrease causing the supply to change by 45. Show the new supply in column 6 in Table 2.18.

f) What will be the new equilibrium price and quantity assuming the original quantity demanded in column 2?
Price: _____ Quantity: _____

Problems for Further Study

Basic (Problems 1–6)

1. **(LO 5)** Circle which of the following factors will lead to an increase in the demand for cranberry juice (which is a normal good).
   a) a decrease in the price of cranberry juice
   b) a decrease in the price of cranberries
   c) the expectation by consumers that the price of cranberry juice is likely to increase
   d) an increase in the price of apple juice
   e) an increase in consumers' average income
   f) an improvement in the juicing process that lowers the cost of producing cranberry juice

2. **(LO 1, 2, 5, 6)** In each of the two graphs in **Figure 2.22**, explain the change in equilibrium from *a* to *b* in terms of:
   1) an increase (or decrease) in demand (or supply)
   2) an increase (or decrease) in the quantity demanded (or quantity supplied)

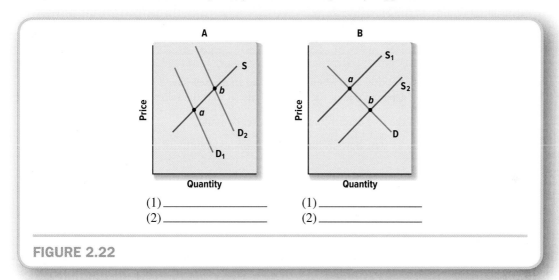

(1) _____   (1) _____
(2) _____   (2) _____

FIGURE 2.22

3. **(LO 4, 5, 6)** Suppose that new medical research strongly indicates that the consumption of coffee can cause cancer of the colon. What effect will this news have on the equilibrium price and quantity traded of the following products?
   a) coffee beans
      Price: _____ Quantity traded: _____
   b) tea, a substitute for coffee
      Price: _____ Quantity traded: _____
   c) Danish pastries, a complement to coffee
      Price: _____ Quantity traded: _____
   d) teapots, a complement to tea
      Price: _____ Quantity traded: _____

4. **(LO 5, 6)** What must have happened to demand or supply to cause the following changes?
   a) The price of guitars falls, but the quantity traded increases.
      Demand/supply must have _____.
   b) The price and quantity traded of saxophones decrease.
      Demand/supply must have _____.
   c) The price of trombones increases, while the quantity traded falls.
      Demand/supply must have _____.
   d) The price and quantity traded of clarinets increases.
      Demand/supply must have _____.

5. **(LO 1, 5)** What is the distinction between demand and quantity demanded?

6. **(LO 1, 4)** Explain the effect of a shortage on prices.

Intermediate (Problems 7–10)

7. **(LO 4, 5, 6)** Consider the effects of each of the events outlined in Table 2.19 on the market indicated. Put a (↑), (↓) or (−) under the appropriate heading to indicate whether there will be an increase, a decrease, or no change in demand (D), supply (S), equilibrium price (P), and the quantity traded (Q).

TABLE 2.19

	Market	Event	D	S	P	Q
a)	Printer inks	A technological improvement reduces the cost of producing printers.				
b)	Butter	New medical evidence suggests that margarine causes migraines.				
c)	Newspapers	Because of worldwide shortages, the prices of pulp and paper increase dramatically.				
d)	Low-quality toilet paper	Consumer incomes rise significantly.				
e)	Movie downloads	Movie theatres halve their admission prices.				
f)	Beef	World price of lamb increases.				

8. **(LO 1, 5)** "The prices of houses rise when the demand increases. The demand for houses decreases when prices increase." Change one of these statements so that the two are consistent with each other.

9. **(LO 5)** Briefly explain the five determinants of market demand.

10. **(LO 4, 5)** Explain, step by step, how an increase in demand eventually affects both price and quantity traded.

Advanced (Problems 11–12)

11. **(LO 4, 5, 6)** Identify any two possible causes and five specific effects involved in the movement from point *a* to *b* to *c* in Figure 2.23.

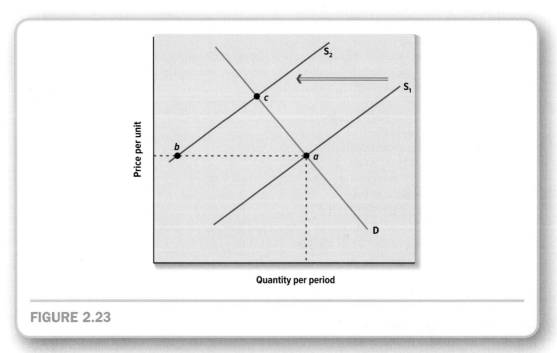

FIGURE 2.23

12. **(LO 6)** Suppose that in response to the high rent and low supply of affordable rental accommodation in the Toronto market, the city constructed 5000 additional rental units and put them on the market at below-equilibrium rents. Draw a supply-and-demand graph showing the effects on the rental market.

Appendix to CHAPTER 2
The Algebra of Demand and Supply

THE ALGEBRA OF THE MARKET

We have described the marketplace in both tables and graphs. This appendix explains how we can also analyze demand and supply algebraically. Suppose that **Figure A1** shows the demand for soya milk in Canada.

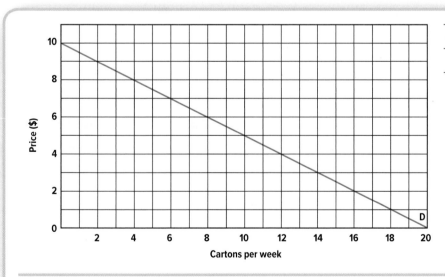

Number of Cartons per Week	
Price ($)	Quantity
0	20
1	18
2	16
3	14
4	12
5	10
6	8
7	6
8	4
9	2
10	0

FIGURE A1

You will remember from the Toolkit that, in general, the algebraic expression for a straight line is

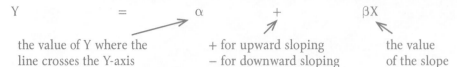

Y   =   α   +   βX

the value of Y where the   + for upward sloping   the value
line crosses the Y-axis   − for downward sloping   of the slope

On our graph, price is shown on the vertical (Y) axis and the quantity demanded on the horizontal (X) axis. Therefore, the general expression for the demand curve is given as

$$P = α + βQ^d$$

Here, the value of α is equal to ($)10. This is where the demand curve crosses the price axis; that is, it is the highest price payable. The value of the slope is the ratio of change, or *rise over run*. In terms of the demand curve, the slope shows by how much the quantity changes as the price changes.

$$\text{The slope} = \frac{Δ \text{ (change in) P}}{Δ \text{ (change in) Q}}$$

For our demand curve, that value equals

$$\frac{1}{-2}$$

This means that each time the price changes by $1, quantity changes (in the opposite direction) by 2 units. The equation for this demand curve, then, is

$$P = 10 - \frac{1}{-2} Q^d \quad \text{or} \quad P = 10 - \frac{1}{2} Q^d$$

Though this is graphically the correct way to express it, in terms of economic logic the quantity demanded is dependent on price rather than the other way around, so let us rearrange the terms, as follows:

$$Q^d = 20 - 2P$$

Now, let us look at the supply side of things. The table and graph in **Figure A2** show the supply of soya milk in the market.

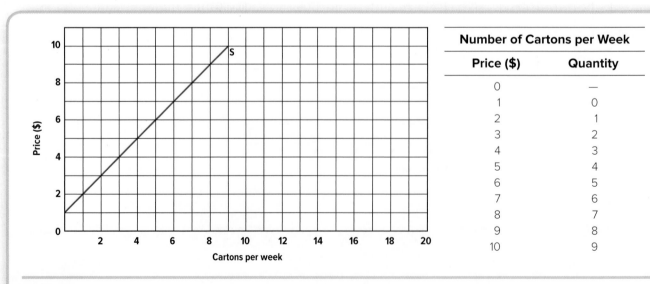

Number of Cartons per Week	
Price ($)	Quantity
0	—
1	0
2	1
3	2
4	3
5	4
6	5
7	6
8	7
9	8
10	9

FIGURE A2

The general equation for the supply curve is

$$P = \alpha + \beta Q^s$$

As with the demand curve, α shows the value where the curve crosses the vertical (price) axis. This happens at a price of $1. The value of the slope is, again, the same as for the demand curve.

$$\frac{\Delta \text{ (change in) } P}{\Delta \text{ (change in) } Q}$$

For this supply curve, it equals

$$\frac{1}{+1}$$

A $1 change in price causes a change of 1 unit in the quantity supplied. The equation for this supply curve, then, is

$$P = 1 + Q^s$$

As we did with the demand curve, let us rearrange this equation in terms of Q^s. Thus

$$Q^s = -1 + P$$

Bringing demand and supply together, in **Figure A3**, allows us to find the equilibrium values. From either the table or the graph, it is easy to see that the equilibrium price is equal to $7. At this price, the quantity demanded and the quantity supplied are both 6 units. Finding equilibrium algebraically is also straightforward. We want to find the price at which the quantity demanded equals the quantity supplied. We know the equations for each, and so we simply set them equal.

$$Q^d = Q^s$$

$$20 - 2P = -1 + P$$

That gives us

$$3P = 21$$

Therefore,

$$P = 7$$

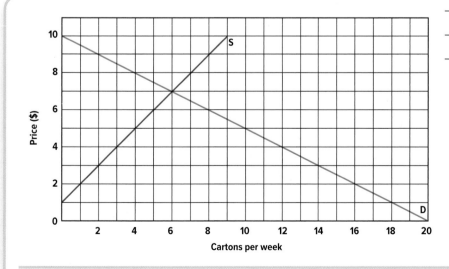

Number of Cartons per Week		
Price ($)	Q^d	Q^s
0	20	—
1	18	0
2	16	1
3	14	2
4	12	3
5	10	4
6	8	5
7	6	6
8	4	7
9	2	8
10	0	9

FIGURE A3

Substituting in either equation (and it is best to do both to make sure you are correct) gives us

$$Q^d = 20 - 2(7) = 6$$

$$Q^s = -1 + (7) = 6$$

Doing things algebraically sometimes makes things easier. For instance, suppose market demand increased by 3 units; that is, the quantities demanded increased by 3 units at every price. What effect would this have on the equilibrium price and quantity? Algebraically, this is quite straightforward to calculate. The increase in demand means that the value of the (quantity) intercept increases by 3 and gives us a new demand equation:

$$Q^d_2 = 23 - 2P$$

The supply has not changed, and so we can calculate the new equilibrium as

$$(Q^d_2 = Q^s)\ 23 - 2P = -1 + P$$

This gives us

$$3P = 24$$

Therefore,

$$P = 8$$

The new equilibrium quantity becomes 7. We can obtain this quantity by inserting the price of $8 into both equations. Thus

$$Q^d_2 = 23 - 2(8) = 7 \text{ and } Q^s - 1 + (8) = 7$$

Study Guide

Problems for Further Study

1. If $Q^d = 40 - 2P$ and $Q^s = 10 + 3P$, what are the equilibrium values of price and quantity?

2. a) If $Q^d = 100 - 5P$ and $Q^s = 10 + P$, what are the equilibrium values of price and quantity?
   b) If demand increases by 12 and price remains the same as in (a), will there be a surplus or a shortage? How much?
   c) If demand increases by 12, what will be the new equilibrium price and quantity?

3. a) If $P = 61 - 0.25Q^d$, what is the algebraic expression for Q^d?
   b) If $P = 16 + 2Q^s$, what is the algebraic expression for Q^s?
   c) What are the equilibrium values of price and quantity?

4. The following table shows the demand and supply of kiwi fruit in Montreal.
   a) What is the algebraic expression for the demand curve?
   b) What is the algebraic expression for the supply curve?
   c) Find algebraically the values of equilibrium price and quantity.

Price per Kilo	Quantity Demanded	Quantity Supplied
$0	675	0
1	575	50
2	475	100
3	375	150
4	275	200
5	175	250

5. Suppose that the demand equation is $Q^d = 230 - 3P$ and the supply equation is $Q^s = -10 + 9P$.
   a) If the price is 15, will there be a surplus or a shortage? How much?
   b) If the price is 22, will there be a surplus or a shortage? How much?

6. Suppose that the demand equation is $Q^d = 520 - 3P$ and the supply equation is $Q^s = 100 + 4P$.
   a) If the quantity presently supplied is 380, what is the price?
   b) At the price in (a), what is the quantity demanded?
   c) At the price in (a), is there a surplus or a shortage?

CHAPTER 3
Demand and Supply: An Elaboration

LEARNING OBJECTIVES

At the end of this chapter, you should be able to:

LO1 Understand that even where markets are not competitive, the forces of demand and supply still apply.

LO2 Explain the effects of simultaneous changes in supply and demand on equilibrium price and quantity traded.

LO3 Explain why markets do not always work well.

LO4 Describe why price ceilings cause shortages.

LO5 Demonstrate that price floors cause surpluses.

LO6 Explain how quotas work and what effect they have on production and prices.

LO7 Explain how sales taxes and subsidies affect markets.

 WHAT'S AHEAD...

We start this chapter by looking at circumstances that might cause simultaneous changes in demand and supply. We then ask how well markets operate and why governments often intervene. We next look at why governments sometimes introduce various types of price controls, and then we try to identify the costs and benefits of such intervention. Next we look at how governments control production and prices through the use of production quotas. Finally, we examine the effect of sales taxes and subsidies on product markets, particularly in the agricultural sector.

A QUESTION OF RELEVANCE ...

You are probably aware that every province in Canada has legislated a minimum wage for hired labour. Do you think that this benefits you as a student looking for work to help pay for your education? Do you think that farmers should be guaranteed minimum prices for the products they sell or that government should effect the levels of agricultural production? Are you living in a province that has rent controls? If so, who do you think benefits from such a policy? These questions sometimes generate a lot of debate. Make a mental note of your answers now, and see if they change as a result of studying this chapter.

When we look at how markets operate, there is a great danger in believing the principles of demand and supply to be immutable scientific laws that are an integral part of the natural universe. Nothing could be further from the truth. As Oser and Brue wrote, commenting on the approach of the economist Alfred Marshall:

> Economic laws are social laws—statements of tendencies, more or less certain, more or less definite.[1]

The collective behaviour of consumers and producers in the marketplace is a result of the society in which we live. Every society has its own history, culture, economic structure, and political environment. The tools of demand and supply are versatile and powerful aids for economists. But while they demonstrate general tendencies, they also have certain limitations. For example, in the previous chapter, we suggested that the price of a product is determined by demand and supply. This is only true under certain conditions. In many cases, the price of products we buy is set by the manufacturers and retailers, not by consumers and producers somehow coming together to form an agreement. Similarly, government determines the price of a number of goods and services that it provides, and as we shall see later in this chapter, it also stipulates the minimum and maximum prices of a number of other products provided by the private sector. In addition, we will look at the effects of government intervention by way of quotas, sales taxes, and subsidies.

3.1 Markets Matter

> **LO1** Understand that even where markets are not competitive, the forces of demand and supply still apply.

We will start by asking the question: Under what circumstances do the forces of demand and supply determine the price of products? Strictly speaking, they do so only in what economists term a "perfectly competitive" market, one in which there are no big dominant firms and no interference by government. (Chapter 8 will look at this type of market in some detail.) It is important to be aware that competitive markets as described in Chapter 2 only work well if they are truly competitive. Bigness in the marketplace, whether in the form of corporations, trade unions, or government, limits the efficient working of the market. In essence, whenever a powerful participant or group of participants is buying or selling in the market, the benefits of competition will be seriously reduced.

But does this also mean that if there are big firms operating, they can ignore the market and charge whatever prices they like? Well, from one point of view, yes they can—but only at their peril. **Figure 3.1**, illustrating the market for the Ford Fusion automobile, makes this clear.

---

[1] J. Oser and S. L. Brue, *The Evolution of Economic Thought*, 4th ed. (New York: Harcourt Brace), p. 273.

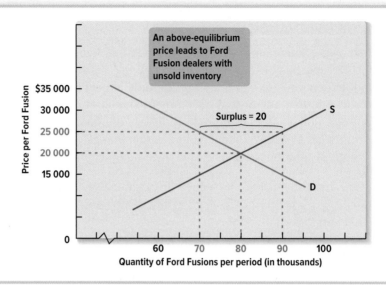

FIGURE 3.1 **An Overpriced Product**

Although Ford Motor Company can price its Fusion at whatever level it wishes, this graph shows that if it wants to sell all of its output, it must sell them at a price of $20 000 or less. If it overprices it at, say, $25 000, the result will be 20 000 unsold vehicles.

GREAT ECONOMISTS: ALFRED MARSHALL

Alfred Marshall (1842–1924) was the son of a tyrannical father who was a cashier at the Bank of England. His father wanted him to put away such frivolous pastimes as chess and mathematics and devote himself to higher pursuits. To this end, he decided that Alfred would study for the church. However, Alfred rebelled, and instead of taking up a scholarship to study divinity at Oxford University, he studied mathematics, physics, and later economics at Cambridge University with financial help from an uncle. Later, as professor of economics at the same school, he influenced a whole generation of economists.

His fame was sealed with the publication of his *Principles of Economics* in 1890. Marshall was a precise and painstaking scholar, and his book was the result of years of study and research. In this text, Marshall established himself as the intellectual leader of neoclassical economics and provided a synthesis of the classical ideas of Smith and Ricardo, with the new idea of marginal analysis (which we will introduce in Chapter 5).

INTERFOTO/Alamy Stock Photo

Despite the fact that Marshall was an expert mathematician, he believed that mathematics should be regarded merely as a useful tool for economists rather than as the provider of fundamental economic truths. He also thought that the "laws of demand" suggest what possible outcomes may result under certain circumstances and that those results may or may not be desirable. Students of economics also owe a debt to Marshall for introducing graphical analysis into the discipline.

In this figure the demand curve, as usual, shows the market demand for the vehicle at various prices. The supply curve shows the outputs that provide the greatest profit for the company at each different selling price. For information, the graph also shows what the equilibrium price would be ($20 000). But this manufacturer can, if it wishes, charge any price it wants. Let us say it charges a price of $25 000 and produces 90 000 Fusions, since this is the quantity that will produce the greatest profit for the firm *at this price*.

Unfortunately, the company will soon discover that consumers are not as excited about this vehicle as it had hoped. At a price of $25 000 it is only able to sell 70 000 units, leaving it with a surplus of 20 000. Obviously, it will eventually have no choice but to drop the price in one way or another, such as by offering rebates to new customers. If it does not, the manufacturer will end up with unsold cars and likely huge losses. The market can be a stern taskmaster.

What this example demonstrates is that even powerful producers (or, for that matter, consumers or governments) must heed market forces, because the market embodies the simple truth that people cannot be forced to buy something they do not want. Similarly, producers cannot be forced to produce products that do not earn them sufficient profits.

This chapter will look at situations in which the market works well and at others in which governments intervene and correct what they perceive to be deficiencies in the market system. As we shall see, markets do not always produce the "right" results for a number of reasons, but in other cases interference by governments may do more harm than good. How well and how fairly markets operate is a central theme in microeconomics, one we will examine from various angles throughout this book.

This chapter is a preliminary exploration of the efficiency of the market system and will help you understand the power of demand and supply analysis. First, however, we need to dig a little deeper into these concepts.

SECTION SUMMARY

a) Markets are most effective in the absence of big corporations, trade unions, or government.

b) Even when a big corporation dominates a particular market, its behaviour is still subject to the demands of buyers since people cannot be forced to buy things they do not want.

3.2   Simultaneous Changes in Demand and Supply

LO2   Explain the effects of simultaneous changes in supply and demand on equilibrium price and quantity traded.

In the last chapter, we looked at the causes of changes in demand and supply, and how they affect both the price and the quantity traded of a product. However, in order to deepen our understanding, we need to be able to explain what will happen if demand and supply change simultaneously—which might well happen in a dynamic, ever-changing economy.

In this next example, we look at the factor market rather than the product market, but the approach remains the same. In particular, we will examine possible changes in the supply of software engineers. The supply of software engineers is definitely increasing these days, since a career in computers is an attractive proposition for many students, and colleges and universities offer a wide range of computer courses. In addition, the demand for engineers by software companies as well as by other businesses and government is steadily increasing. Since both the demand and the supply are increasing at the same time, what can we say about the wage of software engineers and about future job opportunities in the industry? Here it is helpful to think of the wage as the price of labour, with the supply coming from individuals in the labour market and the demand coming from firms, organizations, and governments that hire software engineers. **Figure 3.2** shows the effect of a simultaneous increase in both demand and supply.

© Ayse Ezgi Icmeli | Dreamstime.com

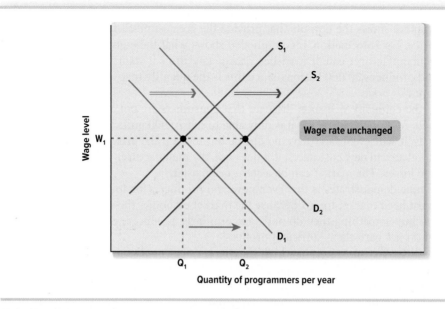

FIGURE 3.2   The Demand for and Supply of Software Engineers

A simultaneous increase in both the demand for and the supply of software engineers will lead to an increase in the number of engineers employed, Q_1 to Q_2, and in this example the wage rate, W_1, is unchanged. However, it is uncertain what will happen to the wage level without knowing exactly how much demand increases in comparison to the increase in supply.

We see that the result is a definite increase in the number of employed engineers from Q_1 to Q_2; however, the wage level W_1 seems not to have changed. In contrast, **Figures** 3.3A and 3.3B give different results.

In **Figure** 3.3A, the shift in the demand curve is greater than the shift in the supply curve, and since demand increases more than supply, the wage level increases from W_1 to W_2. In contrast, **Figure** 3.3B shows a situation in which the supply increase exceeds the demand increase, resulting in a lower

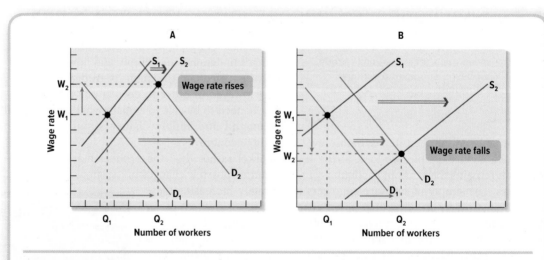

FIGURE 3.3   Simultaneous Increases in Demand and Supply, and the Effect on Wages

In graph A, the increase in demand, from D_1 to D_2, is greater than the increase in supply, from S_1 to S_2. The result is an increase in the wage level, from W_1 to W_2. In graph B, in contrast, the increase in supply, from S_1 to S_2, exceeds the increase in demand, from D_1 to D_2. The result, in this case, is a drop in the wage level, from W_1 to W_2.

> **TABLE 3.1**
> **Determinants of Demand and Supply**

Determinants of Demand	Determinants of Supply
Consumer preferences	Prices of productive resources
Consumer incomes	Sales taxes and subsidies
Prices of related products	Technology
Expectations of future prices, incomes, or availability	Prices of substitutes in production
Population: size, income distribution, and age distribution	Future expectations of suppliers
	Number of suppliers

wage level. Both graphs show, as does the graph in **Figure 3.2**, that the number of engineers employed will increase, but what happens to the wage level depends on the comparative magnitude of the change in demand and supply. In other words, to find out what will happen to the wage level, we need to know the amounts by which demand and supply increase; otherwise the effect is inconclusive—or, as economists say, *indeterminate*.

It is important to remember that many factors can affect the demand for and supply of a product. To refresh your memory about these determinants, **Table 3.1** might be helpful.

Since there are many determinants, it is hardly surprising that more than one might change at the same time. It is important therefore to be able to correctly identify whether demand or supply has been affected, and in what manner.

Whenever multiple shifts are analyzed graphically, the result will always be uncertain unless the amount of each change is known. Because of these indeterminate results, it is often a good idea to analyze the changes in terms of arrows rather than graphs. For instance, from Chapter 2, we know that if the market is initially in equilibrium an increase in demand will produce the following result:

$$\uparrow D \rightarrow \downarrow P \uparrow Q$$

On the other hand, an increase in supply will lead to

$$\uparrow S \rightarrow \downarrow P \uparrow Q$$

As you can see, both changes will tend to push up the quantity traded. However, the increase in demand will push the price up, whereas the increase in supply will push the price down. So, if both changes happen at the same time, the net result on the price is indeterminate. It follows that

$$\left. \begin{array}{c} \uparrow \ D \\ \uparrow \ S \end{array} \right\} \rightarrow \ ? \, P \uparrow Q$$

Similarly, we can analyze the effects of a decrease in both demand and supply:

$$\begin{array}{ccc} \downarrow \ D \ \} & \rightarrow & \downarrow P \downarrow Q \\ \downarrow \ S \ \} & \rightarrow & \underline{\uparrow P \downarrow Q} \\ & & ? \, P \downarrow Q \end{array}$$

In this case, the quantity will definitely decrease; however, the effect on price, as in our last example, is indeterminate.

Next, let us look at what happens when demand and supply move in opposite directions. Suppose that the demand for a product were to increase, while supply decreases—what effect would this have on the market? In terms of arrows, the result is clear, though, as usual, the net result is indeterminate:

$$\begin{array}{ccc} \uparrow \ D \ \} & \rightarrow & \uparrow P \uparrow Q \\ \downarrow \ S \ \} & \rightarrow & \underline{\uparrow P \downarrow Q} \\ & & \uparrow P \, ? \, Q \end{array}$$

It is the change in the quantity this time that is indeterminate; price will definitely increase.

Finally, let us take a look at the last combination—a decrease in demand accompanied by an increase in supply:

$$\downarrow D \;\} \;\rightarrow\; \downarrow P \downarrow Q$$
$$\uparrow S \;\} \;\rightarrow\; \underline{\downarrow P \uparrow Q}$$
$$\downarrow P \;? \;Q$$

As in the previous case, the effect on the quantity is indeterminate; price, however, will definitely decrease.

Returning to our market for software engineers, we can now pose a practical problem that many students have to address: What are the prospects for a good job or a decent salary, given the present trends? The answer depends to a great extent on the number of graduating students and the number of new jobs being created in industry. Suppose, in **Figure 3.4**, that the increase in the supply of graduates exceeds the increased demand.

The initial wage level is W_1, and the quantity of engineers employed is shown as quantity *a*. Suppose that there is a simultaneous increase in demand from D_1 to D_2, and in supply from S_1 to S_2. The increase in the supply of engineers, however, exceeds the increase in demand from the industry. At the present wage level of W_1, the number of new engineers wanted by the industry is represented by the increased quantity *b*; however, the number of qualified engineers has now increased to quantity *c*. There are a number of unemployed engineers (a surplus of engineers) in the amount *bc*. The competition among engineers for jobs may cause the wage level to eventually drop to a lower wage level, W_2. This lower wage level has eliminated the unemployed engineers, some of whom presumably gave up trying to find a job in computers and started looking for other types of work. The workings of the marketplace, therefore, do not ensure that everyone will be happy with the results. The number of employed engineers, however, has definitely increased from quantity *a* to the new equilibrium quantity *d*.

What this software engineer example shows is the way markets operate, and how, by changing the price (the wage level, in this case), surpluses and shortages are eliminated. Does this describe how markets always work? Well, not entirely. Certainly it is true that if the number of graduates exceeds the number of new jobs created, many of these graduates are going to be unemployed. The market's cure for this would be a reduction in wage levels. However, the market solution is not always a popular solution. Throughout the centuries, people have often attempted to circumvent or impede the workings of the market, because they have either doubted the efficiency of the marketplace or have not liked its results. The rest of this chapter investigates this interference.

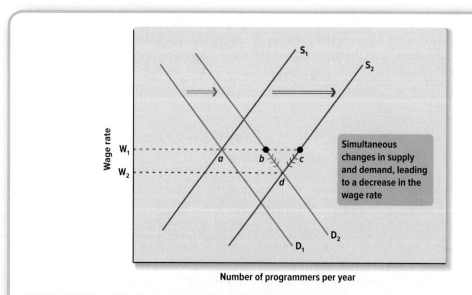

Number of programmers per year

FIGURE 3.4   When the Increase in Supply Exceeds the Increase in Demand

The original wage is W_1, and the number of employed engineers is equal to *a*. Demand and supply now simultaneously increase, from D_1 to D_2 and from S_1 to S_2, respectively. As a result, the number of engineers wanting jobs (*c*) exceeds the number of jobs available (*b*). The surplus of engineers, *bc*, will cause the wage to drop to W_2, and the new equilibrium number of engineers will be quantity *d*.

TEST YOUR UNDERSTANDING

Find answers on the McGraw-Hill online resource.

1. In each of the following cases, explain what effect the changes will have on the equilibrium price and quantity in each market.

Market	Change
a) Day-care services	More mothers with small children are returning to the labour force; at the same time, government decides to introduce subsidies for day-care operators.
b) Marijuana	Government severely increases the penalties for both buying and selling marijuana.
c) DVDs	A new processing method significantly reduces the costs of producing DVDs; at the same time, more consumers download video content directly onto their computers.
d) Organic vegetables	Vegetarianism increases as a result of medical reports extolling its health benefits; at the same time, tighter regulations on the definitions of organically grown products are introduced.

2. If the demand for a product were to decrease more than the supply decreases, will the result be a surplus or a shortage at the original equilibrium price? What will happen to the price level and the quantity traded as a result?

 ## ADDED DIMENSION

Canada's Temporary Foreign Worker Program

The history of Canada's TFW (Temporary Foreign Worker) program began in 1973 when certain foreign high-skill workers and medical specialists were allowed to take jobs in Canada if the employer could demonstrate that no Canadian residents were available for hire. In 2012 the Harper government added a low-skill category which, in many cases, reduced the requirement for demonstration of the unavailability of Canadian workers. This category was then expanded in 2016 by the Trudeau government.

The result was that by 2016 over 4000 Canadian companies had brought in TFWs with a record number of 338 000 arriving in that year alone. The industries involved range from energy and mining to retailers and cell-phone providers to financial firms and railroads.

The program is based on the idea that insufficient Canadian workers are either able or willing to work at prevailing wage rates. (There are suggestions that many Canadian workers are unwilling to take low-skill, low-paying jobs in the retail and food servicing sectors for instance.) If this is the case, the market's usual response to a shortage of labour would be a rise in the price level—in this case, the wage rate for such workers. Wages would rise to the level at which reluctant Canadians would then become willing to work at those jobs. However, rather than allowing the market to do its job, the Canadian government has chosen to eliminate the shortage of workers by increasing the supply of labour, bringing in temporary foreign workers. This will certainly eliminate the shortage, but by increasing the supply it will also keep wage levels down to the benefit of business but to the detriment of Canadian workers.

It is interesting to note that the increase in the influx of TFWs in 2016 came at a time when Statistics Canada reported that job vacancies in the same year had declined from 440 000 to 325 000. This raises the question of whether the decrease in vacancies was a result of the entry of more TFWs (probably) or some other factor such as an uptick in economic growth (unlikely).

There is another aspect of all this. If we focus on the low-skill (rather than the high-skill) component of the TFW influx, it becomes obvious that the employer holds a great deal of power over the worker. This fact was dramatically illustrated by an Ontario Human Rights Tribunal case in which women were being forced to perform sexual acts under the threat of being sent home before their appointed work time expired.

SECTION SUMMARY

a) In a noncompetitive market, a seller is able to set any price desired, but if a price above equilibrium is chosen, a surplus will result and sellers will have to either reduce the price to the equilibrium level or sell less than they would like.

b) The four possible combinations of simultaneous changes in demand and supply are as follows:

- an increase in both demand and supply that results in an increased quantity traded but an indeterminate change in price

- a decrease in both demand and supply that results in a decrease in the quantity traded but an indeterminate change in price

- an increase in demand with a decrease in supply that results in an increase in price but an indeterminate change in the quantity traded

- a decrease in demand with an increase in supply that results in a decrease in price but an indeterminate change in the quantity traded

3.3   How Well Do Markets Work?

LO3   Explain why markets do not always work well.

Imagine, for the sake of illustration, that a devastating tsunami hit a major North American coastal city, resulting in the total destruction of half its housing stock. Let us assume that the population of the city was given advance notice and evacuation efforts were successful, so nobody was killed. However, for the sake of our example, also suppose that half the residents find themselves, in the wake of the receding water, without a place to live. The situation is illustrated in **Figure** 3.5.

Before the tsunami struck, the average monthly value of the housing stock (rented and owned, houses and apartments) was $1000 per month, and the number of occupied units was 100 000. The effect of the tsunami has been to reduce the supply of housing units to 50 000, leading to a shortage

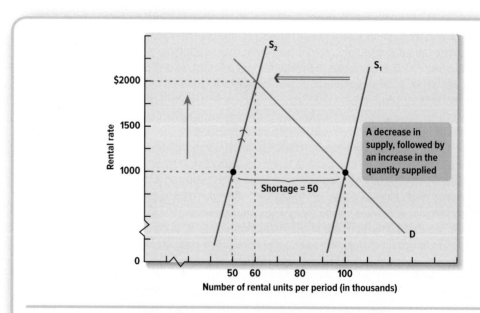

FIGURE 3.5   **Market Adjustment to a Decrease in Supply**

The initial equilibrium rental value was $1000, and the number of rental units occupied was 100 000. A tsunami demolishes half the units, which is reflected in the supply curve shifting left from S_1 to S_2. With a resulting shortage of 50 000 units, rents are forced up, and in time a new equilibrium is reached at a rent of $2000 and with 60 000 units now occupied.

of 50 000 units at the present monthly value of $1000. What we now want to look at is how the market addresses these kinds of changes in supply. The severe shortage of accommodation is definitely going to cause rents to increase appreciably, because many families left homeless are only too willing to pay more than $1000 per month for housing. As the monthly value starts to increase, the quantity supplied will also go up.

This will happen in a variety of ways. Many homeowners will be willing to rent out their basements, some shopkeepers may be willing to convert their shops into rented accommodation, many landlords and tenants will be very happy to subdivide their premises, and at the low end of the accommodation scale, warehouses, stables, sheds, and garages will become available—all at a price. As rents continue to skyrocket, the quantity demanded will fall, since many people will simply be unable to afford the higher rents. (These people will have to find someone to live with, such as a parent or roommate, or live on the streets, or leave the city as happened in New Orleans in 2005–06.) Rents will continue to rise as long as there is a shortage and will stop rising when the market has eliminated that shortage. This occurs, in **Figure** 3.5, when the average value of accommodation has increased to the new equilibrium price of $2000. At this figure, the number of units now occupied has increased to 60 000.

Yet this is not the end of the story. The adjustment process described above probably occurs over a short period, maybe a few months. In the long run, more lasting change will come about in the market. The high value of rents and of property in general will encourage developers to start building more units. As new units are built, the supply of housing will increase, which we could have shown as a rightward shift in the supply curve. In time, as a result of the increased supply, the price of accommodation will drop and the number of housing units on the market will increase. Eventually the number of units might well return to 100 000 and the price of accommodation will revert to $1000, but this would surely take years.

Now consider the question that faces government. Should it sit back and allow the market to cure the problem of the shortage, or should it step in and implement its own cure? Certainly, the competitive market can eliminate shortages, but since it works through economic incentives and disincentives on a voluntary basis, it may not always work fast enough for society's liking. In emergency situations, governments can effect change far more quickly than the marketplace can. In the case of large-scale disasters, such as floods or earthquakes, we expect government to step in immediately and take charge to alleviate suffering. Similarly, in wartime, we take it for granted that government would and should mobilize industry on behalf of the war effort. Governments generally will not rely on market incentives to produce sufficient armaments or military personnel. In other words, we expect government to conscript workers and factories because this is the fastest method of mobilizing resources. On the other hand, it is certainly possible that governments might intervene in situations in which they should not, or use inappropriate methods of intervention.

The earthquake and tsunami in Samoa in 2009 left 3000 people homeless.

Cohen A. Young/USA/US Navy

Markets do not always adjust as quickly as we would like, and this can be a problem. Furthermore, markets do not always produce equitable results, as far as society or government is concerned. Let us look at this aspect.

In our example of the tsunami, the market's short-run solution was to increase the price of accommodation. Suppose (admittedly an extreme scenario) that the destroyed houses were all in the richer section of the city; the houses in the poorer section were all left intact. As the price of accommodation starts to increase, a number of tenants will no longer be able to afford to rent their homes and will be evicted by their landlords, who will gladly see them replaced by new tenants from the rich side of the town. In time, we may well find that the rich now totally inhabit the poor side of the town and that the former tenants are now homeless, forced to double up or relocate. Note in **Figure** 3.5 that when the price of accommodation reaches $2000, there is no longer a shortage, despite the fact that there are now only 60 000 units occupied compared with 100 000 prior to the tsunami. There is technically no shortage of housing despite the fact that 40 000 families have had their lives disrupted. Remember that a shortage means insufficient supply at a particular price. There is sufficient supply at $2000. The fact that many people cannot afford accommodation at $2000 is a different point and is true of many products in our society.

In a sense, the market, like justice, is blind. Resources and products are allocated according to the forces of demand and supply. Whether the results are desirable or not is not the concern of the market. The fact that most people cannot afford everything they would like is a fact of economic life. A number of things are unavailable to most of us, from luxury yachts to summer cabins, from the latest computer to this year's new car model. The market allocates these products according to supply conditions and according to people's desire *and ability* to purchase. The market does not allocate on the basis of who should or who should not get things. That is not the function of markets. However, most people believe that it is the job of governments to see that a certain amount of fairness prevails in society. Throughout history, governments have attempted to correct what they perceive to be inequities in the market. In addition, they often intervene where a competitive market just does not exist.

The problem here is not so much the goals of government (which are obviously a matter of some debate) but the methods used to achieve those goals. It is these methods to which we now turn. We will first take a look at how and why some governments impose maximum and minimum prices on certain goods and services. Then we will look what happens when the government instead imposes production quotas. The final section will examine the effects of sales taxes and subsidies on market prices and outputs.

SECTION SUMMARY

An unregulated market will always find *equilibrium*, but such a result may be seen by some as undesirable either on the grounds of fairness or because the market is sometimes slow to react.

3.4 Price Ceilings

> **LO4** Describe why price ceilings cause shortages.

A favourite method chosen by governments to correct what they see as undesirable market prices is the introduction of **price controls**—legally imposed minimum or maximum prices on various types of privately produced goods and services. Failure to observe these controls usually occasions fines or other punishments for the buyer or seller.

A *price ceiling* is a maximum price at which a product can be sold legally; a *price floor* is a minimum price at which a product can legally be sold.

In both cases, government is establishing limits, not a fixed price. Let us start by looking at price ceilings.

Governments introduce a **price ceiling** primarily when they believe that the present market price of a particular product—usually something thought to be a necessity—is too high for many buyers. One example is rental accommodations. **Figure 3.6** shows the market for apartment rentals in a major Canadian city. Given the demand and the supply, the market rental is presently $1000 and the number of rental units is 100 000. However, government believes that this rent is too high, causing a great deal of financial stress for many poor people. As a result, government decides to impose a form of price ceiling known as **rent control**, which establishes a maximum rent of $600. In reality, there might be a number of ceilings, depending on the size of the accommodation, the number of bedrooms, and so on. (For a price ceiling to be effective, it has to be below the equilibrium price.) Landlords are not allowed to charge a higher rent, though they may charge less, if they wish. However, at a rent of $600, the number of rented apartments demanded has now increased to 120 000 units, since at this lower rate, renting has become a more popular choice than living with roommates or even possibly buying.

The lower rent is good news for renters but decidedly bad news for landlords who will find it difficult to make a profit at this lower rent. Many of them might well decide to sell off their apartments or convert them into condominiums rather than rent them. Or they may convert the apartments into shops or warehouses, if possible, or do what many landlords do in New York and other cities that have introduced rent controls—simply board up their properties and leave them empty because this alternative is more economically attractive than renting them out. The result, in our example, is that the number of apartments available to rent has decreased to 90 000 units. And the consequence of this is a 30 000-unit shortage of apartments.

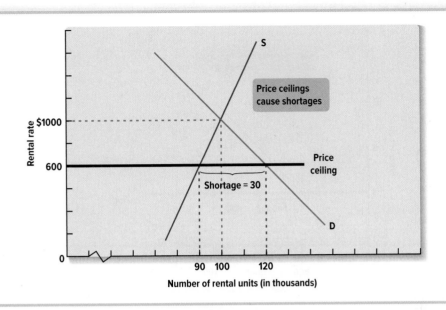

FIGURE 3.6   The Effect of a Price Ceiling on Rented Accommodation

The initial market equilibrium is a rent of $1000 and 100 000 rental units. Establishing a price ceiling of $600 causes the quantity demanded to rise to 120 000 and the quantity supplied to fall to 90 000 units. The result is a shortage of 30 000 units.

This leads to an important conclusion:

Price ceilings cause shortages.

As if all this is not bad enough, there is another serious problem with rent controls. The people currently renting are those who benefit from rent controls because they are paying below-market rents. In addition to those in need, current renters might also include many professionals who could easily afford to pay the market rate. In a market with rent controls landlords are in a very strong position when it comes to choosing new tenants because many people are desperate to find accommodation. However, single mothers, members of visible minorities, low-income students, and other disadvantaged groups will find themselves in a very vulnerable position because landlords can easily avoid renting to these tenants. This leads to a great deal of unfairness and discrimination.

With rent control, abandoning a building may be a better economic option than renting it out.
Denis Tangney Jr./Getty Images

In Canada, there is no federal legislation covering rent controls. The province of Ontario had rent controls between 1944 and 1994. Alberta has never had rent controls but does limit landlords to one rent increase per year.

Another situation in which price ceilings are introduced is during national emergencies, such as wartime. During World War II, many nations felt it necessary to introduce price controls. Wartime economies have to be mobilized for the war effort, which means that productive resources are conscripted by government away from their peacetime activities: certain factories are either taken over directly by government or ordered to start producing armaments and other military requirements; workers are redirected into certain industries or straight into the military. This reduces the amount of resources available to produce civilian goods and services.

The result of this sudden reduction in the supply will be an increase in the prices of most civilian products, including the prices of most foods. Under these circumstances, government may well feel obligated to introduce price ceilings so as to keep prices affordable for most people. The effect of a price ceiling, any price ceiling, will be to cause a shortage, as **Figure 3.7** shows.

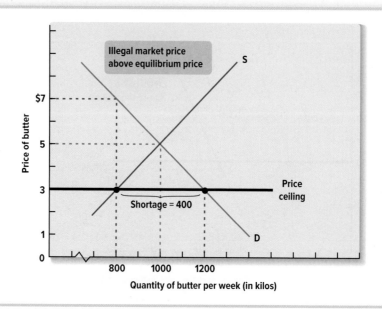

FIGURE 3.7   The Effects of a Price Ceiling on Butter

Equilibrium is at a price of $5 per kilo and a quantity of 1000 kilos. If government introduces a price ceiling at $3, the result is a shortage of 400 kilos. The dashed line, at quantity 800, shows the maximum (illegal market) price at which the quantity supplied could be sold. In this case, it is $7 per kilo.

Assume that the graph illustrates the market for butter. The equilibrium price is $5 per kilo, and the quantity being traded is 1000 kilos per week. Let us suppose that the price is unfortunately far higher than the peacetime price of $3, so government decides to establish a price ceiling for butter at this former price. This lower price is looked on very favourably by consumers, and the quantity demanded rises to 1200 kilos. For many farmers, however, the lower price spells disaster. A number of them are forced to cut back production, and some are forced out of the business of producing butter. At $3, the quantity supplied falls to 800 kilos. The price ceiling, therefore, has caused a shortage of 400 kilos of butter per week.

Shortages, whether or not they are caused by price ceilings, often produce illegal markets. This means that some people who can get their hands on commodities that are in great demand will be willing to risk the fines and penalties from breaking the law and will sell these items above the price ceiling. **Figure 3.7** shows that if illegal marketers were able to get their hands on the total supply of 800 kilos, they could sell this quantity for as high as $7 per kilo—which is above both the price ceiling *and* the equilibrium price.

The butter example demonstrates that if the market is not allowed to allocate goods and services in the normal manner, then someone or something else must perform that task. At the price ceiling of $3 per kilo, the supply of 800 kilos must somehow be allocated to consumers who are demanding 1200 kilos. One way of allocating this short supply is on the basis of a *lottery* whereby everyone has an equal chance of getting one of the 800 kilos. However, this would be a very cumbersome and in-equitable method of distribution. A second method could be to allocate on the basis of **first come, first served**. Again, this is not a fair system, since people who have time on their hands will be able to line up more easily than, say, a parent with young children to look after. Another method is to leave the allocation decision to **producers' preference**, that is, leave it to the seller to decide which customers get what amount of butter and which customers go without. Unfortunately, this method opens itself up to the possibility of favouritism, bribery, and corruption. For instance, sellers may demand extra payments or services from customers before selling, decide to sell only to favourites, refuse to sell to anyone they do not like, and so on.

For this reason, governments are usually forced to undertake the allocation process themselves through the introduction of **rationing**. This means that butter, for instance, would be distributed equally among all families, each family being given ration coupons that allow it to purchase a specified quantity. In our example, each family would get ration coupons entitling it to 2/3 kilo of butter per week. (We are assuming that at $3 per kilo there would be 1200 families each wanting to buy one kilo of butter. Therefore, each family's allocation would be 800/1200, or 2/3 of a kilo.) Certainly, this seems a much fairer method than allowing producers to decide on the allocation. But is it a fair system? On the surface, it would seem so, but we do have the problem of how to define a family—where does a single person living alone fit, for example? Furthermore, realize that people are being given an allowance of butter whether they would normally buy it or not. Imagine the plight of coffee drinkers and smokers if those two products were rationed (beer is not usually rationed in wartime—it is watered down, instead). Their allowance would be the same as that of non-addicts.

In contrast, the market normally takes intensity of desire into account, whereas a rationing system does not. Given these circumstances, it is understandable that people might well trade away coupons they do not want for those they do. But since bartering is a cumbersome exchange method, a market for ration coupons usually develops. This means that people will have to pay to obtain extra coupons as well as having to pay for the product itself.

In summary, the five possible methods of allocation are

- the market
- lottery
- first come, first served
- producers' preference
- rationing

From this, you can see that, even with its faults, the market system usually works better than any alternative. Price ceilings are usually introduced when supplies of a product are limited, and prices consequently are high. But ceilings only address one problem—high prices, and they usually cause the limited supply to shrink even further. Many economists suggest that if the problem is affordability, it might be better attacked by giving direct income relief to those in need rather than helping rich and poor alike by artificially depressing the price.

Let us now see what happens when government introduces price controls, not to depress prices but to increase them.

 TEST YOUR UNDERSTANDING

3. The following graph shows the demand for and supply of milk in the land of Apollo (the quantities are in thousands of litres per day).

   a) Suppose that the government of Apollo introduces an effective price ceiling that is 20 cents below the present equilibrium price. Would the result be a surplus or a shortage? Of what quantity?

   b) If an illegal market were to develop as a result of the price ceiling, what would be the maximum illegal market price?

4. Given the demand and supply shown in the previous question, suppose that the government of Apollo imposed a price ceiling of $1.20 per litre of milk. What impact would this have?

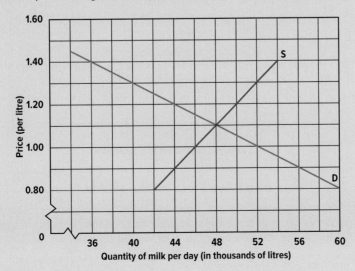

SECTION SUMMARY

a) Price ceilings are government imposed price maximums, often imposed when a product or service is in short supply.

b) Examples of price ceilings are wartime shortages and rent controls.

c) Price ceilings create shortages that force the use of some other form of allocation, such as

- lottery
- first come, first served
- producers' preferences
- rationing

3.5 Price Floors

LO5 Demonstrate that price floors cause surpluses.

Figure 3.8 shows a market in which government believes that the price is, in fact, too low. It has, therefore, introduced a **price floor** above equilibrium, which represents a minimum price. Sellers may sell at a higher price if they wish, but it is illegal to sell at a lower price. In order to be effective, a price floor must be set above the equilibrium price.

It is obvious in this situation that by imposing a price above equilibrium, government is assisting the producers and not the consumers. A higher price is going to mean a higher income for the producers. Which type of producers would government help in this way, and why? The answer is often farmers, because farming has always been regarded as a special type of industry. Agriculture is different from other types of production for a number of reasons. First, unlike, say, manufacturing, supply cannot be totally controlled by farmers. The size of the harvest can fluctuate greatly from year to year, and with it the price of the commodity and the income of farmers. Second, farmers produce a very basic and important commodity: food. Throughout history,

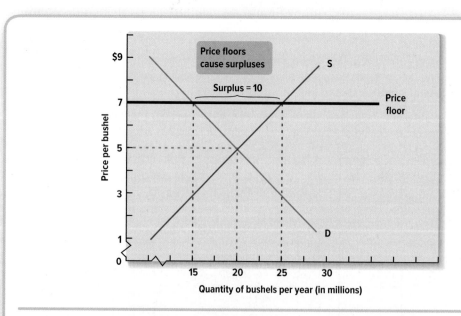

FIGURE 3.8   The Effects of a Price Floor on the Wheat Market

A price above equilibrium will always produce a surplus. In this figure, the price floor of $7 causes a drop in the quantity demanded from the original 20 down to 15; it also causes the quantity supplied to increase from 20 to 25. The result is a surplus of 10 million bushels.

countries have tried to ensure that they are not totally dependent on others for their food supply. If they were so dependent and the supply were interrupted because of war, civil unrest, drought, or other disaster, their position would become precarious. Finally, governments have often been reluctant to allow agricultural land to be traded freely in the marketplace. It is felt that this particular resource is very precious because once it is used for other purposes, such as a housing development or shopping mall, reconverting it to farming is virtually impossible. For these and other reasons, governments in most countries have tried to protect and encourage their agricultural communities. One way of doing this is a price floor on agricultural products, which will guarantee farmers a minimum price.

Price floors cause surpluses.

Figure 3.8 illustrates this basic principle. The graph shows the market for wheat in which the equilibrium price is $5 per bushel and the quantity traded is 20 million bushels per year. It is quite straightforward to calculate the total revenue presently received by farmers:

$$\text{Total revenue (TR)} = \text{price (P)} \times \text{quantity (Q)} \qquad [3.1]$$

In the present case, this works out to $5 × 20 million = $100 million. Now suppose the government introduces a price floor of $7 per bushel. At this higher price, the quantity demanded drops to 15 million bushels, because wheat buyers will look for alternatives to the wheat wherever possible. However, the higher price will induce present farmers to produce more, and others to start up new wheat farms. As a result, the quantity supplied increases to 25 million bushels, so now there is a surplus of 10 million bushels of wheat. This surplus belongs to the government; by introducing the price floor it must take responsibility for any surplus thus created. It also means that the government must buy what the market does not buy. Farmers have received $105 million ($7 × 15 million) in total revenue from buyers; they will also receive an additional $70 million ($7 × 10 million) from the government for the surplus.

Now the government's problem is how to get rid of the surplus a price floor will inevitably produce. A number of possibilities exist. If the surplus is storable, which is true of most grains, it could be stored in grain elevators and used in the future, when the supply may be lower. In this way, the grain elevators are used as reservoirs, taking in grain whenever there is a surplus and releasing it whenever it is in short supply. If the agricultural surplus is perishable, as in the case of milk, eggs, or produce, the government may be able to convert it into other foods or freeze, dry, or can it.

Donating the grain to countries in need is similarly difficult, except in times of natural disasters, because doing so will undermine the receiving country's own agricultural industry or disturb its present trading arrangements. The last option may be simply to destroy the surplus by burning it, burying it, or literally dumping it in the ocean. Understandably, this last alternative is politically embarrassing to governments and is also unacceptable to many people. In summary, there are five ways to deal with a surplus:

All such methods are likely to be expensive. If they are not adopted, the government will have to dispose of the surplus. This is more difficult than it sounds. Selling it to other countries may not be feasible, since in order to do so the price may have to be reduced. But this is **dumping**, a practice forbidden by many international conventions. Donating the grain to countries in need is similarly difficult, except in times of natural disaster, because doing so will undermine the receiving country's own agricultural industry or disturb its present trading arrangements. The last option may be simply to destroy the surplus—burn it, bury it, or literally dump it in the ocean. Understandably, this last option is politically embarrassing to governments and is also unacceptable to many people.

In sum, there are five ways to deal with a surplus:

- store it
- convert it
- sell it abroad at a reduced price (dump it)
- donate it
- destroy it

ADDED DIMENSION

Farm Marketing Boards

Most countries' governments involve themselves in their agricultural sectors; the European Community and Japan do so more extensively than most. In Canada, there are more than 100 farm marketing boards regulating such produce as milk, eggs, wheat, peanuts, grains, and poultry. In total, they exercise control over more than 50 percent of total farm sales in the country and include such federal bodies as the Canadian Wheat Board, the Canada Livestock Feed Board, and the Canadian Dairy Commission. In addition, there are a number of provincial boards. Besides price floors, the other main methods of enhancing and stabilizing farm incomes are quotas (which increase the market price by restricting output) and subsidies granted to farmers (which give them an additional sum of money for each unit of output produced).

Clearly, price floors in agriculture can lead to serious problems. Again, many economists would suggest that, rather than interfering with the market, governments might be better advised to provide direct income assistance to farmers. After all, farmers' income is the main problem they are trying to address.

TEST YOUR UNDERSTANDING

5. The market for corn is described in the figure below.

  a) In equilibrium, what is the total sales revenue being received by producers?

  b) Suppose that government now imposes a price floor of $4 per kilo. What quantity will now be demanded? What quantity will the farmers produce? What quantity will government purchase?

  c) How much will it cost government to purchase the surplus?

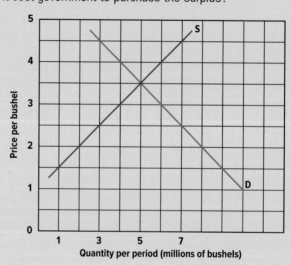

6. Given the same graph, what is the effect of a government-imposed price ceiling of $4?

The Minimum Wage

Finally, we will take a look at another type of price floor used in many countries—a minimum price for labour, or a **minimum wage**. The rationale for minimum-wage legislation is to try to ensure that all working people are guaranteed a minimum level of income on the grounds of compassion and

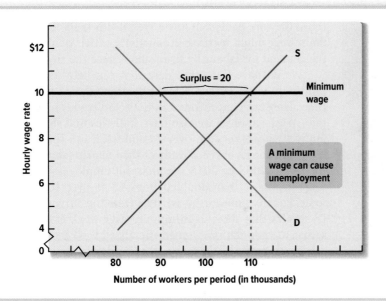

FIGURE 3.9   **Labour Markets and Minimum Wages**

As a result of the minimum wage of $10 per hour, the quantity demanded will drop from 100 000 to 90 000 and the quantity supplied increases from 100 000 to 110 000. The result will be a surplus of 20 000 workers. That is, there will be 20 000 unemployed workers in this particular labour market.

fairness. This goal is generally not criticized by economists, but standard economic theory does question how governments try to achieve it. What is involved here is the principle that when the free workings of the market are interfered with, a number of harmful side effects often result. Let us look at the situation, with the help of **Figure 3.9**.

This figure illustrates a particular labour market in which the demand curve represents the employers' demand for workers (labour), and the supply curve represents the number of individuals wanting to be hired. Suppose the government considers the equilibrium wage ($8 per hour in our graph) to be too low. So it introduces legislation forbidding the payment of any wage below $10 per hour. The higher wage means that employers will have an incentive to economize on labour and consequently they will cut back on employment. This is illustrated by the quantity of labour demanded by firms falling from 100 000 to 90 000. At the same time, the now-higher wage might well attract more workers to this market as seen by the quantity of labour supplied increasing from 100 000 to 110 000. The net result is that there will be a surplus of labour, that is, unemployment of 20 000 workers. The 90 000 workers who have retained their jobs obviously benefit by the minimum-wage legislation—though their working environment might be more intense now that the number of employees has been reduced.

Under the influence of this standard analysis, a number of economists have embraced the idea that a legislated minimum wage set above equilibrium must increase unemployment. Some have gone on on to argue that the poor may be better assisted by income relief that is channelled to them directly by the government rather than indirectly through the marketplace.

However, the idea of a clear link between rising minimum wages and rising unemployment was challenged by two economists whose studied the results of New Jersey's 1992 increase in the minimum wage and concluded that such a link was simply not correct. The discussion was further complicated when another study of the same data by two different economists concluded that the conventional view was valid. Both groups went back and redid their work, with the result that the difference between the two studies was narrowed.

There are two possible explanations for the seemingly contradictory results. The first is a question of one's perspective: Do we look at the total number of people employed in an industry or the total number of hours worked? Since many minimum-wage workers are part-timers, it is possible that the total number of hours does fall, as conventional theory predicts, even if the total number of individuals employed does not. The second is the argument that many workers are not paid low

Young people eating at a fast-food restaurant, a place where some of their friends probably work.

Source: PhotoDisc/PunchStock

wages because they are unproductive, but that they are unproductive because they are paid such low wages. If this is so, the imposition of a minimum wage might increase productivity, which would lead to an increase in the demand for labour by firms and reduce the amount of unemployment.

We do have Canadian data that can help us build a profile of the minimum-wage worker. A majority are under 25 years old and work part time. They are concentrated in the retail trade and food/accommodation industries. However, we also have statistics that show 40 percent of minimum-wage workers are over 25 and work full time. A somewhat alarming trend comes out of a study of the Ontario labour market that showed that from 2003 to 2015 the share of employees working at minimum wage has more than doubled from 4.3 to over 10 percent of the labour force. Equally noteworthy are data from the Survey of Labour and Income Dynamics that show us minimum-wage work is not distributed equally across the population: women, racialized workers, and recent immigrants are much more likely to be working for minimum wage than a white male of any age.

A further point should be noted in this debate. To what extent minimum wage legislation causes unemployment very much depends on the type of market we are looking at. It may be that in markets with many firms and many workers, none of whom have much power to affect the market wage, the result is a degree of unemployment. However, as we shall see in Chapter 12 when we examine non-competitive labour markets, a minimum wage might well decrease rather than increase unemployment.

No matter who is right, the point of this analysis is that any policy that allocates labour across the economy imposes costs, and whether this allocation is done by government or the market, these costs are not always obvious. Economic analysis can help us identify and understand these costs, but this not as easy as it might at first seem.

IT'S NEWS TO ME ...

The new year of 2017 brought raises to millions of low-wage workers in the US. Nineteen states and twenty local jurisdictions raised their minimum wage rates with Arizona's rising to $10 (up 24% from $8.05) and Maine's rising 20% from $7.50 to $9. The city of Seattle set its minimum wage rate at $15 for some workers (those of larger employers who do not pay health benefits) with the promise of extended coverage to all workers with a couple of years.

Economic research is a bit "muddy" when it comes to predictions about the effect on employment from increases in the minimum wage. Much of the confusion revolves around whether the proper measurement of "employment" should be total number of people employed or total number of hours worked. Nonetheless, there is currently little conclusive evidence that increases in the minimum wage are a major job-killer.

However, studies up to this point have been based on minimal hikes on wage rates that were lower than those now coming into effect. In time, this will provide a rush of empirical evidence that may well provide answers to the question: do increases in the minimum wage reduce employment?

Source: *Star Power Reporting*. January 2017.

I. The report says that it is not possible to know the effect of an increase in the minimum wage on unemployment rates in the United States because:

a) Previous increases have been very big.
b) The minimum wage varies between different states.
c) Not all states have minimum-wage legislation.
d) Previous increases have been quite small.

II. Minimum-wage legislation may not cause unemployment in all the following cases except one. Which is the exception?

a) If the demand for labour were to also increase.
b) If the supply of labour were to also decrease.
c) If the increase in the minimum wage is very big.
d) If the minimum wage is set below the market wage rate.

ADDED DIMENSION

The Minimum Wage in Canada

Minimum-wage determination falls under provincial jurisdiction in Canada. A glance at the table below indicates that the rates between the various jurisdictions are remarkably similar—a low of $10.50 in Newfoundland to a high of $13 in Nunavut. This is a very recent outcome—until just a few years ago, the high-to-low range was much wider.

Jurisdiction	Wage ($/hour)	Effective Date	Comments
Alberta	12.20	October 1, 2016	
British Columbia	10.85	September 15, 2016	$9.60 for liquor servers.
Manitoba	11.00	October 1, 2015	Workers involved in construction have a higher starting minimum wage.
New Brunswick	10.65	April 1, 2016	
Newfoundland and Labrador	10.50	October 1, 2015	
Northwest Territories	12.50	June 1, 2015	
Nova Scotia	10.70	April 1, 2016	$10.20 for inexperienced workers (less than three months employed in the type of work they are hired to do).
Nunavut	13.00	April 1, 2016	Currently the highest in Canada.
Ontario	11.40	October 1, 2016	• Students (under age 18, working 28 hours or under per week while school is in session or work when there is a school break): $10.70. • $9.90 for liquor servers.
Prince Edward Island	11.00	October 1, 2016	
Quebec	10.75	May 1, 2016	$9.20 for workers receiving gratuities.
Saskatchewan	10.72	October 1, 2016	
Yukon	11.07	April 1, 2016	Yukon currently pegs annual increases (every April 1) of its minimum wage using the consumer price index.

SECTION SUMMARY

a) *Price controls* imposed on agriculture products are an example of *price floors* and create surpluses that must then be

- stored
- converted into another product
- sold abroad
- given away
- destroyed

b) The *minimum wage* is one example of a price floor. It is controversial because many economists believe that, although it does benefit those who remain working, it may create unemployment that works against those it is mainly intended to help.

3.6   Production Quotas

> **LO6**   Explain how quotas work and what effect they have on production and prices.

Another way governments intervene in markets is by way of **production quotas**.

Here, instead of targeting market prices, the government aims to affect the total output coming onto the market. It does this by introducing legislation to prevent producers from exceeding a stipulated limit on the production or sale of a product. This method is widely used by many countries to restrict imports of certain products—something we will look at in more detail in Chapter 13. However, it is also a very popular method used to control domestic agricultural production; and in many countries, including Canada, it is a more popular method than price floors. As we saw earlier, one of the drawbacks of agricultural price floors is that they often lead to overproduction which generates the problem of dealing with the consequent surpluses. With production quotas, such surpluses never arise. Canada has production quotas on many farm products ranging from eggs and milk to frying chickens, ducks and duck eggs, potatoes, carrots, beets, lettuce, celery, tomatoes, peppers, and cucumbers. Which are controlled varies from province to province. As with price floors, the object is to give farmers a guaranteed and steady income from production. Let's see how this works out.

In **Figure 3.10**, the equilibrium price and quantity produced for raspberries is $4 per pound and 6 million kilos. If the government wanted to improve the lot of the berry farmers by increasing the price *without generating a surplus*, it could impose a quota limiting the overall level of berry production to 4 million kilos, as illustrated by the heavier vertical line. As a result, the price would rise to $6 per kilo. The government would then allocate this quota to individual farmers and make it illegal for any one farmer to sell more. Note that the total revenue to the growers does not change as a result of the increase in price to $6 (4 million kilos times a price of $6 generates the same revenue—$24 million—as 6 million kilos at a price of $4). Nonetheless, the farmers do benefit, since the cost of producing 4 million kilos is lower than that of producing 6 million kilos. The obvious shortcoming of this scheme is the politics involved in allocating the overall quota to individual farmers. Many producers are likely to think that quota is too low and their neighbours' too high.

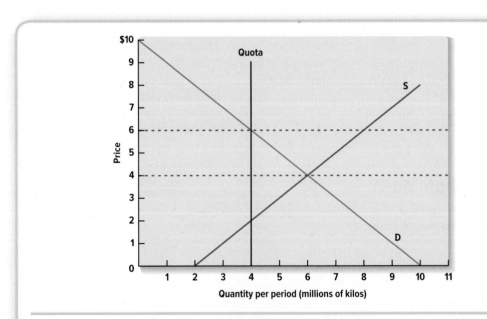

FIGURE 3.10   The Imposition of a Production Quota

The equilibrium price is $4, and the quantity produced is 6 million kilos. Imposing a quota of 4 million will raise the price to $6.

There are other problems associated with production quotas. First, buyers (consumers) are pay-ing a higher price than without the quota. In addition, there is an incentive for farmers to cheat and produce more than their allotted quotas. As **Figure 3.10** shows, the new price is well above the $2 that would normally induce the farmers to produce the quota of 4 million. Every kilo above the quota would reap great profits for the farmer. Preventing this requires production levels to be carefully monitored—an expensive business.

 TEST YOUR UNDERSTANDING

7. The market for soya beans is described in the accompanying figure.

   a) In equilibrium, what is the total sales revenue being received by producers?

   b) Suppose that government now imposes a production quota of 6 million tonnes. What will be the new price per tonne? What will be the total sales revenue?

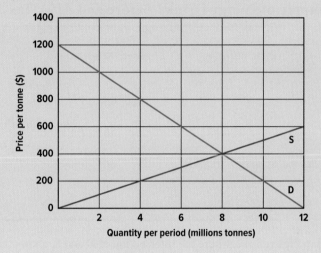

SECTION SUMMARY

a) Production quotas are limits imposed by governments to reduce production or sales of a product. They are often introduced in agriculture.

b) Quotas have the effect of reducing the output of a product and causing an increase in the price. It usually results in an increase in the producers' revenue.

3.7 Taxes and Subsidies

> **LO7** Explain how sales taxes and subsidies affect markets.

Finally, we look at taxation and subsidies, which are methods that governments use to affect market outcomes.

Taxes

The first of these, taxation, we are all familiar with, since almost everything you earn or spend is subject to taxation. Income tax and payroll taxes like EI and CPP are directly deducted from your income by your employer, and sales taxes like the GST and HST are added to the bill when you purchase goods and services. In addition, there are **excise taxes**, which are sales taxes imposed on certain products such as alcohol, cigarettes, and gasoline.

Excise taxes, as with the carbon taxes now levied by most Canadian provinces, generate considerable revenue for the government; but in addition they are often introduced to reduce the production and consumption of these products for either health or environmental reasons. Sales taxes, including excise taxes, are all calculated as a percentage of the sales price of the product and it is the seller who, by law, is responsible for collecting these taxes and actually sending the money to the government. But that need not be the case: the government might instead require that buyers keep a record of all their purchases, calculate the applicable tax, and send their remittance in periodically. However, it is much more expedient—and administratively much cheaper—to monitor the activities of a few thousand sellers than millions of consumers.

Now let us see how the imposition of an excise tax on a particular product impacts that market. We will use the example of a tax on energy drinks imposed to reduce their consumption.

The first three columns of **Table 3.2** show the supply and demand for 6-packs of energy drinks before the imposition of an excise tax. The equilibrium price is initially $8 and the equilibrium quantity is five million 6-packs.

TABLE 3.2
Demand and Supply of Energy Drinks, Before and After Tax

Price per 6-Pack	Quantity Demanded	Quantity Supplied (before tax)	Quantity Supplied (after tax)
5	8	2	0
6	7	3	1
7	6	4	2
8	5	5	3
9	4	6	4
10	3	7	5
11	2	8	6

These are plotted in **Figure 3.11**, where the intersection of D and S_1 shows the initial equilibrium.

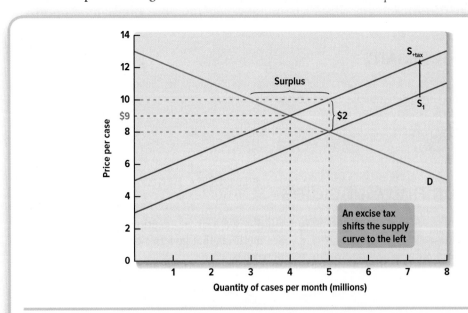

FIGURE 3.11   The Effect of an Excise Tax on the Price and Quantity of Energy Drinks

The effect of a $2 per 6-pack excise tax is to shift the supply curve up from S_1 to S_{+tax}. The result is that equilibrium price increases from $8 to $9 and equilibrium quantity decreases from 5 million to 4 million 6-packs per month.

Now suppose that government imposes an excise tax of $2 on each 6-pack. How will the energy drink market be affected? Well, initially, the 6-pack price will increase from $8 to $10. How many 6-packs would suppliers be prepared to sell at $10? Since the suppliers will have to remit $2 to the government, they will still only receive revenue of $8. The answer, then, is that they will supply the same number of 6-packs—5 million—at the after-tax price of $10, as they did when the price was $8 and there was no tax. In Table 3.2, therefore, we have added a fourth column showing the supply of 6-packs if the price now includes the $2 tax. We can see that if the price is $10 and there is no tax, 7 million 6-packs would be offered; if the price is $10, but this includes the $2 tax, they would only offer 5 million. Effectively the quantities supplied in the table shift down by two rows ($2) after the imposition of the tax. In graphical terms, as we see in Figure 3.11, the new supply curve (S_{+tax}) shifts upward or to the left. This says that at a price of $10 the suppliers will make 5 million 6-packs available, just as they did when the price was $8 with no tax.

Graphically, then, the result of the imposition of a tax is to shift the supply curve to the left (or up) by the amount of the tax. But what about the demand? How is that affected? It is not, in the sense that there is no shift in the demand curve. But customers will certainly react—none too favourably—to the $2 increase per 6-pack caused by the new tax. According to both the table and the graph, the quantity demanded at $10 will be only 3 million 6-packs, leaving a surplus of 2 million 6-packs. This will eventually cause suppliers to reduce prices, and in our example, they will continue to drop prices until the price is $9. At this new equilibrium price, the quantity demanded and supplied will be 4 million 6-packs.

In summary, then:

- The imposition of an excise tax or sales taxes will decrease the supply of the product.

In addition, the tax will cause an increase in its price and a decrease in the quantities traded. Therefore, if the aim of the government is to curtail the consumption of certain undesirable products, the imposition of a sales tax will certainly have the desired effect.

Finally, we might add that if the tax were imposed on the buyer rather than the seller it would cause a decrease in demand. This means that in Figure 3.11, although the market prices would remain unchanged, anyone paying, say, $8 for a 6-pack now has to additionally pay the government a $2 tax. Understandably, the quantities demanded will fall at all prices. In other words, the demand curve would shift to the left, leading to a lower price and a lower quantity traded. So whether the tax is imposed on the buyer or the seller, the impact on the quantity is the same: it will cause a reduction.

 TEST YOUR UNDERSTANDING

8. The market for scallops is described in the following table:

Price per kilo	Quantity Demanded	Quantity Supplied (before tax)	Quantity Supplied (after tax)
$20	600	400	
22	550	450	
24	500	500	_____
26	450	550	_____
28	400	600	_____
30	350	650	_____

a) Before the tax, what are the equilibrium price and quantity?

b) Fill in the Quantity Supplied (after tax) column assuming that a $4 per kilo excise tax is put on the product.

c) What are the new equilibrium price and quantity?

Subsidies

A **subsidy** is a form of financial aid given by a government to an institution, business, or individual with the general aim of promoting economic and social policy. Subsidies come in many different forms, from direct cash grants or interest-free loans to tax breaks, accelerated depreciation, or rent rebates. In Europe and North America many agricultural producers of grain, meat, milk, and eggs receive subsidies. In Canada the forest, mining, and gas and oil industries are also heavily subsidized.

Usually cash subsidies are given per unit produced, so that it pays producers to increase their output levels. For instance, suppose that the market for eggs (in dozens) is shown in **Figure 3.12**.

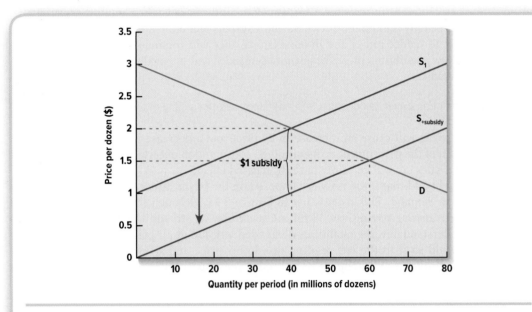

FIGURE 3.12   The Effect of a Subsidy on the Price and Quantity of Egg Production

The effect of a $1 subsidy is to shift the supply curve down (right) from S_1 to $S_{+subsidy}$. The result is that equilibrium price decreases from $2 to $1.50 and equilibrium quantity increases from 40 million to 60 million dozen per period.

The present equilibrium price is $2 per dozen. Now suppose that the government grants a $1 subsidy for each dozen eggs a farmer produces. This means, of course, that instead of receiving $2 per dozen, each farmer now receives $3—$2 from buyers and $1 from the government. In effect, the supply curve shifts down (right) by $1 from S to $S_{+subsidy}$. This can be expressed another way: before the subsidy, farmers needed to receive $2 per dozen eggs to induce them to produce 40 million eggs. After the subsidy, they would be willing to produce that number of eggs for $1 per dozen since they are now receiving an additional $1 subsidy from the government.

The shift in the supply curve means that at the old equilibrium price of $2, producers would like to produce 80 million dozen eggs. However, since nothing has happened to the demand from consumers, there will be a big surplus of eggs, and farmers will eventually be forced to drop the price of eggs until there is no surplus. This will occur at the new equilibrium price of $1.50. As **Figure 3.12** shows, the result will be an equilibrium quantity of 60 million dozen eggs.

In summary, then:

> A subsidy given to producers will increase the supply.

Graphically, the increase in supply will shift the supply curve to the right and cause a decrease in the price of the product and an increase in the quantity traded.

We have seen that if a government wishes to increase the output of a product, a subsidy given to producers will certainly do that. As we shall see in more detail in Chapter 9, there are occasions when it might be preferable to give the subsidy to buyers (consumers) rather than to the producers. If this were the case, it would cause an increase in demand rather than in supply and would cause an increase in the price of the product rather than a decrease. It would, however, have the same effect of increasing the quantity traded.

IN A NUTSHELL ...

When should a government act?

Too much?   **Too little?**

Too high?   **Too low?**

TEST YOUR UNDERSTANDING

9. The market for industrial milk (in millions of hectolitres (1 hectolitre = 100 litres) is described in the following graph:

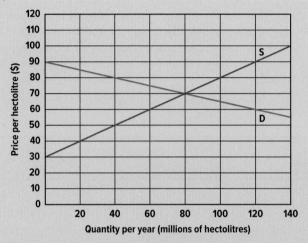

a) If a subsidy of $30 per hectolitre is given to milk producers, draw the new $S_{+subsidy}$ curve on the graph.

b) What will be the new equilibrium price and quantity as a result?

SECTION SUMMARY

a) Sales taxes and subsidies are methods by which a government can affect the quantity produced and sold of a product.

b) The imposition (or increase) in a sales tax imposed on the seller leads to a drop in supply and, graphically, to a left shift in the supply curve. The result is a higher price and a lower output

c) A subsidy given to producers leads to an increase in supply and, graphically, to a right shift in the supply curve. The result is a lower price and a higher output.

Study Guide

Review

WHAT'S THE BIG IDEA?

The first part of this chapter looks at what happens if the demand and the supply change at the same time. Analyzing the results is not too difficult if you remember that when demand changes the price and quantity move in the same direction. So if demand increases (UP), the quantity goes UP and the price also goes UP. On the other hand, when the supply changes, the quantity goes in the same direction as the supply but the price goes in the opposite direction. For example, if the supply increases (UP), the quantity goes UP but the price goes DOWN. It follows that if both demand and supply increase at the same time, both will push the quantity UP but the demand pushes the price UP whereas the supply pushes the price DOWN. As a result, what happens to the price is uncertain (*indeterminate*) unless you know whether the demand change or the supply change is the stronger of the two.

The rest of this chapter looks at three ways governments attempt to correct what they feel are deficiencies in the market. These deficiencies include (but are not limited to) situations in which they feel the price is too high or too low or the quantity produced is too high or too low. Price controls can take the form of either a minimum price (price floor) or a maximum price (price ceiling). The aim of both may be good, but they can create other problems. While price floors increase the price they also create surpluses; and while price ceilings reduce the price they also cause shortages. Production quotas, on the other hand, are simply limits on how much of a product can be produced (without incurring a government fine). Since the supply is reduced, the price of the product will consequently rise. Finally, sales taxes are general percentage taxes on the sale of products (excise taxes are special taxes on particular item like alcohol or gasoline). The effect is to reduce the supply and increase the price. The opposite of a tax is a subsidy where a government will pay a producer a certain amount per item produced. The effect of this is to increase the supply and reduce the price of the product.

NEW GLOSSARY TERMS AND KEY EQUATION

dumping	price ceiling	production quotas
excise taxes	price controls	rationing
first come, first served	price floor	rent control
minimum wage	producers' preference	subsidy

Equation:

[3.1]   Total revenue (TR) = price (P) × quantity (Q)

Comprehensive Problem

(LO 2, 4, 5, 6, 7) **Figure 3.13** depicts the market for rice in the country of Shiva.

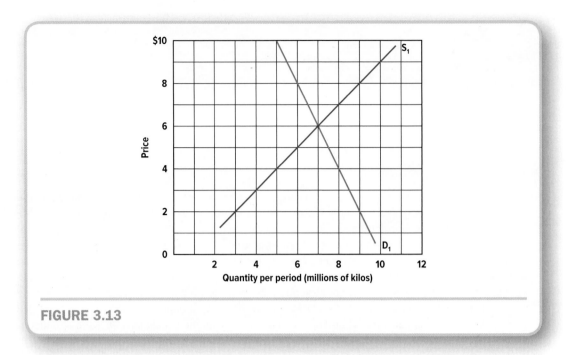

FIGURE 3.13

Questions

a) What is the present equilibrium price and quantity traded in this market?
b) What is the total revenue received by farmers (price × quantity)?
c) Suppose that government introduces a price floor of $8 per kilo. How much, in total, will rice buyers be paying for this quantity?
d) As a result of the price floor, what will be the total amount of the surplus? What will be the dollar amount of this surplus? Who will be responsible for buying this surplus, the government or the farmers? As a result, what will be the total revenue received by farmers?

Answers

a) Price = $6; quantity traded = 7 (million) kilos
   This is where the demand and supply curves intersect.
b) $42 million ($6 times 7 million)
c) $48 million
   At a price of $8 per kilo, the quantity demanded will drop to 6. The total amount now paid by buyers is equal to 6 million kilos times $8 (= $48 million).
d) Surplus: 3 million kilos; $24 million. This surplus is the responsibility of the government to buy. (At $8, the quantity demanded is 6 and the quantity supplied is 9.)
   $72 million ($48 million received from buyers and $24 million from the government for the surplus)

Questions

Suppose that the government is concerned with the size of the surplus and is thinking of replacing the price floor with a production quota of 6 million kilos.
e) If it did so, what would be the new price, quantity, and total revenue of farmers?

Answers

e) Price: $8; quantity: 6 million; total revenue: $48 million. Graphically, insert a vertical line at the amount of the quota of 6 million. This will intersect the demand curve at a price of $8. Total revenue equals the price ($8) times the quantity (6 million) equals $48 million.

Questions

Alternatively, the government is also considering introducing a $3 per kilo subsidy for the rice farmers.
f) If it does introduce the subsidy, what would be the new price, quantity, and total revenue of farmers?
g) Of the three schemes—a price floor, a quota, or a subsidy—which would farmers prefer, and why?

Answers

f) Price: $4; quantity: 8 million; total revenue: $56 million. (Draw a supply-plus-subsidy curve $3 below the supply curve. This curve intersects the demand curve at a price of $4 and a quantity of 8 million. Total revenue from buyers equals $4 × 8 million = 32 million. In addition, the government will pay the subsidy of $3 × 8 million = $24 million. The total revenue therefore is $32 million + $24 million = $56 million.)

g) Farmers would prefer the price floor since they would receive the greatest total revenue ($72 million compared to $48 million for the quota and $56 million for the subsidy).

Study Problems

Find answers on the McGraw-Hill online resource.

Basic (Problems 1–5)

1. **(LO 2)** **Figure 3.14** shows the market for mandarin oranges in Odin for the month of November (in thousands of kilos).

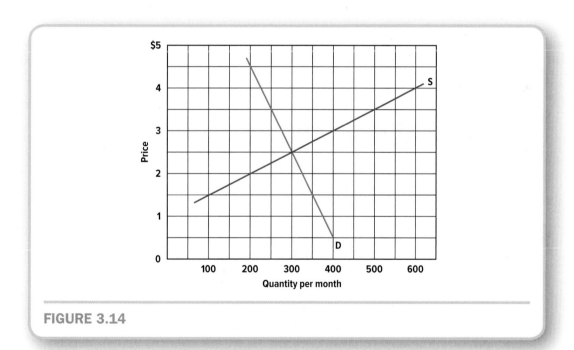

FIGURE 3.14

Suppose that in December the supply of mandarin oranges increases by 350 while the demand increases by 100.
a) Draw and label the new curves D₂ and S₂.
b) What will be the new equilibrium price and quantity?
   Price: _____ Quantity: _____

2. **(LO 2)** **Table 3.3** shows Osiris's market for olive oil (in thousands of litres per month). Suppose that olive oil increases in popularity, and Osiris's buyers are willing to buy an additional 10 units at each of the eight prices in **Table 3.3**. At the same time, as the result of improved technology, oil producers are willing to produce 30 more units at each of the eight prices.

TABLE 3.3

Price ($)	Quantity Demanded	Quantity Demanded 2	Quantity Supplied	Quantity Supplied 2
1	70	——	10	——
2	60	——	20	——
3	50	——	30	——
4	40	——	40	——
5	30	——	50	——
6	20	——	60	——
7	10	——	70	——
8	0	——	80	——

a) Complete Table 3.3.
b) What will be the new equilibrium price and quantity?
New equilibrium price: _____
Equilibrium quantity: _____

3. **(LO 5)** Figure 3.15 shows the rice market in Hatha.

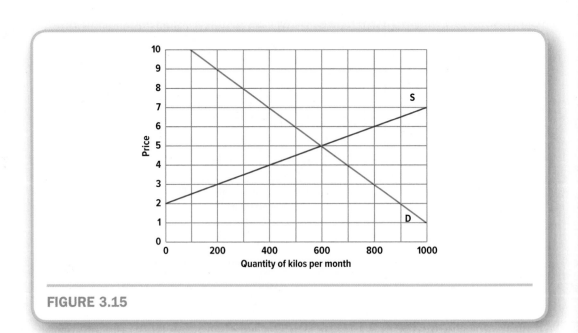

FIGURE 3.15

Suppose that the government of Hatha introduces a price floor of $6.
a) What quantity of rice will buyers purchase? _____
b) How much in total will buyers be paying for the amount in (a)? _____
c) What will be the amount of the rice surplus? _____
d) What is the dollar value of this surplus? _____

4. **(LO 6)** Figure 3.16 depicts the market for industrial milk.

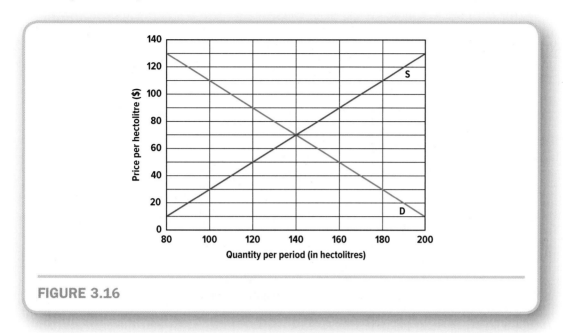

FIGURE 3.16

a) In equilibrium, what is the price, quantity, and total revenue received by milk producers?
Price: $_____ Quantity: _____ Total revenue: $_____

b) Suppose that the government imposes a production quota of 120 hectolitres. What will be the new price, quantity, and total revenue received by milk producers?
Price: $_____ Quantity: _____ Total revenue: $_____

5. **(LO 2)** Figure 3.17 depicts the market for New York steaks.

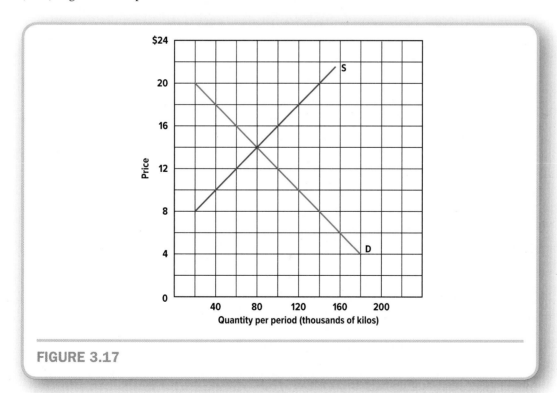

FIGURE 3.17

a) If government were to impose a price floor of $18 per kilo, what would be the result?
Shortage/surplus of _____ kilos

b) If government were to impose a price ceiling of $12 per kilo, what would be the result?
Shortage/surplus of _____ kilos

Intermediate (Problems 6–8)

6. **(LO 7)** Figure 3.18 shows the market for avocados.

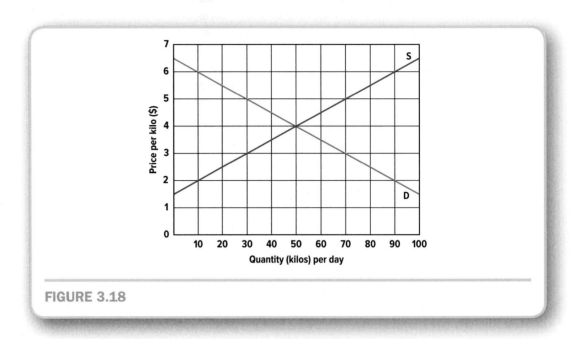

FIGURE 3.18

If the government were to give avocado farmers a $2 subsidy per kilo, what would be the new equilibrium price, quantity, and total amount of the subsidy paid to the growers?
Price: $_____ Quantity: _____ Total subsidy $_____

7. **(LO 2, 4, 5)** Table 3.4 shows the market for mandarin oranges in the country of Preswar.

TABLE 3.4

Price per Kilo	Quantity Demanded	Quantity Supplied
$1.00	850	100
1.10	800	200
1.20	750	300
1.30	700	400
1.40	650	500
1.50	600	600
1.60	550	700
1.70	500	800

a) What are the equilibrium values of price and quantity?
   Price: _____ Quantity: _____
b) Suppose that government imposes a price floor that is $0.20 different from the present equilibrium price. What would be the resulting shortage or surplus?
   (Shortage/surplus): _____ Amount: _____
c) Suppose instead that government imposes a price ceiling $0.20 different from the present equilibrium price. What would be the resulting shortage or surplus?
   (Shortage/surplus): _____ Amount: _____

8. **(LO 7)** Suppose Figure 3.19 depicts the market for smart phones.

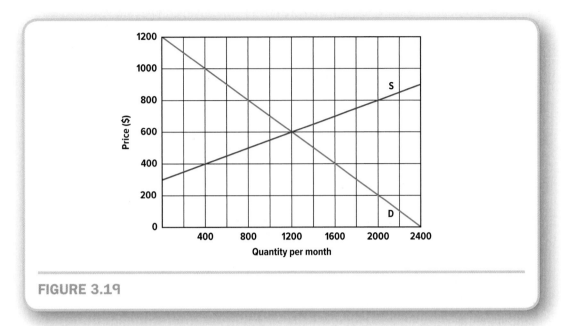

FIGURE 3.19

a) What is the equilibrium price and quantity?
   Price: $ _____ Quantity: _____
b) Suppose the government imposes a $300 excise tax on smart phones. Draw in the new supply
   curve labelled S$_{+tax}$ in Figure 3.19.
c) What is the new equilibrium price and quantity?
   Price: $ _____ Quantity: _____

Advanced (Problems 9–11)

9. **(LO 2, 5)** Table 3.5 shows the market for goat milk in the country of Pegasus (in thousands of litres).
   a) What is the present equilibrium price and quantity traded?
      Price: $_____ Quantity: _____

TABLE 3.5

Price ($)	Quantity Demanded	Quantity Supplied
0.10	520	200
0.15	480	240
0.20	440	280
0.25	400	320
0.30	360	360
0.35	320	400
0.40	280	440
0.45	240	480
0.50	200	520

b) Suppose the government introduces a price floor of $0.40 per litre. What would be the resulting
   shortage or surplus?
c) What would be the result if, after the introduction of the price floor, both the demand and the
   supply were to increase by 20 percent?
d) What would happen if, instead, the demand and supply were to decrease by 20 percent?
   (Shortage/surplus) _____ of _____

10. **(LO 2, 5)** Figure 3.20 depicts the market for blueberries in the country of Roni.

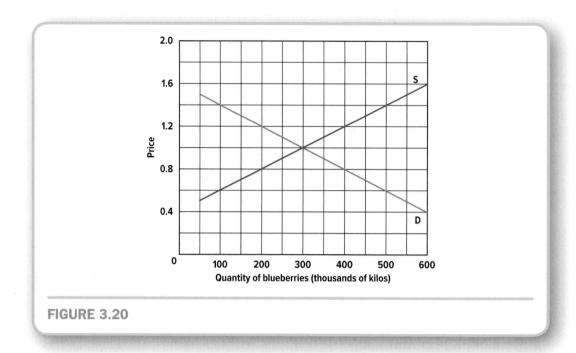

FIGURE 3.20

a) Suppose that, in an attempt to boost the price of blueberries for its farmers, the government of Roni introduces a quota that limits the total amount that farmers can sell to 200 000 kilos. What is the maximum price at which this quantity could be sold? _____

b) What would be the farmers' total revenue as a result of the quota? $ _____

c) What if this government decides, instead of using a quota, to introduce a price floor of $1.20 per kilo? What would be the surplus/shortage and the resulting total revenue of farmers?
Surplus/shortage: _____ Total revenue: $ _____

11. **(LO 7)** The data in Table 3.6 are for kilos of prawns.

TABLE 3.6

Price	Quantity Demanded	Quantity Supplied (before tax)	Quantity Supplied (after tax)
$18	240	180	____
20	220	190	____
22	200	200	____
24	180	210	____
26	160	220	____
28	140	230	____
30	120	240	____

a) What is the present equilibrium price and quantity?
Price: $_____ Quantity: _____ Suppose that the government introduces a $6 excise tax on prawns.

b) Complete the Quantity Supplied (after tax) that results.

c) What will be the new equilibrium price and quantity?
Price: $_____ Quantity: _____

Problems for Further Study

Basic (Problems 1–4)

1. **(LO 2)** In **Figure** 3.21, show graphically how a change of both the demand and the supply curves in the *same direction* can produce the following results.

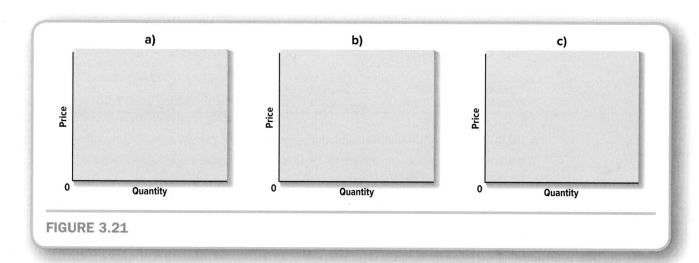

FIGURE 3.21

   a) price decreases, quantity traded decreases
   b) price is unchanged, quantity traded decreases
   c) price increases, quantity traded decreases

2. **(LO 2)** What will be the effect on equilibrium price and quantity if demand for a product increases at the same time that the supply decreases?

3. **(LO 4, 5)** What is a price control? Explain.

4. **(LO 2)** **Figure** 3.22 shows the market for ground coffee in Moncton.

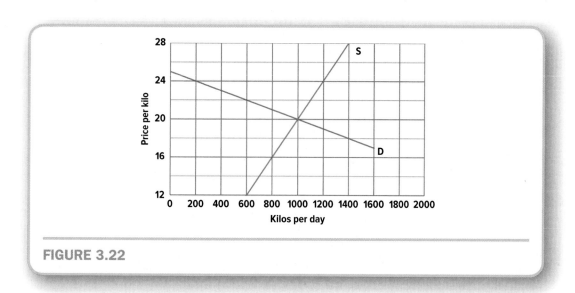

FIGURE 3.22

   a) What would be the new equilibrium price if both the demand and the supply of ground coffee increased by 400 kilos per day?
   b) What would be the new equilibrium price if both the demand and the supply of ground coffee decreased by 400 kilos per day?

Intermediate (Problems 5–8)

5. **(LO 2)** In each of the following markets, explain what effect the change will have on the equilibrium price and the quantity traded.

Market	Change
Orange juice Price: $_____ Quantity: _____	A freeze in Florida occurs at the same time that the price of apple juice rises.
Cigarettes Price: $_____ Quantity: _____	Government introduces an effective anti-smoking policy and increases the tax on cigarettes.
Beer Price: $_____ Quantity: _____	The legal age for drinking is raised at the same time that technological change lowers the cost of brewing beer.
Eyeglasses Price: $_____ Quantity: _____	The cost of producing lenses falls at the same time that wearing eyeglasses becomes quite fashionable.

6. **(LO 5)** Explain how the imposition of minimum-wage legislation might cause unemployment.

7. **(LO 5, 6)** Briefly explain three methods by which a government might help to increase production levels and income of its farmers.

8. **(LO 4)** Explain why a price ceiling imposed above the market price is ineffective.

Advanced (Problems 9–10)

9. **(LO 2)** "Technological improvements over the past five years have so reduced the costs of producing tablet computers that, although they have greatly increased in popularity, the average price has dropped." Illustrate the changes in the tablet market on the graph in **Figure 3.23**.

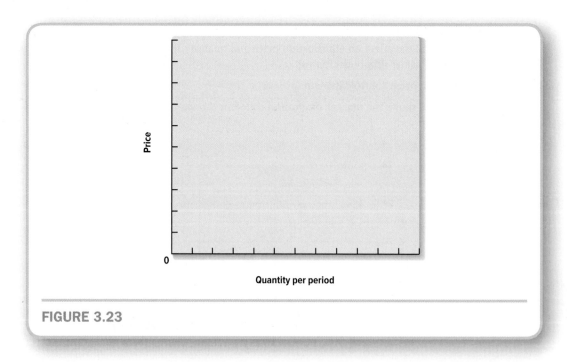

FIGURE 3.23

10. **(LO 7)** What would be the difference in the resulting price and quantity of a sales tax imposed on buyers as opposed to the same tax on sellers? In what way is a sales tax levied on sellers superior to that levied on the buyers of a product?

CHAPTER 4
Elasticity

LEARNING OBJECTIVES

At the end of this chapter, you should be able to:

LO1 Explain price elasticity of demand and its determinants.

LO2 Calculate price elasticity and explain the coefficient of elasticity.

LO3 Describe the relationship between the slope of a demand curve and elasticity, and how this affects the total revenue of the producer.

LO4 Use real-world examples to demonstrate that the concept of elasticity is a powerful tool.

LO5 Describe the meaning and significance of supply elasticity, income elasticity, and cross-elasticity of demand.

WHAT'S AHEAD...

This chapter focuses on how consumers respond to a change in the price of any particular good. Such responsiveness is called *price elasticity of demand*. We begin by showing how the seller's total revenue is directly tied to elasticity. Next, we use the idea of elasticity to analyze four real-life applications that are not generally well understood by the general public. Finally, we see how elasticity is also used in the contexts of supply, income, and inter-product comparisons.

A QUESTION OF RELEVANCE ...

Have you ever noticed that people appear to make some purchases without thinking about them and yet agonize, sometimes for days, over the purchase of other things? We are all aware that almost everything we purchase in Canada is taxed. It may seem clear that an increase in the GST is simply passed on to the consumer, while the retailer and producer are nothing more than disinterested bystanders. But is this really the case? Do the ticket scalpers you see outside high-profile events, such as playoff hockey games or a Lady Gaga concert, always make a profit from the resale of the tickets they hold? Although these questions seem unrelated, they are linked in a way we will explore in this chapter.

Y ou will recall that Chapter 2 introduced the law of demand and established the inverse relationship between price and quantity. Thus, we know that an increase in the price of, say, an airline ticket from Toronto to Montreal would result in a decrease in the quantity of tickets sold. Obviously, this would not be beneficial to consumers, but what we now need to flesh out is whether this would be beneficial to the airline selling the tickets. We introduced the concept of **total revenue** in the previous chapter and now want to ask: "Would the airline receive more or less total revenue as a result of selling fewer tickets at a higher price per ticket?" (It is important to note that we are speaking of the firm's total revenue and not its total profit—that will come later, after we deal with the costs of production in Chapters 6 and 7.) If nothing else is changed, the effect of a higher price would be to increase the airline's total revenue. But something else does change—the higher price will result in the quantity of tickets sold going down, and this will tend to decrease total revenue. So what will be the net effect of these opposing pressures? The answer depends on the concept economists call the price elasticity of demand. The dictionary defines elasticity as "the state of being elastic or flexible," and our focus is on the flexibility of consumers' reactions to a change in price.

4.1 Price Elasticity of Demand

LO1 Explain price elasticity of demand and its determinants.

Price elasticity of demand can be defined as a measure of how much the quantity demanded of a product changes as a result of a change in its price. The measurement of elasticity is obtained by taking the percentage change in quantity and dividing it by the percentage change in price. Note that we use percentage changes, because price is expressed in dollars and quantity is measured in units, so using just the absolute change in quantity divided by the absolute change in price would not work. Also, showing elasticity in percentage terms means we can ignore the units in which the price and quantity are measured.

Let us look at some hypothetical data, shown in Table 4.1.

TABLE 4.1
Total Revenues of Three Products

	BEFORE PRICE CHANGE			AFTER PRICE CHANGE		
	Price	Quantity	Total Revenue	Price	Quantity	Total Revenue
Product A	$5	60	$300	$6	55	$330
Product B	$5	60	$300	$6	50	$300
Product C	$5	60	$300	$6	30	$180

In the three rows of Table 4.1 we have data on three products, A, B, and C, being sold by three different firms that, for the sake of illustration, all have the same price ($5) and the same quantity demanded (60). When we multiply price and quantity we arrive at the same total revenue, $300, for each seller. In the last three columns we see that the price of each product has increased to $6. As a result, the quantity demanded falls but the amount of the decrease differs for each product—5 units in the case of Product A; 10 units in the case of Product B; and a huge drop of 30 units for Product C. It is crucial that you note the effect of these three different responses of quantity changes on the seller's total revenue. In the case of Product A it falls, while it remains unchanged for Product B and rises for Product C. What is being demonstrated here is that these three products have dramatically different price elasticities of demand. Product A has what economists call **inelastic demand**; Product B has **unitary elasticity**; and Product C has **elastic demand**. We will get to the actual calculations of what we call *elasticity coefficients* in the next section, but let us first ask: "Why do consumers react so differently in the case of these three products?" or to use technical language, "What are the determinants of a product's elasticity?"

Determinants of Price Elasticity

If you look back at Table 4.1 you can see that as far as Product A is concerned, customers do not seem unduly concerned about the price increase: the quantity hardly drops at all. You might suggest that, in some sense, the buyers of this product are quite faithful. However, it's altogether a different matter with Product C. It certainly looks like these customers are not too happy with the price increase and purchases drop considerably. They are far from faithful to the product. So what types of products are we looking at here? At first glance, it seems like buyers of Product A are quite indifferent to the price increase, and many of them (though not all) are still buying the same quantities as before. Presumably, Product A is a necessity, a product many customers cannot do without. Product C, on the other hand, looks like a luxury product that customers are more than willing to give up if the price increases. But we must be careful here: it is not uncommon for people to think of products as either luxuries or necessities, so it is tempting to conclude that luxury products are elastic in demand and necessities must be inelastic. While there is undoubtedly validity in this rule of thumb, we must be careful. Food is obviously a necessity for all of us but if you were to list all the foods you purchase from coco-pops to broccoli, from rice to potato chips, not forgetting the coffee, cheese, and frozen pizzas, which are necessities and which luxuries? It wouldn't surprise you to learn that one person's necessity is another's luxury. To some, wine with a meal is an absolute necessity, whereas to others, it is a seldom-bought luxury.

Given this small caution, it still seems that good examples of Product A would be items like illicit drugs or cigarettes. Certainly customers of those products, although they might grumble at a price increase, are still likely to go on buying them regardless. But the real reason for their faithfulness is simply that there are few available substitutes. The availability of close substitutes, then, is the first major determinant of price elasticity. The fewer substitutes there are for a product, the more inelastic its demand. This would be true for such products as alcohol, gasoline, and household electricity.

On the other hand, products for which there are a number of substitutes will have elastic demands. For example, in most people's eyes, almost any other vegetable is a substitute for tomatoes; downloaded and streaming videos and other forms of entertainment are substitutes for theatre movies; pork and beef are close substitutes for lamb. The substitute for a restaurant meal is take-out or a home-cooked meal. Many households find that the substitute for furniture or china and tableware is to simply make do with less of what many consider to be inessential items. If the prices of any of these products were to increase, people can easily switch to their substitutes so the quantities purchased would drop quite a lot.

Before leaving this discussion of the availability of substitutes, we should note that a great deal depends on how the commodity in question is defined. The demand for food is an example of a broadly defined category and, as mentioned, its demand is highly inelastic, since there is no substitute. Yet the elasticity of demand for any one food item, such as green beans, is very elastic because there are many close substitutes. As another example, the elasticity of demand for accommodation is generally quite low because all of us have to live somewhere, whereas the elasticity of demand for home ownership is much greater, since renting is an alternative.

A second determinant of price elasticity is the *percentage of household income spent on the commodity*. In general, we can say that the more money spent on a particular commodity (as a percentage of income), the more elastic the demand for it.

For this reason, the elasticity of demand for a high-priced automobile or for a top-of-the-line home entertainment system will be high. On the other hand, the elasticity of demand for ordinary spices or hand soap will tend to be inelastic, simply because the total percentage of a household's budget spent on such items is small and the price change will have little impact on that budget.

The third determinant of price elasticity is the *amount of time that has elapsed since the price change*. The classic example here is that of oil. When the Organization of Petroleum Exporting Countries (OPEC) oil embargo of 1973 resulted in the halting of (most) oil shipments to North America, the price of oil increased fourfold in just eighteen months. Measurements of elasticity made over this period indicated a very inelastic demand. This was because in the immediate aftermath of such a price shock, very few close substitutes for oil were available. But North Americans (as well as most people around the world) soon became far more energy-conscious and began to find ways to conserve fuel by turning down thermostats and water temperatures in the home and becoming less dependent on the automobile by finding other ways to commute, shop, and take holidays.

When it became apparent that high oil prices were becoming a permanent fact of life, alternative energy sources, such as coal, nuclear, and solar were explored, and in some countries wind turbines started to dot the landscape. As well, oil drilling was embarked upon in some of the less accessible regions of the world, such as the North Atlantic Ocean and the Canadian Arctic. Finally, the North American love affair with big, gas-guzzling automobiles came to an end as smaller, more fuel-efficient cars were introduced. Subsequent measurements of the elasticity of demand for oil ten years after the price shock showed much higher elasticity than what was seen in the first eighteen months. All this leads us to conclude that the longer the time period involved, the greater the elasticity of demand tends to be. In summary, the more elastic the demand for a product,

- the more similar and the more available the number of available substitutes
- the larger the percentage of one's income that is spent on the product
- the longer the period involved

IN A NUTSHELL ...

Prices keep going up!

Big Deal!   **OMG**

Elastic   **Inelastic**

TABLE 4.2
Examples of Products with Different Elasticities of Demand

Commodities That Have Elastic Demands	Commodities That Have Inelastic Demands
Fresh tomatoes	Household electricity
Movies	Eggs
Lamb	Car repairs
Restaurant meals	Food
China and tableware	Household appliances
Automobiles	Tobacco

Finally, Table 4.2 identifies some commodities that typically have elastic demands and some that have typically inelastic demands.

 TEST YOUR UNDERSTANDING

Find answers on the McGraw-Hill online resource.

1. Why is the price elasticity of demand for broccoli so different from that for gasoline?

2. Indicate for the following products in Canda whether you think their demands are elastic or inelastic.

  a) sugar

  b) gasoline

  c) ocean cruises

  d) restaurant meals

  e) women's hats

  f) alcohol

SECTION SUMMARY

a) Price elasticity of demand refers to the ratio of the percentage change in quantity demanded that results from a given percentage change in its price. In percentage terms,

  • if the change in quantity is small, the demand is inelastic

  • if the change in quantity is big, the demand is elastic

  • if the change in quantity is the same as the change in price, the demand is unitary

b) The major determinants of price elasticity are

  • the number of available substitutes

  • the percentage of income spent on the product

  • the time involved in the measurement

4.2　Measuring Price Elasticity

We have just learned that the demand for products can be elastic or inelastic and certain products are more elastic (or more inelastic) than others. In other words, there are degrees of elasticity. In this section, we will look at how we can measure price elasticity and interpret these measures.

In **Table 4.3** we will use the data for the three products we looked at in the previous section, reorganized slightly.

TABLE 4.3
Effect of a Price Change on Three Products

	Original Price	New Price	Original Quantity	New Quantity	Original Total Revenue	New Total Revenue
Product A	$5	$6	60	55	$300	$330
Product B	$5	$6	60	50	$300	$300
Product C	$5	$6	60	30	$300	$150

Let us do some calculations of elasticity in order to obtain the **elasticity coefficient**. We will use the general equation 4.1 below, in which elasticity is symbolized by the Greek lowercase letter epsilon (ε), the subscript p indicates that it is the *price* elasticity of demand that is being referred to, and the Greek uppercase letter delta (Δ) means *change in*.

$$\varepsilon_p = \frac{\%\,\Delta \text{ quantity demanded}}{\%\,\Delta \text{ price}} \qquad [4.1]$$

This basic equation can be expanded as follows:

$$\varepsilon_p = \frac{\dfrac{\Delta Q_d}{\text{average } Q_d} \times 100}{\dfrac{\Delta P}{\text{average } P} \times 100} \qquad [4.2]$$

To obtain the elasticity coefficient for Product A we first need to determine the percentage change in quantity as it changes from 60 to 55. The absolute decrease is 5, and we need to put this over a base to get the percentage increase. This raises the question of whether that base should be the original 60 or the new 55. Since $5 \div 60$ is 0.08 and $5 \div 55$ is 0.09, it clearly does make a difference which base is chosen. To resolve this question, we take the *average* of the original base and the new base, which in this case is 57.5 (simply $60 + 55$ divided by 2). Using averages in this way ensures that we get the same result if the quantity goes down from 60 to 55 or up from 55 to 60.

Thus, the percentage change in quantity is the absolute change of 5 divided by the average base of 57.5 multiplied by 100. Let us show this explicitly:

$$\%\,\Delta Q_d = \frac{5}{57.5} \times 100 = 8.7\%$$

The result of 8.7 percent is the numerator in equation 4.2 above.

Next, we calculate the percentage change in price by dividing the absolute change of $1 by the average of the original and new prices, which is $5.5 (simply $5 + $6 divided by 2). The percentage change in the price is

$$\%\,\Delta \text{ price} = \frac{\$1}{\$5.5} \times 100 = 18.18\%$$

We can now obtain the elasticity coefficient.

$$\varepsilon_p = \frac{\%\,\Delta Q}{\%\,\Delta P} = \frac{8.7\%}{18.18\%} = 0.48$$

Technically, the answer is −0.48, but since we know that price and quantity always move in opposite directions *any* calculation of price elasticity of demand would result in a negative coefficient. Thus, we simply ignore it.

So Product A has an elasticity coefficient of 0.48, which is less than one. A coefficient with a value of less than 1 signifies that the product has an inelastic demand. As we have seen, this means that the quantity demanded is not very responsive to a price change. Specifically, a 1 percent change in price leads to a change of just 0.48 percent in quantity. Note that because the demand is inelastic, total revenue will rise, because the increase in price pushes revenue up more than smaller quantity sold pushes it down. This is borne out in Table 4.3, as we see that total revenue increases from the original $300 to $330. We are now able to make our first generalization involving elasticity:

If demand is inelastic and price rises, total revenue will also rise.

Let us make the same calculation using the figures in the case of Product C. Here, the absolute change in quantity is 30 and the average quantity is 45 (60 + 30 divided by 2).

$$\%\,\Delta Q_d = \frac{30}{45} \times 100 = 66.67\%$$

So the percentage change in quantity is 66.67 percent and is the new numerator in our general equation 4.2 above.

Since the change in the price was the same for Product C as it was for Product A, we can use the same denominator that we calculated for Product A which is 18.18 percent.

To complete our calculation of elasticity, we simply divide the percentage quantity change by the percentage price change, as follows:

$$\varepsilon_p = \frac{\%\,\Delta Q}{\%\,\Delta P} = \frac{66.67\%}{18.18\%} = 3.67$$

Thus, the elasticity coefficient for Product C is 3.67, which is greater than one. Any elasticity coefficient with a value greater than 1 signifies that the product has an elastic demand. Here, the quantity demanded is much more responsive to a change in price. A 1.0 percent change in price leads to a 3.67 percent change in quantity demanded. Since the decrease in quantity, which pushes total revenue down, is stronger than the increase in price, which pushes total revenue up, we would expect the net effect to be a decrease in total revenue. This is verified in Table 4.3 as seen by total revenue decreasing from $300 to $180. We can now make our second generalization about elasticity:

If demand is elastic and price rises, total revenue will fall.

Finally, we should look at the curious case of unitary elasticity, in which the percentage change in both price and quantity are exactly equal. The data for Product B illustrate this. Here, once again, the price decreases from the same $6 to $5, which, as we have seen, is a $1 or 18.18 percent decrease. We also see the quantity sold from rising from 50 to 60. This increase in quantity also happens to equal 18.18 percent (10/55 × 100). The elasticity coefficient is therefore equal to exactly 1 (0.18 percent divided by 0.18 percent). Because the percentage decrease in price is identical to the percentage rise in the quantity sold, the total revenue remains the same. Before the change, the total revenue was $300 (60 quantity at $5 each). After the price decrease, total revenue is still $300 (50 quantity at $6 each).

If the demand is unitary elastic, then a change in price has no effect on total revenue.

We can now make an important generalization:

If the demand is inelastic, price and total revenue move in the same direction. If the demand is elastic, price and total revenue move in opposite directions. If the demand is unitary elastic, total revenue is unaffected by a price change.

Table 4.4 summarizes the effects of a price change:

> **TABLE 4.4**
> **Relationship Between Price and Total Revenue**
>
> | If Demand Is ... | And Price ... | Then Total Revenue ... |
> |---|---|---|
> | inelastic (<1) | rises | rises |
> | inelastic (<1) | falls | falls |
> | elastic (>1) | rises | falls |
> | elastic (>1) | falls | rises |
> | unitary elastic (= 1) | rises | stays the same |
> | unitary elastic (= 1) | falls | stays the same |

 TEST YOUR UNDERSTANDING

Find answers on the McGraw-Hill online resource.

3. This table shows three sets of prices and their related quantities. Calculate the elasticity coefficients for each set.

	Price	Quantity
Set I	$1.50	200
	2.00	100
Set II	120.00	1600
	100.00	1800
Set III	18.50	37
	21.50	43

4. Here are two sets of prices and their related quantities:

	Price	Quantity
Set I	$9	1
	8	2
Set II	2	8
	1	9

a) Calculate the elasticity coefficients for each set.

b) In each set the change in price is $1 and the change in quantity is one unit. Why aren't the coefficients the same?

5. What would happen to total revenue in each of the circumstances below?

a) $\varepsilon > 1$ and price falls.   **d)** $\varepsilon > 1$ and price rises.

b) $\varepsilon < 1$ and price rises.   **e)** $\varepsilon = 1$ and price rises.

c) $\varepsilon < 1$ and price falls.

6. Suppose that the price of four different products all increases by 20 percent. Given the elasticity coefficients shown below, what is the percentage change in the quantity of each product?

a) $\varepsilon = 4$ **c)** $\varepsilon = 1$

b) $\varepsilon = 0.5$ **d)** $\varepsilon = 0$

ADDED DIMENSION

Another Way of Calculating Elasticity

Elasticity of demand measures how consumers react to a price change by measuring the impact of a change in price on the resulting change in the quantity demanded. The basic formulas for calculating elasticity are the ones shown as equations 4.1 and 4.2 in the text. However, when making this calculation we are often obliged to round off both the numerator and the denominator of the formula. The upshot is that the resulting coefficient might be subject to rounding errors. In addition, when doing a number of calculations, it is sometimes faster to use a shortcut that mostly avoids the rounding problem. This computational formula is easy to derive:

$$\varepsilon_p = \frac{\Delta Q/Q \times 100}{\Delta P/P \times 100} = \frac{\Delta Q/Q}{\Delta P/P} = \frac{\Delta Q}{Q} \times \frac{P}{\Delta P} = \frac{\Delta Q \times P}{\Delta P \times Q} \qquad [4.3]$$

Let us work through an example using this formula. Suppose the price of a box of energy bars at Costco increases from \$15 to \$17 and the daily quantity falls from 125 to 95. Summarizing this,

$$P_1 = \$15 \qquad P_2 = \$17 \qquad \text{(Average P = \$16;} \qquad \Delta P = 2]$$
$$Q_1 = 125 \qquad Q_2 = 95 \qquad \text{(Average Q = 110;} \qquad \Delta Q = 30]$$

The resulting elasticity coefficient is

$$\varepsilon_p = \frac{\Delta Q \times P}{\Delta P \times Q} = \frac{36 \times 16}{2 \times 110} = 2.18$$

Elasticity in Action

Suppose that as a summer intern working for Cliff Energy Bars, you have been given the task of advising the marketing manager about the pricing of its two popular energy bars, Almond Energy and Chocolate Energy. The manager is thinking of increasing the price of both bars by 20 percent and wants to get your input. You dig out the company records, and from your research you conclude that the price elasticity of the almond bars is 0.85, whereas for the chocolate bars it is 1.45. So what advice should you give?

You know very well that an increase in the price of the two bars will reduce the sales quantity of both (that's true of all products: a higher price means a lower quantity). But how much will the quantity fall? A simple calculation gives you the answer. For the almond bars, the quantity will fall by 20 percent × 0.85, or 17 percent; for the chocolate bars, the fall will be greater: 20 percent × 1.45, or 29 percent. Since the percentage change in quantity is less for the almond bars than for the chocolate bars, you know right away that the total revenue of the company will increase for the former, but fall for the latter. The marketing manager follows your advice and increases the price only of the Almond Energy bars. The result (you have probably guessed this) was that sales did, in fact, increase. The marketing manager was given a hefty bonus and you received a free box of Almond Energy bars!

TEST YOUR UNDERSTANDING

7. Given the price elasticities and price changes for the following Products A–E, show how much the quantity will change (indicating an increase or decrease) and the resulting effect on total revenue (indicating an increase or decrease).

Product	Price Elasticity	% Δ Price	% Δ Quantity	Δ Total Revenue
A	2	↑ by 5%	——	——
B	0.4	↑ by 10%	——	——
C	0.2	↓ by 20%	——	——
D	1	↑ by 7%	——	——
E	3	↓ by 2%	——	——

> **SECTION SUMMARY**
>
> a) Price elasticity of demand is defined as a measure of how much the quantity demanded changes as a result of a change in price. A standard formula relates the percentage change in quantity demanded to the percentage change in price. Using this formula yields a number called the *elasticity coefficient*.
>
> b) The price elasticity of demand is inelastic if the coefficient is less than 1, it is elastic if the coefficient is greater than 1, and it is unitary elastic if the coefficient is exactly 1.
>
> c) If the price elasticity of demand is inelastic, price and the firm's total revenue move in the same direction. If it is elastic, price and the firm's total revenue move in opposite directions. If it is unitary elastic, a change in price does not affect total revenue.

4.3 Price Elasticity Graphically

LO3 Describe the relationship between the slope of a demand curve and elasticity, and how this affects the total revenue of the producer.

In this section we will take this concept of elasticity and give it graphical representation. We will continue to use the same three products we used as examples in the last two sections.

If you recall, the price of Product A increased from $5 to $6 and as a result the quantity decreased from 60 units to 55 units. This is illustrated in **Figure 4.1A**.

The quantity does not decrease by very much and the elasticity coefficient we measured in the last section was equal to 0.48. This means that this product is inelastic, and as a result the demand curve plots fairly steeply.

With **Figure 4.1B**, the quantity demanded of Product B changed from 60 to 50 units which yielded an elasticity coefficient of exactly one—unitary elasticity. (Note that the resulting demand curve is not a 45-degree line but a rectangular parabola.)

Finally, the curve in **Figure 4.1C** is fairly flat and illustrates the fact that the demand here is elastic. In the case of this third product, the quantity demanded has changed a whopping 30 units, from 60 to 30, and its coefficient is equal to 3.67.

Although it seems generally possible to identify the elasticity of demand in terms of the slope, we must be very careful here, since the slope of a demand curve is not the same thing as elasticity. Let us explain this important point using **Table 4.5** using some new hypothetical data.

TABLE 4.5
Demand, Total Revenue, and Elasticity Schedule

Price	Quantity	Total Revenue (price × quantity)	Elasticity	
$10	0	0		
9	1	9	19.0	
8	2	16		Elastic
7	3	21	3.0	
6	4	24		
5	5	25	1.0	Unitary
4	6	24		
3	7	21	0.33	
2	8	16		Inelastic
1	9	9		
0	10	0	0.05	

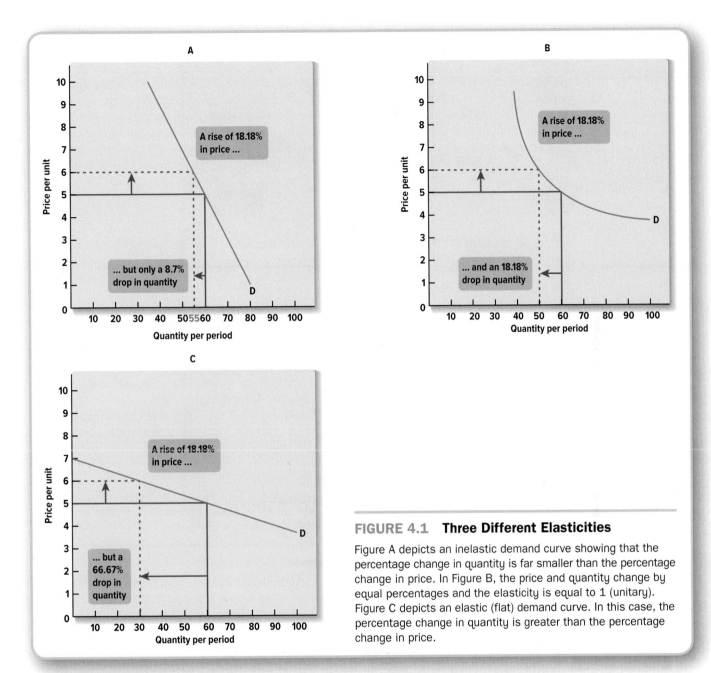

FIGURE 4.1   Three Different Elasticities

Figure A depicts an inelastic demand curve showing that the percentage change in quantity is far smaller than the percentage change in price. In Figure B, the price and quantity change by equal percentages and the elasticity is equal to 1 (unitary). Figure C depicts an elastic (flat) demand curve. In this case, the percentage change in quantity is greater than the percentage change in price.

Note how total revenue *rises* from $0 to $25 as the price decreases from $10 to a price of $5. Since price is falling and total revenue is rising, we know this means that demand must be elastic. This is confirmed by the elasticity coefficients in the last column. Further, as price continues to fall from $5 to $0, total revenue *falls* from $25 back down to $0, indicating that demand is inelastic in this range of the demand curve. The price/quantity combination of $5 and 5 units is also of particular interest because total revenue is at its maximum.

It is also evident that this $5 price is the midpoint of the demand curve. This is no coincidence. If total revenue ceases to rise as price falls, we can no longer be on the elastic portion of the demand curve. If total revenue has not yet begun to fall as price decreases, we cannot yet be on the inelastic portion of the demand curve. Thus, if demand is no longer greater than 1 and not yet less than 1, it can only be exactly equal to 1. From this we can conclude that:

The upper half of any straight-line demand curve is elastic and the lower half is inelastic.

Furthermore, the midpoint is where we experience unitary elasticity. Again, this means that the percentage change in quantity is exactly equal to percentage change in price, and thus total revenue does not change. As we can see, it also means that at this point total revenue is at a maximum.

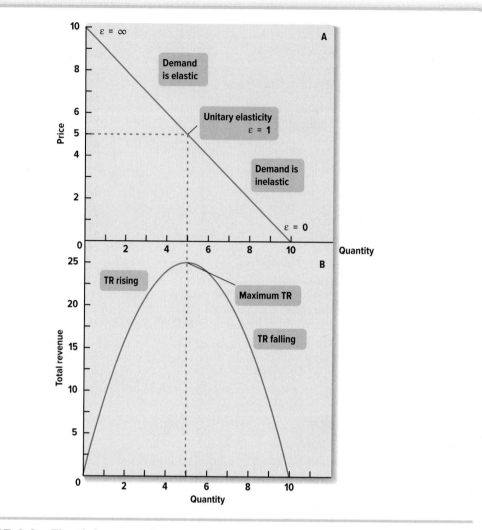

FIGURE 4.2   Elasticity and Total Revenue

In Figure A, at the top half of the demand curve, the demand is elastic. Figure B shows that as the price drops from $10 to $5 total revenue increases. At the midpoint, at a price of $5, demand is unitary and total revenue is maximum. As prices are reduced below $5 Figure A shows that demand is inelastic, and Figure B shows that total revenue falls.

These ideas are graphed in **Figure 4.2**. We see that at the top of the demand curve, the demand is very elastic (at its extreme, infinite). As the price drops, so too does the elasticity. And as the bottom graph shows, as the price drops total revenue rises. At the midpoint of the demand curve, elasticity is one (unitary elasticity) and total revenue is at its maximum. Thereafter, as the price drops, both elasticity and total revenue fall until they are equal to zero at price zero.

It is clear, then, that the slope of the demand curve is not the same thing as its elasticity, and as we have seen, elasticity itself has different values at different points on the demand curve. Given that, you might wonder why we suggested earlier that a product with an elastic demand has a flat demand curve and one with an inelastic demand has a steep curve. The answer is that in the case of a shallow-sloped demand curve, what we are looking at is the upper half of what would be a much longer curve if extended all the way to the horizontal axis of the graph—and the upper half of any demand curve is elastic.

Since the upper half of any straight-line demand curve is the elastic portion, we can look at the demand curve in **Figure 4.1C** and say that it is an elastic demand curve because we know that the lower half of the curve (most of which we do not see) is the inelastic portion. Similarly, when we look at a steep demand curve such as the one in **Figure 4.1A** we are looking at the lower portion of a much longer demand curve, and this lower portion is inelastic.

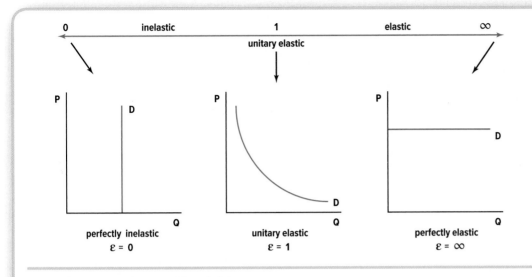

FIGURE 4.3   Range of Elasticities

A vertical demand curve illustrates a perfectly inelastic demand. The centre graph shows a rectangular hyperbola, illustrating unitary elasticity. The right graph shows a horizontal line, illustrating a perfectly elastic demand.

Finally, we present the full range of price elasticities in **Figure 4.3**. The perfectly inelastic demand plots as a vertical line, which shows that a change in price has no effect upon quantity demanded. Demands with elasticities between 0 and 1 are inelastic. We have already seen that a unitary elastic demand curve plots as a rectangular hyperbola. The essence of this curve is that every price/quantity combination produces the same total revenue. The demands for products with elasticities above 1 are elastic. At its extreme of infinite elasticity, the demand is said to be perfectly elastic. Such a demand plots as a horizontal straight line, and it suggests that even a small increase in price results in nobody buying the product whereas a tiny decrease would encourage everybody to buy.

 TEST YOUR UNDERSTANDING

8. a) Graph a demand curve using the data from the accompanying demand schedule (make each square on both axes equal to 2).

b) What is the slope of this demand curve?

c) How might you demonstrate that the elasticity of demand was not the same as the slope?

Price	Quantity
1	18
2	16
3	14
4	12
5	10
6	8
7	6
8	4
9	2

Elasticity and Total Revenue, Graphically

We have seen the importance of price elasticity to any firm in the business of selling products. Our calculations of the elasticity coefficients for our Products A, B, and C showed that how (or whether) a firm's total revenue will increase or decrease as the result of a price change depends solely on the elasticity of demand of the product.

We bring this section to a close by graphically showing this same, crucially important point using **Figure 4.4**.

Since Total Revenue = Price × Quantity, we can show this on the graph in terms of areas. In **Figure 4.4A**, the blue-lined rectangle shows the original total revenue ($5 × 60); the red-dashed-lined rectangle shows the new total revenue ($6 × 55). The area of the new rectangle is bigger than the original one, showing that total revenue is greater. You can see this in terms of what the firm loses in revenue and what it gains as a result of increasing the price. In **Figure 4.4C**, the top wedge shows the gain in revenue as a result of increasing the price; the amount is $1 × 55, or $55. The loss is the vertical wedge and is equal to $5 × 5, or $25. The gain of $55 is greater than the loss of $25. Overall the firm gains $30 in total revenue.

Figure 4.4B illustrates the gain and loss in revenue when the elasticity of demand is unitary. Here, we see that the gain in total revenue of $50 ($1 × 50) is exactly equal to the loss in total revenue

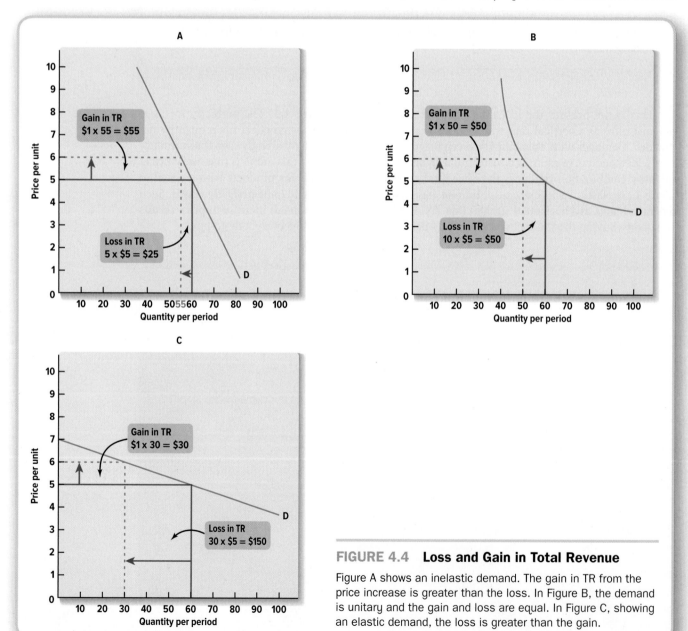

FIGURE 4.4   Loss and Gain in Total Revenue

Figure A shows an inelastic demand. The gain in TR from the price increase is greater than the loss. In Figure B, the demand is unitary and the gain and loss are equal. In Figure C, showing an elastic demand, the loss is greater than the gain.

of $50 (10 × $5). The area lost is exactly equal to the area gained. The result is no change in total revenue.

In the final graph, **Figure 4.4C**, the gain in total revenue of $30 ($1 × 30) is far less the loss of $150 ($5 × 30). The overall loss, therefore, is $120. This illustrates an elastic demand.

In summary:

> An increase in price will increase total revenue if the demand is inelastic, decrease total revenue if the demand is elastic, and leave it unchanged if the demand is unitary elastic.

Conversely:

> A decrease in price will decrease total revenue if the demand is inelastic, increase total revenue if the demand is elastic, and leave it unchanged if the demand is unitary elastic.

 TEST YOUR UNDERSTANDING

9. A firm's total revenue was $1200 when the price of its product was $30 and increased to $1500 when the price was dropped to $25. Is the demand for this product, elastic, inelastic, or unitary elastic?

SECTION SUMMARY

While it can be easily demonstrated that the *slope of a demand curve* and its elasticity are not the same thing, we can nonetheless generalize, and say that

- a relatively steep demand curve is mostly inelastic
- a relatively shallow demand curve is mostly elastic

An increase in price will raise the seller's total revenue if demand is inelastic but lower total revenue if it is elastic. A decrease in price will have the opposite effect. Total revenue is unaffected if the demand is unitary elastic.

4.4   Applications of Price Elasticity

> **LO4**   Use real-world examples to demonstrate that the concept of elasticity is a powerful tool.

Who Pays Sales Taxes?

In Chapter 3 we saw how a sales tax levied on a product will increase its price and reduce the quantity traded. We also noted that in most countries sales taxes (including **excise taxes**) are levied on the seller rather than the buyer. In other words, the *impact* of such taxes falls on the seller. However, the more interesting question is: Who bears the *incidence* of these taxes? In other words, who really pays these taxes—the seller or the consumer? Most people believe it is the consumer, because they assume that the seller simply adds whatever amount the tax might be on to the price of the product and thus passes the tax on. But is this correct?

The answer to who pays for sales taxes is actually quite straightforward:

- If the price of the product increases the same amount of the tax, it is the customer who pays.
- If the price of the product does not increase at all, it is the seller who pays.

As you probably suspect, these are extreme instances. In most cases, the price generally increases but seldom by the amount of the tax. In other words, the incidence of the tax is generally on *both* the buyer and the seller. But who pays the major portion depends upon the elasticity of demand.

Figure 4.5 shows how differences in elasticity affect the outcome. In both graphs, the shift in supply, S_1 to S_{+tax}, is the same. However, the demand D in graph A is inelastic, whereas in graph B it is

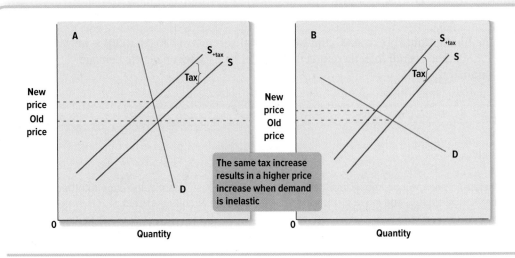

FIGURE 4.5   The Effect of an Excise Tax on Two Different Demand Curves

Here, the supply curve shifts by the same amount, from S to S$_{+tax}$, in both graph A and graph B, as a result of the imposition of a sales tax. The two demands, however, are quite different—inelastic in the case of graph A and elastic in the case of graph B. The resulting increase in price is much greater in graph A than in graph B.

 TEST YOUR UNDERSTANDING

10. The accompanying graph shows the demand and supply for headphones.

    a) What are equilibrium price and quantity, assuming demand schedule D and supply schedule S?

    b) Suppose that a \$30-per-unit excise tax was placed on this product. Draw in the new supply curve labelled S$_{+tax}$.

    c) What are the new equilibrium price and quantity?

    d) What proportion of the tax is paid by the consumer, and what proportion is paid by the seller in this case?

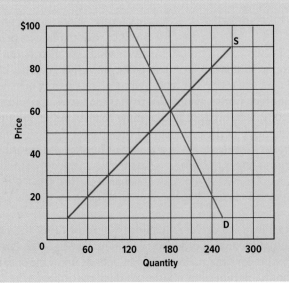

elastic. The initial price in both instances is the same. But note how much more the price increases in the circumstances illustrated in graph A than in those in graph B. Since the price increase is a result of the sales tax, consumers are paying a larger percentage of the tax in graph A than they are in graph B. It follows that the larger the percentage paid by the consumers, the smaller the percentage of the tax paid by the sellers of the product.

Thus, we can generalize to say:

> The more inelastic the demand for a product, the larger the percentage of a sales (or excise) tax the consumer will pay.

Another way to look at this is that since there are few substitutes for products with inelastic demand, the higher price will not have a significant effect on the quantity demanded by consumers and they will be more willing to pay a larger percentage of the tax and a higher price. On the other hand, if the demand for a product is elastic, many consumers will look unfavourably at the price increase and therefore the seller will have to absorb a good portion of the tax by keeping the price increase as small as possible.

Why Do Governments Impose "Sin Taxes"?

The price of cigarettes in Canada today ranges from $10 to $15 per pack—the price varies because both the federal and provincial governments impose taxes and the rate of taxation varies from province to province. Generally, the tax on a pack of cigarettes is between $4 and $5. In addition, about 80 percent of the price of beer, wine, and other types of alcohol is tax.

The reason for these high "sin taxes," as they are called, is not complicated. While it is true that governments may want to reduce the sale—particularly to young people—of what they consider to be harmful products, these products also have very inelastic demands, and governments discovered a long time ago that they could raise their tax revenues by simply raising the tax rate.

The graphical effect of increasing the tax rate on a product with an inelastic demand is illustrated in **Figure 4.6**. A higher tax rate shifts the supply curve to the left, and the price goes up much more than the quantity traded goes down.

What this shows is that a tax on any product will cause the equilibrium price to go up and the equilibrium quantity to fall. However, as we have seen, for a product with an inelastic demand, the fall in quantity is comparatively small, so it does not greatly affect government's tax revenues. To see why, let us consider what would happen if government increased the tax on two different products: a $2 tax on both a packet of salt (a product with a fairly inelastic demand because there are few substitutes) and a kilo of fresh tomatoes (a product that has an elastic demand because there are a number of substitutes). To keep things simple, let us suppose that 10 million units are sold every year, so that government is reaping tax revenues of $20 million from each product. Now, what would happen if government, to increase its revenues, increased the tax on both salt and tomatoes by $1 per unit?

A block from Parliament, where government is working on anti-smoking legislation, teens in the Rideau Centre shopping mall light up. Eleven percent of Canadian teenagers smoke, according to a 2012 Canadian Tobacco Use Monitoring Survey.
© Digital Vision

In both cases, the quantity sold is going to fall due to the resulting increase in price (the actual prices are not relevant). However, the sales of tomatoes will drop a lot more than the sales of salt. Suppose sales fall to 9 million and 6 million units respectively. The result is an increase in the tax revenue of $7 million ($20 to $27 million) in the case of the salt, but a drop in tax revenue of $2 million (from $20 to $18 million) in the case of the tomatoes. We can summarize the results in **Table 4.6**.

Clearly, then, if a government wants to maximize its tax revenues, it is better to impose taxes on those products that have inelastic demands: cigarettes, alcohol, and gasoline. (They seldom tax salt these days, though Britain infamously taxed salt during its colonial rule of India.)

In summary, we can conclude that although some members of government may have a genuine concern for people's health, the main reason governments put "sin taxes" on goods with inelastic demands is because they can increase their tax revenues.

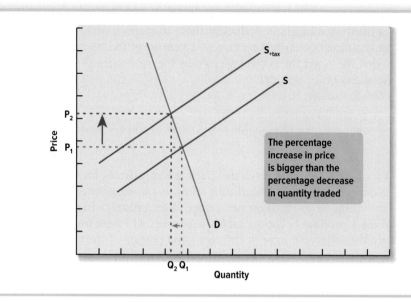

FIGURE 4.6 **The Effect of an Increase in the Tax on Cigarettes**

An increase in the tax on cigarettes has the effect of shifting the supply curve to the left, from S to S_{+tax}. Since the demand for cigarettes is inelastic, the resulting increase in price, P_1 to P_2, is greater than the decrease in the quantity demanded, Q_1 to Q_2.

TABLE 4.6
The Effect of a $1 Increase in the Tax on Salt and Tomatoes

TAX REVENUES BEFORE THE TAX INCREASE	
Salt	Tomatoes
10 million units @ $2 each = $20 million	10 million units @ $2 each = $20 million
TAX REVENUES AFTER THE TAX INCREASE	
9 million units @ $3 each = $27 million	6 million units @ $3 each = $18 million

Why Might a War on Drugs Increase Crime Rates?

Drug paraphernalia, including cocaine on a mirror, a razor, marijuana, and a pipe.

© JupiterImages/Comstock/Getty Images

Most people feel that crime rates in North American society are high and (mistakenly) seem to rise year after year. Furthermore, the effects of crime appear to be spreading into the middle class and are no longer confined to the underworld. The general public is becoming more intolerant of this, so some politicians are calling for tougher criminal laws.

What often gets targeted in any get-tough-on-crime campaign is the selling of illegal drugs such as cocaine and heroin, and of illegally obtained prescription drugs such as amphetamines. But such a focus ignores the fact that heroin and cocaine have highly inelastic demands. This has serious consequences, considering that even if the policy is somewhat effective, the supply of illegal drugs will never be eliminated; see **Figure 4.7**.

Let us assume that D is the (inelastic) demand for cocaine and that S_1 is the original supply that results in a price of $100 per gram and a quantity traded of 500 000 grams per week.

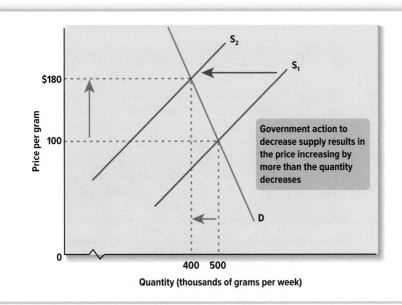

FIGURE 4.7   **The Cocaine Market**

If D and S₁ are the demand and supply curves for cocaine, the equilibrium price and quantity will be $100 per gram and 500 000 grams per week. A campaign against the drug trade will reduce the supply of cocaine, that is, the supply curve will shift to the left, as in S_2. This will greatly increase the price to $180.

Next, let us assume that the government cracks down on drug imports with the result that the supply decreases, as illustrated by the curve shifting back to S_2. This causes the price of cocaine to rise to $180 per gram, while the quantity demanded decreases to 400 000 grams per week.

So the quantity of heroin on the streets is reduced a little. However, what is important in all this is the amount spent by the consumers of cocaine in the two instances. When the price is $100 per gram, a total of $50 million per week is spent ($100 × 500 000), while $72 million is spent after the rise in price caused by the decrease in supply ($180 × 400 000). A large percentage of this money is obtained by the users of cocaine through various types of crime, such as robberies, car thefts, muggings, and holdups, as well as white-collar crimes such as embezzlement and fraud. In our example, $22 million more per week is spent on cocaine than before the decrease in supply. We must conclude that it is highly likely more crime will be committed to obtain these additional funds.

Hence the seeming paradox that a policy aimed at reducing crime in fact increases the its incidence. This provides insight into why some types of crime seem to continue to rise despite our anti-crime policies and the efforts of our police forces.

As a footnote, here are some alarming statistics on drug use in the United States (the number one country in the world for illegal drug use). Since President Richard Nixon proclaimed a War on Drugs in 1971, the U.S. has spent over $1 trillion on combating drug use. However, the sale of illegal drugs in the U.S. (and the world) has since skyrocketed. In fact, sales of illegal drugs worldwide is estimated at $340 billion annually, which exceeds the GDPs of all but the top twenty economies in the world. Along with the increased sales of drugs and increased spending by government to fight drug trading, the number of people incarcerated in U.S. jails has steadily increased every year from 40 000 in 1980 to 2.2 million today. A Pew study says that it costs the U.S. government approximately $31 000 a year to incarcerate a prisoner. Note that the annual cost to fund a public school student is less than $12 000.

When Is a Good Harvest Bad for Farmers?

A good harvest is one in which crop yields are high and farmers are able to bring large quantities of what they grow to market. For example, a typical wheat farmer might harvest 20 000 bushels in an average year, whereas in a good year, he might harvest 25 000. Would not a good harvest then be cause for celebration on the part of the farmer? Not necessarily, and the reason involves the price elasticity of demand.

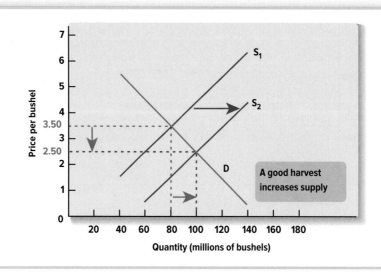

FIGURE 4.8   The Effect of a Good Harvest on the Wheat Market

A good harvest increases the supply of wheat and shifts the supply curve from S_1 to S_2. Given the inelastic demand for wheat, the decrease in price is substantial and the total revenue going to farmers as a group decreases.

The demand for some agricultural products—tomatoes, lettuce, and plums, for example—is certainly elastic, since many close substitutes are available. However, the elasticity of demand for the more basic commodities, such as wheat and rice, is less so.

If we combine an inelastic demand with the fact that a good harvest would increase supply and shift the supply curve to the right and thus decrease price, the total revenue that would flow to the farmers as a group would decline. This is illustrated in Figure 4.8. Here we see that the equilibrium price and quantity in a normal year is $3.50 per bushel and 80 million bushels. This would give wheat farmers total revenue of $280 million (the red-dashed rectangle). In a good harvest year, the supply curve shifts to the right, and the new equilibrium price and quantity are $2.50 and 100 million bushels (the blue-lined rectangle). This results in the price dropping far more than the quantity increases so that the total revenue decreases to $250 million. The good harvest results in farmers' losing $30 million in revenue. This illustrates the adage that farmers ask the gods for a poor harvest—for everyone except themselves.

 TEST YOUR UNDERSTANDING

11. The data on the right are for economy-line bicycles.

   a) What are the equilibrium price and quantity?

   b) What is the total expenditure (= total revenue) at equilibrium?

   c) If the supply were increased by 50 percent, what would be the new equilibrium price and quantity?

   d) What is the total expenditure (= total revenue) at this new equilibrium?

   e) What is the price elasticity of demand between these two equilibrium points?

Quantity Demanded (D_1) per Week	Price per Unit	Quantity Supplied (S_1) per Week
2 000 000	$260	800 000
1 800 000	320	1 200 000
1 600 000	380	1 600 000
1 400 000	440	2 000 000
1 200 000	500	2 400 000

SECTION SUMMARY

The four applications of the concept of price elasticity of demand show that

- the more inelastic the demand curve, the larger the proportion of a sales tax consumers pay
- governments raise a great deal of revenue from excise taxes on products with high inelastic demand, such as cigarettes
- any attempt to crack down on crime by focusing on the supply of illegal drugs will likely increase crime
- a good harvest is not always good news for farmers

4.5 Other Elasticity Measures

LO5 Describe the meaning and significance of supply elasticity, income elasticity, and cross-elasticity of demand.

The concept of elasticity can be applied to supply as well as to demand. The definition of **elasticity of supply** is analogous to that of demand.

$$\varepsilon_s = \frac{\%\Delta \text{ quantity supplied}}{\%\Delta \text{ price}} \qquad [4.4]$$

$$\varepsilon_s = \frac{\dfrac{\Delta Q_s}{\text{average } Q_s} \times 100}{\dfrac{\Delta P}{\text{average } P} \times 100} \qquad [4.5]$$

As we did with the demand curve, we can make some generalizations about the elasticity of supply from the position and slope of the curve as seen in **Figure 4.9**. Here, we have two supply curves, S_1 and S_2, and a common price change from \$2 to \$3. In the case of supply curve S_1, the quantity

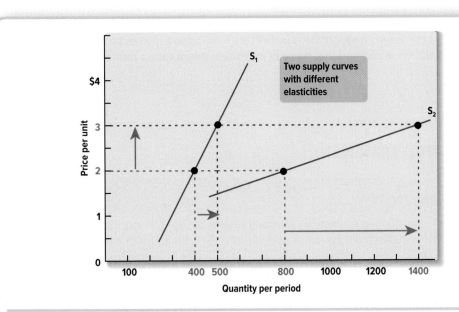

FIGURE 4.9 Elasticity of Supply

Supply curve S_1 is inelastic, as can be seen from the fact that only a small quantity change (from 400 to 500) results from the price increasing from \$2 to \$3. S_2, on the other hand, is an elastic supply curve, since quantity increases from 800 to 1400 as a result of the same price increase.

supplied rises from 400 to 500, and in the case of supply curve S_2 the quantity supplied almost doubles from 800 to 1400. We can therefore legitimately conclude that the elasticity of supply of S_2 must be larger than that in S_1. In the case of S_1, the supply elasticity is

$$\frac{\frac{100}{450} \times 100}{\frac{1}{2.5} \times 100} = \frac{+22.2\%}{+40\%} = +0.55$$

And for S_2, its supply elasticity is

$$\frac{\frac{600}{1100} \times 100}{\frac{1}{2.5} \times 100} = \frac{+54.5\%}{+40\%} = +1.36$$

This allows us to generalize that the elasticity of supply of more shallow curves is greater than that of steeper curves, although we again caution that elasticity does change as we move along any supply curve, just as it did in the case of the demand curve.

Given that producers would like to increase the quantity they supply as much as they can in response to an increase in price, what might explain the kind of difference in response indicated by S_1 and S_2? The first possible explanation involves the *level of technology* in use. If it is a sophisticated technology, such as one that requires complicated tool and die making, then S_1 is probably more representative. The use of a very simple technology, such as in cardboard carton production, would more likely be represented by S_2. Implied in this explanation, however, is an even more important determinant of supply elasticity, the *time involved*.

The famous nineteenth-century British economist Alfred Marshall recognized the importance of time in the determination of supply elasticity with his famous fish market example. In **Figure 4.10A** we see a perfectly inelastic supply curve. This represents what Marshall called the *momentary market period*, now usually referred to simply as the *market period*. As an example, he talked about the day's catch of fish, in the quantity of Q_1, having landed at the docks. This is all the fish that will be supplied until the next day (momentary supply), no matter how high the price might go. Marshall called the supply curve S_2 in **Figure 4.10B** the *short-run supply curve*; it is more elastic than S_1 and reflective of the various responses fishers might be able to make in the short run to a higher price. These responses include hiring extra crew, staying out longer, or using more nets. The supply curve in **Figure 4.10C** is the *long-run supply curve*, reflecting long-term adjustments to higher price, such as training additional crew and building more boats, which might take a number of months or years to accomplish.

 ADDED DIMENSION

Supply Elasticity for Milk

The International Farm Comparison Network released a study of supply elasticities for milk in various countries in 2005. The data collected covered a three-year period and included the following:

United States	0.86
United Kingdom	0.70
Netherlands	0.37
Canada	0.34
Poland	0.27

You will notice that all five of these elasticity measures are less than one, which means that the supply elasticity of milk is generally inelastic.

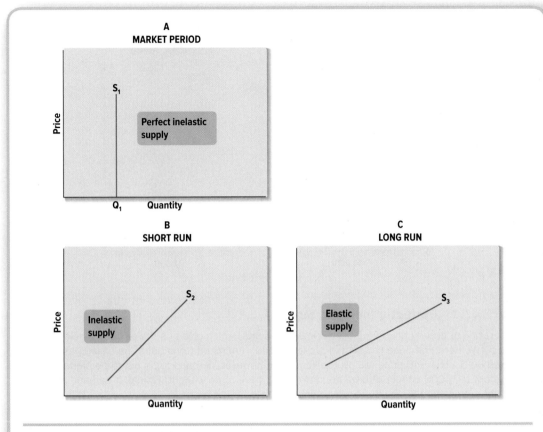

FIGURE 4.10   **Supply Elasticity in Three Periods**

Supply is perfectly inelastic in graph A. Marshall called this the momentary or market period. In graph B, the short run, supply is still inelastic but not perfectly inelastic. In graph C, the long run, supply is elastic.

From Marshall's fish market example, we can conclude that:

The longer the time frame involved, the more elastic will be the supply.

 TEST YOUR UNDERSTANDING

12. Calculate the price elasticity of supply in the $2 to $3 range if the quantity supplied increases from 35 to 45.

Ticket Scalping

An interesting application of supply elasticity involves *scalping*. This occurs when individuals who have purchased tickets for an event at the regular price then resell them at a higher price. Consider a hockey playoff or a high-profile concert, for which only a limited number of tickets are available. The owners of the home team (or the promoters of the event) must set the regular ticket price in advance by trying to estimate, as best they can, the demand for the event. **Figure 4.11** gives us three possibilities.

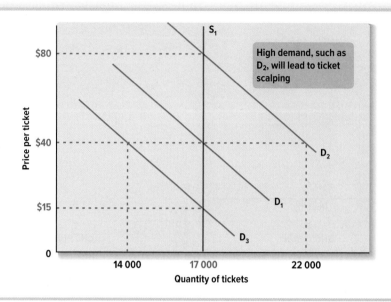

FIGURE 4.11   **Perfectly Inelastic Supply**

A concert hall or hockey rink has a fixed number of seats, which gives us the perfectly inelastic supply curve. Here, the price per seat is preset at $40. If demand turns out to be exactly as indicated by D_1, this $40 price will be equilibrium. If, however, demand turns out to be higher than anticipated, D_2, 5000 people who wanted tickets will have to do without. Finally, if demand proves to be that represented by D_3, there will be unsold seats for the event.

Scalpers hope that their team plays well enough that the demand for tickets remains high.

© Jeff Greenberg 3 of 6/Alamy

The fact that there is a limited number of tickets for sale (in this case, 17 000) results in the supply curve being perfectly inelastic, as reflected by S_1. Now assume that the price, which must be fixed before the tickets go on sale, is set at $40. If the demand for tickets to this event happens to be that represented by D_1, we would have equilibrium with 17 000 tickets sold and would congratulate the promoters for their correct guesstimate. If, instead, demand turns out to be higher, as represented by D_2, the general public will wish to buy 5000 more tickets than are available for sale. These are the circumstances of a shortage that scalpers thrive on; they get in line to buy tickets as early as possible and then buy as many as they can, to resell at a higher price. (As **Figure 4.11** shows, with a demand of D_2, the equilibrium price is $80.) Whether such activity is legal varies from province to province in Canada but it undoubtedly goes on everywhere.

Does scalping always pay off? Not if both the ticket-price setters and the scalper overestimate the demand. This situation is represented by D_3 in **Figure 4.11**. Here, at the $40 price, 3000 tickets will remain unsold and the scalper will have no option but to dump the tickets at a greatly reduced price. (As **Figure 4.11** shows, the ticket price should be $15 to clear the market.) This probably does not often happen, however, because there is evidence that event organizers prefer to set the official price a little below what they think people will actually pay; they prefer to reap the publicity when there are big lineups for tickets. In any case, it is clear that the phenomenon of a perfectly inelastic supply curve and a fixed preset price does generate some interesting twists in our analysis and leads to the conclusion that:

If the supply of a product is fixed, then only the demand determines the equilibrium price.

IT'S NEWS TO ME ...

After listening to the woeful cries of Tragically Hip fans who felt burned by scalpers when they tried to buy tickets to the iconic Canadian band's final concert in the summer of 2016, Ontario Attorney General Madeleine Meilleur says she's looking into ways to regulate the online ticketing industry better.

However, just a year ago, the government quietly opened the floodgates to allow scalpers to resell tickets online when it changed regulations in the Ticket Speculation Act in the summer of 2015. Scalping tickets had been illegal in Ontario but the new regulations were changed to allow resellers to make a profit—if the tickets were "authenticated."

From the Attorney General's perspective, opening the doors to authenticated ticket reselling could only help consumers. Instead of turning to the black market, where they were often ripped off, consumers could go to legal, legitimate resellers who could provide assurance that the ticket they bought could get them in the door.

However the idea of helping consumers turned sour when it became clear that these resellers have access to tickets the general public never gets a chance to buy. Such sentiment seems to be legitimized by the fact that when the tickets for the concert were put online for the public to buy they were all snapped up within 30 seconds of being offered.

The speculation is that industry insiders are able to use ticket-buying "bots" to siphon off tickets from the general public and then resell them for sometimes as much as 10 times their face value.

So what might Attorney General Meilleur do now? One proposed idea is to legislate the selling of high profile concert and sports tickets so as to follow the airline ticket model. Here, tickets would be sold online, one at a time, to individuals whose name would be on the ticket and could not be resold. And what about the price of the ticket? Perhaps sellers could use the auction model of selling to the highest bidders until all the limited number of tickets are sold.

Source: *Star Power Reporting,* July 2016.

I. What is the underlying economic reason that allows for the possibility of scalping?

   a) a perfectly elastic demand curve
   b) a perfectly inelastic demand curve
   c) a perfectly elastic supply curve
   d) a perfectly inelastic supply curve

II. Which of the following possible methods of allocation underlies the current system of ticket selling?

   a) lottery
   b) first come, first served
   c) producers' preference
   d) none of the above

TEST YOUR UNDERSTANDING

13. Rihanna is scheduled to perform at Centennial Hall, which seats 5000. Ticket prices for this one-night concert are set at $50 each and go on sale two weeks in advance.

  a) Suppose that many more than 5000 people want a ticket at the set price. Draw a graph showing both the supply curve and the demand curve.

  b) Is the ticket price above or below the equilibrium price?

Income Elasticity

As we have seen, the concept of price elasticity of demand involves the responsiveness of the quantity demanded to a change in price. Another important idea is the responsiveness of quantity demanded to a change in income (with the price being held constant), which is called **income elasticity** (of demand). As we saw earlier in this chapter, in the case of price elasticity, our measurement involves

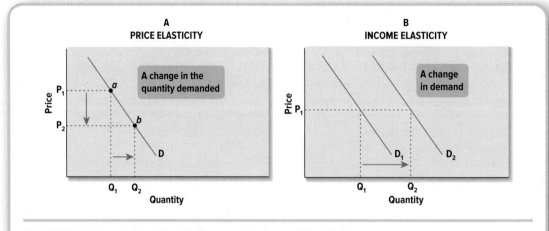

FIGURE 4.12   Price Elasticity and Income Elasticity

In Figure A, the movement along the demand curve from point *a* to point *b* involves the price elasticity of demand. In contrast, income elasticity of demand involves a shift in the demand curve, such as D_1 to D_2 in Figure B.

moving up or down on a single demand curve as illustrated in **Figure 4.12A**. In contrast, in the case of income elasticity the whole demand curve shifts, since, as you recall from Chapter 2, a change in income causes a change in demand.

The increase in the quantity demanded in **Figure 4.12B** is a result of the shift in the demand curve from D_1 to D_2, and the higher the income elasticity, the greater this shift will be.

$$\varepsilon_Y = \frac{\%\Delta \text{ quantity demanded } (Q_d)}{\%\Delta \text{ income } (Y)} \qquad [4.6]$$

$$\varepsilon_Y = \frac{\dfrac{\Delta Q_d}{\text{average } Q_d} \times 100}{\dfrac{\Delta Y}{\text{average } Y} \times 100} \qquad [4.7]$$

Once again, if this coefficient turns out to be greater than one, the demand is said to be *income elastic*; if it is less than one but greater than zero, we say demand is *income inelastic*. Examples of products that tend to be income elastic are air travel, restaurant meals, hairstyling services, and private swimming pools. Examples of products that tend to be income inelastic are tobacco, food, and prescription medicines.

Most products, whether income elastic or inelastic, have an income elastic coefficient greater than zero and are therefore the *normal* products defined in Chapter 2. However, for *inferior* products, the quantity demanded of the product actually declines in response to an increase in income, and therefore the income elasticity is negative. Staple foods, such as rice, flour, and potatoes, are the most likely examples of inferior products.

If these examples suggest to you that the distinction between products that are income elastic (greater than 1) and income inelastic (less than 1) is one of luxuries and necessities, you are correct. Households with limited incomes tend to buy mostly necessities. If the household's income rises, almost all of that additional income would be spent on the luxuries that previously could not be purchased. An undeniable characteristic of a postindustrial economy is that as income rises the percentage of total consumption of services rises, while that of physical goods declines. This is a reflection of the fact that most people consider such services as travel, dining out, and hiring a gardener as little ways they might give themselves a treat, and

---

TABLE 4.7

Differences in Spending Between the Richest and Poorest Groups in Canada, 2012

	INCOME INELASTIC			INCOME ELASTIC	
Category	Lowest Income Percentile	Highest Income Percentile	Category	Lowest Income Percentile	Highest Income Percentile
Food	14.2%	11.2%	Transportation	13.9%	18.1%
Shelter	32.9	22.6	Recreation	4.5	7.1
Health care	4.3	3.0	Insurance and pension contributions	1.4	9.0
Household operation	7.2	6.4			
Tobacco and alcohol	2.7	1.8			

Source: Adapted by the authors based on Statistics Canada, Spending Patterns in Canada, 2012. Table number 203-0022 extracted March 14, 2014. http://www.statcan.gc.ca/bsolc/olc-cel/olc-cel?lang=eng&catno=62-202-X.

this kind of expenditure undoubtedly becomes a greater part of one's total expenditures as income rises.

Table 4.7 shows how the proportion of after-tax income spent on different categories of goods varied from one income group to another in Canada in 2012. It is a truism that rich people spend more on almost everything than poor people do, but the proportion that they devote to the necessities of life is smaller, while the proportion they spend on luxury items is much greater.

All the items on the left are income inelastic. For instance, 47.1 percent of total spending by the poorest income groups went to food and shelter (14.2 percent on food and 32.9 percent on shelter). For the richest group, food and shelter represented only 33.8 percent of total spending (11.2 percent on food and 22.6 percent on shelter). The items on the right are all income elastic, which means that higher-income groups spend more both in absolute terms and proportionately on such things as transportation, recreation, and insurance.

 TEST YOUR UNDERSTANDING

14. You are given the following data and may assume that the prices of X and Y do not change.

Income	Quantity Demanded of X	Quantity Demanded of Y
$10 000	200	50
15 000	350	54

   a) Calculate the income elasticity for products X and Y.

   b) Are products X and Y normal goods?

Cross-Elasticity of Demand

Finally, in addition to price elasticity of demand, elasticity of supply, and income elasticity, we also need to understand the concept of **cross-elasticity of demand**—the way in which the quantity demanded of a product responds to a change in the price of a related product. Here, we are comparing how the quantity demanded of one product, A, responds to a change in the price of another product, B.

$$\varepsilon_{AB} = \frac{\%\Delta \text{ quantity demanded of Product A}}{\%\Delta \text{ price of Product B}}$$ [4.8]

$$\varepsilon_{AB} = \frac{\dfrac{\Delta Q_d^A}{\text{average } Q_d^A} \times 100}{\dfrac{\Delta P^B}{\text{average } P^B} \times 100}$$ [4.9]

Consider butter and margarine. An increase in the price of margarine will lead to an increase in the demand for butter, as indicated in **Table 4.8**.

TABLE 4.8
Cross-Elasticity of Margarine and Butter

MARGARINE		BUTTER	
Price	Quantity Demanded per Week (lb.)	Price	Quantity Demanded per Week (lb.)
$1.50	5000	$3.00	1000
2.10	3200	3.00	2000

Given the data in **Table 4.8**, it seems clear that the increase in the demand for butter is the result of the change in the price of margarine, since the price of butter remains unchanged but the quantity demanded increases. The cross-elasticity of demand of butter for margarine, therefore, is

$$\varepsilon_{AB} = \frac{\dfrac{+1000}{1500} \times 100}{\dfrac{+0.60}{1.80} \times 100} = \frac{+67\%}{+33\%} = +2$$

When we are looking at cross-elasticity, the sign of the coefficient is important. The fact that the coefficient is a positive number confirms that these two goods are substitutes and reinforces something we learned in Chapter 2: a rise in the price of a product (margarine) will increase the demand of a substitute product (butter).

 TEST YOUR UNDERSTANDING

15. Think of a Mars bar and a Snickers bar. Do you think the cross-elasticity of these two products is positive or negative? Do you think the coefficient would be high or low? Next, think of beer and beer nuts. Do your answers to the two questions change, and if so how?

It stands to reason that if substitute products have a positive cross-elasticity, complementary products will have a negative cross-elasticity. We can easily verify this. What would happen to the demand for computer games as a result of a *decrease* in the price of computers? Surely, it would increase, and as a result the cross-elasticity calculation between the two would have a negative sign, as we would expect in the case of complementary products.

As we have seen, elasticity is a concept of wide application, and one that extends our understanding of supply/demand analysis in many useful ways. You may find the following graphical summary of the various elasticity measures helpful.

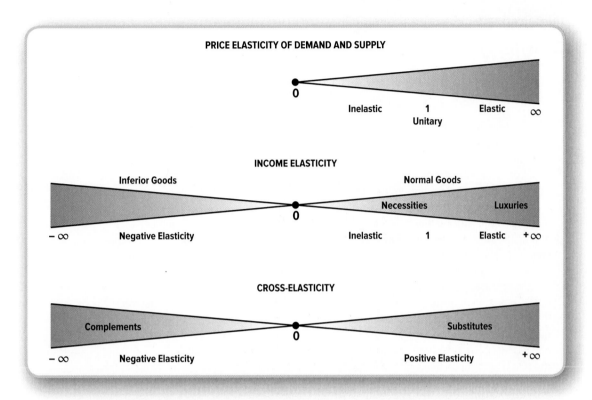

SECTION SUMMARY

a) The elasticity of supply depends primarily on the time involved, so

- supply is perfectly inelastic in the market period
- supply is inelastic, but not perfectly so, in the short run
- supply is elastic in the long run

b) The case of ticket scalping is a classic application of the concept of supply elasticity.

c) Income elasticity involves a shift in the demand curve as a result of a change in income (rather than a movement along the demand curve as in the case of price elasticity of demand). A negative coefficient indicates an inferior product. A positive coefficient that is less than one indicates a necessity. A positive coefficient that is more than one indicates a luxury product.

d) Cross-elasticity of demand involves the percentage change in the quantity demanded of one product as a result of a percentage change in the price of another product. A positive elasticity coefficient indicates a substitute product. A negative coefficient indicates a complementary product.

Study Guide

Review

WHAT'S THE BIG IDEA?

This chapter is all about how people react to changes in economic variables. Four different measures are introduced: three of them relate to how consumers' demand for a particular product is affected by a change in its price (price elasticity), a change in their incomes (income elasticity), or a change in the price of other products (cross elasticity). The fourth measure examines how producers react to a change in the price of the product they are selling (supply elasticity). In some cases, people have a strong reaction to the change—an elastic response. In other cases they hardly react at all—an inelastic response. Measuring this reaction is not too difficult if you remember that in the various equations the cause of the change (price or income) goes in the denominator and the effect of the change (a change in the quantity either demanded or supplied) goes in the numerator. In addition, the changes must always be expressed in percentage terms.

One of the important applications of price elasticity of demand is to figure out how much the total revenue of sellers (or total amount paid by consumers) is affected by a price change. We know that if the price of a product decreases, the quantity will rise. That's true for all products. But more importantly, if the demand is elastic, the increase in quantity is going to be very big, meaning total revenue will increase. With an inelastic demand, the rise in quantity is small compared to the decrease in the price, so total revenue will fall. This is important when looking at products like oil, or many agricultural products. Generally speaking, the higher the price, the greater the total revenue; the lower the price, the lower the total revenue. With elastic demands, it's the exact opposite.

Finally, as the Added Dimension box on calculating elasticity shows, the value of the elasticity coefficient can be calculated by multiplying the (inverse of) the slope of the demand curve by the ratio of the price divided by the quantity. This means that even if the demand curve is a straight line (a constant slope), the value of the elasticity coefficient will vary according to which point (which price/quantity ratio) on the demand curve you're looking at. Generally, the higher the price, the greater the elasticity.

NEW GLOSSARY TERMS AND KEY EQUATIONS

cross-elasticity of demand
elastic demand
elasticity coefficient
elasticity of supply

excise tax
income elasticity
inelastic demand
price elasticity of demand

total revenue
unitary elasticity

Equations:

[4.1] $\varepsilon_p = \dfrac{\% \Delta \text{ quantity demanded}}{\% \Delta \text{ price}}$

[4.2] $\varepsilon_p = \dfrac{\dfrac{\Delta Q_d}{\text{average } Q_d} \times 100}{\dfrac{\Delta P}{\text{average } P} \times 100}$

[4.3] $\varepsilon_p = \dfrac{\Delta Q/Q \times 100}{\Delta P/P \times 100} = \dfrac{\Delta Q/Q}{\Delta P/P} = \dfrac{\Delta Q}{Q} \times \dfrac{P}{\Delta P} = \dfrac{\Delta Q \times P}{\Delta P \times Q}$

[4.4] $\varepsilon_s = \dfrac{\%\Delta \text{ quantity supplied}}{\%\Delta \text{ Price}}$

[4.5] $\varepsilon_s = \dfrac{\dfrac{\Delta Q_s}{\text{average } Q_s} \times 100}{\dfrac{\Delta P}{\text{average P}} \times 100}$

[4.6] $\varepsilon_Y = \dfrac{\%\Delta \text{ quantity demanded } (Q_d)}{\%\Delta \text{ Income (Y)}}$

[4.7] $\varepsilon_Y = \dfrac{\dfrac{\Delta Q_d}{\text{average } Q_d} \times 100}{\dfrac{\Delta Y}{\text{average Y}} \times 100}$

[4.8] $\varepsilon_{AB} = \dfrac{\%\Delta \text{ quantity demanded of Product A}}{\%\Delta \text{ price of Product B}}$

[4.9] $\varepsilon_{AB} = \dfrac{\dfrac{\Delta Q_d^A}{\text{average } Q_d^A} \times 100}{\dfrac{\Delta P^B}{\text{average } P^B} \times 100}$

Comprehensive Problem

(LO 2, 4, 5) Assume that there is only one movie theatre and only one video streaming outlet in a small mining town in northern Manitoba. The weekly demand, by all the townspeople, for movies and streamed video rentals is given in **Table 4.9**.

TABLE 4.9

Prices of Movies	Quantity of Movies Demanded	Total Revenue	Prices of Videos	Quantity of Streamed Videos Demanded	Total Revenue
$3	450	_____	$2.00	950	_____
4	400	_____	2.50	900	_____
5	350	_____	3.00	825	_____
6	300	_____	3.50	750	_____
7	250	_____	4.00	650	_____
8	200	_____	4.50	550	_____
9	150	_____	5.00	425	_____

Questions

a) Fill in the total revenue columns.
b) What prices for movies and for streamed videos would maximize the seller's total revenue?
c) What is the price elasticity of demand for movies if the theatre changes the price from $6 to $5, and what is the change in total revenue? What is the price elasticity of demand if the price changes from $6 to $7 and what is the change in total revenue?
d) What conclusions can you draw from your answers in (c)?

Answers

a) See the following table:

TABLE 4.9 (COMPLETED)

Prices of Movies	Quantity of Movies Demanded	Total Revenue	Prices of Videos	Quantity of Streamed Videos Demanded	Total Revenue
$3	450	$1350	$2.00	950	$1900
4	400	1600	2.50	900	2250
5	350	1750	3.00	825	2475
6	300	1800	3.50	750	2625
7	250	1750	4.00	650	2600
8	200	1600	4.50	550	2475
9	150	1350	5.00	425	2125

b) $6 for movies and $3.50 for videos.

c) The elasticity of demand for the price change from $6 to $5 is

$$\frac{(50/325 \times 100)}{(1/5.5 \times 100)} = 15.4/18.2 = 0.85$$

The change in total revenue is −$50.
For the price change from $6 to $7,

$$\frac{(50/275 \times 100)}{(1/6.5 \times 100)} = 18.2/15.4 = 1.18$$

The change in total revenue is −$50.

d) For movie prices below $6, demand must be inelastic, since reducing price results in a decrease in total revenue. For prices above $6, demand must be elastic, since raising price also results in a decrease in total revenue. Therefore, $6 is the point of unitary elasticity and is the price that maximizes total revenue for the seller. (Calculations of price changes for streamed videos from $3.50 to $3 and from $3.50 to $4 would lead us to the same conclusion for streamed videos.)

Questions

e) Suppose that the streaming video outlet was charging the price that maximized total revenue, but the city government imposes an excise tax on *videos* that results in the price of streamed videos rising to $4.50. As a result, the demand for *movies* increases by 20 at each price. Complete Table 4.10.

TABLE 4.10

Price of Movies	(New) Quantity of Movies Demanded	Total Revenue
$3	————	————
4	————	————
5	————	————
6	————	————
7	————	————
8	————	————
9	————	————

f) Would the theatre now want to charge the same price for movies?

g) Given the circumstances in (e), what is the cross-elasticity of movies for streamed videos? What does this say about the relationship between the two products?

Answers

e)

TABLE 4.10 (COMPLETED)		
Price of Movies	(New) Quantity of Movies Demanded	Total Revenue
$3	470	$1410
4	420	1680
5	370	1850
6	320	1920
7	270	1890
8	220	1760
9	170	1530

f) Yes. As can be seen in the table, total revenue is still maximized when price is $6.

g) At the $6 price for movies, the quantity demanded rises from the original 300 to 320 as a result of the price of videos increasing from $3.50 to $4.50. Thus, the cross-elasticity of movies for videos is

$$\frac{+(20/310 \times 100)}{(+1/4 \times 100)} = +6.4/+25 = 0.26$$

Since the coefficient is positive, the two products are substitutes.

Questions

h) Referring to the original data in **Table 4.9**, assume now that the average weekly earnings of the townspeople rise from $500 to $550 with the result that demand for movies increases 20 percent. If the price being charged is $6, what is the income elasticity of demand? What does this suggest about the product, movies?

Answers

h) At the $6 price for movies, the quantity demanded for movies rises from 300 to 360 (by 20 percent) as incomes rise from 500 to 550 so the income elasticity of movies is

$$\frac{(+60/330 \times 100)}{(+50/525 \ 100)} = +18.18/+9.52 = +1.91$$

Since the coefficient is positive, movies are a normal good and, in addition, since it is greater than one, movies are a luxury good.

Study Problems

Find answers on the McGraw-Hill online resource.

Basic (Problems 1–5)

1. **(LO 2, 4)** Suppose that the price of a kilo of bananas drops from $4.50 to $3.50, and as a result the quantity sold increases from 85 to 115 kilos.
   a) What is the value of total revenue before and after the price change? $ _____
   b) What is the percentage change in the price? _____

c) What is the percentage change in the quantity? _____

d) What is the value of the price elasticity of demand? _____

e) Is the demand elastic or inelastic? _____

2. **(LO 5)** If the quantity of bread supplied increased by 12 percent when the price increased by 10 percent, what is the value of the elasticity of supply? _____

3. **(LO 5)** Suppose that household incomes in Sherbrooke rose from $48 000 to $52 000, and that, assuming no change in price, the quantity of Kraft macaroni and cheese rose from 156 to 164 cases per week.

   a) What is the value of the income elasticity of demand for Kraft macaroni and cheese? _____

   b) What does this suggest about this product? _____

4. **(LO 5)** Suppose that the price of President's Choice macaroni and cheese decreased from $9 to $7 per case, and at the same time the quantity of Kraft macaroni and cheese dropped from 192 to 128 cases.

   a) What is the cross-elasticity of demand between the two products? _____

   b) What is the relationship between the two products? _____

5. **(LO 2)** Given the price elasticities and price changes for the following Products A–E in Table 4.11, show how much the quantity will change (indicating an increase or decrease) and what effect this will have on total revenue (indicating an increase or decrease).

TABLE 4.11

Product	Price Elasticity	% Δ Price	% Δ Quantity	Δ Total Revenue
A	0.5	↑ by 10%	_____	_____
B	1.4	↓ by 5%	_____	_____
C	0.4	↓ by 20%	_____	_____
D	1	↑ by 3%	_____	_____
E	3	↑ by 4%	_____	_____

Intermediate (Problems 6–11)

6. **(LO 3)** See the demand curve in Figure 4.13.

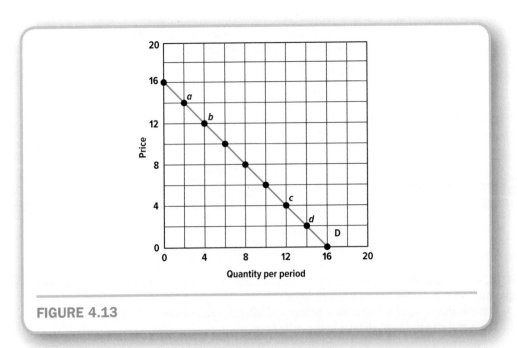

FIGURE 4.13

a) What is the value of the slope of the demand curve?

b) What is the elasticity of demand between points *a* and *b*, and between points *c* and *d*?

    a and *b*: _____

    c and *d*: _____

c) At what price is the elasticity of demand equal to one? $_____

d) At what price would consumers spend the most on this product? $_____

e) Between what prices is demand inelastic? _____ and _____

7. **(LO 3)** Table 4.12 is the demand schedule for poetry booklets in the town of Never Ending.

TABLE 4.12

Price	Quantity	TR
$20	0	_____
18	3	_____
16	6	_____
4	9	_____
2	12	_____
10	15	_____
8	18	_____
6	21	_____
4	24	_____

a) Calculate the total revenue of the seller at each quantity.

b) At what quantity and price is total revenue maximized?

    Quantity: _____ Price: $ _____

c) In **Figure 4.14A** draw the demand curve and indicate the point of unitary elasticity.

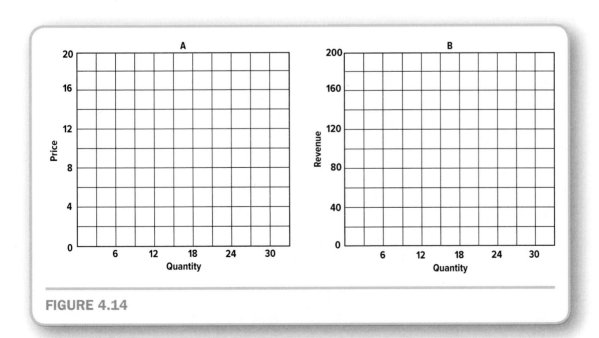

FIGURE 4.14

d) In **Figure 4.14B** draw the total revenue curve and indicate the point of maximum total revenue.

8. **(LO 3, 4)** Figure 4.15 shows the market for oats.

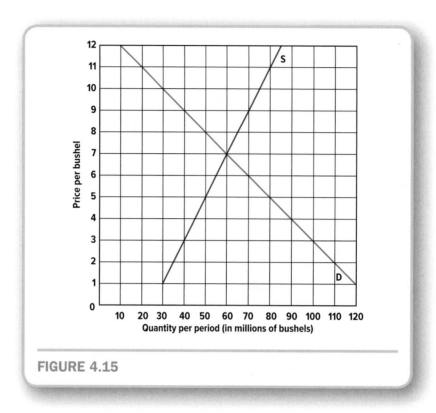

FIGURE 4.15

a) At the present equilibrium, what is the total revenue received by farmers (in millions of dollars)?
$ _____

b) Suppose that the oat industry had a very good harvest and the supply increased by 30 million bushels. Draw the new supply curve in **Figure 4.15**.

c) What will be the new total revenue received by farmers (in millions of dollars)? $ _____

d) What does this suggest about the elasticity of demand for oats? _____

9. **(LO 1, 2, 3)** Table 4.13 shows the demand for haircuts from seniors and other customers on an average weekday in the local hairdressing shop.

TABLE 4.13

Price of Haircut	Quantity Demanded by Seniors	Quantity Demanded by Other Customers
$20	1	9
18	4	10
16	7	11
14	10	12
12	13	13
10	16	14
8	19	15
6	22	16
4	25	17
2	28	18

a) Between the prices of $16 and $20, which of the two demands is more elastic? _____

b) What price would give the shop the greatest sales revenue? $_____

10. **(LO 1, 2)** Adam makes specialized garden figurines in a small shop on his property, and his monthly total sales revenue is $800 when he charges $20 for each figurine. One month, he tried lowering his price to $18, and his total sales revenue that month dropped to $756. On the basis of these data, what is the price elasticity of demand for Adam's product? _____

11. **(LO 3)** The data in Table 4.14 are for electricity, measured in megawatts.

TABLE 4.14

Price	Quantity Demanded
$ 97	103
98	102
99	101
100	100
101	99
102	98

a) At what price is the total expenditure by consumers at a maximum? $_____

b) What is the price elasticity of demand at this price? _____

Advanced (Problems 12–15)

12. **(LO 2, 5)** Table 4.15 relates to a particular market.

TABLE 4.15

Year	Average Income	Price of M	Quantity of M	Price of N	Quantity of N
1	$50 000	$2.50	100	$20	800
2	50 000	2.80	90	20	750
3	50 000	2.80	80	30	700
4	55 000	2.80	90	30	720

a) What is the price elasticity of demand for Product M? _____

b) What is the price elasticity of demand for Product N? _____

c) What is the income elasticity of demand for Product M? _____

d) What is the income elasticity of demand for Product N? _____

e) What is the cross-elasticity of demand of Product M for a change in the price of Product N? _____

13. **(LO 3)** Trader Tom delivers boxes of tomatoes (and sometimes other perishable items) to two remote towns in northern Alberta. The demand schedules for tomatoes in each of the towns are shown in Table 4.16.

TABLE 4.16

	TOWN A				TOWN B	
Price	Quantity Demanded	Total Revenue	Price	Quantity Demanded	Total Revenue
$ 5	15	_____	$ 5	11	_____
10	14	_____	10	10	_____
15	13	_____	15	9	_____
20	12	_____	20	8	_____
25	11	_____	25	7	_____
30	10	_____	30	6	_____
35	9	_____	35	5	_____
40	8	_____	40	4	_____
45	7	_____	45	3	_____
50	6	_____	50	2	_____
55	5	_____	55	1	_____
60	4	_____	60	0	_____
65	3	_____	65		_____
70	2	_____	70		_____
75	1	_____	75		_____

a) If during a particular week Tom has only four boxes to deliver, how many boxes should he deliver to each town if he wishes to maximize his total revenue? _____

b) What would your answer be if Tom had six boxes the next week? _____

c) How many boxes should Tom deliver to each town—if available—to maximize his total revenue? _____

14. **(LO 1, 4)** The data in Table 4.17 are for 5 kilo boxes of lobsters.

TABLE 4.17

Price	Quantity Demanded	Quantity Supplied (before tax)	Quantity Supplied (after tax)
$100	900	820	_____
110	880	840	_____
120	860	860	_____
130	840	880	_____
140	820	900	_____
150	800	920	_____

a) Before the tax, what are the equilibrium price and quantity?
   Price: $_____ Quantity: _____

b) Fill in the Quantity Supplied (after tax) column, assuming that a $20-per-unit excise tax is put on the product.

c) What are the new equilibrium price and quantity?
   Price: $_____ Quantity: _____

d) What portion of the $20-per-unit excise tax is paid by the seller, and what portion is paid by the consumer?
   Paid by seller: _____%
   Paid by consumer: _____%

15. **(LO 3, 4)** Table 4.18 contains data for the demand for a box of blueberries in two different markets.

TABLE 4.18

| | MARKET 1 | | MARKET 2 | |
| | Quantity | Quantity | Quantity | Quantity |
Price	Supplied	Demanded	Supplied	Demanded
$9.50	800	560	800	480
9.00	760	580	760	520
8.50	720	600	720	560
8.00	680	620	680	600
7.50	640	640	640	640
7.00	600	660	600	680

a) What is the equilibrium price and quantity in each market?
   Market 1 price: ——————— Quantity: ———————
   Market 2 price: ——————— Quantity: ———————
b) What is the total revenue earned by suppliers in each market?
   Market 1: ——————— Market 2: ———————

Now, assume that government has imposed a quota of 560 in both markets.

c) In which market would the blueberry growers be happier? ———————
d) In which market is the price elasticity of demand more inelastic? ———————

Problems for Further Study

Basic (Problems 1–4)

1. **(LO 1)** Define the term *price elasticity of demand*. What does it mean if a calculation of the price elasticity of demand turns out to be less than one?

2. **(LO 1)** Why is the price elasticity of demand for carrots so different from that for cigarettes?

3. **(LO 5)** Which of the following types of income elasticity
   (i) negative elasticity
   (ii) zero elasticity
   (iii) positive inelasticity
   (iv) positive elasticity

   is suggested by each of the following responses to a decrease in income?

   a) People buy a lot less of a product.
   b) People buy the same quantity of a product.
   c) People buy a little less of a product.
   d) People buy more of a product.

4. **(LO 2)** Do you think the income elasticity of each product listed below is high, low, or negative?
   a) skiing holidays
   b) postage stamps
   c) potatoes
   d) scuba diving equipment
   e) prescription drugs
   f) low-priced, single-ply toilet paper

Intermediate (Problems 5–7)

5. **(LO 1)** Explain the three factors that determine the price elasticity of demand. Which is most important?

6. **(LO 4)** Explain why a bad harvest might be good for farmers.

7. **(LO 5)** Categorize each of the products listed in (a) to (e) below in terms of their income elasticity ((i) to (iv)).
   (i) positive, inelastic
   (ii) positive, elastic
   (iii) zero
   (iv) negative

   a) salt
   b) weekend getaway
   c) milk
   d) generic macaroni and cheese mix
   e) cigarettes

Advanced (Problems 8–11)

8. **(LO 4)** Under what conditions will the consumer pay all of the excise tax placed on a particular product?

9. **(LO 3)** Which of the demand curves in **Figure** 4.16, D_1 or D_2, is more elastic at price P_1? At price P_2?

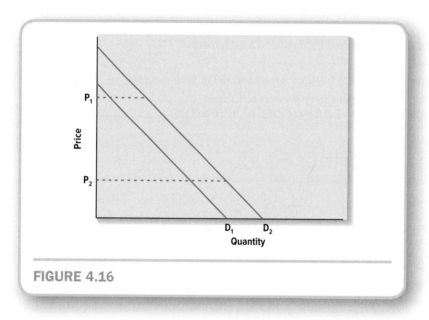

FIGURE 4.16

At price P_1: _____% At price P_2: _____%

10. **(LO 1, 5)** The dean of arts at a large university recently said she felt that the demand for postsecondary education must be very inelastic because enrollment has decreased very little despite a doubling in tuition fees (after inflationary effects have been removed) over the past ten years. Do you agree with the dean? Why, or why not?

11. **(LO 2)** Suppose you are a researcher attempting to calculate the price elasticity of demand for Products A and B. Your research associate has collected the data in **Table** 4.19 to assist you. Suppose you use these data to calculate the price elasticities of demand for Products A and B. Comment on the validity of your calculations.

TABLE 4.19

Year	Price of Product A	Quantity Traded of Product A	Price of Product B	Quantity Traded of Product B	Average Consumer Income
1	$ 8	1000	$25	300	$32 000
2	10	1100	22	350	34 000

CHAPTER 5
Consumer Choice

LEARNING OBJECTIVES

At the end of this chapter, you should be able to:

LO1 Explain the law of diminishing marginal utility.

LO2 Derive a consumers' purchasing rule that ensures satisfaction is maximized.

LO3 Explain how marginal utility theory is applicable to real-world examples.

LO4 Provide a theoretical rationale for downward-sloping demand curves.

LO5 Explain why consumers generally value a product more than the purchase price they pay.

LO6 Explain why some sellers charge different prices to different consumers for the same product.

WHAT'S AHEAD ...

This chapter looks at the approach to consumer behaviour known as *marginal utility theory*. This theory helps us better understand how the rational consumer allocates income toward the purchase of various products. It also provides a deeper understanding of demand and why consumers are willing and able to purchase more at lower prices. We explain the idea of consumer surplus and look at attempts by producers to acquire this surplus through price discrimination.

A QUESTION OF RELEVANCE …

Suppose the government of Canada gave a $200 bonus to every citizen of the country, with the proviso that it must be spent immediately. What are the odds that any two individuals would buy exactly the same products? One in a thousand? One in a million? Probably more like one in twenty million. Every individual is unique, and this is reflected in each person's tastes and spending behaviour. What determines individual tastes is more a subject for the psychologist than the economist, but how taste translates into purchases is very much the province of the economist and is the subject of this chapter.

You do not need to be a student of economics to appreciate that people's tastes differ; one person's paradise is another person's prison! And even when people buy the same products, we cannot be sure that they receive the same amount of satisfaction from them. Yet our formulation of an individual's demand is predicated on the assumption that it measures, or at least indicates, their desire and ability to purchase. An increase in either would presumably cause that person to purchase more. Measuring ability to purchase is easy enough: it can be gauged by individuals' income and wealth. But how do we measure intensity of desire? Well, a number of economists in the latter part of the nineteenth century attempted to do just that. In doing so, they introduced an important new idea called the **marginal**.

The marginal revolution shifted the focus of economists away from totals, such as total profits or total costs or total utility, and toward the margin, which means the extra or additional profit or cost or revenue. English economist Alfred Marshall believed that concentrating on people's actions *at the margin* provided a better understanding of their behaviour. If we are trying to understand why a consumer buys one particular basket of goods rather than any other, it is more instructive conceptually to look at each purchase one at a time, rather than trying to evaluate the total result of a morning's shopping. The basket of goods is, after all, the result of a number of individual decisions, not one single decision.

Using this approach, Marshall developed the concept of *marginal utility* and with it the important law of diminishing marginal utility. The theory of consumer behaviour, which uses this concept, is the focus of this chapter. Before we look at it, we should mention that the idea of the margin is not always easy to grasp at first. It is definitely worth the effort, however, since it lies at the heart of so much economic analysis and is the basis of many of the ideas contained in later chapters.

5.1   The Law of Diminishing Marginal Utility

LO1   Explain the law of diminishing marginal utility.

Suppose I wished to communicate to you the immense satisfaction I get from my first beverage of the day. I could use words like "greatly" or "fantastically" or even "indescribably" refreshing, but no words could accurately capture the degree of my pleasure, or **utility**, as economists call it. Suppose, instead, that I assign a number to indicate the amount of my utility, say 100 utils. Does this communicate my pleasure any more accurately? Probably not, since you have no idea what a util is and we have no instrument with which to measure it. However, if I then tell you that the second beverage of the day gives me only 50 utils of pleasure, you have a very clear indication of how I rate these two drinks.

On the other hand, my friend Cleo might suggest that she gets 200 and 100 utils from her first two drinks. Since neither of us can objectively measure the amount of utility, we cannot conclude that she derives twice as much utility as I do. In other words, we cannot make interpersonal comparisons of utility. Nevertheless, we can still draw some interesting conclusions about consumer behaviour by pursuing this idea of utility.

For example, assume that a frantic student, Anna, is at her local coffee bar, beginning an all-night cram session for her finals. Suppose also that she keeps score of the amount of pleasure (measured in utils) she derives from the successive lattés that keep her going through the night. (Of course, this is her subjective evaluation, and it might change from time to time.) It seems reasonable to suppose that the very first latté would give her the greatest satisfaction, and each one afterward would give less and less pleasure, as shown in Table 5.1.

TABLE 5.1
Total Marginal Utility

Quantity	Marginal Utility (MU)	Total Utility (TU)
1	45	45
2	36	81
3	25	106
4	21	127
5	12	139
6	0	139
7	−6	133

The column headed **marginal utility** (MU) shows the amount of pleasure or satisfaction, measured in utils, that Anna derives from each latté consumed. We can express marginal utility in terms of an equation:

$$\text{Marginal utility (MU)} = \frac{\Delta \text{ total utility}}{\Delta \text{ quantity}} \qquad [5.1]$$

Since Table 5.1 shows that the quantity changes by one unit each time, the denominator in equation 5.1 is equal to one. It can be seen that Anna's MU decreases as she drinks more lattes. Although every latté, at least until the sixth cup, gives her positive marginal utility, she derives less and less MU from successive units. This is known as the **law of diminishing marginal utility**. It seems reasonable to suppose that this law holds for most of us most of the time. Our knowledge of life and our personal experiences alone support the idea that more may be better, but additional units do not give the same degree of pleasure. In summary:

Although TU increases, MU diminishes with successive units.

Furthermore, at some point more becomes worse. For Anna, that point comes with the seventh cup where her MU is −6. Since the first unit of anything we consume gives us positive utility, and the last gives us negative utility, MU must be declining with successive amounts consumed.

The last column in Table 5.1 shows Anna's total utility (TU) derived from consuming the various quantities. TU can be found by summing the marginal utility from each unit. For example, the TU from consuming 5 units is

$$TU_{5 \text{ units}} = MU_1 + MU_2 + MU_3 + MU_4 + MU_5 \qquad [5.2]$$

From Table 5.1, we can see that the TU from 5 units is

$$TU_{5 \text{ units}} = 45 + 36 + 25 + 21 + 12 = 139$$

You can see, looking Table 5.1, that Anna's TU increases with the amount consumed, but the rate of increase slows down with increasing quantities. This is the same thing as saying that MU diminishes, a point illustrated in Figure 5.1.

The TU curve goes up as more of this product is consumed—at least, up to the sixth unit. However, the rate at which it increases gets smaller and smaller, that is, the slope of the TU curve gets smaller (or the curve gets flatter). The slope of the TU curve is the same thing as the MU. In other

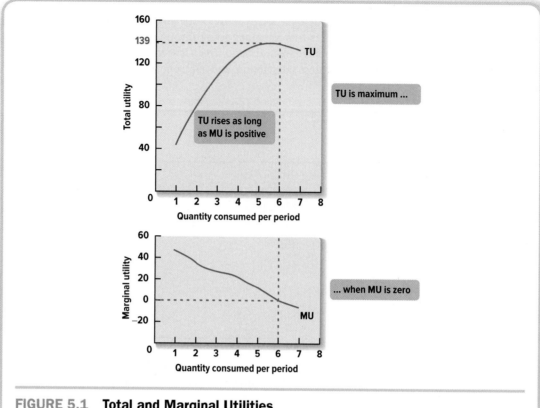

FIGURE 5.1   Total and Marginal Utilities

The TU curve increases as the quantity consumed increases. But it increases at a declining rate: that is, the slope gets smaller and becomes zero at a quantity of 6. This is where TU is at a maximum (of 139). Since the slope of the TU curve is driven by MU and MU is declining, we know that the slope of the TU curve is also declining.

words, starting from a high of 45 utils when one unit is consumed, the MU declines with increased consumption until it eventually becomes zero with the consumption of the sixth unit. Note that the TU curve is at a maximum when MU equals zero.

Before we start to develop this theory of utility a bit further, it is important to state the conditions under which it operates. First of all, we take it for granted that the consumers we are describing act rationally. By this, we mean that they will wish to consume more as long as total utility increases. This point bears repeating. A rational consumer will want to consume more only so long as increased consumption adds to total satisfaction:

> The objective of the consumer, it is assumed, is to maximize the pleasure derived from consumption, that is, to maximize total utility.

In addition, this idea of diminishing marginal utility makes sense only if we are considering consumption over a relatively short time period. If Anna were to consume the seven lattés over seven evenings, her marginal utility would likely remain constant or even increase. Finally, as Alfred Marshall pointed out, certain products are indivisible; thus, a small quantity may be insufficient to meet certain special wants. For example, three automobile tires would not give a great deal of utility without the fourth. In summary, marginal utility theory applies when

- the consumer is behaving rationally
- the consumer's objective is maximum satisfaction
- purchases and consumption take place over a short period
- the units purchased may sometimes be sets of items

TEST YOUR UNDERSTANDING

Find answers on the McGraw-Hill online resource.

1. Complete the table, which shows Michelle's utility for milkshakes.

Quantity	Total Utility (TU)	Marginal Utility (MU)
1	20	___
2	35	___
3	___	10
4	___	8
5	58	___
6	60	___
7	___	0
8	___	−5

SECTION SUMMARY

a) *Marginal utility* is the amount of extra satisfaction derived from the consumption of one more unit of a product. It can be expressed as

$$MU = \frac{\Delta \text{ total utility}}{\Delta \text{ quantity}}$$

It can be measured in hypothetical numbers of utils.

b) The *law of diminishing marginal utility* states that the extra satisfaction derived from one more unit of a product declines as more of that product is consumed.

5.2   Optimal Purchasing Rule

LO2   Derive a consumers' purchasing rule that ensures satisfaction is maximized.

From the information contained in Table 5.1, it is apparent that even if Anna had unlimited income or if the refreshment were free, there would still be a limit to how much she would drink. She would never drink more than six lattés, since no rational consumer would consume a unit that gives negative marginal utility. In other words, if we wanted to develop some rule of rational consumer behaviour, we might suggest that a person with unlimited income should consume every product to the point of total satiation! The problem with this little rule is that it does not apply to any known consumer, because all people, no matter how rich or poor, have limited incomes (not to mention limited time) and therefore have to make choices.

To derive a more relevant rule of consumer behaviour, let us suppose that Anna has a limited budget of $24 and is choosing between two products: lattés and pieces of pastry, each costing $4. The utility of both products is shown in Table 5.2.

The question now is: How should Anna best allocate her evening's budget if she wishes to maximize her total utility? She certainly cannot consume both products to the point of maximum total utility, since that would cost $24 for the 6 cups of latté and $24 for 6 pieces of pastry, a total of $48—double her budget. We need to figure out (on her behalf) what combination of the two goods, costing $24, will produce the maximum total utility. One way to do this would be to work out every possible combination, given the

How much marginal utility does this cup produce?

Brand X/Getty Images

TABLE 5.2
Comparison of the Utilities of Lattés and Pieces of Pastry

	LATTÉ			PIECES OF PASTRY	
Quantity	Marginal Utility	Total Utility	Quantity	Marginal Utility	Total Utility
1	45	45	1	64	64
2	36	81	2	52	116
3	25	106	3	40	156
4	21	127	4	26	182
5	12	139	5	10	192
6	0	139	6	0	192
7	–6	133	7	–7	185

$24 constraint, and see which particular combination maximizes utility. The procedure is a little tedious, but not particularly difficult, as Table 5.3 shows.

TABLE 5.3
Utility Obtained from Combinations of Lattés and Pastries

	LATTÉS	PIECES OF PASTRY		BOTH
Quantity	Total Utility	Quantity	Total Utility	Total Utility
0	0	6	192	192
1	45	5	192	237
2	81	4	182	263
3	106	3	156	262
4	127	2	116	243
5	139	1	64	203
6	139	0	0	139

Since she can only make 6 purchases, one possible combination might be 0 lattés and 6 pieces of pastry. This would give Anna a total utility of 192. But another feasible—and better—way of spending $24 would be on 1 latté and 5 pieces of pastry for a total utility from both products of 237 utils. The table shows every possible combination of the two products costing $24. A glance at the last column of Table 5.3 shows that the best combination is 2 cups of latté and 4 pieces of pastry, because this yields the maximum total utility of 263 utils.

But most of us do not allocate our budget this way. In Anna's case, it is unlikely that she would sit down in advance and try to figure out which combination is best for her. She is more likely to make her choices one at a time—that is, marginally. This approach will give us the same results as looking at every single combination as we just did, and is less tedious and far more instructive.

Suppose that on entering the coffee bar, Anna takes $4 from the $24 out of her purse and walks up to the counter to place an order. What should she buy? Table 5.2 shows us that a pastry looks more attractive because the marginal utility of the first pastry (64 utils) exceeds that of the first latté (45 utils). Having eaten her pastry, should Anna now buy her *second* pastry or should she buy her *first* latté? Well, the *second* pastry is worth 52 utils to her, while the *first* latté is worth 45 utils, so she should buy a pastry. Now, what about her third purchase? Should it be a *third* pastry or her *first* latté? Since the *first* latté, at 45 utils, is better than the *third* pastry at 40 utils, she should buy her first latté. On to her fourth purchase. Should it be a *second* latté (36) or a *third* pastry (40)? It should be a third pastry. We continue in a similar fashion until Anna's $24 has been exhausted. This is shown in Table 5.4.

TABLE 5.4
Successive Purchase Choices

	Product	Total Spent	Marginal Utility	Total Utility
First purchase	First pastry	$ 4	64	64
Second purchase	Second pastry	8	52	116
Third purchase	First latté	12	45	161
Fourth purchase	Third pastry	16	40	201
Fifth purchase	Second latté	20	36	237
Sixth purchase	Fourth pastry	$24	26	263

At the end of the evening, Anna will have purchased a total of 2 lattés and 4 pieces of pastry, and in doing so, she will have maximized her utility at 263 utils. We have already seen from Table 5.3 that this combination will ensure maximum utility. (Another quick way of getting the answer is to simply ask: Which are the 6 biggest MUs in Table 5.2? The answer, as we know, is the first two lattés and the first four pastries. But as we are about to see, we need to be very careful here, because this method only works if the prices are the same.)

From this knowledge, we could perhaps adopt a new optimal purchasing rule: *In order to maximize total utility, a consumer should allocate spending by comparing the marginal utility of each product and purchasing the product that gives the greatest marginal utility.* There is, however, a very serious defect in this rule. Suppose that I were to compare the marginal utilities of the two following products and, according to this rule, purchase the one that gives the greatest marginal utility:

First bottle of beer: MU = 120 utils

First Porsche car: MU = 10 000 000 utils

So I would buy the Porsche because it has a higher marginal utility for me! The only problem is that I cannot quite afford it. Our purchasing rule obviously needs a little more refinement, since we need to take the price of products into consideration. In order to make a rational decision, what we really need to compare is not marginal utils but the amount of **marginal utility per dollar spent**. Or, more colloquially, we are trying to find out which product gives the most bang for the buck! In terms of a formula, it is

$$\text{MU per \$ spent} = \frac{\text{MU}}{\text{price}} \qquad [5.3]$$

For instance, suppose we are trying to decide whether to buy a $2 slice of pizza that gives us 40 utils or a $1.50 pop that gives 36 utils. Figuring out the MU per dollar spent gives us

$$\text{MU per \$ spent on pizza} = \frac{40}{2} = 20$$

$$\text{MU per \$ spent on pop} = \frac{36}{1.50} = 24$$

Clearly then, buying the pop would be a more sensible decision.

What this suggests is that a rational consumer would continue to purchase a product as long as its marginal utility per dollar spent was greater than that of any other product. Of course, as the consumer increases the consumption of any given product, its marginal utility per $ spent is going to fall, and so some other product will then become a more attractive proposition.

IN A NUTSHELL ...

So what varieties? And how many of each?

Let us stay with the latté/pastry example, but this time, in Table 5.5, assume that the management of the coffee bar decides to decrease the price of lattés to $3 but leaves the price of pastry unchanged at $4. Now, how would Anna spend her budget of $24?

TABLE 5.5
Marginal Utility per Dollar Spent

	LATTÉS			PIECES OF PASTRY	
Quantity	MU	MU per $ (price = $3)	Quantity	MU	MU per $ (price = $4)
1	45	15	1	64	16
2	36	12	2	52	13
3	25	8.3	3	40	10
4	21	7	4	26	6.5
5	12	4	5	10	2.5
6	0	0	6	0	0

To figure out the optimal allocation of Anna's $24 budget, we will proceed as before, by looking at each separate purchase; but since lattés and pastries have different prices, we need to do some calculations to make them comparable. We do this by dividing the marginal utility of lattés by three and the marginal utility of pastries by four, as shown in Table 5.5. To start with, the first pastry gives a higher marginal utility per dollar spent than the first latté (16 compared with 15), so this would be her first purchase. The first latté gives a higher MU per dollar spent (15) than the second pastry (13), so that is her second purchase. We can continue in this fashion, purchase by purchase, and the results are summarized in Table 5.6.

> **TABLE 5.6**
> **Choice of Lattés and Pieces of Pastry, Purchase by Purchase**
>
> | | Product | Total Spent | Marginal Utility per $ Spent | Marginal Utility | Total Utility |
> |---|---|---|---|---|---|
> | First purchase | First pastry | $ 4 | $16 | 64 | 64 |
> | Second purchase | First latté | 7 | 15 | 45 | 109 |
> | Third purchase | Second pastry | 11 | 13 | 52 | 161 |
> | Fourth purchase | Second latté | 14 | 12 | 36 | 197 |
> | Fifth purchase | Third pastry | 18 | 10 | 40 | 237 |
> | Sixth purchase | Third latté | 21 | 8.3 | 25 | 262 |
> | Seventh purchase | Fourth latté | 24 | 7 | 21 | 283 |

The best way for Anna to spend her $24 is to purchase four lattés and three pieces of pastry. This would give her (check back to **Table 5.2**) a total utility of 283 (127 + 156) utils, which is higher than could be produced by any other combination that could be purchased with $24. Note also the effect of this decrease in the price of lattés: the number of lattés purchased increased from two to four, whereas the quantity of the related product, pieces of pastries, dropped from four to three.

We can draw two important conclusions from this exercise. The first is that it allows us to develop an optimal purchasing rule. It suggests that whenever the marginal utility per dollar spent on Product A is greater than that for Product B, we would buy and consume more of A. As this is done, of course, the marginal utility per dollar spent on Product A starts to decline, until we get to the point where Product B becomes more attractive:

$$\text{if } \frac{MU_A}{P_A} > \frac{MU_B}{P_B} \Rightarrow \text{consume more A}$$

$$\text{if } \frac{MU_A}{P_A} < \frac{MU_B}{P_B} \Rightarrow \text{consume more B}$$

Our conclusion:

> We should buy and consume products to the point at which the marginal utility per dollar spent on each product is more or less equal for all products.

However, more than just two products are competing for our spending. If we discover, for instance, that some third or fourth product offers a greater MU per dollar, we would switch some of our spending away from Products A and B in favour of these other products. In other words, we allocate our spending between products so that we have no advantage to be gained from further switching, and this happens when their MUs per dollar are all equal. The optimal purchasing rule, then, is

$$\frac{MU_A}{P_A} = \frac{MU_B}{P_B} = \ldots \ldots \frac{MU_Z}{P_Z} \qquad [5.4]$$

Now this does not mean that we will end up buying the same quantities of each product. Far from it. Suppose, for example, that we have finished shopping at the supermarket with our money all spent and look down at our basket to find we have six granola bars, two frozen pizzas, three kilos of apples, and five bottles of energy drinks. Now if, on further consideration, we think perhaps that we don't need that second pizza but could certainly use a few more granola bars, we would reallocate our spending accordingly. We would do this until we were happy with the mix—that is, that the last kilo of apples, the last pizza, the last pack of granola bars and the last energy drinks give us the same MU per dollar spent.

The second important conclusion to our latté-pastry example is that it helps us to underpin the theory of demand. You will recall that when the prices of lattés and pastries were $4 each, we spent our $24 budget buying two lattés and four pastries. We then examined what would happen if the price of lattés were to drop to $3 each. It turned out we would reallocate our spending by increasing our purchases of lattés to four and reducing the quantity of pastries to two. Why? The answer is that the lower price of

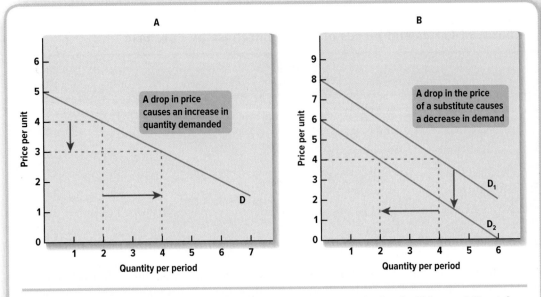

FIGURE 5.2   The Effect of a Price Fall on the Demands for Lattés and Pastries

In Figure A, the drop in price of lattes leads to an increase in the quantity demanded. In Figure B, the lower price of a substitute product (lattes) causes a left shift in the demand curve for pastries.

lattés *increases* the MU per dollar spent on them and so they become a more attractive alternative to the pastries, causing us to buy more lattés and few pastries. **Figure 5.2** illustrates exactly what happened.

But what about the demand for pastries? The price of pastries remained the same as did Anna's budget of $24. However, her purchases of pastries dropped from 4 to 3. The reason why this happened, as we saw in Chapter 2, is the result of a decrease in the price of a substitute product which causes a drop in demand of the product in question. This is illustrated by a left shift in the demand curve in **Figure 5.2B**.

   ADDED DIMENSION

Behavioural Economics

With the advent of the desktop computer beginning in the 1970s, the economics profession became deeply invested in trying to prove that it was as "scientific" as the pure sciences of physics and chemistry. Therefore, to achieve the same mathematical precision of those sciences, mainstream economists made the radically simplifying hypothesis that all human behaviour was driven by people who were "optimizers," and thus their behaviour was as predictable as the speed of a physical body falling through space. Such a hypothesis is, of course, rooted in Marshall's marginal utility theory.

Yet we all know that economic outcomes are the result of human decision making. One of the major players in what has become known as *behavioural economics* is Richard Thaler, who has spent his career challenging the idea of rational human optimizers (he calls these *econs*) by studying the radical notion that the central agents in the economy (whom he calls *humans*) are individuals who are often quite irrational and error-prone. Two of his more popular books are *Nudge* (co-authored with Cass Sunstein) and *Misbehaving: The Making of Behavioral Economics*.

In the latter work, Thaler takes on a huge range of topics, ranging from retirement savings to house insulation, from the draft strategy of NFL teams to corporate leadership. His treatment of these topics, woven into the idea of econs supposedly being the players, is truly hilarious.

Thaler makes lists of observed behaviours that are obviously inconsistent with the view that people are utility maximizers. Some of the behaviours are given names—for example, the "endowment effect," whereby individuals systematically value things they already own much more than the identical item in someone else's hands.

TEST YOUR UNDERSTANDING

2. Given the marginal utilities and prices of the four products in the following table, which product would a rational consumer choose as her next purchase?

	Apple	Beer	Ice Cream	Hot Dog
Marginal utility	120	300	140	150
Price	$1.50	$4.00	$2.00	$3.00

3. Melissa's marginal utility per dollar spent for apples and pears is given in the following table. How many of each kind of fruit would she purchase if she were to make only nine purchases?

Pears	MU per Dollar Spent	Apples	MU per Dollar Spent
1	9	1	18
2	8	2	14
3	7	3	10
4	6	4	6
5	5	5	2
6	4	6	0

4. Niki is considering buying some fruit. His total utility from apples and bananas is shown in the following table:

	APPLES			BANANAS	
Quantity	Total Utility	Marginal Utility	Marginal Utility per $	Total Utility	Marginal Utility
1	40	——	——	30	——
2	70	——	——	54	——
3	88	——	——	72	——
4	104	——	——	82	——
5	118	——	——	90	——
6	130	——	——	95	——

a) Complete the marginal utility columns.

b) If Niki has a budget of $8 and the prices of both apples and bananas are $1 each, how many of each will he purchase?

c) Suppose that the price of apples increases to $2. Complete the marginal utility per $ column for apples.

d) After the price change, how many apples and bananas will he now purchase?

e) Draw the demand curves for apples and bananas reflecting the changes.

SECTION SUMMARY

a) The marginal utility per dollar spent is:

$$\frac{MU}{price}$$

b) The *optimal purchasing rule* can be expressed as

$$\frac{MU_A}{P_A} = \frac{MU_B}{P_B} = \cdots \frac{MU_Z}{P_Z}$$

c) A drop in the price of a product increases its MU per $ spent resulting in consumers buying more of the product and less of a substitute product.

5.3 Applications of Marginal Utility Theory

LO3 Explain how marginal utility theory is applicable to real-world examples.

Marginal utility theory, as esoteric as it might at first appear, does provide us with some interesting insights into consumer behaviour. It can explain some obvious and some not-so-obvious activities.

Why Our Favourite Things Are Not Always Our Favourites

We all have our favourite food, whether it is steak or lobster, pizza or something else, that we love over all others. So why is it that we don't spend all of our food budget on that single favourite? The answer is simple: even our favourite product is only a favourite *up to a point*. After consuming a certain quantity, its marginal utility per dollar spent drops to the point where other things become more attractive.

What Determines Your Priority Spending?

It is an interesting experiment to imagine how one would spend additional increments of income starting off with, say, a basic $100 per week, and increasing it by increments of $100. Let's say you did have only $100 per week. What would you spend the money on? Presumably, you would spend it on those things that have the greatest marginal utility for you. For most of us, this would mean using our money on food and shelter. Income would need to increase appreciably before any allocations are made for clothes, and higher still before any entertainment dollars are spent.

How we adjust our purchases to higher income levels is what is meant by *income elasticity*, a concept we encountered in the Chapter 4. You can imagine that products with low income elasticities (water, food) have the highest initial marginal utilities and thus will be highest in terms of priority. Similarly, those products with high income elasticities (air travel, movies) will have lower initial marginal utilities and must be of a lower priority. Research has consistently demonstrated that poorer families spend by far the largest proportion of their incomes on basic necessities such as food and shelter (often well over 50 percent), whereas richer families spend proportionately less (sometimes less than 30 percent).

Don't Some Things Improve with Age?

Another intriguing aspect of marginal utility theory involves those situations in which the law of diminishing marginal utility may not apply. The law is applicable to all products and all people, but maybe not at all times. For example, it is certainly possible to think of certain things for which the marginal utility seems to increase the more they are consumed. (Think of a new music album; it often takes repeated hearings before you get full enjoyment from it.) This may be true also of fine wines and paintings and so on. However, as we mentioned earlier, Alfred Marshall cautioned that the idea of diminishing marginal utility only makes sense if the product is consumed over a reasonably short period. Furthermore, the rule applies only to the purchasing of the product, not to its repeated "consumption," as is the case with music and artwork.

Shouldn't Incomes Be More Equally Distributed?

Diminishing marginal utility takes another interesting twist when we look at the fascinating subject of money. Is money also subject to the law of diminishing marginal utility? In other words, is it true that the more money you have, the less valuable additional amounts become for you? Since money is just one form of wealth, often the question is amended as follows: Does the marginal utility of wealth or income decline as more is obtained? For example, imagine a rich person and a poor person walking toward each other on the street; halfway between them lies a $10 bill.

Which of them would gain the greater utility from its possession—the rich person, for whom it might be the hundred-thousandth $10 bill of the year, or the poor person, for whom it could be the difference between a good week and a bad one? Intuition suggests that the marginal utility of the poor person is likely to be far higher than that of the rich person, for whom the gain (or loss, for that matter) of $10 might well go unnoticed. Here, intuition seems to confirm the law of diminishing marginal utility even for the product money. If this is so, some might argue that this is strong grounds for advocating a more equitable distribution of income and wealth, since the gain in marginal utility by the poor would greatly exceed the loss of marginal utility by the rich so that overall utility (or social welfare) is increased.

Note that the above idea need not imply an equal distribution, only a more equitable or fairer one. The idea would be to take from the rich and give to the poor as long as the marginal utility of the former is smaller than the marginal utility of the latter. This would continue until (figuratively) the screams of the rich person (who may no longer be quite so rich) are equal to the whoops of joy coming from the poor person (who may no longer be quite so poor). It may well be that their marginal utilities become equalized when the rich person now has an income reduced to $5000 per week, while that of the poor person has been increased to $500.

However, you might protest such a scheme. After all, you may well ask, what is fair about a system that takes income from one person, who may have worked extremely hard to earn it, and gives it to another who may have done nothing to deserve it? Nevertheless, modern governments do try to increase the overall well-being of their communities by transferring income from the rich to the poor. It is most likely that those individuals with higher incomes (a lower marginal utility of money) tend to save more and receive, in turn, relatively more of their income from their investment sources. Governments have typically imposed higher taxes on this type of income, which is a de facto acceptance of the argument that these marginal income dollars yield a lower marginal utility for their recipients than the higher marginal utility gained from labour by lower income earners when they sell their labour.

TEST YOUR UNDERSTANDING

5. The table below shows the total utility that two children, Jan and Dean, derive from various amounts of weekly allowance.

Amount of Weekly Allowance	Jan's Total Utility	Dean's Total Utility
$ 1	200	400
2	380	500
3	540	595
4	680	685
5	800	770
6	900	850
7	980	925
8	1040	995
9	1080	1060
10	1100	1120

As their parent, you can afford to pay them a total allowance of only $10. How would you divide this amount between the two children so as to maximize their combined total utility? What will be the combined total utility?

There is, however, another issue in all of this. As pointed out earlier, we simply cannot compare utilities between people. Thus, while we might well be inclined to believe that the rich person's marginal utility is less than the poor person's, there is simply no way of measuring this.

From all of this, however, we should not conclude that the theory of marginal utility is of little use or that it should be discarded. One of its most important uses is to give a strong underpinning to the law of demand, which is the topic of the next section.

SECTION SUMMARY

Marginal utility theory helps us understand why we do not spend all of our income on our single favourite product and why we have priorities in our purchasing decisions. It also encourages us to think of the reasoning behind a more equitable distribution of income.

5.4   Marginal Utility and Demand

> **LO4**   Provide a theoretical rationale for downward-sloping demand curves.

We saw earlier, in our latté/pastry example, that marginal utility theory suggests that a decrease in the price of one product leads to an increase in the quantity purchased of that particular product while decreasing the quantity purchased of the competitive product. We need to look at this in more detail.

We know that the particular numbers we assign to utility are quite arbitrary; any set of numbers would do. However, there is one particular measuring unit with which we are all familiar, and that is money. We could, if we wished, measure utility in dollars. For instance, Akio could suggest that his first drink of power-juice after a hard game of tennis gives him, say, $8 worth of utility. Another way of expressing it would be to say that, irrespective of its actual price, he would be willing to pay $8 for that power-juice. Let us examine Akio's utility for his favourite drink in terms of *dollar marginal utility* (*$MU*) in Table 5.7.

TABLE 5.7
Akio's Dollar Marginal Utility

Quantity Consumed	$MU
1	8
2	5
3	4
4	3
5	2
6	1
7	0

Although they look similar, do not confuse our previous term, *marginal utility per dollar spent,* which measures the number of utils obtained for each dollar spent, with *$MU,* which is measuring utility itself in terms of dollars. Table 5.7 shows that Akio's $MU declines with increasing quantities; this simply reflects the law of diminishing marginal utility. However, with this information, we can work out exactly how much Akio would purchase at different prices. Suppose, for instance, that the price of his power-juice was $10 a bottle. How much would he purchase? The answer must be zero, since even his first drink of the day is worth only $8 for him. So why would he pay $10 for the product? We would get the same result if the price was $9. What if the price dropped to $8? How many would he buy now? The answer is one, since he would surely pay $8 for something he felt was worth $8. However, he would not purchase a second drink, since he rates it at only $5, which is less than the price. Let us continue to drop the price. Say the price is $7. How many will he purchase now? Presumably, he still would not be prepared to buy more than one, since the price is still higher than his valuation of the second drink. The same is true at $6. Not until the price drops to $5 would Akio be prepared to buy two power-juices. Continuing to drop the price by $1 each time would produce the results in Table 5.8. This table spells out Akio's demand schedule, which relates the quantities demanded at various different prices, graphed in Figure 5.3.

The derivation of the demand curve in this manner provides a very different perspective on demand. In a sense, it shifts the emphasis away from the price and onto the quantity. Instead of asking, "How many would you buy at this price?" it asks, "What is the maximum price you would pay to buy this quantity?" From Akio's point of view, the price cannot be more than $8 to induce him to buy one power-juice. In order to get him to buy two power-juices, the price of the second power-juice must drop, simply because we know that the marginal utility of his second power-juice will be lower. In other words, to induce people to buy increasing quantities of any product that they value less and

TABLE 5.8
Demand Curve, Derived

Price of Power-Juices	Quantity Demanded
$10	0
9	0
8	1
7	1
6	1
5	2
4	3
3	4
2	5
1	6

less, the price must be lower. To get Akio to buy six power-juices, the price must be as low as $1. In a sense, it is the value of the last one purchased and not the total value of them all that determines how much is bought.

The fact that it is the marginal utility of the last unit purchased that determines the price you are prepared to pay for a product and the quantity you want to buy is a very subtle idea, one that is difficult to grasp at first. But it really does have some important implications in today's business world.

For example, how frustrating must the situation be if you are the seller of these power-juices? What our analysis shows is that in order to induce Akio to buy 6 bottles, you will have to drop the price to $1. But that doesn't seem right! After all, assuming you could get inside Akio's head, you know

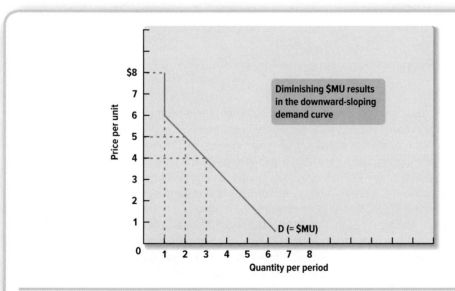

FIGURE 5.3   Marginal Utility and the Demand Curve

To induce Akio to buy one power-juice, the price cannot be higher than $8, since that is how much he values the first power-juice. To get him to buy a second power-juice, the price must drop to $5 because that is his evaluation of the second power-juice. If the price drops to $4, Akio would be prepared to buy three power-juices. The price must continue to drop in order to encourage Akio to buy more. His $MU curve is the same thing, then, as his demand curve.

that the value that he places on these 6 power-juices comes to $23 ($8 for the first, $5 for the second, and so on). And yet Akio gets to enjoy these 6 power-juices for a grand total of $6—for just $6, he can buy 6 power-juices that he values at $23. In other words, Akio is getting a big bonus. Economists call this bonus the *consumer surplus*. Let us look at this topic in more detail.

ADDED DIMENSION

The Famous Diamond–Water Paradox

The diamond–water paradox was first mentioned by Aristotle and introduced by Adam Smith in his famous 1776 work, *The Wealth of Nations*. Smith was interested in finding out what determines the value of products, and realized that the rather elusive term *value* is used in two different ways. It might mean what he termed "value in use," which is what we mean by utility, that is, the amount of satisfaction that individuals derive on the basis of their individual evaluation. Alternatively, the word might mean what Smith termed "value in exchange." This is the value the market places on the product—in exchange for other products or for money.

Most things we buy have similar values in use and in exchange. However, a number of products, like water, have a very high value in use but are worth almost nothing in exchange. Conversely, other products like diamonds have a very high exchange value but quite a low value in use. Smith tried, unsuccessfully, to resolve this seeming paradox. It took almost a century and the introduction of marginal utility theory before economists were able to provide a solution.

In the following example, instead of considering diamonds, let us look at the contrast between water and another very precious commodity, oil. Suppose we are comparing the utilities derived from 50 litre drums of each. The following table presents the preferences of Karl, an average consumer.

The Utilities of Water and Oil

WATER			OIL		
Quantity	$MU	$TU	Quantity	$MU	$TU
1	$1000	$1000	1	$110	$110
2	500	1500	2	100	210
3	300	1800	3	90	300
4	200	2000	4	80	380
5	150	2150	5	70	450
6	60	2210	6	60	510

The first striking observation is how highly valuable water is when compared with oil. Its total utility (value in use) far exceeds that of oil. Suppose that you literally had no water. How much would you be prepared to pay for it? Karl would pay almost anything—$1000 for the first drum of water. This may be his whole income, but he would pay it to stay alive. But note how dramatically the $MU of water drops. After five drums Karl not only has enough to drink, but enough to wash his clothes, his body, and his car, and he still has plenty left over to water the garden. The value of a sixth drum of water to Karl is only $60. In contrast, though, note how gradually the $MU of oil drops.

Now, suppose that Karl has a budget of $1200 and that the price of both oil and water is $100, so that he is able to make a total of 12 purchases. How much of each would he purchase? You can see that his first $500 would be spent on 5 drums of water, but the next $500 would go on 5 drums of oil. After spending $1000, he values the oil and water equally and he would buy one of each, for a total of 6 drums of water and 6 drums of oil. The marginal value of the 6th drums are equal for water and for oil despite the fact that the first 5 drums of water have given him a total dollar utility of $2150 compared with only $450 for oil—nearly 5 times as much. But the total utility is irrelevant when deciding on the next purchase, and Smith's idea of value in exchange centres on the marginal and not the total utility.

The answer to Smith's paradox, then, is that value in use is reflected in the total utility of a product, whereas value in exchange (the market price) is determined by its marginal utility.

5.5   Consumer Surplus

> **LO5** Explain why consumers generally value a product more than the purchase price they pay.

The surplus that Akio derived in our last example is not a sum of money received but the additional satisfaction that we all receive for free. It comes about from the fact that normally we can obtain as much or as little of a product as we want at a single constant price. Akio could, after all, obtain 1 or 6 or 100 power-juice drinks, and they would still cost him just $1 each. However, except for the last one, every unit he buys is worth more than the price. He obtains a **consumer surplus** on each, as Table 5.9 shows.

TABLE 5.9
Marginal and Total Consumer Surplus

Drinks	$MU	Price	Marginal Consumer Surplus	Total Consumer Surplus
First	$8	$1	$7	$ 7
Second	5	1	4	11
Third	4	1	3	14
Fourth	3	1	2	16
Fifth	2	1	1	17
Sixth	1	1	0	17

The marginal consumer surplus is the difference between the dollar marginal utility of a unit and the price paid for that product—or, put another way, it is the difference between how much a person would be prepared to pay and how much a person actually pays for a unit, that is,

$$\text{Marginal consumer surplus (MCS)} = \$MU - \text{price} \tag{5.5}$$

And total consumer surplus is the sum of the marginal consumer surplus derived from each successive unit consumed (5 units in this case):

$$\text{Total consumer surplus} = MCS_1 + MCS_2 + MCS_3 + MCS_4 + MCS_5 \tag{5.6}$$

In conclusion, Akio gets a consumer surplus of $17 from these six power-juices. His *total* $ utility comes to $23, but his bill comes to only $6.

Since all of us derive consumer surplus from our purchases, we can illustrate the idea in terms of the market demand. For instance, **Figure 5.4** shows the demand curve for daily ski passes at a local ski resort. The curve shows the maximum price that could be charged at various different quantities; for example, 2000 passes could be sold at a price of $100 each, 4000 could be sold at $90, and so on. The demand curve, therefore, represents how much people would be willing to pay.

Let us assume the price is $100. The vertical distance between the price line and the demand curve represents the amount of consumer surplus at each quantity. For instance, 2000 people would have been prepared to pay $100 for a ticket. The fact that they only have to pay $60 means that each of them obtains a consumer surplus of $40. If, instead, the price had been $90, then 4000 people would have bought a pass. But we already know that 2000 of those 4000 would have paid $100; the

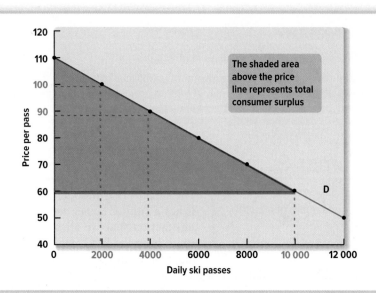

FIGURE 5.4   Consumer Surplus, Graphically

For each quantity, the vertical distance between the price line and the demand curve represents the amount of (marginal) consumer surplus. For instance, at a quantity of 2000 the price is $60, but those customers would be prepared to pay $100, so the difference of $40 is the marginal consumer surplus. At a quantity of 4000 the price is still only $60, and these customers are willing to pay $90, so the marginal consumer surplus is $30. Adding all the marginal consumer surpluses gives the total consumer surplus (the shaded area).

other 2000 were not prepared to pay $100, but they were willing to pay $90. Members of this latter group, then, are enjoying a consumer surplus of $30 each. If we continue this exercise down to the $60 price level and assume the ski resort only charges passes in $10 increments, we will discover that the total consumer surplus is $200 000, as shown in Table 5.10. (Theoretically, if purchases could be made in any quantities, including partial units, and if they could be sold at any price, even fractions of a cent, we could calculate the total consumer surplus as the area of the triangle between the demand curve and the price line. In our example, that amounts to $1/2 \times 10\ 000 \times \$50 = \$250\ 000$.)

This consumer surplus, then, can be represented by the triangular area below the demand curve and above the price line, as shown in Figure 5.4. A higher price will, of course, mean that consumers will enjoy a smaller total consumer surplus; a lower price will mean a higher total consumer surplus.

The amount of consumer surplus depends on the type of product, and more particularly is determined by its demand elasticity. For instance, Figure 5.5 shows that consumers enjoy a bigger consumer surplus from products with inelastic demands than from those that have elastic demands.

If the price is P_1, the quantity purchased of each of the two products is quantity Q_1. At lower quantities, however, buyers of Product 1 (demand curve D_1) in Figure 5.5A would be prepared to pay higher prices than would buyers of Product 2 (demand curve D_2) in Figure 5.5B. The area between the price line and the demand curves represents the total amount of consumer surplus. The graph shows that this area is much greater in the case of the inelastic demand curve, D_1, than it is with the elastic demand curve, D_2.

The idea that consumers derive a greater surplus from products with inelastic demands conforms to our idea of what is meant by inelastic, which is that buyers are not particularly affected by a price change, presumably because they think that the value of the product far exceeds its market price. For most smokers, the benefit they get from cigarettes far exceeds even the very high prices they have to pay for them.

So what's a day on the slopes worth?

Pixtal/AGE Fotostock

TABLE 5.10
Calculating Consumer Surplus

Consumers	Would Have Paid:	But Only Pay:	Therefore Get a Marginal Consumer Surplus Of:	For a Total Consumer Surplus Of:
1st 2000	$100	$60	$40	$80 000
2nd 2000	90	60	30	60 000
3rd 2000	80	60	20	40 000
4th 2000	70	60	10	20 000
5th 2000	60	60	0	0

It is easy to see why producers would like, if they could, to capture this consumer's surplus for themselves. At the present price of $60 per day pass, ski mountain operators in our last example (see **Figure 5.4**) are deriving revenues of 10 000 × $60 = $600 000 from daily sales. However, as **Table 5.10** shows, consumers are enjoying an additional psychological benefit, or consumer surplus, of $200 000. The temptation for sellers to try to capture this surplus is great. Let us examine the ways sellers might try to do this.

One way is to figure out just how much individual consumers are prepared to pay for the product. This can be done through consumer questionnaires and auctions such as those on eBay. In an auction, customers bid up the price to the point where (ideally from the seller's point of view) the sole remaining customer is being forced to pay what she really thinks it is worth. Examples of this are the many e-commerce websites. A "Dutch auction" works even better from the seller's point of view and captures even more of the consumer surplus. Here, the auctioneer starts the bidding at a very high price, which is then lowered, step by step, until someone indicates she is willing to pay the last price mentioned. In order to avoid missing out on a purchase, customers may well end up paying the maximum they are prepared to spend. For instance, suppose that I want to bid on a pair of titanium skis at an auction and I happen to be the keenest buyer. In fact, I would be prepared to go as high as $500, whereas the next-keenest bidder would go no higher than $300. At a regular auction, I could buy the ornament for $301, but at a Dutch auction, I would likely bid my maximum of $500.

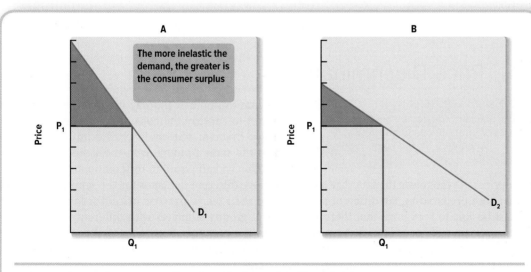

FIGURE 5.5   Consumer Surplus Varies with Elasticities

The demand curves in graphs A and B both have the same price (P_1) and quantities (Q_1). However, demand curve D_1 is steeper (the demand is more inelastic) than D_2 (the demand is elastic). As a result, the total consumer surplus (the shaded area) is bigger in A than in B.

TEST YOUR UNDERSTANDING

6. Given Akio's utility for beverages as shown in **Table 5.7**, what quantity would he purchase if the price was $2, and what would his total consumer surplus be as a result?

7. The demand for chocolate-covered kumquats is quite small and is shown in the table here.

Price	Quantity
$10	1
9	2
8	3
7	4
6	5

Assuming partial units cannot be bought, what is the marginal consumer surplus for each unit bought, and what is the total consumer surplus if the price is $6?

In addition, note that an auctioneer with four identical items to sell will sell them one at a time, so as to get the maximum consumer surplus from each. Another way of capturing this surplus is to recognize that consumers value the first item purchased far more than they do subsequent items. A seller of winter tires, then, might charge $95 for a single tire but sell two for $170 and a set of four for $300, and so on. You might think of this as receiving a discount from bulk buying, but you might also look on it as having to pay a premium for buying small quantities.

SECTION SUMMARY

The fact that consumers are able to buy all they want of most products at a fixed price, but base their decisions on how much to buy on marginal utility, leads to the concept of *consumer surplus*, which is the difference between the consumer's evaluation of a product and the price paid for it.

5.6   Price Discrimination

LO6   Explain why some sellers charge different prices to different consumers for the same product.

A final example of the way in which producers attempt to capture the consumer surplus is through **price discrimination**. Price discrimination means that the same product, with the same costs of production, is being sold to different consumers at different prices. It recognizes the fact that consumers have different demands for the same product and are therefore prepared to pay different prices. As we shall see, to practise price discrimination, sellers must be able to recognize that there are different groups of buyers with different demand elasticities, and somehow be able to distinguish between those groups. Furthermore, if people are being charged different prices, the seller must try to find a way to prevent resales of the product. In addition, the sellers must have control over the price they charge.

Suppose that you are the owner of an independent movie theatre and you estimate that the demand for movie tickets is as shown in **Table 5.11**. At present you are charging $12 admission and receiving a daily revenue of $2400. Of course, you would like to increase your revenue by attracting more customers. You realize, however, that a number of people are not willing to pay $12 on a regular

TABLE 5.11
Demand for Movie Tickets

Price of Admission	Number of Daily Tickets Sold	Total Revenue
$12	200	$2400
9	250	2250
6	300	1800

basis and that the only way to attract them is to reduce the price. The trouble is that if you do reduce the price, your total sales revenue will fall to $2250 at $9 (that is, $9 × 250) and to $1800 at $6 ($6 × 300). This is because, if you do reduce the price in order to sell more tickets, you will have to reduce the price for everyone.

Or will you? What if you could charge different prices to different groups of people? Well, in order to do that, first you need to identify the people who are reluctant to pay $12 but would be willing to pay, say, $6. (There are 300 people prepared to pay $6 but only 200 prepared to pay $12. Thus, there are 100 people not prepared to pay this extra $6.) Included in this group are low-income people, many of whom would happily visit the theatre for $6 but are unable to afford $12. You have no way of recognizing such people, but certain identifiable groups are generally poor, such as young or retired people.

So what you would do is charge a lower price for these groups but continue the high price for your regular patrons. In this way, you can increase your revenue appreciably. Your regular 200 patrons continue to pay $12, but you attract an additional 100 patrons who each pay $6. Your total revenue increases by $600 per day as a result. On the surface, it looks as though you are offering discount prices to certain identifiable groups and, of course, that is how you would probably advertise it. The truth of the matter is that you are charging a premium price to the other identifiable group (the higher-income group).

Figure 5.6 shows how the movie theatre owner is able to capture some of the consumer surplus by practising price discrimination. The blue rectangle shows the total revenue received if a single price of $6 is charged to all the moviegoers. With two-tier pricing, the total revenue is increased and the pink area is the part of the consumer surplus captured by the theatre owner.

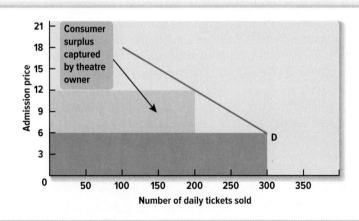

FIGURE 5.6   **Price Discrimination and Consumer Surplus**

The blue area shows the total revenue received if the owner wishes to have 300 clients at a single price. By practising price discrimination he can still have 300 clients, but 200 of those now pay $12 each. The result will be extra income as a result of capturing some of the consumer surplus, shown as the pink area.

In order to practise price discrimination, then, it is necessary to

- identify groups of customers with different demand elasticities
- separate them from the others
- ensure that those obtaining the lower prices cannot resell the product
- ensure that the seller has control over the price

These features exist for theatre admissions because a young person cannot resell the seat to an older person. For this reason, price discrimination is mostly practised with personal services rather than goods. Other examples of discrimination on the basis of age occur in the area of transportation, where, in most countries and cities, seniors and students travel at reduced fares on buses, trains, and planes.

Besides price discrimination based on age, it is often also practised on the basis of gender. Men have a good deal on haircuts, for example, where they often pay considerably less for a cut than women despite the fact that their hair may be twice as long! On the other hand, women generally get a break at nightclubs where they are often admitted free of charge before 10 p.m. while men often have to pay a big fee to enter.

Price discrimination is also practised on the basis of *time*. Suppose I own a coffee shop and I have no trouble attracting customers between 7 and 10 o'clock in the morning, the time when most people are desperate for coffee. However, business falls off considerably after 10 o'clock. In order to attract more customers in the off-peak periods, I would have to drop my prices, but why should I give everyone the benefit of lower prices when they are quite happy to pay my regular prices? The answer, of course, is to have two-tiered prices: a higher price in peak periods than in off-peak periods. Again,

IT'S NEWS TO ME ...

A recent report released by Consumers' Research and Protection provides insight on how airlines set their ticket prices. The report focuses on the point that today's airlines employ a very high-tech strategy called yield management which intentionally aims to charge different prices to different passengers in order to maximize the total revenue collected for each departing flight. But how can they do that? When the airline starts to sell tickets for a given flight, which may be months in advance, they start with what their experience tells them is a medium price (half way between the highest and lowest of the past). However, the airlines will, initially, limit the number of seats available at that initial price level—usually just a very few, say, 4—and wait for the general public to respond.

At this point, the airline's computer program will kick in and, using a sophisticated algorithm, constantly monitor the selling of tickets. This program is able to change the number of seats available at any minute and any of the various price levels that their past booking patterns indicate might sell a few tickets. Quite literally, in any one 24 hour period the posted price could have a range of hundreds of dollars—say $369 (2 tickets sold at 10:30 a.m.) to $640 (1 ticket sold at 11:49 p.m.). Does this always work as planned by the airlines? The most likely answer to this question is "probably."

Source: *Star Power Reporting*, February 2017.

I. Which economic concept is key to understanding the pricing policies of airlines?

a) the law of diminishing returns
b) consumers' surplus
c) the optimal purchasing rule
d) $MU

II. Which of the following is true?

a) The airlines are simply trying to sell out the available seats on every flight.
b) The airlines are pursuing price discrimination in order to maximize TR.
c) The airlines are using price discrimination to give customers what they want.
d) The airlines are pursuing the auction method of selling tickets.

this method is practised by many transport companies and other businesses, such as hairdressers and movie theatres, that have times of the day or the week when sales are sluggish. Similarly, many telephone and hydro companies have different rates at different times of the day. Other examples would be airlines that give discounts to travellers who spend weekends away from home and long-distance phone companies that charge lower prices for calls at certain hours.

In fact, when it comes to airline fares, there is a great deal of price discrimination. It is not unusual to find that for any flight route in Canada (or around the world for that matter) there are as many as ten or more different fares being charged to passengers. Here are just some of the causes of price discrimination.

Advance purchase: The cheapest fares usually require that you purchase the tickets at least 14 days in advance.

Minimum stay: Many flights require that you stay at your destination at least two nights (often including a Saturday stopover).

Departure day: Flights are generally cheaper if you fly on a Tuesday, Wednesday, or Saturday—the slowest flight days.

Flight time: The very first or very last flights of the day are cheapest, with "red eye" flights being cheapest of all.

The prices for coffee may vary before and after 10 o'clock in the morning.

Brand X Pictures/PunchStock

Season: Summer months and holiday times—Christmas, Thanksgiving, and spring break—mean high-season rates.

Seats on the plane: Exit and bulkhead seats (with extra leg room) are more expensive.

Children and infants: Parents pay a lower price for children's tickets.

Restrictions: Tickets that can be easily cancelled or changed are usually more expensive.

In fact, when it comes to airline fares, there is a great deal of price discrimination. It is not unusual to find that for any flight route in Canada (or around the world for that matter) there are as many as ten or more different fares being charged to passengers. Here are just some of the causes of price discrimination. *volume of purchases.* As we saw earlier, it is typical for a single item to cost more than the per-item cost for, say, a dozen. However, this practice may not always be price discrimination, since the costs per unit in terms of packaging, storing, and merchandising are often much higher for single items than for bulk. In a sense, when you buy in bulk, the costs are lower per item for the seller, and as a result, the savings are passed on to the buyers (witness the success of warehouse-style stores opening up in many countries). On the other hand, it is certainly true that big customers often get charged lower fees for many services, such as banking and legal services, than do small customers, who use these services infrequently or not extensively. These are almost certainly examples of price discrimination.

To sum up, price discrimination is typically practised on the basis of

- age
- gender
- time of purchase
- time of use
- volume of purchases

It is important to understand what price discrimination involves, since as we shall see in Chapter 10, many monopolists can and do discriminate on the basis of price.

TEST YOUR UNDERSTANDING

8. The following table shows the demand for haircuts on an average weekday in your hairdressing salon. Investigation into the market has revealed to you that the demand from seniors differs greatly from that of your other customers.

Price of Haircut	Quantity Demanded by Seniors	Quantity Demanded by Other Customers
$20	1	9
18	4	10
16	7	11
14	10	12
12	13	13
10	16	14
8	19	15

a) If you could only charge one price to all customers, which price would give you the greatest sales revenue?

b) Suppose you charged seniors a different price than you charge other customers. What prices would you charge each group in order to maximize your sales revenue?

SECTION SUMMARY

a) If sellers could price-discriminate by charging a higher price to certain groups and a lower price to others, most (all) consumer surplus would be exploited. In order to do this, the seller would have to

- identify customers with different demands
- separate them from the other customers
- ensure that those obtaining the lower prices cannot resell the product
- have control over the price

b) Price discrimination is practised on the basis of a number of things, including

- age
- gender
- time of purchase
- time of use
- volume of purchases

Study Guide

Review

WHAT'S THE BIG IDEA?

The most important idea in the chapter is that marginal utility is what lies behind the demand curve. This is based on two common-sense principles: first, that any one individual's tastes varies according to the quantity of a product that she has bought and consumed; and second, that tastes vary from person to person. Wrapped up in the first principle is the idea of diminishing marginal utility: the value (MU) that we place on a product varies according to the amount we are buying/consuming and will decrease as we acquire more. This means that our favourite product is only our favourite up to a certain point; soon our second-favourite becomes our favourite until it too is replaced. The implication of this is that if sellers want to get consumers to buy more of a product, they must be prepared to drop the price. That's the reasoning behind the "Buy two, get one for half-price" and other volume discounts.

These two reasons underpin the market demand curve: as the price of a product drops, people buy more, and more people buy. This means that a lower price will induce (and is necessary to induce) people to buy more of a product, given that their MUs drop with increased amounts. It also means that a lower price will encourage people who weren't previously buying the product to now make a purchase. Further, since consumers will purchase increased units of a product up to the point where the value of the last unit is equal to the market price, it follows that they must value all previous units purchased more than the price. This is what is meant by consumer surplus, and it is the basis for price discrimination. Sellers will try to get some of this consumer surplus by charging different prices to different consumers and, if they can, different prices for different units. For instance, in our ski example in the chapter, besides giving a discount to seniors and students (discrimination by buyer) they might also decide to charge different rates for the number of days skied (discrimination by unit). For example, they might charge $100 per for the first day, $75 for the second, $50 for the third, and $30 for each subsequent day. In this way, they would be hoping to charge skiers and boarders a price equal to the $M of the average snow lover.

NEW GLOSSARY TERMS AND KEY EQUATIONS

consumer surplus	marginal	price discrimination
law of diminishing marginal utility	marginal utility	utility
	optimal purchasing rule	

Equations:

[5.1] $\text{Marginal utility (MU)} = \dfrac{\Delta \text{ total utility}}{\Delta \text{ quantity}}$

[5.2] $\text{TU}_{5 \text{ units}} = \text{MU}_1 + \text{MU}_2 + \text{MU}_3 + \text{MU}_4 + \text{MU}_5$

[5.3] $\text{MU per \$ spent} = \dfrac{\text{MU}}{\text{price}}$

[5.4] $\dfrac{\text{MU}_A}{\text{P}_A} = \dfrac{\text{MU}_B}{\text{P}_B} = \text{.......} \dfrac{\text{MU}_Z}{\text{P}_Z}$

[5.5] $\text{Marginal consumer surplus (MCS)} = \$\text{MU} - \text{price}$

[5.6] $\text{Total consumer surplus}_{5 \text{ units}} = \text{MCS}_1 + \text{MCS}_2 + \text{MCS}_3 + \text{MCS}_4 + \text{MCS}_5$

Comprehensive Problem

(LO 2) Suppose that you are vacationing at a resort in the Caribbean and are trying to determine how to spend your time and money on two activities, windsurfing and snorkelling, which both cost $10 per hour. The marginal utility of the activities are shown in Table 5.12.

TABLE 5.12

	WINDSURFING			SNORKELLING		
No. of Hours	Marginal Utility	Marginal Utility per $ Spent	Total Utility	Marginal Utility	Marginal Utility per $ Spent	Total Utility
1	85	_____	_____	100	_____	_____
2	80	_____	_____	90	_____	_____
3	65	_____	_____	75	_____	_____
4	60	_____	_____	70	_____	_____
5	55	_____	_____	50	_____	_____
6	40	_____	_____	25	_____	_____
7	30	_____	_____	20	_____	_____
8	5	_____	_____	10	_____	_____

Questions

a) Complete the columns of total utilities.
b) Assume that you have a budget of $60. To maximize your total utility, how many hours would you spend on the two activities? What is the resulting total utility?
c) At the end of the day, you dig deep into your pocket and discover an extra $20. Now, how many hours would you spend on the two activities so as to maximize your total utility? What is the resulting total utility?

Answers

a) See the following table:

TABLE 5.12 (COMPLETED)

	WINDSURFING			SNORKELLING		
No. of Hours	Marginal Utility	Marginal Utility per $ Spent	Total Utility	Marginal Utility	Marginal Utility per $ Spent	Total Utility
1	85	8.5	85	100	6.67	100
2	80	8.0	165	90	6.0	190
3	65	6.5	230	75	5.0	265
4	60	6.0	290	70	4.67	335
5	55	5.5	345	50	3.33	385
6	40	4.0	385	25	1.67	410
7	30	3.0	415	20	1.33	430
8	5	0.5	420	10	0.67	440

b) $20 and 2 hours on windsurfing and $40 and 4 hours on snorkelling. Tw hours of windsurfing produces 165 utils and 4 hours of windsurfing gives 335 utils. The total therefore is 500 utils.

To find the best allocation, look at the marginal utility of each activity in turn. 1st hour: snorkelling (100 utils); 2nd hour: snorkelling (90); 3rd hour: windsurfing (85); 4th hour: windsurfing (80); 5th hour: snorkelling (75); 6th hour: snorkelling (70).

c) The extra $20 would be spent on windsurfing to give a total of $40 and 4 hours on windsurfing, and $40 and 4 hours on snorkelling. Four hours of windsurfing produces 290 utils and 4 hours of snorkelling gives 335 utils. The total therefore is 625 utils.

Since you have already worked out the first 6 hours of activities, continue from that point and work out the 7th and 8th hours. 7th hour: windsurfing (65); 8th hour: windsurfing (60).

Questions

d) Suppose that your utility from the two activities remains unchanged the next day, when you arrive with $80 in your pocket. Unfortunately, you discover that the hourly charge for snorkelling has increased to $15. Complete the marginal utility per $ columns in Table 5.12.

e) How many hours would you spend on the two activities in order to maximize your total utility, assuming that partial hours cannot be purchased? What is the resulting total utility?

f) Show the effects of the change in the price of snorkelling in Figure 5.7.

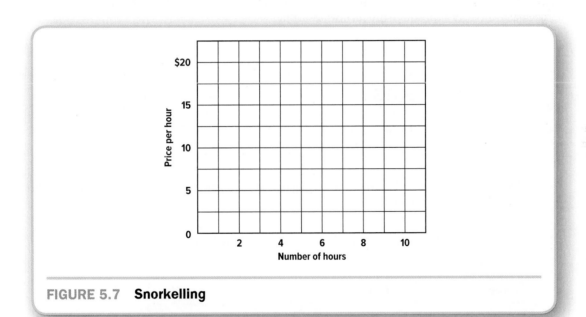

FIGURE 5.7   **Snorkelling**

g) What has happened to the demand/quantity demanded for windsurfing?

Answers

d) See Table 5.12 (Completed).

e) $50 (5 hours) on windsurfing and $30 (2 hours) on snorkelling. Five hours of snorkelling produces 345 utils and 2 hours of windsurfing gives 190 utils. The total therefore is 535 utils.

Comparing the MU per dollar purchase by purchase gives:

1st hour: windsurfing (8.5) 2nd hour: windsurfing (8.0)

3rd hour: snorkelling (6.67) 4th hour: windsurfing (6.5)

5th hour: snorkelling or 6th hour: windsurfing or windsurfing (6.0) snorkelling (6.0)

7th hour: windsurfing (5.5)

f) See Figure 5.7 (Completed).

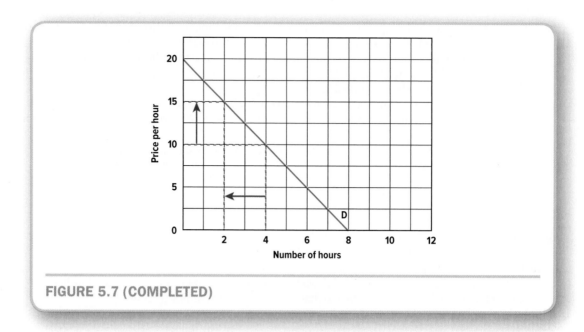

FIGURE 5.7 (COMPLETED)

g) An increase in the price of snorkelling causes an increase in the demand (a rightward shift in the demand curve) of a substitute product (windsurfing).

Study Problems

Find answers on the McGraw-Hill online resource.

Basic (Problems 1–5)

1. **(LO 1)** Given Jan's total utility from consuming packets of potato chips in Table 5.13, calculate her marginal utility for each unit.

TABLE 5.13

Quantity	Total Utility	Marginal Utility
1	60	_____
2	110	_____
3	140	_____
4	155	_____
5	167	_____
6	177	_____
7	186	_____
8	192	_____
9	195	_____
10	196	_____

2. **(LO 2)** Given Jon's marginal utility from consuming packets of potato chips in Table 5.14, calculate his total utility for each quantity.

TABLE 5.14

Quantity	Total Utility	Marginal Utility
1	_____	38
2	_____	26
3	_____	22
4	_____	18
5	_____	14
6	_____	10
7	_____	8
8	_____	5
9	_____	3
10	_____	2

3. **(LO 2)** Erika cannot decide whether to buy a packet of potato chips, cheese whirls, or nacho chips, whose marginal utilities are 50, 36, and 42, respectively. The prices of the snacks are $1.25, $0.80, and $1.20, respectively.

   a) Calculate the MU per dollar spent for each of the three products. _____; _____; _____

   b) If Erika can afford to buy only one packet, which should she buy?

4. **(LO 2)** Erika's evaluation of packets of nacho chips in terms of $MU is shown in Table 5.15.

TABLE 5.15

Quantity of Chips	$MU	Price	Marginal Consumer Surplus	Total Consumer Surplus
1	$3.00	_____	_____	_____
2	2.50	_____	_____	_____
3	1.80	_____	_____	_____
4	1.50	_____	_____	_____
5	1.25	_____	_____	_____

If the price of nacho chips is $1.20, and June buys five packets, calculate her marginal consumer surplus for each packet and the total consumer surplus from all five to complete Table 5.15.

5. **(LO 4)** Table 5.16 shows Daniel's demand for giant slurpees.

TABLE 5.16

Quantity	MU	TU
1	50	_____
2	_____	90
3	_____	125
4	25	_____
5	20	_____
6	_____	188
7	_____	200
8	6	_____
9	_____	206
10	_____	200

a) Complete Table 5.16.
b) At what quantity is total utility maximized?
c) What is marginal utility at this quantity?

Intermediate (Problems 6–10)

6. **(LO 4)** Figure 5.8 depicts Christian's $MU for ice creams and for giant chocolate cookies.

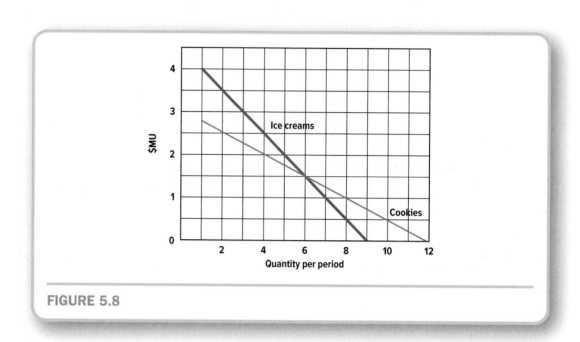

FIGURE 5.8

a) Complete Table 5.17.

TABLE 5.17		
Quantity	**Ice Cream $MU**	**Cookies $MU**
1	_____	_____
2	_____	_____
3	_____	_____
4	_____	_____
5	_____	_____
6	_____	_____

b) If Christian's budget only allows him to make a total of six purchases, how many units of each product would he buy? Ice cream: _____ Cookies: _____
c) If he found he could afford 10 units, how many of each product would he buy?
   Ice cream: _____ Cookies: _____

7. **(LO 2)**
   a) Chika has calculated the marginal utility that she derives from her paid employment and from leisure. This is presented in Table 5.18. In her ideal world, where she could work as few or as many hours as she wished, how would she allocate her sixteen waking hours? (She does need to sleep.)

TABLE 5.18

Hours	MU Paid Employment	MU Leisure
1	100	80
2	90	75
3	80	70
4	70	65
5	60	60
6	50	55
7	40	50
8	30	45
9	20	40
10	10	35

b) Unfortunately, Chika begins to realize that unless she gets an education she will not enjoy a high salary and therefore will not be able to afford more leisure time. She therefore decides to spend six hours each day studying (in addition to her eight hours of sleep). How will she now divide the remaining hours between work and leisure? Work: _____ Leisure: _____

8. **(LO 2)** Maria has $7 to spend on breakfast. Unfortunately, the snack bar in the building where she works has only three items: muffins at $1 each, soup at $1.50, and cappuccinos at $2 each.
a) Given her total utility figures in Table 5.19, complete the MU columns.

TABLE 5.19

Quantity	Muffins TU	Muffins MU	Muffins MU per $	Soup TU	Soup MU	Soup MU per $	Cappuccinos TU	Cappuccinos MU	Cappuccinos MU per $
1	60	_____	_____	120	_____	_____	70	_____	_____
2	110	_____	_____	186	_____	_____	130	_____	_____
3	140	_____	_____	234	_____	_____	160	_____	_____
4	160	_____	_____	273	_____	_____	170	_____	_____
5	162	_____	_____	291	_____	_____	175	_____	_____

b) How should she allocate her budget?
Muffin(s): _____ Soup: _____
Cappuccino(s): _____

9. **(LO 6)** Sam's drive-in movie theatre attracts two main groups of customers: teenagers and parents with young children. The demand of the two groups is shown in Table 5.20.
a) Complete the total revenue columns in Table 5.20.
b) If Sam charges a single admission price and wants to maximize his total revenue, what price should he charge, and what will be his total revenue?
Price: $_____ Total revenue: $_____
c) Suppose, instead, that Sam is able to price-discriminate between the two groups and charge different prices to each. How much would he charge each, and what would be his total revenue now?
Price to teenagers: $_____ Price to parents: $_____ Total revenue: $_____

TABLE 5.20

TEENAGERS			PARENTS	BOTH	
Admission Price ($)	Quantity Demanded	Total Revenue ($)	Quantity Demanded	Total Revenue ($)	Total Revenue ($)
8	100	_____	0	_____	_____
7	150	_____	5	_____	_____
6	180	_____	15	_____	_____
5	200	_____	30	_____	_____
4	210	_____	55	_____	_____
3	215	_____	80	_____	_____
2	218	_____	100	_____	_____
1	220	_____	150	_____	_____

10. **(LO 2)** Jeremy loves eating toast and drinking cans of pop. Table 5.21 shows his marginal utility measured in terms of dollars, that is, in $MU.

TABLE 5.21

PIECES OF TOAST		POP	
Pieces	$MU	Cans	$MU
1	3	1	1.50
2	2.50	2	1.40
3	2	3	1.00
4	1.20	4	0.60
5	0.20	5	0.20
6	−0.50	6	−0.20

Suppose that Jeremy has a budget of $7 and the price of both the toast and the pop is $1.
a) How many of each item will Jeremy buy to maximize his total utility? Pieces of toast: _____
   Cans of pop: _____
b) How much $ total utility will he derive?
c) How much total consumer surplus will he obtain from each item? Toast: _____
   Pop: _____
Now, suppose that Jeremy moves back to his parents' home, where he considers eating to be a free activity.
d) How much of each item will he now consume? Pieces of toast: _____
   Cans of pop: _____
e) How much total consumer surplus will he now obtain from each item? Toast: _____
   Pop: _____

Advanced (Problems 11–16)

11. **(LO 2)** Christina has decided to spend her evening eating sushi and watching videos. Each piece of sushi and each video costs $2. Her total utility for the two products is shown in Table 5.22.

TABLE 5.22

	VIDEOS			SUSHI PIECES	
Number	Total Utility	Marginal Utility	Number	Total Utility	Marginal Utility
1	48	_____	1	45	_____
2	86	_____	2	85	_____
3	112	_____	3	115	_____
4	130	_____	4	134	_____
5	142	_____	5	150	_____
6	150	_____	6	158	_____

a) Complete the marginal utility columns in Table 5.22.
b) How should Christina allocate a budget of $10 to achieve utility maximization, and what will be her total utility? Videos: _____ Pieces of sushi: _____ Total utility: _____
c) Suppose that the sushi shop offered a deal whereby Christina can buy a four-piece pack for $6. How will Christina allocate her budget, and what will be her total utility now?
Videos: _____ Pieces of sushi: _____ Total utility: _____

12. **(LO 6)** In Mt. Pleasant, the consumption of green tea seems to be related to political party membership. The demand for kilograms of tea per month by party affiliation is shown in Table 5.23. A single firm supplies green tea in Mt. Pleasant.

TABLE 5.23

Kilogram of Tea Price	Liberals Quantity	Liberals Total Revenue	Conservatives Quantity	Conservatives Total Revenue	NDP Quantity	NDP Total Revenue	Total Quantity	All 3 Parties Total Revenue
$6.00	4	_____	6	_____	8	_____	_____	_____
5.40	5	_____	7	_____	9	_____	_____	_____
4.80	6	_____	8	_____	10	_____	_____	_____
4.20	7	_____	9	_____	11	_____	_____	_____
3.60	8	_____	10	_____	12	_____	_____	_____
3.00	9	_____	11	_____	13	_____	_____	_____

a) Complete Table 5.23.
b) What single price should the firm charge everyone if it wants to maximize its total sales revenue and what will be its total revenue? Price: $_____ Total revenue: $_____
c) Suppose that the government of Mt. Pleasant allows the firm to price-discriminate on the basis of political affiliation. If the firm wishes to maximize its total sales revenue, how much should it charge each group and what will be its total revenue? Liberal price: $_____ Conservative price: $_____ NDP price: $_____ Total revenue: $_____
d) What is the price elasticity of demand for these three groups between the prices of $6 and $5.40?
Liberal: _____ Conservative: _____ NDP: _____
e) What is the relationship between elasticity and the prices charged?
The greater the elasticity, the (higher/lower) _____ the price charged.

13. **(LO 5)** Figure 5.9 indicates Alberto's demand for tickets for the amusement park ride called the Twisted Bender.

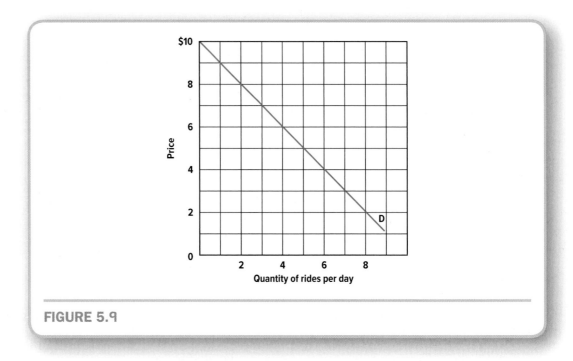

FIGURE 5.9

a) What is Alberto's total consumer surplus if the price per ticket is $6? _____

b) What is Alberto's total consumer surplus if the price per ticket is $2? _____

14. **(LO 2)** **Figure** 5.10 indicates Marshall's marginal utility for two products, A and B.

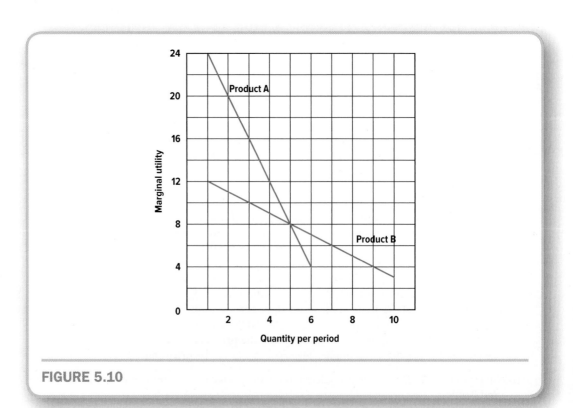

FIGURE 5.10

a) From **Figure** 5.10, complete columns 2 and 4 of **Table** 5.24.

TABLE 5.24

| (1) | (2) | (3) Product A | (4) |
Quantity	Product A MU	MU per $ (at $2)	Product B MU
1	_____	_____	_____
2	_____	_____	_____
3	_____	_____	_____
4	_____	_____	_____
5	_____	_____	_____
6	_____	_____	_____

b) If the price of both products is $1, what quantity of each good would Marshall purchase if his budget was $8?
   Quantity of A: _____ Quantity of B: _____
c) Suppose that the price of Product A increases to $2. Complete column 3 of **Table** 5.24.
d) If Marshall's budget remained the same, what quantities of each good would he now purchase?
   Quantity of A: _____ Quantity of B: _____

15. **(LO 5)** Suppose that **Figure** 5.11 depicts the demand for grape oil, which can be purchased in any quantities and sold at any price.

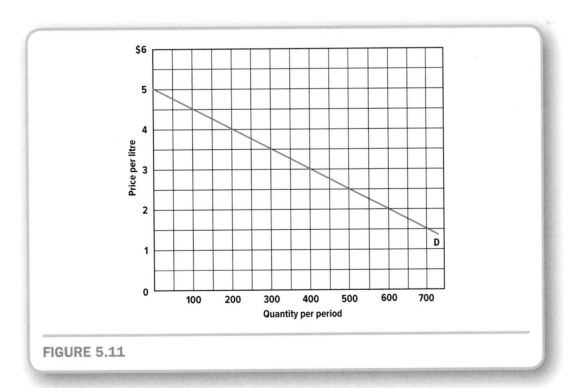

FIGURE 5.11

a) What is the total consumer surplus if the price per litre is $4? _____
b) What is the total consumer surplus if the price per litre is $2? _____ (*Hint:* Area of a triangle?)

16. **(LO 4)** **Figure** 5.12 shows the demand for haircuts at the Uppercuts Hairdressing Salon.

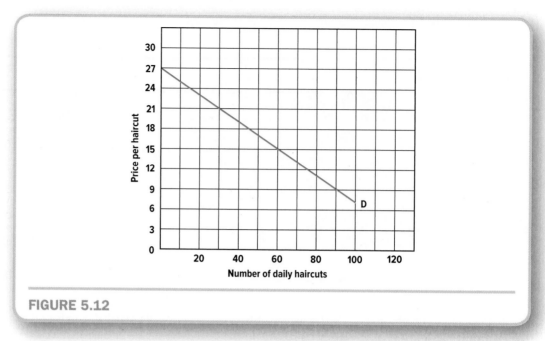

FIGURE 5.12

a) If the salon charges a single price of $9, what will its total daily revenue be? $_____

b) Suppose, instead, that the salon practises price discrimination and now charges $15 for haircuts to regulars but only $9 to retirees and economics instructors. What will its new total daily revenue be? $_____

c) What is the value of consumer surplus that the salon has captured as a result of price-discriminating? _____

d) Show in **Figure 5.12** the area that represents the value of consumer surplus captured.

Problems for Further Study

Basic (Problems 1–4)

1. **(LO 1)** Your local pizzeria is having a special on medium pizzas. The first pizza will cost you $10, but if you buy a second pizza it will only cost you $5. What aspect of consumer theory does this illustrate?
2. **(LO 1)** What does *marginal utility* mean, and what is the *law of diminishing marginal utility*?
3. **(LO 3)** Explain why a rational consumer does not spend all of her income buying only her favourite product.
4. **(LO 4)** Suppose you had five 50 litre containers of water. Name a different purpose for each container. Now list them in order of marginal utility.

Intermediate (Problems 5–7)

5. **(LO 1, 4)** Explain the relationship between the marginal utility of a product and the demand for it.
6. **(LO 6)** What does price discrimination mean? Give three examples of price discrimination.
7. **(LO 1)** "If marginal utility is decreasing, total utility must also be decreasing." Is this correct?

Advanced (Problems 8–10)

8. **(LO 5)** The more inelastic the demand of a product, the greater will be the consumer surplus. Explain, with examples of products why this is/or is not correct.
9. **(LO 4)**
   a) Suppose that Daniel is willing to pay a maximum of $5 for his first slice of pizza. For each additional slice, he would be prepared to pay up to 50 cents less. If Daniel could obtain the pizza for free, how many slices would he eat?
   b) If the price of a slice of pizza happened to be $2, how many slices would he purchase (assuming his budget allowed it)? What would be his total consumer surplus as a result?
      Number of slices: _____ Consumer surplus: $_____
10. **(LO 1)** "The marginal utility a person derives from the consumption of a product is unrelated to its price." However, the substitution effect suggests that when the price of one product declines it becomes more attractive to consumers, that is, its marginal utility increases. How can you reconcile these two statements?

Appendix to CHAPTER 5
Indifference Curve Analysis

Sasha was a financially struggling student who spent all his hard-earned savings (plus the proceeds of his student loans) on the bare essentials of life—food, rent, tuition, books, bus pass, and so on. Then, one day, he received a very pleasant surprise in the mail. An understanding aunt wrote to tell him that henceforth she would send him $64 per month on the condition that he spend all of it only on whatever gave him a little pleasure. Since Sasha loved both music (he had been given a CD player to take with him to college) and movies, he decided that he would spend this monthly gift on only those two items. Sasha was a little out of touch with prices but he did know that CDs cost more than movies, and so he asked himself what would be his ideal combination to purchase. He felt that five movies and three CDs sounded right (combination B). But then he thought a little more about it and asked himself, "If I wanted to buy one more CD, how many movies would I be prepared to sacrifice?" The answer was only one, since the prospect of fewer than four movies per month was not appealing (combination C). Sasha then asked the same question in reverse: "If I had to sacrifice one of these CDs, how many more movies each month would compensate me?" He decided that the answer to this question was three (combination A). In effect, Sasha now identified three combinations of the two goods that gave him equal satisfaction (or pleasure) as summarized in Table A1.

TABLE A1		
Combination	CDs	Movies
B	3	5
C	4	4
A	2	8

THE INDIFFERENCE CURVE

An economist, observing Sasha's thought process, would say that Sasha was attempting to maximize total utility from his spending on entertainment and had identified three points on his **indifference curve**. **Figure A1** illustrates this curve.

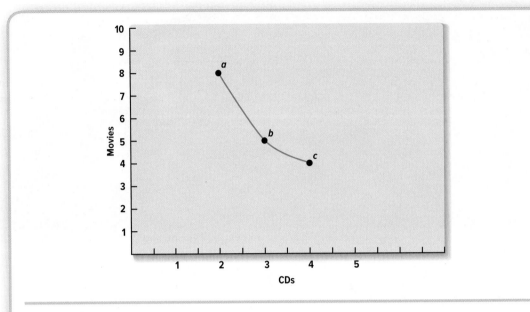

FIGURE A1

Sasha's preferences for movies and CDs are such that he is indifferent among the three possible combinations indicated by points *a*, *b*, and *c*. Connecting these points yields an indifference curve.

There are two important aspects of this indifference curve that we need to emphasize. First, it is downward sloping, which is to say that Sasha will be willing to give up CDs only if he gets more movies and vice versa. This seems eminently reasonable. Second, the rate at which he is willing to give up movies for a CD or CDs for a movie is crucial. Economists call this the **marginal rate of substitution**, or, as we will call it, the MRS.

If we focus on point *a* in **Figure A1**, we see that this is the combination of 8 movies and 2 CDs. If we move from point *a* to point *b*, we see that Sasha is willing to give up 3 movies (8 down to 5) to gain one more CD (2 up to 3). Between these two points, the value of Sasha's MRS of a CD for movies is 3/1 or 3. Note, however, what happens as we move from point *b* to *c*. Here, Sasha is willing to give up only one movie (5 down to 4) to gain one more CD (3 up to 4). Thus, here, the value of his MRS of CDs for movies is only 1/1 or 1. What we have just identified is the **law of diminishing marginal rate of substitution**. This is quite analogous to the law of diminishing marginal utility that we encountered in Chapter 5 and reflects the fact that the more CDs that Sasha already has, the fewer movies he is willing to give up to gain yet another CD. Again, this seems reasonable because we know that Sasha loves both CDs and movies.

The effect of the law of diminishing MRS is that the indifference curve will be bowed in (convex), and because we have already established that it is downward sloping, we now have the basic shape of all indifference curves. Furthermore, we can point out two more things about the indifference curve: its slope is equal to the MRS, and this slope becomes less steep as we move down the curve, since the MRS of CDs for movies diminishes the more CDs Sasha has. We thus know that Sasha's indifference curve in **Figure A1** would become less steep to the right of point *c* and more steep to the left of point *a*.

THE BUDGET LINE

Let us now return to Sasha's story to report that he has just made a trip downtown to price both CDs and movies (remember his previous financial situation had made him a little out of touch). He was surprised, and more than a little disappointed, to learn that movies were now $8 and the type of CDs that he wanted averaged $16. He then returned to his dorm and made **Table A2**, which lists the combinations of the two goods that he could afford to buy with his budget of $64 per month.

TABLE A2	
Movies	**CDs**
8	0
6	1
4	2
2	3
0	4

We can now graph the data in Table A2 and obtain what economists call the budget line (BL) or budget constraint line, since Sasha's limited budget constrains him to only these combinations (he could, of course, buy fewer quantities of either goods, but his aunt's condition was that he spend all of the $64). The budget line is illustrated in Figure A2.

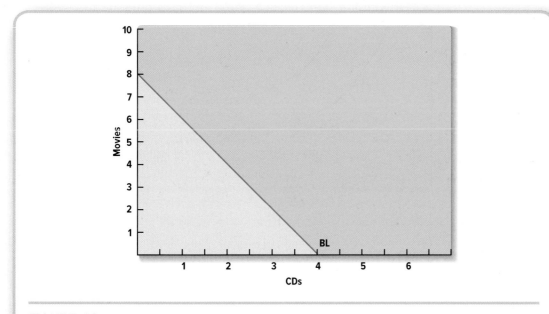

FIGURE A2

The budget line, BL, identifies the various combinations of movies and CDs that Sasha is able to afford given his financial constraint of $64. The budget line begins with the combination of 8 movies and zero CDs and has a slope of –2. Any combination of the two goods in the pink-shaded area is unobtainable.

We need to point out that the slope of the budget line is a reflection of the prices of the two goods. If we put the price of CDs, which is $16, over the price of movies, which is $8, we get 16/8 or 2. Technically, this slope needs to be expressed as –2 because the budget line must be downward sloping.

It was clear to Sasha that he simply could not obtain any of the combinations he had first listed in Table A1. He would, therefore, need to construct another indifference curve, which, although it would result in lower total utility, would fit his budget. He could see that a combination of 4 movies and 2 CDs per month was within his budget, and so he started there (combination E). He then asked himself how many more movies would compensate him for reducing the number of CDs from 2 to 1. He decided that this would be 3 movies, giving him a second combination of 7 movies and one CD (combination D). He then asked himself how many movies would he sacrifice in order to have 3, rather than 2 CDs. The answer is only one, which gives him a third combination (F) of 3 movies and 3 CDs. These new combinations are summarized in Table A3.

TABLE A3

Combination	Movies	CDs
d	7	1
e	4	2
f	3	3

Since Sasha is indifferent among these three (new) combinations, we can take this information and plot a new indifference curve (I_2) on **Figure A3**.

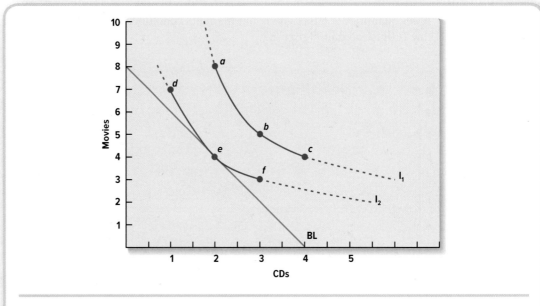

FIGURE A3

Sasha is indifferent to the combinations represented by points *d*, *e*, and *f* because they all are on the same indifference curve, I_2. Given his budget line, BL, only combination *e* is affordable.

Let us examine what **Figure A3** is telling us. First, points *d*, *e*, and *f* are all combinations of the two goods to which Sasha is indifferent, since they are all on the same indifference curve, I_2, and give him equal utility. Second, Sasha would prefer any combination of the two goods on indifference curve I_1 since it higher than (or is to the right of) I_2. Third, he is limited by his budget to the points, that lie on the budget line, BL. And finally, of all these points only *e* is within Sasha's budget, and this will, then, be his obvious choice.

UTILITY MAXIMIZATION

There is something very fundamental about point *e* that you need to fully understand. At this point, the indifference curve and the budget line are tangent, and this means that their slopes are the same. Since we know that this slope is –2 and since we have established that the budget line is equal to the relative prices of the two goods and that the slope of the indifference curve is equal to the MRS, we have

$$\frac{P_{CDs}}{P_M} = MRS$$

Furthermore, we know that the MRS is a reflection of Sasha's marginal utility for the two goods. Therefore, the above equation can be expressed as

$$\frac{P_{CDs}}{P_M} = \frac{MU_{CD}}{MU_M}$$

This second equation can be rewritten as

$$\frac{MU_M}{P_M} = \frac{MU_{CD}}{P_{CD}}$$

You will recognize that this is the optimal purchasing rule that we obtained in Chapter 5. Sasha will maximize his utility, given a budget constraint, by equating the marginal utility per dollar spent on movies with the marginal utility per dollar spent on CDs. What is different about the indifference curve approach, however, is that we got here without having to assign values for the marginal utilities of either good. Interesting, isn't it?

THE INCOME AND SUBSTITUTION EFFECT

In Chapter 2, we learned that if the price of a particular good increases, then the quantity demanded will decrease for two reasons—the income effect and the substitution effect. This can be illustrated nicely using indifference curves, as illustrated in **Figure A4**.

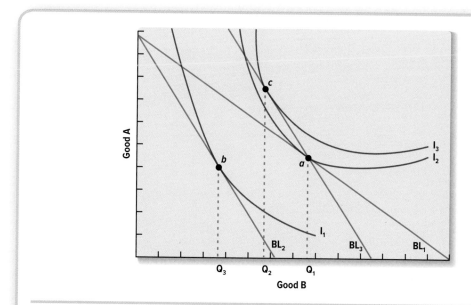

FIGURE A4

Point *a* illustrates the original maximization of utility, which results in the consumer purchasing quantity Q_1 of good B. An increase in the price of good B results in the budget pivoting from BL_1 to BL_2 and a new maximization illustrated by *b*. Budget line BL_3 passes through the original combination *a* but is now tangent to a higher indifference curve, I_3, at point *c* and quantity purchased of Q_2. Thus, Q_1 to Q_2 is the substitution effect, and Q_2 to Q_3 is the income effect.

Given budget line BL_1 and indifference curve I_2, the consumer's maximization point is *a*, which results in quantity Q_1 of good B being purchased (as well as some of good A). An increase in the price of good B pivots the budget line to the left, as seen in BL_2, and the consumer's purchases change to point *b* and quantity Q_3. This is quite consistent with the idea that an increase in the price of good B will lead to a decrease in the quantity demanded.

But how much of the decrease (Q_1 down to Q_3) is because the consumer's real income has decreased, and how much is due to the consumer substituting the now relatively cheaper good A for good B? To answer this question, we conceptually give the consumer enough additional income to enable her to purchase the original combination of the two goods. This is illustrated by budget line BL_3, which has been shifted right and passes through the original combination at point *a*. You should note that BL_3 is parallel to BL_2, since BL_3 represents the same price level as BL_2 with a higher income level. BL_3 is tangent to a higher indifference curve, I_3 at point *c*. Note that the consumer could purchase the original combination *a* but has instead chosen combination *c*. This latter combination must yield a higher level of utility and is thus on a higher indifference curve. The point of tangency between BL_3 and I_3, point *c*, yields quantity Q_2. Thus, this consumer has decreased her purchases of good B from Q_1 to Q_2 because she is substituting good A for good B, which is the substitution effect. The decrease in the quantity of good B purchased, Q_2 to Q_3, is the result of the decrease in real income and, thus, is the income effect.

This completes our brief discussion of indifference curve analysis.

Study Guide

Review

NEW GLOSSARY TERMS

indifference curve   law of diminishing marginal rate of substitution   marginal rate of substitution

Study Problems

Find answers on the McGraw-Hill online resource.

1. **Table A4** shows three indifference schedules for Barbara. The price of each fruit is $1, and Barbara's budget is $12.

TABLE A4

INDIFFERENCE CURVE 1		INDIFFERENCE CURVE 2		INDIFFERENCE CURVE 3	
Apples	Bananas	Apples	Bananas	Apples	Bananas
9	2	10	4	12	6
6	3	6	6	8	7
5	5	5	9	6	8
4	9	4	13	5	11
3	14	3	18	4	16

a) Draw the three indifference curves and the budget line on **Figure A5**.

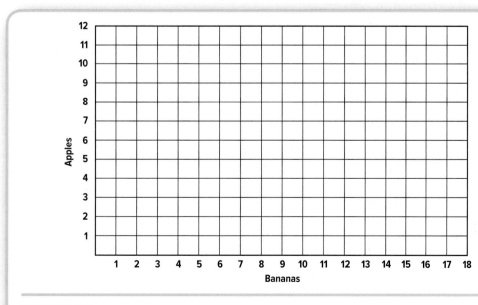

FIGURE A5

b) What quantities of each will maximize Barbara's total utility if she spends all of her budget?
   Apples: _____ Bananas: _____
   Suppose that the price of apples increases to $1.50.
c) Draw the new budget line in **Figure A5**.
d) What quantities of each will now maximize Barbara's total utility if she spends all of her budget?
   Apples: _____ Bananas: _____

2. **Figure A6** shows an indifference map for Alan. A's cost $3, and B's cost $2. Alan has a budget of $30.
   a) Draw Alan's budget line in **Figure A6**.

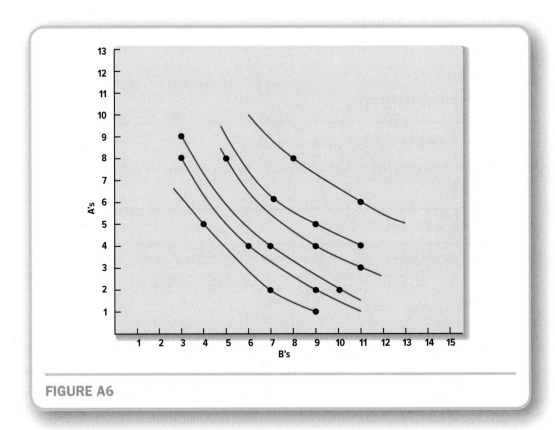

FIGURE A6

b) What quantities of each product will maximize Alan's total utility if he spends all of his budget?
   A's: _____ B's: _____

Suppose that the price of B's increases to $3.
c) Draw in the new budget line in **Figure A6**.
d) What quantities of each will maximize Alan's total utility if he spends all of his $30 budget?
   A's: _____ B's: _____
e) In **Figure A6**, draw a budget line (BL$_3$) which reflects the new price but with the same real income as before the price change.
   A's: _____ B's: _____
f) How much does the quantity of B decline due to:
   The substitution effect? _____
   The income effect? _____

CHAPTER 6
A Firm's Production Decisions and Costs in the Short Run

LEARNING OBJECTIVES

At the end of this chapter, you should be able to:

LO1 Explain what a firm is and list the different types of firms.

LO2 Describe how and why economists and accountants measure costs differently, and distinguish between the accountants' and economists' views of profits.

LO3 Explain the crucial relationship between productivity and costs.

LO4 Demonstrate the important difference between fixed costs and variable costs.

LO5 List and graph the seven specific cost definitions used by economists.

LO6 Explain the meanings of *increasing productivity* and *cutting costs*.

 WHAT'S AHEAD ...

In this chapter, we look at the costs of production faced by a typical firm. First, we make a distinction between explicit cost and implicit cost. Later, we see that there are seven ways to measure costs and that each interrelates with the others in specific ways. This enables us to study the behaviour of firms in different market structures in subsequent chapters. To understand the costs of production, we must first understand *productivity* because a firm's productivity underlies its costs. Finally, we explore what is meant by a reduction in a firm's cost of production.

A QUESTION OF RELEVANCE ...

Have you even been given a free ticket to a concert or ball game? Did it cost you anything? Did it cost the person who gave it to you anything? Did it cost the organizers of the event anything? Who said (besides the Beatles) that the best things in life are free? And does this include a free lunch? In this chapter, we will discuss how to identify free goods and economic goods, and how to measure the cost of economic goods.

Chapters 4 and 5 looked in some detail behind the demand curve. In this chapter and the next, we will explore the derivation of the supply curve, and so our focus shifts from the behaviour of consumers to that of producers. To do this, we will need to look in some detail at what constitutes the costs of production for the firm and what causes those costs to change. We must be careful here that when we use the term *costs* we are not looking at things from the consumers' perspective but from the producers.' For instance, if we suggest that a new car costs $30 000, we do not mean that this is the price of the car, but that this is how much it costs the manufacturer to produce it.

6.1   The Role of the Firm

LO1   Explain what a firm is and list the different types of firms.

In this section, we take a look at the business organization—what economists call the **firm** a term which embraces a number of different types of organizations including:

- *sole proprietorship*, whose owner/manager is responsible for all activities of the firm
- *partnership*, which has two or more joint owners (in a limited partnership, some of the partners have no part in running the firm and are not liable for its debts)
- *corporation*, whose owners are not personally responsible for debts and not personally involved in its operations
- *state-owned enterprise* (also known as *Crown corporation* in Canada), which is owned by the government and generally run by appointed officials
- *nonprofit organization*, which is organized to achieve certain goals by providing goods and services, but not with the intention of making a profit

Firms face a long list of decisions they must make, ranging from deciding what to produce to deciding where production should take place. Economists, however, focus on the two issues they consider of primary importance: how firms decide on the price they will charge for their output and how they determine the right level of production. To examine these issues, we will look at short-run costs in this chapter and long-run costs in Chapter 7. This will lay the groundwork for Chapters 8, 9, and 10, where we consider how firms operate in different market structures with different levels of competitive intensity.

Production is the activity of a business organization or firm using inputs to obtain output of some product. One sees examples of it every day. Think of Ocean Concrete or Lafarge using sand, gravel, cement, water, machines, and labour (all of which are *inputs*) to produce concrete (or other *outputs*). Of course, the inputs used in production have to be paid for, and this payment becomes the firm's *costs*.

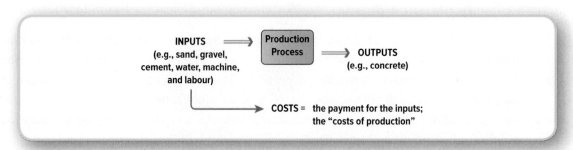

When most students hear the word "costs," they think of the dollars and cents actually paid out by the firm. Many costs can be thought of in just this way, but this is by no means the whole story. For example, a firm might buy a machine for $200 000 that it expects to be able to use for eight years. What is the cost of this machine in the first year of its use? Surely, the answer is not the full $200 000. Instead, the cost could be thought of as that portion of the machine used up or worn out during the year. The annual amount of this wear is called **depreciation**. In this example, the cost of depreciation might be equal to, say, one-eighth of $200 000, or $25 000.

 ADDED DIMENSION

Why Do Firms Exist? The Coase Answer

One of the truly intriguing questions in economics is: Why do firms exist? Ronald Coase (1910–2013), a Nobel laureate who taught for many years at the University of Chicago, offered an elegant answer in the late 1930s. Consider this situation: I want a new house. I could find a lot and arrange to buy it. Then I could hire someone to prepare the lot for construction, locate and hire someone to dig a hole for the basement, hire still someone else to prepare and pour the concrete foundation, hire others to frame the building (after someone else has been found to design the structure), and hire still others to do the roofing, plumbing, electrical, and finishing work.

At each stage, I would have to seek bids, negotiate prices, decide on product types and schedules, and hope that everyone delivered on what they promised. All of this would take a lot of time and money—that is, it has *transactions* costs.

Alternatively, I could simply buy a house that some firm has put on the market. In putting a house up for sale, the firm has absorbed all the transactions costs, and since it has produced dozens (hundreds) of houses, including the one I buy, it has been able to reduce the per-house transactions costs. That is why a firm exists—it is more efficient.

SECTION SUMMARY

a) A firm is a business organization that transforms inputs into outputs

b) The five different types of business organizations are

- sole proprietorship
- partnership
- corporation
- state-owned enterprise
- nonprofit organization

6.2   Explicit and Implicit Costs

LO2   Describe how and why economists and accountants measure costs differently, and distinguish between the accountants' and economists' views of profits.

As an introduction to costs, let us use the example of a mom-and-pop firm, in which the owners often contribute their own money and time to the firm. Is the contribution of money to the firm free? Should we consider the time put into the firm by its owners as having no costs? The answer to both questions is no, and this once again raises the concept of opportunity costs, which was introduced in Chapter 1.

Imagine that two hypothetical owners, Otto and Melissa, inherit $96 000 and put it into their tote bag company, Total Totes. The costs to the firm, economists would argue, must include what this couple might have done with the $96 000 instead of putting it into their business. One clear alternative would be to buy some mutual funds, from which they could earn, let us say, 10 percent per year. Therefore, the cost to the firm of using this $96 000 is the sacrifice of the lost return of $9600 per year (or $800 per month).

Similarly, we might ask what Otto and Melissa could do instead of putting sixteen hours a day (eight hours each) of work into their business. Well, both might hire their labour out to someone else in a similar business who wanted the skills Otto and Melissa possess. Let us assume that the going market wage for this type of labour is $100 per day. We should then assign to the firm a cost of this couple putting their time into the business of $4000 per month (two people times $100 per day times twenty days). The important thing to note is that neither the $9600 in interest per year nor the $4000 per month in wages need necessarily be actually paid out by the firm, but each is a legitimate cost of doing business using the concept of opportunity cost. In other words, to an economist, there is a cost involved—even if no payment is made—if an activity involves the use of productive resources, since those resources might have been used elsewhere.

We can see that there are two distinct types of costs in our example of Total Totes. **Explicit costs** are the costs paid to non-owners, such as wages to employees and payments to suppliers. **Implicit costs** are the costs of using the owners' resources when no payment is made. If the owners did choose to take a payment for their implicit wage costs, we might think of this as *wages paid to self* and this would change the implicit cost into an explicit cost.

Table 6.1 shows a typical month's accounting of the business activity for Total Totes.

TABLE 6.1
Total Totes: Profit and Loss Statement (for a typical month)

Total Revenue:	Cash sales (excluding sales tax)		$20 000
Explicit Costs:	Rent	$ 1 500	
	Materials and supplies	4 200	
	Utilities	1 000	
	Hired labour	10 000	
	Depreciation on equipment	500	
Total Explicit Costs:		$17 200	
Accounting Profit:			$ 2 800
Implicit Costs:	Opportunity costs of the $96 000 put into the business	800	
	Labour put in by owners	4 000	
Total Implicit Costs:		4 800	
Total Explicit and Implicit Costs:		$22 000	
Economic Profit or (Loss):			$(2 000)

We should mention that an accountant and an economist would calculate the depreciation on equipment differently. Assume that the $500 depreciation expense is the maximum amount that the tax laws allow monthly, and that this is the figure used by the accountant. The economist would argue, however, that the actual cost of equipment this year is the decline in its market value that results from its being one year older. This might or might not be equal to $500, but for expediency, we will assume that it is.

As you can see from Table 6.1, if we considered only direct out-of-pocket expenses (explicit costs) we would conclude that Otto and Melissa had made a profit of $2800 in this month. In fact, here is how an accountant would report the month's activities:

$$\text{Total accounting profit} = \text{total revenue} - \text{total explicit costs} \qquad [6.1]$$

Economists, however, recognizing the concept of opportunity cost, would calculate that rather than making a $2800 profit, Total Totes lost $2000 in this month:

$$\text{Total economic profit} = \text{total revenue} - \text{total costs (implicit and explicit)} \qquad [6.2]$$

In other words, if Otto and Melissa had put their money into a mutual fund and hired themselves out at the going market wage rate, they would have received an income of $4800 rather than the $2800 that they did receive. In other words, they are $2000 worse off. What this means is that the two of them need to earn at least $4800 per month to make their business venture worthwhile. This is what economists refer to as a **normal profit**: the amount that has to be earned in order to keep an entrepreneur in that line of business over the long haul. In other words—and as strange as it sounds—economists regard this normal profit as a cost, no different from any other cost. You can perhaps work out that Total Totes needs to have sales of $22 000 (assuming no change in costs) just in order for Otto and Melissa to make a normal profit.

Now suppose business really picks up (and, for simplicity's sake, costs remain the same) and sales increase to $25 000. With explicit costs of $17 200 plus implicit costs (or normal profits) of $4800, there would now be a surplus of $3000. This surplus is what economists refer to as **economic profit**. This surplus over and above the normal profits is sometimes referred to as *supernormal profit* (normal profit is a necessary cost of production and must be earned in order for the entrepreneur to stay in business). Economic profit, on the other hand, is unnecessary (though desirable) in the sense that it does not have to be earned to keep the entrepreneur in business. It can be regarded as the reward for the risk the entrepreneur takes. This means that even if Otto and Melissa earned zero economic profit, they would still be happy to stay in the tote bag business as long as they can earn a normal profit. The graphic here illustrates these ideas.

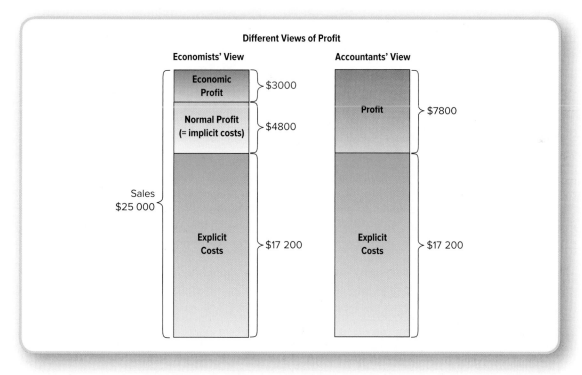

There is another interesting aspect of opportunity cos. Consider the following scenario. Walking through the local mall, you come upon the food court and decide to eat. At first, you are torn between a taco platter for $6.99 and a sou p-and-sandwich combo for the same price. You are aware that the opportunity cost of the one is the sacrifice you make by not buying the other, but there is more. Assume that you decide on the taco platter and sit down to enjoy your purchase. After a single bite, you realize that you have made the wrong choice and you really do not want to eat even another bite. What is the cost of leaving the platter uneaten and simply walking away? To an economist, the answer is zero because the $6.99 you spent on the taco platter is a **sunk cost**, the amount you spent to purchase something that has no current resale value. Sunk costs are absolutely irrelevant to decision making. Even if a firm has spent millions of dollars on equipment, if that money has already been spent and the equipment has no resale value, throwing it away has no cost.

What we are really saying here is that if an asset is a sunk cost, it no longer carries any opportunity cost. Other examples of sunk costs would be fees paid to a consultant or money spent on market research.

ADDED DIMENSION

Urban Encroachment on Agricultural Land

An interesting application of the concept of implicit cost involves the phenomenon of the growing pressure of urbanization on our nation's farmland. As our population continues to grow, our cities have spread out into land used for farming. This drives up the implicit costs of agricultural activities, since land used for housing or urban support activities such as gas stations or golf courses carries a far higher price than land used for farming. This increased implicit cost intensifies the pressure on farmers to sell out to developers.

TEST YOUR UNDERSTANDING

Find answers on the McGraw-Hill online resource.

1. Judy is presently working as an activities facilitator at a local community centre, where she earns $1000 per month after tax. However, she is not happy with her job and is thinking of returning to college to do a two-year program to upgrade her skills. She has estimated the costs as follows:

Annual costs of tuition and textbooks	$2800
Annual cost of board and lodging (same as her present costs)	8000
Additional transportation costs per year	700

   What would be an economist's estimate of the cost of Judy taking the two-year program?

2. Abdi recently gave up a job that paid $1500 a month after tax to open up his own convenience store. He works full time in the store, which had a total revenue of $105 000 last year. His total (explicit) costs amounted to $65 000. He reckons his store is now worth $200 000, and if he were to sell it and invest the proceeds in his dad's supermarket he would earn himself an 8 percent annual return. What is Abdi's economic profit during the year?

SECTION SUMMARY

The chapter begins by distinguishing between explicit costs (payments to non-owners) and implicit costs (any use of the owners' resources that does not require a payment). This distinction enables us to define *normal profit*, which subtracts only explicit costs from total revenue and *economic profit*, which subtracts both explicit and implicit costs.

6.3   Theory of Production

LO3   Explain the crucial relationship between productivity and costs.

Let us now turn our attention to the theory of production. It is clear that increased production will involve higher total costs, and this output/cost relationship is one that we need to explore fully. First, however, we need to understand some basic relationships *within* the concept of production itself.

Total, Average, and Marginal Product

Common sense seems to indicate that if more inputs are added to the production process, more output would be obtained. Yet, to leave things at that would skirt over some of the most important aspects of the production process.

Not all inputs can be increased at the same time. For example, a farmer can add more variable inputs, such as water and fertilizer, to his fields this season, but he cannot increase the size of his fields. Thus, we need to recognize that, within any given period, some inputs will be fixed. This leads us to a very important point: as long as any one input is fixed, we are in what economists call the **short run**. This chapter will be entirely in the context of the short run. The Chapter 7 will look at the long run, in which all inputs are considered variable. What we mean by "variable," then, is that the amount of input varies with the amount of output. Simply put, the more produced, the greater the number of variable inputs required.

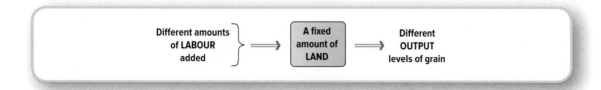

Let us now look at a simple model of production. In Table 6.2, we show what happens to the number of tote bags Otto and Melissa can produce each day in their small factory when they employ different amounts of labour. In this case, the fixed factor is the size of their premises. The variable factor is labour (which we assume is provided with the necessary materials). Table 6.2 shows what happens as Total Totes employs an increasing number of employees.

The second column in Table 6.2 indicates the output, which is what economists call **total product** (TP). Here, we see what happens to total product as we add successive units of labour. It is important to note that total product does not rise proportionately with the increase in labour. This change in total product is what economists call the **marginal product** (MP)—the extra production that results from adding another unit of input, in this case labour. The marginal product of labour is simply the extra output from each additional worker. Formally, the marginal product of *labour* is

$$MP_L = \frac{\Delta TP}{\Delta L} \qquad [6.3]$$

The marginal product is different from the **average product** (AP), which is nothing more than total product divided by the number of inputs. Average product is often called *productivity per worker*, or the average product of the average worker. Formally, the average product of labour is

$$AP_L = \frac{TP}{L} \qquad [6.4]$$

TABLE 6.2
Marginal and Average Product Data

Units of Labour	Total Product (TP)	Marginal Product (MP)	Average Product (AP)
0	0	/	/
1	4	4	4
2	16	12	8
3	36	20	12
4	60	24	15
5	75	15	15
6	84	9	14
7	84	0	12
8	72	−12	9

Let us go to Table 6.2 to examine these new concepts in detail. The data in the third column indicate that the marginal product of the first unit of production is four, whereas that of the second production unit is twelve. Why might the marginal product of labour rise? Does it mean that the second worker is better than the first? No, because we assume that each worker is equally good. So what is the explanation?

An analogy may help here. Can you imagine trying to build a fence by yourself? It could be done, but it would be slow and awkward. You would have to set each post temporarily with a stake and support, step back to see if it was straight, then readjust the support and step back again, and so on. Two people (each with tools and material) could likely build a fence *more than* twice as fast as one could. That is to say, the marginal product of the second person would be higher than that of the first person due to the rewards of specialization.

Adam Smith referred to this phenomenon as the **division of labour**. In his famous example, Smith marvelled at the fact that a state-of-the-art factory in eighteenth-century England, which employed only ten workers, was able to produce 48 000 ordinary straight pins in a single day by dividing the process of pin-making into ten distinct functions in which each worker performed only one task. The emphasis here is on the word *process*, as distinct from the situation where each worker separately and independently would make a whole pin from start to finish. In Smith's estimation, if each worker made complete pins, the factory would produce fewer than 1000 pins in a day.

IN A NUTSHELL ...

INPUTS	produce	OUTPUT
Must be paid	results in	costs of production

So what specifically lies behind the advantages of the division of labour? Adam Smith saw five distinct reasons for what he called "the productive power of the division of labour":

1. the enhanced ability to fit the best person to the right job
2. the increased dexterity achieved when that best worker becomes specialized in performing a single operation
3. the time saved when workers do not have to change tools or switch machines because they are performing a single aspect of the process
4. the time saved that would otherwise be lost moving from one operation to another (what we would today call assembly-line production)
5. the machine specialization that can be developed around specific, discrete operations

This last aspect is by far the most important, and proved to be a vital step in the industrial revolution. Without the division of labour, the extensive use of more and more specialized machines that has occurred over the past two centuries simply would not have been possible and the world would be a very different place.

We can now see how the marginal product of labour will at first increase as more labour is added to a production process. However, we need to ask why marginal product at some point declines—as can be seen in Table 6.2, beginning with the addition of the fifth unit of labour. We might also ask why the benefits of specialization do not continue indefinitely.

The answer to both these questions raises one of the most important concepts in all of microeconomics: the **law of diminishing returns**, a concept first developed by David Ricardo. This law states that, as more and more units of a variable resource (in this case, labour) are added to a production process, at some point the resulting increase in output (MP) begins to decrease, assuming that at least one other input (in this case, the factory size) is fixed. The reason for the decreasing marginal product of labour is simply that a fixed-size factory will eventually become overcrowded with workers. A more accurate term would be the *law of diminishing marginal productivity*, but in this chapter we will stick with the more commonly used term.

This production line is a modern-day example of Adam Smith's division of labour.

John A. Rizzo/Getty Images

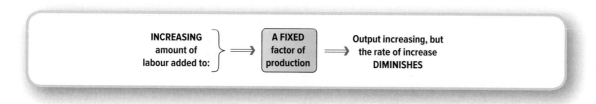

When one stops to think about it for a moment, the law of diminishing returns is a technological reality that must be valid; otherwise, we could grow the world's food in a flowerpot by simply adding more and more variable inputs until production rose to the necessary level. We cannot do this, and the reason we cannot is the law of diminishing returns.

We now need to make four points of clarification. First, while the fixed input in our example above happens to be the size of the factory, it could have been *any* input—for the law of diminishing returns to apply, the only necessity is that at least one input be fixed. Second, our example had only one variable input—labour—and we illustrated the law of diminishing returns by showing that the marginal product of labour declines. However, if there had been two variable inputs instead of one, both would have manifested diminishing returns. Third, any discussion of the law of diminishing returns assumes that technology is unchanging. If technological change does occur, we get a new set of output numbers, but those numbers are still subject to diminishing returns. Finally, while our example is in the context of manufacturing, the law applies in all productive activities, including agriculture.

It is very important to note that even when diminishing returns set in, the total product *continues to rise*. However, the *rate of increase* in the total product begins to fall. If you are familiar with calculus, you may recognize that marginal product is the first derivative of total product, in other words, it is the slope of the TP curve. Even without calculus, it is important to recognize that total product can continue to rise even though marginal product has started to decline. As you can see from Table 6.2, when the eighth worker is added, the total product declines, indicating that the marginal product of additional workers is negative. The table's data can also be put into graphical form. This is illustrated in Figure 6.1A.

Note three things about the TP curve. First, total product rises quickly at first because of the advantages gained from the division of labour. Second, at the point of diminishing returns (after the use of the fourth unit of labour), the rate of increase in the curve decreases, Third, the rise in

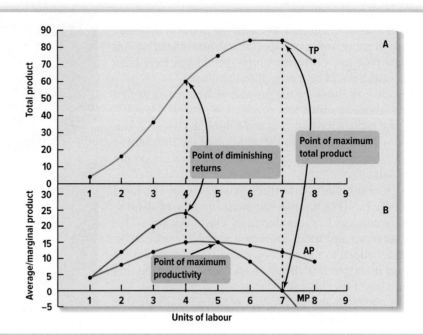

FIGURE 6.1   **The Total, Average, and Marginal Product Curves**

As more units of the variable input labour are used (up to 6 units), total product rises, but the rate of increase slows with the use of the fifth unit of labour. This is the point of diminishing returns. Maximum total product of 84 is reached when 7 units of labour are employed (where MP = 0). When the marginal product curve is above the average product curve, the latter rises. Similarly, when the marginal product curve is below the average product curve, the average declines. At the point where the marginal product curve intersects the average product curve, the average is at its maximum: 15 tote bags per unit of labour.

total product continues despite having passed the point of diminishing returns. You may also notice that there is a small "kink" in the TP curve when the fourth unit of labour is added. This reflects the fact that the MP curve has reached its maximum with the use of four units of labour and declines thereafter.

Let us now turn to a discussion of average product. There is a marginal/average relationship reflected in the data in Table 6.2 that needs to be emphasized. All students intuitively know what this relationship is without being aware of it. Imagine that you are taking a course in which your class mark is made up of ten quizzes worth ten points each. You know that if you got a score of four on the first quiz and six on the second quiz, your average is, at that point, five. You also know that in order to raise your average score, you will have to get a score above five on the third quiz. That mark is the marginal mark, and if the marginal is above the average, the average will rise. If, however, your third test score is less than five, your average of all three quizzes would fall; that is, if the marginal is below the average, the average will fall.

Let us take this marginal/average relationship and look back at the data in Table 6.2. Note that the second, third, and fourth units of labour all have a marginal product that is above the average product, and therefore average product rises. The addition of the fifth unit of labour, which has a marginal product that is exactly the same as the previous average (15), results in the average product neither increasing nor decreasing but remaining constant at 20. The sixth unit of labour has a marginal product of 9, which is below the average, and therefore average product falls to 14. We can generalize as follows:

Average product will rise if marginal product exceeds it and will fall if marginal product is less.

Figure 6.1B illustrates this relationship graphically. You can see that marginal product is at a maximum when four units of labour are used. Further, when marginal product equals average product, average product is at its maximum. Because of the way these particular sets of numbers work out, this maximum average product *appears* (see Table 6.2) to occur with the addition of the fourth unit of labour. But we must be careful here, because, technically speaking, it is with the fifth unit that average product is maximized, since this is where average product is equal to marginal product.

We have now identified three maximums: maximum total product, which was achieved with the addition of the seventh unit of labour; maximum marginal product, which was achieved with the addition of the fourth unit of labour; and maximum average product, which was achieved with the fifth unit of labour. So which is the most productive point? When economists use the term *most productive* or mention *highest productivity*, they are referring to maximum *average* product. This is an engineering concept that refers to the point at which the most output *per unit of input* is achieved.

A similar question is: What is the best output to produce? But we cannot answer that question without knowledge of the costs of the inputs and the price of the output. We will leave discussion of the price of output for Chapter 8. Here, we will now take up the topic of the costs of production.

 TEST YOUR UNDERSTANDING

3. Assume that the amount of capital is fixed.

a) Fill in the blanks in the table.

b) With the addition of which unit of labour do diminishing returns begin?

Units of Labour	TP	MP of Labour	AP of Labour
0	0	/	/
1	80	___	___
2	170	___	___
3	___	80	___
4	310	___	___
5	___	___	70
6	370	___	___
7	370	___	___

c) How many units of labour are used in the average product of labour at a maximum?

d) What is the value of marginal product when total product is at a maximum?

4. Given the data in the table, calculate both the MPL and the APL for each unit of labour used.

Quantity of Labour	Total Product	Marginal Product of Labour	Average Product of Labour
1	400	___	___
2	1000	___	___
3	1500	___	___
4	1800	___	___
5	1900	___	___

SECTION SUMMARY

a) Total product (output) is the end result of *adding inputs* to the production process, and from this we get

$$MP_L = \frac{\Delta TP}{\Delta L}$$

$$AP_L = \frac{TP}{L}$$

b) Advantages gained from the *division of labour* (specialization) explain why MP initially rises as more inputs are used; the *law of diminishing returns* explains why MP eventually declines as more units of input are used.

c) AP will

- rise if MP is above it
- fall if MP is below it

6.4 Marginal and Variable Costs

> **LO4**   Demonstrate the important difference between fixed costs and variable costs.

We now want to forge a link between the quantity of output produced and the cost of producing it. While production relates the number of units produced to the amount of labour used, costs relate dollars to the number of units produced. One of the important questions Otto and Melissa want to address in their company is: How much does it cost us to produce a tote bag? As we shall see, the answer is not a single figure but depends on the level of production; that is, it depends on how many workers they employ and the level of total product (output).

Table 6.3 reproduces the first four columns from Table 6.2 and adds three more, the first of which is **total variable cost** (TVC), which is the sum of all costs that vary directly with the level of output. Variable costs would normally include the cost of variable inputs, such as materials, power, and labour. However, in our simplified example, we have assumed that labour is the only variable cost. Suppose that Otto and Melissa can obtain labour for $120 per unit per day. The figures in the total variable costs column are then obtained by simply multiplying the number of units of labour by $120.

TABLE 6.3
Cost Data for a Firm

(1)	(2)	(3)	(4)	(5)	(6)	(7)
Units of Labour	TP	MP	AP	TVC	MC	AVC
0	0	/	/	0	/	/
1	4	4	4	$120	$30.00	$30.00
2	16	12	8	240	10.00	15.00
3	36	20	12	360	6.00	10.00
4	60	24	15	480	5.00	8.00
5	75	15	15	600	8.00	8.00
6	84	9	14	720	13.33	8.60
7	84	0	12	840	/	10.00

The sixth column introduces the very important concept of the **marginal cost** (MC). Marginal cost is the increase in total variable cost as a result of producing one more unit of output. Ignore the seventh column for the moment.

To obtain the value for marginal cost, we need to emphasize that the definition of marginal cost involves the cost of each additional *unit* of output produced. Therefore, we need to divide the $120 increase in total variable cost, which results from using one more unit of labour, by *marginal product* in order to find the cost of an additional *unit of output* produced. For example, the first unit of labour can produce 4 units of output at a cost of $120. Each unit, therefore, costs $120 divided by 4, or $30 per unit.

Similarly, the second unit of labour increases total product by (has a marginal product of) 12 at a cost of $120. This yields a marginal cost of $10 ($120 divided by 12). The third unit of labour has a marginal product of 20, and therefore the marginal cost of production when 3 inputs are employed is $6, and so on.

In summary, each unit of labour hired costs an identical $120. However, the amount of additional output that each unit produces (MP) is different. The cost of producing additional units of output (the marginal cost), therefore, will also vary.

We will see later, in this and subsequent chapters, that this concept of marginal cost is at the centre of a great deal of microeconomics analysis. The formal definition of marginal cost can be expressed as

$$MC = \frac{\Delta TVC}{\Delta \text{total output}}$$ [6.5]

Let us now look at the seventh column of our data in Table 6.3. Here, we have **average variable cost** (AVC), which is simply the total variable cost divided by the total output. Formally, this is

$$AVC = \frac{TVC}{\text{total output}}$$ [6.6]

To illustrate this calculation, in Table 6.3, we see that when 5 units of labour are being used, the output is 75 and the total variable costs are $600. Dividing the $600 by 75 yields an average variable cost of $8.00.

We should point out that the same marginal/average relationship we discussed in reference to the marginal and average products also applies to marginal and average costs. Thus, just as the average product was at a *maximum* when it was equal to marginal product, average variable cost will be at a *minimum* when it is equal to marginal cost. **Figure** 6.2, which uses the data from Table 6.3, will help you understand this.

In **Figure** 6.2A, you see the marginal product and average product curves. They are, roughly, two inverse U-shaped curves with the marginal product curve intersecting the average product curve at the latter's *maximum* point. This occurs when five units of labour are being used and is the firm's *most productive* point for this size of plant. Next, look at the graphing of the marginal cost and average variable cost curves in **Figure** 6.2B. What you see there are two U-shaped curves, with marginal cost intersecting average variable cost at the latter's *minimum* point. This is at an output of 75, which is the output that 5 units of labour are able to produce. In short, when the average product is at a maximum, the average variable cost will be at its minimum. It is also true that when the marginal product is at a maximum, marginal costs will be at a minimum.

As mentioned above, this is not a coincidence. Average variable cost and marginal cost are upside-down images of average product and marginal product. That is:

> Variable costs of production are a reflection of productivity.

This is what lies behind the observation that an increase in productivity is equivalent to a decrease in costs.

This relationship bears repeating. We can see in either Table 6.3 or **Figure** 6.2 that as marginal product (MP) initially *increases*, marginal cost (MC) *decreases*. Similarly, as average product (AP)

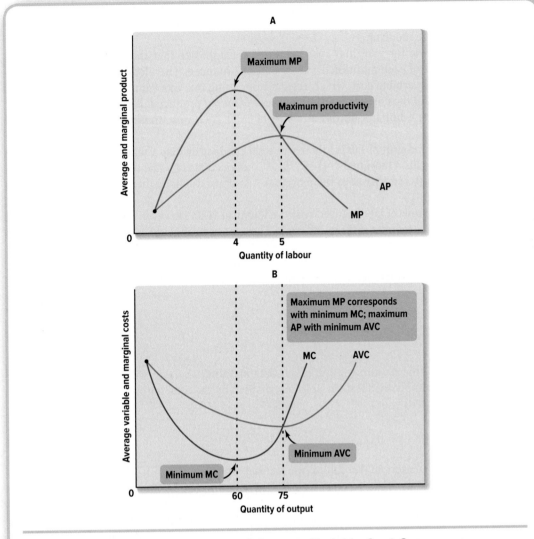

FIGURE 6.2   The Marginal Cost and Average Variable Cost Curves

In Figure A, the MP curve intersects the AP curve at its maximum point when 5 units of labour are being used. In Figure B, the MC curve intersects the AVC curve at its minimum, which occurs at an output of 75. This is the output that 5 units of labour can produce.

increases, average variable cost (AVC) declines. This is a result of the division of labour. However, at some point diminishing returns set in. When this happens, marginal product (and average product) starts to *decrease*. As a result, marginal cost (and average variable cost) starts to *increase*. A diagrammatic summary might be useful:

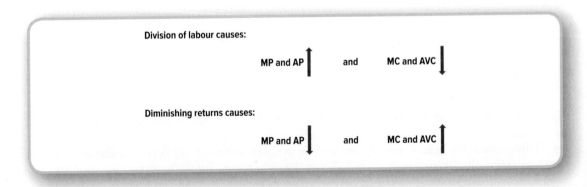

TEST YOUR UNDERSTANDING

5. a) Assuming that all units of labour cost the same, fill in the blanks in the table here.

  b) When is marginal cost at a minimum?

  c) What is the marginal product of labour when 4 units of labour are used?

Units of Labour	Total Output	TVC	MC	AVC
0	0	0	/	/
1	100	200	___	___
2	220	___	___	___
3	320	___	___	___
4	400	___	___	___
5	460	___	___	___
6	480	___	___	___

SECTION SUMMARY

a) *Total variable cost* is the dollar amount of variable inputs incurred in producing output, and from this we get

$$MC = \frac{\Delta \text{ TVC}}{\Delta \text{ total output}} \quad \text{or} \quad \frac{\Delta \text{ TC}}{\Delta \text{ total output}}$$

$$AVC = \frac{\text{TVC}}{\text{total output}}$$

b) Two very important *relationships* are as follows:

 • MP is at a maximum when (the number of inputs being used are able to produce an output where) MC is at a minimum.

 • AP is at a maximum when (the number of inputs being used are able to produce an output where) AVC is at a minimum.

6.5   Total Costs and Average Total Costs

LO5   List and graph the seven specific cost definitions used by economists.

We have established the fundamental relationship between productivity and costs. Our next step is to complete our discussion of costs by reminding ourselves that in the short run, any production process involves at least one fixed factor, so we need to add the concept of fixed cost to our analysis. **Total fixed costs**, in contrast to variable costs, do not vary with the level of output. In fact, fixed costs remain the same, whether output is 0, 100, 1000, or 100 000. Examples of fixed costs are a long-term lease, a business licence, and an insurance policy.

The data we derived for Total Totes were helpful in understanding the important relationship between productivity and costs. However, they are less useful when we add in the fixed costs. This is simply because we need to see what happens, not when we add in an additional amount of an *input* like an extra worker, but when a firm produces another unit of *output*. That being the case, we are now going to introduce a new set of figures—those experienced by Rosemary, who runs a small pottery business out of her home, and faces very low fixed costs because she is able to rent kiln time at the local school.

TABLE 6.4
The Complete Table of Costs

1	2	3	4	5	6	7	8
Output (per week) (Q)	TVC	AVC	MC	TFC	AFC	TC	ATC
0	0	/	/	$30	/	$ 30	/
1	$ 20	$20.00	$20	30	$30.00	50	$50.00
2	28	14.00	8	30	15.00	58	29.00
3	42	14.00	14	30	10.00	72	24.00
4	60	15.00	18	30	7.50	90	22.50
5	82	16.40	22	30	6.00	112	22.40
6	110	18.33	28	30	5.00	140	23.33
7	148	21.14	38	30	4.28	178	25.43
8	198	24.75	50	30	3.75	228	28.50

Note that the new data in **Table 6.4** (unlike **Table 6.3**) show what happens to costs as we increase *output* one unit at a time rather than investigating the effects of increasing *inputs* one unit at a time. This will make our calculations much easier.

The first column is simply the output (or total product) per week of the large vases that Rosemary specializes in. Columns 2, 3, and 4 have been explained. Column 5 is the total fixed cost. In this example, we assume it to be $30 per week. Next, we have **average fixed costs** (AFC), which are simply

$$AFC = \frac{TFC}{\text{total output (Q)}} \qquad [6.7]$$

Looking down column 6, we see that average fixed cost declines continuously as output rises. To obtain **total cost** (TC) (column 7), we simply do a summation.

$$TC = TVC + TFC \qquad [6.8]$$

Total cost rises continuously as output rises, and the *rate* of rise also begins to increase once diminishing returns set in.

Finally, **average total cost** (ATC) is

$$ATC = \frac{TC}{\text{total output (Q)}} \qquad [6.9]$$

We know that

$$TC = TVC + TFC$$

If we divide both sides by output (Q), we obtain

$$\frac{TC}{Q} = \frac{TVC}{Q} + \frac{TFC}{Q}$$

which is the same as

$$ATC = AVC + AFC \qquad [6.10]$$

Two more equations are useful to know. First, since marginal cost is the change in (or addition to) total variable cost, if we add up all the additions, we get

$$\Sigma MC = TVC \qquad [6.11]$$

(Σ means "the summation of.")

Note that since fixed costs do not change with output, any change in total variable costs will also change total cost by exactly the same amount. Given this, we have the last of our formulas:

$$MC = \frac{\Delta \text{ total cost } (\Delta TC)}{\Delta \text{ total output } (\Delta Q)}$$ [6.12]

You will note that we have two equations for marginal cost (MC): equations 6.5 and 6.12. You may use either one—they are equivalent, because the only change that occurs to total cost is as a result of a change in total variable cost.

Furthermore, the relationship between marginal cost and *average variable cost* that we stressed earlier in this chapter also applies to the interaction between marginal cost and *average total cost*. As long as marginal cost is below average total cost, average total cost will fall (as it does for the first units of output in Table 6.4). But as soon as marginal cost rises above average total cost, the latter will begin to rise. Given this basic relationship, it is also true that the marginal cost curve will intersect the average total cost curve at the latter's minimum point. This can be seen at point *b* in Figure 6.3, where we now put the quantity of output on the horizontal axis and dollar costs on the vertical.

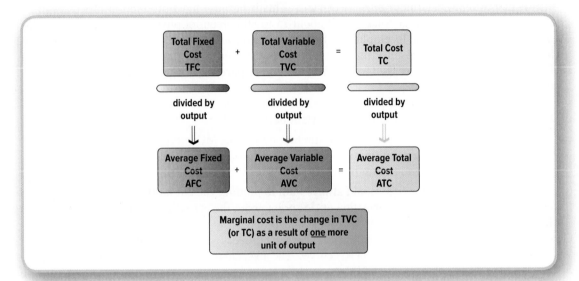

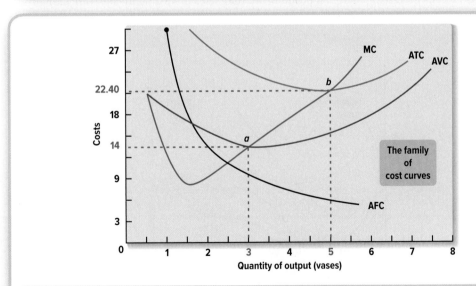

FIGURE 6.3   The MC, ATC, AVC, and AFC Curves

The U-shaped marginal cost curve intersects the average variable cost curve at its minimum point (*a*), which is an output of 3 units and a cost of \$14. It also intersects the average total cost curve at its minimum point (*b*), which is 5 units and \$22.40. The average fixed cost curve declines continuously.

Using this figure as a visual representation, let us pull things together:

- Both the U-shaped marginal cost curve and the saucer-shaped AVC curve reflect the advantages of the division of labour as it declines and then, as it rises, the law of diminishing returns.
- Marginal cost is initially below the average variable cost curve and the average total cost curve but then rises above each of these, which explains their basic saucer shape.
- The marginal cost curve intersects the average variable cost curve at its minimum point and the average total cost curve at its minimum point.
- The average fixed cost curve continuously declines.

Let us now focus on point *a*, the minimum point of the average variable cost curve. Note that this occurs at an output of 3 vases. Since the average variable cost curve is an upside-down image of the average product curve, we know that the average product curve must be at its maximum. Next, note that the minimum point on the average total cost curve is at an output of 5 vases (point *b*). Such an output level is defined by economists as **economic capacity**. Graphically, this simply means the lowest point on the average total cost curve. Economic capacity does not mean that the firm is operating at maximum *physical* capacity. This is because most production processes probably reach minimum average total cost at about 75 to 80 percent of physical capacity. Comparing points *a* and *b* enables us to emphasize that the most productive point (point *a* on the graph), where average product is at a maximum, is *not* the lowest average cost point (point *b* on the graph). This is simply a reflection of the fact that fixed costs are part of average total costs, but not part of average variable costs.

To help you get a good grasp of these various points, **Figure 6.4** shows a standard version of the three most important curves and three important output levels:

- the point of diminishing returns (minimum point of the MC curve)
- the most productive point (minimum point of the AVC curve)
- economic capacity (minimum point of the ATC curve)

Can we conclude that a firm would always want to produce the output that minimizes ATC? Not necessarily, since we have no information at this point about the price the firm receives when it sells the product. We will sort this out in Chapters 8, 9, 10, and 11.

Let us now look at the corresponding total curves. **Figure 6.5** graphs the total cost (TC), total variable cost (TVC), and total fixed cost (TFC) curves. The TVC curve starts at the origin because variable costs are zero when output is zero and rises slowly at first which reflects the declining average variable cost (which also means increasing marginal product) but then rises more quickly later (reflecting rising

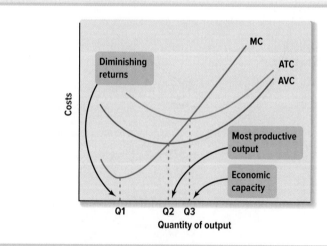

FIGURE 6.4   **Three Important Cost Curves**

Q_1 is the point of diminishing returns where MC is lowest (and where MP is highest). The most productive output is Q_2 where AVC is lowest (AP is highest). Q_3 is economic capacity where ATC is lowest.

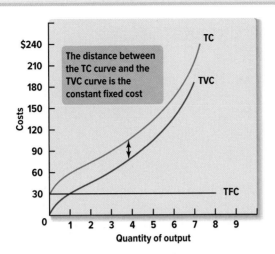

FIGURE 6.5   The TC, TVC, and TFC Curves

The total cost curve begins at $30 (the amount of fixed cost) and rises from there. The total variable cost curve starts at the origin, since variable cost is zero when there is no output. The total fixed cost curve is horizontal, reflecting the fact that the fixed cost of $30 does not vary with output. The difference between the TC and TVC is this constant $30.

average variable cost). The TC curve starts at $30 because total fixed costs are equal to this level even when output is zero. In fact, the TC curve looks just like the TVC curve; it is simply shifted upward by the amount of fixed cost. The TFC curve starts at the same $30 and does not vary with output.

Let us now take a look back at the data in Table 6.4 and ask how many vases per week Rosemary would want to produce. The lowest ATC is achieved when she produces five a week. Would she ever choose to produce six, seven, or even more? The answer to this question, once again, is simply that it depends on how much she gets for each vase when she sells them. For example, if she is able to sell her vases for $30 each, she would be willing to produce more than just five vases despite the fact that her ATC would be higher than when five are produced.

 ADDED DIMENSION

Zero Marginal Costs

There is currently a debate about whether marginal costs exist when it comes to software engineering products sold as apps for use on cell phones and tablets. On the one side of the debate is the idea that the next download of Angry Birds or Evernote has zero incremental cost to the parent firm that engineered these applications. Thus there are no marginal costs.

In contrast, others argue that more apps sold means that the cost of email and phone support provided to users obviously rises, and this clearly fits the definition of marginal costs. Furthermore, as sales of the apps increase, the likelihood of needed updates increases, and this is a variable cost directly tied to sales (output) and thus to marginal costs.

So do we have any clear-cut examples where marginal costs are clearly zero (or at least very close to zero)? The answer is "of course." Think of the MC of selling one more ticket to a partially full movie theatre or one more ticket on an airplane flight that has empty seats. Other examples are one additional admittance to a flower garden or an amusement park. A recent intriguing event is the release of Jeremy Rifkin's new book *The Zero MC Society*, which invites the reader to imagine a world in which almost everything produced has a marginal cost approaching zero. His radical conclusions—foretelling the eclipse of our current economic system and the rise of the "collaboratists"—promise to generate much debate.

TEST YOUR UNDERSTANDING

6. Fill in the blanks in the table below:

Output (per day)	TC	TVC	AVC	TFC	AFC	ATC	MC
0	$200	0	/	___	/	/	/
1	280	___	___	___	___	___	___
2	340	___	___	___	___	___	___
3	420	___	___	___	___	___	___
4	520	___	___	___	___	___	___
5	640	___	___	___	___	___	___
6	780	___	___	___	___	___	___

SECTION SUMMARY

a) *Total cost* is

$$TC = TVC + TFC$$

From this, we get

$$AFC = \frac{TFC}{total\ output}; ATC = \frac{TC}{total\ output}$$

and

$$ATC = AVC + AFC$$

b) Graphically, the *MC curve* is U-shaped and intersects

- the AVC curve at its minimum, indicating the most productive output
- the ATC curve at its minimum, indicating economic capacity

c) Three important outputs are

- lowest minimum MC (where diminishing returns start)
- lowest AVC (most productive output)
- lowest ATC (economic capacity)

6.6   How Can a Firm Cut Costs?

> **LO6**   Explain the meanings of *increasing productivity* and *cutting costs*.

There is occasional discussion in the media about the need for firms to cut costs. Unfortunately, this phrase is, by itself, ambiguous. A firm can always cut *total* cost by decreasing output. But surely this is not what is meant by the urgent calls for reductions in costs. When firms speak of cutting costs, what they mean is a reduction in *average* costs rather than total costs. But first, we need to make one point clear. So far, our presentation of costs is based on the assumption that the firm is already producing at the lowest possible cost *for each output level*. In other words, it is producing efficiently. (We will have more to say about efficiency in Chapter 9.) Given this, is it possible for average costs to get any lower? Yes, if the firm is able to buy its inputs cheaper. The firm often has little control over the prices of the inputs it buys, but these prices can and do change from time to time. It is possible that the price of either the fixed or the variable inputs might change. Let us consider the effect of a decrease in the price of a variable input.

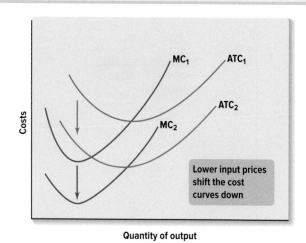

Quantity of output

FIGURE 6.6   A Shift in the Marginal and Average Total Cost Curves

The shift down in the marginal cost curve—MC_1 to MC_2—and in the accompanying average total cost curve—ATC_1 to ATC_2—is the result of input prices decreasing.

In graphical terms, such a decrease would shift down the marginal, average variable, and average total cost curves. For our analysis, we isolate the average total and the marginal cost curves in Figure 6.6 to illustrate such a shift.

In Figure 6.6, the marginal cost curve shifts down as a result of a decrease in the input price of the variable input such that the minimum point of the curve occurs at a lower dollar cost but at the same level of output. There is also a corresponding shift in the average total cost curve. We have not shown the average variable cost curve, but if we had, it would also shift down. The basic shapes of the curves remain unchanged, however, since the law of diminishing returns still applies. Would the average fixed cost curve also shift down? Only if the price of the fixed input(s) decreased. Similarly, the curves would shift up if input prices increased.

There is another possibility. Recall that the marginal cost of output is determined by the marginal product of the factor inputs. What if marginal product were to increase? This would decrease marginal cost, which would pull both average variable and average total cost down as well. And what might cause this increase in productivity leading to a decrease in costs? It might be something as simple as replacing older, inefficient machines with newer, more efficient ones. For example, a new photocopier might make the small staff of a law firm more productive. To put it more generally, costs could fall as a result of introducing a smarter way of producing. In other words, **technological improvement**, as long as it does not involve a new-size plant, will have a significant impact on productivity and therefore on a firm's costs.

However, as mentioned, we do need to be careful here, since often applying a new technology does often involve a new size of plant. That takes us to the subject of the long run, which we deal with in Chapter 7. We can say, however, that if the marginal product of a productive process increases, the cost of production will decrease, even in the short run.

A firm's cost will fall if factor prices decrease or a technological improvement is introduced.

If neither resource prices nor productivity change, is there any other way that a firm can reduce average costs? Certainly this will *not* be possible if the firm is already producing the output that results in the lowest average cost—that is, if it is at economic capacity.

Would firms ever want to operate at an output that is less than economic capacity? No. But firms are sometimes forced to reduce output because of market conditions. The consequences of this are illustrated in Figure 6.7. Here, we assume that market conditions have forced the firm to choose an output of Q_2 with average total costs of ATC_2, which are higher than they would be at economic capacity (ATC_1). This is what economists describe as **excess capacity**, defined as the situation in which the firm's output is less than economic capacity. Excess capacity is inefficient in the sense that average total costs are not at a minimum. In summary, if a firm has excess capacity, average costs could

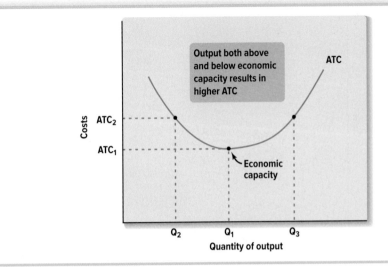

FIGURE 6.7   A Firm Experiencing Excess Capacity

If market conditions force a firm to operate at output level Q_2, its average total costs (ATC_2) will be higher than they would be if the firm operated at economic capacity (Q_1). Similarly, a firm will have a higher average cost if it is operating above economic capacity, such as Q_3.

be cut by *increasing* output. However, this option may not be available to the firm if it does not have sufficient orders for its product. We will refer to this concept again in Chapter 11.

Conversely, would firms want to operate at an output level above this capacity, say output Q_3, despite the higher average cost? Perhaps in the short run they would, if demand and prices were particularly high, but no firm wants to produce above economic capacity indefinitely. The cost in terms of overtime pay and wear and tear on machinery can become prohibitive. Given this, it is likely that the firm will soon be looking to move into larger premises. (This is what we mean by the long run, the subject of the next chapter, Chapter 7.)

IT'S NEWS TO ME ...

Researchers at the University of Twente (Netherlands) just released an update on their work on developing computer models that can make industrial-production processes significantly more accurate and therefore cheaper. These models (which can be purchased for a relatively modest one-time expenditure which then become a sunk cost) use engineered software that, like a weather prediction model, can predict the simulated outcomes of various sets of circumstances. This enables detection of abnormalities in the metal forming process such as the effects of wear and tear in the machinery, or variations in the blend of lubrication, used to mass produce parts for things like automobiles or airplanes. The result is the mass production of parts that have consistent quality and thereby reduces the need to re-machine parts that fail to meet pre-determined specifications.

One engineer-observer from the BMW auto corporation said: "This is a significant step forward in the use of IT in our industry and will result in significant cost savings."

Source: *Star Power Reporting,* February 2017.

I. Which of the following is true as a result of the application of the computer model?

    a) Marginal cost would be unaffected.

    b) Fixed cost would be unaffected.

    c) Both average variable cost and average fixed would decrease.

    d) Fixed cost would increase and average variable cost would decrease.

II. How would the application of the above computer model affect the firm's cost curves?

    a) It would shift the ATC curve down.

    b) It would shift the MC curve down.

    c) It would shift both the AVC and the MC curves down.

    d) None of the above.

TEST YOUR UNDERSTANDING

Inputs	Total Output	TC_1	MC_1	ATC_1	TC_2	MC_2	ATC_2
0	0	$150	/	/	——	/	/
1	10	175	——	——	——	——	——
2	25	200	——	——	——	——	——
3	35	225	——	——	——	——	——
4	40	250	——	——	——	——	——
5	42	275	——	——	——	——	——

7. a) Fill in the blanks in the MC_1 and ATC_1 columns above.

   b) Assuming that the price of the variable inputs decreases by $5, fill in the TC_2, MC_2, and ATC_2 columns.

8. Given the graph shown here:

   a) At what output do diminishing returns begin?

   b) What is the most productive output?

   c) What output is economic capacity?

   d) When output is 250, what does *ab* represent?

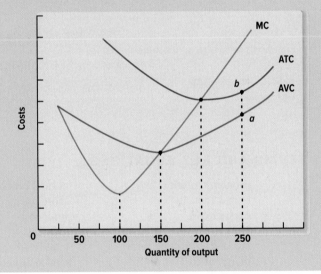

SECTION SUMMARY

a) MC, AVC, and ATC decrease (and, graphically, their respective curves shift down) if prices of variable input fall.

b) Only the ATC will decrease if the price of the fixed input falls.

c) The two factors that will cause a drop in costs are

   • a fall in input prices

   • an improvement in technology

Study Guide

Review

WHAT'S THE BIG IDEA?

The key term in this chapter is *average total costs*. This is because in later chapters we will be comparing this to the price at which the firm sells its products. The selling price is the amount of revenue the firm receives for each unit it sells, so comparing this with the unit, or average, cost makes sense. The interesting aspect of average (total) cost is that it varies according to the level of production. This means that it really isn't possible to state how much it costs a firm to produce, say, a car, a computer, or even a case of beer, because it all depends how much is being produced. If the firm produces only a small quantity, its average costs are likely to be very high.

There are two reasons for this. First, the fixed costs have to be spread over only a small number of units. (If a car manufacturer has fixed costs of $1 billion and only produces one car, that's going to be the most expensive car ever produced!) Second, with only a small level of production, it is not really possible to enjoy all the benefits of the division of labour. It follows that the more the firm produces, the lower the average cost of production, as it will be able to practise the division of labour and at the same time the share of fixed costs per unit will continue to fall.

So higher production levels mean lower average costs of production. However, there is a limit to this. At some point, diminishing returns kick in. All this means is that if the size of the manufacturing plant is fixed (and this is true in the short run), eventually it will become too small and productivity will start to fall. This will cause the average costs to begin rising.

It is therefore possible both for a firm to produce too little and for it to produce too much. If we ignore the price of the product, the best output is one at which average cost is at its lowest. And this is what is meant by the economic capacity.

NEW GLOSSARY TERMS AND KEY EQUATIONS

average fixed cost	economic profit	normal profit
average product	excess capacity	short run
average total cost	explicit cost	sunk costs
average variable cost	implicit cost	total cost
depreciation	law of diminishing returns	total fixed costs
division of labour	marginal cost	total product
economic capacity	marginal product	total variable cost

Equations:

[6.1]   Total accounting profit = total revenue − total explicit costs

[6.2]   Total economic profit = total revenue − total costs (implicit and explicit)

[6.3] $MP_L = \dfrac{\Delta TP}{\Delta L}$

[6.4] $AP_L = \dfrac{TP}{L}$

[6.5] $MC = \dfrac{\Delta TVC}{\Delta \text{total output}}$

[6.6] $AVC = \dfrac{TVC}{\text{total output}}$

[6.7] $AFC = \dfrac{TFC}{\text{total output}}$

[6.8]   TC = TVC + TFC

[6.9]   ATC = $\dfrac{\text{TC}}{\text{total output}}$

[6.10] ATC = AVC + AFC

[6.11] ΣMC = TVC

[6.12] MC = $\dfrac{\Delta \text{ total cost}}{\Delta \text{ total output}}$

Comprehensive Problem

(LO 3, 4, 5) Last summer Daniel started the Custom Made Pot Company, which specializes in earthenware pots. The number of pots produced each week varies with the number of workers he employs as shown in Table 6.5.

TABLE 6.5

Number of Workers	TP	MP	AP
1	4	——	——
2	16	——	——
3	36	——	——
4	50	——	——
5	60	——	——
6	60	——	——

Questions

a) Fill in the marginal and average product columns in Table 6.5.
b) On the graph in Figure 6.8, plot and label the two curves.

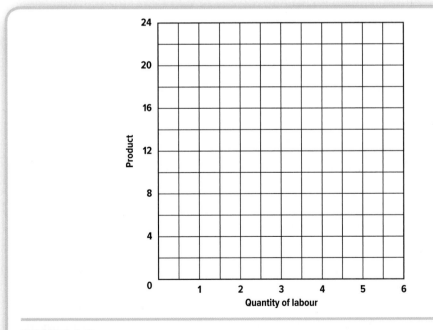

FIGURE 6.8

Answers

a) See Table 6.5 (Completed).

TABLE 6.5 (COMPLETED)

Number of Workers	TP	MP	AP
1	4	4	4
2	16	12	8
3	36	20	12
4	50	14	12.5
5	60	10	12
6	60	0	10

b) See **Figure** 6.8 (Completed).

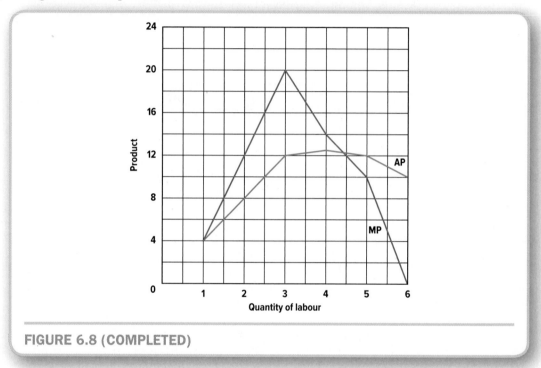

FIGURE 6.8 (COMPLETED)

Questions

c) Assuming that each worker costs $300 a day (wages and materials), and Custom Made Pot has weekly fixed costs of $480, fill in Table 6.6.

TABLE 6.6

Number of Workers	TP = Output	TVC	TFC	TC	AVC	ATC	MC
1	4	—	—	—	—	—	—
2	16	—	—	—	—	—	—
3	36	—	—	—	—	—	—
4	50	—	—	—	—	—	—
5	60	—	—	—	—	—	—
6	60	—	—	—	—	—	—

d) On the graph in **Figure** 6.9, plot the following points showing the quantity and dollar amounts. Mark each plot with the corresponding letters:

- point of diminishing returns (D)
- most productive point (P)
- economic capacity (E)

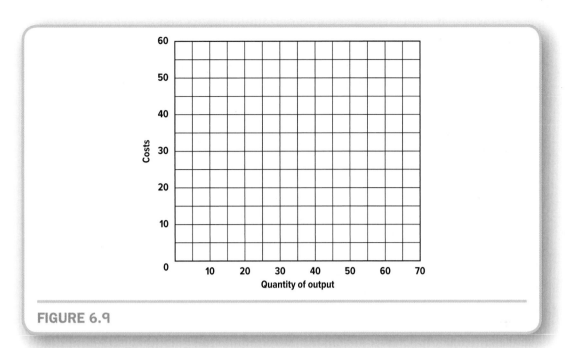

FIGURE 6.9

Answers

c) See Table 6.6 (Completed).

TABLE 6.6 (COMPLETED)

Number of Workers	TP = Output	TVC	TFC	TC	AVC	ATC	MC
1	4	$300	$480	$ 780	$75	$195	$75
2	16	600	480	1080	37.5	67.5	25
3	36	900	480	1380	25	38.3	15
4	50	1200	480	1680	24	33.6	21.4
5	60	1500	480	1980	25	33	30
6	60	1800	480	2280	30	38	∞

d) See Figure 6.9 (Completed).

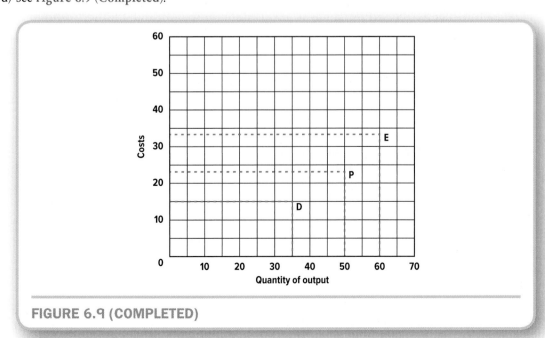

FIGURE 6.9 (COMPLETED)

Study Problems

Find answers on the McGraw-Hill online resource.

Basic (Problems 1–5)

1. **(LO 3)** Table 6.7 shows the total product for a firm. Complete the average and marginal products.

TABLE 6.7

Units of Labour	Total Product	Average Product	Marginal Product
0	0	——	——
1	12	——	——
2	30	——	——
3	54	——	——
4	68	——	——
5	80	——	——
6	84	——	——
7	77	——	——

2. **(LO 5)** Table 6.8 shows the total fixed and variable costs of a firm. Complete the table.

TABLE 6.8

Output	TFC	TVC	TC	AFC	AVC	ATC	MC
1	1200	400	——	——	——	——	——
2	1200	600	——	——	——	——	——
3	1200	720	——	——	——	——	——
4	1200	800	——	——	——	——	——
5	1200	1500	——	——	——	——	——
6	1200	3000	——	——	——	——	——
7	1200	5250	——	——	——	——	——

3. **(LO 3)**
   a) Complete Table 6.9 for Bannister Inc.

TABLE 6.9

Number of Workers	Total Product	Average Product	Marginal Product
1	2	——	——
2	5	——	——
3	——	3	——
4	——	——	3
5	14	——	——
6	——	——	1
7	15	——	——

b) How many workers are being used when the point of diminishing returns is first apparent?
_____

c) How many workers are being used when total product is at a maximum? _____
d) What is the most productive output? _____

4. **(LO 5)** The data in Table 6.10 are for the Quite Small Blueberry Farm. The quantities are for the number of tonnes of berries per year.

TABLE 6.10	
Quantity	**Total Cost**
0	$2000
1	2400
2	2700
3	2800
4	2860
5	3000

a) What is the amount of TFC? _____
b) What is the MC of the third tonne produced? _____
c) What is the TVC of producing 4 tonnes? _____
d) What is the ATC of producing 2 tonnes? _____

5. **(LO 2)** Emily recently graduated with a B.A. in economics and was offered a job with a small but growing company for $38 400 per year. About the same time, Emily inherited $60 000. She decided to pass up the job and use her inheritance to purchase a bubble tea shop rather than put the money into a bond fund (as her uncle suggested), which would have paid 5 percent per year interest. Emily works full time at her new business, and at the end of the year she had revenues of $81 000 and total explicit costs of $42 000.
a) What was Emily's accounting profit or loss for the year? _____
b) What was her economic profit or loss for the year? _____

Intermediate (Problems 6–9)

6. **(LO 5)** Table 6.11 shows some of the costs of production for a the Clean-Cut Chain Saws manufacturing company.

Output	Total Cost ($)	Total Variable Cost	Marginal Cost	Average Total Cost	Average Variable Cost	Average Fixed Cost
0	2520	___	/	/	/	/
1	3420	___	___	___	___	___
2	4040	___	___	___	___	___
3	4500	___	___	___	___	___
4	4920	___	___	___	___	___
5	5220	___	___	___	___	___
6	5520	___	___	___	___	___
7	6300	___	___	___	___	___
8	7320	___	___	___	___	___
9	9720	___	___	___	___	___

TABLE 6.11

a) Complete the table.
b) What is the value of total fixed cost? $_____
c) What is the most productive level of output? _____
d) At what output is economic capacity? _____
e) If TFC doubled, what is the marginal cost of the 8th unit? $_____

7. **(LO 5)** Table 6.12 shows data for Big Bob's Brewing Company. The quantities are for large vats of beer.

TABLE 6.12

Output	TFC	TVC	TC	MC	AFC	AVC	ATC
0	$210	0	—	/	/	/	/
1	—	—	—	$100	—	—	—
2	—	—	—	60	—	—	—
3	—	—	—	50	—	—	—
4	—	—	—	80	—	—	—
5	—	—	—	100	—	—	—
6	—	—	—	126	—	—	—
7	—	—	—	156	—	—	—
8	—	—	—	190	—	—	—

a) Fill in the blanks in the table.
b) At what level of output is average product at a maximum? _____
c) What is the value of average total cost at this output level? _____
d) What is the output at economic capacity? _____
e) If fixed costs were to double, what would be the marginal cost of the fifth unit of output?
   $_____

8. **(LO 4, 5)** Table 6.13 gives data for a firm named Crystal Clear Speech Writing Services. Fill in the blanks in the table.

TABLE 6.13

Output	AFC	AVC	ATC	MC	TVC	TC
1	—	—	—	40	—	—
2	—	—	—	—	70	—
3	—	—	90	—	—	—
4	40	—	—	—	—	320
5	—	—	—	70	—	—
6	—	55	—	—	—	—
7	—	—	—	—	480	—
8	—	—	—	—	—	840

9. **(LO 5)**

a) Fill in the blank columns in Table 6.14 for the firm Bannister Railings, assuming that the cost of variable inputs decreases by 50 percent.

TABLE 6.14

Output	TVC_1	TVC_2	AVC_1	AVC_2	MC_1	MC_2
1	$ 44	——	$44.00	——	$44.00	——
2	64	——	32.00	——	20.00	——
3	78	——	26.00	——	14.00	——
4	88	——	22.00	——	10.00	——
5	100	——	20.00	——	12.00	——
6	120	——	20.00	——	20.00	——
7	150	——	21.42	——	30.00	——
8	200	——	25.00	——	50.00	——

b) In **Figure** 6.10 sketch in the AVC_1, MC_1, AVC_2, and MC_2 curves. (You need not plot in each point, but place each curve with its lowest point in the correct position on the grid.)

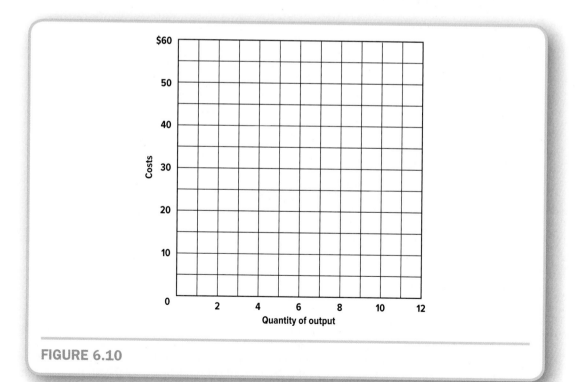

FIGURE 6.10

Advanced (Problems 10–12)

10. **(LO 3)** Figure 6.11 is for the Grow 'Em Right Nursery.

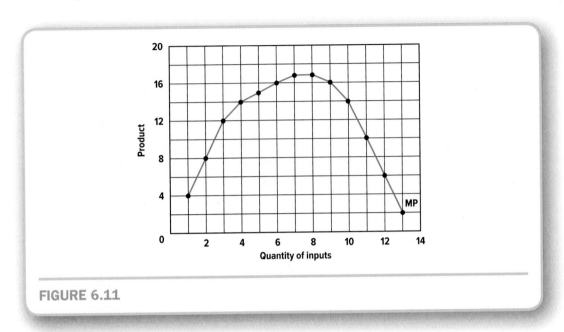

FIGURE 6.11

a) Fill in the Marginal, Total, and Average Product columns in Table 6.15.

TABLE 6.15

Quantity	Marginal Product	Total Product	Average Product
1	——	——	——
2	——	——	——
3	——	——	——
4	——	——	——
5	——	——	——
6	——	——	——
7	——	——	——
8	——	——	——
9	——	——	——
10	——	——	——
11	——	——	——
12	——	——	——
13	——	——	——

b) Add the AP curve to Figure 6.11
c) What is the value of maximum AP? _____

11. **(LO 6)** A firm has a choice of two different technologies to produce its product. The first technology has a total fixed cost of $1200 and a constant marginal cost of $200. The second has a total fixed cost of $2000 and a constant marginal cost of $60. Use Table 6.16 to gather the information needed to determine the output levels at which Technology I would give the lowest total cost, and those output levels at which Technology II would give the lowest total cost.

TABLE 6.16

Output	TC I	MC I	TC II	MC II
0	——	——	——	——
1	——	——	——	——
2	——	——	——	——
3	——	——	——	——
4	——	——	——	——
5	——	——	——	——
6	——	——	——	——
7	——	——	——	——
8	——	——	——	——
9	——	——	——	——
10	——	——	——	——

12. **(LO 3, 4, 5)** Table 6.17 shows the cost data of a furniture manufacturer named Cindy's Custom Made.

TABLE 6.17

Output of Chairs	Total Hours	Average Hours per Chair	Marginal Hours per Chair	TVC	AVC	TFC	TC	ATC	MC
1	5	——	——	——	——	180	——	——	——
2	9	——	——	——	——	——	——	——	——
3	12	——	——	——	——	——	——	——	——
4	18	——	——	——	——	——	——	——	——
5	25	——	——	——	——	——	——	——	——
6	36	——	——	——	——	——	——	——	——

a) Complete the table, assuming that labour and materials cost $12 an hour.
b) What is the most productive output? _____
c) What are AVC and ATC at this quantity? _____
d) What is the output at economic capacity? _____

Problems for Further Study

Basic (Problems 1–4)

1. **(LO 4, 5)** Which of the following are fixed costs (F) and which are variable costs (V)?
   a) a business licence _____
   b) the setup costs for a computerized payroll accounting system _____
   c) production cost for materials and supplies _____
   d) production staff wages _____
   e) leasehold costs for the firm's land and buildings _____

2. **(LO 2)** Distinguish between explicit cost and implicit cost.

3. **(LO 3)** Define the terms *total product, average product,* and *marginal product.*

4. **(LO 1)** Name and describe *three* different types of private, for-profit firms (business organizations).

Intermediate (Problems 5–7)

5. **(LO 3)** What is the relationship between the AP/MP curves and the AVC/MC curves?

6. **(LO 3)** What is excess capacity?

7. **(LO 4)** Given the cost curves in Figure 6.12:
   a) At what output do diminishing returns begin? _____
   b) What is the most productive output? _____
   c) What output is economic capacity? _____

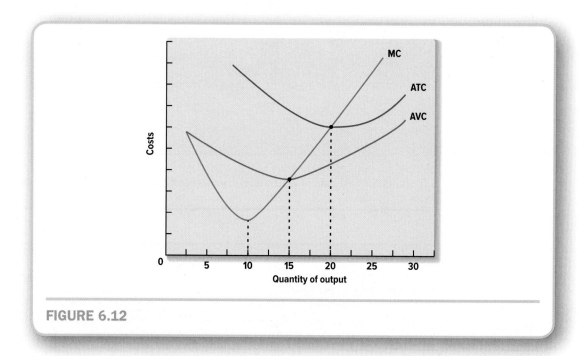

FIGURE 6.12

Advanced (Problems 8–11)

8. **(LO 2, 3)** It has been observed that all the members of farming families in developing countries often work intensively on small pieces of land. Is this rational?

9. **(LO 2)** What is the cost for the Toronto Maple Leafs to give a local girls' and boys' club fifty free tickets to a hockey game? Does it matter for what game the tickets are offered?

10. **(LO 2)** David recently graduated with a B.A. in economics and was offered a job with a large company that pays $44 000 per year. At about the same time, David's grandfather died and left him an inheritance of $45 000. David decided to pass up the job, and using $39 000 from the inheritance he purchased a tool rental business. (David put the other $6 000 into a savings account that pays 9 percent annual interest.) He put his full effort into the new business, and in the first three months of operation he had total sales revenues of $29 500 and total explicit costs of $14 260.
    a) What is David's accounting profit for the period? _____
    b) What is David's economic profit for the period? _____

11. **(LO 3)**
    a) What output corresponds to the point of diminishing returns?
    b) What output corresponds to the point of maximum productivity?
    c) What output corresponds to the point of economic capacity?

CHAPTER 7
Costs in the Long Run

LEARNING OBJECTIVES

At the end of this chapter, you should be able to:

LO1 Distinguish between the short run and the long run.

LO2 Explain why medium-sized firms are sometimes just as efficient as big firms.

LO3 Demonstrate why big firms sometimes enjoy great cost advantages.

LO4 Demonstrate why firms can sometimes be too big.

LO5 Explain what is meant by the right size of firm.

LO6 Explain the effect of technological and input price changes on a firm's cost.

LO7 Explain why markets can sometimes be too small.

WHAT'S AHEAD...

In this chapter, we continue discussing costs but shift the focus from the short run to the long run. We define what economists mean by the long run and explain how it relates to the size of the firm. We show why there are great advantages for a firm to be big, but also look at what happens when firms get too big. Finally, we discuss the idea of the right size of firm by looking at the concept of minimum efficient scale.

A QUESTION OF RELEVANCE ...

If we think of all the different products you and I purchase, it is apparent that we could produce some for ourselves—tomatoes, cookies, and even a birdhouse. So why do we buy the things we could make ourselves? And why is it that something as comparatively simple to make as a cardboard box is produced in giant factories, whereas highly complex computers are produced in small workshops that dot the countrysides of Asian countries? Why, for that matter, aren't furniture factories as big as car assembly plants, and why aren't aluminum smelters as small as dairy plants? The answers to these questions involve the concept of economies of scale, the central theme of this chapter.

This chapter rounds out our discussion of the costs of production. The focus is on the long run, which allows us to address two significant issues: the role of technology in raising productivity and enabling economic growth and the importance of economies of scale (which we will define in Section 7.3) in explaining the dramatic rise in international trade.

7.1   The Short and the Long Run

> **LO1**   Distinguish between the short run and the long run.

In the discussion about the costs of production in the previous chapter, we made the assumption that at least one factor of production, in any given production process, was fixed. This is what we referred to as the short run. In contrast, economists define the **long run** as a period in which the producing firm has the option of changing *all* of its inputs. In other words, in the long run there are no fixed factors and all inputs are variable.

There is a technique to thinking about the long run. You should recognize that at *any one point in time*, the firm is always in the short run. Imagine a factory manager as she steps out of her office onto the shop floor. Are any of the factor inputs used in production fixed? Of course. At least one, and probably several, will be: the square footage of the plant, the number of machines, or the quantity of some crucial raw material. Firms are always operating in the short run, and as a result the reality of diminishing marginal product is present.

Now, imagine that manager walking back into her office and closing the door as she sits down to ask herself: Where do we want to be in five years? As she proceeds to answer this question, she is able to treat all inputs as variable. She is able to conceptualize the long run. It is in this sense that economists describe the long run as a planning horizon:

> In real time, all production processes operate in the short run, and diminishing marginal productivity is an unavoidable reality.

> In the conception of the long run, there are no fixed factors, and diminishing marginal productivity does not apply. All costs are variable.

It is important to note that the distinction between the short run and the long run is not made in terms of specific periods of time. Suppose you are a manufacturer of window blinds operating from a medium-sized plant and are pleased to note that the number of orders has increased dramatically over the past month. How do you react? Well, you obviously need more resources to increase production. Getting more material supplies presents no great difficulty: it really entails nothing more than picking up the phone and increasing your normal order from your supplier. You have a number of options as far as increasing the amount of labour is concerned: you can ask your staff to work overtime or come in at weekends, or you can even hire more workers, temporarily or permanently. It may be just as easy to buy or rent extra machines, as long as they are not too specialized. These are all variable factors that in most cases are easy to increase or decrease. The one factor that may be very difficult to change is the size of your premises. There are two major reasons for this. First, it will probably be very expensive in terms of moving costs and in the disruption of business. Second, and more importantly, most firms lease their premises, which means that they are not able to leave— except at the cost of a big penalty—until the lease is up. If the lease ends in three months, this is the short-run period for our firm; however, if there are still five years to go, that is the length of the short run. In other words, it is often difficult to get more of certain factors of production, be it a special-iszed machine or worker or extra production space. The short run, then, is the period of time during which these particular factors are fixed, and this period will vary from firm to firm.

We now need to elaborate on this very important short-run/long-run distinction by carefully developing the **long-run average cost curve** (LRAC). Note that for the balance of this chapter we will use the term *average cost* to refer to the short run (rather than *average total cost* as we did in the previous chapter) and *long-run average cost* for the long run.

SECTION SUMMARY

a) The short run is a period of time in which at least one factor of production is fixed.

b) The long run is a period of time in which there are no fixed factors of production; all factors are variable.

c) In most cases, the size of the premises is the fixed factor. It is difficult to quickly move because

- it is expensive to move and business will be interrupted
- the firm cannot move until it comes to the end of its lease

7.2 Constant Returns to Scale

> **LO2** Explain why medium-sized firms are sometimes just as efficient as big firms.

We begin this discussion by imagining a firm, Rising Sun Products Limited, that produces high-storage-capacity USB flash drives and operates in a small-sized plant, which we shall call plant 1. Further, we will assume that there are also three other plant sizes available to Rising Sun: plant 2, which is exactly twice the size of plant 1; plant 3, which is exactly three times the size of plant 1; and plant 4, which is exactly four times the size of plant 1. Some short-run average cost data are presented in Table 7.1.

TABLE 7.1
Rising Sun's Plant Size Alternatives

Output of Flash Drives per Day	AC in Plant 1	AC in Plant 2	AC in Plant 3	AC in Plant 4
100	$ 6.00	$ 7.00	$7.50	$8.00
200	5.00	6.00	6.50	7.10
300	6.00	5.50	6.00	6.50
400	8.00	**5.00**	5.70	6.00
500	11.00	5.50	5.30	5.80
600	15.00	6.00	**5.00**	5.50
700	20.00	7.00	5.30	5.20
800	26.00	8.00	5.70	**5.00**
900	33.00	9.50	6.00	5.20
1000	41.00	11.00	6.50	5.50

Remember from the previous chapter that economic capacity is defined as the output at which (short-run) average costs are at a minimum. From Table 7.1, we can see that in plant 1 (the present plant), economic capacity is achieved with an output of 200 flash drives per day. However, Rising Sun's reputation for producing a state-of-the-art product has been steadily growing within the industry, and it has increased production to 400 a day for the past couple of months just to meet customers' orders. The consequence of this strong demand, which the firm welcomes, is that its average costs have been running at $8 per unit, far above the minimum average cost level of $5. Something has to be done. Rising Sun must either refuse some customers' orders, which is undesirable; raise prices, which might have negative long-run consequences; or build a bigger plant that can handle the 400-per-day output and yet maintain average costs of $5.

Suppose the firm decides to build a larger plant. This decision leads to a management debate about the size of the new plant. One option is to think conservatively and opt for plant 2, which achieves minimum average costs of $5 at the current output level of 400 units per day. The second option is to anticipate even more growth in the future and opt for plant 3, which would require an output of 600 units a day to achieve the desired minimum average costs of $5. There are, however, two drawbacks associated with plant 3. The first is that it is more expensive to build, and the second is that if plant 3 is chosen, the current rate of production of 400 per day would only lower average costs to $5.70. Thus, building plant 3 would prove to be the right decision only if orders increase sufficiently to justify a production run that is higher than the current level. Since no one can predict the future with certainty, let us assume that a conservative decision is made to build plant 2.

In time the new plant is ready, and Rising Sun is able to handle the runs of 400 units per day at a reduced average total cost of $5. But the story does not end here. Our firm's fortunes continue to

Inventory is just one of the costs of production.

Source: Ryan McVay/Getty Images

grow, and sales rise to the point that production runs of 600 units a day are needed to keep up with commitments made to customers. As we can see in Table 7.1 (plant 2 column), this raises average cost to $6 in new plant 2, and Rising Sun is again faced with a major decision about the correct plant size for its operations. It could upgrade to plant 3 and reduce average costs (at current rates of output) to $5, or it could make the bold decision to build a new plant—plant 4—in anticipation of even more sales growth in the future. If Rising Sun does this, it faces the risk that future sales will decline, and it could again face high average costs.

As you can see, the long run involves planning—firms must try to anticipate the future. This is risky. Businesspeople do not always like taking risks, but doing so is often unavoidable.

Figure 7.1 is a graphical presentation of the average costs data from Table 7.1. Points *a*, *b*, *c*, and *d* in Figure 7.1 identify economic capacity in each of the four plant sizes, that is, where (short-run) average costs are at a minimum. By connecting these points, can we obtain a long-run average cost curve? Technically no, if these four different-sized plants are the *only* options. However, if we assume there are many other possible plant sizes, there would exist many other AC curves that have not been shown. Each of these would have a minimum point, and connecting all these points would give us something close to a horizontal LRAC curve, as shown in Figure 7.1. Let us make this assumption, and proceed with our focus remaining on the four plant sizes we've already mentioned.

In its long-run planning, Rising Sun must choose one of these four points as its daily production target. Which one it chooses would, of course, depend on its estimates of long-run production requirements, and that would depend on its estimates of future sales. However, once a decision is made, be it plant 1, 2, 3, or 4, the firm finds itself on one of the four (short-run) average cost curves. That is, it finds itself in the short run, where, at output levels above economic capacity, average cost rises. Thus, we say once again:

A firm can *plan* as if it is in the long run, but it always operates in the short run.

Returning to Figure 7.1, notice that the horizontal long-run average cost curve shown is a reflection of the concept of **constant returns to scale**. This term, used only in the context of the long run, refers to the situation in which output increases in exact proportion to an increase in inputs.

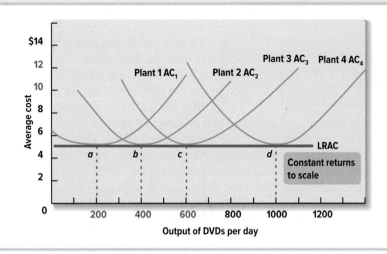

FIGURE 7.1   Average Costs of Production in Four Plant Sizes

Points *a*, *b*, *c*, and *d* are all points of minimum average costs in four different plant sizes. By connecting them, we obtain the long-run average cost curve.

Recall that, in this example, we assumed that plant 2 was exactly twice as large as plant 1. If we also assume that the amount of labour and materials being used in plant 2 is also exactly twice the quantity used in plant 1, and if we assume that the prices of these inputs do not change, the total cost of producing 400 units per day would be exactly twice the total cost of producing 200 units. This means the average costs will be the same in both cases. You can verify this by looking back at Table 7.1. Here, you will see that the minimum average cost for all the plants is the same—$5. These are the conditions that result in a horizontal long-run average cost curve, that is, constant returns to scale.

 TEST YOUR UNDERSTANDING

Find answers on the McGraw-Hill online resource.

1. The table here shows the average costs associated with three different plant sizes.

   a) Which plant is best suited to produce an output of 4 units?

   b) What is the value of long-run average cost?

Output	Plant 1 Average Cost	Plant 2 Average Cost	Plant 3 Average Cost
1	$45	$62	$80
2	36	47	63
3	42	36	49
4	55	44	36
5	70	68	52

SECTION SUMMARY

Constant returns to scale exist when an increase in a firm's inputs result in a proportional increase in output. The result is a horizontal LAS curve. In these cases, a medium-sized firm can be as efficient as a big firm.

7.3   Economies of Scale

LO3 Demonstrate why big firms sometimes enjoy great cost advantages.

To take our discussion of long-run costs one step further, we introduce a new firm, Deep Sea Concrete, which is currently producing 1000 cubic metres of concrete a day in plant 1. We will assume that the total cost of doing this is $40 000, which means that Deep Sea's average cost of production is currently $40 per metre.

Now let us assume that Deep Sea builds a larger plant that is exactly double its present size, which results in its total cost exactly doubling. What will happen to the average costs of production as a result? The answer very much depends on what happens to the level of output. With our last example, Rising Sun, a doubling of inputs led simply to a doubling of output. But in reality, this may or may not happen. In fact, in many cases, output could more than double and cause average costs to fall. This is what economists term **economies of scale**. Let us see how this works out in the case of Deep Sea.

Economies of scale in production have dramatically increased global trade.

Digital Vision

Let us assume that as a result of doubling its inputs, Deep Sea's output level increased from the original 1000 cubic metres up to 2500 cubic metres per day. Remember that total costs have doubled from $40 000 to $80 000. If we divide the new output level of 2500 cubic metres into $80 000, we obtain a new per-cubic-metre cost of $32, well below the original average cost of $40. This is illustrated in **Figure 7.2**. The original plant's average costs are shown as AC_1. At its original output, it was producing an output of 1000 cubic metres at an average cost of $40 per metre. Plant 2 is exactly double the size of plant 1, and yet it achieves certain economies of scale enabling it to produce an output of 2500 at a lower cost of $32.

Firms in industries characterized by assembly-line production of standardized products, such as automobiles, television sets, refrigerators, and railway cars, are likely to experience declining long-run average cost. In these cases, such firms become formidable competitors because increased output means lower per-unit costs. As we will discuss in later chapters, this is the reason why these industries are often dominated by a few large firms.

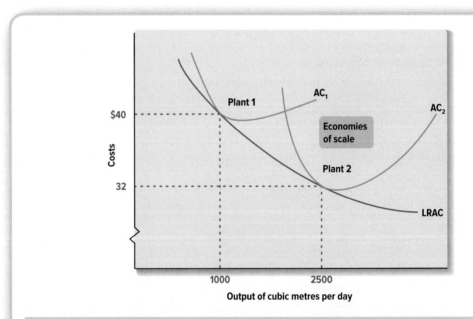

FIGURE 7.2 **Long-Run Average Costs Under Conditions of Economies of Scale**

AC_1 (plant 1) and AC_2 (plant 2) are both (short-run) average cost curves. We have identified one point on each curve representing two output levels used in our example. Connecting these two points gives us a portion of the long-run average cost curve, which declines as output rises.

Now, we need to understand these economies of scale and why many larger firms are able to produce at lower average costs than smaller firms. Broadly speaking, there are two reasons. The first is what we call *technical economies of scale*, which are very closely related to the advantages gained from the division of labour, discussed in Chapter 6. In many contexts, production workers save time if they do not have to switch job functions during the day, or if they develop special skills as a result of performing only one particular operation. Small plants also use division of labour, but big firms are able to exploit it on a far greater scale.

Large-scale production also encourages *management specialization*. Two examples of management specialization are a supervisor who is just as capable of handling twelve workers as eight, or an accounting department that does not grow in size despite a 30 percent increase in the output of the firm. Further, as a firm grows in size, rather than increasing the number of general managers, it makes sense for the firm to hire specialized managers, such as controllers, marketing managers, production managers, and so on.

In addition, as firms grow in size they are able to benefit as a result of *machine specialization*. A classic example is the use of robots on an expensive assembly line, something that would probably not be an option for a firm with a small output. But in general, when a firm grows in size it doesn't just obtain more of the same machines and equipment. What it will tend to do is improve the quality of its physical capital and buy machines better suited to its operations. Whatever the method used to achieve them, technical economies of scale mean an increase in inputs leading to a proportionally greater increase in output, and therefore average cost of production goes down. We call this phenomenon **increasing returns to scale**. The language can get tricky here, but we are simply saying that increasing returns to scale exist because of the presence of technical economies of scale.

The second explanation for economies of scale is that big firms also enjoy other advantages in the form of the *pecuniary economies* of doing business. These come in four forms.

- First, big firms with large outputs often need to borrow large sums, and their *cost of borrowing* (the interest rate they have to pay on the loan) is often lower than the rate charged smaller firms when they borrow—assuming the small firms are able borrow at all, which for many firms may be difficult to do.
- Second, high-volume firms can also *buy inputs in bulk*, which also often means at a lower per-unit price. In addition, bulk selling lowers their per-unit sales cost.
- Third, bigger firms produce in large volumes and so are able to sell previously wasted *by-products*—think of wood chips from a lumber mill that can be used to make particle board. It may even be possible, in some cases, for the firms to themselves start also processing and selling the by-products.
- The fourth and final advantage for large firms is that they have economies of scale in *marketing and advertising*. A thirty-second national television advertisement costs the big firm no more than it does the small firm, but the per-unit output cost of the advertisement is much lower.

The following graphic illustrates this idea of economies of scale.

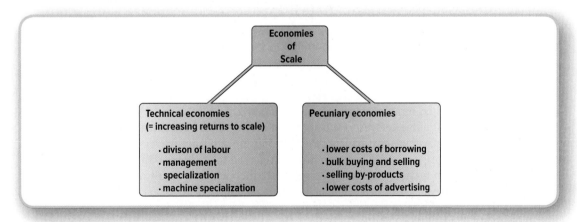

In summary, our original company, Rising Sun Products, experienced constant returns to scale, which meant it did not enjoy any economies of scale and its long-run cost remained the same, whatever its size. Thus its long-run average cost curve was horizontal. However, for our second firm, Deep Sea Concrete, long-run costs are falling and the long-run average cost curve is downward sloping, which reflects the existence of economies of scale.

TEST YOUR UNDERSTANDING

2. Indicate the presence of either constant returns to scale or increasing returns to scale in each set of data.

	Total Cost	Output
Set 1	$ 30 000	175
	60 000	375
Set 2	450 000	100
	900 000	200

SECTION SUMMARY

a) *Technical economies* of scale (resulting in increasing returns to scale) occur as a result of

- division of labour
- management specialization
- machine specialization

b) *Pecuniary economies* of scale (in which large firms have a significant advantage) include

- lower cost of borrowing
- bulk buying and selling
- the selling of by-products
- lower costs of advertising

7.4   Diseconomies of Scale

LO4   Demonstrate why firms can sometimes be too big.

The Deep Sea Concrete example illustrated economies of scale. It is also possible for **diseconomies of scale** to exist. When diseconomies of scale are present, average costs of production will increase rather than decrease as output is increased. When this happens, big firms are at a serious disadvantage. Assume, for instance, that Deep Sea, as in our previous example, doubled its plant size with a consequent doubling of its total costs from $40 000 to $80 000. Now suppose that its output was unable to keep pace, and instead increased only by 60 percent from 1000 to 1600 cubic metres. The result would be an increase in its average costs from $40 ($40 000 divided by 1000) to $50 ($80 000 divided by 1600). This is illustrated in **Figure 7.3**. Here, we see that the original output of 1000 cubic metres in plant 1 resulted in an average cost of $40. Plant 2 is twice as big. However, the output has only increased to 1600 cubic metres, resulting in an average cost curve that is higher than that of plant 1. As a result, the average cost has increased to $50. Since output increased by less than inputs, diseconomies of scale are present. These can also be referred to as **decreasing returns to scale**.

But why might productivity fall and average costs increase as a result of a firm's growth? The answer lies in the bureaucratic inefficiencies in management that all larger firms (as well as nonprofit organizations and governments) experience. This is due to size and does not necessarily imply incompetence. Such diseconomies can result because communication must pass through more channels, becoming subject to interpretation by many more people. Since the lines of communication increase exponentially with the number of personnel, the cost of communication can increase dramatically. Misinterpretation also becomes more likely, especially if the information is complicated and technical in nature. Further, as the management organization within the firm becomes larger, the lines of responsibility and decision making become blurred. If the problem of miscommunication and uncertain responsibility become serious enough, diseconomies of scale occur.

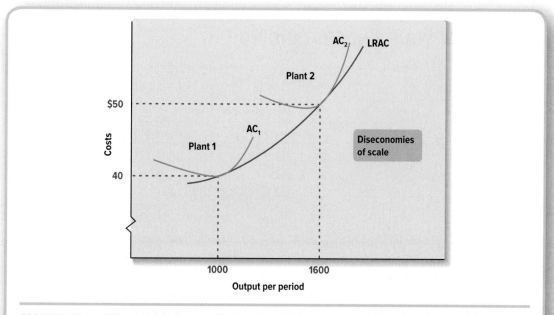

FIGURE 7.3   The LRAC Curve Under Conditions of Diseconomies of Scale

Plant 2 is twice the size of plant 1. However, because of diseconomies of scale, output only increases from 1000 to 1600 cubic metres. The result is an increase in average cost from $40 to $50.

If such technical diseconomies of scale outweigh the pecuniary economies of scale that might be present, diseconomies of scale result and the long-run average cost curve begins to rise. The graphic here illustrates what might happen to physical output when inputs are doubled.

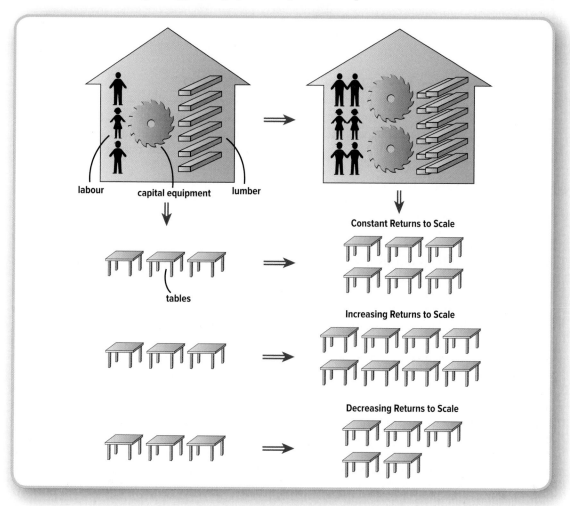

TEST YOUR UNDERSTANDING

3. Decide in each of the following cases (A–D) whether constant returns to, economies of, or diseconomies of scale exist.

	Inputs 1	Inputs 2	Output 1	Output 2
A	6	12	240	480
B	46	92	275	650
C	18	27	500	800
D	260	540	1240	2480

4. Assume that a firm's total cost of producing an output of 600 units is currently $24 000. If total cost increases to $48 000 and the price of inputs and technology remain unchanged, calculate the change in average cost, and state whether constant returns and economies or diseconomies of scale exist for each of the three cases:

a) Output increases to 1100.

b) Output increases to 1250.

c) Output increases to 1200.

SECTION SUMMARY

Diseconomies of scale can occur if bureaucratic inefficiencies within large firms are significant.

7.5   What Is the Right Size of Firm?

LO5   Explain what is meant by the right size of firm.

In Chapter 6, when we looked at a firm's operations in the short run, we pointed out that it is crucial for firms to decide their best output level. In similar fashion, we can ask:

In the long run, what is the best size of firm?

Can a firm be too small? Can it be too big?

In previous sections of this chapter, we looked at the concepts of constant returns to scale, economies of scale and diseconomies of scale. So the question arises: Which of these three does the average firm experience? The not-so-obvious answer is: In most cases, all three. Firms in many industries do not necessarily experience only constant returns to scale, *or* only economies of scale, *or* only diseconomies of scale; in fact, for the majority of firms, all three may be present over different output ranges.

Figure 7.4 will help. Here we see that the LRAC is a curve that envelopes each of the possible short-run average cost curves. What this suggests is that as a firm grows in size it will initially experience economies of scale, at least up to an output level of Q_1. As it continues to grow, and produces output levels greater than Q_1 but less than Q_2 it is subject to constant returns to scale. Finally, when it becomes quite large and produces an output level above quantity Q_2 it becomes subject to diseconomies of scale.

If this long-run average cost curve were typical for a particular industry, we would conclude that any firm that has an output level below quantity Q_1 is probably too small. Output levels below Q_1

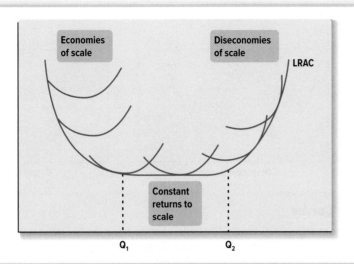

FIGURE 7.4   **The Complete Long-Run Average Cost Curve**

Economies of scale exist for output levels up to Q_1. Constant returns to scale prevail for output levels between Q_1 and Q_2. Finally, diseconomies of scale prevail for output levels above Q_2.

could put any firm at a cost disadvantage compared with its competitors. Similarly, we would also conclude that any firm whose output level was above quantity Q_2 was probably too big and could lower its average cost of production by scaling down the size of its operations.

Note that the long-run average cost curve in **Figure 7.4** has the same general U shape as the short-run average cost curve we developed in the previous chapter—but for quite different reasons. The shape of the short-run average cost curve is influenced by the division of labour and diminishing marginal productivity. The long-run average cost curve takes on its shape as the result of economies and diseconomies of scale and the possibility of constant returns to scale.

Another important way to view the issue of the right size of firm is to ask: Is bigger always better? We will see that it really depends on the industry in question. Appropriate-sized firms are able to take advantage of any economies of scale that exist without becoming too big and experiencing diseconomies. This is what we mean by **minimum efficient scale** (MES). This refers to the smallest size a firm can be while still enjoying all the economies of scale but not so big that it is suffering diseconomies. In other words, it is the smallest size of plant capable of achieving the lowest long-rum average cost of production.

The next figure shows three possible LRAC curves for different industries, each resulting in a different minimum-efficient scale. **Figure 7.5A** illustrates the case where the MES occurs at a large output, which means that a firm would have to be quite large to capture all of the economies of scale available. In this type of industry, small- and medium-sized firms, because of their comparatively higher average costs, are simply not able to compete with larger firms. Thus, this type of industry tends to be dominated by a few large firms. Examples are the automobile (General Motors, Ford), pipeline (Enbridge, Kinder Morgan), satellite data transmission (Telesat, Globalstar), cable distribution (Bell TV, Cable Axion), television transmission (Cogeco, Shaw Media), and petrochemical industries (ARC Resources, Irving Oil).

In **Figure 7.5B**, the MES occurs at output Q_1 but we can imagine a variety of different-sized firms capable of producing outputs up to Q_2, are all able to capture economies of scale. This is because costs remain constant over a wide range of outputs, so an appropriate-sized firm could be either relatively small or large. Examples here would be such industries as computer software (Open Text), real estate services (Royal LePage, MacDonald Realty Group), and meat packing (J.M. Schneider Inc., Conestoga Meat Packers).

Finally, **Figure 7.5C** illustrates an industry in which the MEC occurs at a low output level and means that only relatively small firms would be appropriate. This is the case with vegetable farming and small-scale retailing, such as the local dollar store.

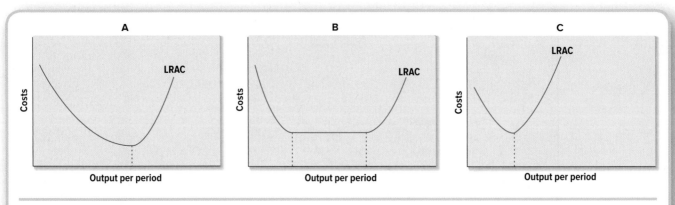

FIGURE 7.5   **Three Possible LRAC Curves**

Given the LRAC curve in Figure A, the minimum efficient scale (MES) would need to be large. In Figure B, the MES is at output Q_1 although a variety of firm sizes capable of producing up to output Q_2 would be appropriate. However, the LRAC curve in Figure C shows that the MEC occurs at a low output and only small firms would be appropriate.

IT'S NEWS TO ME ...

The Future Institute has just released a report on two small, but very interesting, artificial intelligence (AI) companies. The first one, Maluuba, is a new small firm based in Waterloo with just over 50 employees. Its co-founder Mohamed Musbah says that his firm is focused solely on training computers to understand language, whether in conversation with a human, or when reading a document or other source of text.

The second is a Montreal-based firm called Automat which is headed by co-founder Andy Mauro. It is working on making it easier for anyone to build a bot (a web robot) that uses artificial intelligence and human expertise to enable conversations.

Mauro calls the current rush to find AI talent as a "land grab"—big-name players such as Amazon, Uber and Apple have paid hundreds of thousands of dollars in yearly compensation to poach star researchers and engineers. Yet, he has still been able to hire very good people. This is a reflection, he believes, that the industry's talent has divided into two camps. "There are people that want to work at big companies and have that stability but there are also people that want to be pirates and chose to work at the startups."

Source: *Star Power Reporting,* January 2017.

I. The fact that new small firms seem able to compete with very large established multinational firms in attracting new talent indicates that the LRAC curve in the industry is consistent with:

  a) significant economies of scale
  b) constant returns to scale
  c) some diseconomies of scale

II. Which of the following is likely to occur as the AI industry continues to make breakthroughs in developing computers that can understand language?

  a) More firms in other industries will find useful applications for these breakthroughs.
  b) The keyboards on our current laptops, iPods, and cell phones will gradually be replaced with voice commands.
  c) Court recorders will become obsolete.
  d) All of the above.

SECTION SUMMARY

a) The firm's LAS envelops all of the AS curves.

b) A firm can be considered to be of the *right* size only if it is big enough to capture economies of scale but not so big as to suffer diseconomies. The right size is called the *minimum efficient scale.*

7.6   Changes in Short- and Long-Run Costs

LO6   Explain the effect of technological and input price changes on a firm's cost.

We saw in the last section that the long-run average cost curve (LRAC) is a curve that envelops all the short-run cost curves (AC). This means that if the short-run costs were to change, then so too would the long-run costs. We pointed out at the end of Chapter 6 that the two factors that could cause such a change are a change in input prices or the introduction of an improved technology. Either of these would affect both the short-run average cost, as well as marginal cost. In addition, a change in these factors would also change the long-run costs. So if the short-run cost curves were to shift, so too would the long-run average cost curve.

Figure 7.6 shows what would happen if, for instance, a firm were to either experience a drop in input prices or be able to introduce an improved technology. This would affect the costs of production at all output and plant sizes. The result would be a shift down in all the short-run curves (AC) and accordingly also in the long-run cost curve (LRAC). Conversely, if the firm were to experience an increase in input prices, the whole range of short-run costs would increase resulting in both those curves and the long-run supply shifting up.

While a change in input prices and a change in technology can both affect costs of production, the change in technology is usually of far more significance. This is because a change in input prices is generally beyond the control of the individual producer and such prices can just as easily and quickly decrease as increase. Technological improvement is a different manner: it is usually in the producer's power to introduce or not, and can have a more lasting impact on business. This emphasizes the importance of technological improvement for the firm in this modern, competitive world. Improved technology (in the economic sense) means lower costs of production, and lower costs of production mean more success.

We can add one more point to the discussion of reducing costs. As you are aware, corporate takeovers and mergers between firms are quite prevalent these days. Why is this? One explanation involves fixed costs. If the new, larger firm that results from a takeover or merger can keep its fixed

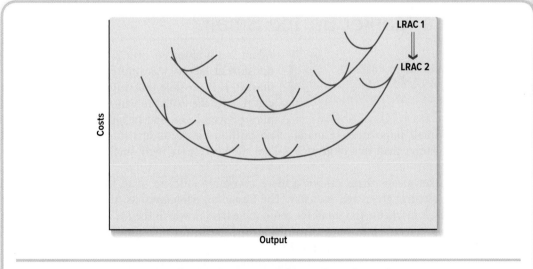

FIGURE 7.6   A Decrease in the Long- and Short-Run Cost Curves

A drop in input prices or the introduction of an improved technology will shift the cost curves of every possible plant size and thus shift down the long-run average cost curve from $LRAC_1$ to $LRAC_2$.

cost below the *combined* fixed costs of the original two firms, average costs of production will have been reduced and the profitability of the new firm will be enhanced.

ADDED DIMENSION

Increased Rates of Productivity Growth

One of the truly phenomenal trends in the years just before the recession of 2008 was the impressive growth rates in output per capita in the United States. Underlying this trend were increases in labour productivity in the 2.5–3 percent range, something that has not been seen for decades. Such statements as "productivity growth is the cornerstone of economic growth and wealth creation" were found in popular publications as well as in academic journals.

Most economists agree that at the root of these productivity increases is the *technological change* associated with the computer and information "revolution." Nonetheless, Canada's rates of productivity increase have consistently lagged behind those of the United States. In 2009, research by John Baldwin and Wulong Gu (both with Statistics Canada) concluded that Canada's lagging productivity rates had three causes: a reluctance of Canadian firms to meet foreign competition head-on, inadequate spending on new capital equipment, and a failure of firms to grow large enough to capture minimum efficient scale. The same conclusions were reached by a Conference Board of Canada study in 2012. However, there was a small glimmer of good news in that the Canada–U.S. growth-in-productivity gap narrowed a bit in 2014–16.

SECTION SUMMARY

Both short-run and long-run average costs can *decrease* if

- the price of factor inputs decreases
- technological improvement occurs
- mergers reduce the average fixed costs of the new firm

7.7   Can a Market Be Too Small?

> **LO7**   Explain why markets can sometimes be too small.

Adam Smith observed, over 200 years ago, that the division of labour was limited by the size of the market. Is it possible that a limited size of market can restrict the extent to which firms enjoy economies of scale? Yes, and in fact this is the case in Canada, with its small population (Canada's 36.5 million people is less than the population of California and no larger than that of greater Tokyo) and correspondingly small market, at least for some industries.

If a small market means firms cannot achieve minimum efficient scale, then inefficiency can become widespread throughout the industry. The Canadian economy has historically faced this problem. Its domestic market is too small for those industries in which the MES dictates that a large output is necessary to minimize average cost. As a result, such firms are inefficient by world standards. This situation is illustrated in **Figure 7.7**.

A small market may force a firm to limit its output to Q_1 and experience average total cost of AC_1 as illustrated in **Figure 7.7**. This is above the level of minimum long-run average cost. A larger market would allow the firm to build a larger plant, as represented by the AC_2 curve, and thereby achieve minimum long-run average costs.

Thus, we can see that Adam Smith was correct in his observation that the division of labour can be limited by the size of the market in both the short run and the long run. In the short run, a

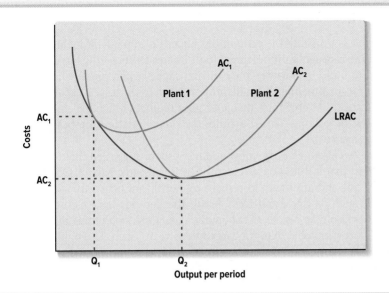

FIGURE 7.7 Minimum Efficient Scale

If a small market limits the firm's output to Q_1, then its average cost, AC_1, is not able to achieve minimum efficient scale. A larger market that allowed an output of Q_2, and thus a larger firm as represented by AC_2, would enable that firm to achieve its minimum efficient scale.

limited-size market can force a firm to produce at an output below economic capacity. More significantly, a limited-size market can prevent firms in the long-run from building large-scale plants and capturing available economies of scale through increased output levels. This inability to increase output levels limits the firm's ability to gain all of the possible economies of scale. As we will see in Chapter 13, this is one of the strongest arguments for free trade between nations—to expand the size of the market.

IN A NUTSHELL ...

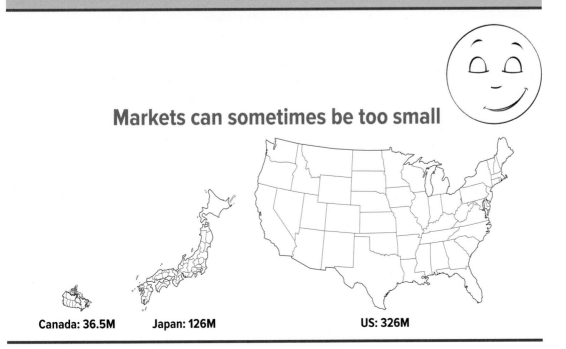

Markets can sometimes be too small

Canada: 36.5M   Japan: 126M   US: 326M

Does Size Matter Anymore?

Let us consider what is probably the economist's favourite example of technical economies of scale. The cost of a pipeline is roughly proportional to its circumference—the larger the circumference, the more steel needed to build it. However, the carrying capacity of a pipeline is determined by its area, which means that larger pipelines have disproportionately increased capacity and thus lower per-unit costs. For instance, a twelve-inch-diameter pipe requires twice the steel of a six-inch pipe but can carry *four* times the volume. This illustrates the classic relationship between bigger volume and lower long-run average cost.

For most of the twentieth century, conventional wisdom suggested that the bigger a firm became, the more likely it was that it would be successful. The Royal Bank, Barrick Gold, Imperial Oil, and IBM are big and successful, and are likely to remain so. But things began to change when, in the 1990s, specialty channels such as CNN and ESPN broke the decades-long stranglehold of the big three American TV networks on the market. At about the same time, small mini-mill companies in the steel industry became more profitable than the large mainstream firms. Large multinational corporations started to make deals with small software-engineering startups to hedge their bets on the future.

What is happening here? Don't economies of scale count anymore? In many cases, they still do, but that is not the whole story.

For new firms, changing technology is lowering the barriers to entry into some industries despite the presence of economies of scale. Financial capital is much more mobile and therefore more available to small firms. In addition, as technology advances, smaller and smaller computers can do what could previously only be done with a room-sized mainframe. As a result, increased efficiency comes from a reduction in the size of the means of production. This new concept, that smaller is better, fits well with emerging evidence that market demand for many products is shifting away from standardized products toward customized products. More and more, consumers are demanding unique products that meet highly specialized needs. Thus production must become much more flexible, and the emphasis is shifting to customized products.

 ADDED DIMENSION

The Rise of the On-Demand Economy

The traditional explanation of why firms exist revolves around the idea of the high transaction cost involved when individuals try to do complicated tasks. As an example, it explains why most people buy their new house from a contractor rather than building it themselves. Today's corporations are the legacy of the huge companies that emerged from the industrial revolution and defined capitalism for over a century—beginning about 1880.

But the end of the second decade of the twenty-first century is upon us, and things are shifting very quickly. Now, most people carry powerful computers in their pockets and the ramifications are now becoming apparent. Uber, founded in one city in 2009, now operates worldwide, and its annual sales are now well over $1 billion. The company Handy will supply labour and services to individual households on demand. Instacart will do an individual's grocery shopping and deliver to the door. TaskRabbit will quickly find and deliverer a last-minute gift. There are even firms that will do a person's laundry. What we now have is what is termed the "on-demand economy."

More significantly, however, this phenomenon is extending beyond consumer services. Appirio supplies businesses and professionals with freelance software coders, and Axiom employs hundreds of lawyers who service thousands of corporations, some very large. Amazon's Mechanical Turk gathers an array of specific needs received from hundreds of clients, repackages them into similar sets, and then invites freelancers to choose which ones they want to put in a bid to work on. This process accesses spare time and spare cognitive ability around the world. The actual work is usually done "at home," eliminating the need for offices and for full-time employees who generally require health insurance and retirement plans.

The result has been described as "hyperspecialization" that extends the division of labour far beyond Adam Smith's pin factory.

Next, consider the fact that networks of small computers can quickly be expanded or scaled back. Thus, firms can deploy *many* assembly lines, each turning out a customized variant of the same basic product rather than only *one* huge assembly line that stamps out a standardized product in massive volumes.

An interesting example of the trend toward smaller-scale production is the rise in the use of specialized types of green energy. For example, the use of marginal agricultural land in many of the more northern parts of Canada can grow what are known as short rotation coppice (SRC) trees. The harvested trees are dried and then fed into a process that produces diesel fuel. In addition to the environmental advantage of this method—it is carbon-neutral (the carbon released in the burning of the wood is exactly equal to that sequestered from the atmosphere as the trees grew)—it is as cheap as diesel fuel made in the traditional way from oil. The future may well see scores of relatively small-scale diesel plants scattered across the nation's agricultural regions.

This raises a fundamental question: Will this new technology alter the scale of the firm that uses it? In other words, as production becomes more customized and computers become more sophisticated, will efficient production mean smaller firms? These days, it seems that huge corporations are finding it cheaper to farm out work to lower-cost specialists, which are often more flexible, than to retain the bureaucratic organizational structure necessary to manage the entire process within a single operation.

Evidence for such downsizing comes from the fact that small automotive-parts firms have been growing in the last decade, while large automobile manufacturers have been just holding their own. This leads some economists to argue that as production becomes significantly more specialized and products more customized, the growth in the numbers of efficient small firms will come at the expense of giant firms.

Not all economists agree that this is the trend. They point out that what can be done efficiently in a small firm can also be done in the corner of a General Motors plant. However, if smaller does prove to be better, then a great deal will change, and this chapter on long-run average cost and the related advantages of economies of scale will have to be rewritten.

Computer chips like these are getting smaller and more powerful every year.

Mitch Hrdlicka/Getty Images

 TEST YOUR UNDERSTANDING

5. Draw a graph showing short-run and long-run average costs curves that illustrates a firm producing both below economic capacity and at less than minimum efficient scale.

SECTION SUMMARY

A market can be *too small* if it limits the size of the firm to an output level that is

- below economic capacity in the short run
- below minimum efficient scale in the long run

Study Guide

Review

WHAT'S THE BIG IDEA?

One thing that some have difficulty understanding is this distinction between the short run and the long run. Economists do not define these ideas in terms of a certain number of months or years. Instead they look at things from the point of view of: "How long does it take a firm to change its level of production?" This will vary from industry to industry and from firm to firm. For a manufacturer whose production methods are uncomplicated, who does not employ sophisticated or specialized equipment or workers, and buys supplies that are plentiful and easy to obtain, the answer would presumably be: "Not long at all." But for other firms, who would find it extremely difficult to obtain more resources, such as a very specialized technician or a custom-made machine, the short run might be a matter of years. But whatever the complexity of a firm's operations, the major stumbling block may well be the legal or financial difficulties involved in moving to the new premises that a change in the level of production would require. Again, the short run might be measured in years rather than months.

The other difficult idea for many is the whole concept of the long-run average cost and its graph. What the long-run curve shows are the absolute lowest cost at which a firm could produce for every possible output. It assumes that for each output level there is an ideal size of premises in which are employed exactly the optimum number of staff, machines, and supplies. This means that each output is associated with a different premises size. From that point of view, it is obviously an "ideal" rather than a practical option.

NEW GLOSSARY TERMS

constant returns to scale
decreasing returns to scale
diseconomies of scale

economies of scale
increasing returns to scale
long run

long-run average cost curve
minimum efficient scale
technological improvement

Comprehensive Problem

(LO 3, 4, 6) Table 7.2 contains short-run cost data for five different plant sizes for the R2D2 Robotics Company.

TABLE 7.2

Output	Plant 1	Plant 2	Plant 3	Plant 4	Plant 5
10	$ 8.00	$10.50	/	/	/
20	7.00	9.00	/	/	/
30	6.00	7.50	$10.00	/	/
40	6.50	6.00	8.00	/	/
50	7.50	5.00	6.50	$10.30	/
60	9.00	5.80	4.00	8.50	/
70	10.50	7.00	4.90	7.00	/
80	/	8.20	6.00	5.10	$6.50
90	/	10.00	7.80	4.00	6.00
100	/	/	8.50	4.30	5.40
110	/	/	/	5.60	5.00
120	/	/	/	7.70	5.30
130	/	/	/	10.00	6.00
140	/	/	/	/	7.10

Questions

a) On the grid in **Figure** 7.8, sketch in the five short-run cost curves (you do not have to plot each point) placing the lowest point of each curve in the correct position.

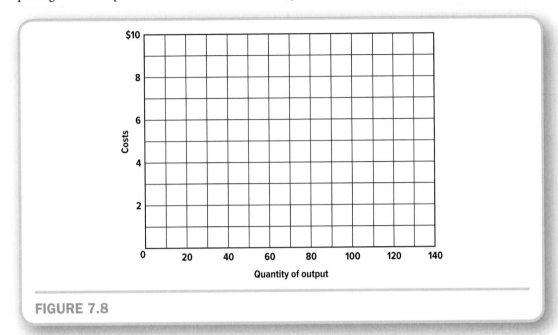

FIGURE 7.8

b) Fill in **Table** 7.3 showing the best size of plant for the given outputs.

TABLE 7.3

Outputs	30	40	50	60	70	80	90	100	110	120
Plant #	__	__	__	__	__	__	__	__	__	__

c) Roughly sketch the long-run average cost curve in **Figure** 7.8.

Answers

a) See the following figure:

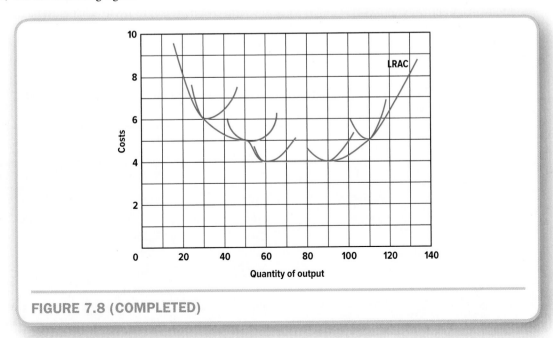

FIGURE 7.8 (COMPLETED)

b) See Table 7.3 (Completed).

TABLE 7.3 (COMPLETED)

Outputs	30	40	50	60	70	80	90	100	110	120
Plant #	1	2	2	3	3	4	4	4	5	5

c) See Figure 7.8 (Completed).

Questions

d) What plant size would the firm need in order to achieve minimum efficient scale (MES)?
e) What is the output level that achieves MES?
f) If R2D2 is producing an output of 80 in plant 4, does excess capacity exist?
g) What is the economic capacity of plant 5?
h) Given the LRAC curve in **Figure 7.8**, between what output levels are economies of scale present?
i) Given the LRAC curve in **Figure 7.8**, between what output levels are constant returns to scale present?
j) Given the LRAC curve in **Figure 7.8** between what output levels do diseconomies of scale exist?
k) If R2D2's sales are limited to 50, for which plant sizes we can say that the market is too small?

Answers

d) Plant 3 (minimum efficient scale is the smallest size of plant at which a firm is able to minimize long-run average cost).
e) Minimum long-run average cost is achieved at an output of 60.
f) Yes (excess capacity exists because an output of 80 is below the output, 90, at which minimum average cost of $4 is achieved).
g) Output of 110 (economic capacity is where short-run average costs are minimized).
h) Between the outputs of 0 and 60, where long-run average costs are declining.
i) Between the outputs of 61 and 90, where long-run average costs are constant.
j) Above the output of 90, where long-run average costs are increasing.
k) The market is too small for plant sizes 3, 4, and 5, since all have economic capacity at outputs above 50.

Study Problems

Find answers on the McGraw-Hill online resource.

Basic (Problems 1–5)

1. **(LO 3, 4, 6)** Suppose that Jump A Lot Inc. can produce 16 trampolines a day for a total cost of $1920. If technology and input prices remain the same and total cost increases to $3840, what must be the new quantity of output per day under conditions of
   a) constant returns to scale? _____
   b) economies of scale? _____
   c) diseconomies of scale? _____

2. **(LO 2, 3, 4, 5, 6)** Table 7.4 contains average cost data for four different-sized plants—1, 2, 3, and 4—which are the only four sizes possible.

TABLE 7.4

Output	Plant 1	Plant 2	Plant 3	Plant 4
40	$60	$70	$90	$110
50	55	60	80	95
60	60	50	70	80
70	65	60	60	65
80	70	70	50	55
90	80	80	60	45
100	90	90	70	55

a) At what output is economic capacity for each of the four plants?
Plant 1: _____ Plant 2: _____
Plant 3: _____ Plant 4: _____

b) In which plant and at what output is minimum long-run average cost achieved?
Plant: _____ Output: _____

c) Which plant is the right size to produce an output of 60?

d) Which plant is the right size to produce an output of 80?

3. **(LO 2, 4, 5)** Figure 7.9 illustrates a series of short-run average cost curves, numbered AC_1 through AC_5, that correspond to five different plant sizes, which are the only sizes possible.

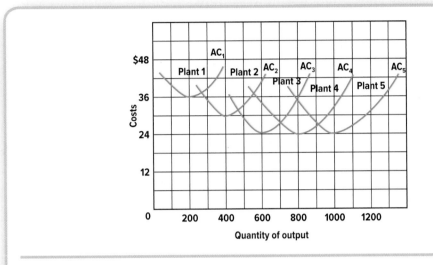

FIGURE 7.9

a) What is true about output levels 200, 400, 600, 800, and 1000?

_____

b) What is the right size of a plant to produce an output of 500? _____

c) Between what output levels do economies of scale prevail?

_____

4. **(LO 2, 3, 4)** Assuming that technology and the prices of all inputs remain fixed, decide, in each of the four cases (A–D) in **Table 7.5**, whether economies of, diseconomies of, or constant returns to scale exist.

TABLE 7.5

	Inputs 1	Inputs 2	Output 1	Output 2
A	7	14	21	42
B	26	52	230	420
C	38	57	300	500
D	360	432	2200	2750

Case A: _____ Case B: _____
Case C: _____ Case D: _____

5. **(LO 2, 3, 4)** Assuming that technology and the prices of all inputs remain fixed, decide, in each of the four cases (A–D) in **Table 7.6**, whether economies of, diseconomies of, or constant returns to scale exist.

TABLE 7.6		
Case	Total Cost	Output
A	$ 12 500	50
	25 000	100
B	6 000	20
	12 000	42
C	450 000	225
	980 000	450
D	80 000	40
	150 000	80

Case A: _____ Case B: _____
Case C: _____ Case D: _____

Intermediate (Problems 6–8)

6. **(LO 5, 7)** Table 7.7 shows average cost data for three different-sized plants—1, 2, and 3—which are the only three sizes possible.

TABLE 7.7			
Output	Plant 1	Plant 2	Plant 3
100	$12	$15	$19
200	11	12	16
300	10	8	12
400	11	11	9
500	12	15	10

a) In what plant size is MES achieved? _____
b) What is economic capacity for plant 3? _____
c) What is the right-size plant to produce an output of 400? _____

7. **(LO 2, 3, 6)** Figure 7.10 illustrates a series of short-run average cost curves, numbered AC_1 through AC_4, which correspond to the only four different automobile plant sizes possible.

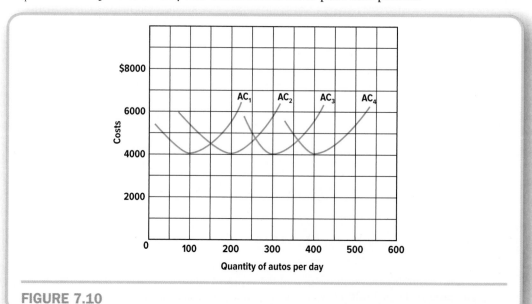

FIGURE 7.10

a) What can you say about returns to scale? _____
b) Are economies of scale present? _____
c) If, in this automobile plant, it takes 40 workers and 100 units of capital to produce 200 automobiles a day, how much labour and capital is involved in producing 400 automobiles a day? _____

8. **(LO 2, 3, 4)** Table 7.8 shows the long-run total costs for three different firms.

TABLE 7.8

JAD			HAFIZ			YNARI		
Output	Total Cost	Average Cost	Output	Total Cost	Average Cost	Output	Total Cost	Average Cost
10	$ 300	____	20	$12 000	____	100	$ 2 000	____
20	600	____	40	23 200	____	200	4 200	____
30	900	____	60	33 900	____	300	6 900	____
40	1200	____	80	44 400	____	400	10 400	____
50	1500	____	100	55 000	____	500	15 000	____
60	1800	____	120	65 760	____	600	21 000	____

a) Complete the average cost columns in Table 7.8.
b) Are these three firms experiencing economies of, diseconomies of, or constant returns to scale?
Jad: _____
Hafiz: _____
Ynari: _____

Advanced (Problems 9–12)

9. **(LO 2, 3, 6)** Figure 7.11 illustrates a series of five short-run average cost curves, numbered AC_1 through AC5, which correspond to the only five different automobile plant sizes possible.

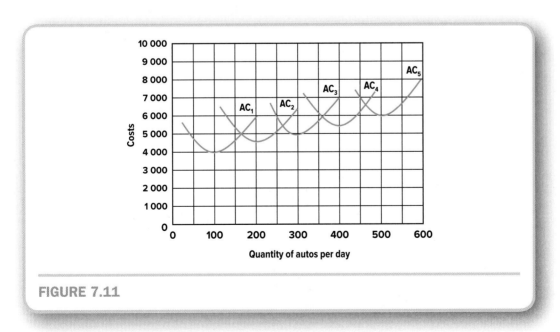

FIGURE 7.11

a) What type of returns to scale is this firm experiencing? _____
b) If, in this automobile plant, it takes 20 workers and 50 units of capital to produce 200 automobiles, what can you say about the amount of labour and capital needed to produce 400 automobiles?
_____

10. **(LO 3)** The inputs and outputs for Carbon Credits Inc. are as shown in Table 7.9.

TABLE 7.9

Output	INPUTS		Total Cost	LRAC
	Capital	Labour		
100	1	5	____	____
200	2	8	____	____
300	3	11	____	____
400	4	12	____	____
500	5	22	____	____
600	6	37	____	____

a) Assuming capital costs $50 per unit and labour costs $10 per unit, fill in the blanks in the table.
b) With what output does increasing returns come to an end? _____

11. **(LO 3)** The inputs and outputs for Yogi Soft Drinks Inc. are as shown in Table 7.10.

TABLE 7.10

Output	INPUTS		Total Cost	LRAC
	Capital	Labour		
100	1	3	____	____
200	2	5	____	____
300	3	7	____	____
400	4	11	____	____
500	5	18	____	____
600	6	30	____	____

a) If capital costs $30 per unit and labour costs $15 per unit, fill in the blanks in the table.
b) When are increasing returns to scale present? _____
c) At what output is MES achieved? _____

12. **(LO 5)** Table 7.11 shows average cost data for three different-sized plants—1, 2, and 3—which are the only three sizes possible.

TABLE 7.11

Output	Plant 1	Plant 2	Plant 3
10	$2000	$1800	$2700
20	1500	1400	2400
30	900	1000	1800
40	1200	800	1200
50	1800	1200	1000
60	2500	1800	1300

a) What is the value of AC at economic capacity in each of the three plants? $_____
b) What does your answer to (a) say about the shape of the LRAC curve? _____
c) In which plant size is MES achieved? _____

Problems for Further Study

Basic (Problems 1–3)

1. **(LO 1)** Define what is meant by the term *long run*.

2. **(LO 2)** What is the shape of the LRAC curve for a firm enjoying constant returns to scale?

3. **(LO 4)** What is the major cause of diseconomies of scale?

Intermediate (Problems 4–7)

4. **(LO 7)** On the graph in **Figure 7.12**, sketch both short- and long-run average cost curves that illustrate a firm producing both below economic capacity and at less than minimum efficient scale. Label the output Q_1.

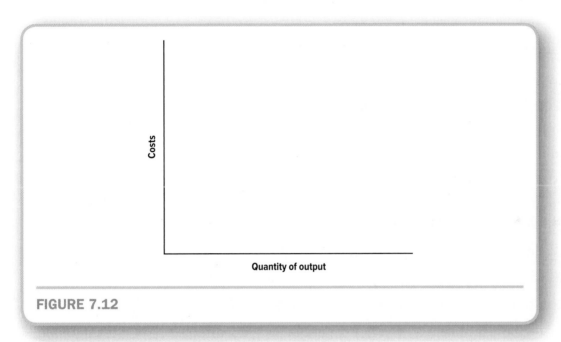

FIGURE 7.12

5. **(LO 5)** In what sense might a firm be too small?

6. **(LO 7)** Define the term *minimum efficient scale*.

7. **(LO 7)** Is the idea of a right-sized firm a short-run or long-run concept?

Advanced (Problems 8–11)

8. **(LO 3)** Discuss the distinction between *technical economies of scale* and *pecuniary economies of scale*. Give two examples of each.

9. **(LO 4)** What is the difference between *diminishing returns* and *decreasing returns to scale*? Which of the concepts refers to the long run and which to the short run?

10. **(LO 7)** Sketch a graph (remember to label the axes) that shows a firm achieving both MES and economic capacity.

11. **(LO 1)** What problems would a firm encounter when relocating its business?

CHAPTER 8
Perfect Competition

LEARNING OBJECTIVES

At the end of this chapter, you should be able to:

LO1 Distinguish among a firm, an industry, and a market.

LO2 Explain what is meant by perfect competition and the market system.

LO3 Use two approaches to explain how a firm might maximize its profits.

LO4 Explain what is meant by break-even price and shutdown price.

LO5 Explain how a firm's supply curve is derived.

LO6 Explain the effect of a change in market demand or market supply on both the industry and the firm.

 WHAT'S AHEAD...

In this chapter, we take our first look at market structures using what economists call the *perfectly competitive* model. After describing some examples of perfect competition, we look at the behaviour of the individual firm, how it decides on its production level, and how profits are affected. We derive rules for determining the output level at which the producer breaks even, the level at which it will make the most profit, and the level at which it might be advised to shut down operations. The rest of the chapter shows how the market and the individual producer react to changes in demand, technology, and input costs.

A QUESTION OF RELEVANCE ...

Market systems are dynamic and always changing. New industries are born, and established industries die on a fairly regular basis. Are new firms guaranteed a profit? Would you be a fool to look for a job in a declining industry, or an even bigger fool to join the multitudes looking for jobs in the growing industries? Is it possible for a firm caught in the drag of a dying industry to redefine itself and become successful doing something else? Is there some kind of common denominator that we can use to study "the market"? In this chapter, we will find out.

We have now completed our look at the firm's revenue side (in the demand-focused Chapter 4) and the firm's cost of production (in the supply-side-focused Chapters 6 and 7). We are now ready to put the demand side and the supply side together in this chapter and continue the process in Chapters 9, 10, and 11. We will examine what economists call *market structure* with the focus on the firm's two most important output decisions: What output will a firm choose to produce, and what price will prevail? To answer these questions, we need to know a lot about the market in which the product will be produced and sold.

8.1 Characteristics of Different Markets

> **LO1** Distinguish among a firm, an industry, and a market.

Let us clarify some terminology before we go any further. *Industry* is the collective name for all the firms producing a similar product. The different firms in the industry may or may not know each other well, they may or may not be members of some sort of common association, and they may or may not agree on various types of collective action. What they have in common is that they produce a similar product, usually using the same technology. A *market*, you will remember from Chapter 2, refers to the interactions of both producers and consumers. In other words:

> An industry is the name for a group of producers; a market refers to the interaction of producers and consumers.

Economists see two main ways in which markets differ. The first is in the types of products sold. Do all the producers sell an identical product, or are there variations between one firm's product and those of other firms? The second difference reflects the numbers of buyers and sellers interacting in the market. Is it populated by many firms and consumers, or is it dominated by a few big players? The number of competing firms and what they produce indicates just how much power any one firm might have in the marketplace and how easy or difficult it is for a new firm to enter a market.

For instance, if there are lots of firms in an industry and their products are almost identical, no single firm will have much influence over the price and it will be easy for new firms to join the industry. Economists call this type of market *perfect competition*, which is the focus of this chapter. But in other types of markets, there may be very few firms, and each may produce an easily identified product that's different from those of its competitors. Table 8.1 shows each of the four types of markets that we will be studying.

TABLE 8.1
Characteristics of the Four Markets

| Type of Product | NUMBER OF FIRMS IN THE INDUSTRY | | |
	Many	Few	One
Identical	Perfect competition	Undifferentiated oligopoly	Monopoly
Differentiated	Monopolistic competition	Differentiated oligopoly	

In essence, then, there are four major types of markets, as presented in **Table 8.2**: *perfect competition*, such as commodity markets, in which many producers all produce an identical product; *monopolistic competition*, in which there are also lots of producers, each selling a slightly different product—convenience stores for example; *oligopoly* (either *differentiated* or *undifferentiated*), in which a few large producers dominate the market, as in the oil refining business; and finally, *monopoly*, in which there is a single producer in the market, as in the public utility industries of most provinces.

TABLE 8.2
The Different Types of Markets

Market	Number of Sellers	Type of Product	Ease of Entry to Market	Seller's Control over Price	Examples
Perfect competition	Numerous	Identical	Easy	None	Commodities, such as wheat
Monopolistic competition	Many	Differentiated	Easy	Low	Convenience stores, restaurants
Oligopoly: undifferentiated	Few	Identical	Difficult	Moderate	Oil refining, lumber
Oligopoly: differentiated	Few	Differentiated	Difficult	Substantial	Automobiles, soft drinks
Monopoly	One	Unique	Very difficult	Substantial	Public utilities, cable companies

 TEST YOUR UNDERSTANDING

Find answers on the McGraw-Hill online resource.

1. In what type of market will you find the following types of firms/products?

a) hairdressing salons

b) industrial chemicals in Canada

c) commercial breweries in Canada

d) world market for coffee

e) Rogers Cable in Ontario

SECTION SUMMARY

a) Firms make up an industry, and this industry operates within the context of a market, where producers and consumers interact.

b) Markets are differentiated by

• the number of firms

• the type of product

c) There are four types of markets:

• perfect competition

• monopolistic competition

• oligopoly

• monopoly

8.2   Perfect Competition and the Market System

> **LO2**   Explain what is meant by perfect competition and the market system.

Features of Perfect Competition

Perfect competition is defined as a market in which the participants are all *price takers*. That is, no single consumer or producer can have any significant influence in the market; the actions of a single firm or individual will have no perceptible effect on the price of the product or its quantity produced. A perfectly competitive market thus provides a level playing field for all of its participants.

For this level field to exist, four conditions must be fulfilled. First, there must be a *large number of buyers and sellers*, and all must be small in relation to the whole market. When each producer is relatively small, a decision by any particular producer to, say, double its output (or to produce nothing at all) will not have much impact on the market. Similarly, a decision by any particular consumer to increase or decrease her purchases will have no perceptible effect on the total quantity sold. Also, in such market collusion between groups of consumers (such as cooperatives) or producers (such as closed associations) cannot exist, nor can there be any involvement by big corporations, trade unions, or government. The market-determined price is a given—a take-it-or-leave-it proposition.

The second feature of a perfectly competitive market is that, in it, *no preferences are shown*. This means that the consumer does not care (and probably does not know) where the product comes from because the producers all make identical (or undifferentiated) products. Similarly, producers show no preference toward any particular consumer. For them, all consumers are the same.

The third defining feature of a competitive market is that *there should be easy entry into and exit from the market*, for both producers and consumers. This is sometimes rephrased to say that there are no significant *barriers to entry*. This implies that for the prospective producer, it is reasonably easy to set up in business: the amount of financial capital is relativity small and easy to obtain and no licence or entry fee is required. On the other side, easy entry means consumers are not required to pay a membership fee or join a club in order to buy a product.

The fourth and final feature of a perfectly competitive market is that *producers have all the market information necessary to make rational production and purchasing decisions*. This means that knowledge about what is being sold and the technology used to make it is available to all concerned.

In summary, the four conditions for a perfectly competitive market are as follows:

- many small buyers and sellers all of whom are price takers
- no preferences shown by consumers
- easy entry and exit by both buyers and sellers
- the same market information available to all

If these four conditions exist, the anonymous forces of demand and supply determine both the price of the product and the quantity traded, and since demand and supply are almost always changing we should expect to see the price change quite frequently. Conversely, if for any particular product the price seldom changes, this is evidence that that market is not perfectly competitive.

Let us see, now, if we can find some examples of perfectly competitive markets in our economy.

Examples of Perfectly Competitive Markets

Before looking for examples of perfectly competitive markets, we should emphasize that the first condition (many small buyers and sellers) does not require every producer to be small in its scale of operations, only *small in relation to the total market*. It is just as possible, then, to have some reasonably big competitive firms as it is to have one single, small monopolist. For example, a 1000 hectare wheat farm in Manitoba might be considered large—say $400 000 in annual sales—but it is not even close to being a monopolist, given the enormous size of the world's wheat market with its annual sales in the billions of dollars. On the other hand, a small gas station with only $40 000 in sales might be a monopolist in a remote northern town.

The second condition, that no preference be shown by consumers, immediately rules out such examples as travel agents, hairdressers, gas stations, and so on, since customers do show preferences in their buying patterns.

Another important point is that it is not the number of products that makes the market competitive but the number of individual producers. For example, although there are more than a hundred different breakfast cereals on the market, most are produced by just two or three giant firms, which means the market is not perfectly competitive.

Given these cautions, are there good examples of perfectly competitive markets these days? Well, the closest we will come is a situation in which the market is very big and the product is generic—for example, the world markets for such commodities as coca, rubber, wheat, and so on. These are all examples of homogeneous products: and the prices of these products change hourly in response to changing supply and demand conditions around the world.

IT'S NEWS TO ME ...

Commodities Watch has just released its February report which highlighted unusual world price movements in two key commodities—cocoa and wheat.

Cocoa prices continued a several-month-long trend to reach new four year lows on the news that good weather in the West Africa countries of Ghana and Ivory Coast promises a very good harvest this year. These two countries are major producers of the key ingredient in making chocolate.

In contrast, the world wheat price was up 4.5% on news that unusually dry weather in the US wheat belt was causing stress on the winter wheat crops and expectations of a poor harvest intensified.

In short, your box of chocolate will probably be cheaper this year but your loaf of bread may well be more expensive.

Source: *Star Power Reporting.* March 2017.

I. Which of the following statements is correct?

a) The market supply curve for cocoa has shifted to the right.
b) The market supply curve for cocoa has shifted to the left.
c) The market supply curve for wheat has shifted to the right.
d) Both (a) and (c) have occurred.

II. Regarding the demand curve facing the individual firm, which of the following statements is correct?

a) The perfectly elastic demand curve facing cocoa producers has shifted up while it has shifted down for wheat producers.
b) The perfectly elastic demand curve facing cocoa producers has shifted down while it has shifted up for wheat producers.
c) The demand curves of both commodities are unaffected, since this is a supply issue.
d) None of the above.

The world markets for commodities tend to be very competitive.

(Cows) Reimar Gaertner/Age Fotostock; (Coffee beans) STOCK4B-RF/Glow Images; (Vegetables) Pixtal/Age Fotostock; (Corn) Getty Images/stock photo; (Apples) Shutterstock/Teri Virbickis; (Pumpkins) Shutterstock/Loren L. Masseth; (Oil rig) Oleg Kozlov/Alamy

A Canadian producer of a particular commodity, however big it may be in this country, is unlikely to have much impact on the world supply. In most respects, then, world markets for commodities are reasonably competitive. But what about inside Canada—are there any perfectly competitive markets domestically? Well, the stock market is often cited as an example of a perfect market, in which the prices of products (stocks and bonds) often change minute by minute. However, on closer inspection, it falls short of being perfectly competitive because the action of a single large buyer or seller can and does affect the price of shares. This runs counter to our criterion that no single buyer or seller can affect the market price. In addition, you need to use the services of an agent or broker and pay a commission to buy a share of anything, which means access to the market is not perfectly free.

In truth, there are few examples of perfectly competitive markets in the modern world, compared with the situation in the eighteenth century, when Adam Smith first wrote about market characteristics. In Smith's day, all producers were small, and the output of most producers was very similar to that of the competition. This is no longer true.

Given this fact, it is reasonable to ask why economists continue to talk about and analyze a market structure that hardly exists. There is a very good answer. Economists use the construction of the perfectly competitive market structure as an ideal model of how a market acts in its pure (perfect) sense. Then, once they have figured out how perfectly competitive markets work, they have a benchmark against which to judge and compare real-world markets.

In this sense, the economist is no different from the physicist who explains what will happen in ideal situations and then revises his conclusions for other circumstances. Galileo, for example, investigated the behaviour of falling bodies and concluded that they all fall at identical rates of acceleration. It is surprising that many people have learned this snippet of theory, forgetting that it is true only in the idealized situation of a vacuum. They will argue vigorously that a kilo bag of feathers and a kilo bag of lead, if thrown from a high building will both hit the ground at the same time. (They won't, as a matter of fact! A kilo bag of feathers is far bigger than a kilo of lead and encounters more air resistance.) In short, the physicists' vacuum is like the economists' "perfectly competitive" market.

Finally, it should be said that the economists' definition of perfect competition differs greatly from the everyday understanding of the term *competition*. Most people, asked to give examples of vigorous competition, would cite Pepsi-Cola and Coca-Cola or Reebok and Nike or the competition in the automobile industry. To economists, however, this is about as uncompetitive as you can get, since each of these producers is very powerful and exerts a great deal of influence in its own market. In other words, though the rivalry between Pepsi and Coke might be intense, the competition is weak. As explained above, something closer to true competition exists between a wheat farmer in Alberta and another farmer she has never met in Manitoba, hundreds of kilometres away.

ADDED DIMENSION

Perfect Competition and the Market System

A perfectly competitive market system is part of what economists refer to as the *market economy* and what others refer to as *free enterprise*. Yet both these terms involve much more than most people realize. In fact, lying beneath the surface are four cornerstones.

The first is the reality that for competition to be effective *trade must be fluid and free*. Furthermore, for trade to even take place, one party must have a surplus of something and, in order to have that surplus, must have produced more than it wishes to consume.

In other words, the economy and its people must practise *specialization*—which is the second cornerstone. And we know that specialization can increase productivity enormously and help make a country wealthy.

Put another way, if a self-sufficient country or individual does not trade, an efficient market system is not necessary. But few if any historical groups have used self-sufficiency effectively. Specialization is the key to high levels of productivity, and specialization requires trade. Therefore, a bigger market means more specialization and more trade, and this means a wealthier nation.

The third cornerstone of a market economy is the institution of *private property*. The desire for increased wealth provides a big incentive for people to work hard and be innovative, and the risk of losing what they already have is usually a sufficient deterrent to laziness and incompetence. In other words, without private property, government itself must provide rewards and penalties in order to promote economic efficiency. But leaving this up to the whim of government officials opens up the system to all sorts of abuse, corruption, and failure.

The final cornerstone of a successful market system is what Adam Smith called "a legal and social foundation." What this means is that rules of minimally acceptable conduct must be present so that people have trust in the system. The market system has often been compared to sports, in which individuals (and producers) need a certain amount of hard work, skill, and good luck to come out on top. And competition requires that all contestants be treated equally—that there be a level playing field. For this to happen, there must be rules applied consistently and impartially by officials. A true superstar in any sport (or industry), the one who earns the big salary and endorsements, is the one who does things differently from anyone who has ever played the sport before. But this originality cannot extend to breaking the rules of the game. A soccer player who, in the name of innovation, decides that instead of kicking the ball he will pick it up and throw it into the goal would not be lauded for his originality but get red-carded! Soccer without rules would be pointless. Similarly, free enterprise without regulation would simply descend into anarchy, lawlessness, and corruption. Government's role is to lay down simple, basic regulations within which firms must operate—and governments must be ready to prosecute firms that infringe the rules.

 TEST YOUR UNDERSTANDING

2. In what way(s) does the stock market represent a good example of perfect competition? In what way(s) does it represent a bad example?

SECTION SUMMARY

The four conditions that must exist for an industry to be *perfectly competitive* are

- many small sellers and buyers, all of whom are price takers
- no preferences shown by either buyers or sellers
- easy entry and exit by both buyers and sellers
- the same market information available to all

8.3   The Competitive Industry and Firm

> **LO3**   Use two approaches to explain how a firm might maximize its profits.

As we have seen, in perfectly competitive markets, individual producers (and consumers) have no control over the price at which the product is bought and sold. The price is determined by the collective action of thousands, if not millions, of separate participants in the market. The forces of demand and supply determine the price, and once the price is established, it becomes a take-it-or-leave-it proposition for each individual. This is illustrated in **Figure 8.1**, using grommet manufacturing as an example and assuming no intervention from the government.

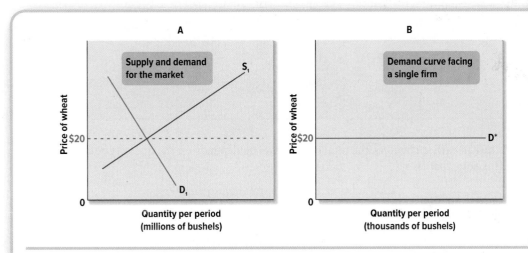

FIGURE 8.1   **The Competitive Industry and Firm**

The market demand, D_1, shown in Figure A, is the total demand from the many buyers of grommets, and the supply of grommets, S_1, comes from thousands of individual manufacturers. The individual manufacturer depicted in Figure B produces a tiny part of the supply, S_1. The market price of $20 applies to all buyers and sellers, including this particular manufacturer, who can then sell as much or as little as she wishes at this price.

In **Figure 8.1A**, given the market demand and supply curves for grommets, the equilibrium price is $20 per unit. This is the market price, the only price at which grommets will be bought and sold. From the individual manufacturer's point of view, shown in **Figure 8.1B**, the price will remain at $20, irrespective of how much or little this manufacturer decides to produce. In a sense, as far as the manufacturer (we will call her Wallis) is concerned, this price line represents the (perfectly elastic) demand curve, D*, for her grommets. She cannot sell the grommets for a higher price because nobody will buy them if they can purchase grommets elsewhere for $20; nor would she want to sell them at a lower price, because she can sell as much as she wants at $20 anyway. Wallis is very much at the mercy of the market.

Since the individual manufacturer cannot affect the price, the only decision is to figure out what quantity will provide the greatest profit. Before we do this, however, we need to look a bit deeper at the possible sales revenue for the manufacturer.

Total, Average, and Marginal Revenues

So, given the market price of $20 per unit, Wallis needs to decide how much to produce. Table 8.3 shows what sales revenues she will receive for different quantities sold.

TABLE 8.3
Deriving Average and Marginal Revenue

Output	Price	Total Revenue (TR)	Average Revenue (AR)	Marginal Revenue (MR)
0	$20	$ 0	$ /	$ /
1	20	20	20	20
2	20	40	20	20
3	20	60	20	20
4	20	80	20	20
5	20	100	20	20
6	20	120	20	20
7	20	140	20	20
8	20	160	20	20
9	20	180	20	20
10	20	200	20	20

As we saw in earlier chapters, the total (sales) revenue depends on the quantity sold and the price at which it is sold, that is,

$$\text{Total revenue (TR)} = \text{output (Q)} \times \text{price (P)}$$

The **average revenue** she receives per unit is simply the total revenue divided by the quantity sold.

$$\text{Average revenue (AR)} = \frac{\text{total revenue (TR)}}{\text{output (Q)}} \text{ or } \frac{Q \times P}{Q} = P \qquad [8.1]$$

Finally, the **marginal revenue** is the additional total revenue derived from the sale of an additional unit:

$$\text{Marginal revenue} = \frac{\Delta \text{ total revenue (TR)}}{\Delta \text{ output (Q)}} \text{ or } \frac{\Delta Q \times P}{\Delta Q} = P \qquad [8.2]$$

The concept of "the marginal" is of great importance in economics, so we need to clearly understand what is meant by marginal revenue. This refers to the amount that total revenue changes as a result of selling an additional unit of the product. In the case of a perfectly competitive firm, how much it receives from selling another unit is simply the price of the product, but as we shall see in later chapters, this is not true for firms in other types of markets.

In Table 8.3, you can see that the price, average revenue, and marginal revenue all equal $20. The equality of these three measures of revenue holds for all competitive firms. To state it in the form of an equation,

$$\text{Price} = \text{average revenue} = \text{marginal revenue}$$

This simply says that the average amount Wallis receives for selling a unit of grommets is the price she sells it for, and this remains a constant $20. Similarly, the marginal revenue (the amount she receives for selling an additional unit) is also a constant $20, that is, the same as the price. Although this might all seem unnecessarily complicated, the concept of the marginal lies at the heart of economic analysis. Also, as mentioned, the price and marginal revenue are not the same in other market situations. We will look at this in later chapters.

Let us look at these variables graphically in **Figure 8.2**. We see in **Figure 8.2A** that the total revenue curve is a straight, upward-sloping curve; its steepness depends on the marginal revenue (or price) of the product. The greater the price, the steeper the slope of the total revenue curve. Since average and marginal revenues are equal, they are represented by a single curve, as we already saw in **Figure 8.1B**. This curve is horizontal to the output axis.

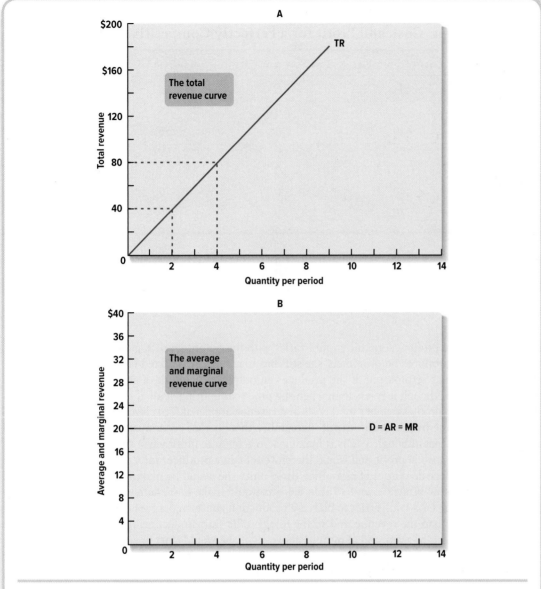

FIGURE 8.2   Revenue Curves

The total revenue curve is upward sloping, which means that the more grommets sold, the greater the total revenue. It also has a constant slope (a straight line) because each additional unit sold increases the total revenue by the same amount, in this example by $20.

The average revenue, the marginal revenue, and the price are all equal to $20, and all remain constant, regardless of the quantity sold. This horizontal line is also the demand curve faced by the individual firm.

Price, Profit, and Output Under Perfect Competition

We have seen that the price at which the manufacturer can sell her grommets is a given; she has no control over it. She has only one decision to make. What output level will produce the maximum profit? (Economists generally assume that profit maximization is the prime goal of the firm. Whether this is a legitimate assumption, and what other goals might be considered, is a discussion we will leave until Chapter 11.)

Profit maximization depends on both the revenue and the costs of production. Table 8.4 repeats the revenue information from Table 8.3 and adds to it the costs of production in Wallis's workshop.

Total profit is the difference between total revenue and total costs:

$$T\pi = TR - TC \tag{8.3}$$

TABLE 8.4
Total Revenue, Cost, and Profit for a Perfectly Competitive Producer

Output (Q)	Price (AR = MR)	Total Revenue (TR)	Total Cost (TC)	Total Profit (Tπ)
0	$20	$ 0	$ 30	$−30
1	20	20	48	−28
2	20	40	58	−18
3	20	60	60	0
4	20	80	63	17
5	20	100	70	30
6	**20**	**120**	**90**	**30**
7	20	140	120	20
8	20	160	160	0
9	20	180	220	−40
10	20	200	300	−100

The amount of profit—economic profit—varies with the output level. A glance at Table 8.4 shows that when Wallis produces no grommets, she still has to contend with fixed costs of $30 and so would make a loss of $30 at zero output. If she produces an output of one unit of grommets, she would still make a loss (of $28), though it is less than when she produces nothing at all. If she produces three units, she will make zero profit, since her total costs and revenue are equal. This level of output is referred to by economists as the **break-even output**. Remember, though, that economists regard a normal profit as part of costs, so that although Wallis is making zero economic profit when she produces three units, she is still making normal profit, and would therefore remain a producer rather than go out of business. If she were to produce an output of more than three units, she would be making not only normal profit but also the economic profit shown in Table 8.4. She would make maximum economic profit of $30 at an output of six units. As Wallis tries to increase production above an output of six units, her total costs start to rise faster than the revenue, and so the total profits start to decline. At an output of eight she would again be breaking even, and at outputs above eight she would start to encounter losses.

Wallis will maximize her profit at 6 units, where (Total revenue − total cost) is greatest. This idea is illustrated in Figure 8.3. Because of fixed costs, total costs are always higher than revenues at low output levels. Until break-even is reached at an output of 3 units, the total cost curve is above the total revenue curve, and Wallis would be making a loss; this is shown in the total profit curve at the bottom of the graph. Break-even occurs where the two curves (TC and TR) intersect, at outputs of 3 and 8, and where the total profit curve crosses the horizontal axis. At these two output levels, total profit is zero. At outputs above 8, Wallis would again be taking a loss, but any output between 3 and 8 would produce a profit. Graphically, the distance between the two curves shows the amount of profit or loss, and the greatest profit is realized when the gap between the two curves is greatest, and this occurs at an output of 6. (It also occurs at an output of 5 units, but for reasons we will soon explain, 6 units is the "real" maximum profit point.) This is shown explicitly in the total profit curve.

Now, let us see what happens if the price of grommets increases. In that case, Wallis will enjoy higher total revenue at every price. Figure 8.4 shows the effect graphically of a price increase from $20 to $30. A higher price pivots the total revenue curve to the left (it gets steeper) from TR_1 to TR_2. You can see that the total revenue at a quantity of 10 grommets has increased from $200 (10 × $20) to $300 (10 × $30).

A higher price therefore leads to three things:

- higher profits (or smaller losses) at every output level
- a wider range of profitable outputs (in Figure 8.4 the break-even outputs previously at 3 and 8 are now at 2 and 10)
- an increase in the firm's output (in our example from 6 to 7 grommets)

A decrease in price, on the other hand, will mean a flatter TR curve and will lead to the opposite result.

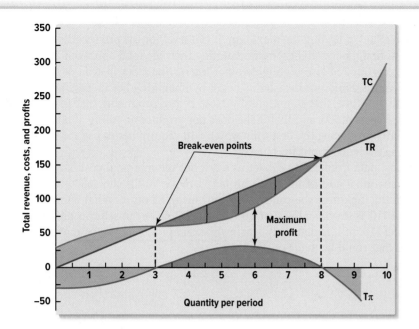

FIGURE 8.3   Total Revenue, Costs, and Profits

If Wallis produces either 0, 1, or 2 units, she will take an economic loss, illustrated as the distance between the TR curve and the TC curve and shown explicitly at the bottom in the total profit curve. At an output of 3 and 8 units, the two curves intersect, which are the break-even outputs. Any output between 3 and 8 will produce an economic profit. Maximum profits occur at the point where the distance between the two curves is greatest—at an output of 6 units. Outputs greater than 8 would result in a loss, since the TR curve is below the TC curve.

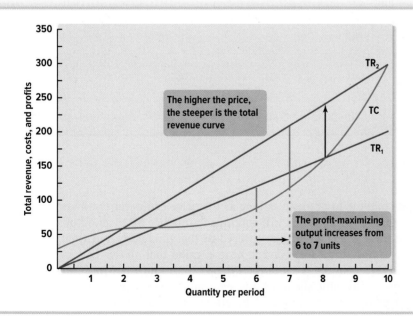

FIGURE 8.4   The Effect on Production and Profits of a Change in Price

The higher the price of a product, the greater the total revenue at each output. An increase in price will shift the total revenue curve from TR_1 to TR_2. The result will be greater profits and an increase in the profit-maximizing output from 6 to 7 units.

The Marginal Approach to Profitability

An alternative method of finding the maximum profit level for the producer is in terms of marginals. This approach, at first glance slightly more daunting than the total approach, is a far more revealing way of looking at profit and also highlights other interesting facts. Instead of looking at every possible output that Wallis could produce, let us begin by imagining her increasing production of grommets by one unit at a time, that is, marginally. Now, before producing that first unit Wallis is aware that she has fixed costs of $30, and that if she does not produce anything at all she will sustain a loss of $30. So she starts producing the first unit, which will require her to pay for supplies, wages, and so on (not forgetting a normal profit for herself).

Using the cost data from Table 8.4, let us work out the marginal cost of each unit. In Table 8.5 we see that the marginal cost of the first unit is $18. Since Wallis can sell this unit for $20, it is certainly worth producing, since she can make a surplus of $2 on it. What about the second unit? Its marginal cost, at $10, is less than the first unit. Again, if Wallis can sell this grommet for $20, she will make a surplus of $10, so it is definitely worthwhile. Table 8.5 shows the marginal cost of each unit and the surplus that could be made on each.

TABLE 8.5
Marginal Cost and Marginal Revenue

Output (Q)	Total Cost	Marginal Cost	Marginal Revenue = Price	Marginal Surplus/Deficit	Total Profit/Loss
0	$ 30				$−30
1	48	$18	$20	$ 2	−28
2	58	10	20	10	−18
3	60	2	20	18	0
4	63	3	20	17	17
5	70	7	20	13	30
6	90	20	20	0	30
7	120	30	20	−10	20
8	160	40	20	−20	0
9	180	60	20	−40	−40
10	200	80	20	−60	−100

Wallis will continue to produce as long as the price can cover the marginal cost of each unit. Table 8.5 therefore tells us that she will continue to produce up to an output of 6 units. That is because each unit up to 6 has more than covered its marginal cost. And what about this sixth unit? Well, although she only breaks even on it, bear in mind that all our cost curves include a normal profit for the producer, so she is more than happy to produce it. More importantly, although she makes no surplus on this unit, she has made a surplus on every single unit up to this one. However, she would never produce the seventh unit, because its marginal cost ($30) exceeds its marginal revenue (price) of $20.

This result confirms what we already know from Table 8.4—but puts it in a very different light and suggests that

If marginal revenue > marginal cost → produce more

If marginal revenue < marginal cost → produce less

Therefore, to maximize its total profit, the firm should increase production to the point at which marginal revenue is equal to marginal cost. In other words,

A firm maximizes its total profits by producing an output at which the marginal cost equal marginal revenue.

We can illustrate this important point in **Figure 8.5**, which shows the marginal revenue (price) for Wallis, the grommet maker. Here we see that the line indicating MR = AR = price is above the marginal cost curve for each unit up to number 6. After that point, each unit costs more to produce than its price. The maximum that should be produced is 6 units.

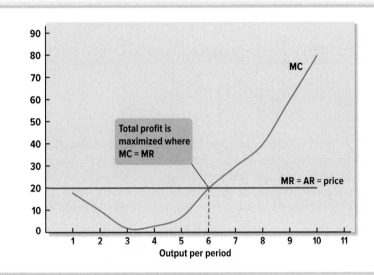

FIGURE 8.5 **Marginal Revenue and Marginal Cost**

A firm will continue to increase production as long as the MR (price) is greater than (above) the MC. Here, production will increase to 6 units. Although this last unit makes no surplus, all previous units have. The producer would not produce a seventh unit, as that unit would result in a loss.

 TEST YOUR UNDERSTANDING

3. Given the accompanying data for Marshall's Meat Ltd., calculate the level of total profits at each output. What are the break-even and profit-maximizing outputs?

Marshall's Meat Ltd.		
Output (Q)	Price (P)	Total Costs (TC)
0	$50	$ 40
1	50	135
2	50	180
3	50	220
4	50	230
5	50	250
6	50	280
7	50	350
8	50	450

SECTION SUMMARY

a) The demand curve for a firm in a perfectly competitive environment is perfectly elastic and is horizontal at the market-determined price.

b) Break-even output occurs where TR = TC, and this is a situation in which a firm is making normal profits only, with no economic profits.

c) A firm will maximize its economic profits where MC = MR or TR − TC is greatest.

d) A firm should increase its output if MR > MC, and decrease its output if MR < MC. To maximize total profit, a firm should produce an output at which MR = MC.

8.4 Break-Even Price and Shutdown Price

> **L04** Explain what is meant by break-even price and shutdown price.

So far, we have established that the best output to produce is that at which the marginal revenue (price) and the marginal cost are equal, assuming the firm will produce at all (something we will look at in a moment). But we need to figure out a few other important benchmarks. For instance, we know that a higher price will encourage the firm to produce more and will increase its profitability; conversely a lower price will reduce output and profitability. Our next task is to find out what price level will result in neither a profit or loss for the firm; in other words, what is the firm's **break-even price**? To help us do this we need to revisit the firm's costs, particularly its average costs. This is done in Table 8.6.

TABLE 8.6
Average and Marginal Costs

Output (Q)	AVC	ATC	Price = AR = MR	MC
0	/	/	$20	/
1	$18	$48	20	$18
2	14	29	20	10
3	10	20	20	2
4	8.25	15.75	20	3
5	8	14	20	7
6	10	15	20	20
7	12.8	17.1	20	30
8	16.25	20	20	40
9	21.3	24.6	20	60
10	27	30	20	80

We know that a firm will break even if its total revenue is equal to its total costs, that is, TR = TC. If we divide both the revenue and costs by the quantity, we can restate that break-even occurs where:

$$TR/Q = TC/Q$$

or where

$$\text{Average revenue (AR)} = \text{average cost (ATC)}$$

It follows then that if the average revenue (or price) is greater than average costs, the firm will make a profit. Conversely, if average costs are greater than average revenue, the firm will make a loss.

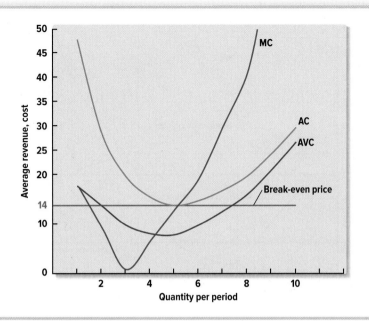

FIGURE 8.6 Break-Even Price

The break-even price is located at the point of minimum average total cost (AC). For Wallis, this is equal to $14. If the price is above $14, the firm can make a profit; below this, it will take a loss.

Graphically, a price level above average cost will mean a profit; a price level below will result in a loss. Therefore, the break-even price is the price level that is just equal to the minimum average total cost.

If you look at Table 8.6 you can see that the lowest average total cost at which Wallis can produce is $14. Her break-even price, then, is $14. This is depicted in Figure 8.6. We can now state that any price above the break-even price of $14 will enable Wallis to make an economic profit, and any price below $14 will result in a loss.

Now, suppose the price happens to be $20. This is illustrated in Figure 8.7. Remember that to maximize profits, the firm should produce the output at which the marginal revenue and marginal costs are equal. Figure 8.7 shows that this occurs at an output of 6 units. This is confirmed in Table 8.6 where we see that the marginal cost is equal to a price of $20 at output of 6. At this output level, the average cost is $15 so the **average profit** is simply the difference between the average revenue (price) and the average cost:

$$A\pi = P (= AR) - AC \text{ or } \frac{T\pi}{Q} \qquad [8.4]$$

So Wallis makes an average profit of $5 ($20 – $15) when she produces 6 units. If we multiply the average profit of $5 by the output of 6, it gives us a total profit of $30. Graphically the total profit is shown as the shaded rectangle with a width of $5 (the average profit) and a length of 6 (the output).

We should also note that for any given price, the break-even *outputs* occur where TR = TC. In terms of averages, this also occurs where AR (or P) = AC. The two break-even outputs are at outputs of 3 and 8, as shown in Figure 8.7.

Now let's consider what would happen if the price happens to be less than the break-even *price* of $14. We know that this means Wallis would be taking a loss. The question now is: Would Wallis, or any firm, ever willingly produce at a loss? In many cases, the answer is yes.

In the short run, given that the size of its operations is fixed, and faced with a price that is less than average cost, the competitive firm has only two choices: continue to produce, but at a loss, or temporarily shut down. In either case, the firm will continue to exist, hoping that the market will eventually pick up. (If it does not, in the *long run*, it may have little choice but to

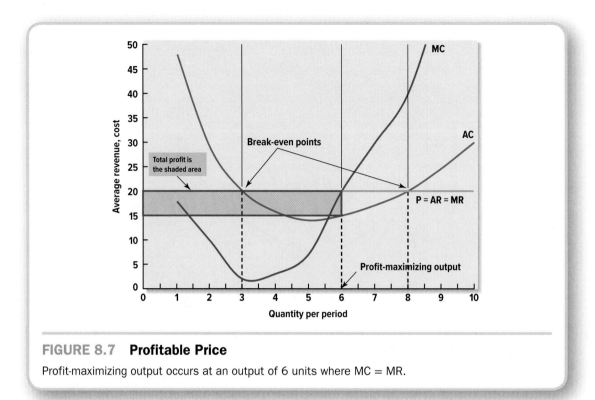

FIGURE 8.7   Profitable Price

Profit-maximizing output occurs at an output of 6 units where MC = MR.

shut down permanently.) So if the price is below the break-even price, what should it do? Produce or shut down? The answer will depend on whether the loss from producing is bigger or smaller than the loss from shutting down. And what loss will be incurred if the firm decides to shut down? This would be the amount of its total fixed costs. We can thus conclude that:

> As long as the losses from production are less than its total fixed costs, the firm should continue to produce.

If the total fixed costs of a firm are, say, $10 000 per week, then the worst loss that the firm can incur is $10 000, which will result from shutting down and producing zero. What this says, in terms of an operational rule, is that since the firm can do little about its fixed costs, because these costs are sunk costs that have already been incurred, it should at least try to ensure that it can cover its variable costs, such as wages, materials, and so on. If the firm is unable to cover even its variable costs, let alone its fixed costs, it would be foolish to produce at all because this will just make its loss even bigger. However, if it can at least cover the variable costs with a little surplus left over, this surplus can help pay for some of the fixed costs.

All of this suggests that the aim of the firm must always be to cover its variable costs (at minimum), and if it cannot it should shut down. Table 8.6 indicates that the lowest AVC ($8) occurs at an output of 5 units. This is illustrated in Figure 8.8, with the **shutdown price** at $8 which is located at the lowest point of the average variable cost curve. If the price is above $8, Wallis will produce even if it entails a loss because she can more than cover her variable costs. And the best output to produce will be the amount at which the price is equal to the marginal cost. This will at least ensure the smallest loss. If the price falls below the shutdown price, Wallis should shut down temporarily and absorb the loss, which will be equal to her total fixed costs.

A decision to temporarily close its doors and cease operations is not a decision a firm will make lightly; and how long it can stay closed will depend on a number of factors, particularly its ability to finance its losses. If it becomes unable to finance its losses, the temporary closure may well become permanent.

You can now see that the firm needs to make different decisions and that different cost curves are used to make these decisions. The average variable cost curve is used to decide whether to

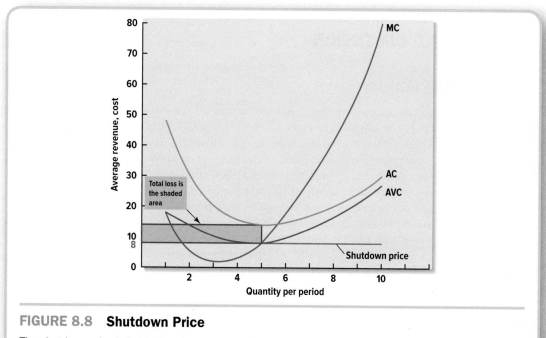

FIGURE 8.8   Shutdown Price

The shutdown price is located at the minimum of the average variable cost (AVC) curve. In this case, it is equal to $8. If the price is above $8, the firm will produce; below this, it will (temporarily) shut down.

produce at all or shut down, the marginal cost curve is used to decide the best output, and the average cost curve is used to determine the level of profit or loss.

Since some of these ideas can seem a little confusing at first, let us summarize what we have said so far in a graphic:

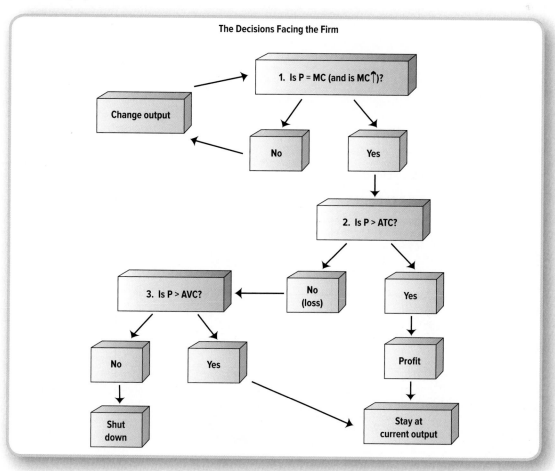

ADDED DIMENSION

Marginal Pricing in Action

The concepts of marginal costs and marginal revenue, far from being esoteric ideas with no relevance in the business world, play a very important part in determining prices and total profits for many major companies. For example, fixed costs are very high for most airlines. To fly a 747 from Toronto to Los Angeles is an expensive proposition, costing tens of thousands of dollars in terms of flight crew, fuel, insurance, landing fees, and so on. The increased variable cost—the marginal cost per passenger—on the other hand, is very low, because it consists of a prepackaged meal, perhaps a drink or two, the cost of replacing a headset, and a little more fuel because of the extra weight. Rather than cancel a flight, which an airline cannot do if it is a scheduled flight, it is entirely reasonable for the airline to offer seats below their full cost to at least cover the marginal costs. In other words, as long as the price is above the marginal costs, it will be worthwhile to take on one more passenger.

 TEST YOUR UNDERSTANDING

4. The following data are for Garden Pots Ltd.

Output (Q)	Average Cost (AC)	Marginal Cost (MC)
0	/	/
1	$45	$15
2	25	5
3	20	10
4	18.75	15
5	19	20
6	20	25
7	22	34
8	25	46

If the price of a pot is $20, what are the break-even levels of output and what is the profit-maximizing output?

5. See the following graph for a perfectly competitive firm.

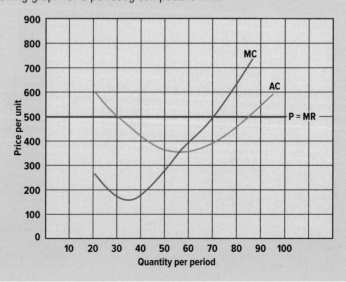

a) What is the profit-maximizing output, and what is the amount of profit at that output?

b) On the graph, shade in the area depicting the firm's total profit.

6. The following graph shows the costs of production for Smith Industries, a perfectly competitive firm.

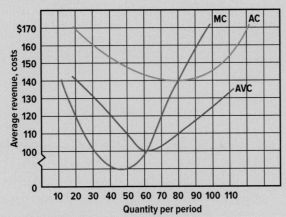

a) What is the break-even price?

b) What is the shutdown price?

SECTION SUMMARY

a) The *break-even price* is equal to the lowest minimum ATC. If the price is above this, the firm will make a profit; below it, the firm will make a loss.

b) For any given price, the *break-even outputs* occur where AR (price) = ATC.

c) The minimum point of the AVC curve is significant for two reasons:

- If the market-determined price is below this, the firm should shut down and limit its losses to TFC.

- The portion of the MC curve that lies above this point is the firm's supply curve.

8.5 The Firm's Supply Curve

> **LO5** Explain how a firm's supply curve is derived.

Let us now put some flesh on these ideas by working through an example, and in doing so help derive a supply curve for a firm. For a change of pace, let us look at some of the costs of an apple cider producer, as shown in **Table 8.7**. Assume that the output is in quantities of 10 litre jugs.

First of all, let us confirm some important benchmarks for this producer. A glance at **Table 8.7** shows that the lowest average total cost is $29. This is the value of the break-even price. If the price is higher than $29, he can make a profit; if it is lower than $29, he will make a loss. Next, look at the average variable cost column in **Table 8.7**. This shows that the lowest average variable cost is $20. This is the value of the shutdown price. If the price is between $20 and $29, the producer will take an economic loss but the cider is still worth producing; however, below $20, the producer should shut down operations, at least temporarily. Given this basic information, let us figure out the supply curve for this producer, relating the quantities he would like to produce at different prices.

Suppose that the price is $15. We have already decided that the firm would not produce anything at this price. By even producing nothing, it will still incur a loss and this loss will be equal to his total fixed costs of $40. (This is the value of total costs when output is zero.) Now let us see what happens at a price of, say, $25. We know he will make a loss at this price, but let us confirm the best output and the size of the loss. To do this, we look down the MC column. As long as the price the

TABLE 8.7
Deriving the Firm's Supply Curve

Output (Q)	Total Costs (TC)	Marginal Costs (MC)	Average Variable Costs (AVC)	Average Total Costs (ATC)
0	$40	/	/	/
1	65	$25	$25	$65
2	85	20	22.50	42.50
3	100	15	20	33.33
4	120	20	20	30
5	145	25	21	29
6	180	35	23.33	30
7	225	45	26.43	32.14
8	280	55	30	35

cider producer receives can cover the cost of each additional unit, it will be worthwhile producing the cider. Bear in mind that the additional costs of producing each unit involve variable costs only. Given this, then, the first five units are definitely worthwhile, since the marginal cost of each unit is less than $25. However, production of the sixth unit results in a marginal cost of $35, which exceeds the price of $25. The cider manufacturer should therefore produce only five units at a total cost of $145 and receive 5 × $25 = 125 in total revenue, thereby making a loss of $20:

$$\text{Total loss } (-\$20) = \text{TR } (5 \times \$25 = \$125) - \text{TC } (\$145)$$

This is certainly preferable to the shutdown loss of $40.

Let us try a third price of $35. We know in advance that the producer should be able to make a profit at this price. Again, the profit-maximizing output is where the price is equal to the MC. Looking at Table 8.7, we can see that this occurs at an output of 6, where the MC is also $35. The total cost at this output is $180, and total revenue is equal to 6 × $35 = $210. The profit, therefore, is

$$T\pi \ (\$30) = \text{TR } (6 \times \$35 = 210) - \text{TC } (\$180)$$

We could continue in similar fashion for other prices, say $45 and $55. The results are tabulated in Table 8.8.

TABLE 8.8
The Firm's Supply Schedule

Price (P)	Output (Q)	Profit/Loss
$15	0	$ −40
25	5	−20
35	6	+30
45	7	+90
55	8	+160

You can see from this table that the higher is the price of the cider, the higher is the chosen level of production and the more profitable is production. The table relates the various quantities that the producer would produce at different prices; in other words, it is the producer's supply schedule. Since the producer will always equate the price with the MC, the supply curve of the firm is in fact identical to its MC curve, as **Figure 8.10** makes clear. Here, we see that the profit-maximizing (or loss-minimizing) output occurs where the MR (or price) equals the MC. At a price of $25 profit maximization is at an output of 5, at $35 it is at an output of 6, at $45 it is at an output of 7, and so on. These points all occur along the MC curve, which is therefore synonymous with the firm's supply curve; that is, the MC curve is the supply curve. However, if the price is below $20, the firm could not cover its AVC. It would, therefore, shut down and produce 0. The supply curve is therefore not the whole of the MC curve, but that portion above the AVC curve. Because of the equality between the price and MC:

> The supply curve for the firm is the portion of its MC curve that lies above its average variable cost curve.

As we noted before, if the price is lower than the minimum AVC, the firm would simply not produce.

IN A NUTSHELL ...

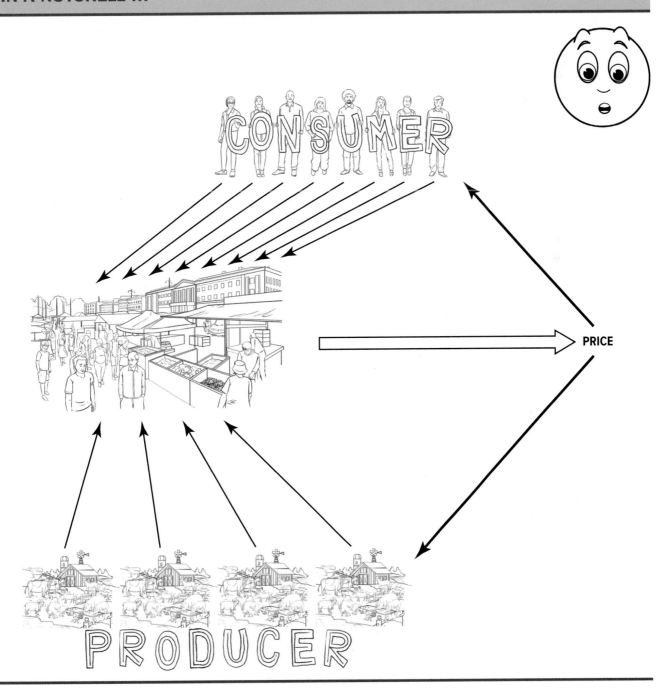

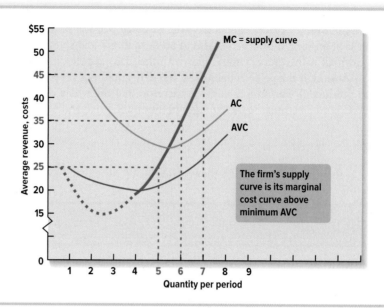

FIGURE 8.10   The Firm's Supply Curve

To maximize profits, the firm equates the price with MC. Therefore, if the price is $25, it is equal to MC at a quantity of 5. At a price of $35, they are equal at a quantity of 6; at $45, an output of 7; and so on. Below $20, the quantity is 0 because this is the shutdown price.

 TEST YOUR UNDERSTANDING

7. See the accompanying data for a competitive firm.

   a) What are the firm's break-even and shutdown prices?

   b) What will be the firm's output and profit or loss at a price of $25? $40? $60?

Output	Total Costs	Marginal Costs	Average Variable Cost	Average Total Cost
0	$ 60	/	/	—
1	100	$40	$40	$100
2	120	20	30	60
3	150	30	30	50
4	190	40	32.5	47.5
5	240	50	36	48
6	300	60	40	50

SECTION SUMMARY

In order to maximize profits the firm produces an output where MC = MR (P). Since higher outputs imply higher MCs, they are also associated with higher prices. Thus, the firm's MC curve (above the AVC) is also its supply curve.

8.6   The Industry Demand and Supply

> **LO6**   Explain the effect of a change in market demand or market supply on both the industry and the firm.

The total supply of cider for the *whole industry* is derived by adding together the supply of each individual cider producer. For instance, if there were ninety-nine other similar-sized producers in the industry, the total supply would be equal to 100 times the quantities shown in **Table 8.8**.

The firm's supply curve is plotted in **Figure 8.11A**. The industry supply curve in **Figure 8.11B** is the horizontal summation of the supply curves of the 100 cider producers. For instance, at a price of $35, the individual firm shown in **Figure 8.11A**, would produce 6 units and the total production of the industry shown in **Figure 8.11B** would be 600 units. Since we know that each firm's supply curve is identical to its MC curve, the industry supply curve is identical to the MC curve of the whole industry. **Figure 8.11B** also shows the market demand for cider. Given the demand and supply, the equilibrium price for cider is therefore $35 per jug. This price is the same for each cider producer, and we can see in **Figure 8.11A** that, at this price, the average producer will produce an output of 6 jugs.

Table 8.8 confirms that at this output, the average firm will make a profit of $30. (The industry profit is therefore 100 × $30, or $3000.) In this way, the fortunes of the industry and the individual firm are totally interrelated. Let us pursue this further by examining what happens when the demand for cider changes.

Long-Run Effects of an Increase in Demand

We now need to recall what is meant by short run and long run from the perspective of both the firm and the industry. As we saw in Chapter 7, the short run for the firm is a period during which it can do nothing to affect the size of its premises. The economic capacity of the firm is therefore fixed. From the industry's point of view, the short run also means that the size of the industry is fixed (because the number of firms in the industry and the size of each firm are fixed). From the firm's point of view, the long run is the amount of time it takes to change the size of its premises, whereas for the industry the long run is the amount of time it takes for present firms to quit or new firms to enter the industry.

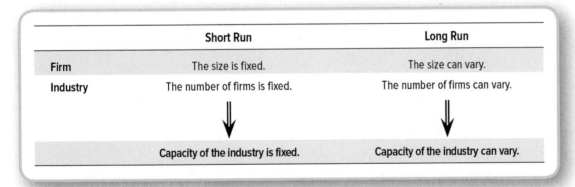

	Short Run	Long Run
Firm	The size is fixed.	The size can vary.
Industry	The number of firms is fixed.	The number of firms can vary.
	Capacity of the industry is fixed.	Capacity of the industry can vary.

Let us now work through the effects of an increase in the demand for cider in both the short run and the long run. Suppose new medical evidence suggests that cider reduces cholesterol levels and the result of this information is a big increase in the demand for cider. From the industry point of view, the effect of this news is an increase in the price of cider.

Figure 8.12A shows that the increase in demand leads to an increase in price and an increase in the quantity produced—a movement from point *a* to point *b*. Suppose that the firm shown in **Figure 8.12B** is a representative cider producer and is initially breaking even, that is, making only normal profit. As the price of cider starts to rise, this firm and the other producers realize they can increase profit by increasing production. The increased production in the industry (from point *a* to *b* in **Figure 8.12A**) is the result of the present firms producing more (from point *a* to *b* in **Figure 8.12B**) with their present facilities. Each producer, previously making only normal profit, now finds itself making economic profit.

This situation is unlikely to last indefinitely. New firms will be attracted by the economic profit being made in the cider industry and will enter the industry, thus increasing the number of firms. This is shown by a shift in the supply curve from S₁ to S₂ in **Figure 8.12A**. The effect of this increased

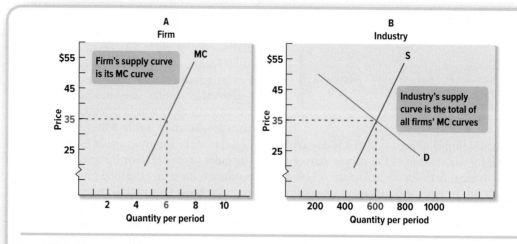

FIGURE 8.11   Industry Supply and Market Equilibrium

The supply of the firm shown in Figure A is based on **Table 8.9**. If the industry consists of 10 identical firms, the market supply would be that shown in Figure B. Given the demand curve shown in that figure, the equilibrium quantity is 600 and the market equilibrium price will be $35. Figure A shows that at a price of $35 this average firm will produce 6 units, and since there are 100 firms in total, this confirms the industry output of 600.

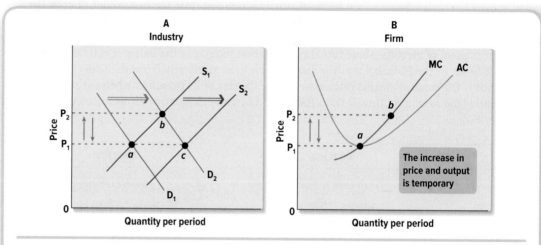

FIGURE 8.12   The Effects of an Increase in Demand on the Industry and Firm

The industry was initially in equilibrium at point *a* in Figure A (D_1S_1), and at the equilibrium price, P_1, the average firm was breaking even and producing an output of *a* in Figure B. As a result of the increase in the demand from D_1 to D_2, both the price and the industry output increase to point *b* in Figure A. However, in the long run, new firms enter, and the market supply increases from S_1 to S_2. As a result, the market price drops, and point *c* becomes the new equilibrium. The average firm finds the price falling and reduces its output back to point *a* in Figure B.

competition in the industry will be a fall in the price of cider and a new equilibrium being established at point *c*. For the older firms, this drop in the price of cider will force a cutback in production and profit until they are back where they started at point *a* in **Figure 8.12B**. Although in the long run the price, profitability, and production levels for the average firm have remained the same, there is one significant difference: the industry is now much bigger, and the larger number of firms means increased industry production.

There may well be an additional change to consider. The first effect of the increase in demand was an increase in price, which stimulated firms to produce more. However, the maximum production of each firm was limited by the size of its premises and by the fact that costs would increase significantly as the firm approached its physical limits. If the average firm believed that the higher demand was likely to be maintained in the future, it would have every incentive in the long run to increase the size of its facilities. In other words, in the long run, the capacity of the industry may increase not only because there are more firms but also because firms are larger. The chain of events is diagrammed below.

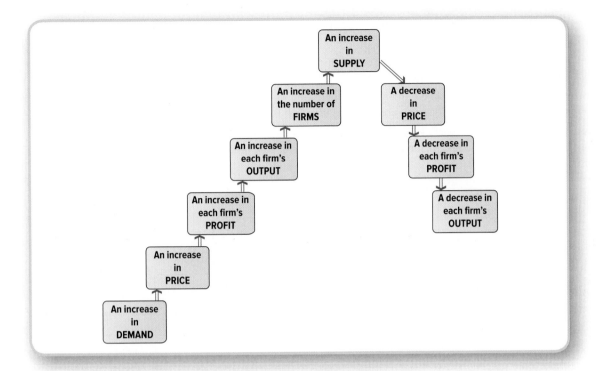

Long-Run Effects of a Decrease in Demand

As in the last example, we will assume that initially the average cider producer is just making normal profit. Suppose that new medical evidence suggests that while cider may reduce cholesterol levels, it also causes tooth decay and constipation. Faced with this new information, consumers drastically reduce their purchases of cider. The decrease in demand is shown in **Figure 8.13A**.

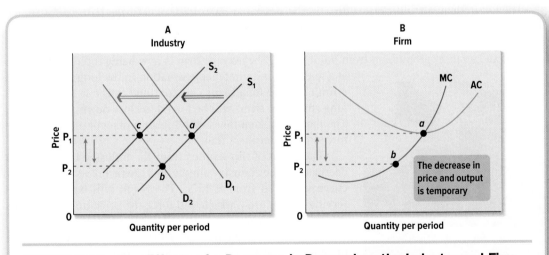

FIGURE 8.13 **The Effects of a Decrease in Demand on the Industry and Firm**

The drop in demand from D_1 to D_2 reduces the output level and the price from point a to point b in Figure A. Output drops because the average firm is forced to cut back production as the price falls. This is shown in the movement from a to b in Figure B. Since the average firm is now producing at a loss, in the long run some firms will be forced out of business. This is shown by a leftward shift in the supply curve from S_1 to S_2 in Figure A, which will cause the price to recover to point c. From the existing firm's point of view, the higher price will cause it to return to point a in Figure B, where it will again be breaking even.

TEST YOUR UNDERSTANDING

8. The following graphs show the market demand and supply for orange swizzlers (A) and the costs for a single firm in the industry (B).

a) What is the equilibrium price and what quantity will the firm produce? Show the price line on graphs A and B. Suppose that the demand for orange swizzlers increases by 600.

b) What will be the new price and quantity in the market, and how many will the representative firm produce? Show the new demand and price on graph A and the price and quantity on graph B.

c) Suppose that, as a result of the increase in demand, the supply increases with the result that the price returns to its original level. Show the new supply on graph A and the resulting changes on graph B.

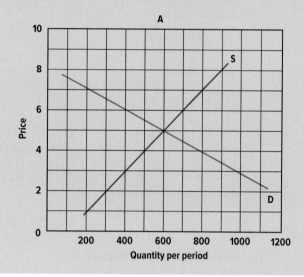

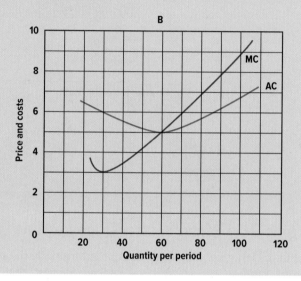

The fall in demand will cause a drop in the price and quantity traded in the industry, as shown in the movement from point *a* to point *b* in **Figure 8.13A**. This reduction is the result of changes forced on the average cider producer, as shown in **Figure 8.13B**. Here, the drop in price causes a fall in profit and a fall in production from point *a* to *b*. The average firm is now being forced to produce at a loss. This is an untenable situation in the long run. There is a limit to how long firms can continue to incur losses. In the long run, some firms will be forced to close down permanently. The more inefficient ones with higher costs will presumably be forced out of business first.

The effect of this exodus from the industry is shown as a decrease in the industry supply in **Figure 8.13A**. The supply curve shifts left from S_1 to S_2. The result will be fewer firms serving the industry, which will force the price up until the industry losses disappear. This will occur when the representative firm is no longer making a loss, that is to say, when the price level returns to its original level at point *c*. From the firm's viewpoint, **Figure 8.13B** shows that as the price starts to recover, production and prices will follow suit, and so eventually the firm is back at production level *a*.

The representative firm in the long run is back where it started, having suffered lower production and profit in the meantime. However, in the long run, the size of the industry shrank following the exit of a number of firms.

Canadian Auto Workers union members create a picket line blocking access to the General Motors Canada head office in Oshawa, Ontario, on June 4, 2008, in protest of the announced closing of the Oshawa truck plant.

Mark Spowart/The Canadian Press

ADDED DIMENSION

Competition and the Internet

A number of commentators have suggested that the Internet has made the economic system more competitive. For instance, in its March 20, 2000, edition, *The Economist* said, "the Internet cuts costs, increases competition, and improves the functioning of the price mechanism. It thus moves the economy closer to the textbook model of perfect competition."

Economists have identified a number of reasons why this may be the case. First, the Internet increases the amount of information about products and prices that is available to buyers. Second, it reduces the transactions cost for consumers to obtain this information because it cuts out the traditional middlemen, who hamper economic efficiency. Third, it increases the transparency of markets (everything is open to public scrutiny) and so intensifies the amount of competition. Finally, it reduces the technical barriers to entry for new firms, since setting up a website and accessing the market is much easier and cheaper than using the traditional methods of the past.

SECTION SUMMARY

a) When an industry that is initially in equilibrium experiences an *increase in market demand*, the following will occur:

- Market price will increase.
- Each firm's profit will increase.
- Output of each firm will increase.
- New firms will enter the industry.
- Market supply will increase.

A *decrease in market demand* will have the opposite effect.

8.7   Long-Run Supply of the Industry

The above analysis of the long-run effects of a change in the demand for a product suggests that it leaves the price of the product unchanged, although it has an impact on the size of the industry and on levels of production. However, this may not be true if changes in the industry size affect the firm's costs of production. For instance, as the industry grows in size with the entrance of new firms, its demand for all sorts of resources, including labour, will similarly grow. The result may be that the price of these resources, and therefore, the costs of production for the representative firm, will increase. This is known as an **increasing-cost industry**, and its *long-run supply curve* will look like the one in **Figure 8.14A**. For example, if the cider industry consumes a big proportion of all apples sold in the market, it is likely that as the cider industry grows, and with it the demand for apples, the price of apples and therefore the industry's own costs of production will start to rise. The long-run supply curve for that product, then, would be upward sloping, which means that an increase in the size of the industry is accompanied by an increase in the price of cider.

If we suppose, on the other hand, that the cider industry purchased only a very small fraction of the output of the apple industry (or if, in general, the cost of apples was only a tiny fraction of the total costs of producing cider), the cider industry could grow without having any impact on apple prices. It would then be categorized as a **constant-cost industry**, and its supply curve would be horizontal as shown in **Figure 8.14B**. This is what happened in our example in Section 8.6.

Next, let us ask if it is possible that costs might decrease in the long run. This could happen if, say, the expansion of both the cider and the apple industry caused more competition in the apple industry or if apple growers started to enjoy economies of scale. In either case, apples might well

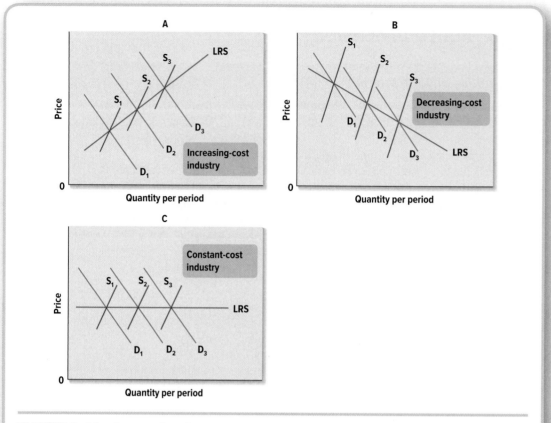

FIGURE 8.14   Increasing-Cost, Decreasing-Cost, and Constant-Cost Industries

In all three cases, A, B, and C, the increases in demand from D_1 to D_2 to D_3 are accompanied in the long run by increases in supply from S_1 to S_2 to S_3. If this expansion has no impact on the costs in the industry, as in Figure C, the price is unaffected, with the result that the long-run supply curve is horizontal. In Figure A, however, costs increase as the industry expands so that the long-run supply curve is upward sloping. In Figure B, as the industry expands, the costs of production falls, resulting in a downward-sloping, long-run supply curve.

become cheaper, thus lowering the costs in the cider industry. The industry would then be a **decreasing-cost industry**, with a corresponding downward-sloping long-run supply curve as shown in **Figure 8.14C**.

We can find a number of examples of each type of industry in the real world. Perhaps the classic example of a decreasing-cost industry is the computer industry, which originated in Silicon Valley (south of San Francisco). As the market for computers (particularly personal computers) grew rapidly, the demand for components—chips, boards, and so on—grew apace. Whole industries developed to serve manufacturers of computers, and the increased competition among these suppliers led to a dramatic decrease in the costs of inputs to the computer industry. The same trend can be found in most electronics, from HD TVs to tablets, from smart phones to entertainment centres.

An example of an industry in which costs and therefore prices have *increased* over the years is the National Hockey League. As the sport developed rapidly, particularly with the expansion of franchises to new American cities in the 1990s, the demand for NHL players grew along with it. The result was an escalation of players' salaries—by far the largest expense for hockey clubs. The result has been an increase in both the costs of operating an NHL team and the prices to attend games.

Finally, a constant cost industry would be one where the major input was content (music, books, information) that is available at a more or less constant price. A radio station or a book publisher would be examples.

In summary, we can see from these examples that competitive markets are dynamic, interrelated, and self-adjusting. A change in demand is translated into price changes, which affect production, profitability, and the size of the industry. Needless to say, each of these changes will also affect employment and the purchase of resources, which, in turn, will bring about changes to the suppliers of both complementary and competing industries. Changes in costs and technology will also affect the profitability of firms and cause the exit or entry of firms, which will then affect the production and profitability of the industry and the price.

In this way, perfectly competitive markets could be called perfectly sensitive markets because they respond quickly and efficiently to the smallest of changes. As Chapter 9 will show, they also produce a number of other significant benefits. But that chapter will also point out the ways in which a perfect market can sometimes fail to respond to change and ways in which responding to change might produce unfavourable results.

The prices of most electronics are a fraction of what they were just five years ago.

Kviktor/Dreamstime.com

TEST YOUR UNDERSTANDING

9. Suppose that initially the market demand and supply for a product are as shown in the accompanying graph.

a) Now assume that the demand increases by 30 units at every price and, as a result, new firms enter, causing the supply to increase by a similar 30 units. Label the new curves D_2 and S_2. Identify the new equilibrium. What are the new price and quantity?

b) Assume that, as a result of the industry expansion, the costs of production increase by $6 per unit. (The supply curve shifts up by $6.) Label the new supply curve S_3. What are the new price and quantity? Identify the equilibrium, and draw in the industry's long-run supply curve.

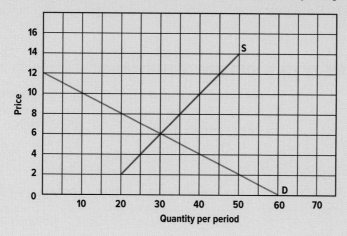

SECTION SUMMARY

The *long-run* supply curve for an industry can be one of the following:

- upward sloping, which is called an increasing-cost industry
- downward sloping, which is called a decreasing-cost industry
- horizontal, which is a constant-cost industry

Study Guide

Review

WHAT'S THE BIG IDEA?

Two important aspects of the chapter need a bit of explaining. The first is the idea of the break-even. Suppose, for example, that you are given the price of a product. You can then easily determine the total revenue for every output. If you know the total costs, then the *break-even outputs* (and there are usually two) occur where the total cost and revenue are equal. (Or, if you are dealing with averages, it is those outputs where the average revenue [price] equals the average cost.) The *break-even price* is different. It's a benchmark price at which the firm can just break even, and it is equal to the value of lowest average total cost. If the price is higher than this, the firm will make a profit; below this it will make a loss. It is important not to confuse these two break-evens with the idea behind the profit-maximizing output. This occurs where the MC equals the MR. Now, it's true that on the last unit produced the firm will "break even," but it's only true for that unit; on every other unit produced up to that point, the firm has a made a profit.

The other aspect that can cause difficulty is finding the profit-maximizing output for the firm when you are given the price. If you know the average and marginal costs, your first job should be to calculate the break-even price and the shutdown price. Once you have those, you know that if the given price is below the shutdown price, the firm is going to take a loss (which will be equal to the value of its total fixed costs). On the other hand, if the price is above the shutdown price but below the break-even price, the firm should produce even though it will take a loss. If the price is above the break-even price, the firm should definitely produce, because it will make a profit. Assuming that the firm is going to produce, look at the marginal costs starting with the first unit; as long as the price is above the MC it will continue to produce. Continue this process until the price is equal to the MC or until the MC is greater than the price. Stop at that point: this will be the profit-maximizing output.

NEW GLOSSARY TERMS AND KEY EQUATIONS

average profit
average revenue
break-even output
break-even price

constant-cost industry
decreasing-cost industry
increasing-cost industry

marginal revenue
perfect competition
shutdown price

Equations:

[8.1] $AR = \dfrac{TR}{Q}$

[8.2] $MR = \dfrac{\Delta TR}{\Delta Q}$

[8.3] $T\pi = TR - TC$

[8.4] $A\pi = \dfrac{T\pi}{Q}$

Comprehensive Problem

(LO 3, 4, 5, 6) Table 8.9 shows the cost data for Farmer Mill, a barley farmer.

TABLE 8.9

Quantity	Total Cost	Total Variable Cost	Marginal Cost	Average Cost ($)	Average Variable Cost ($)
0	$ 6	0	/	/	0
1	10	$ 4	$ 4	___	___
2	12	6	2	___	___
3	16	10	4	___	___
4	22	16	6	___	___
5	30	24	8	___	___
6	40	34	10	___	___
7	52	46	12	___	___

Questions

a) Complete Table 8.9.
b) What are the values of the break-even and shutdown prices?

Answers

a) See Table 8.9 (Completed).

TABLE 8.9 (COMPLETED)

Quantity	Total Cost	Total Variable Cost	Marginal Cost	Average Cost	Average Variable Cost
0	$ 6	0	/	/	/
1	10	$ 4	$ 4	$10	$4
2	12	6	2	6	3
3	16	10	4	5.3	3.3
4	22	16	6	5.5	4
5	30	24	8	6	4.8
6	40	34	10	6.67	5.67
7	52	46	12	7.43	6.57

b) Break-even price $5.30 (lowest AC); shutdown price $3 (lowest AVC)

Questions

c) Given the prices shown in column 1 of Table 8.10, complete columns 2, 3, 4, and 5. (Assume that partial units cannot be produced.)

TABLE 8.10

(1)	(2)	(3)	(4)	(5)	(6)	(7)	(8)
Price	Output	Total Revenue	Total Cost	Profit (+)/ Loss (−)	Quantity Supplied 1	Total Quantity Demanded	Quantity Supplied 2
$ 2	___	___	___	___	___	800	___
4	___	___	___	___	___	700	___
6	___	___	___	___	___	600	___
8	___	___	___	___	___	500	___
10	___	___	___	___	___	400	___

Answers

c) See Table 8.10 (Completed).

TABLE 8.10 (COMPLETED)

(1)	(2)	(3)	(4)	(5)	(6)	(7)	(8)
Price	Output	Total Revenue	Total Cost	Profit (+)/ Loss (−)	Total Quantity Supplied 1	Quantity Demanded	Total Quantity Supplied 2
$ 2	0	$ 0	$ 6	$ −6	0	800	0
4	3	12	16	−4	300	700	450
6	4	24	22	+2	400	600	600
8	5	40	30	+10	500	500	750
10	6	60	40	+20	600	400	900

To find output levels at which she will produce, you need to find the output at which the marginal cost equals (or is greater than) the price. At a price of $4, the output will be 3; at a price of $6, the output will be 4; and so on.

Questions

d) Suppose that there are a total of 100 farms in the barley market, including and identical to Farmer Mill's. Show the total supply in column 6 of Table 8.10.

e) If the market demand for barley is as shown in column 7, what will be the equilibrium price and quantity traded?

f) At the equilibrium price, what quantity will Farmer Mill produce, and what will be her profit? What will be the industry profit?

g) As a result of your answer in (f), will firms enter or leave this industry?

h) Suppose that, in the long run, the number of firms increases by 50 percent. Show the new totals in column 8 of Table 8.10. As a result, what will be the new equilibrium price? What quantity will Farmer Mill produce, and what will be her profit? What will be the industry profit?

Answers

d) Column 6 is derived by multiplying column 2 (Farmer Mill's supply) by 100.

e) Price of $8 and a quantity traded of 500 (where quantity supplied 1 equals quantity demanded)

f) Quantity = 5 units (column 2); firms' profit = $10 (column 3); industry profit = $1000

g) Enter (because the average firm in the barley industry is making economic [above normal] profits).

h) See column 8 in Table 8.10 (Completed) (column 6 times 1.5).
   Equilibrium price = $6;   Quantity = 4
   Firm profit = $2;   Industry profit = $300 (150 firms @ $2 each)

Study Problems

Find answers on the McGraw-Hill online resource.

Basic (Problems 1–6)

1. **(LO 3)** Assuming the price of oats is $3 per kilo, calculate the total revenue and the total profit (or loss) at the quantities shown in Table 8.11.

TABLE 8.11

Quantity (kilos)	600	700	800	900	1000
Total revenue	——	——	——	——	——
Total cost	$2000	2150	2400	2650	2910
Total profit	——	——	——	——	——

2. **(LO 3)** A grommet-maker sold 45 grommets last week and received total revenue of $1215. This week, he sold 48 grommets and received total revenue of $1296. What are the average and marginal revenues of grommets?

Average: _____ Marginal: _____

3. **(LO 3)** Complete Table 8.12, which shows the total profits from producing grommets.

TABLE 8.12

Quantity	11	12	13	14	15	16
Total profit	$220	$264	$325	$336	$345	$352
Average profit	——	——	——	——	——	——

4. **(LO 3, 4)** Figure 8.15 shows the TC and TVC curves of Galbraith's Globes Inc., a perfectly competitive firm.

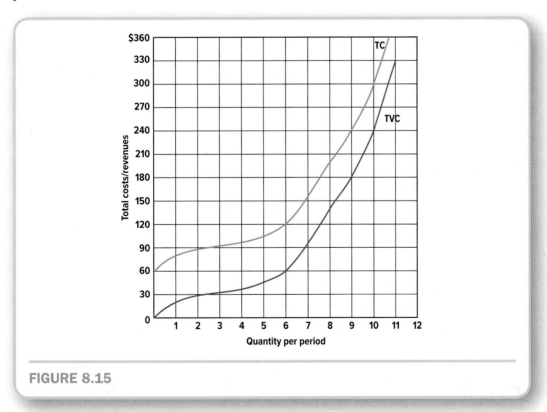

FIGURE 8.15

a) Assuming the price is $30, draw in the total revenue curve, and label it TR₁.

b) At this price, what are the break-even output(s), the profit-maximizing output, and the level of profits at that output?

Break-even output(s): _____ and _____

Profit-maximizing output: _____

Total profit: $_____

5. **(LO 3, 4, 5, 6)** In **Figure** 8.16, graph A shows the *market* demand and supply in a competitive market, and graph B shows the cost curves of a representative *firm* in that industry.

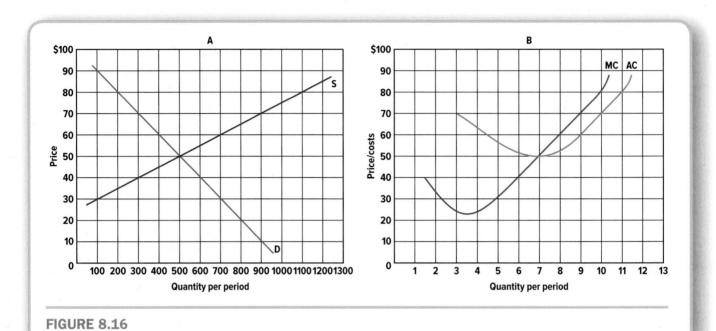

FIGURE 8.16

a) What are the market equilibrium price and quantity?
   Price: _____ Quantity traded: _____
b) At equilibrium, what quantity is the firm producing? What is its total profit or loss?
   Quantity: _____ Profit (+)/loss (−): _____

6. **(LO 3, 4)** **Figure** 8.17 shows the average and marginal cost curves for Kandi Keynes, a perfectly competitive firm.

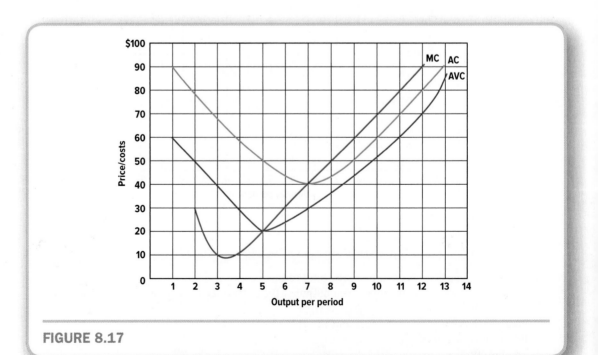

FIGURE 8.17

a) Assuming the price is $60, draw in the marginal revenue curve, and label it MR_1.

b) At this price, what are the break-even output(s), the profit-maximizing output, and the level of total profits at that output?

Break-even output(s): _____ and _____

Profit-maximizing output: _____

Total profit: $_____

c) Draw a marginal revenue curve, labelled MR_2, which ensures that, at best, the firm breaks even.

d) What is the corresponding break-even price? $_____

e) Draw a marginal revenue curve, labelled MR_3, which ensures that, at best, the firm just remains in operation.

f) What is the corresponding shutdown price? $_____

Intermediate (Problems 7–9)

7. **(LO 3)** You are given the following information for a producer of organic grommets, in a perfectly competitive market.

TFC = $8   Market price = $10

The marginal cost of production appears in Table 8.13.

TABLE 8.13

Output	MC ($)
1	7
2	6
3	5
4	7
5	9
6	12

What is the profit-maximizing output? Is the firm making a profit or loss? How much?

Output: _____ Profit/loss: _____ of $_____

8. **(LO 4)** Table 8.14 shows the cost data for Smith's Snuff, a perfectly competitive firm.

TABLE 8.14

Output	Total Cost	Marginal Cost
0	$120	/
1	_____	$30
2	_____	20
3	_____	30
4	_____	40
5	_____	50
6	_____	60
7	_____	70
8	_____	80

a) Complete Table 8.14.
b) What is the total amount of the shutdown loss? That is, what loss will Smith's Snuff incur if it does not produce at all? $_____
c) Assuming no partial units, complete Table 8.15 showing how much Smith's Snuff will produce and what its profit or loss will be at the various prices given.

TABLE 8.15

Price ($)	Output	Total Revenue	Total Cost	Profit (+) or Loss (−)
$20	_____	_____	_____	_____
40	_____	_____	_____	_____
60	_____	_____	_____	_____
80	_____	_____	_____	_____

9. **(LO 4)** The cost data in Table 8.16 are for Marshall's Meats, a perfectly competitive firm.

TABLE 8.16

Output	Average Variable Cost	Average Total Cost	Marginal Cost	Total Cost
0	_____	/	/	$ 80
1	_____	_____	_____	110
2	_____	_____	_____	130
3	_____	_____	_____	160
4	_____	_____	_____	200
5	_____	_____	_____	250
6	_____	_____	_____	310
7	_____	_____	_____	42

a) Complete Table 8.16.
b) What is the break-even price? $_____
c) What is the shutdown price? $_____
d) If the market price of the product is $50, what quantity will Marshall's Meats produce? What will be its profit or loss?
Quantity: _____ Profit or loss: _____
e) If the market price of the product is $110, what quantity will Marshall's Meats produce? What will be its profit or loss?
Quantity: _____ Profit or loss: _____

Advanced (Problems 10–12)

10. **(LO 3, 4, 5, 6)** Table 8.17 shows information for Hayek's Maps, a perfectly competitive firm.

TABLE 8.17

Output	TC	MC
0	$ 100	/
1	200	____
2	290	____
3	370	____
4	468	____
5	575	____
6	700	____
7	870	____
8	1090	____

a) Complete the MC column in Table 8.17.
b) Given the prices in Table 8.18, fill in columns 2, 3, 4, and 5. (Assume that partial units cannot be produced.)

TABLE 8.18

(1)	(2)	(3)	(4)	(5)	(6)	(7)
Price	Output	Total Revenue	Total Cost	Profit/Loss	Total Supply	Total Demand
$ 89	____	____	____	____	____	800
98	____	____	____	____	____	700
107	____	____	____	____	____	600
116	____	____	____	____	____	500
125	____	____	____	____	____	400
134	____	____	____	____	____	300

c) Suppose there are 100 firms identical to this one. Show the total supply in column 6 of Table 8.18.
d) If the market demand is as shown in column 7 of Table 8.18, what will be the equilibrium price? What quantity will be traded in the market?
   Price: _____ Quantity traded: _____
e) At equilibrium, what quantity will this firm produce? What will be its profit or loss?
   Quantity produced: _____ Profit or loss: _____
f) As a result of your answer in (d), will firms enter or leave this industry? _____

11. **(LO 3, 4)** Suppose that the total fixed cost for a particular competitive firm is $6. The marginal cost for the first unit produced is $10 and decreases by $2 for each of the next two units produced. Thereafter marginal cost increases by $2 for each additional unit.
   a) Complete Table 8.19.

TABLE 8.19

Units	Total Cost	Marginal Cost	Total Variable Cost	Average Variable cost	Average Total Cost
0	____	/	/	/	/
1	____	____	____	____	____
2	____	____	____	____	____
3	____	____	____	____	____
4	____	____	____	____	____
5	____	____	____	____	____
6	____	____	____	____	____

b) What is the shutdown price? What is the break-even price?

Shutdown: _____ Break-even: _____

c) If the market price is $10, what is the firm's profit-maximizing output? What is the firm's total profit or loss?

Output: _____ Profit or loss: _____

12. **(LO 3, 4)** You are given the following cost and revenue data for Parkin's Pickles, a perfectly competitive firm at its current output level.

TR = $1430   TFC = $440   MC = $20
AFC = $4   AVC = $8

a) Is the firm making a profit or a loss? How much?

Profit or loss: _____ Amount: $_____

b) Is the firm producing the optimal output? If not, should it produce more, less, or none at all? _____

Problems for Further Study

Basic (Problems 1–3)

1. **(LO 1)** Explain the difference between an *industry* and a *market*.

2. **(LO 2)** What are the four main features of perfectly competitive markets? Explain each.

3. **(LO 3)** From a firm's point of view, what are three implications of a rise in the price of a product?

Intermediate (Problems 4–7)

4. **(LO 7)** Explain what will happen to the output and price of a constant-cost industry if there is an increase in market demand.

5. **(LO 4)** What is meant by *break-even price*?

6. **(LO 4)** Explain why a firm will continue to operate as long as its loss is no greater than its total fixed costs.

7. **(LO 3, 4)** In each of the following cases (a) through (c), you are given certain cost and price information for a number of competitive firms at their present output levels. Assuming the short run, and that marginal costs are increasing in all cases, indicate whether each firm should
    i) produce more
    ii) produce less
    iii) shut down
    iv) cannot be determined without more information

    a) Total variable cost exceeds total revenue. _____
    b) Total fixed cost exceeds total revenue. _____
    c) Total cost exceeds total revenue. _____

Advanced (Problems 8–10)

8. **(LO 7)** What is the long-run supply curve of the industry? How might it be upward sloping? Downward sloping? Horizontal?

9. **(LO 2)** What four conditions are necessary if the market system is to work effectively? Briefly explain each.

10. **(LO 1)** Although it is true that stock prices change constantly, the stock market is in fact not a good example of a perfectly competitive market. Give three reasons for this.

CHAPTER 9
An Evaluation of Competitive Markets

LEARNING OBJECTIVES

At the end of this chapter, you should be able to:

LO1 Explain how perfectly competitive markets encourage technological improvement and growth in the size of firms.

LO2 Explain the benefits of perfectly competitive markets.

LO3 Examine the five reasons perfect competition might fail to achieve desirable results.

LO4 Describe how governments try to deal with external costs, such as pollution.

LO5 Explain how governments try to encourage production of goods and services, such as education, that carry external benefits.

 WHAT'S AHEAD...

This chapter examines the successes and the failures of competitive markets and how, to use the words of Adam Smith, the producer is "led by an invisible hand to promote an end which was no part of his intention."[1] Out of this comes the concept of efficiency, which we formally define and explain. We look at some of the other benefits of competition and then examine various situations in which competitive markets fail. Finally, we look at the reasons for the failure and explore some of the ways that these problems can be addressed, either through government intervention or by helping the market find its own solutions.

---

[1] Adam Smith, *The Wealth of Nations* (Edwin Cannan edition, 1877), p. 354.

A QUESTION OF RELEVANCE ...

It is commonly recognized that competition leads to efficiencies and that we all benefit as a result. But these benefits also carry a cost. Canada is one of the richest countries in the world, and yet it has been estimated that over five million Canadians live in poverty. This poverty, as well as the ugliness and deprivation that come with it in the midst of plenty, beauty, and affluence, highlights both the huge success of the market economy and, at the same time, one of its failings. This chapter may enable you to better understand these issues.

We saw in Chapter 8 how competitive firms react to changes in prices and profitability. Each change causes an adjustment by the firm and by the whole industry, as well. This chapter will continue to examine this theme of adjustment and will evaluate the results.

Adam Smith popularized the compelling and (at that time) original idea that an economy, thus a society, functions best if government leaves it alone. The pursuit of self-interest, it seemed to Smith, would lead people, as if directed by an *invisible hand*, to create a harmony of interests. It should be remembered that in Smith's time, interference by governments in the lives of ordinary people was often arbitrary, discriminatory, and despotic. Both these points led Smith, along with other writers at the time, to suggest that political and economic interference by the government should be limited. In other words, he advocated the doctrine of **laissez-faire**.

For Smith, political and economic liberties went hand in hand. He argued that people should be free to decide their own economic actions, to work wherever and in whatever firm or location they wish, and to produce, sell, and buy whatever products they desire. He tried to explain that not only was such a doctrine morally correct but, just as importantly for our purposes, it was economically sound. An economy works best, he believed, if it is left unplanned, uncoordinated, and undirected. Interference by government is undesirable; if a government tries to direct you to buy certain types of goods that it feels you want, you will probably resent its interest in your welfare. After all, you know better than any government what you want. Such interference is also unnecessary. You certainly do not need any government to persuade you to buy more of a product if it becomes cheaper; you will probably do so anyway. Similarly, entrepreneurs do not need to be told that it is a good idea to open a business in a profitable industry rather than in a declining industry; they already know this. The market works perfectly well, Smith would have suggested, without a manager or a controller or a planning committee to direct it.

The doctrine of laissez-faire raises several questions, however. Will the pursuit of self-interest result in the best of all possible economies? Will it help generate what most people would consider a good society? Might laissez-faire result in a society of greedy and selfish individuals who are unconcerned about their neighbours, a society in which one person's gain is at the expense of another? Furthermore, is it possible that an unplanned economy may result in chaos and anarchy?

The major thrust of this chapter is to look at these questions to see just how effective a perfectly competitive economy (as envisioned by Smith) is, how well it reacts to economic changes, and how desirable the resulting changes are. Thus, what we first need to look at is how changes are accommodated by a perfectly competitive market.

9.1 How Competitive Markets Adjust to Long-Run Changes

LO1 Explain how perfectly competitive markets encourage technological improvement and growth in the size of firms.

We begin this chapter by looking at how firms adjust to long-run changes, such as technological change and growth in the size of firms.

Technological Improvement and Perfect Competition

If an industry (or an economy for that matter) is to grow and prosper, its environment must encourage and stimulate innovation. Let us see how well perfect competition encourages change by looking at how it accommodates the most economically important type of change: technological change.

Suppose that Bobby Brewer discovers an improved brewing method that speeds up the fermentation process by 50 percent so that beer can now be produced more quickly and therefore more cheaply. The result for Bobby will be higher profits. Will the other brewers (assuming there are no patent restrictions) be inclined to introduce this new process? Some will, and some will not. Regardless of this, as word of the new process spreads, it is likely that a number of new brewers, sensing the prospect of economic profits, will join the industry. The whole industry will start to grow. However, the result of this influx of new brewers is a long-run increase in supply and a resulting decline in price. And what will happen to the older breweries that did not introduce Bobby's new technology? Faced with a fall in the price, they will be forced to introduce it; otherwise, their accumulating losses will force their exit from the industry. Eventually, only firms that use the new process will survive. Producers in competitive markets are therefore forced to be innovative; if they are not, competition from new, more progressive firms will force them to change or go the way of the dodo. To emphasize an important point:

> Competitive markets encourage innovation.

The Effect of Perfect Competition on the Size of the Firm

In Chapter 8, we observed that in the short run, an increase in demand for the firm's output increases both its price and profitability. This will stimulate the firm to increase production. If the firm believes that the industry is likely to remain both high-demand and high-profit, it will be encouraged to grow in size, especially if this leads to economies of scale. This idea is illustrated in **Figure 9.1**.

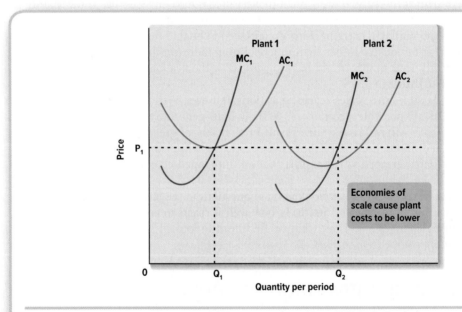

FIGURE 9.1   Long-Run Equilibrium for the Competitive Firm

Suppose that a firm is operating out of plant 1 and the present market price is P_1. The profit-maximizing output in this case will be quantity Q_1, where, in fact, the firm is just breaking even. However, if we assume that there are economies of scale to be obtained in this industry, it will pay the firm to move to a bigger plant, such as plant 2, and increase its level of production to Q_2 (where $P = MC$) and thereby earn economic profits.

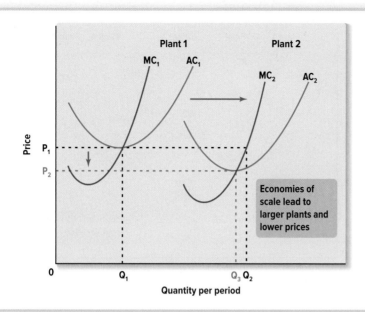

FIGURE 9.2   Plant Growth and Its Effect on the Market

The existence of economies of scale will encourage firms to grow in size. Assume that at present the price is P_1 and the firm is operating out of plant 1 where it is breaking even. In the long run, it will wish to move into a bigger plant, say, plant 2, where it can now enjoy economic profits at Q_2 if the price stays the same. However, if all firms do the same, the market supply will increase, causing the price eventually to drop to P_2, where the firm is once again making only normal profits, that is, breaking even.

If the firm is operating out of plant 1 and the present price is P_1, then the best it can do is break even by producing an output of Q_1. It is not worth trying to produce a higher output than this because the average costs will be higher, and the result will be a loss. However, if there are economies of scale to be obtained in this industry it will pay the firm to increase the size of its operations in the long run. For instance, if it were to operate out of plant 2, it could now make economic profits because the average costs of production will be lower. In plant 2, profit maximization occurs at an output of Q_2. In time, then, firms will tend to grow in size if there are economies of scale to be enjoyed.

Unfortunately, what is true for the individual firm is also true for all firms in this industry: they will all be encouraged to grow in size. The effect on the market is the same as new firms entering the industry; that is, the capacity of the industry will expand, which means that market supply increases, and this will result in a reduction in price. The result of this expansion is illustrated in **Figure 9.2**.

Suppose that the price of the product is initially at P_1 and the average firm's cost curves are shown as AC_1 and MC_1 in **Figure 9.2**. In the short run, the firm is making only normal profits; that is, it is breaking even. However, higher profits can be made through growth because economies of scale can be obtained. This will cause the representative firm to move into a bigger plant, such as plant 2, and since other firms will do the same, the price will drop as the industry supply increases. As this firm and others grow in size, their costs drop—and so does the price. In time, the eventual price of the product will drop to price P_2 in **Figure 9.2**. All of which means:

In the long run, competitive firms will not make economic profits.

Figure 9.3 extends this idea. As we saw, over a period of time, competitive firms will tend to grow in size if there are economies of scale to be obtained. This causes the price to drop and economic profits to be squeezed out. When the typical firm in this industry has grown to plant size 3, it will have no further incentive to grow because plants bigger than plant size 3 will experience diseconomies of scale. For plant size 3, the optimum output will be Q_3. The two forces combined—firms growing in

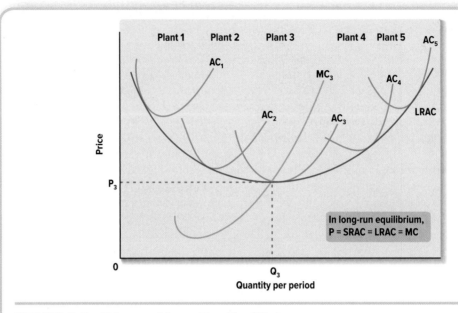

FIGURE 9.3 Price and Long-Run Equilibrium

Because of economies of scale, the average firm will increase in size from plant 1 to plant 2 and to plant 3, which is the lowest-cost plant. But as this happens, the price will drop until the firm is making normal profits only at P_3.

size and falling market price—will result in the typical firm producing an output of Q_3 in a plant of size 3 in **Figure** 9.3 and the price level settling at P_3. This leads to a very important conclusion:

> In the long run, in perfectly competitive markets, equilibrium price will be equal to the firm's long- and short-run average costs (both of which are at their minimums) and also to the marginal cost.

We now need to look at the implications of this important conclusion.

 TEST YOUR UNDERSTANDING

Find answers on the McGraw-Hill online resource.

1. Exactly why should a firm downsize if it is suffering diseconomies of scale?

SECTION SUMMARY

a) Competitive markets adjust to *technological change* very well; firms that do not keep up with desirable changes will often simply fail to remain in business.

b) As firms grow in size, both average cost and price will drop in the long run.

9.2 The Benefits of Perfect Competition

LO2 Explain the benefits of perfectly competitive markets.

We have just seen one of the major benefits of perfectly competitive markets: they encourage innovation by offering the reward of short-term economic profits. Conversely, they penalize firms that refuse to innovate by causing them to incur economic losses, which will ultimately force them out of business. Competition is the spur that brings about this result.

Extending our analysis, let us develop the idea that perfect competition forces firms to be both productively and allocatively efficient.

Productive and Allocative Efficiency

Concentrating on the average costs in **Figure 9.3** for a moment, we can see that in the long run the firm will produce at the point where price equals both short-run average cost and long-run average cost.

This conclusion illustrates the concept of productive efficiency. This means that a product is being produced at the lowest possible average cost, that is, in the most efficient plant size and at the most efficient output level for that particular plant size. Furthermore, customers are the main beneficiaries of this because they are paying a price just equal to this lowest possible average cost. This means that the firms are making normal profits only.

> Productive efficiency is achieved at the output where P = minimum AC.

Productive efficiency is one way in which economists try to evaluate all forms of markets. They ask: Does this particular system result in goods and services being produced at their lowest costs, and does the price of the product reflect that cost? You can see from our analysis so far that in the long run a perfectly competitive market passes this test.

But producing products at their lowest costs is not much use if nobody wants to buy those products or if customers are buying them only because no alternatives are available. There is a second, equally important test of how well a market performs, and that is to ask: Given their tastes and incomes, are consumers getting the products they want? In other words, is the best possible bundle of goods being produced?

For instance, an economy that produced only black-and-white TVs or a vegan society that produced lots of beef or pork would hardly be considered efficient, even if these things were produced at the lowest cost possible. On the other hand, a society that takes into consideration the tastes of people (as well as their incomes and the capabilities of the economy) is said to possess *allocative efficiency*—that is, the very best allocation of resources and products has been achieved, and no other combination of products would achieve a better result for society.

Suppose, for example, that society would benefit more from a new primary school than from an additional parking structure. In that case, the building of the school would be an allocatively efficient use of resources, while building the parking garage would not. Ideally, we would like to ensure that these scarce resources are allocated to various firms and industries in a way that the total output yields the greatest satisfaction to consumers. What the market needs to do is, in a sense, weigh the cost of using the resources in a particular manner against the satisfaction that the resulting products yield. This means that the marginal cost of production should, in some sense, be measured against the marginal utility from consumption. As you will recall from Chapter 5, consumers are purchasing their "best bundle" of goods when the marginal utility per dollar spent is equal for all products (the optimal purchasing rule). We also know that in order to maximize profits, perfectly competitive firms will produce an output at which the price is equal to marginal cost. And what price will ensure both that consumers maximize total utility and firms maximize total profits? The answer is the equilibrium price, at which quantity demanded and quantity supplied are equal. Allocative efficiency implies, then, not only the maximization of consumers' utility but also the maximization of producers' profits. It also means:

> Allocative efficiency occurs at the output where P = MC.

In short, allocative efficiency balances the tastes and incomes of consumers against the availability of the economy's resources.

What perfectly competitive markets do is adjust production and consumption among different products until no further gain could accrue to either producers or consumers from any other combination of goods. This is the essence of productive and allocative efficiency, and is a major characteristic of perfectly competitive markets. **Figure 9.4** illustrates this outcome.

Figure 9.4A shows that in a perfectly competitive environment the typical firm produces an output where both short-run and long-run costs are at a minimum and price equals marginal costs. If we were to sum each firm's output at the various levels of its marginal cost, we would get the market supply curve in **Figure 9.4B**. When we add the market demand curve, we get the equilibrium price of $6 and an equilibrium quantity of 3000 as determined by the interaction of supply and demand.

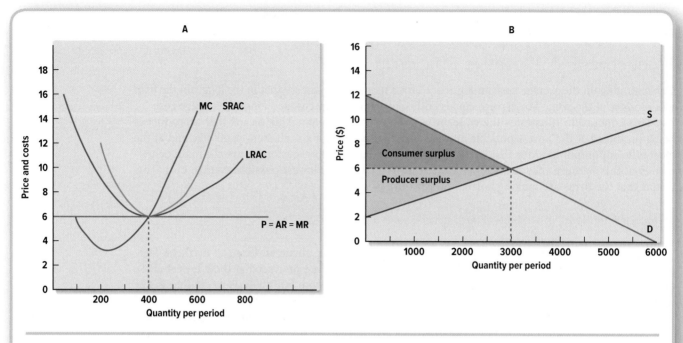

FIGURE 9.4   **Producer and Consumer Surplus in Long-Run Equilibrium**

In Figure A we see the typical firm in long-run equilibrium at an output of 400 that minimizes both short-run and long-run average costs and P = MC = $6. In Figure B we see the whole market, which is determined by summing the marginal cost curves of each firm to get the market supply curve and then adding the market demand curve. The market equilibrium price is $6, and quantity is 3000.

The dark-shaded triangle in **Figure 9.4B** above the price line but below the demand curve represents consumer surplus, as we discussed in Chapter 5. It is the difference between what consumers are willing to pay and the actual price of the product. In the case of **Figure 9.4B** the value of this consumer surplus is not difficult to measure, as it is equivalent to the area of the dark triangle, that is, $9000 (1/2 × $6 × 3000). In a very similar sense, the light-shaded triangle represents **producer surplus**, since producers received a price for each unit supplied, up until the very last one, which exceeds the amount that they would be willing to accept. Again, we can easily measure its value in **Figure 9.4**. The area of that triangle gives us $6000 (1/2 × $4 × 3000). Therefore, another way of thinking of productive and allocative efficiency is to realize that it means consumer and producer surplus has been maximized. The addition of consumer and producer surplus gives us what economists call **economic surplus** which can be thought of as the benefit that society as a whole receives from the production and consumption of a product. The value of the economic surplus in our example is $15 000 ($9000 consumer surplus plus $6000 producer surplus). The important point is that the economic surplus produced in perfectly competitive markets is greater than in any other type of system.

In summary, we can say that in the long run perfectly competitive markets produce an output of goods

- from the most efficient plant size for their industry (lowest LRAC)
- at the most efficient output level for that particular plant size (lowest SRAC)

The significance of this is that both productive and allocative efficiencies have been achieved and economic surplus has been maximized.

Other Benefits of Competitive Markets

Productive efficiency and allocative efficiency are the two main standards by which economists try to evaluate markets, but they are not the only benefits that result from competition. As we have previously mentioned, another advantage that the market system (whether highly competitive or not) has over a planned economy is that markets are a collection of the interaction of millions of producer and consumer decisions happening all at once. There is no one coordinating them and no government organization framing them. That is, the system is automatic and is free of expensive administrative costs. In this sense, the system has no cost.

We also need to add the intuitive argument that perfect competition encourages innovation. It is not hard to imagine active, energetic businesspeople who continuously try to break out of the market constraints of normal profits by introducing innovative, cost-cutting techniques (shifting both the MC and the AC curves down). In a competitive market, such an advantage will not last long, however, since competitors will quickly try to imitate the innovation.

One more supposed benefit of the market system is definitely open to debate. Many people would suggest that any idea of freedom is meaningless unless people are guaranteed economic freedom. A quote from Adam Smith will help give meaning to the term *economic freedom*:

> Every man, as long as he does not violate the laws of justice, is left perfectly free to pursue his own interest in his own way, and to bring both his own industry and his own capital into competition with those of any other man, or order of men.[2]

This theme has been taken up in modern days by many proponents of laissez-faire capitalism, who argue that freedom is impossible in a socialist state because the state directs where and how people are to employ their labour and capital. In addition, socialist states usually forbid the private ownership of capital, and so the individual has no control over how the country's capital will be used. This group argues that while capitalism does not guarantee freedom, it is a necessary condition for it. It follows that they believe all free states are capitalistic, though not all capitalist states are free.

We are now left with the four strengths of the perfectly competitive market system:

- It maximizes economic surplus because both productive and allocative efficiency is achieved.
- It does this automatically (is free of administrative costs).
- It encourages innovation.
- It promotes economic freedom.

This is the case for a laissez-faire approach by government toward the market system. However, note once again that we are speaking only in the context of a *perfectly* competitive market system.

GREAT ECONOMISTS: RICHARD LIPSEY

Richard Lipsey (1928–) received his three degrees from the University of British Columbia, the University of Toronto, and the London School of Economics, and has taught at Essex, Yale, and Simon Fraser University where he is now Professor Emeritus. He has served as the Senior Economic Advisor at the C.D. Howe Institute and has received the Order of Canada. He is best known for his paper "The General Theory of the Second Best" and as a prolific author. His *An Introduction to Positive Economics* is now in its thirteenth edition and has been translated into eighteen languages with total sales well over 6 million copies.

Globe and Mail/Fernando Morales

A bibliography by the Canadian Economics Association concludes by saying that he has had a bigger impact on Canadian economic policy than anyone outside of government. It has been observed that of the three greatest post–World War II economists—Samuelson, Friedman, and Lipsey—he is the least known, almost certainly because of his decision never to exaggerate his accomplishments or influence.

Despite his fame and achievements Richard Lipsey has always been ready to serve, as evidenced by his willingness to address the annual meetings of the BC College Economists or manning a Salvation Army's Christmas kettle.

---

[2] Ibid., p. 651.

TEST YOUR UNDERSTANDING

2. Given the following graph:

   a) At what output(s) is the firm productively efficient?

   b) At what output(s) is the firm allocatively efficient?

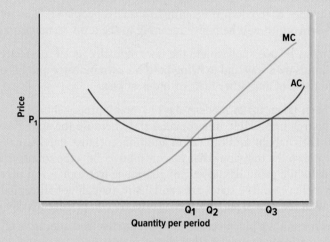

3. Given the following graph of a competitive market:

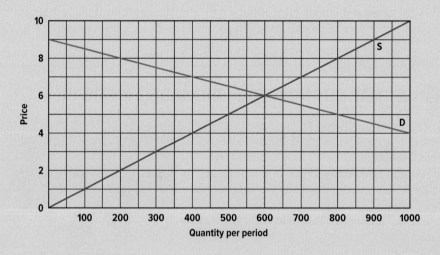

What are the values of the consumer surplus, the producer surplus, and the economic surplus?

SECTION SUMMARY

Other direct *benefits* of a competitive market are that

• it maximizes economic surplus because both productive and allocative efficiency are achieved

• it does this automatically (is free of administrative costs)

• it encourages innovation

• it promotes economic freedom

9.3 Market Failures

> **LO3** Examine the five reasons perfect competition might fail to achieve desirable results.

Despite the advantages of the market system, it has been criticized over the years on many grounds. The remainder of the chapter will examine some of these criticisms, called **market failures**. We will look at five types of market failures.

First, it is said that the market is no guarantor of fairness, and *income and wealth inequalities* often seem endemic to competitive markets. Second, *competitive markets are often unstable* and periodically seem to move, without warning, from an expansionary boom to a recessionary slump. Third, competitive markets seem to contain the seeds of their own destruction because they easily admit *forces that work to destroy competition*. Fourth, competitive markets do not ensure the production of a number of important goods and services known as public goods. Finally, competitive markets often encourage the overproduction of some products and the underproduction of other products because the market has difficulty integrating what are known as *externalities*.

We will look at each of these criticisms in turn and try to understand why many observers think that governments have an important role in correcting some of these deficiencies.

Income and Wealth Inequalities

When evaluating a particular economic system, the question of fairness is particularly pertinent. Critics of competitive markets point out that allocative efficiency, while desirable in some ways, does not guarantee fairness. Allocative efficiency means that resources are allocated in the most efficient manner *given the income distribution that prevails at that point in time.*

However, it is a simple truth that the competitive market system expresses no concern about what that income distribution actually is. In other words, if the income distribution were to change in ways that most consider undesirable, the competitive market system would automatically adjust the allocation of resources to also make the new allocation efficient. Even a society that has a vast number of poor people and a very few very rich people could have an economy that was allocatively efficient. In short, competition is blind to the fate of its participants.

For most people, an important aspect of fairness is that the rewards are commensurate with the amount of effort expended. In many respects, competitive markets do reward greater effort with greater incomes. However, the competitive market system does not always guarantee that this will be so. In particular, many people earn great rewards without putting forth any effort because they are owners of resources. Resource ownership is not evenly distributed in competitive societies and is handed down from generation to generation. The result is that the incomes that flow from this wealth are sometimes the result of parentage rather than effort. In short, competitive markets may perpetuate existing inequalities.

Most populations include people with no marketable resources, and who without government intervention would be left destitute by the competitive market. This is the case when people do not have even their own labour to sell, perhaps because they are mentally unhealthy or physically infirm, are too young or too old, or must look after family members full time. The perfectly competitive market would normally fail to provide such people with any income at all. The result may be a distinctly skewed distribution of incomes and wealth, causing a big disparity between the earnings of the very rich and the very poor.

Income disparities certainly exist in Canada, and have in fact been rising. In constant (2014) dollars, between 1995 and 2014 average after-tax incomes increased by nearly 33 percent (from $51 200 to $68 000). However, for the lowest 10 percent of families, average income in fact declined from $9 400 to $9 300 whereas the top 10 percent saw their incomes rise by almost 46 percent (from $128 100 to $186 500). Put another way, in

The disparity between the rich and the poor is often conspicuous and obvious.

© Ginasanders/Dreamstime.com

1995 the top 10 percent of families earned 13.6 times the amount earned by the lowest 10 percent. By 2014, that figure had risen to 20 times.

One graphic way of showing the wide disparity between the rich and the poor in Canada is using the metaphor of the *parade of the giants*, first described by the Dutch economist Jan Penn. Suppose everybody in Canada were to march past you in a two-hour parade with the marchers organized in terms of income, the poorest going first and the richest last. Now, suppose the heights of the people are proportional to their income, those with twice the average income being twice the height of the average. What would the parade look like? Well, it is easy to imagine a parade in which the people get steadily taller. But that would miss out some of the important details. In fact, the parade of giants would be more like a parade of dwarfs.

At first, you would have great difficulty peering down at the people, as they would be just a few inches in height—old people, youngsters, and welfare recipients. After 15 minutes, the height of the dwarfs is still less than 10 inches. Next come the lower-skilled members of the work force—manual labourers and retail workers—all of them below waist height. In fact, it would take over 50 minutes for them all to pass, there are so many of them. Halfway through the two-hour parade, you would expect to be looking people in the eye—people of average height should be in the middle. But that is not so. In fact, it is only in the last 40 minutes or so that you encounter people of your own height. After that, heights begin to surge with the arrival of doctors, lawyers, and senior civil servants 20 feet tall and more. The real excitement, though, only begins in the last few minutes as the bankers, stockbrokers, and successful corporate executives arrive, peering down from 50, 100, 500 feet above you. Only in the last seconds do you get a fleeting glimpse of pop stars, movie stars, and the super-rich. At least, you can see parts of them; their heads are way up in the sky, a mile above you.

You might ask: But don't our tax and income transfer programs counteract the tendency of income disparity in Canada? One way to answer this question is to look at the effect of the tax and transfer system and compare average income levels of the poorest and richest groups before and after taxes and transfers. In 2011 the richest group had over 24 times as much before-tax-and-transfer income as those in the poorest group. Then in the same year, after adjusting for the effect of taxes and transfers, the richest group had only 9 times as much income as the poorest group. This means that government taxes and transfers are reducing income inequality. However, it is also true that the tax and transfer system is not reducing the income disparity gap as much as it once did. In 1989, the richest group had 7 times more income after taxes and transfers than the poorest group. As we just saw, this figure has grown to be over 9 times. Therefore the answer to our question above is: Yes, but not as much as it used to.

In summary:

> The fair distribution of income is an issue that the market simply does not address.

IT'S NEWS TO ME ...

A recent report from the Conference Board of Canada indicates that income inequality in Canada has increased over the past 20 years. The report said that after hitting a low of 28 in 1989, Canada's Gini coefficient [a measure of income or wealth distribution, used to measure inequality] began to rise in the 1990s to over 30 (the range is from 0, for absolutely equal income distribution, to 100 for total inequality). So far it has remained around 32 in the 2000s with the just released latest estimate of 33 for 2016.

Why has this happened? The conventional explanation is that market forces, particularly skill-biased technical change and increased globalization, are increasing the demand for highly skilled labour in developed countries such as Canada. At the same time, these developed countries are importing more low-skills-intensive goods with the result that jobs in the low-skilled industries are lost. A leading economic journal echoes this view by noting that new technologies have pushed up demand for the brainy and well-educated and at the same time hit the rich world's less educated folk with unaccustomed competition.

An alternative explanation, put forward by economist Paul Krugman, is that the increase in inequality can be attributed to institutional forces, like declines in unionization rates, stagnating minimum wage rates, deregulation, and national policies that favour the wealthy. In Canada, Armine Yalnizyan notes that falling top marginal tax rates are part of the explanation for the rise of the richest 1 per cent of the population.

Source: *Star Power Reporting*, March 2017.

I. Which of the following is consistent with the conventional explanation of Canada's rise in the Gini coefficient?

a) a decrease in the demand for highly skilled workers
b) an increase in the supply of less educated workers
c) a decrease in imports of low-skills-intensive goods
d) advances in skill-based technology

II. Which of the following statements is invalid?

a) Unionization rates in Canada have declined.
b) The marginal tax rate for higher incomes has fallen.
c) Canada's Gini coefficient has been stable for most of the 2000s.
d) Minimum wage rates have been increasing steadily.

 ADDED DIMENSION

The Rich and the Poor

There are a number of ways to measure income inequality. One is the Gini index, which measures the difference between how a country's income is distributed and a base of zero that assumes perfectly equal distribution. (Perfectly unequal distribution would be 100%.) Using this method, the country with the most even income distribution is Ukraine, with a coefficient of 24.1. Others with relatively equal distributions are Norway (25.9), Sweden (27.3), and Belgium (27.6). Countries with less equal distributions (higher coefficients) are the United States (41.1), China (42.2), and Brazil (51.5). South Africa (63.4) has the most unequal distribution.

Rank	Country	Gini Coefficient	Rank	Country	Gini Coefficient
1	Ukraine	24.1	47	Australia	34.9
2	Slovenia	25.6	50	Italy	35.2
3	Norway	25.9	55	Spain	35.9
4	Slovak Republic	26.1	72	United States	41.1
5	Czech Republic	26.1	74	Russia	41.6
18	Denmark	29.1	78	China	42.2
19	Germany	30.1	97	Mexico	48.2
35	United Kingdom	32.6	98	Bolivia	48.4
37	France	33.1	109	Colombia	53.5
40	Canada	33.7	113	South Africa	63.4

Source: *World Development Indicators*, World Bank, 2017.

continued

Another way of looking at income distribution within a country is to measure the percentage of income received by the highest 10 percent of income earners. Here are some examples.

Rank	Country	% of Total Income	Rank	Country	% of Total Income
1	Slovak Republic	20.5	43	Italy	26.3
2	Ukraine	20.6	47	Australia	26.5
3	Norway	20.9	53	France	26.8
4	Slovenia	21.1	74	United States	30.2
5	Sweden	21.5	84	China	31.4
20	Denmark	23.5	89	Russia	32.2
21	Germany	23.7	122	Mexico	39.7
25	United Kingdom	24.7	130	Colombia	42.2
27	Japan	24.8	136	South Africa	51.3
39	Canada	25.7	137	Namibia	137

Source: World Development Indicators, World Bank, 2017.

Ukraine and Norway's income distributions are the most equal in the world and, as you can see, Canada's income distribution is more equal than that in most countries of the world.

Instability of Competitive Markets

Since the dawn of the industrial age, observers have noticed that competitive economies do not grow at a steady pace despite a general upward trend in production and incomes. Instead, they seem to be prone to business cycles of booms and slumps. A period of rapid economic growth and full employment eventually comes to an end, followed by a period of low or even negative growth and high unemployment. In other words, recessions seem endemic to the market system. Such fluctuations are unpredictable and not fully understood. They can, and often do, cause great distress for some, and for this reason governments generally need to intervene in the economy to minimize these fluctuations. Such intervention has often been criticized, but the truth remains that the competitive market by itself fails to prevent such harmful booms and recessions. Since the attempts of government policy to manage the economy make up a large part of the subject of *macro*economics, we will not pursue this idea any further in this text.

The Forces of Uncompetition

As we saw in Chapter 8, the market system encompasses the idea that producers and consumers are free to buy and sell whatever they wish, whenever and wherever they choose. Laissez-faire implies freedom from government constraint. But the troubling question for many observers is this: Does this freedom mean that firms can choose *not* to compete with one another? Adam Smith was always wary of businesspeople:

> People of the same trade seldom meet together, even for merriment and diversion, but the conversation ends in a conspiracy against the public, or in some contrivance to raise prices.[3]

However, having raised the possibility that firms might collude, he quickly dismissed the idea. He believed that should a number of firms collude or one big firm try to dominate an industry, it would lead to profitable opportunities for those firms that refused to collude. They could simply undercut the prices of the big firms.

But Smith ignored the fact that big firms have an advantage over smaller firms. They can achieve economies of scale, and can therefore operate at lower costs; thus, they can undercut the prices of small firms and drive them out of business. Once this is done, the competitive market ceases to exist.

[3] Ibid., p. 129.

In the automobile, oil refining, and hydroelectric industries, for instance, the benefits from economies of scale can be enormous. The twentieth century saw a tremendous increase in the number of very big firms, and many industries today are dominated by a few giant companies. All of this forces us to conclude that the *ideal* of a perfectly competitive market may not be possible, given the dynamics of the *actual* market, and therefore may not produce the benefits that we have looked at. An important consequence when the forces of imperfect competition take hold in the economy is that the size of the economic surplus—made up of consumer and producer surplus—will decline as prices of goods rise and quantities produced fall. We will have more to say about this in Chapter 10.

 ADDED DIMENSION

The Theory of Second Best

In the 1950s, Canadian economist Richard Lipsey raised a serious challenge to idea that competition in the marketplace actually yields the impressive benefits that the model implies. The restricting assumptions that underlie the perfectly competitive market model—the absence of market power for large firms to influence prices, no uncertainty about the future and perfect information—are obvious. Nonetheless, many proponents of laissez-faire capitalism argue that even though perfect competition is always an abstraction and never a reality, the closer we can move markets toward the state of perfect competition, the better off we will all be. They are saying that any increase in the level of competition within a particular market is an improvement and the social benefits of such a movement are always positive.

Lipsey successfully discredited this view using an elaborate mathematical model. We can borrow an analogy from Joseph Heath to illustrate how. Imagine that you really want to go to Hawaii for a winter holiday but you have a fixed budget that you must adhere to. You check with your travel agent about prices only to discover that you simply cannot afford to go to Hawaii. You then begin to think about an alternative destination and discover that your budget will allow you to go to Las Vegas for a few days. Las Vegas is only half as desirable as Hawaii, but you simply cannot afford Hawaii so you settle for the second-best alternative.

Then, out of the blue, your agent calls back to say that she has found a package that will fly you 90 percent of the way to Hawaii for a price within your budget. In the abstract, 90 percent of your first choice is preferable to the second-best alternative, which is only half as desirable. But—and this is a big but—90 percent of the way to Hawaii is nonsense. You would spend the holiday in the ocean somewhere!

The point of this analogy is that while the proponents of free-market capitalism admit that perfect competition is not possible, they continue to argue that any move toward getting the economy closer to fulfilling the conditions of perfect competition is an improvement. Not necessarily so, according to Lipsey. An example here would be the opening up of the North American market to free trade in automobiles in the 1970s. This was a move toward a more competitive economy. Whether it made North American societies better places in which to live is an open debate.

Provision of Public and Quasi-Public Goods

Many goods and services consumed in Canada are provided by government. Some of these products could just as easily be provided by the private market. In many other countries, they are. So why do governments, in general, feel that they should be responsible for providing *any* goods and services, especially when doing so requires the imposition of taxes? In a sense, the provision of public goods is a retreat from the idea of personal freedom because it means, for instance, that you and I do not have complete freedom to choose what we want to buy or not buy.

Nonetheless, there are a number of compelling reasons that throughout history, governments have felt it desirable to provide certain products. The most obvious case is the one in which private firms would simply not provide them because they would not be able to make a profit doing so. To understand why, we need to look in more detail at what exactly economists mean by a public good (some economists prefer the term "collective good").

Strictly defined, **public goods** have two features that distinguish them from **private goods**. First, all public goods are **nonrival goods**. For example, my watching a popular TV show every week does not in any way prevent you from enjoying the same show: the quality of the broadcast signal remains the same no matter how many people are watching it at the same time. With a private good, the situation is very different. If, for example, you help yourself to a can of beer (a private good) from my fridge during a commercial, one less can is available to me.

Other examples of public goods that are nonrival are knowledge and fresh air. If I acquire more knowledge of a subject or breathe more deeply, it does not diminish the amount of those valuable resources available to others. As far as a government-provided service is concerned, military defence is also an example of a nonrival good, since the fact that I am defended does not reduce the amount by which you are defended.

The second feature of all public goods is that they are **non-excludable**. A classic example of a good that is non-excludable is a lighthouse. Imagine a small fishing village where the fishers are often coming to grief because of the hidden presence of a reef just offshore. Someone, quite rightly, decides that the construction of a lighthouse would provide sufficient warning. A lighthouse company constructs the needed building and charges a fee to all the fishers who are going to use its services. But you can easily see that in this situation, there will be no need for individual fishers to pay such a fee, because it will be very difficult for the lighthouse company to exclude nonsubscribers from looking at the lighthouse. That being so, the lighthouse company will soon go out of business, and the only way a future lighthouse could be built is by government financing it out of tax revenues (or through voluntary contributions).

A lighthouse is a public good.

Perry Mastrovito/Creatas/PictureQuest

Another example of a non-excludable good is policing. If the amount of crime in a town is reduced because of efficient policing, all citizens of the town will benefit. To sell policing as a private good would be very difficult because it would be impossible to prevent those people who were not prepared to pay for the services from receiving a benefit. (This is often referred to as the *free rider* problem.)

Many products are both nonrival and non-excludable, including lighthouses, military defence, and policing, as well as snow removal from highways, swamp clearance, and the provision of laws and the court system. As a result, these are truly public goods and must be provided by governments, since the market system would be unable to provide them. But lest you should think that all products that are nonrival are also non-excludable, think, for instance, of cable television or an art gallery. In both these cases, it is certainly possible to prevent nonsubscribers from enjoying these services (thus they are excludable), but in each case, the addition of one more user does not really affect the provision of services to others (thus they are nonrival). It is also possible for something to be rival but non-excludable. For example, fisheries on the high seas are definitely rival (overfishing will certainly deplete the fish stock), but it is almost impossible to exclude fishing vessels from the high seas. In short:

A public good is one that is both nonrival and non-excludable.

While it is true to say that public goods must be provided by government, it does not follow that all goods actually provided by government are public goods—some, in fact, are private goods! For example, education is not a public good. Indeed, most countries have a private-school sector, since it is easy to exclude nonsubscribers. The same is true of private health services (treatment by doctors and hospitals), postal delivery, and the provision of social infrastructure, such as highways and harbours. All these might be produced by the private sector but are often provided by government. Such goods do not meet the strict definition of a public good. Thus, if they are provided by government, they are known as **quasi-public goods** (they "look like" public goods).

An F18 fighter jet of the Canadian Air Force prepares to take off.

© Maurice Morwood/Alamy

There are three main reasons why governments decide to provide these quasi-public goods. First, the costs (to the firm and to consumers) of collecting revenues in a private market might be prohibitive. This is the case with urban roadways, for example. Although a toll charge could be imposed on major highways, it would be expensive to install toll booths (or some other collection device) on all urban and suburban streets or on little-used country roads.

To prevent this possibility, the provision and maintenance of roads is usually financed through taxation. Or consider the case of Canada's health care system. If one accepts the validity of universal health care coverage, Canada's single-payer system has proven itself very efficient, as is evidenced by the fact that the administration costs of health care expenditures are 7.5 percent of GDP in the United States but only 2.5 percent in Canada.

A second reason for the provision of quasi-public goods by government is a situation in which competition is inefficient because it would involve wasteful duplication. This is particularly true when large economies of scale are involved. Rather than allow a number of competing electricity distribution and public transportation systems, for instance, a government might take sole responsibility for providing such services.

The final, and probably the most important, reason governments provide health and education services is that these quasi-public goods are important not only to the people who currently use the services but to society as a whole. These services involve what are known as external costs and benefits, a subject to which we now turn.

Externalities

The fifth failure of the competitive market is its inability to take into account the costs and benefits, not just to producers and consumers of products but to the rest of society as well. The true social costs of any product include the private costs of production as well as the **external costs**. Similarly, the true social benefits include both the private benefits enjoyed by the users of the product as well as the **external benefits** enjoyed by others. The production of most products involves a certain amount of these **externalities**, but with some products the externalities are so great that by ignoring them the market totally distorts the prices and quantities produced.

Let us look at some examples of externalities and see why they arise. First, it should be pointed out that when you pay for a product you likely assume you are paying the full costs of producing it. Often, however, this is not the case. Suppose fishers cast their nets and earn their livelihoods downstream from a pulp mill. What is to prevent the mill from maximizing its profits by discharging its effluent by the cheapest method possible—by simply dumping it into a nearby river? This has enormous implications for the fishers (not to mention the fish). It also means that customers of the pulp mill are not really paying the full costs of the product.

There are any number of examples of external costs besides the obvious ones of water and air pollution. Noise pollution is experienced by anyone living near a major airport or near the lines of an urban railroad or on a busy street. Aesthetic pollution is suffered by anyone whose scenic views from home or office are suddenly destroyed by a new monster house or skyscraper. It is now acknowledged that these external costs to society are as important as the private costs of production.

And it is not just with *production* that external costs occur. The *consumption* of products can also impose external costs on others. For example, we are all aware these days of the harmful effects of cigarette smoking, not just to smokers but also to those forced to breathe second-hand smoke. Similarly, the consumption of alcohol combined with driving can also impose great harm on others. The competitive market, however, does not include these additional costs in the overall costs of production. The result of this is that the prices of many products are *lower* than they would otherwise be and the quantity demanded is higher, and thus too much of certain products are being produced. In a sense, then, producers and consumers of these polluting products are enjoying a benefit partly at the cost of other members of society.

It is true that the production and consumption of certain products cause external costs, but there are many cases where the production and consumption of other products may well lead to external *benefits*. For instance, if I spend money on having my front yard landscaped, I enjoy the benefits of greater aesthetic enjoyment and an increase in the value of my property. But my neighbours would also enjoy an increase in property values—they receive an external benefit. However, this is usually a "free" benefit, unless I go door to door asking for contribution. Not a good idea—at least not in my neighbourhood!

Another example of an external benefit would be the symbiotic relationship between an orange orchard and a neighbouring honey farm. The

Air pollution from a pulp and paper mill is just one of many examples of external costs.

Photodisc/Getty Images

production of oranges produces a clear external benefit for the honey farm, since the bees get a ready source of nectar. But the orchard also derives a benefit from the convenient proximity of the farm; by pollinating the blossoms, the bees increase the orange crop. However, it is more usual that *consumption* of goods gives rise to external benefits. For instance, it is clear that if you were given a flu vaccine you would derive a benefit, but it also helps others because their chance of contracting the illness from you is reduced. We all derive enormous external benefits when our fellow citizens are healthy and well educated.

But probably the most important example of external benefits are those related to health and education. It is a simple truth that individually each of us gains enormous benefits from being healthy and well educated; but it is equally true that I and the rest of society gain from the fact that you and others are also healthy and well educated.

IN A NUTSHELL ...

The World of Perfect Competition Has Some Flaws

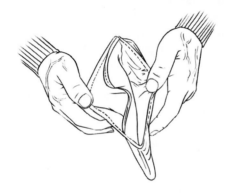

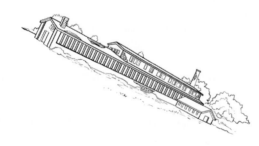

We can now summarize the five types of market failures:

- The market creates gross inequalities of income and wealth.
- A market economy may be quite unstable.
- Competition, the market's internal regulator, may disappear.
- The market is unable to provide public goods.
- The market ignores externalities.

TEST YOUR UNDERSTANDING

4. Which of the following goods are nonrival, and which are non-excludable?

a) art galleries

b) high-seas fisheries

c) national defence

d) a seat in a movie theatre

e) highways

Are any of these *both* nonrival and non-excludable?

ADDED DIMENSION

Canada's Record on Greenhouse Gas (GHG) Emissions

There is a growing consensus that climate change is now the most serious global environmental threat facing humankind. The consequences of climate change include global warming, a rise in the world's sea levels, an increase in the number of extreme-weather events such as tornados, hurricanes, and tsunamis, and altered rainfall patterns across continents.

The vast majority of scientists who study this problem are convinced that climate change is a direct consequence of higher greenhouse gas (GHG) concentrations in the atmosphere. Since burning fossil fuels produces GHG, how we produce the energy that we use to generate electricity, move people and goods about, heat our water and homes, and so forth, is of great importance. The challenge facing us is to make economic growth less dependent on carbon-based energy by finding much more efficient ways of using the old type of energy and developing and adapting new, cleaner types of energy as quickly as possible.

So how has Canada done compared to other countries in meeting this challenge? The sad truth is that it is one of the world's largest GHG emitters—it ranks fifteenth out of seventeen OECD countries on GHG emissions per capita, only the U.S. and Australia having higher per capita emissions. In 2014, Canada's GHG emissions were 15.9 tonnes per capita, significantly higher than the seventeen-country average. In 1992, Canada signed the United Nations Framework Convention on Climate Change (UNFCC), under which it committed to stabilizing GHG emissions at 1990 levels by 2000. Yet by 2000 Canada's absolute GHG emissions were 22 percent higher than ten years earlier. Canada went on to ratify the multinational Kyoto Protocol (the first binding agreement to limit GHG) in 2002, in which it pledged to reduce GHG emissions to 6 percent below 1990 levels between 2008 and 2012. But by 2010 absolute GHG emissions remained 17 percent above 1990 levels.

Then, in December 2011, Canada announced its withdrawal from the Kyoto Accord only one day after negotiators from nearly 200 countries meeting in Durban and South Africa at the United Nations Climate Change Conference completed a marathon of climate talks to establish a new treaty to limit carbon emissions.

The latest international attempt to limit GHG emissions was the Paris Agreement in December of 2015. It was described as a historic turning point that included 195 countries including Canada. Our performance under these new standards will be closely watched, as Canada's record on controlling the growth of GHG emissions has been far less than stellar.

SECTION SUMMARY

A competitive market can *fail* because it

- may create gross income and wealth inequalities
- can be quite unstable
- cannot prevent the rise of monopolies
- is unable to provide certain desirable goods, called *public goods*, that are nonrival and non-excludable
- ignores external costs and benefits

9.4   Dealing with External Costs

> **LO4**   Describe how governments try to deal with external costs, such as pollution.

It is clear that, since we are social animals, every person's behaviour affects others—for good or for ill. It is also clear that to address each and every externality is impossible. However, when the externality is of particular importance, some kind of action is required. In these cases, the difficult task for policy makers is to estimate the value of the externality and then attempt to integrate this into the production process—what economists term *integrating external costs*. There are three basic ways to do this:

- legislative controls
- taxation
- cap and trade

One very important externality is *pollution*. Let us look at each of these methods in turn as they apply to this concern.

Legislative Controls to Limit Pollution

Legislative control is one method of curtailing the production of pollutants. For instance, government might impose quotas on the levels of production or of pollutants; it might set up pollution emission standards, and fine or prosecute producers who exceed the limits; or it might decree that certain types of anti-pollution devices be installed at the polluters' expense.

Each of these methods has been tried, with varying degrees of success. However, the offences are sometimes difficult to detect, prove, or successfully prosecute. Many attempts to enforce pollution control regulations end up in long courtroom battles that give law firms more business but do not help the environment much at all. Furthermore, a serious drawback to legislative controls is the fact that there is no incentive for producers to go beyond the minimum standard and reduce the level of their pollution further.

In Canada, the protection of health and the environment is covered by the 1999 *Canadian Environmental Protection Act* (CEPA), which comprises a set of regulations concerning ocean dumping, waste reduction, the reduction of acid rain, the production of fuels, the protection of the ozone layer, and the control of toxic chemicals. These and other provincial and municipal regulations protect individuals and the environment from banned substances, including PCBs, asbestos, mercury, and DDT; restrict such things as the use of leaded gasoline and the outdoor burning of garden waste; and require emissions controls on cars.

Taxation to Limit Pollution

A second method of integrating the costs of pollution into the overall cost of production (and thus its price) is by *imposing taxes on the polluter*. This can be done by way of an excise tax, or general "pollution tax," that varies with the amount of production.

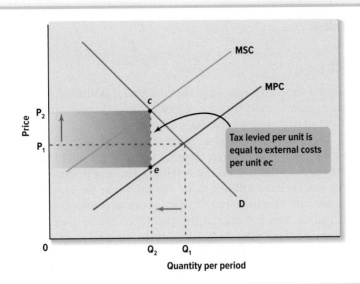

FIGURE 9.5   Marginal Private Costs and Marginal Social Costs

The MPC curve shows the marginal private costs of production. Given the demand for product D, the market price is P_1 and quantity is Q_1. Adding the external costs equal to ce gives us the curve labelled MSC (marginal social costs). If government imposes a pollution tax of ec, the new supply curve would be synonymous with the MSC curve, the new price would be P_2, and the new quantity would be Q_2.

Suppose that the marginal costs of production in a particular industry are as shown in **Figure 9.5**. If you recall, this is the same as the firm's supply curve. However, we have relabelled it here as the **marginal private costs**, or MPC, curve to reflect the fact that these are the internal costs incurred by the private producer of the product.

But these may not be the only costs associated with producing this product; this industry may impose serious costs on the rest of society in the form of air and water pollution. We call these additional societal costs *external costs*. Suppose we were able to measure these extra costs and estimated that they were equal to a per-unit amount of external cost, as shown in **Figure 9.5**.

If we add both the marginal private costs *and* the external costs, *ec*, then the total costs to society are represented by the higher curve labelled *MSC*, or **marginal social costs**. These are the true costs of production—the direct production costs and the costs of the associated pollution. If the firms do not have to worry about these external costs, the resulting price, P_1, is too low and the production level, Q_1, is too high from society's point of view. One way to force producers to recognize these costs would be to impose an excise tax equal to the external costs, *ec*.

The effect of the tax will be to increase the price from P_1 to P_2 and reduce production from Q_1 to Q_2. Just how much the price increases or the output decreases will depend on the elasticities of demand and supply. This, in turn, will determine how much of the tax is paid by consumers of this product in the form of higher prices and how much is absorbed by producers in the form of lower profits. However the tax is split, those people most directly involved with the product are being forced to pay the true cost. In addition, government will be deriving a tax revenue equal to the rectangular shaded area, which it could use to clean up some of the effects of pollution or help those suffering as a result of pollution.

In late 2016 Prime Minister Justin Trudeau announced an example of the application of this approach when he unveiled plans for a new national carbon tax that puts a per-tonne tax on the burning of fossil fuels.

What Trudeau called his "pan-Canadian approach to pricing carbon pollution" will see a $10 a tonne tax applied to carbon emissions starting in 2018. The tax rate will rise by $10 per year until it hits $50/t in 2022. This will be imposed on all provinces that are not already pricing carbon at an equivalent rate—British Columbia is collecting its own carbon tax (with a current rate of $30/t) and

Alberta plans on introducing one in 2017, so both will be exempt from the federal tax as long as they meet or exceed the federal rate.

Cap and Trade

A third way society might choose to deal with the problem of pollution is called the *cap-and-trade system*, which provides economic incentives for achieving reductions in pollution. The overall goal of this approach is to minimize the cost of meeting a predetermined emissions target called the *cap*. It is usually envisioned that this cap would start off near the current level of admissions and then be lowered from one year to the next. Thus, over time, total emissions would be reduced.

A governmental body sets the cap on the total amount of a pollution that will be allowed—say, the amount of carbon emissions that can be released into the atmosphere. Individual companies would then be allocated their share of this total cap in the form of carbon credits ensuring that the sum of the credits does not exceed the cap. Once the system is up and running, companies that want to increase their actual emissions to accommodate increased production would then have to buy additional carbon credits from one of two sources. The first is other firms that have reduced emissions below their allocated amount through the installation of less-polluting equipment or have simply reduced their output. The second is companies that have earned credits as a result of their environmentally friendly activities. An example of the second source would be a company that creates plantations of purposely grown trees or grasses. These vast plantations, in effect, pull carbon out of the atmosphere and deposit it in the plants and the ground.

The buying and selling of such carbon credits is the *trade* part of the program. In this system, buyers pay a charge for exceeding their pollution allowance, while sellers are rewarded for reducing overall emissions.

Currently Quebec is a partner with California in a cross-border carbon trading system called the Western Climate Initiative (WCI). Ontario plans to join the WCI soon. Nova Scotia has indicated that it might set up its own stand-alone cap-and-trade system. Those provinces that use cap and trade are exempt from the carbon tax introduced in by the government in late 2016.

The two approaches to controlling the emissions of GHG (greenhouse gases) reflect distinct characteristics. Provinces with fast-growing economies and a focus on carbon-intensive industries (B.C., Alberta) will lean toward a tax, since overall emissions can rise as the tax is paid. Provinces with slow or declining economic growth (Quebec, Nova Scotia) will prefer cap and trade, since deindustrialization automatically reduces emissions and makes the cap easier to reach.

This has the makings of trouble, since it is predicted that by 2022 the tax per tonne in the carbon-tax provinces could be as much as twice the rate in cap-and-trade provinces. This could lead to a national debate over "fair" carbon pricing, which could become a political quagmire.

Another, similar example of cap and trade would be a cap on the dumping of waste water into a particular river and the issuancd of a quantity of pollution permits that equalled the total cap. These permits would then be auctioned off each year.

Both the tax and the cap-and-trade approach use the market to address the problem of controlling pollution, and thus are sometimes called forms of *free-market environmentalism*.

In the cap-and-trade approach, organizations that do not pollute could be entitled to participate. Thus, environmental groups could purchase and retire credits or permits—and drive up the market price of the remaining credits or permits in accordance with the law of demand. The result, of course, is less total pollution.

Interestingly, one of the first applications of cap and trade was a joint effort between Canada and the United States in the 1980s to reduce acid rain in the Great Lakes region of the two countries. It is widely accepted that this is an example of a very successful application of policy.

 TEST YOUR UNDERSTANDING

5. What are three ways to integrate external costs?

SECTION SUMMARY

The classic example of an *external cost* is pollution, the effects of which can be addressed by

- legislative controls on pollution levels
- a per-unit pollution tax (such as a carbon tax) on production
- a cap-and-trade system to control pollution emissions

9.5   Integrating External Benefits

LO5   Explain how governments try to encourage production of goods and services, such as education, that carry external benefits.

The government has a number of methods to encourage the production of goods and services that provide a lot of external benefits. Two of the more popular ways are the direct provision by the government of those goods and services and the provision of subsidies by the government to encourage private firms to produce them.

The Provision of Quasi-Public Goods

It would be wrong to suggest that the prime reason most governments provide public education and public medical care is that they recognize the extent of external benefits. The truth is that in many cases, people over the centuries have demanded and even fought for access to the basic "right" to free public education and medical care. Such services have usually been regarded as necessities, as much as, say, food, housing, or clothing. The interesting result of this political process is that, to a certain extent, how well a person is dressed, fed, or accommodated is usually regarded as a matter of private concern, whereas the health and education of people are regarded as being of public concern.

Many governments responded to these demands after World War II and dramatically increased the provision of government services and products. As the public sector increased appreciably, it often extended access from what was considered basic coverage. Public education began to include postsecondary education; health service coverage was extended to dental, chiropractic, and psychiatric medicine; transportation began to include not only the building and maintenance of highways and harbours but also the provision of airports; communication started to include not just postal services but also telephone, radio, and television services.

In addition to this, many countries began to nationalize their major industries including hydroelectricity and mining. In other countries, governments started competing with private industry in the provision of gasoline, concert theatres, and racetracks. This massive proliferation of public services led to a public outcry in the 1980s, and the movement back toward private ownership began. The balance these days between the provision of public and private goods varies considerably from country to country, and is in a state of flux as countries search for the ideal mixture.

Providing Subsidies

The direct provision of goods and services is not the only way that government can encourage more production of certain products; it can also offer subsidies to private firms. As we saw in Chapter 2, a subsidy is merely a reverse tax, in which government pays the producer a certain amount for each unit produced.

As an example, suppose that government is convinced that the provision of day-care services involves not only benefits for the children and parents who use them but also external benefits to the rest of society. In **Figure 9.6** our conventional demand curve has been relabelled as the **marginal private benefits**, or MPB, curve. A demand curve represents how much of a product people are willing and able to purchase at different prices. But it also reflects the value that people put on a product. This figure shows, for instance, that parents are willing to buy 50 000 spaces in day care at a monthly fee of $800. It also suggests that parents feel that a space in the day care is worth at least $800 to them; that is, they would each receive a private benefit equivalent to at least $800. Let us say that, in

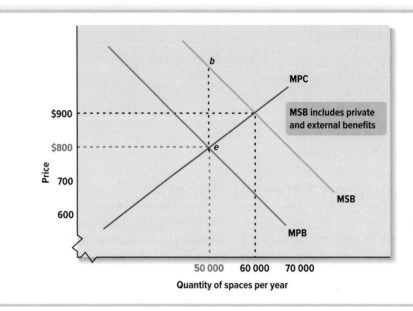

FIGURE 9.6   Marginal Private Benefits and Marginal Social Benefits

The demand curve for a product, MPB, shows the benefits users derive from it. The amount of benefits that nonusers enjoy is shown as the amount *eb*. The total of the private and external benefits gives us the marginal social benefits (MSB). Given the supply curve MPC, the equilibrium quantity and the price are 60 000 spaces and $900 respectively, if external benefits are included.

addition, it has been determined that there are external benefits to day-care spaces that equal amount *eb* for each child. The total benefits, both private and external, are shown as the higher curve labelled MSB, or **marginal social benefits**.

MPC, the supply curve, represents the marginal private costs. If both external and private benefits are considered, giving us the marginal social benefits curve, we have the equilibrium price of $900 and quantity of 60 000 day-care spaces. On the other hand, if only private benefits are taken into consideration, the result is a lower equilibrium price and lower number of spaces—50 000 and $800, respectively. Thus, ignoring social benefits results in both a quantity and a price that are lower than the socially desirable levels.

One way to encourage the provision of more day-care spaces would be to subsidize them. But should the subsidy be given to parents or to the day-care centres? Does it make any difference? Suppose government wants to increase the number of day-care spaces from 50 000 to 60 000 per our last example and decides to give a subsidy to day-care operators that will induce them to build extensions to their premises and employ additional staff. Say the amount of the subsidy comes to $200 per child per month. The introduction of such a subsidy would be represented graphically by a rightward shift in the supply (or MPC) curve, to the MPC-plus-subsidy curve, as shown in **Figure 9.7**. This would have the desired effect of increasing the number of spaces to 60 000. But note that it would also lead to a *decrease* in the monthly day-care charge to $700. So who gains? Well, society gains by having an additional 10 000 spaces, but who gains financially from the subsidy? It is true that the day-care centres are receiving $200 from government, but because of the increased supply the price has dropped by $100 to $700. In other words, they end up with a net gain of $100. The same is true for parents; they, too, gain $100, since fees are now that much lower.

What would happen if the same subsidy were given to the parents instead? Since it is parents who are receiving it, the effect graphically will be to increase the demand (the MPB) curve by the amount of the subsidy, from MPB to MPB-plus-subsidy as shown in **Figure 9.8**. The result would again be an increase in the amount of spaces from 50 000 to 60 000, but the higher demand from parents would result in the price increasing from $800 to $900. As with the case of the subsidy to day-care operators, parents will gain $100, since they are receiving a subsidy of $200 directly from government but have to pay an extra $100 in fees. Similarly, the day-care centres gain $100, the amount of the increased fees. (In reality, how the $200 would be shared between parents and day-care centres depends on the elasticities of demand and supply.)

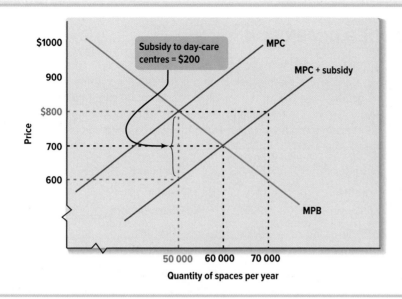

FIGURE 9.7   Subsidizing Day-Care Operators

One way in which government could increase the number of day-care spaces from 50 000 to 60 000 would be to grant a subsidy to day-care operators. In this graph, the subsidy amounts to $200 per month for each day-care space. The result of the subsidy will be to increase the number of spaces and also to reduce the day-care fee from $800 to $700 per month.

In summary, then, it does not really matter too much who receives the subsidy, since both parents and day-care centres will gain, as will society because it will have more available day-care spaces. However, if we are concerned that the price of products should more accurately reflect the real value (including externalities) of products, the subsidy should be given to parents because that would produce a higher price.

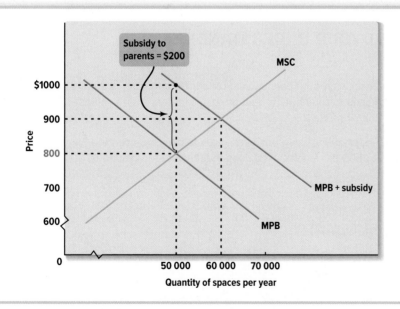

FIGURE 9.8   Subsidizing Parents Who Use Day-Care Centres

A subsidy of $200 per child to parents shifts the demand for day-care spaces (MPB) to the right, resulting in the MPB + subsidy curve. This results in the socially desirable price and quantity of $900 and 60 000 spaces, respectively.

ADDED DIMENSION

Child-care costs in Canada are the highest of any of the OECD countries in the world—except in Quebec. The table below shows the 2016 monthly costs for infant care (ages 0-2) in ten cities—the five most expensive cities and the five least expensive. The $175 for Montreal is the standard across the province, while rates in the other provinces vary, the more rural areas usually being less expensive. Rates for ages 2–5 are somewhat lower, but the trend is the same.

Toronto	$1730	Saskatoon	$850
St. John's	1400	Regina	800
Vancouver	1225	Charlottetown	742
London	1183	Winnipeg	650
Calgary	1083	Montreal	175

In Toronto, St John's, and Vancouver the child-care costs for an infant are higher than tuition for a postsecondary student. Across the OCED countries the average two-income family spends 15 percent of its after-tax income on child care while in Canada it is over 22 percent.

Why are Quebec's rates so low? The answer is that its provincial government provides generous subsidies to child-care centres while in the other provinces subsidies are very selective or nonexistent. Other factors—the varying cost of rental space for the facility, differences in the minimum wage rates and the availability of child-care centres—do come into play, but the presence of a subsidy is most significant.

The economic implications of these high child-care rates are profound. In the case of households with more than one under-age-five child, it simply does not pay for the second parent to go to work—unless a professional income is the opportunity cost.

This means the stay-at-home parent is out of the labour force for several years of her or his wage-earning life and will probably face difficulty re-entering the job market later. This means a smaller labour force and a lower level of GDP than would otherwise be the case.

TEST YOUR UNDERSTANDING

6. If a cash subsidy is given to parents with children in day care, is there a danger that the money might not be used to contribute toward the day-care fee, and might instead be used for other purposes? Does it matter?

7. In **Figure 9.7**, after the subsidy has been given to day-care operators, how many spaces would be offered at $800 per month? Why does the monthly fee drop to $700 after the subsidy?

SECTION SUMMARY

a) Government can integrate external benefits by

- directly providing public (or quasi-public) goods
- subsidizing private firms to encourage the provision

b) The day-care example illustrates how subsidies could be used to incorporate external benefits that the perfectly competitive market would otherwise ignore. This can be done in two ways:

- a subsidy to day-care operators, which would raise the quantity traded and lower the price
- a subsidy to parents, which would raise the quantity traded and raise the price

Study Guide

Review

WHAT'S THE BIG IDEA?

One of the difficult concepts for students to grasp is the idea of externalities—the costs and benefits that come about as a by-product from the production or consumption of a product. These costs and benefits are experienced by society in general rather than just the producers or consumers. This means they are not included in the market price, and so as a result many products are underpriced. It also means that those products with lots of external costs are overproduced and those with lots of external benefits are underproduced.

One way of addressing the external costs like pollution or discarded waste is for the government to tax those products whose production causes the problem. (Graphically this causes a left shift in the supply curve.) The result will be a higher price that more accurately reflect the true costs. It will also lead to lower levels of production. On the other hand, to stimulate production of those products that have external benefits to the rest of society, the government might offer subsidies to either the producers or the consumers of those products. (If given to the consumers, subsidies would shift the demand curve to the right.) The other difficult concept relates to the producer and consumer surpluses. The producer surplus is what producers save because for any output (up to the equilibrium quantity) they would have accepted a lower price than they actually receive (the market price). (Graphically it is the difference between the supply curve and the market price.) The consumer surplus is the savings that consumers make because for all the quantities (up to the equilibrium quantity) they would have happily paid a higher price than the actual market price. (Graphically it is the difference between the demand curve and the market price.)

NEW GLOSSARY TERMS

economic surplus   marginal private costs   nonrival goods
external benefits   marginal social benefits   private goods
external costs   marginal social costs   producer surplus
externalities   market failures   public goods
laissez-faire   non-excludable   quasi-public goods
marginal private benefits

Comprehensive Problem

(LO 4, 5) The graph in **Figure 9.9** shows the marginal private benefits and the marginal private cost per year of a program at a flight-training school in London. Suppose that research indicates that the marginal external benefits from having well-trained pilots is $6000 per student.

Questions

a) Draw in the new marginal social benefits curve in **Figure 9.9**, and label it MSB.
b) Given the new MSB curve, what is the ideal number of students in this program?
c) Now suppose that further research indicates that there are marginal social costs equal to $3000 per student due to more traffic and congestion at the college. Draw in the MSC curve in **Figure 9.9**.

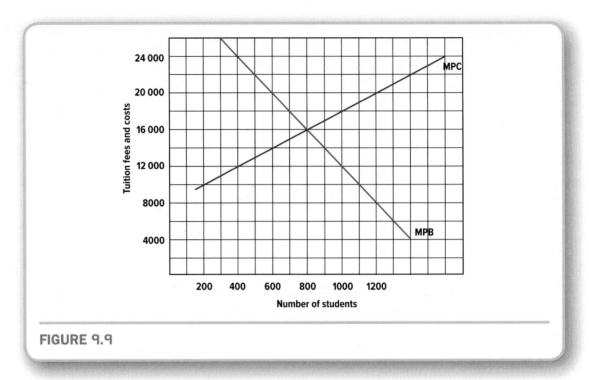

FIGURE 9.9

d) Now what is the optimum number of students in this program when both marginal social benefits and costs are considered?

Answers

a) See **Figure 9.9 (Completed)**.

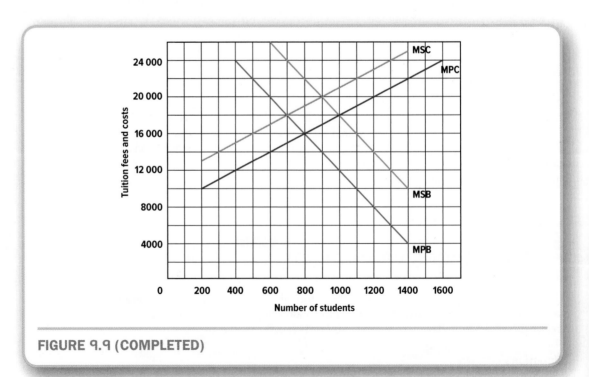

FIGURE 9.9 (COMPLETED)

b) Ideal number of students: 1000. (Where the MSB intersects the MPC curve.)
c) See **Figure 9.9 (Completed)**.
d) Optimum number of students: 900. (Where the MSB intersects the MSC curve.)

Study Problems

Find answers on the McGraw-Hill online resource.

Basic (Problems 1–4)

1. **(LO 3)** In Canada today, which of the following products is a private good, a public good, or a quasi-public good?
   a) military defence _____
   b) domestic airline flights _____
   c) the post office _____
   d) cable TV _____

2. **(LO 5)** Figure 9.10 shows the market for polio vaccinations in Narnia. The market is presently in equilibrium.

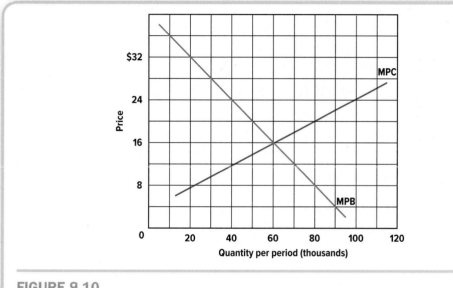

FIGURE 9.10

   a) Assuming the marginal external benefit is estimated at an additional $12 per vaccination, draw in the MSB curve.
   b) What are the optimal price and quantity from society's point of view?
      Price: $_____ Quantity: _____

3. **(LO 1)** Table 9.1 shows the average production costs per bushel of corn in five different sizes of farms operating under perfectly competitive conditions. Assume the industry is in long-term equilibrium.

TABLE 9.1

Output	Size 1	Size 2	Size 3	Size 4	Size 5
100	$6.50	/	/	/	/
200	5.30	6.00	/	/	/
300	5.25	5.50	6.00	/	/
400	5.70	5.00	5.00	6.00	6.50
500	6.25	5.15	4.75	5.00	5.75
600	7.50	5.70	4.90	4.50	5.25
700	/	6.25	5.40	4.75	4.75
800	/	/	6.00	5.25	5.00

a) What size of farm will the representative farm operate out of? _____

b) What output of corn will it produce and what will be the price of corn?
Output: _____ Price: $_____

4. **(LO 4)** The Government of Malaca has decided to sell pollution permits that will allow people to discharge pollutants into its largest freshwater lake. Each permit represents the right to discharge one tonne of pollutants. Malaca has determined that the lake will tolerate a maximum of 40 tonnes of pollutants per year and has decided to sell the permits using a Dutch auction—that is, one that starts at a very high price that is reduced in steps until the price reaches a level that will result in all 40 tonnes of pollution permits being sold at the same price. The results of the bidding are shown in Table 9.2.

TABLE 9.2

Price per Pollution Permit	Bidder A	Bidder B	Bidder C	Bidder D	Bidder E
$6000	2				
5500	4	6			
5000	6	6	1	1	1
4500	8	7	2	2	2
4000	10	7	4	3	3
3500	12	9	6	3	4
3000	14	10	8	3	5
2500	16	11	9	4	6
2000	18	12	10	4	7

a) What will be the price of pollution permits as a result of this auction? _____

b) Suppose bidder E happened to be an environmental protection group. If this group had not participated in the auction, what would the price of pollution permits have been, and what difference would there have been in the amount of pollutants discharged into the lake?
Price: $_____ Difference in quantity of pollutants: _____

Intermediate (Problems 5–8)

5. **(LO 4)** Within the remote nation of New Hope, total industrial production is currently creating a constant level of GDP that results in 2400 million tonnes per year of carbon being released into the atmosphere. The government announced three years ago that a cap on carbon emissions of 2220 million tonnes would be imposed. This triggered the creation of new firms that began to plant large plantations of trees grown specifically to absorb carbon from the atmosphere and thus earn carbon credits that they would sell to the highest bidder. See Table 9.3 for the supply of these earned carbon credits available when the program begins.

TABLE 9.3

Price of Carbon Credits	Quantity of Credits Created
$ 900	40
1000	60
1100	90
1200	120
1300	150
1400	180
1500	210

a) What will be the initial price for carbon credits? _____

b) Assume that new technology enables the same level of GDP to be achieved with 5 percent less carbon emissions. Now what is the price of carbon credits? $_____

ADDED DIMENSION

Patents and Exclusive Rights

Patent legislation provides the original inventor with a period during which the invention is protected from competition so that the inventor will be able to make monopoly profits through direct sales or by charging others a royalty when they use the invention. The reason for this is that new products or technologies are often very expensive to bring to market, and through such legislation it is hoped that research and development will be encouraged. In Canada, registered patents are granted twenty years of protection.

A number of problems associated with patents, however, deserve at least brief mention. For instance, if the registered description of the invention is too narrow, it will allow others to introduce and try to patent something that is merely a slight modification of the original. For this reason, many firms seeking patent protection try to define the patent as broadly as possible ("a motorized conveyance with four wheels," for instance) so as to keep out all competition. However, patent offices tend to dismiss patents that are too widely defined, such as "computers," or those in the form of broad ideas or theories, such as "the theory of relativity," for example. Additionally, if patent protection is granted for only a short time, it tends to inhibit research, but if it is extended too much it might well inhibit competition.

Finally, it should be noted that in order to register a patent, the inventor must give complete disclosure of the product and the process. But since this might reveal far too much to the competition, a number of inventions (such as the specific formula for Coca-Cola) have never been registered but remain instead trade secrets.

 TEST YOUR UNDERSTANDING

Find answers on the McGraw-Hill online resource.

   1. Entry into the following industries is very difficult. What type of barrier to entry is involved?

   a) computer operating systems

   b) commercial aircraft manufacturing

   c) west coast wild salmon fishing

production and leave it to the market to determine the maximum price at which that output can be sold. Therefore:

> The monopolist can determine either the price *or* the quantity sold; it cannot determine both the price *and* quantity sold.

All this can be expressed another way: since the monopolist and the industry are one and the same, it faces the market demand for the product, and that demand is represented by a downward-sloping demand curve. From the consumers' point of view, this means that if the price drops, they will buy more. From the monopolist's perspective, it means that in order to sell more the monopolist must lower the price. A monopolist cannot sell all it wants at any given price; it is forced to decrease the price in order to sell more.

This has important implications for the monopolist's revenues. As a result, it has a downward-sloping demand curve, whereas a perfectly competitive firm has a perfectly elastic, horizontal demand curve. We should note that, throughout our analysis, we are assuming that the monopolist is selling all of its units at a single price; in other words, it is not practising price discrimination. Later in this chapter, we will look at the implications of the monopolist charging different prices to different customers.

Fillup.ink is the only printer ink refill company in a small town in northern Ontario. The first two columns of **Table 10.1** show the number of daily ink refills Fillup.ink performs at various prices; that is, they represent the demand for ink refills.

TABLE 10.1
Total, Average, and Marginal Revenues of the Monopolist

Quantity	Price	Total Revenue	Average Revenue (AR)	Marginal Revenue (MR)
1	$20	$ 20	$20	$20
2	19	38	19	18
3	18	54	18	16
4	17	68	17	14
5	16	80	16	12
6	15	90	15	10
7	14	98	14	8
8	13	104	13	6
9	12	108	12	4
10	11	110	11	2
11	10	110	10	0
12	9	108	9	−2

The terms *total, average,* and *marginal revenues* were introduced in Chapter 8. Note that as with the competitive firm, the average revenue (TR/Q) is the same thing as the price. Note also that the total revenue increases with quantity sold but only up to a point. Here, that point is a quantity of 10. If Refill.ink wishes to increase the number of refills sold to 11, it must drop the price to $10. This move will have no effect, however, on the total revenue, which remains at $110. Should this monopolist wish to increase output and sales to 12, the price will have to come down to $9, with the result that total revenue will start to fall. Unlike a competitive firm, then, the monopolist is faced with a maximum sales revenue.

Table 10.1 also shows that for the monopolist the marginal revenue (ΔTR/ΔQ) is not equal to the average revenue. The extra (marginal) sales revenue that the monopolist receives for selling one more unit is not equal to the price. This is because when the monopolist sells one more unit, it *gains revenue* equal to the price at which it sells that unit, but it *loses revenue* because it is forced to drop the price, not only on the additional unit sold but on *every* unit it sells.

Suppose, for instance, that Fillup.ink is presently selling 5 refills at a price of $16 each, for a total revenue of $80. If it reduces the price to $15, it will be able to sell 1 more refill and so gain revenue equal to 1 × $15 = $15. However, it will lose revenue because it is dropping the price by $1 on the previous 5 refills it was selling; that is, it will lose revenue equal to $1 × $5 = $5. It gains $15 but loses $5 so that its net gain is only $10, which is its extra revenue for the additional one refill sold. Because the demand curve is downward sloping, the extra amount of revenue the monopolist gains from an additional sale will always be less than the price. In summary:

In order to increase its sales, a monopolist is forced to reduce its price, not just on the last units sold but on the whole of its output.

These points are illustrated in **Figure 10.1**. In **Figure 10.2**, we bring together graphs of the total revenue and of the average and marginal revenues to show the relationships between them.

Up to an output of 10, the total revenue curve is upward sloping, but the slope gets smaller and smaller with increasing output. The slope, which is the same thing as the marginal revenue, measures the rate at which total revenue changes. In other words, as **Figure 10.2B** shows, the marginal revenue decreases as the output increases. Note that the total revenue curve rises to a maximum at an output

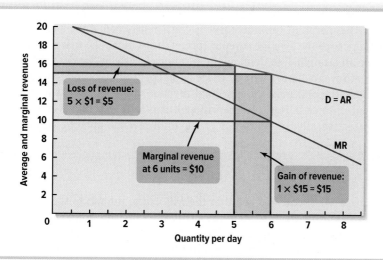

FIGURE 10.1   Average Revenue and Marginal Revenue

In cutting the price by $1, the producer is losing $1 times his present output of 5 = $5. However, it gains from the fact that it increases output sales by 1 refill at the lower price of $15 = $15. The marginal revenue is the net gain of $10 which is lower than the price of $15.

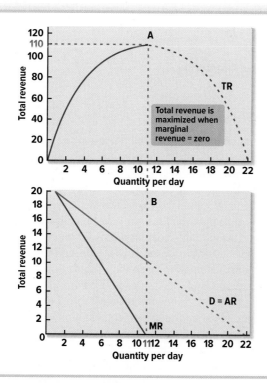

FIGURE 10.2   Total, Average, and Marginal Revenues

Up to a point, the total revenue of the monopolist increases as more units are sold. However, the rate of increase (the slope of the TR curve) declines throughout. The total revenue reaches a maximum at an output of 11. After that, the total revenue starts to decline.

The average revenue curve is identical to the demand curve, which means that additional units can only be sold if the price is lowered. In this graph, the price must drop by $1 in order to increase sales by one unit; that is, the slope of the demand curve has a value of 1. The slope of the MR curve, however, is 2, since it drops by $2 for each additional unit sold. This means that the MR curve drops twice as steeply as the AR curve.

of 11 (and 10) and thereafter declines. Note also that the average revenue curve is the same thing as the demand curve. The marginal revenue curve is consistently below the average revenue curve and is twice as steep; every time the average revenue (price) drops by $1, the marginal revenue drops by $2.

This is true for all straight-line demand curves: however steep the demand (AR) curve, the corresponding marginal revenue curve will be twice as steep. (It also means that wherever the demand curve intersects the horizontal axis, the marginal revenue curve will cross it at half that value.) As long as the marginal revenue is positive, even though it is falling, total revenue must be increasing. When it becomes negative, after an output of 11, the total revenue must be falling. Thus:

> Total revenue is at a maximum when the marginal revenue is neither positive nor negative, that is, when it is zero.

If you examine **Figure 10.2**, you will see that the MR curve intersects the horizontal axis (that is, MR = 0) exactly at the output (of 11) where the TR is at its highest point (TR is at a maximum).

Fillup.ink, the monopolist, will never produce an output greater than 11 units, because a higher output will presumably increase the total costs but lower total revenue; at outputs greater than 11, marginal revenue is negative. Graphically, in **Figure 10.2**, this means that the monopolist will produce an output of less than 11—in other words, on the upper portion of the demand curve. Since the top portion of any demand curve is elastic, it means that:

> A monopolist will produce only where the demand is elastic.

In order to analyze the behaviour of monopolists a bit more thoroughly, we need to know exactly at what output a monopolist will produce. To do this, we need to know not only the revenue but also the costs and therefore the profitability of the monopolist.

 ADDED DIMENSION

Monopolies Under the Radar

There are a number of examples of monopolies that just don't come to the attention of the general public. One of these is Luxottica, an Italian company that makes almost all of the sunglasses available on the market. Luxottica began buying every glasses-making company it could in the early 1980s and now completely dominates the industry.

Similarly, Simmons Pet Foods acquired the Canada-based company Menu Foods in late 2016 and now has near-control of the canned pet food market in North America.

We know that corn syrup is everywhere in our diet—it is in almost every candy or soda on the market. But it is also in, for example, ethanol gasoline, rubber tires, and even drywall. This gives Monsanto, a U.S. biotech company, tremendous power, since they supply 80 percent of the corn seed supply. Since plants produce their own seeds why do farmers have to purchase from Monsanto? The answer is that, unlike regular seeds, Monsanto seeds are resistant to the (very popular) pesticide Round Up, used to kill weeds in the corn fields, and they also contain a gene that automatically sterilizes the plant so it can't make any more seeds. Farmers then have no choice but to buy from Monsanto.

Finally, there is InBev, which dominates the world's mass-market beer industry (not the local craft breweries). Their brands include Budweiser, Labatt, Corona, Beck's, and Löwenbräu to name just five.

 TEST YOUR UNDERSTANDING

2. Suppose that a monopolist was charging a price of $50 for its product and was selling 15 units. It has now lowered its price to $48 and is selling 16 units. What is the marginal revenue? What is the price elasticity of demand over this price range?

10.2   Profit-Maximizing Output for the Monopolist

> **LO2**   Describe how the profit-maximizing output and price are determined for a monopolist.

In the short run, the cost structure for the monopolist is no different from that of the competitive producer. This means that the monopolist similarly enjoys the advantages of the division of labour as it produces more and later faces diminishing returns as it is constrained by the size of its operations. In Table 10.2, we have added the total costs of Refill. ink (which has a TFC of $30) to the total revenue data from Table 10.1 to calculate the total profits at the various output levels.

TABLE 10.2
Calculating Total Profits of the Monopolist

Quantity (refills per day)	Price (= AR)	Total Revenue (TR)	Total Cost (TC)	Total Profit (Tπ)
1	$20	$ 20	$ 40	$−20
2	19	38	48	−10
3	18	54	54	0
4	17	68	56	14
5	16	80	62	18
6	15	90	72	18
7	14	98	87	11
8	13	104	104	0
9	12	108	124	−16
10	11	110	150	−40

Given the data in Table 10.2, the profit-maximizing output for Fillup.ink is an output of either 5 or 6. (There are technical reasons, which we will explain in a moment, why the "correct" answer is an output of 6.) The price at this output level would be $15 per refill, which will give the monopolist a total profit of $18. These points are shown on the graph in Figure 10.3. Break-even outputs are at 3 and 8. The maximum profit point is at an output level of 6, where the vertical distance between the two total curves is at its greatest. Additionally, the maximum profit point is shown explicitly on the total profit curve, where it occurs at the highest point.

The point of maximum total profits also occurs where the slopes of TR (which is the same as MR) and TC (which is the same as MC) are equal.

Now, we need to look at things using the perspective of the average and marginal revenues and costs. This view is not quite so straightforward, but it does reveal some interesting information. Table 10.3 shows the average and marginal costs for Fillup.ink as well as repeating the revenue data used earlier.

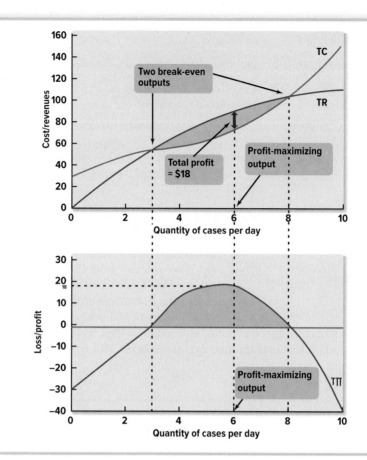

FIGURE 10.3 **Total Costs, Revenues, and Profits for the Monopolist**

Break-even occurs where the TR and TC curves intersect, that is, at outputs of 3 and 8. Between those two outputs, TR is greater than TC, and therefore, any output will be profitable. Maximum profits occur at an output of 6. At this output, the vertical distance between the two curves is greatest. In the bottom graph the total profit curve (TΠ) shows explicitly the amount of economic profit at each output and confirms these points.

TABLE 10.3
Calculating Total Profits of the Monopolist Using the Marginal Approach

Quantity	Price (= AR)	Total Revenue (TR)	Total Cost (TC)	Average Cost (AC)	Marginal Cost (MC)	Marginal Revenue (MR)	Total Profit (Tπ)
1	$20	$ 20	$ 40	$40.00	10	20	$−20
2	19	38	48	24.00	8	18	−10
3	18	54	54	18.00	6	16	0
4	17	68	56	14.00	2	14	14
5	16	80	62	12.40	6	12	18
6	15	90	72	12.00	10	10	18
7	14	98	87	12.44	15	8	11
8	13	104	104	13.00	17	6	0
9	12	108	124	13.78	20	4	−16
10	11	110	150	15.00	26	2	−40

The two columns on which we will concentrate are marginal cost and marginal revenue. The rule for profit maximization, which was developed in the context of perfect competition in Chapter 8, applies, regardless of the type of market we are looking at. Just to remind you of that rule:

Profits are maximized (or losses minimized) at an output where MR = MC.

Looking at those two columns confirms that profit maximization occurs at an output of 6, since at this output both marginal revenue and marginal cost are equal to $10. (This is why we prefer to identify the output level of 6 rather than 5 as the profit-maximizing output, although they produce the same total profit.) The important difference between a monopoly and a perfectly competitive market is that in a monopoly market, marginal revenue is not the same thing as price (or average revenue). Indeed, as we have seen, at an output of 6 units, the price will be $15—far greater than the marginal revenue of $10. **Figure 10.4** plots the various average and marginal curves.

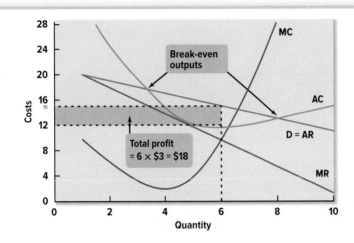

FIGURE 10.4   **Average and Marginal Costs and Revenues for the Monopolist**

Break-even occurs where TR = TC. This must also be where AR = AC, that is, at outputs of 3 and 8. Every output between those two points is profitable. Maximum profit occurs where the MC and MR curves intersect. This is at an output of 6, where MC = MR = $10. This output would be sold at a price of $15, that is, where the vertical line from the output of 6 intersects the demand curve.

The break-even points occur where total revenue and total cost are the same. This is also where the average revenue equals average costs. As we saw before, these points are at an output of 3 and 8. At any outputs between the break-even points, the monopolist will make a profit. Profit maximization occurs where the marginal cost curve intersects the marginal revenue curve, and this is at an output of 6. At that output, the average cost of an ink refill is $12, and the selling price is $15, and so Fillup.ink is making an economic profit of $3 per refill. Since it is selling 6 refills, we can confirm that the total profit is $18 (6 times $3). This is the blue-shaded area in **Figure 10.4**.

Note that unlike the situation with a perfectly competitive industry, there is no supply, and no supply curve, for the monopolist. This is because there is no unique relationship between price and quantity. Looking at **Table 10.3**, you can see it does not make sense to ask how much this monopolist would produce at, say, a price of $18, since, given its cost structure, an output level of 3 at a price of $18 is a combination that the monopolist would never choose. For each demand faced by the monopolist, there is only a single appropriate price and a single appropriate quantity.

We should mention that being a monopolist does not guarantee profitability. If you return to **Table 10.3** and assume that average costs were increased by $5 at every output level, you can see that no output would be profitable. Therefore, it is simply not true, as many believe, that monopolists are always profitable, almost by definition. Though many are, monopolists can and do sustain losses from time to time.

TEST YOUR UNDERSTANDING

3. Complete the following table for Onan, the monopolist, and indicate the break-even outputs and the profit-maximizing output.

Quantity	Price (= AR)	Total Revenue (TR)	Total Costs (TC)	Total Profit (Tπ)
20	$100	_____	$2060	_____
21	98	_____	2080	_____
22	96	_____	2112	_____
23	94	_____	2142	_____
24	92	_____	2177	_____
25	90	_____	2216	_____
26	88	_____	2257	_____
27	86	_____	2322	_____
28	84	_____	2417	_____
29	82	_____	2530	_____

4. Using the data below, complete the table.

Quantity	Price	Total Revenue (TR)	Total Costs (TC)	Average Costs (AC)	Marginal Costs (MC)	Marginal Revenue (MR)
20	$100	$2000	$2067	_____	_____	_____
21	98	2058	2087	_____	_____	_____
22	96	2112	2112	_____	_____	_____
23	94	2162	2142	_____	_____	_____
24	92	2208	2177	_____	_____	_____
25	90	2250	2216	_____	_____	_____
26	88	2288	2257	_____	_____	_____
27	86	2322	2322	_____	_____	_____
28	84	2352	2417	_____	_____	_____
29	82	2378	2530	_____	_____	_____

a) Now show that at break-even outputs the average revenue (= price) is equal to the average costs.

b) Find the profit-maximizing output and price.

SECTION SUMMARY

a) The profit-maximization output for a monopolist is where MC = MR, and the price the monopolist will charge for this output is the maximum possible price, given the market demand curve.

b) Total revenue is maximized at an output where MR is zero.

c) A monopolist produces an output where the demand is elastic.

10.3   What Is So Bad About Monopoly?

> **LO3**   Explain five grounds on which monopolies can be criticized.

Let us return our focus to a profitable Fillup.ink. If this was an example of a competitive firm, we know what would happen in the long run in response to economic profits. As we saw in Chapter 8, the effect would be to attract many new firms into the industry so that eventually economic profits would be competed away. However, since this is a monopoly market, there is no competition, and because of this, a profitable monopolist can continue to make economic profits indefinitely.

Furthermore, the monopolist is reasonably secure, because it is protected by various barriers to entry. Of course, like any firm, monopolists might incur losses, which could not be sustained indefinitely and would eventually force the monopolist out of business. However, the existence of monopoly profits do not lead to any change, except to make the monopoly owners richer. This implies that the monopolist is both productively and allocatively inefficient. Let's examine this important point.

Remember from Chapter 9 that *productive efficiency* means the producer is producing the product at the lowest possible average cost. This is not true for the monopolist. A glance back at **Figure 10.3** shows that Fillup.ink, like all monopolists, will produce an output below economic capacity, and so have average costs higher than minimum average cost. But in addition, the price being charged is above even these high costs. This means consumers pay a higher price than would be the case in a competitive industry, because the average cost is higher than is possible and because the monopolist is making economic profits. We'll look at this in more detail in section 4.

Besides consumers, society as a whole loses out, because the existence of monopolies may lead to a more unequal distribution of income and wealth. With competitive industries, the (lower) profits are spread among many producing firms, whereas with a monopoly the (higher) profits may be concentrated in the hands of only a few owners.

In addition, as **Figure 10.3** shows, at the profit-maximizing output (where MC = MR) the price is above the marginal cost. This means that the monopoly is also *allocatively inefficient* and that consumers' desire for this product at the margin, as measured by the price, is higher than its cost. In other words, they would be willing to pay for more additional units than the monopolist would be happy to accept. However, the monopolist restricts the quantity available in order to increase its profit. In contrast, *if* this market were competitive a greater quantity would be produced.

Apart from these criticisms, one other aspect of monopolies is cause for concern: their ability to practise price discrimination. This, although perhaps less damaging than some of the other charges against monopolies, does tilt the balance of power away from consumers and into the hands of the monopolist. Let us look at why.

Price Discrimination

As we saw in Chapter 5, price discrimination is how producers attempt to capture at least some of the existing consumer surplus, by selling a product to different people at different prices. To do this, each individual producer exercises a degree of market power, some control over the price. Firms in all forms of imperfectly competitive markets thus practise product discrimination. But it is a significant feature of many monopoly markets as well: we often see it in the fields of transportation (buses, railroads, and airlines) and communications (telephones and so on).

IT'S NEWS TO ME …

A recent article in the *Hollywood Reporter* argues that Netflix's deep pockets and willingness to spend big on original series may be the early signs of a monopoly. Netflix's $6 billion annual content budget (three times the size of its main competitors HBO and Amazon) and the growing success of its original productions has some Hollywood executives very worried.

continued

This year, the company will release 30 original series making up 600 hours of scripted content which is a dramatic increase from just 1 series in 2013. This fact alone has led to one industry executive to wonder out loud if Netflix isn't on the road to dominating the world of storytelling.

Furthermore, Netflix is not cutting corners on paying for high profile talent to star in its productions. One new series with Will Smith in the lead has a budget of $90 million and Brad Pitt will get $20 million to star in another one.

Source: *Star Power Reporting.* March 2017.

I. Netflix is trying to become dominant in its industry by establishing:

a) technical barriers to entry
b) legal barriers to entry
c) economic barriers to entry
d) a new, unique, approach to TV viewing

II. If Netflix does become a dominant (near-) monopoly, which of the following is most likely to follow?

a) Graphically, Netflix's marginal cost curve will shift down.
b) Viewership ratings for the established TV networks will increase.
c) The subscription price for Netflix will rise.
d) Sports channels viewership ratings will fall.

There are two major forms of price discrimination: discrimination among units purchased and discrimination among buying groups. Discrimination among units purchased arises because of the law of diminishing marginal utility, which suggests that buyers do not value all units of a product equally; the first unit purchased has greater value than the second, the second more than the third, and so on. For example, one consumer might value a first giant pizza at $16, but a second pizza may be worth, say, only half of that, or $8. The only way this consumer might be induced to buy two pizzas would be if the price were $8 each. This means the pizza shop would receive a total revenue of $16. But this is true only if there is a single price for pizzas. But what if, instead, the shop charged a different price for each pizza? How could it do this? Simple. It would sell a single pizza for $16 but would offer a second, bonus pizza for the low price of $6. That certainly sounds like a deal, especially since the customer values a second pizza at $8. As a result, the pizza shop is able to increase its total revenue to $22.

Discrimination among units purchased occurs whenever you see a two-for-one sale ("Get a second meal for free" or "A 50-percent discount when a first meal of equal value is purchased") or when you get a card punched and receive, say, a free coffee for every six purchased. There are many other examples like this, in which the consumer is able to buy additional units for a lower price. However, we must be careful here—just because a consumer can obtain a lower price by buying in large volumes does not necessarily mean the seller is practising price discrimination. Price discrimination exists only when a product is being sold at different prices for reasons *not associated with costs*. Sellers generally would prefer to sell by the case, since it is cheaper for them in terms of storage and transaction costs and it pays them to pass on some of these savings to the customer.

Discrimination among buyer groups occurs because different groups of consumers have different demands for products and so they value products differently. Some people are desperate to see first-run movies, and accordingly are willing to pay more for the pleasure. Others are willing to wait until the movie has been out for a few weeks, when they can see it at reduced prices. Similarly, many new products, including video game consoles, cell phones, and HD TVs are initially sold at high prices because the manufacturers realize that many people are prepared to pay premium prices in order to be the first kid on the block to own the latest toy. Generally, it is often only a matter of months before the price drops to the point at which the average customer is willing to buy. Finally, as we noted in Chapter 5, in addition to the fact that the price discriminator has control over the price

IN A NUTSHELL ...

Price Discrimination Can Take Many Forms

and different groups of consumers have different elasticities of demand, there is a third condition for price discrimination: there must be no possibility of resale.

We also saw in Chapter 5 that there are a number of ways groups differ: age, gender, when they want to buy or use a service, and so on. Being able to charge different prices to different groups will undoubtedly increase the sales revenue of the seller. This is illustrated in **Figure 10.5**, which shows the demand for haircuts at the Hair Today, Gone Tomorrow barber shop.

Figure 10.5A shows the daily demand by adults, **10.5B** the demand by seniors, and **10.5C** the total demand. The demand by adults is more inelastic than for seniors, since the latter are perhaps not so self-conscious about their appearance. If Hair Today could only charge a single price, its sales revenue would be maximized at a price of $15, which would attract 50 adults and 30 seniors. Its total revenue would be equal to $1200 (a total of 80 customers at $15 each), as illustrated in **10.5C**.

However, if Hair Today were to charge different prices to the two groups, it could increase its total revenue from both groups and therefore overall. Because the demand by adults is fairly inelastic, it will increase its total revenue by *raising* the price to, say, $18. Its customer base would only drop to 45 customers, resulting in a higher total revenue of $810 (45 at $18) compared with previous $750 as can be seen in **10.5A**. Conversely, since the demand from seniors is fairly elastic, Hair Today will

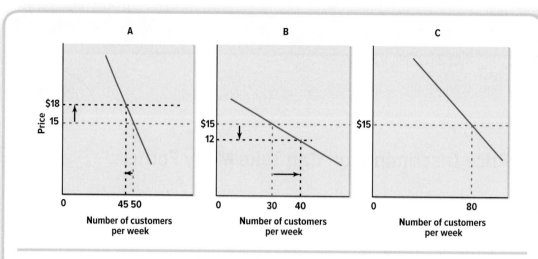

FIGURE 10.5   The Demand for Haircuts by Two Different Groups

Figure A shows the demand for haircuts by adults and is inelastic. Figure B is the demand by seniors and is elastic. The total demand by both groups is shown in Figure C. If only one price could be charged, Figure C shows that the price that maximizes revenue is $15, which would produce revenue of $1200 ($15 × 80). If price discrimination is practised, the barber's shop should increase the adults' price to $18 in Figure A, giving a revenue of $810 ($18 × 45), and lower the price for seniors to $12 in Figure B (for a revenue of $480). Its total revenue from the two groups would then be $1290.

gain increased revenue by *decreasing* the price for them. **Figure 10.5B** shows that a reduction of the price to $12 increases the number of customers to 40, resulting in a new total revenue of $480 (40 at $12) compared with the previous $450 (30 at $15). Consequently, the overall total revenue increases to $1290 compared with the $1200 of total revenue earned with a single price.

As we saw in this example, charging different prices to the two groups increases the total revenue of the seller. However, if the seller could divide up the client base even further into three, four, or five groups it would gain even more revenue. To take it to an extreme, if it could charge every single customer a separate price—the maximum each is prepared to pay—it could really boost its business. But **perfect price discrimination** is a sellers' dream rather than a reality.

That said, many companies these days do try to subdivide their clientele into as many different groups as ingenuity allows. The result, as we saw in Chapter 5, is that on a flight from Vancouver to Toronto it is not uncommon to find as many as twenty different fares charged to passengers, with prices ranging from as little as $350 to as high as $3000. The amount that individual customers pay depends on their age, when they booked, who they booked with, when they fly, how long they are staying at their destinations, whether they are staying over a weekend, and so on.

Similarly, smart phone companies offer a bewildering variety of options designed to tailor a specific package for each of its customers. Now, of course, some of these options do mean a higher cost to the smart phone firms, but most do not. As a result, you get to choose the type of phone you would like, its ring tones, the term of the lease, and an array of other options.

The result of price discrimination is higher revenues and profits for the firm and a loss of consumer surplus for the consumer. However, balanced against that is the fact that output is greater than it would be for the single-price monopolist. In addition, the consumer may have a greater variety of options to choose from, although it may take a great deal of time to weigh the various costs of those options.

The array of options and prices is sometimes bewildering.

© Hupeng | Dreamstime.com

In summary, monopolies are criticized for

- being able to make economic profits indefinitely
- being both productively and allocatively inefficient
- creating a more unequal distribution of income and wealth within society
- using their power to practise price discrimination

TEST YOUR UNDERSTANDING

5. The following table shows the demand for haircuts at Quick Cuts Inc.

Price	Quantity
$20	1
19	2
18	3
17	4
16	5
15	6

a) If this were a single-price barber, what would be the total revenue for doing six haircuts?

b) If this barber were able to practise perfect price discrimination by charging each customer the maximum he or she would pay, what would be the total revenue for doing six haircuts?

SECTION SUMMARY

Monopolies can be criticized for

- being able to make economic profits even in the long run
- being both productively and allocatively inefficient
- creating a more unequal distribution of income
- using their power to practise price discrimination

10.4   Monopoly and Perfect Competition Contrasted

> **LO4**   Explain the significant difference between monopoly and perfect competition.

We can show the comparison between a monopoly and a perfectly competitive industry graphically. Suppose that **Figure 10.6** illustrates a perfectly competitive mushroom industry that consists of 100 small mushroom growers all producing an identical type of mushroom. The supply curve represents the total supply of mushrooms from these growers, and the demand curve is the total market demand from millions of mushroom eaters. The competitive price of mushrooms is $6 per kilo, and the total production is 60 000 kilos per month.

Suppose that a monopolist were to buy out all the mushroom growers in the area. Having consolidated all the farms into one big combine, the monopolist sets out to maximize profits. How does it do this? By finding the output at which marginal cost is equal to marginal revenue. This will be the

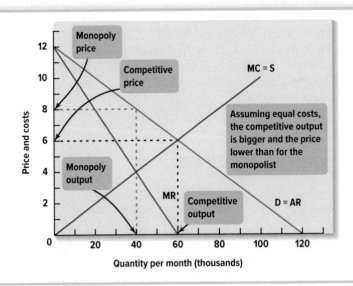

FIGURE 10.6   Monopoly and Perfect Competition Contrasted

The competitive market's equilibrium occurs where the quantities demanded and supplied are equal. This occurs at a price of $6 and an output of 60 000 kilos. If, on the other hand, this were a monopoly industry, the monopolist would produce at the point where MR equals MC. The profit-maximizing output for the monopolist, then, is at an output of 40 000 kilos, which could be sold at a price of $8 per kilo.

profit-maximizing point. Graphically, the supply curve of the perfectly competitive industry, you may remember, is synonymous with its marginal cost curve. Deriving the marginal revenue curve is reasonably straightforward because the demand curve is the same thing as the average revenue curve. Given the straight-line demand curve in **Figure 10.6**, the marginal revenue can be drawn as a curve falling twice as steeply. In other words, since the demand (average revenue) curve crosses the horizontal axis at an output of 120, the marginal revenue curve will cross it at half that value, that is, 60.

The intersection of the marginal cost and revenue curves occurs at an output of 40 000 kilos. To find the maximum price at which this quantity could be sold, we graphically extend the output curve up to the demand curve, which establishes that this quantity could be sold at a maximum price of $8 per kilo.

In simple terms, the monopolist can make maximum profits by restricting the output, thereby pushing up the price of the product. In summary:

- Monopolies charge higher prices than perfectly competitive firms.
- Monopolies produce lower outputs than perfectly competitive firms, and these outputs are below economic capacity.

Recall that monopolies are both productively inefficient and allocatively inefficient. That is to say, a monopolist will produce an output at which the price is well above the average cost of production: it is productively inefficient. It also produces an output at which the price is above the marginal cost: it is allocatively inefficient.

Let us elaborate a little on that last point. As we saw in Chapter 9, perfectly competitive markets are supremely efficient in the sense that the equilibrium output maximizes the amount of economic surplus. In contrast, the amount of economic surplus in the case of monopoly is considerably less, as **Figure 10.7** shows.

You will recall from Chapter 9 that the economic surplus is the total of the consumer and producer surplus. In the case of the perfectly competitive market depicted in **Figure 10.7A**, the consumer surplus amounts to $180 000 (60 000 × $6/2) and the producer surplus is also $180 000, for a total economic surplus of $360 000. However, the monopolist shown in **10.7B** will produce at a lower output of 40 000 kilos and sell this quantity at a price of $8 per kilo. The consumer surplus in this case has been reduced to $80 000 (40 000 × $4/2) and the producer surplus has increased to $240 000

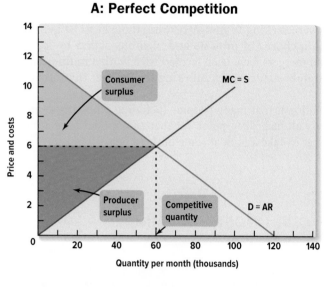

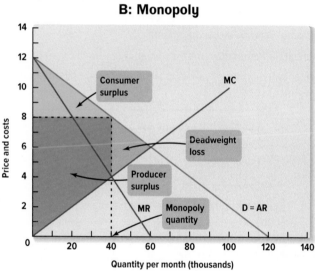

FIGURE 10.7 Economic Surplus: Perfect Competition Versus Monopoly

In Figure A, the competitive price is $6 and the quantity is 60 000. The consumer surplus (the green triangle) is equal to $180 000. The producer surplus (the blue triangle) is also $180 000. The economic surplus is therefore the total of $360 000. In Figure B, the monopoly price is $8, and the quantity is 40 000. The consumer surplus (the green triangle) is equal to $80 000, and the producer surplus (the blue area) is equal to $240 000. The economic surplus is therefore $320 000, leaving a deadweight loss (the small triangle) of $40 000.

for a total economic surplus of $320 000. This means consumers have lost $100 000 in consumer surplus and the monopolist has gained $60 000 in producer surplus. The result is that the economic surplus (the total of both) is $40 000 less in the case of the monopolist than it would be in the case of perfect competition. This loss in economic surplus, referred to as the **deadweight loss**, is equal to the size of the small triangle ($40 000) in **10.7B**. The deadweight loss is the total surplus lost, compared with an efficient market, due to market imperfections. Those imperfections result in either the over- or the underproduction of a product and may be the result of such things as taxes, price controls, or imperfect markets (of which monopoly is a prime example).

We begin to see why governments have often interceded in the market by regulating monopolies and have at times outlawed private monopolies or broken up existing ones. Nevertheless, it is fair to say that the history of anti-monopoly legislation and its enforcement in North America over the past century shows a singular lack of consistency. In certain periods, even the slightest suggestion that some firms were seeking to merge, or were thought to be behaving in an uncompetitive way, was greeted with a chorus of protests and vigorous action by legislators; in other periods, trusts, monopolies, and mergers have been treated with benign indifference by governments. What is the reason for this ambivalence, even allowing for the fact that other political considerations may be at work?

One major explanation is that many people—including economists—are not convinced that monopolies are necessarily all bad. They point out that monopolies have a number of advantages over competitive markets. Let us take a look at some of these benefits.

 TEST YOUR UNDERSTANDING

6. In **Figure 10.6**, what would be the total revenue earned by the perfectly competitive industry? What would be the total revenue earned by the monopolist industry? In the light of your answer, explain why the monopolist is not charging the same price as the competitive industry.

7. Use the graph below to answer these questions.

   a) If this graph depicts a competitive market, what is the equilibrium price and quantity?

   b) If this graph depicts a monopolist, what is the equilibrium price and quantity?

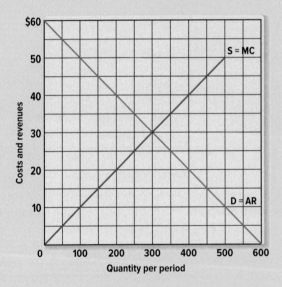

8. a) If the graph above depicts a perfectly competitive market, what are the values of the consumer surplus, the producer surplus, and the economic surplus?

   b) If the graph above depicts a monopolist, what are the values of the consumer surplus, the producer surplus, the economic surplus, and the deadweight loss?

SECTION SUMMARY

Compared with a perfect competitive firm, the monopolist charges a higher price and produces a smaller output, all things being equal. In addition, monopoly entails a deadweight loss, which means that the economic surplus is less than under perfect competition.

10.5   In Defence of Monopoly

> **LO5** Explain three grounds on which monopolies can be defended.

We can focus on one of the possible benefits of monopoly by returning to our mushroom industry and considering what happens when it is monopolized. Some would argue that the conclusions made earlier, with their negative implications, are not valid, because if a competitive industry were monopolized, the costs of production would likely change. A monopolist is unlikely to preserve 100 separate mushroom farms, each a replica of the others, with the resulting duplication of many functions. More likely, it will rationalize the industry in an attempt to achieve *economies of scale*. It would certainly not require 100 managers, 100 accountants, 100 crating machines, and so on.

If it is true that costs are lower under a monopoly, then, graphically, this would mean that the whole average cost curve will be lower, resulting in a correspondingly lower price and a larger output than is shown in **Figure 10.6**. In fact, if costs were significantly lower, the profit-maximizing price could be lower and the output larger than under perfect competition. Economies of scale in some industries are so extensive that in order for a firm to reduce costs sufficiently to make a profit, it may have to produce an output that is very big relative to the size of the market. Under these conditions, the market may only be able to support a single firm. It is cases like this—in which *competing firms simply would not be profitable*—that give rise to what are called **natural monopolies**. This situation is illustrated in **Figure 10.8**.

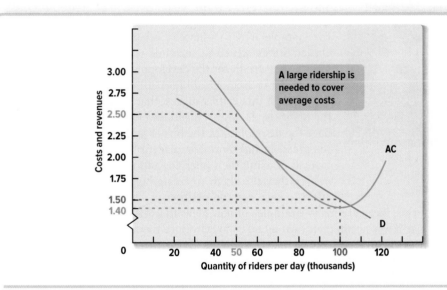

FIGURE 10.8   **Natural Monopoly**

The graph shows that extensive economies of scale result in minimum AC at 100 000 riders. If the rail fare is set at $1.50, the quantity demanded will be 100 000 and a single transit company could make a profit, since at this level of ridership the average cost is $1.40. If the market were shared between two rail companies serving, say, 50 000 riders each, the average cost would be $2.50, which is well above the fare of $1.50.

Suppose **Figure 10.8** illustrates the demand and costs for an urban rail system in a particular city. Because of the very high costs of the railbed and all the rolling stock, the system needs to operate with at least 100 000 users a day to reduce the average cost enough for the system to be profitable. With 100 000 users, it can charge a price of $1.50 per ride, and since this is above the average cost of $1.40 the system will be profitable. (For the sake of simplicity, the MC curve has been omitted.)

However, given the size of this particular market, it would be impossible for it to support two competing firms. If each firm had a ridership of 50 000, the average costs for each firm would be $2.50 per ride, well above the $1.50 price that would attract 100 000 users. Because two firms could not make a profit in this market, we have a natural monopoly. Natural monopolies occur whenever

GO Transit is an example of a natural monopoly.

© Yelena Rodriguez | Dreamstime.com

Joseph Schumpeter and John Kenneth Galbraith both thought big firms have advantages in terms of research and development.

PhotoLink/Getty Images

startup costs in an industry are so high that the market can support only one profitable firm. A small city in Canada simply could not support more than one urban rail system, whereas Tokyo possesses a number of competing companies, some private and one publicly owned.

In most small urban markets (and in a number of large ones), such industries as water, electricity and natural gas supply, urban bus and rail transportation, and telecommunications tend to be natural monopolies. Since they are also extremely important to a community, they may become publicly owned and are often referred to as **public utilities** (or public goods). To put it another way, in certain types of markets competition may well be costly and wasteful.

A second suggested benefit of being big (and many monopolies are very big) accrues to both the monopolist and society as a whole and occurs because of more extensive *research and development*. A number of economists, including Joseph Schumpeter and John Kenneth Galbraith, have written extensively on the advantages that big firms have in terms of research and development. Small competitive firms are simply not capable of doing extensive research and development, the scale and costs of which tend to be prohibitive. Many innovations were brought about by big businesses in the twentieth century. For example, AT&T (American Telephone and Telegraph) in the United States, which at the time was a monopolist, has been given major credit for the development of transistors and lasers, both major technological breakthroughs.

Against this, critics suggest that while big firms might have the *ability* to do research and development, they do not always have the *desire*. In fact, the bigger and more dominant they are, the greedier and more complacent they might get. As a result, instead of using their energies and resources to improve technology, they use them to create bigger barriers to entry in an effort to keep out competition.

Even worse than this, there are many examples of new ideas that have, in fact, been suppressed by big business because it was not in their own interests to introduce them. For instance, it was a long time before fluorescent tubing came on the market, despite the fact that the technology had been known for a long time. What incentive does a manufacturer have to introduce a bulb that can last for years when incandescent bulbs burn out every few months?

A third and final advantage that large corporations, such as monopolies, may have over smaller firms is that they can *offer better salaries and conditions to their employees* and as a result attract a higher quality of staff. In addition, perhaps because their size makes them conspicuous or because they have the finances, big corporations often have better labour practices and are open to more consumer scrutiny than are their smaller cousins.

Many observers, recognizing these benefits of monopoly, suggest that government should take a laissez-faire attitude toward it. There are, they suggest, other ways of curbing possible excesses. Monopolists are not all-powerful; they will always be at the mercy of consumers, who may simply choose not to buy. Fear of possible public scrutiny of their operations and the resulting bad publicity often serve as a sufficient brake on abuses. In addition, while the monopoly, by definition, does not have to worry about any present competition, it does have to worry about possible future competition. In other words, the barriers to entry are seldom totally insurmountable, and the attraction of high profits may be a sufficient incentive to newcomers to try to overcome these barriers. In summary, the existence of monopolies can be defended on the following grounds:

- They capture large economies of scale in production.
- They engage in extensive research and development into new techniques of production and new products.
- They attract high-quality staff by offering relatively high wages and good working conditions.

TEST YOUR UNDERSTANDING

9. In **Figure 10.8**, suppose there are two competing rail companies, each capturing 50 percent of the market. What would be the total profit or loss of each firm if they both charged a fare of $1.50?

GREAT ECONOMISTS: JOHN KENNETH GALBRAITH

John Kenneth Galbraith (1908–2006) was an economist who earned a reputation as a critic of orthodox economic theory. Born in rural Ontario, Galbraith was educated at the University of Toronto and the University of California, Berkeley. During his varied career, he played many different roles, including advisor to the U.S. government during World War II, member of the board of directors of *Fortune* magazine, and U.S. ambassador to India during the Kennedy administration. He was for decades a respected teacher at Harvard University, and a recognized expert on Far Eastern art. His prolific writings include *The Affluent Society* and *The New Industrial State*, in which he criticizes American big business for creating consumer demand through advertising rather than simply satisfying existing demand. He received honorary degrees from six Canadian universities.

(AP Photo)/Cpimages

His writings often first presented what he termed the "conventional wisdom" (a phrase he coined) on some question and then proceeded to tear it apart with cutting wit and analysis.

SECTION SUMMARY

Monopolies can be defended on the grounds that

- they capture large economies of scale, and are therefore efficient
- they engage in extensive research and development into new technology and new products
- they offer relatively good wages and working conditions for their employees

10.6   Controlling the Monopolist

> **LO6**   Discuss ways that governments can change the behaviour of monopolies.

In the past, governments have seldom been persuaded that public scrutiny or the threat of competition are in themselves sufficient to address the possible damage that can be caused by monopoly. They therefore feel impelled to take more direct action. We will consider three possible courses of direct action: taxation, price setting, and nationalization.

Government's aim in regulating monopoly is usually to bring about a more competitive result: ideally, to force the monopolist to reduce its price and profits, and increase its output. As we shall see, a number of measures have been attempted with varying degrees of success. Let us look at the first of these: taxation of the monopolist.

Taxing the Monopolist

Two major types of taxes a government can levy on the monopolist are a lump-sum profits tax and a monopoly sales tax. The distinction between these is that the lump-sum tax is a fixed cost and therefore does not affect marginal cost, whereas the sales tax is a variable cost and will increase marginal cost. This distinction is important in how it affects the monopolist's output price and profits.

Suppose that before the imposition of the tax, the monopolist in **Figure 10.9A** was had a profit-maximizing output of 160 units, which were being sold at $60 per unit. Let's see what will happen if the government imposes an annual lump-sum profits tax of $3200. The average cost curve will reflect this new tax by shifting up $20 at the present output of 160 from $AC_{before\ tax}$ to $AC_{after\ tax}$ in **Figure 10.9A**. However, since the variable costs are unaffected by this tax, the marginal cost curve does not change. As a result, the profit-maximizing output remains unaffected. Given the new costs, the best output level is still 160 units and the best price is still $60 per unit. The only thing affected is the profitability.

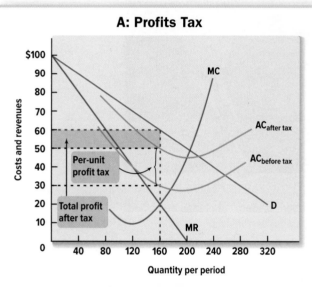

A: Profits Tax

B: Monopoly Sales Tax

Before the imposition of the profits tax, the monopolist was maximizing its profits at the point where MC = MR, producing an output of 160 units at a selling price of $60 per unit. The effect of a fixed tax of $3200 will be to increase the average costs of the monopolist, by $20 per unit. As a result, the monopolist will continue to produce 160 units at a price of $60. However, its profits will decline by the $3200 tax.

In Figure B, prior to the tax, the monopolist was producing where the MC and MR curves intersect— at an output of 160. This gives a selling price of $60. Imposing a $20 per unit sales tax means that MC increases by $20 at every output level. This is shown by an upward shift in the MC curve from MC_1 to MC_2. The new profit-maximizing equilibrium now occurs at the point where the MC_2 curve intersects the MR curve, that is, at an output of 140. The resulting price at which this output can be sold is $65.

FIGURE 10.9   Taxes Levied on a Monopolist

Since the output and price levels are unaffected by a lump-sum profit tax, such a policy has its limitations, though it does at least return some of the excess profits to society by way of increased tax revenue to government. The provincial government in British Columbia imposed this type of tax on the mining industry in the 1970s. The industry's response was to reduce its presence in the province considerably and a new government quickly reversed the policy.

Now let's see what happens in the case of a per-unit sales tax being imposed on the monopolist. In **Figure 10.9B** we see that prior to the tax the output level was 160 (where the marginal cost and revenue are equal) and the price was $60. Now suppose the government levies a monopoly sales tax of $20 per unit. The result will be that the marginal cost curve will shift upward by $20 at every level of output, from MC_1 to MC_2. As a result, the new profit-maximizing output is reduced to 140, and the new price will be $65. Part of the new tax of $20 does get passed on to the customer, since the price has increased by $5. The other $15 is absorbed by the monopolist.

The extent to which the monopolist is able to shift the tax onto the consumer depends, in good part, on the price elasticity of demand. In most cases, the cost is shared between the producer and consumer, and as a result, the total profit of the monopolist will be reduced. However, this type of tax fails abysmally to reduce prices and increase output—in fact, it has just the opposite effect. The province of Alberta raised the royalty rate on the Athabasca Oil Sands project near Fort McMurray in 2007. Since this royalty is calculated by multiplying output times price times the royalty rate, its effect is the same as a sales tax.

Government Price Setting

In Canada, large monopolies are often regulated by commissions, such as the Canadian Radio-television and Telecommunications Commission (CRTC), the Ontario Hydro Commission, and the Canadian Transport Commission. Such commissions are made up of representatives from government, industry, and the public and have the power to approve, or not, any price change the monopoly might propose.

Often, such commissions counter the effects of monopoly power by the more direct method of *price setting*. For example, airports are often seen as monopolies, and, as such, are subject to price regulation on the fees airline companies must pay to land their planes. Also, there is evidence that price regulation by the federal government on new pharmaceutical drugs (when the manufacturer enjoys a monopoly position via a patent) results in a lower price than would result from an unregulated market.

Governments, in theory, have the power to force the monopolist to sell at any price as long as this does not impose losses on the monopolist (and thus force it out of business). However, some prices are better than others. From society's point of view, the most allocatively efficient solution would be to force the monopolist to charge a price equal to the marginal cost of production—that is, the **socially optimum price**. This is illustrated in **Figure 10.10**.

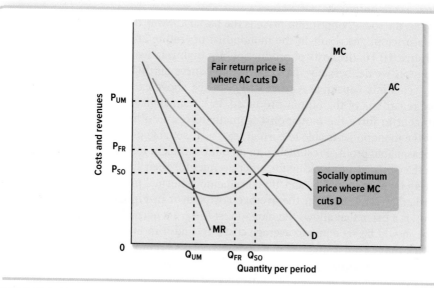

FIGURE 10.10   The Socially Optimum and Fair-Return Prices

With no intervention by government, the monopolist would maximize profits where MC = MR. This occurs at the output marked Q_{UM} and at a price of P_{UM}. The socially optimum price is that at which price is equal to MC at an output of Q_{SO} and a price of P_{SO}. However, this price is below AC, so the monopolist would be forced to incur a loss. Instead, government might impose a fair-return price, at which price is equal to AC. This occurs at the point AC intersects the demand curve and produces the output Q_{FR} and a price of P_{FR}.

Suppose that without government regulation, the monopolist would produce the quantity Q_{UM} (unregulated monopolist) at a price P_{UM}. Assume now that government decides to regulate the monopolist and forces it to charge a price equal to its marginal cost. If you think of the demand curve as being the price curve, it is easy to find the socially optimum price because it is located at the point where the MC curve cuts the demand curve. (You might recall from an earlier discussion that if this were a perfectly competitive industry, marginal cost is the same as supply so that the socially optimum position is equivalent to the perfectly competitive equilibrium between demand and supply.)

ADDED DIMENSION

Government and Monopolies: An Uneasy Relationship

Since monopolies produce both benefits and costs, governments have often differed in their approach to them. Unlike the United States, Canada has tended to look at monopolists not so much as problems in themselves but as part of a wider problem of restrictive practices, in which firms often combine to restrain competition. The first anti-combines legislation in Canada, passed in 1889, not only sought to prevent the formation of monopolies or near-monopolies but also forbade collusion among firms to raise prices or restrict supplies to their customers, or to do anything that would "unduly lessen competition."

Over the years, this legislation has been revised and updated, the last revision coming in the form of the 1986 *Competition Act*. This act forbids actions that would lessen competition, but not mergers or monopolies per se, only the "abuse of dominant position." In fact, it explicitly recognizes that some mergers may be warranted as in the public interest if, for example, this would allow Canadian firms to compete better in world markets.

The socially optimum price, therefore, is P_{SO}, and at this price, the quantity purchased will be Q_{SO}. This regulated price will have the desired effect of reducing the price (and profits) of the monopolist and inducing an increase in output.

Wherever possible, the socially optimum price is the best. However, in certain circumstances the imposition of such a price might result in the monopolist operating at a loss. This is particularly true where, as in **Figure 10.10**, the costs of production are high relative to the demand at the relevant price. (In this graph, we deliberately show the demand curve cutting the average costs curve at an output less than economic capacity.) A price of P_{SO} in the above example is below the average costs of production, regardless of the output produced. In circumstances like this, it would not be possible for government to force the monopolist to incur losses. In other words, government will need to ensure that the monopolist is able to earn at least a reasonable profit.

And what is a reasonable profit? Presumably, an amount sufficient to keep the company in business and to prevent the owners from looking for other avenues for their financial investment. This is what economists mean by normal profits; and, if you remember, normal profits are regarded as a cost of production and therefore included in the average cost shown in **Figure 10.10**. A **fair-return price**, in other words, is a price that allows the monopolist to earn a normal profit and no more. This means that the price should be set equal to average costs. To find it in **Figure 10.10**, we need to locate the point at which the AC curve cuts the demand curve. This occurs at a price of P_{FR}, and at this price, the quantity purchased is equal to an output of Q_{FR}. You can see that the fair-return price tends to be something of a compromise between the unregulated monopolist's position and the socially optimum position. In many cases, however, a government may have no choice but to compromise.

Nationalization

A final way in which governments attempt to deal with monopolies is to nationalize them. This means that the state acquires the monopoly reluctantly (sometimes) or eagerly (often), either by compulsory and uncompensated acquisition (seldom) or by a buyout of the owners (usually). It then operates the enterprise (as a Crown corporation in Canada) on whatever terms it sees fit. It may or may not operate the enterprise to make a profit; it may or may not charge the socially optimum price.

There is no guarantee, however, that the monopoly will be any more efficient or socially responsible simply because is operated by the state.

Attempting to ensure that certain monopoly and oligopoly industries act in the public interest, some countries have gone to the extreme measure of taking over the industries completely (with or without compensation). Supposedly, government can then appoint its own managers, who will presumably have full knowledge about the costs of production and can ensure that "fair" prices and a "proper" level of production are maintained. In the United Kingdom, after World War II, a number of industries, such as coal mining, steel, and railways, were nationalized by the then-ruling Labour government and run by government-appointed boards. In contrast, in the United States, these and other industries were left in private hands but regulated by government-appointed bodies.

As might be expected, Canada has a more flexible approach to this question. Some firms and whole industries have been nationalized, some are still privately owned but regulated, and some remain privately owned and unregulated. The nationalized firms include federally controlled corporations such as the CBC and Canada Post. Former Crown corporations, such as Canadian National (CN), Air Canada, and Petro-Canada, have now been privatized. In addition, many provinces have Crown corporations producing electricity, while at the municipal level, urban transit, the water system, and garbage collection are usually public enterprises.

 TEST YOUR UNDERSTANDING

10. The accompanying figure shows the costs and revenue for a monopolist. On the graph, indicate the following:

   a) the price (P_{UM}) and quantity (Q_{UM}) if the monopolist is unregulated

   b) the price (P_{SO}) and quantity (Q_{SO}) if the monopolist is required to charge the socially optimum price

   c) the price (P_{FR}) and quantity (Q_{FR}) if the monopolist is required to charge the fair-return price

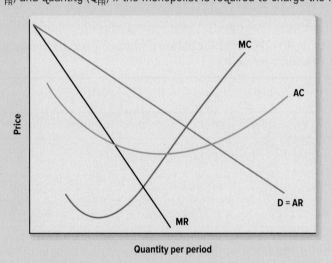

SECTION SUMMARY

Governments can attempt to change the behaviour of monopolies in three ways:

- They can tax the monopolist, using either a lump-sum tax or a per-unit sales tax. In the first case, price and quantity are unaffected; in the second case, the price increases and the quantity decreases. In both cases, the monopolist's profits are reduced.

- They can require that the monopolist sell at a specific price, either a socially optimum price (where P = MC) or a fair return price (where P = AC).

- They can nationalize the monopolist, for example converting it into a Crown corporation.

Study Guide

Review

WHAT'S THE BIG IDEA?

One of the most important ideas in this chapter is that a monopolist, unlike the competitive firm, has control over the price and can choose whatever price it likes. However, it is still the buyers who decide what quantities they are willing to purchase. Thus, in effect, the monopolist faces the market demand. The big implication of this is that in order to sell more units, the monopolist has to drop its price. As a result, the extra sales revenue earned from selling one more unit (at the lower price) is offset by the amount lost by having to reduce the price on all units sold. This extra revenue (the marginal revenue) will always be less than the price.

Like a competitive firm, a monopolist's profit-maximizing output occurs where the marginal revenue and marginal cost are equal. However, this output level is always less for the monopolist than for the competitive firm, and it can be sold at a higher price. The result is that the economic surplus (the total of the consumer and producer surplus) is always less than for the competitive firm.

NEW GLOSSARY TERMS

barriers to entry	monopoly	public utilities
deadweight loss	natural monopoly	socially optimum price
fair-return price	perfect price discrimination	

Comprehensive Problem

(LO 2, 4, 6) Table 10.4 depicts the metal keg industry, which is perfectly competitive. (All units, apart from the price are in thousands per week.)

TABLE 10.4

Price ($)	Quantity Demanded	TR ($)	MR ($)	MC ($)	AC ($)	TC ($)	Tπ ($)
30	0	——	/	/	/	28	——
28	1	——	——	20	48	48	——
26	2	——	——	11	29.5	59	——
24	3	——	——	8	22.3	67	——
22	4	——	——	16	20.75	83	——
20	5	——	——	17	20	100	——
18	6	——	——	18	19.7	118	——
16	7	——	——	20	19.7	138	——
14	8	——	——	25	20.4	163	——
12	9	——	——	30	21.4	193	——

Questions

a) Complete Table 10.4.
b) What are the equilibrium values of price, quantity traded, and total profit (or loss) in the industry? (Recall that the supply for a perfectly competitive industry is the same as the marginal cost.)
c) Suppose instead that the table depicts a monopolist. What will be the profit-maximizing price, quantity, and profits?

Answers

a) See Table 10.4 (Completed).

TABLE 10.4 (COMPLETED)

Price ($)	Quantity Demanded	TR ($)	MR ($)	MC ($)	AC ($)	TC ($)	Tπ ($)
30	0	$ 0	/	/	/	28	$–28
28	1	28	$28	20	48	48	–20
26	2	52	24	11	29.5	59	–7
24	3	72	20	8	22.3	67	+5
22	4	88	16	16	20.75	83	+5
20	5	100	12	17	20	100	0
18	6	108	8	18	19.7	118	–10
16	7	112	4	20	19.7	138	–26
14	8	112	0	25	20.4	163	–51
12	9	108	–4	30	21.4	193	–85

b) Price: $18; quantity: 6000; profit/loss: loss of $10 000. (The price is equal to MC at a quantity of 6000. Price [equals the marginal cost] of $18. At this level of output, there is a loss of $10 000.

c) Price: $22; quantity: 4000; profit/loss: profit of $5000. (To maximize profits, a monopolist will produce that output at which marginal revenue is equal to marginal cost. This occurs at an output of 4000. This quantity will be sold at a price of $22. The table shows that at this output, total profit is equal to $5000.

Questions

d) Now suppose that the government is not satisfied with the monopolist's situation and decides to impose a lump-sum monopoly tax of $3000. What will be the price, quantity, and profits?

e) Instead of the tax, the government decides to impose a socially optimum price. What will be the price, quantity, and profits?

f) Finally, suppose that instead of the socially optimum price, the government imposes a fair-return price. What will be the price, quantity, and profits?

Answers

d) Price: $22; quantity: 4000; profit/loss: profit of $2000. (A tax of $3000 is a fixed cost. Therefore it will have no effect on the marginal costs. It will increase the total costs and reduce profits by $3000 at every output level. The best output level is the same as before; the monopolist would simply be making $3000 less profit at this output.)

e) Price: $18; quantity: 6000; profit/loss: loss of $10 000. (The socially optimum price is that at which P = MC, that is, where the demand curve intersects the MC curve. This is the same as D = S, which you calculated in (b).)

f) Price: $20; quantity: 5000; profit/loss: $0. (The fair-return price is that at which the price equals the AC.)

Study Problems

Find answers on the McGraw-Hill online resource.

Basic (Problems 1–5)

1. **(LO 2)** Figure 10.11 shows the demand and marginal cost curves for the monopolist Mr. Peanut.

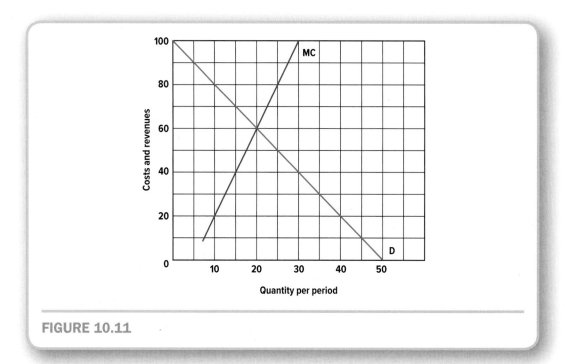

FIGURE 10.11

a) Draw in the marginal revenue curve.
b) What are the values of the profit-maximizing output and price?
   Output: _____ Price: $_____
c) What are the values of output, price, and total revenue, when the firm's total revenue is maximized?
   Output: _____ Price: $_____
   Total revenue: $_____

2. **(LO 2)** Figure 10.12 refers to the monopolist Ms. Get It Right.

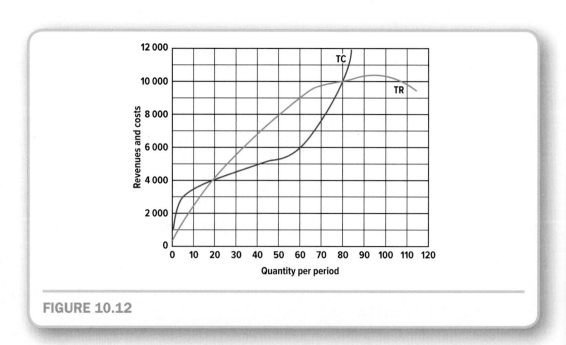

FIGURE 10.12

a) At what output(s) does the firm break even?
   _____ and _____

b) At what output does the firm maximize its profits? _____

c) What is the amount of this profit? $_____

3. **(LO 2)** Figure 10.13 shows the cost and revenue curves for IchiBan Inc., a monopolist.

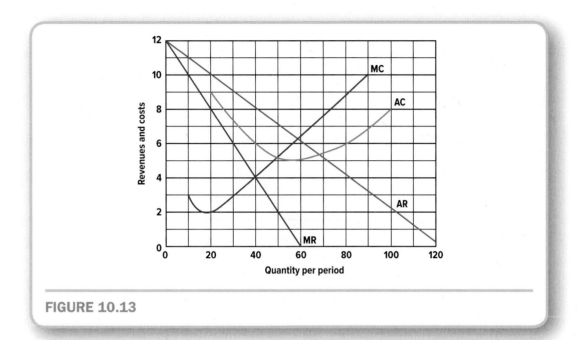

FIGURE 10.13

a) What is the monopolist's profit-maximizing output and price?

   Output: _____ Price: $_____

b) What will be the monopolist's total profit? $_____

4. **(LO 2)** Figure 10.14 shows the demand for the product of Primo the monopolist.

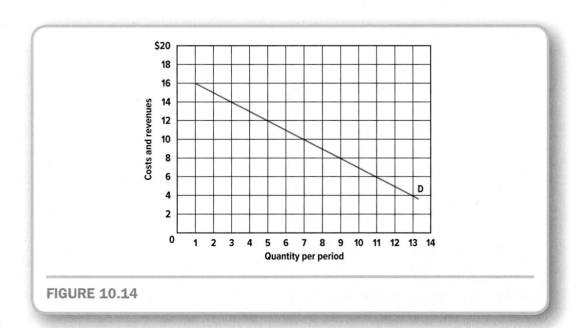

FIGURE 10.14

a) From this information, complete Table 10.5, and add the MR curve to Figure 10.14.

TABLE 10.5

Quantity Demanded	Price = AR ($)	TR ($)	MR ($)
1	___	___	___
2	___	___	___
3	___	___	___
4	___	___	___
5	___	___	___
6	___	___	___
7	___	___	___
8	___	___	___
9	___	___	___
10	___	___	___
11	___	___	___

b) At what output level is total revenue maximized? What is the marginal revenue at this output?
Output (units): _____ Marginal revenue: $_____
c) What is the maximum output the monopolist would produce? _____
d) What is the elasticity of demand for outputs greater than the quantity in (c)? _____
e) What general rule can you derive from these observations? _____

5. **(LO 2)** The monopolist Mr. Pop It Right is considering whether it is worthwhile producing an additional 20 units per day of his large bags of popcorn. Doing so would cost him an additional $42 in total. He is currently selling 48 bags per day at $4 each. In order to sell the additional 20 bags every day, however, he would have to lower his price to $3.50. What do you recommend? _____

Intermediate (Problems 6–9)

6. **(LO 2, 4)** Table 10.6 shows the costs and demand for the clove oil industry.

TABLE 10.6

Quantity	Price	Total Revenue	Marginal Revenue	Marginal Cost	Total Cost	Total Profit
0	$20	___	/	/	$ 9	___
1	19	___	___	___	23	___
2	18	___	___	___	33	___
3	17	___	___	___	48	___
4	16	___	___	___	64	___
5	15	___	___	___	82	___
6	14	___	___	___	102	___
7	13	___	___	___	124	___
8	12	___	___	___	148	___

a) Complete Table 10.6.
b) If this industry was perfectly competitive, what would be the output, price, and total industry profit?
Output: _____ Price: $_____ Profit: $_____
c) If this industry was a monopoly industry, what would be the output, price, and total industry profit?
Output: _____ Price: $_____ Profit: $_____

7. **(LO 2, 4)** Sol-Motors is the only auto manufacturer in West Lidia, a country that prohibits the importation of cars. **Figure 10.15** shows the demand and the costs for Sol-Motors.

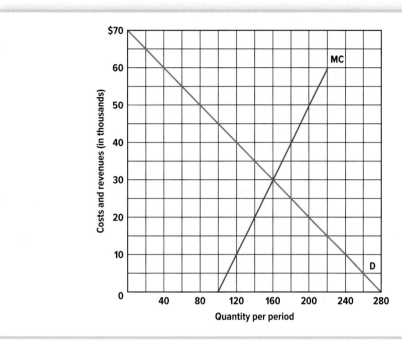

FIGURE 10.15

a) Add the marginal revenue curve to the graph (starting at zero).
b) What are Sol-Motors's price-maximizing output and price?
   Output: _____ Price: $_____
c) Suppose that the government of Lidia imposes a price ceiling of $20 000 per car. What is the firm's profit-maximizing output now? _____
d) What would be the output if **Figure 10.15** represented a perfectly competitive industry rather than a monopoly? _____

8. **(LO 2, 6)** **Figure 10.16** shows the cost and revenue information for Shitotsu the monopolist. What are the levels of price, output, total (sales) revenue, and total profits if the monopolist were to produce at the positions (a) through (d) indicated in **Table 10.7**?

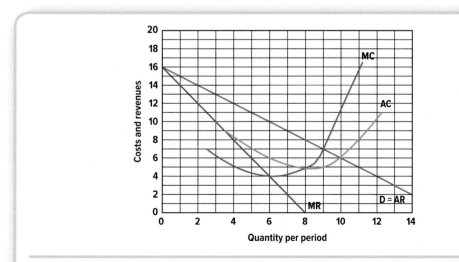

FIGURE 10.16

TABLE 10.7

	Price ($)	Output	Total Revenue ($)	Total Profits ($)
a) Total revenue maximization	_____	_____	_____	_____
b) Profit maximization	_____	_____	_____	_____
c) Socially optimum price	_____	_____	_____	_____
d) Fair-return price	_____	_____	_____	_____

9. **(LO 3)** Ivan runs a small independent movie theatre in Scarborough, which presently attracts 1200 customers per week at a ticket price of $8. His customer base comprises 1000 adult customers and 200 seniors. He would like to increase his total revenue by practising price discrimination. He knows that the demand by adults is fairly inelastic and that a change in the admission price of $1 would change the quantity by 80 customers. He also recognizes that the demand by seniors is fairly elastic and a $1 change in the price would result in a change of 50 customers.
   a) From this information, complete Table 10.8.

TABLE 10.8

	ADULTS		SENIORS	
Price	Quantity	Total Revenue	Quantity	Total Revenue
5	_____	_____	_____	_____
6	_____	_____	_____	_____
7	_____	_____	_____	_____
8	_____	_____	_____	_____
9	_____	_____	_____	_____
10	_____	_____	_____	_____
11	_____	_____	_____	_____
12	_____	_____	_____	_____

   b) What is Ivan's present total revenue?
   c) Should he increase or decrease the price for adults? Should he increase or decrease the price for seniors?
   d) What price will maximize the total revenue from adult customers?
   e) What price will maximize the total revenue from seniors?
   f) What will be the total revenue from both groups?

Advanced (Problems 10–13)

10. **(LO 2)**
   a) Complete Table 10.9, which shows the costs and revenues of Solo the monopolist. (You may assume that the demand curve is a straight line.)

TABLE 10.9

Quantity per Period	Price	TR	MR	MC	TC
0	/	/	/	/	$ 65
1	$32	____	____	$ 8	73
2	____	____	____	7	80
3	28	____	____	6	86
4	____	____	____	5	91
5	____	120		6	97
6	____	____	____	7	104
7	20	____	____	8	112
8	____	____	____	9	121
9	____	____	____	10	131
10	____	____	____	12	143

b) What are the values of the profit-maximizing output, price, and total profit or loss?
   Output: _____ Price: $_____ Total profit/loss: _____ $_____
c) At what output will total revenue be maximized, and what will be the value of total revenue?
   Output (units): _____ Total revenue: $_____
d) What is the value of MR when profits are maximized and when total revenue is maximized?
   MR is _____ when profits are maximized.
   MR is _____ when total revenue is maximized.

11. **(LO 2)** Table 10.10 shows the cost and revenue data for Molly the monopolist.

TABLE 10.10

Quantity per Period	Price	Total Revenue	Marginal Revenue	Marginal Cost	Total Cost
0	$30	____	/	/	$ 4
1	28	____	____	____	32
2	26	____	____	____	54
3	24	____	____	____	72
4	22	____	____	____	86
5	20	____	____	____	98
6	18	____	____	____	112
7	16	____	____	____	134
8	14	____	____	____	160
9	12	____	____	____	192

a) Complete Table 10.10.
b) What are Molly's profit-maximizing output and price, and what will be the amount of her profit?
   Output: _____ Price: $_____ Profit: $_____

c) Suppose that the demand for Molly's product increased by three units at every price level. Complete Table 10.11.

TABLE 10.11

Quantity per Period	Price	Total Revenue	Marginal Revenue	Marginal Cost	Total Cost
____	$30	_____	/	_____	_____
____	28	_____	_____	_____	_____
____	26	_____	_____	_____	_____
____	24	_____	_____	_____	_____
____	22	_____	_____	_____	_____
____	20	_____	_____	_____	_____
____	18	_____	_____	_____	_____
/	16	/	/	/	/
/	14	/	/	/	/
/	12	/	/	/	/

d) What will be her new profit-maximizing output and price, and what will be the amount of her profit?

Output: _____ Price: $_____ Profit: $_____

12. **(LO 2, 3)** Figure 10.17 shows the demand curve facing Jill the monopolist, who cannot sell partial units.

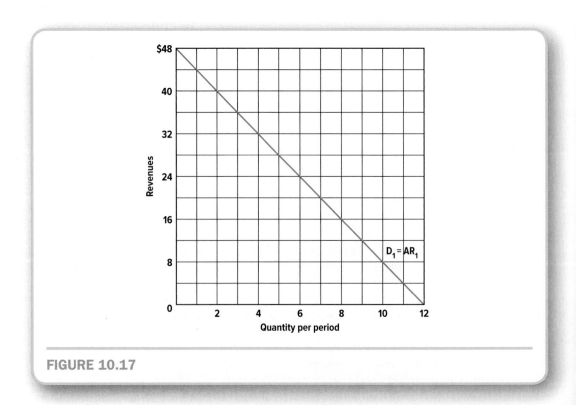

FIGURE 10.17

a) Using Figure 10.17, fill in columns 2, 3, and 4 in Table 10.12.

TABLE 10.12

(1) Quantity	(2) AR_1	(3) MR_1	(4) TR_1	(5) AR_2	(5) MR_2	(7) TR_2
1	___	___	___	___	___	___
2	___	___	___	___	___	___
3	___	___	___	___	___	___
4	___	___	___	___	___	___
5	___	___	___	___	___	___
6	___	___	___	___	___	___
7	___	___	___	___	___	___
8	___	___	___	___	___	___
9	___	___	___	___	___	___
10	___	___	___	___	___	___
11	___	___	___	___	___	___
12	___	___	___	___	___	___

b) Draw in the MR_1 curve in **Figure 10.17**.

c) What is the level of output when Jill's total revenue is maximized? What is her total revenue?

   Output: _____ TR: _____

d) Suppose that Jill could practise perfect price discrimination by selling each unit at a different price (the first at $44, the second at $40, the third at $36, etc.). Fill in columns 5, 6, and 7 in **Table 10.12**.

e) Now, what is Jill's maximum total revenue? _____

13. **(LO 4)** Suppose that **Figure 10.18** depicts a perfectly competitive market.

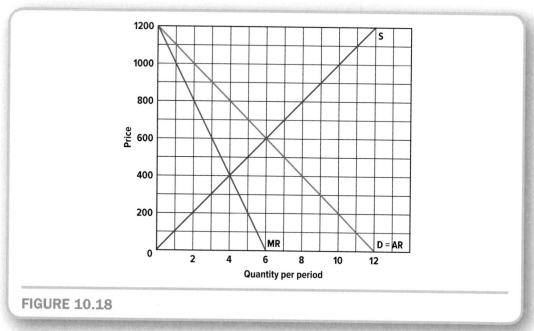

FIGURE 10.18

a) What are the equilibrium price and quantity? At that equilibrium, what are the values of the producer surplus, the consumer surplus, and the economic surplus?

   Price: $_____ Quantity: _____ Producer surplus: _____

   Consumer surplus: _____ Economic surplus: _____

b) Suppose instead that **Figure 10.18** depicts a monopoly. What would be the monopolist's price, quantity, producer surplus, consumer surplus, economic surplus, and deadweight loss?

   Price: $_____ Quantity: _____ Producer surplus: _____

   Consumer surplus: _____ Economic surplus: _____

   Deadweight loss: _____

Problems for Further Study

Basic (Problems 1–3)

1. **(LO 3)** What are the four main criticisms of monopoly? Explain each.

2. **(LO 5)** Explain three good features of monopoly.

3. **(LO 1)** What is meant by *barriers to entry*? What are the three types of barriers? Give an example of each.

Intermediate (Problems 4–7)

4. **(LO 4)** Explain what is meant by the deadweight loss.

5. **(LO 3)** Explain the difference between discrimination among units and discrimination among buying groups.

6. **(LO 1)** Explain why the average revenue of the monopolist is not the same thing as the marginal revenue.

7. **(LO 6)** Why would a lump-sum tax have no impact on either the price or the output of a monopolist?

Advanced (Problems 8–10)

8. **(LO 2)** Tom, the only steel drum manufacturer in Narnia, can sell a single drum for $30. However, for every extra drum he wants to sell, he is forced to reduce the price (for all his customers) by $2. The total fixed costs in his workshop are $15, and the variable cost of the first drum produced is $25. For each extra drum thereafter, the cost drops by $5, up to and including the fifth drum. After that, the cost of each extra drum increases by $5.

   a) Draw the AR, MR, AC, and MC curves in **Figure 10.19**.

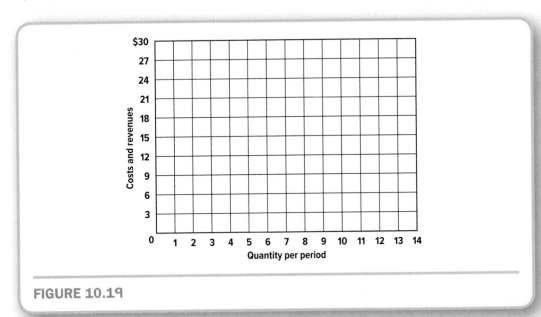

FIGURE 10.19

   b) What is Tom's profit-maximizing output, price, and total profit or loss?
   Output: _____ Price: $_____ Profit/loss: $_____

9. **(LO 1)** A monopolist would never produce in the price range at which the demand was inelastic. Why not?

10. **(LO 2)** In terms of both totals and averages/marginals, identify the profit-maximizing output for the monopolist.

CHAPTER 11
Imperfect Competition

LEARNING OBJECTIVES

At the end of this chapter, you should be able to:

LO1 Explain the importance and effects of product differentiation, including advertising.

LO2 Differentiate between the two types of imperfect competition.

LO3 Explain why monopolistically competitive firms tend to have excess capacity and are unlikely to earn long-run economic profits.

LO4 Describe the main characteristics of oligopoly markets.

LO5 Explain why large firms are often tempted to collude and form cartels.

LO6 Explain price leadership and why oligopolistic firms are reluctant to change prices very often.

WHAT'S AHEAD ...

This chapter looks at the behaviour of firms operating in two types of imperfectly competitive markets, referred to as *monopolistic competition* and *oligopoly*. We begin by looking at their common features, and see how firms try to distinguish their products through advertising and other means. We then look at equilibrium in both markets and evaluate how the results compare with those of perfect competition. In the case of the monopolistically competitive firm, we show why the distinction between the short run and the long run is important. In the case of the oligopolistic firm, we emphasize the importance of interdependence among firms. This means there is no single theory of oligopoly, and the behaviour of the oligopolistic firms depends upon whether they collude.

A QUESTION OF RELEVANCE ...

Baseball caps, video cameras, haircuts, beer, books, TV programs, cell phones, cigars, calculators, and airline flights—what do all these have in common, apart from the fact that they are of interest to most students and their professors? They are all produced by firms that are neither perfect competitors nor monopolies. Instead, all the firms associated with these products operate in a market structure that economists call *imperfect competition*.

In previous chapters we examined two market structures: monopoly and perfect competition. There are only a few examples of a pure monopoly, and as we have seen, the model of perfect competition is more of an abstraction (albeit a very useful one) than a description of our present world. Lying between these two extremes is the market for a multitude of common products that millions of people buy. The term **imperfect competition** is used by economists to refer to these more familiar market situations, and it describes much of modern capitalism reasonably well. As we shall see, there are two different forms of imperfect competition: *monopolistic competition* and *oligopoly*. We will discuss the differences between the two shortly. Many of the ideas in this chapter were developed independently in the 1930s by Edward Chamberlin of Harvard University and Joan Robinson of Cambridge University.

 GREAT ECONOMISTS: JOAN ROBINSON

Joan Robinson (1903–83) was a long-time professor of economics at Cambridge University and a student of Alfred Marshall's. Although neither a member nor a founder of any particular school of thought, she made significant contributions to economic theory, including a critique of Marxist economics from the position of a friendly detractor. Her most important contribution, however, was *Economics of Imperfect Competition* (1933). The book filled a huge void in economics: the analysis of market structures that lie between the extremes of monopoly and perfect competition.

Her work was published at the same time as that of the American economist Edward Chamberlin, who wrote on the same theme. The two provided similar, though not identical, analyses. Chamberlin praised imperfect competition for adding increased consumer choice. Robinson criticized it, concluding that firms in imperfect competition are likely to reduce output in order to maintain price, and this results in a great deal of idle capacity and the waste caused by underutilized resources. Consequently, she believed government should intervene to discourage this form of market structure.

© Peter Lofts Photography/National Portrait Gallery, London

11.1   Product Differentiation

LO1   Explain the importance and effects of product differentiation, including advertising.

Imperfect competition is competition between firms based on some factor other than price—one example of this type of competition is **product differentiation**. Product differentiation is the attempt by a seller to offer a product that is *seen* by the consumer as different, and presumably of better value than the others on the market. There are several ways this may be done. A recognizable logo is a popular form of product differentiation.

Nearly everyone recognizes the Nike "swoosh" seen on television ads, T-shirts, baseball hats, and billboards. To many consumers, the widely recognized symbol adds to the desirability of owning a pair of Nike shoes. This increases the demand for Nike products and enables the company to charge a higher price than its rivals do. The golden arches of McDonald's are perhaps the world's most recognizable symbol. The success of this company speaks volumes about the rewards of effective product differentiation.

Besides using a logo, firms try to create a special image for their products through distinctive brand names. Several highly successful examples are: a Hoover is a vacuum cleaner, Kleenex is really a facial tissue, a Band-Aid is an adhesive dressing, Saran Wrap is quite ordinary plastic sheeting, and Scotch tape is just one of many types of adhesive tape. In each case, the brand name is so familiar that it has come to be used to refer a generic product. Besides the use of recognizable symbols or brand names, firms sometimes try to differentiate their products through distinctive packaging of different sizes, colours, shapes, or textures. Infants, for instance, can recognize their own favourite brands of cereal or candy long before they are able to read.

Product differentiation may also take a different form. Think of a business, such as a retail outlet, in which location and service are often significant differentiators. This explains, for example, why some dry-cleaning shops do brisk business while others do not, or why a supermarket chain retains a strong presence in older neighbourhoods where it has attractive, long-established locations and a reputation for service.

Roadside signs are one way sellers try to differentiate their products.

Royalty-Free/CORBIS

Another type of product differentiation occurs through *product development*, in which firms introduce a new and supposedly improved version of their product. A prime example occurs annually in the auto industry, where new models are introduced every year and each new version is reported to be an improvement that will better meet customer needs. This phenomenon has spread to other industries, resulting in, for example, the annual new models of television sets or, almost unbelievably, of mattresses.

Finally, let us look in some detail at the way firms attempt to differentiate their products through advertising. There may actually be no difference between two brands of motor oil, but if people think there is a difference, product differentiation has occurred. Successfully convincing consumers that one motor oil is better than another often involves an extensive advertising effort.

Advertising by rival firms can be thought of as a very expensive and very important form of nonprice competition. In many people's minds, the word *advertising* conjures up images of expensive TV commercials, which only very large firms can afford. However, it comes in many other forms, from flyers delivered directly to households to signboards in a mall. These are how smaller firms attempt to differentiate themselves from their rivals.

There is debate within the discipline of economics over the benefits of advertising to society as a whole. Let's now look at both sides of the argument.

Supporters point out that advertising provides the consumer with vital information about the availability, quality, and location of products, which helps greatly to cut down on the consumers' search time in acquiring information. For instance, it would be very inefficient if you had to obtain information about buying a car by driving from dealer to dealer because there was no advertising.

A second argument in favour of advertising is that it increases the degree of competition in the market because new firms are better able to enter an industry when they can announce their entry through advertising. For example, imagine the near-impossibility of a firm such as Hyundai breaking into the North American car market without engaging in national advertising. An extension of this argument is that the development and introduction of new products is also greatly enhanced by the presence of advertising. The point is sometimes made that advertising creates an atmosphere that encourages new-product development so that technological change is nurtured.

The third argument of supporters is that extensive advertising can actually lower the price of many products, for two reasons. First, increased competition, mentioned above, would be expected to heighten consumer knowledge about prices and thereby force down prices and decrease profit margins for the representative firm. Second, it has been argued that advertising enables a firm to expand and thereby enjoy economies of scale in production. This lowers average costs and ultimately the price.

Another benefit credited to advertising is that it helps support many other industries, including websites, print publications, and TV shows which are all financed by sponsors' ads. Whether this improves our overall standard of living is a value judgment best left up to the reader.

In summary, supporters of advertising believe it is beneficial because it

- provides the consumer with vital information
- enhances competition between firms
- lowers the prices of products
- finances magazines and TV shows

 ADDED DIMENSION

Too Many Breakfast Cereals?

A trip to the local supermarket yields interesting insights into product differentiation and competition. A bewildering choice of products is on display: 20 types of laundry detergent, a dozen brands of coffee, 50 different and tempting types of cookies, and at least 30 different breakfast cereals. This really is competition in action. Or is it? Although we have spent time in this text looking at the markets for various products and figuring out what determines the price and output of each, it is firms—not products—that compete.

A closer look at the cereal aisle reveals that while there may well be 30 brands on display, the majority are produced by only four competing firms: General Mills, Quaker, Post, and Kellogg. Combined, they account for 80 percent of sales. General Mills manufactures Cheerios, Cinnamon Toast Crunch, and Wheaties among many others; Quaker is responsible for Life and Quaker Oats; Post sells Raisin Bran, Cap'n Crunch, and Shreddies; and Kellogg produces their famous Cornflakes, as well as Vector, Froot Loops, Rice Krispies, Special K, and so on.

In all, these four companies produce well over a hundred brands. But why would a company sell more than one brand—in essence competing against itself? The companies themselves would suggest that are simply catering to consumer demands and increasing the choices available. However, the real answer lies in simple arithmetic. Suppose, for instance, that you are trying to enter the breakfast cereal industry, and suppose further that each of the four major companies produced only one brand each. With luck and good sales promotion you are hoping to take market share away from the others with your new brand of appealing, nutritious cereal. Assume that you are successful and you are now one of the Big Five, and as a result the older companies have seen their market share drop from 25 percent to 20 percent each and you have captured 20 percent.

Now back to the real world. What if you entered the market with your new product and faced competition from 50 other brands? Probably, the best you can expect to capture is a proportional share of the market—just 2 percent. Multi-branding, in other words, is just one way for firms to establish and maintain market share. As such, it acts as a big barrier for new entrants into the market.

In rather dramatic contrast, critics of advertising argue that it is wasteful. Suppose that all advertising is eliminated tomorrow. What do you think would happen to total consumption expenditures in the whole economy? They would suggest that it's very unlikely it would fall. Expenditure patterns might well change—as fewer products that had been highly advertised are bought—but more of other products would be purchased, so total consumer spending would be little affected. This argument also goes on to state that the billions of dollars spent trying to persuade consumers to buy a certain brand of product could then be spent in much more socially desirable ways. This argument downplays the informational value of advertising by pointing out that most advertising (TV in particular) is aimed at persuasion, and its effectiveness is cancelled out by a rival firm's large expenditures with the same goal in mind. For instance, millions of dollars are spent by both Procter & Gamble and its rival Johnson & Johnson as they go head to head in the shampoo wars on television. We might ask if, after all is said and done, the consumer is any better off as a result.

Critics of advertising also challenge the idea that it increases competition by arguing that it is just as likely that huge advertising budgets used to promote brand loyalty can create a barrier to entry that could encourage the emergence of monopoly tendencies.

Finally, critics hold that expenditures on advertising must raise the price of products. Someone pays for the billions of dollars spent every year on advertising, and that someone must be either the producer or the consumer. If the producer ended up paying, it would seem logical for it not to advertise. But, the argument goes, it is the consumer who pays, and it is very unlikely that anyone's hair is cleaner or more beautiful because of advertising—but the shampoo is probably more expensive than it would otherwise be.

In summary, many criticize advertising because it

- is mostly noninformational and wasteful
- encourages concentration within industries
- raises prices to the detriment of consumers

As you can see, points on both sides of this argument seem persuasive, and empirical studies have not succeeded in ending the debate.

Let us bring this discussion on product differentiation to a close by summarizing the ways that firms attempt to do this:

- developing a recognized brand name, product logo, or packaging
- securing a superior location or developing a reputation for exceptional service
- engaging in product redevelopment and improvement
- developing an effective advertising strategy

SECTION SUMMARY

a) Product differentiation is a characteristic of imperfect market structures (though some oligopoly industries are made up of firms that sell identical products).

b) There is debate within economics about the benefits of advertising. Supporters believe advertising is beneficial because

- it provides the consumer with vital information
- it enhances competition among firms
- it lowers prices of products
- it finances magazines and television shows

Critics of advertising argue that

- it is mostly noninformational and wasteful
- it encourages concentration within industries
- it raises prices to the detriment of consumers

11.2   The Difference Between the Two Types of Imperfect Competition

LO2 Differentiate between the two types of imperfect competition.

Let us now distinguish between two types of market structures that come under the general heading of imperfect competition. **Monopolistic competition** is a market containing many relatively small firms, whereas **oligopoly** is a market with a few large firms. One way of emphasizing this distinction is to compare industry **concentration ratios**—which measure the percentage of an industry's total sales that the largest few (for example, four) firms control. Suppose that the combined sales revenue of the four biggest firms in the asphalt industry is $320 million and the total sales revenue of the whole industry is $400 million. The concentration ratio in that industry would therefore be $320/$400 × 100 = 80 percent.

High concentration ratios often occur when large output levels are required for a firm to capture economies of scale. For example, the automobile, aluminum, oil refining, beer, soft drink, and airline industries are all oligopolies. On the other hand, industries in which economies of scale are not significant tend to have low concentration ratios. These industries, such as real estate agencies, brake and muffler shops, travel agencies, hair salons, and dry-cleaning shops, contain many small firms and are therefore monopolistically competitive.

Table 11.1 provides some data on selected Canadian industries that are highly concentrated and whose markets are, therefore, oligopolistic. An industry with a concentration ratio above 40 percent is regarded as highly concentrated and therefore oligopolistic. The figures indicate the percentage of total industry output produced by the largest four firms in the industry.

TABLE 11.1
Highly Concentrated Canadian Industries

Industry	CONCENTRATION RATIO OF TOTAL INDUSTRY SALES % (top four producing firms)	
	1990	2005
Motor vehicles	87.2	100.0
Petroleum	75.6	99.9
Tobacco	98.8	99.8
Cement	72.0	99.7
Fertilizers	56.7	99.4
Tires	86.2	99.3
Breweries	90.6	99.2
Sugar and confectionary	47.8	98.7
Household appliances	61.6	98.5
Coffee and tea	76.5	97.8
Sporting and athletic goods	22.7	92.8
Wineries	48.5	92.2

Source: Statistics Canada, *Concentration Ratios in the Manufacturing Industries*, Catalogue 31C0024.

It should be noted that some oligopoly industries, breweries for example, may contain not only a few dominant firms but also a number of small firms. Deciding whether a particular industry is an example of monopolistic competition or an oligopoly is a matter of degree and a question of fact. In other words, when looking at any industry, we need to ask, "Would the total supply of this industry be seriously affected by the exit of its largest firm?" If yes, it is clearly an oligopoly industry. If no, it is monopolistically competitive.

 TEST YOUR UNDERSTANDING

Find answers on the McGraw-Hill online resource.

1. The Canadian grummit industry consists of ten companies whose annual sales are as shown.

a) Calculate the (four-)firm concentration ratio for this industry.

b) In what type of market does the grummit industry operate?

Company	Sales (in $millions)
A	22
B	6
C	17
D	12
E	8
F	15
Next four companies (total)	12

SECTION SUMMARY

A concentration ratio measures the percent of an industry's sales controlled by the top four firms.
A high concentration ratio is a characteristic of oligopoly markets.

11.3   Monopolistic Competition

> **LO3**   Explain why monopolistically competitive firms tend to have excess capacity and are unlikely to earn long-run economic profits.

Let us now look in detail at the market structure we call monopolistic competition—the third type of market structure after perfect competition and monopoly. Some examples of monopolistically competitive markets were mentioned above. Others include almost all retailing, from ladies' clothes stores to gasoline retailing; almost all of the services that are provided directly to the retail consumer, including travel agents, hairdressing, shoe repair, and tax accounting; almost all services aimed at the homeowner, such as roofers, plumbers, carpet layers, and painters; most of the growing cottage-industry sector, from software designers to authors and proofreaders; and some manufacturing markets, such as the textile, footwear, and furniture industries.

A monopolistically competitive industry has four characteristics. The first is that the industry is made up of *many relatively small firms* that act independently of each other. Across any metropolitan area are dozens of shops, agencies, and small businesses, each of which tries to distinguish itself from its competition. Similarly, across the whole economy are dozens of T-shirt or chair manufacturers acting in the same way.

Second, there is *freedom of entry* into the industry for new firms. This is analogous to the perfect-competition model. Free entry does not mean that entry requires no money. What it does mean is that there are no significant barriers to entry, such as those we discussed in Chapter 10.

Hairdressing is an example of a monopolistically competitive industry.
© Iakov Filimonov | Dreamstime.com

Third, firms within a monopolistically competitive industry have *some control over the price* of the products they sell. This is unlike the firms in a perfectly competitive industry. Despite such control, there is often very little price competition among firms. Instead, competition centres on attempts by individual firms to differentiate the products they sell.

The fourth characteristic of a monopolistically competitive industry is the fact that each firm sells a differentiated product. Many would suggest that product differentiation is the major defining characteristic of monopolistic competition. This is because a new entrant into the market has a degree of control, not only over the price it charges but also over the product itself. In contrast, a new corn farmer, for instance, has little choice but to sell its corn at the same price as every other corn farmer. But further than that, the farmer has almost no chance of making his product unique. Corn is corn. However, if you are thinking of opening a new restaurant you not only have control over the prices of the menu items but can also decide what type of food to serve and what clientele to appeal to.

In summary, the characteristics of a monopolistically competitive industry are

- many small firms
- freedom of entry
- some control over price
- differentiated products

The Short-Run and Long-Run Equilibrium for the Monopolistically Competitive Firm

The costs of production of firms in a monopolistically competitive industry tend to be very similar—the cost (other than, possibly, rent) of running one hair salon is not much different from the cost of another. On the other hand, the presence of nonprice competition and product differentiation does mean that the demand faced by one firm can be quite different from that facing another. This is why our analysis of this type of market structure focuses on the role of the demand faced by the individual firm. Usually, the individual firm faces a highly elastic demand curve, although it is not perfectly elastic as in the case of the perfectly competitive model.

There are, in fact, two main factors that determine the elasticity of demand for a monopolistically competitive firm: the number of competitive firms and the amount of product differentiation between those firms. If there is very little competition for a firm or if its product is very different from the competition's, the demand will be inelastic. At the opposite extreme, if there is extensive competition and the product is indistinguishable from that of the competition, the demand would be perfectly elastic, and we would be describing perfect competition. Generally speaking, since there is not a great deal of competition and not much difference between competing firms in monopolistically competitive industries, the average firm faces a fairly elastic demand. However, should a new firm arise that offers something a little different, it may have an edge in the short run.

For example, imagine that a new fusion restaurant called Bella Sushi has just opened with its imaginative selection of sushi pizzas. So successful is it that it is soon making enviable economic profits, as illustrated in **Figure 11.1**.

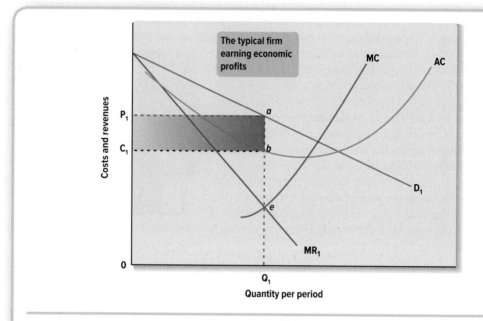

FIGURE 11.1   The Monopolistically Competitive Firm in Short-Run Equilibrium

D_1 is an elastic demand curve with its associated marginal revenue curve MR_1. AC and MC are the normal U-shaped cost curves. The area P_1aQ_10 represents total revenue. Similarly, C_1bQ_10 represents total costs. If we subtract costs from revenue, we get economic profits, represented by area P_1abC_1.

Figure 11.1 shows the restaurant's fairly elastic demand curve (D_1) with its associated marginal revenue curve (MR_1) along with the average cost curve (AC) and marginal cost curve (MC). These last two curves are the same as those developed in Chapter 6. You will notice that the graph is identical to that for a monopolist and for every firm that is not perfectly competitive. Much of what we said about the monopolist will apply here, too.

Given its costs and demand, our Bella Sushi needs to figure out two things: the right output level at which to operate and the right price to charge. The answer to the first question is that it is the output level that maximizes total profits, which in **Figure 11.1** is quantity Q_1. This is the point where the marginal cost equals marginal revenue (point e). The right price is the highest price that the firm can charge and still sell the optimum quantity—in this case, price P_1.

To find out the amount of total profit the restaurant is making, remember that total revenue equals price times quantity. This is represented on the graph by the area P_1aQ_10. Similarly, total cost equals average cost times quantity, and this is represented by the area C_1bQ_10. Total revenue less total cost is total profit, and this is represented by the area P_1abC_1. Remember that these are economic profits, since normal profits by definition are incorporated in the costs.

We now come to the crucial point in understanding how monopolistically competitive industries function. What will be the response of outsiders not yet in the industry to the fact that Bella Sushi is making economic profits? The answer is that some of these outsiders will want a share of these profits and will try to duplicate its success by opening up their own sushi pizza restaurants. And what will be the effect of this entry?

The first noticeable effect will be that prevailing prices in the industry will fall as the available supply increases. Bella Sushi, shown in **Figure 11.1**, will notice that business just is not as good as it used to be. At its current price, it will find that it now has fewer customers. In graphical terms, the demand curve that the restaurant faces (the same one we saw in **Figure 11.1**) shifts to the left and also becomes more elastic. The reason is that Bella Sushi must now share the market with new competitors. This will continue as long as Bella Sushi and the other new restaurants are making economic profits.

So when will this come to an end? The answer is: when all the economic profits have been squeezed out so that the average firm is just breaking even. Graphically this occurs where the demand curve is exactly tangent to the average cost curve as illustrated in **Figure 11.2**.

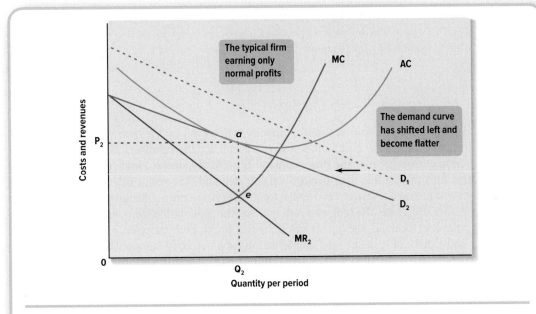

FIGURE 11.2   The Long-Run Equilibrium for the Firm

The equilibrium price and quantity are P_2 and Q_2. Further, since the demand curve is tangent to the average cost curve at point a, the area P_2aQ_2O represents both total revenue and total cost. This is the case of zero economic profit.

As always, the firm's best output level is at the point where marginal cost equals marginal revenue (point e), which occurs at quantity Q_2. The best price is the highest that can be charged and still sell quantity Q_2. This is price P_2. In other words, the best that the Bella Sushi can now do is to break even at point a. Given this point of tangency between the AC curve and the demand curve (which is also the average revenue curve), the area P_2aQ_2O represents both the restaurant's total revenue and its total cost. Therefore, economic profits are zero. Another way of stating this is that the firm is making only normal profits.

We are now ready for the main conclusion from our analysis of the monopolistically competitive industry model:

In the long run, the representative firm in a monopolistically competitive market makes only normal profits.

In other words, in the long run there are no economic profits to be made in, say, the dry-cleaning, shoe repair, hardware retailing, or textile manufacturing businesses. Think of it this way: If there were economic profits to be made in doing something as simple as running a dry-cleaning shop, wouldn't some of you start doing that? And if enough of you did open your own shops, what would happen to those economic profits? They would disappear.

Now, this last point should not be interpreted to mean that there are *no* monopolistically competitive firms that make economic profits in the long run. We are probably all aware of some travel agent or gas station or convenience store that seems, even in the long run, to be so busy it must be making an economic profit. Such exceptional firms do exist, and usually the reason can be summed up in two words: product differentiation. This might be the result of an excellent location, exceptional service, or another, similar reason. However, for every one of these success stories there are three or four other stories of firms that entered the same industry, hung on until the owner's money was gone, and then went out of business. If we subtract these firms' losses from the profits of the successful firms, we would more closely approximate zero economic profits in the long run in the *whole industry*.

 TEST YOUR UNDERSTANDING

2. Since there are hundreds of small family-owned restaurants in any large Canadian urban area, why are these markets considered to be monopolistically competitive and not perfectly competitive?

3. Assume that a representative firm in monopolistic competition is experiencing economic losses. What series of events will occur to return this firm to its long-run equilibrium?

Appraisal of Monopolistic Competition

You may recall from Chapter 6 that economic capacity is achieved by the firm when output is produced at minimum average cost. This is an automatic result for the representative firm in the long run in perfect competition because the firm's demand is perfectly elastic. However, the monopolistically competitive firm faces a less than perfectly elastic demand. The result is that the point of tangency between the demand curve and the average total costs curve cannot be at the latter's minimum point. **Figure 11.3A** illustrates the long-run outcome for the monopolistically competitive firm.

Given its costs and demand, the best it can do is just break even (at point *a*). This occurs at an output of Q_{MC} and a price of P_{MC}. The long-run situation for a perfectly competitive firm is different, as illustrated in **Figure 11.3B**. Since it faces a perfectly elastic demand curve (equal to the price, P_{PC}), it would produce an output of Q_{PC}. This output occurs where average cost is at its lowest, and this,

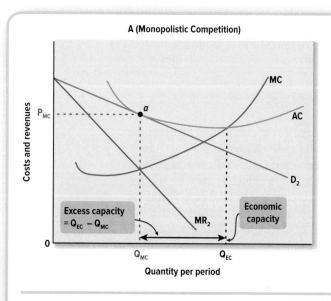
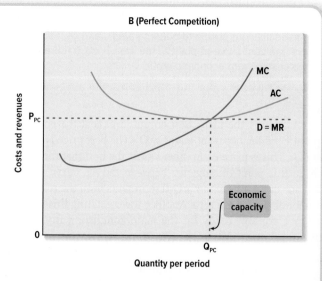

FIGURE 11.3 Excess Capacity

Figure A shows that the long-run equilibrium for a monopolistically competitive firm is at quantity Q_{MC}, which is less than economic capacity (Q_{EC}). The difference in the two outputs $Q_{EC} - Q_{MC}$ is referred to as excess capacity. Figure B shows that the long-run equilibrium for a perfectly competitive firm with a perfectly elastic demand curve, D = MR, is at economic capacity, Q_{EC}.

you will recall, is referred to as *economic capacity*. The monopolistically competitive firm, on the other hand, produces an output less than this. Consequently, it does not achieve productive efficiency, because the long-run equilibrium price does not equal minimum average total cost. This difference between output Q_{MC}, which is produced, and Q_{EC}, which would be produced given productive efficiency, is the amount of excess capacity.

In addition, the price that the monopolistically competitive firm will charge is P_{MC}, which is greater than marginal cost and is also above the perfectly competitive price of P_{PC}. Since this price exceeds marginal cost, we can also conclude that the firm does not achieve *allocative efficiency* as defined in Chapter 9.

At the root of this excess capacity is product differentiation. Each firm's attempt to differentiate itself, or its product, from all the others in the market results in the overall market being fragmented. Excess capacity is the result.

The fragmentation of the market means that the representative firm in each industry finds its profit-maximizing output to be one at which average total costs are not at the minimum. This means that the total output of a monopolistically competitive market could be produced at a lower cost. It also means that each firm is underutilizing its resources and could produce a far greater output than it actually produces. For instance, during off-peak hours, many gas stations—often located at each end of the compass at busy intersections—are often less than half full. The same is true at the many hair salons, restaurants, and travel agencies that dominate the urban landscape.

Japanese schoolgirls do not exhibit diverse consumer choice in choosing which clothes to wear each morning.

© Deco Images II/Alamy

Does this mean public policy should somehow restrain firms from fragmenting the market by attempting to differentiate themselves? Almost certainly not. Not only would this be difficult to do, but also we need to recognize the benefits that arise from differentiation. The most important of these is the fact that consumers have a wide choice of variations of the same general product, which makes it more likely that diverse consumer tastes will be fully satisfied. There are many gasoline stations, convenience stores, and shoe styles available to choose from in our economy. Most people see this as a strength of the market system rather than a weakness. However, it does come at a cost to the consumer: production could be technically more efficient if the representative firm could raise its output to the level at which average costs are at a minimum.

 TEST YOUR UNDERSTANDING

4. Consider the following graph for a monopolistically competitive firm.

   a) What output will this firm produce?

   b) How much excess capacity exists at this output level?

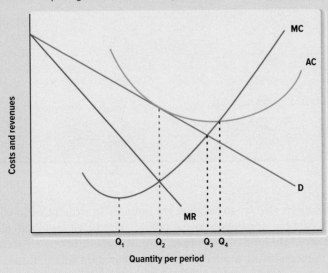

Explaining the Franchise Phenomenon

It should be clear from the discussion so far that there are no economic profits in a monopolistically competitive industry in the long run, because it is easy for new firms to enter the industry. We can turn this observation around and deduce that if entry could somehow be blocked, the chances for most firms to experience economic profits would be greatly increased. How might it be possible to block entry, to make a monopolistically competitive industry less competitive?

Well, one way is through a **franchise** organization. A franchise is a form of business wherein a successful firm (the *franchiser*) allows others (*franchisees*), under licence and for a fee, to use its trade name, proprietary knowledge, and processes. Besides the fee, the franchisee also has to pay a percentage of its sales and agree to purchase its supplies from the franchiser. In return, the franchisee gets the exclusive rights to sell the product within an agreed-upon territory. That exclusive right, in effect, blocks entry of new, competing firms, even if the product becomes very popular. We find such groupings in the fast-food industry, real estate agencies, auto repair specialists, and convenience stores, among others.

The many potential advantages to franchising include bulk purchasing, national advertising, and in particular brand identification. In addition, it allows individuals to own their own businesses without having to accumulate the large sums it would take to get started on a national level. If such brand identification becomes so strong that, for example, going out for a hamburger is redefined as going out to McDonald's, the meaning of the term "industry" is changed. This means that entry can be controlled, since each franchise holder has a contractual commitment from the franchiser that entry into his or her territory is blocked.

Now, there is no guarantee that a rival selling a similar but not identical product will not enter the same territory, but entry by a new firm selling the same differentiated product is controlled. Proof that even this limited blocking of entry is valuable is found in the fact that the purchase price of an established franchise firm is often quite high—in the hundreds of thousands of dollars.

Every year, Franchise Direct publishes its list of the world's top 100 franchises. As Table 11.2 shows, the majority are in the hospitality sector (hotels and restaurants), a prime example of monopolistic competition. Interestingly, of the top 100 global franchises, 80 are registered in the U.S. (5 in Canada) and one-third are in the fast-food industry.

TABLE 11.2
Top Global Franchises

Rank	Franchise Name	Country	Industry
1	McDonald's	U.S.	Fast food
2	KFC	U.S.	Chicken
3	Burger King	U.S.	Fast food
4	Subway	U.S.	Sandwiches and bagels
5	711	U.S.	Convenience stores
6	Hertz	U.S.	Car rental
7	Pizza Hut	U.S.	Pizza
8	Marriott International	U.S.	Hotels
11	RE/MAX	U.S.	Real estate
14	Carrefour	France	Convenience stores

Professional associations also try to redefine the industry in which their members practise. They do this by trying to create the perception in the public's mind that members of the association are better qualified to do a certain kind of work than nonmembers. If hiring an accountant is redefined, through advertising, to mean hiring a certified general accountant (CGA), the demand for CGAs will increase. If the professional association is also able to limit the number of new certifications that it issues (so restricting entry), those who already hold certification receive benefits in the form of higher fees.

Blocked Entry as a Result of Government Policy

Entry into a monopolistically competitive industry may be blocked by government law or regulation. A classic example here is that entry into the taxi business in Vancouver requires one to have a special driver's licence, a car, a kilometrage meter, a sign, and a government-issued licence. Unlike ordinary business licences, taxi licences in Vancouver are issued in a limited quantity. As a result, the only way to buy one is to purchase it from an existing holder. This, of course, can be done, but the price, until recently, was very steep—approximately $800 000 in 2014.

But then came the worldwide Uber phenomenon, and just the threat of its entry into Vancouver sometime in the future has driven down the price of an existing Vancouver taxi license, which in 2017 fell to $250 000.

The price of an existing taxi licence (whether $800 000 or $250 000) is a result of policy of the city government to limit the total number of taxi licences. Government-regulated quotas on such agricultural products as chickens, cheese, and milk have the same effect—the existing holders can sell their quota for a (sometimes high) price. If such entry ceased to be blocked because of a change in government policy (or a new phenomena such as Uber), the price of an existing licence or quota would immediately drop to equal the government's fee for a new licence.

In summary, a purely monopolistically competitive industry will experience zero economic profits in the long run. Free entry by new firms ensures this. On the other hand, if product differentiation and a redefinition of an industry are successful, what was free entry becomes controlled entry, and economic profits might exist in the long run. Similarly, if government pursues a policy of limiting entry by new firms into a particular industry, this too will result in long-run economic profits.

SECTION SUMMARY

a) Monopolistic competition is a market in which

- there are many small firms
- there is freedom of entry by new firms
- firms have some control over price
- firms sell differentiated products

b) In the long run, the typical firm in monopolistic competition

- makes no economic profit
- charges a price above minimum average cost and is therefore not productively efficient
- charges a price above minimum marginal cost and is therefore not allocatively efficient

11.4   Oligopoly

LO4   Describe the main characteristics of oligopoly markets.

Let us now turn to the last of our four market models—oligopoly. As mentioned earlier, an oligopoly is characterized, first of all, by the fact that the industry is made up of a *few large firms that dominate the market,* which means that the concentration ratio is high.

Oligopolies can be found both in industries that produce differentiated products and in industries that produce a standardized product. Examples of oligopolistic industries in which the products are differentiated are tobacco, breweries, automobiles, major appliances, electronic goods, and batteries. Examples of industries in which the few firms produce a standardized product are steel, aluminum, lumber, and pulp. Individual oligopolistic firms are usually large enough to be commonly known by most people. They include all the Generals—General Motors, General Foods, General Tire, General Electric, General Paint—plus a host of other household names from Phillips to Nikon to Apple.

New firms do occasionally enter an oligopoly industry. Yet, and this is our second characteristic, *entry is difficult*—much more so, for example, than in a monopolistically competitive industry. Let us examine why this is so.

Note that the firms mentioned above concentrate on the production of physical products, such as cars, tires, TV sets, or boxes of cereal. This is no coincidence: the production of almost any physical product involves economies of scale, and such economies result in falling average cost as output is increased. Thus, at the early stages of a new industry, firms able to increase the size of operation will gain a tremendous advantage over rivals that lag behind. This leads to the dominance of an industry by the few firms that grew fastest in the beginning. Thus, once the industry has grown beyond its early stages, barriers to entry become more significant.

As discussed earlier in the chapter, such oligopoly firms as those in monopolistic competition engage in a great deal of *nonprice competition*. This is especially so when product differentiation is present. This can be considered the third characteristic.

The fourth characteristic is the ability of the firm to have significant control over the price that it charges for its product. We are not talking about total control, because it is consumers who determine how much to buy and therefore how successful the firm will be. In addition in determining the price it sets for the product it sells, the oligopolist's control is also limited by what is called **mutual interdependence**, which is the fifth characteristic of this market structure. Mutual interdependence exists when one firm, before it makes a decision, feels it is necessary to consider the reactions of rival firms. It is this phenomenon of mutual interdependence that, more than any other characteristic, distinguishes oligopoly from the other types of market structures.

IN A NUTSHELL ...

Your Success Depends on What The Others Do

For example, picture a typical oligopolistic industry in which a large percentage of the total output is produced by only two firms (the soft-drink industry in North America is a typical example). Each firm is large and powerful and would presumably be able to set the price of its own product. Yet any pricing decision that either firm makes might generate a response from the rival firm. Thus, the power of firm A is very much constrained by the anticipated reaction of firm B. Such interdependence plays a crucial role in any oligopoly environment. Because of this mutual interdependence and because of the uncertainty about how competitors will react to pricing and output changes, there is no single oligopoly theory of price and output. As a result, a number of theories have been developed to explain oligopoly markets.

In summary, an oligopoly industry has five characteristics:

- It is dominated by a few large firms.
- Entry by new firms is difficult.
- Nonprice competition between firms is widely practised.
- Each firm has significant control over its price.
- Mutual interdependence exists between firms.

 TEST YOUR UNDERSTANDING

5. Since both oligopoly and monopolistically competitive firms practise price differentiation and have control over their own prices, in what ways are they different?

SECTION SUMMARY

Oligopoly is a market in which

- there is domination by a few large firms
- entry by new firms is difficult because of barriers to entry
- nonprice competition among firms is widely practised
- each firm has significant control over price
- mutual interdependence exists among firms

11.5   The Temptation to Collude

LO5   Explain why large firms are often tempted to collude and form cartels.

To a large extent, the world of oligopoly is a struggle between cooperating and competing. It pays for oligopoly firms to cooperate because that is how they can make the most *joint* profits. But even when they cooperate, there is still the incentive to compete and outdo the rival, which could result in even greater *individual* profits for one of the firms. Cooperation among rivals is called **collusion**, which is an agreement or understanding among firms for purposes of setting prices and/or dividing up the market. As we shall see later in this chapter, collusion often means that the colluding firms tend to act as though they are a single monopolist with the results we saw in the last chapter: productive and allocative inefficiency. Societies are poorly served by such arrangements and so collusion between firms is illegal in most countries and usually carries stiff fines or other penalties. However, collusion between countries is a different matter, as we shall see, and is impossible to prosecute.

To help you understand this "compete versus cooperate" dilemma, imagine an isolated village in a remote, mountainous region of ancient Persia, which possesses an abundant supply of drinking water from the local well to which, until now, the villagers have free access.

Now suppose that the village sheik, whose name is Aman, is granted ownership of the well in return for exceptional services rendered to the empire's sultan. Aman has completed a course in economics and is eager to put some of those ideas into practice; in addition, as the new monopoly owner, he is trying to decide how he can maximize his profits. First, he knows that the marginal cost of the water is zero; and since it is identical to the supply curve, it plots as a horizontal straight line in **Figure 11.4**. This is done by simply drawing the MC = S curve along the horizontal axis.

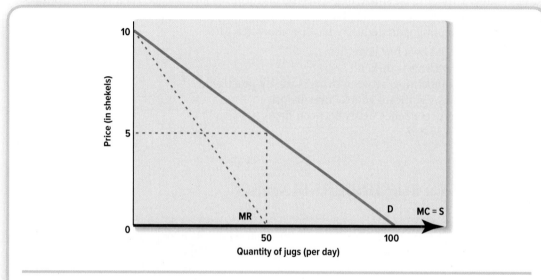

FIGURE 11.4   The Demand for Drinking Water in an Ancient Persian Village

The maximum price for water is 10 shekels, and the maximum quantity is 100 jugs. Given this demand curve, the marginal revenue drops twice as steeply and crosses the quantity axis at 50 (half of 100). This is the revenue- (and profit-) maximizing output; that is, total revenue is maximized where MR = 0. The maximum price for this quantity is 5 shekels (half the maximum price of 10 shekels). The total revenue equals 250 shekels (50 × 5 shekels).

Now all Aman needs to do is figure out the revenue side and decide which price will give him the maximum revenue (and therefore maximum profits).

Some quiet research he has brought him to the conclusion that the maximum anyone would pay for the water is 10 shekels per jug. In addition, he has observed that the maximum daily usage is 100 jugs per day. So he knows the two end points of his demand curve and, assuming the curve is a straight line, he adds that to his graph. The demand and supply curves intersect at a price of zero and a quantity of 100 jugs. (This is the perfectly competitive equilibrium.) Aman's economics course has taught him that total revenue is maximized where the marginal revenue is zero; so he proceeds to add the MR curve to his graph, knowing it is twice as steep as the demand curve and bisects the axis at the halfway point of 50 jugs. His analysis is complete: the best quantity is 50 jugs and the maximum price he can charge for that quantity is 5 shekels per jug. His total revenue, which is equal to his total profits, is therefore 250 shekels (50 jugs at 5 shekels per jug).

All goes well for a time and Aman is pleased with both his analysis and the profits he is making.

Now suppose that a few weeks later, a village shepherd, Omar, while digging large stones out of the ground to give his sheep better access to a nearby mountain trail, discovers a bountiful spring of fresh water. Knowing that Aman is charging 5 shekels a jug, he decides that he would like a piece of the action; he offers his water for sale to the villagers at 4 shekels per jug. The result is that all the villagers turn their backs on the village well and start buying from Omar. Understandably, Aman is furious and decides to drop his price to 2 shekels. Omar retaliates and drops his price even lower, 1½ shekels. A price war has broken out, and it is clear that the price may well continue to drop. But how low can it go? Well, since the cost of the water is zero, we already know that the competitive price will eventually fall to zero. But Aman and Omar also realize this and so decide to hold a summit meeting. At a shady spot between the well and the newly found spring, a truce is declared in the price war. They come to an agreement to divide the market equally between them. Aman explains that the revenue- and profit-maximizing price is 5 shekels and the maximum output should be 50 jugs. So they decide to limit the output to 25 jugs per day each, which will earn each of them a profit of 125 shekels.

All goes fine for a few more weeks until Aman gets a bit greedy. Although 125 shekels are better than something close to zero, which would have been the outcome if the price war had continued, it is, nevertheless, only half of what he used to earn. He starts to wonder what would happen if he were to renege on his promise to Omar and increase his output by 10 jugs, to 35 jugs. He realizes that the total output would rise to 60 jugs (25 by Omar and 35 by himself), which would cause the price to drop to, say, 4 shekels. But that would still give him greater revenue, since 35 jugs at 4 shekels amounts to 140 shekels, 15 more than his present earnings. (It would be tough luck for Omar, whose revenue, as a result, would drop to 100 shekels—25 jugs at 4 shekels each.) However, unfortunately for Aman, Omar has been thinking exactly the same thing and has also concluded that an increase in output to 35 jugs would be in his best interests.

So, as rational profit-maximizers, what should they do? We can present their choices by making use of a technique economists call **game theory**. Game theory was first developed by economists John Neumann and Oskar Morgenstern in the 1940s to analyze (military) strategic behaviour. This idea can be applied not just to oligopoly theory but also to any situation wherein people seek to work out the best possible action, taking into consideration the possible reactions of rivals. The various strategies and outcomes (or payoffs) are usually presented in the form of a matrix. The payoff matrix for Aman and Omar is shown in **Figure 11.5**.

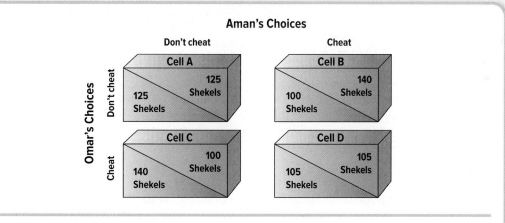

FIGURE 11.5   **The Payoff Matrix for Aman and Omar**

Cell A shows the outcome if Aman and Omar stick to their agreement. This is the best outcome for them jointly. Cell B shows the result if Aman cheats but Omar does not (better for Aman but worse for Omar). Cell C shows what happens if, instead, Omar cheats but Aman does not (better for Omar, but worse for Aman). Cell D shows the likely outcome when they both cheat, which produces the worst joint outcome for them.

There are four possible payoffs, labelled cells A through D. Cell A shows the results if neither of them cheats and they stick to their original agreement to produce an output of 25 jugs each. Cell B shows what will happen if Aman cheats but Omar sticks to the agreement. Cell C shows, on the contrary, what will happen if Omar cheats but Aman sticks to the agreement. Finally, cell D shows what would happen if they both cheat.

If both Aman and Omar stick to the agreement, the payoff, as shown in cell A, is 125 shekels to each of them. If, on the other hand, Aman cheats and increases his output to 35, but Omar sticks to the agreement, cell B shows the outcome would be a profit of 140 shekels to Aman but a profit of only 100 shekels to Omar. Cell C shows the results if the positions were reversed and Omar cheats but Aman sticks to the agreement. Now, Omar would end up with 140 shekels, with Aman's dropping to 100. Finally, cell D shows what would happen if they both cheat. In this case, if they both decide to increase output by 10 jugs, the total output would increase to 70 jugs causing the price to drop to 3 shekels, with the result that each would receive 105 shekels.

It is clear that the best option for them would be to stick to the agreement, since the monopoly position definitely guarantees the greatest joint profits. But is that likely to happen?

 GREAT ECONOMISTS: JOHN NASH

In the early 1950s, a young graduate student at Princeton University, John Nash, wrote a series of articles and mathematical proofs that laid the groundwork for the game theory revolution that swept through economics in the 1980s and 1990s. Nash became a tenured faculty member at the Massachusetts Institute of Technology at the unbelievably young age of 29 in 1958.

That same year, he was struck by paranoid schizophrenia, and as a result lost his faculty position. He wandered around Europe and North America—in and out of mental institutions—for the next few decades.

Reuters/Alamy Stock Photo

The effects of his illness began to recede in the early 1980s. Nash returned to Princeton, but was seen or spoken with only rarely and thus came to be known as the Phantom of Fine Hall. Nevertheless, in 1994 he received the Nobel Prize in Economics for his work of 40 years earlier. Hollywood's version of his story is told in the movie *A Beautiful Mind*.

Look at things from Aman's point of view. He is thinking: "What if Omar does stick to the agreement? Then the best thing from my point of view would be to cheat, since I would earn 140 shekels instead of 125 shekels. On the other hand, if Omar cheats, what's my best option? Again, I should cheat, since I would earn 105 shekels rather than 100 shekels. In other words, irrespective of what Omar does, my best option is to cheat!" But, as you can guess, Omar has come to the same conclusion: he should also cheat! So, what will happen? They will both cheat despite the fact that this is, by far, the worst result for them jointly. This result is what is referred to as a **Nash equilibrium**, named after Nobel Prize winner in Economics John Nash.

This story highlights some important aspects of oligopoly markets. First, competition may well lead to a price war, causing prices to drop to the point where oligopolists may not be able to make profits or may even make losses. Second, cooperation, in contrast, can offer far greater rewards for oligopoly firms—it can offer them the prospect of making monopoly profits. The temptation to collude, therefore, is very high despite the fact that collusion is illegal and is banned in most countries. Third, these collusive agreements seldom last long, since the temptation for one (or all) of the parties to cheat is too attractive. Since collusion implies cheating on consumers, it is perhaps only a further small step to cheating on your business partners. Or, as the saying goes, there is no honour among thieves.

The existence of interdependence and the possibility of collusion among firms results in oligopoly theory that is complex and a little messy. For this reason, there is not a single oligopoly model but rather several possible variants, each of which has a different focus. We will investigate a couple of examples of collusive oligopoly and then look at two examples of how oligopoly firms behave, assuming that they do not collude.

PRISONERS' DILEMMA

A classic example of game theory is provided by the story of the two criminals, Al and Bob, well known to the police, who were caught driving a stolen car. During interrogation, the police become convinced that the pair are also guilty of a multimillion-dollar bank robbery that took place last month. However, not having sufficient evidence to charge them, the prisoners are put in separate rooms and given the following offer:

- If both criminals confess to taking part in the robbery, they will each receive a seven-year sentence.
- If one criminal confesses but his friend doesn't, he will receive a one-year sentence and his friend will get a ten-year sentence.
- If neither confesses, each will receive a three-year sentence.

The choices facing the two prisoners can be summarized in the following matrix:

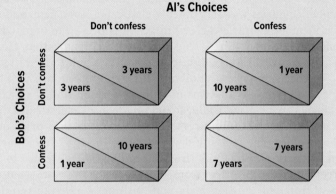

So what to do? Clearly, the best joint outcome for the two of them is to keep quiet and not confess which would result in each getting a three-year sentence. But Al starts thinking and comes up with: "Suppose Bob doesn't confess. Then the best thing I should do is confess because I will then only get one year as opposed to three. Then again, what if Bob does confess? In that case, the best for me again is to confess, since I will get seven years instead of ten. It's a no-brainer: whatever he does, I'm best off if I confess." Of course, Bob is going through the same reasoning and comes to the same conclusion. Predictably, the result is that they both confess and end up with the worst of all joint outcomes: seven years each!

 TEST YOUR UNDERSTANDING

6. Assume that two firms dominate the running-shoe industry. One of them hires a high-profile sports figure to endorse its product by appearing in its advertising.

   a) What would you expect the other firm to do in response, and why?

   b) After the second firm has reacted in the way you said it would, what do you think each firm's relative share of the market would be?

   c) Given your answer in (b), what might these two firms be tempted to do?

Collusive Oligopoly

If rivals decide that they are going to collude instead of competing, the collusion can take many different forms.

Firms might divide up the market on the basis of geography (you stay south of the river, and we will stay north). Alternatively, the whole market could be divided up according to existing

It is nearly impossible to know what the price of gasoline will be in the future.

Ivansabo/Dreamstime.com

client lists, or simply by general agreement on an output quota for each firm. The most obvious form of collusion, of course, is for the firms to agree on a fixed price. When both price fixing and quotas are used, the firms are acting as if they were a single monopolist. This means that they need to determine the profit-maximizing output for the group as a whole and then divide up this output in some agreed-on fashion. Whether the collusion is out in the open or secret, the term **cartel** is used to describe a formal agreement of cooperation among firms.

The classic example of an open cartel is that of the Organization of the Petroleum Exporting Countries (OPEC), which came into existence in 1961. Within a few years, it controlled more than 85 percent of the world's oil exports.

OPEC did not draw much worldwide attention until 1973, when the member countries agreed to restrict their (combined) output, thereby decreasing the market supply of oil. To accomplish this they set a total output target and then assigned each member a quota based on that (restricted) quantity. This had a dramatic effect on world markets. Some straightforward elasticity analysis will help us understand why.

Up to this point in OPEC's history, the demand faced by any one of the twelve member countries was undoubtedly elastic. But *world* demand for oil is inelastic, and once member countries agreed to act in concert, the organization created a near-monopoly on oil exports. Thus OPEC, as an organization, faced a highly *inelastic demand*. **Figure 11.6** shows the effect of OPEC's policy of restricting the output of oil.

The decision to restrict oil output is represented by a shift to the left in the supply curve from S_1 to S_2. Remember that our definition of supply is the amount that producers are able and *willing* to put on the market at various different prices. What we are saying here is that the OPEC producers were, at each and every price, only willing to put on the market less than before. The inelastic demand curve in **Figure 11.6** means that a relatively modest 20 percent restriction in quantity (from 30 million barrels a day to 24 million) causes a dramatic 400 percent increase in price (from $2 a barrel to $8). Note what happened to OPEC's revenues. They rose from $60 million a day (30 million × $2)—the red-dashed rectangle—to $192 million a day (24 million × $8)—the blue-lined rectangle.

Each of the twelve member nations was selling less oil than before, but combined they were receiving over three times the previous revenue. This was the beginning of a very significant shift in wealth among the world's economies, and it all came about because former rivals acted cooperatively

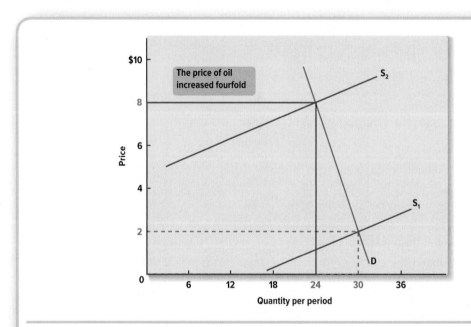

FIGURE 11.6   The Effect of OPEC's Policy on the World Market for Oil

By forming a cartel, the twelve members of OPEC were able to reduce the world's supply of oil, which resulted in the supply curve shifting to the left, from S_1 to S_2. Since the world demand for oil is inelastic, this resulted in a dramatic increase in the price of oil from $2 to $8.

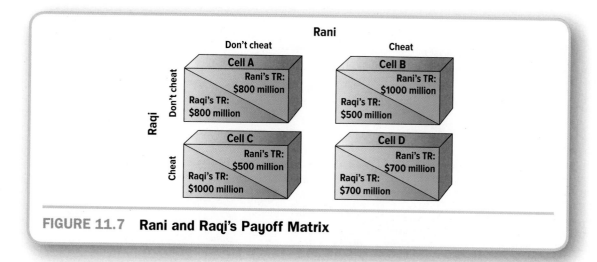

FIGURE 11.7   Rani and Raqi's Payoff Matrix

and behaved like one big monopoly. How long could this last? Seemingly, as long as each of the twelve stuck to their assigned quotas and *trusted* that others were doing the same.

However, like most things, OPEC's stranglehold on the world oil-export market changed. On the supply side of things, the high price of oil (it peaked at about $35 a barrel in the early 1980s) brought new productive capacity to the market by countries not in OPEC but keen to enter the market at these high prices. In addition, the world's demand for oil was reduced as a result of conservation efforts that prompted some new technology and through the development of alternative sources of energy.

All of this caused the world price of oil to start to drop. As this tendency intensified, the price of oil began to plummet even further, and the OPEC countries found that cutting their quotas again and again did not stop the trend toward much lower prices. Oil revenues to the OPEC-12 fell dramatically, which was quite a shock given that these countries had come to assume they would enjoy fantastic revenues forever and were spending accordingly. In the face of falling revenues and growing excess capacity, various members of OPEC began to cheat. They sold their quota at the official (agreed-upon) price and then also tried to sell additional quantities under the table at a reduced price. The net effect of this was a further increase in the world's supply of oil and an even greater downward pressure on the price.

Each member country had to choose between cooperating (sticking to the agreement) or competing (breaking the agreement). We can again analyze this fundamental dilemma using game theory. In Figure 11.7, we set up a simple payoff matrix in which we assume there are only two countries, Rani and Raqi.

 ADDED DIMENSION

The Escalating Price of Oil

The following graphs help to put oil prices into some context. The first graph shows how oil prices have escalated over the past forty years.

continued

The next graph shows comparative gasoline prices and how much of the price is attributable to excise taxes. Note that the cost of gasoline varies from 49 to 85 cents per litre. However, taxes vary from a low of 32 cents in the U.S. to $1.32 in the U.K.

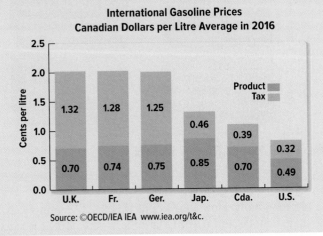

International Gasoline Prices
Canadian Dollars per Litre Average in 2016

Source: ©OECD/IEA IEA www.iea.org/t&c.

The figures in each cell show the (hypothetical) total revenues resulting from the four possible outcomes. (Again, these figures are simply made up; but not to worry, as it is how they change that matters.) Joint revenue between the countries is maximized at $1600 million ($800 million each), as seen in cell A, and can be achieved if both countries cooperate and stick to the agreement.

Cell B shows us what will happen if Rani cheats on the agreement but Raqi does not. In this case, Rani's revenue will increase to $1000 million, while Raqi's will drop to $500 million. Their situation would be reversed, however, if it was Raqi that cheated and Rani did not, as seen in cell C. If they both cheated, they will each see their revenues drop to $700 million, as shown in cell D.

It is clear that the best outcome for them jointly would be to stick to the agreement and earn a total combined income of $1600 million. The worst outcome would be if they *both* cheated. Then, they would end up with a combined income of only $1400 million.

So what do they do? You have probably guessed the answer: they will cheat! Think of things from Rani's point of view. Since the country's fortune depends on what Raqi does, it asks, "What is the best thing that can happen to my country if Raqi does, indeed, stick to the agreement? If we also stick to the agreement we will earn $800 million, but if we cheat we will earn $1000 million. No question, we should cheat. But what if Raqi cheats? Then, the worst outcome is that we do not cheat and earn $500 million. The best option is if we do cheat. Then, we will earn $700 million." So, irrespective of what Raqi does, Rani's best option would be to cheat. Raqi will, of course, have figured things out the same way. As a result, they will both end up cheating.

You can now see why cartels are difficult to hold together; the temptation to cheat is just too great. As a result, by 1985, OPEC officially abandoned its system of quotas, and the power of the most significant cartel of the century was weakened. In summary, we can say that:

Cartels work to the advantage of members only if there is no cheating among the participants.

Our next example of collusion comes from the world of advertising. Suppose that in Canada, two big breweries, Eastern and Western, presently advertise extensively and are splitting the market equally. However, they realize that the effect of much of this advertising is self-cancelling and that if neither firm were to advertise, they would still split the market equally but their costs would be considerably lower and their profits higher. Given this, suppose that they come to an agreement to reduce their advertising budgets to the bare minimum.

The outcome is illustrated in **Figure 11.8**. Cell A shows that each firm receives $500 million in profits per year. There is, however, an enormous potential reward involved if either firm decides to cheat on the agreement, as can be seen by examining the results in cells B and C. If either firm chooses a large-budget strategy and its rival chooses a small-budget strategy, then its profits will increase significantly, while its rival's profits decrease.

As we saw in previous game theory examples, the mostly likely outcome will be that they both use the large budget strategy and end up only making $300 million each (cell D). Again, you might well ask,

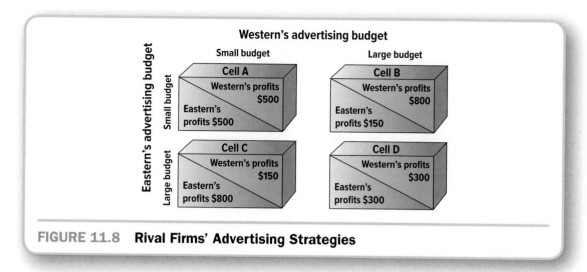

FIGURE 11.8 **Rival Firms' Advertising Strategies**

wouldn't it be advantageous for the two firms to stick with the agreement and not use the large-budget strategy? On the surface the answer would seem to be yes, but for this solution (represented by cell A) to persist, both firms must trust each other, and as we saw in earlier examples, this is unlikely.

There are numerous real-life examples of collusion between competitors on record. In the mid-eighties, it was widely accepted that Major League Baseball (MLB) owners were restricting players' salaries to increase their profits. This led to a long strike by the players, and eventually to a new contract that included a free-agency clause for players. Another example involves the conviction of several food manufacturers in the United States for conspiring to fix the prices of food services to the U.S. Army and to U.S. colleges and universities. Not that many years ago, three Canadian companies—Hershey Canada Inc., Mars Canada Inc., and Nestlé Canada Inc.—were charged in court with conspiracy to fix the price of chocolate bars, through clandestine meetings between executives at various coffee shops, restaurants, and industry conventions over the previous five years.

 TEST YOUR UNDERSTANDING

7. Suppose that Spartan Inc. and Trojan Ltd., the only two firms in the industry, have entered into a collusive agreement to share the industry's total profits of $50 million equally. If one of them cheats, the cheater will increase its profits by $10 million at a cost of $10 million to the other firm. If both cheat, they will each reduce their profits by $5 million.

   a) Construct a matrix showing the various options.

   b) Which option will they likely chose?

SECTION SUMMARY

a) Oligopoly firms sometimes collude in order to avoid the risk of a price war. However, such illegal agreements are seldom long-lasting because of the temptation to cheat on the agreement.

b) Game theory is a method of analyzing firm behaviour that highlights the mutual interdependence between firms. Its first application in the chapter was to analyze two possible advertising strategies between two firms.

c) Cartels involve overt collusion between firms and can be analyzed effectively using game theory.

   • The OPEC example explained why the member countries found it to their collective advantage to agree to quotas and why those countries later found it to their individual advantage to cheat on the agreement.

   • The advertising example shows why rival oligopolists often have big advertising budgets, even though much of it is self-cancelling and therefore ineffective.

11.6 Noncollusive Oligopoly

LO6 Explain price leadership and why oligopolistic firms are reluctant to change prices very often.

Both the OPEC example and the advertising example suggest that although cooperation through collusion produces the greatest joint rewards, individual rivals still end up competing because the incentive to cheat is strong. Will this always be the result? No. Certainly, it will not be the result if rivals learn from bitter experience. This is particularly true when competition takes the form of price cutting. Often, such activity has led to an outright price war. Such price rivalry leads to "death by a thousand cuts," causing great losses and bankruptcies. There are a couple of ways firms can avoid this. The first is through the practice of price leadership.

IT'S NEWS TO ME ...

The U.S. Court of Appeals for the Federal Circuit has just reopened a longstanding patent lawsuit related to Samsung copying the design of the iPhone nearly six years ago.

The court will seek to determine the exact amount Samsung owes Apple for infringing upon the iPhone's patented design, including its rectangular front face with rounded edges and grid of colorful icons on a black screen.

Apple's damages could be calculated based on Samsung's entire profit from the sale of its infringing Galaxy smartphones.

It will now be up to the appeals court to decide. Apple last month said the lawsuit, ongoing since 2011, has always been about Samsung's "blatant copying" of its ideas, adding that it remains optimistic that the U.S. Court of Appeals will send a powerful signal that stealing isn't right.

Samsung's defense centered on the insides of its phone being a different technology but many design companies, including Calvin Klein, filed briefs in support of Apple, arguing the iPhone maker is entitled to all profits Samsung has earned from infringing on iPhone's design. As a precedent, they cited a 1949 study showing more than 99% of Americans could identify a bottle of Coca-Cola by shape alone.

Source: *Star Power Reporting.* March 2017.

I. The two firms, Apple and Samsung, are firms operating in what type of market?

    a) monopolistic competition
    b) perfect competition
    c) oligopoly
    d) monopoly

II. If the courts impose a substantial monetary settlement against Samsung, which of the following statements are valid?

    a) Apple will enjoy stronger barriers to entry in the cell-phone manufacturing industry.
    b) Samsung will likely go out of business.
    c) The two companies will merge.
    d) None of the above.

Price Leadership

In a number of cases, industrial history and a process of trial and error have led the firms in a number of industries to concede price leadership to a single firm—usually the largest or most efficient one. The leader monitors its cost and revenue patterns with the long view in mind—ignoring the day-to-day fluctuations in demand and costs. When conditions change sufficiently that a price increase seems urgent, the leader will balance the advantages of a large increase with the risks of creating a tempting opening for a new entrant into the industry. Having decided on a price increase that is profitable but not too high to risk new entry, the leader announces this price increase in some very public way, and the rival firms in the industry quickly follow suit by also increasing their prices by a similar amount. In this way, rival firms engage in what amounts to price-fixing without there being overt collusion and without doing anything technically illegal. This also allows firms in an industry to adjust prices without triggering a price war. At various times in the past, Canada Cement Ltd., Canadian General Electric, American Airlines, and Tesco supermarkets (in the United Kingdom) have been price leaders in their industries.

The Kinked Demand Curve

In certain circumstances, the choice of action by an oligopoly firm is not clear-cut. Sometimes rival firms may want to compete, and other times to cooperate. This is the case with the model known as the *kinked demand curve*, developed in the 1930s by economist Paul Sweezy to explain price rigidities often observed in oligopoly markets. The basic proposition of this model is that any one interdependent firm, say Wonder Inc., will reason that if it increases the price of its product, rival firms will see this as a golden opportunity to gain market share at the expense of Wonder by simply *not* increasing their prices.

Technically, what this reaction by rivals means is that the demand curve that Wonder faces for all prices above the prevailing price is quite elastic, and we know that increasing the price of a product that has an elastic demand is not advantageous to the firm because its total revenue would fall. On the other hand, Wonder Inc. reasons that if it were to lower its price, its rivals may well interpret this as a very aggressive move on Wonder's part to attempt to steal customers from them. They would have no option, Wonder reasons, but to compete by matching the lower price, and the overall distribution of market share between firms would not change. This means that Wonder's lower price would attract very few new customers; in effect, the demand curve that Wonder faces for all prices below the prevailing price is inelastic. Of course, lowering the price of a product with inelastic demand is not advantageous because this, too, would decrease total revenue.

In other words, the behaviour of its competitors is not symmetrical. They will match any price decrease, but ignore any price increase. This leads to the conclusion that the demand curve faced by Wonder Inc., given its view of how rivals would react to any price change it might initiate, is kinked at the prevailing price. This is illustrated in **Figure 11.9**.

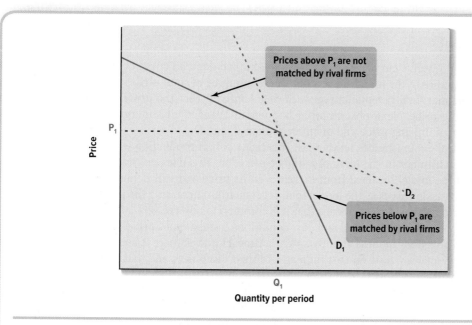

FIGURE 11.9   **The Kinked Demand Curve**

Wonder Inc. thinks that any price decrease it might initiate will be matched by its rivals, which will result in inelastic demand below the prevailing price. Further, it thinks that if it raises the price of its product, its rivals will not raise their prices, which will result in elastic demand above the prevailing price. Thus, Wonder Inc. views its demand curve as kinked at the prevailing price of P_1. The dotted portions of the two curves are not relevant to our analysis.

Given this, then, it is a case of "damned if you do, and damned if you don't." The best action Wonder Inc. could take is no action at all. This is an explanation of the often-observed phenomenon of oligopoly rivals charging very similar prices for competing products. Furthermore, these prices do not change often. What is of additional interest about the kinked demand curve is that the marginal revenue curve associated with this peculiar demand curve has a discontinuity, as shown in **Figure 11.10**.

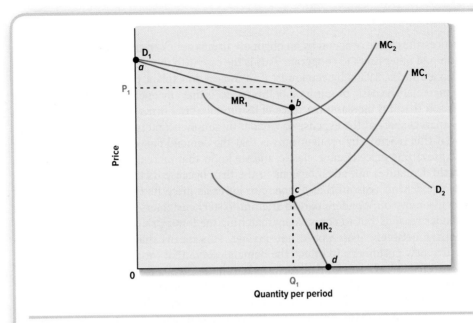

FIGURE 11.10   **The Kinked Demand Curve and Marginal Revenue Curve**

The discontinuity in the marginal revenue curve is the result of the kink in the demand curve. MC_1 is the original marginal cost curve. Quantity Q_1 is the profit-maximizing output that results in price P_1. An increase in marginal cost from MC_1 to MC_2 results in no change in equilibrium price or quantity.

The marginal revenue curve associated with the kinked demand curve D_1D_2 is *abcd*. It turns out that this discontinuity in the marginal revenue curve might be of some significance. The intersection of MC_1 with the marginal revenue curve, *abcd*, at *c* confirms that the prevailing price of P_1 is the profit-maximizing price. Next, observe what happens if Wonder Inc.'s marginal cost rises to MC_2. Wonder's profit-maximizing price and quantity remain P_1 and Q_1.

Now, in normal circumstances, an increase in a firm's cost of production will be (at least partially) passed on to the customer in the form of a higher price. But this does not happen here, because the firm is afraid of the loss of business from increases in its price and will be forced, reluctantly, to absorb the higher costs. In this case, the loss of total revenue from increasing the price is greater than the amount of the increased costs. This means that it is common to observe very stable prices in oligopoly industries despite changes in demand and cost conditions. For example, prices of some cars or fridges can remain unchanged for months, if not years, at a time. However, there is another simple reason big firms are often reluctant to pass on cost increases to their customers, and that is that changing prices in itself can be very expensive. These *menu costs*, as they are called, include the costs of reprinting brochures and price lists and of updating prices in cash registers and computers. Such changes can be prohibitively expensive and therefore might be done only infrequently and reluctantly.

One rather serious qualification about the kinked demand theory needs to be added before we leave it. If you go back and quickly reread this section, you will notice that nowhere in the analysis did we explain why the prevailing price was P_1 to begin with. We just stated it. Thus, although it is a rather neat and logical explanation for price rigidity, it cannot explain how that price came about.

An Appraisal of Oligopoly

From an overall economic point of view, how do oligopolies measure up? Are they an efficient form of market structure? The typical oligopoly firm possesses a degree of market power, which means that its demand curve is downward sloping. Thus, as we saw in **Figure 11.3**, it will not operate on the minimum point of its average cost curve. This means that it will not achieve economic capacity. Moreover, an oligopoly firm will charge a price that exceeds average cost. These two points lead us to our first conclusion: an oligopoly firm does not achieve productive efficiency. Second, an oligopoly firm will charge a price higher than its marginal costs. Thus, it will also not achieve allocative efficiency. When we compare these realities with those of firms in perfect competition, we see that oligopolies do not stack up very well at all.

Some people have even gone so far as to argue that monopolies are preferable to oligopolies. At least it is politically feasible to regulate monopolies, whereas oligopoly industries, which often produce very similar outcomes to those in monopoly industries, go unregulated.

On the other hand, it has been argued that oligopolies operate in an environment highly conducive to the vital research and technological change that our economy needs to remain competitive by world standards. John Kenneth Galbraith, a leading proponent of this view, pointed out that modern research is very expensive. For this reason, large oligopoly firms are the most likely ones to be able to finance it. In addition, the barriers to entry they enjoy give them some assurance they will be able to recover the cost of research before the new technology or new product is imitated by others.

If this view is correct, it will mean that an oligopoly industry, over the long haul, will foster technological change and improvement. This would reduce its average cost, with the result that prices would fall and output levels would rise. On the other hand, many suggest that oligopoly industries, because they are protected by barriers to entry, may well become greedy and complacent and lose their competitive edge. In addition, they often spend their time and energy in nonprice competition, such as advertising (thereby creating even higher barriers to entry) rather than in initiating research and development.

Once again, you can see a sharp point of debate within the discipline:

> Some believe that oligopolies are too powerful and produce inefficiently; others take the view that oligopolies are at the cutting edge of new technological development and, in the long run, push the average costs of production down.

Are Firms Profit Maximizers?

John Kenneth Galbraith's work is also at the centre of another point of debate within the discipline. All four market models—from perfect competition to oligopoly—contain an underlying assumption that we need to examine. This is the assumption that the firm behaves in a way that maximizes its profits. If demand, costs, or taxes change, then the firm will adjust its output level and (if it can) its price level so as to continue making maximum total profits. This assumption underlies the concept of firm equilibrium and is at the heart of microeconomics. This can be seen by the following quote from the University of Chicago's George Stigler:

> [Profit maximization is] the strongest, the most universal, and the most persistent of the forces governing entrepreneurial behaviour.[1]

Galbraith challenged this fundamental assumption in his work *The New Industrial State* (1967), in which he pointed out that a characteristic feature of the large multinational corporation of today is that management and ownership have become divorced. Ownership of publicly traded companies is typically very diverse and is often unknown to the hired managers who make corporate decisions, whom Galbraith calls the *technostructure*. Galbraith goes on to say:

> So long as earnings are above a certain minimum, it would be agreed that management has little to fear from the stockholders. Yet [the discipline of economics assumes that] it is for these stockholders, remote, powerless and unknown, that management seeks to maximize profits.[2]

Most would find, argued Galbraith, that the proposition that individual managers seek to maximize their own return—to make as much income for themselves as possible—is reasonable and sound. For managers to maximize the profits of the corporation, they would have to show great restraint in what they pay themselves. In effect, they would have to forgo personal reward in order to enhance it for others. Galbraith says:

> Accordingly, if the traditional commitment to profit maximization is to be upheld, they [the managers] must be willing to do for others, specifically the stockholders, what they are forbidden to do for themselves.[3]

[1]George J. Stigler, *The Theory of Price*, rev. ed. (New York: MacMillan, 1952), p. 149.

[2]John Kenneth Galbraith, *The New Industrial State* (Boston: Houghton Mifflin Co., 1967), p. 115.

[3]Ibid., p. 117.

ADDED DIMENSION

The World's Largest Economic Entities

The following is a list of the world's 80 largest economic entities. Countries are ranked by 2015 GDP and corporations by 2015 revenue, both in billions of American dollars.

Rank	Entity	Value ($billions U.S.)	Rank	Entity	Value ($billions U.S.)
1	United States	18 037	41	Philippines	292
2	China	11 008	42	Colombia	292
3	Japan	4 383	43	Ireland	284
4	Germany	3 363	44	Royal Dutch Shell (NL/U.K.)	272
5	United Kingdom	2 858	45	Pakistan	271
6	France	2 419	46	Exxon Mobil (U.S.)	246
7	India	2 095	47	Chile	241
8	Italy	1 821	48	Volkswagen (Germany)	237
9	Brazil	1 775	49	Toyota Motor (Japan)	237
10	Canada	1 551	50	Apple (U.S.)	234
11	Korea, Rep.	1 379	51	Finland	232
12	Australia	1 339	52	BP (U.K.)	226
13	Russian Federation	1 331	53	Berkshire Hathaway (U.S.)	211
14	Spain	1 200	54	Portugal	199
15	Mexico	1 144	55	Bangladesh	195
16	Indonesia	862	56	Greece	195
17	Netherlands	750	57	Vietnam	194
18	Turkey	718	58	McKesson (U.S)	192
19	Switzerland	671	59	Peru	189
20	Saudi Arabia	646	60	Czech Republic	185
21	Argentina	583	61	Kazakhstan	184
22	Sweden	496	62	Iraq	180
23	Walmart (U.S.)	482	63	Romania	180
24	Nigeria	481	64	Samsung (Korea Rep.)	177
25	Poland	477	65	New Zealand	174
26	Belgium	455	66	Glencore Xstrata (Switzerland)	170
27	Thailand	395	67	Industrial & Commercial Bank (China)	167
28	Norway	387	68	Algeria	167
29	Austria	377	69	Daimler (Germany)	166
30	United Arab Emirates	370	70	Qatar	165
31	Egypt	331	71	United Health Group (U.S.)	157
32	State Grid (China)	330	72	CVS Health (U.S.)	153
33	South Africa	315	73	EXOR Group (Italy)	153
34	Hong Kong, China	309	74	General Motors (U.S.)	152
35	Israel	299	75	Ford Motor (U.S.)	150
36	China National Petroleum (China)	299	76	China Construction Bank (China)	148
37	Malaysia	296	77	AT&T (U.S.)	147
38	Denmark	295	78	Total (France)	143
39	Sinopec (China)	294	79	Hon Hai Precision (China)	141
40	Singapore	293	80	General Electric	140

Source: Fortune 500; World Bank, *World Development Indicators*.

If the behaviour of today's modern corporations is not driven by profit maximization, how might one understand their behaviour? Galbraith believed the *multiple* goals of today's corporations included earning sufficient profits to keep the shareholders happy; obtaining autonomy of decision making; developing state-of-the-art technology; achieving high rates of growth; and even such social goals as designing and manufacturing a superior space vehicle, which would greatly enhance the company's image and give management a great sense of pride. There need not be any hierarchy in such a list, because one corporation's ranking of goals may not be the same as another's. The point is that modern management is often motivated to pursue a number of goals rather than solely to maximize profit.

Again, we neither feel any particular ability nor see any particular need to try to resolve this issue. We do, however, find it important and interesting that something as fundamental as the assumption of profit maximization has not gone unchallenged. This is evidence that the discipline of economics is alive and that its ideas continue to be debated and developed.

 TEST YOUR UNDERSTANDING

8. Given the following graph:

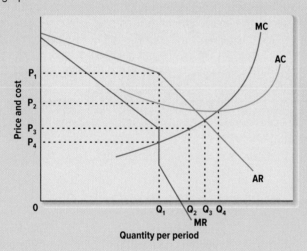

a) What output should this firm produce in order to maximize its profits?

b) What price should this firm charge?

9. a) Explain how one might argue that the existence of oligopolies means higher prices for consumers.

b) Explain how one might argue that the existence of oligopolies means lower prices for consumers.

SECTION SUMMARY

a) Price leadership involves tacit collusion between firms. Kinked demand curve theory is effective in explaining the often-observed phenomenon of stable prices within oligopoly industries.

b) Oligopolies are productively and allocatively inefficient, though some argue they foster technological change.

c) Galbraith and others believe that profit maximization is not the sole or even the most important goal for many corporations. They posit other motives behind firm behaviour.

Study Guide

Review

WHAT'S THE BIG IDEA?

The game theory examples and problems can cause some difficulty. Remember that the game theory matrix is no more than a table showing the two possible options available to each of two players. It does not matter which option is shown in which column or row. For instance, in many cases the options facing each player is "cheat" or "not cheat." You could put "cheat" in the first or second column for the first player or in the first or second row for the second. As a result, you can't come to the conclusion that the "answer" is always in the bottom right square! It all depends on how you have set up the matrix. There is no one way of solving these problems; the best approach is to ask "If the other player does this, what is my best option?" and then ask "On the other hand, if he does that, what is my best option?" It usually results in you cheating (and the same goes for the other player!).

As far as the kinked demand theory is concerned, the important point is that it is based on the idea that your competitors will behave differently according to whether you increase or decrease your price. If, on the other hand, they always match you whether you increase or decrease the price, your demand curve will be inelastic. On the contrary, if your competitors totally ignore you if you change your price, your demand will be elastic. However, the likely thing in these oligopoly markets is that the competition will *ignore* you if you increase the price but *match* you if you lower it. This means the top half of your demand curve is elastic and the bottom half inelastic.

NEW GLOSSARY TERMS

cartel	game theory	Nash equilibrium
collusion	imperfect competition	oligopoly
concentration ratio	monopolistic competition	product differentiation
franchise	mutual interdependence	

Comprehensive Problem

(**LO 3**) The graph in **Figure 11.11** is for Chic and Sharpe Ltd., a firm in the women's garment industry, which is monopolistically competitive.

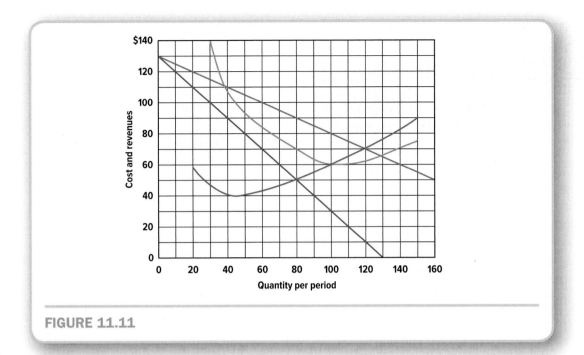

FIGURE 11.11

Questions

a) Label the four curves in **Figure 11.11**.
b) What is the profit-maximizing output and price?

Answers

a) See **Figure 11.11** (Completed).

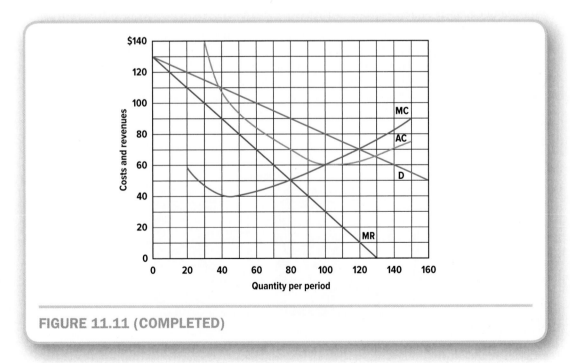

FIGURE 11.11 (COMPLETED)

b) Output = 80 (where MC = MR); price = $90 (where a vertical line from an output of 80 meets the demand curve)

Questions

c) At the output in (b), what are the amounts of total cost, total revenue, and economic profit?
d) How much excess capacity exists?
e) What will the presence of economic profits do?
   (i)   result in entry of new firms into the industry
   (ii) have no effect on the number of firms in the industry
   (iii) result in the exit of firms from the industry
f) As a result of your answer to (e), the demand curve in **Figure 11.11** will
   (i)   shift to the right
   (ii) shift to the left
   (iii) not shift

Answers

c) Total cost = $5600 (80 × average cost of $70)
   Total revenue = $7200 (80 × price of $90)
   Economic profit = $1600 ($7200 − $5600)
d) Excess capacity = 20 (the difference between economic capacity of 100—lowest AC—and actual output of 80)
e) (i) result in entry of new firms into the industry (because the average firm is making economic profit)
f) (ii) shift to the left

Study Problems

Find answers on the McGraw-Hill online resource.

Basic (Problems 1–3)

1. **(LO 5)** Assume that the only two firms in the industry, Sundance Inc. and Moondance Ltd., have entered a collusive agreement to reduce their advertising budgets to a minimum. If either of them cheats, the cheater will increase its profits by $30 million at a cost of $30 million to the other firm. If they both cheat, they will each reduce their profits by $15 million.
  a) Complete the matrix in **Figure 11.12** showing the options facing the two firms.

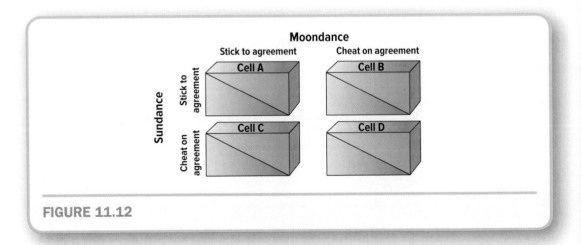

FIGURE 11.12

  b) Explain which option they will likely choose, and why. _____

2. **(LO 2)** The Costa Rican gimble industry consists of 14 firms whose annual sales are as shown in Table 11.2.

a) What is the (four-) firm concentration ratio for this industry? _____

TABLE 11.2

Firm	Sales (in $millions)
A	18
B	5
C	6
D	8
E	10
F	12
Next eight firms (total)	21

b) In what type of market does the gimble industry operate? _____

3. **(LO 3)** Aruna owns Pottery Plus, a small firm that produces terra cotta pots for sale in the Edmonton area. Figure 11.13 represents Aruna's situation. Pottery Plus has two rival firms. Aruna is convinced that she dare not raise her price because her rivals will not raise their prices, and she dare not decrease her price because her rivals will simply match her lower price.

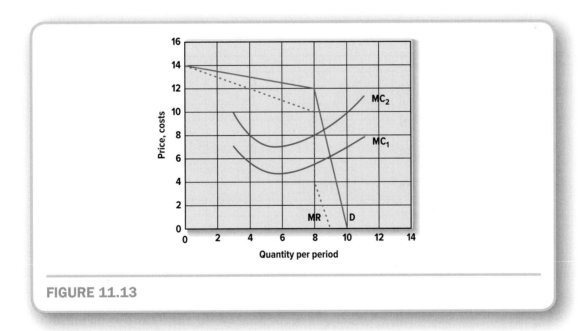

FIGURE 11.13

a) What price does Aruna charge? $_____

b) What quantity does she produce? _____

c) If her marginal costs are MC_1 is she producing the optimal output? _____

d) If her marginal costs increase to MC_2 will she reduce her output? _____

Intermediate (Problems 4–7)

4. **(LO 3)** Table 11.3 contains some revenue and cost data for the Rising Moon T-shirt Company (quantities for packets of a dozen shirts), which is in long-term equilibrium.

TABLE 11.3

Quantity	Price	TR	MR	TC	MC	AC
0	/	$ /	/	$122	/	/
1	___	64	___	154	___	___
2	___	124	___	184	___	___
3	___	180	___	216	___	___
4	___	232	___	250	___	___
5	___	280	___	286	___	___
6	___	324	___	324	___	___
7	___	364	___	364	___	___
8	___	400	___	406	___	___

a) Complete Table 11.3.
b) What is the profit-maximizing price and output for Rising Moon?
   Price: $_____ Output: _____
c) At the profit-maximizing output, what are MC and MR?
   MC: _____ MR: _____
d) At the profit-maximizing output, what are AC and AR?
   AC: _____ AR: _____
e) Given your answers above, what type of market must Rising Moon be operating in?

5. **(LO 5)** The graph in Figure 11.14 shows the demand for Cosmic shampoo.

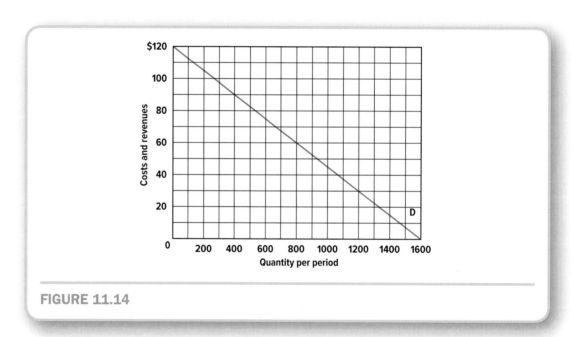

FIGURE 11.14

Suppose there are no fixed costs and marginal cost is a constant $60.
a) What are the perfectly competitive price and output?
   Price: $_____ Output: _____
b) What are the cartel (monopoly) price and output?
   Price: $_____ Output: _____
c) If there are only four firms in the cartel, what are the price and output of each firm, assuming equal shares?
   Price: $_____ Output of each firm: _____

6. **(LO 5)** **Figure 11.15** shows the daily demand curve for fresh spring water in a remote mountain village in the land of Far Country. The only spring is controlled by the village chief, who earns revenue from the sale of water in order to cover the costs of running the village. The villagers bring their own jugs and pay a price per jug as they leave.

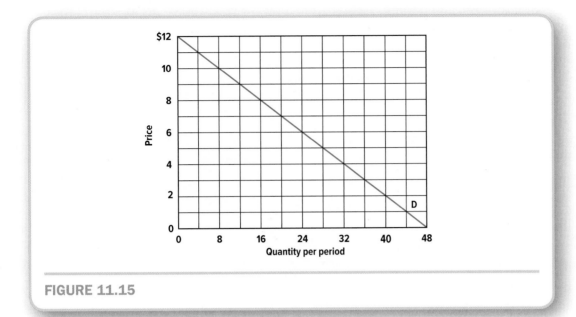

FIGURE 11.15

a) What quantity of jugs would be sold each day in order to maximize his total revenue? _____
b) What price would the chief charge? $_____
c) What is MR at this price and quantity? _____
d) What price would the chief charge in order to maximize his total profits? $_____

7. **(LO 3)** Answer the following question based on **Figure 11.16**, which is for Blue Smooth Yoga Mats Ltd.

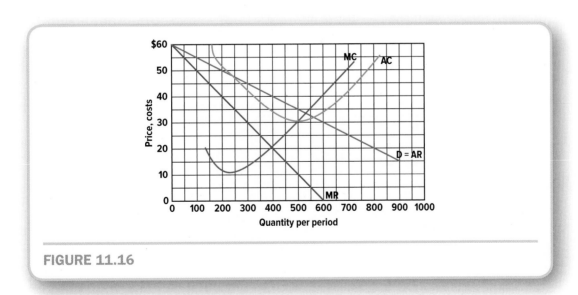

FIGURE 11.16

a) What is the profit-maximizing output? _____
b) What price will the firm charge? $_____
c) How much excess capacity exists at the output in (a)? _____
d) Is Blue Smooth making economic profits? _____
e) Is the current situation long-run equilibrium? _____

Advanced (Problems 8–10)

8. **(LO 5)** Table 11.4 is the demand faced by The Tienshan Company, a monopolist, which enjoys zero variable cost in its production.

TABLE 11.4

Price	Quantity Demanded	Total Revenue = Total Profit
$5.00	30	$_____
4.50	45	_____
4.00	60	_____
3.50	75	_____
3.00	90	_____
2.50	105	_____
2.00	120	_____
1.50	135	_____
1.00	150	_____
0.50	165	_____
0	180	_____

a) Complete Table 11.4.
b) What price will Tienshan charge, and what quantity of output will it produce?
   Price: $_____ Output: _____

Suppose that Endless Journey Inc., which also has zero variable cost, enters this industry and assumes that Tienshan will continue to produce its current output as in (b).
c) Complete Table 11.5.

TABLE 11.5

Price	Quantity for Tienshan	Quantity for Endless	TR = Profit for Endless
3.00	_____	_____	_____
2.50	_____	_____	_____
2.00	_____	_____	_____
1.50	_____	_____	_____
1.00	_____	_____	_____
0.50	_____	_____	_____

d) What output will Endless Journey choose to produce, and what will be the new market price, given both firms' output?
   Endless Journey's output: _____ New price: $_____

9. **(LO 5)** Figure 11.17 shows the market for oil in the kingdom of Bernai. In order to boost its revenues, the country decides to reduce the supply by 6 (million) barrels.

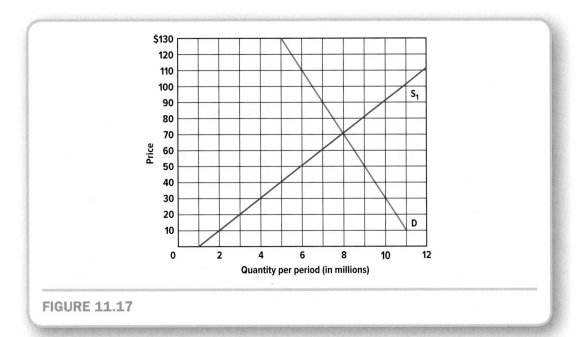

FIGURE 11.17

a) Draw in the new supply curve, labelled S₂.

b) What is Bernai's initial total revenue? $_____

c) What is Bernai's new total revenue? $_____

10. **(LO 5)** Figure 11.18 shows the demand for nectar in Gardenia.

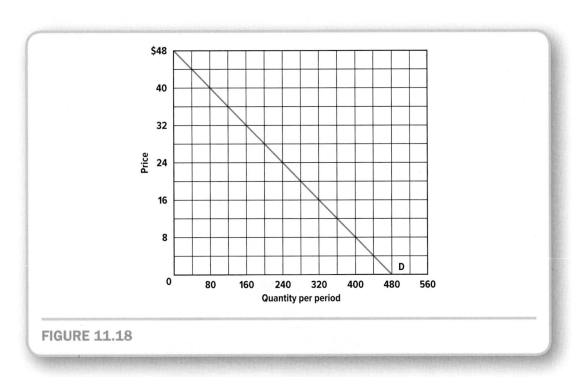

FIGURE 11.18

Suppose that there are only two firms, Ace and Pace, producing nectar, and they decide to act as a cartel (monopoly) and share the market equally.

a) What price and output will maximize their joint total *revenue*, and what amount is that?

Price: $_____ Output: _____ Total revenue: $_____

b) In the payoff matrix in **Figure 11.19**, show in cell A the amount of total revenue each will receive if they stick to the agreement.

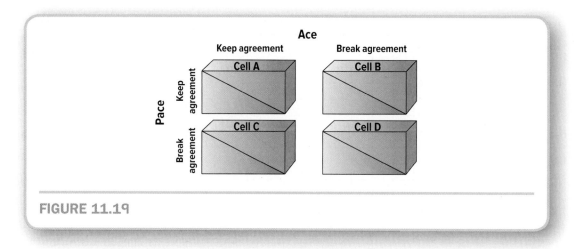

FIGURE 11.19

c) Suppose that Ace believes Pace will honour the agreement by maintaining his present output. However, Ace decides to cheat and increase his output by one-third. What will be Ace's and Pace's total revenues? Show Ace's and Pace's results in cell B.

d) Now assume that the positions are reversed and that Pace decides to cheat while assuming Ace will stick to the agreement. Show Ace's and Pace's resulting revenues in cell C.

e) Finally, in cell D show the total revenue of Ace and Pace that would result if they *both* cheated.

Problems for Further Study

Basic (Problems 1–3)

1. **(LO 1)** Explain four methods of product differentiation.

2. **(LO 5)** What is a cartel?

3. **(LO 4)** What is meant by *mutual interdependence*?

Intermediate (Problems 4–6)

4. **(LO 5)** Popsi and Cuke entered into an (illegal) agreement whereby each agreed to reduce the amount spent on advertising by 50 percent. After a year of apparent success, Popsi is uneasy about the agreement and begins to wonder whether it should continue to abide by the agreement or instead go back to its pre-agreement level of advertising. The payoff matrix, expressed in millions of dollars of profits per year, for Popsi and Cuke's choices is shown in **Figure 11.20**. What do you think Popsi should do, and why?

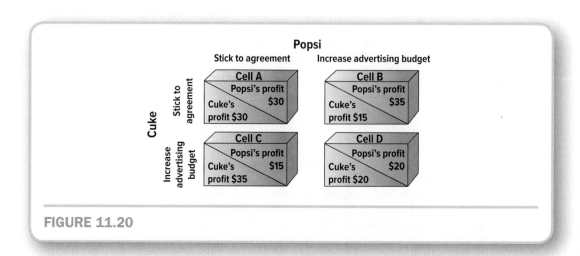

FIGURE 11.20

5. **(LO 3)** In the short run, is it possible for the typical monopolistically competitive firm to make an economic profit?

6. **(LO 1)** Discuss the pros and cons of advertising.

Advanced (Problems 7–10)

7. **(LO 3)** The graph in Figure 11.21 is that of Do Drop In, a shop in the dry-cleaning industry.

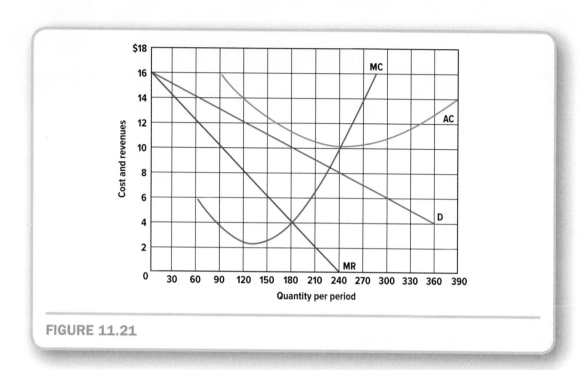

FIGURE 11.21

a) At the optimal output, what price will Do Drop In charge and what will be its output?
   Price: $_____ Output: _____

b) At the optimal price and output, what will be its total revenue, total cost, and total loss?
   TR: $_____ TC: $_____ Total loss: $_____

c) If this firm made a rational decision to continue to produce, despite the loss, average variable cost must be below what level?
   Less than $_____

8. **(LO 3)** Suppose that, in long-run equilibrium, a monopolistically competitive firm's AC equals price. Given this, why hasn't it achieved productive efficiency? How is excess capacity related to your answer?

9. **(LO 6)** "High risks means high profits." Would this likely be the motto of the technostructure? Why, or why not?

10. **(LO 5)** Explain why cartels often lose their effectiveness in keeping the price of their products high.

CHAPTER 12
The Factors of Production

WHAT'S AHEAD ...

In this chapter, we shift our focus from the market for goods and services to the market for the factors of production. The key concept here is the productivity of those factors, whether labour, land, or capital. You will learn that both productivity and the prices of the output produced lie behind the demand for any factor. We also examine the supply of each of the factors, putting particular emphasis on the supply of labour, and we explain the reasons behind different wage rates.

A QUESTION OF RELEVANCE ...

Like most students today, you probably spend a lot of time wondering about what kind of job you will end up with and spend even more energy worrying about whether the job will be satisfying and well paid. There are a number of other questions students sometimes ask as well. Is it a good idea to chase the elusive dollar, or should you sacrifice some income to gain a satisfying career? You might also wonder if it makes sense to take risks while you are young and leave caution for middle age. Or perhaps you wonder why professional athletes get paid so much and day-care workers so little. This chapter will give you some insights into these questions and others like them.

The first eleven chapters of this book wove their way through the topics of supply and demand, costs, and market structure. There was a common theme to all of this discussion. The focus was on the **product market**, for example the demand for orange juice and gasoline, the supply of automobiles by oligopolistic firms, and the supply of or demand for shoes from a monopolistically competitive firm.

We now shift the focus to the **factor market** and look at the supply of and demand for the factors of production—labour, natural resources (land), capital, and enterprise—as well as some of the more interesting issues that arise from this discussion. One comment about the demand for factors can be made now. Factor demand is a derived demand; that is, since people want automobiles, there is a demand for auto workers.

12.1 The Competitive Labour Market

> **LO1** Demonstrate that the competitive market wage is determined by both the demand for and the supply of labour.

In this section we will be looking at competitive labour markets. Our definition of perfect competition as it relates to the factor market is not greatly different from that of the perfectly competitive product market. The first ingredient is that the suppliers (employees) and the demanders (employers) of labour should all be comparatively small, so that none are able to significantly affect either the quantities or the price of labour (the wage rate). Second, it means that employers in particular show no preferences as to which employees they hire, since all are equal in terms of skills and abilities. You might think here of fast-food workers or bakery employees, who are in plentiful supply and whose skills are interchangeable. To see what determines the wage rate and the numbers employed in perfectly competitive labour markets, let us first examine the demand for labour.

The Demand for Labour

To ask what determines the demand for labour is equivalent to asking what factors an employer considers when deciding whether to hire one more employee or pay for more hours of labour. The discussion in Chapter 6 on marginal productivity is key to formulating an answer. What the employer has to keep in mind in making such a decision is how the benefit derived from one more hour of labour compares with the cost of employing that person. If the benefit outweighs the cost, the additional hour will be bought. If, however, the cost outweighs the benefit, no new work will be created.

Suppose we are looking at a small bakery. What does it gain from one more hour (or day or week) of labour? The answer is that it gains from what that labour can produce (loaves of bread), that is, its marginal product. In money terms, it gains revenue as a result of selling that bread (marginal product). In other words, it benefits as a result of receiving **marginal revenue product**, which is equal to the marginal product times the price at which the marginal product is sold. That is,

Marginal revenue product (MRP) = marginal product (MP) $\times$ price (P) [12.1]

Now, since the marginal product is equal to $\Delta Q/\Delta L$, where Q is the quantity of output and L is the quantity of labour, we could rewrite the last equation as

$$\text{Marginal revenue product (MRP)} = \frac{\Delta Q \times \text{price (P)}}{\Delta L}$$

Given that $\Delta Q \times P$ is the same thing as the change in total revenue, an alternative way of defining the marginal revenue product is

$$\text{Marginal revenue product (MRP)} = \frac{\Delta \text{ total revenue } (\Delta \text{TR})}{\Delta \text{ labour}} \qquad [12.2]$$

In other words, the marginal revenue product is the additional revenue that the bakery earns from the output produced by an additional unit of input (bakery employee).

And what is the cost of employing this labour? It is simply the (hourly, daily, weekly) wage rate of the bakery employees. We can envision the employer balancing the cost, for instance, of one more hour of hired employment, with the marginal revenue product of the person supplying that extra hour. Table 12.1 will help clarify this.

TABLE 12.1
Marginal Revenue Product of Labour Data

Hours of Labour	Total Product	Marginal Product of Labour	Unit Price of Product	Total Revenue	Marginal Revenue Product of Labour
0	0	/	$1.50	0	/
1	10	10	1.50	$ 15.00	$15.00
2	25	15	1.50	37.50	22.50
3	45	20	1.50	67.50	30.00
4	75	30	1.50	112.50	45.00
5	100	25	1.50	150.00	37.50
6	120	20	1.50	180.00	30.00
7	135	15	1.50	202.50	22.50
8	145	10	1.50	217.50	15.00
9	150	5	1.50	225.00	7.50
10	150	0	1.50	225.00	0

The concepts contained in the first three columns of Table 12.1 were introduced in Chapter 6 and need no comment. The fourth column indicates that the per-unit price of the product (in this case, loaves of bread) is $1.50 and, further, that this price does not change as more and more bread is produced and sold. (We are assuming that the producer is selling its output in a perfectly competitive market, which is usually the case in the bakery market.) The figures in the Total Revenue column are obtained by multiplying the total product by the $1.50 price per unit. The marginal revenue product of labour figures can be obtained by using either equation 12.1 or 12.2.

For instance, using equation 12.1, when the eighth hour of labour is employed, the MRP is equal to

$$\text{MRP} = \text{MP (10)} \times \text{P ($1.50)} = \$15$$

Or, using equation 12.2 gives us

$$\text{MRP} = \frac{\Delta \text{TR}(\$217.50 - \$202.50)}{\Delta \text{ labour (1)}} = \$15$$

Having identified the marginal revenue product of labour, we now want to know how many hours of labour the baker would hire if the wage rate for bakery employees was, for example, $15 per hour. Suppose we are considering employing one hour of labour. Is that worth it? Yes, because the

MRP is at least equal to the wage rate. What about a second hour? Definitely, since the MRP of $22.50 is greater that the $15 it would cost to employ a person for that hour. And the third hour? Even better, since the MRP of $30 is much greater than the $15 wage rate. We continue in this fashion until we get to the eighth hour, where again the MRP and wage rate are equal. The ninth hour of labour would not be hired, because its marginal revenue product ($7.50) is less than the hourly wage of $15. In other words, we would hire 8 hours of labour.

We are now in a position to make a significant generalization. An employer, operating under conditions of a perfectly competitive labour market, will hire up to the point at which the marginal revenue product of labour equals the wage rate. Profit maximization occurs when for the last unit of labour employed

$$MRP_L = W \qquad\qquad [12.3]$$

In fact, we can generalize by saying that *any* factor (capital, labour, or land) will be bought up to the point where its MRP just equals its price. If the marginal revenue product of capital, for example, is $600 per unit and its price is $550, it will be bought. If, however, its marginal revenue product is only $500, it will not be bought. Generally, as long as the marginal benefit (MRP) of employing or purchasing an additional unit of a factor exceeds its marginal cost (price), the firm should employ it. This idea is analogous to the optimal purchasing rule we saw in Chapter 5, where we concluded that consumers would maximize utility by equating the marginal utility per dollar spent on each product with its price. Here, the firm, not the consumer, is maximizing profits rather than utility.

Now, let us return to the data in Table 12.1 and ask how many hours of labour would be hired if the wage rate decreased to, say, $7.50? We can see that the MRP_L of the ninth hour of labour is also $7.50 and, applying the rule above, 9 hours of labour would be hired.

Let us now turn to Figure 12.1, where we graph the marginal revenue product data from Table 12.1. The MRP curve has the same shape as the familiar MP curve, since it is derived by multiplying MP by the constant price. If the wage rate was, say, $15, the firm would hire 8 hours of labour. A ninth hour of labour would be hired only if the wage rate dropped to $7.50. In general, the demand by firms for any factor depends on that factor's marginal revenue product, which is illustrated by the downward-sloping portion of its MRP curve. But why hire 8 hours, as opposed to 1, since they have the same MRP of $15? The answer is that, as Table 12.1 shows, it would not

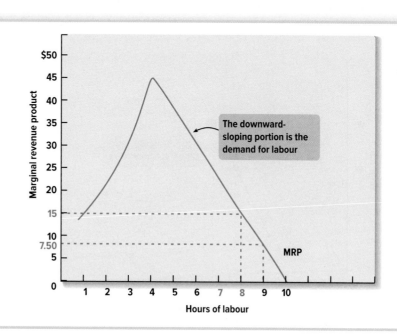

FIGURE 12.1   The Firm's Marginal Revenue Product of Labour

The downward-sloping portion of the firm's MRP_L curve represents its demand for labour. For instance, when the wage rate is $15, eight hours of labour will be hired. At a wage rate of $7.50, nine hours of labour will be hired.

be wise to stop at 1 hour, since for all subsequent hours up until the eighth, the MRP is above the wage rate. This is similarly the case for all hours up until the fourth. In other words, the upward-sloping portion of the MRP curve is irrelevant. In fact:

> The downward-sloping portion of the MRP curve is the firm's demand curve for that factor.

The above illustration of the firm's demand for labour assumed that the firm was selling its output in a perfectly competitive product market. Would our analysis change if the firm operated in, say, an oligopolistic product market? The basic answer is no, since the only change would be that the marginal revenue product of labour would decline faster. This is because using more of any factor always increases output, and this increase in output would mean that the firm would be forced to decrease the price of that output in order to sell the increased quantities. That is to say, the marginal revenue for competitive firms is constant and equal to price, whereas for imperfectly competitive firms it declines with output, driving marginal revenue product down faster.

As we have seen, a single firm's demand for labour curve is determined by that firm's marginal revenue product. If we want to know the *market* demand for labour, say for bakery employees, we could do as we did in Chapter 2, and horizontally sum each baker's demand to obtain a market demand for labour curve.

The Supply of Labour

Now let us examine the other side of the market; the supply of labour. What determines the supply of bakers for instance? Well, bakery employees are just a small part of the economy's **labour force** which is simply the number of people over the age of 15 who are willing and able to work at paid employment. The total amount of hours that these people are willing to work is the **labour force supply**.

We know that the labour force supply tends to expand as the wage rate increases, as illustrated in **Figure 12.2**. There are two explanations for this upward-sloping supply of labour. First, as the wage rate increases, the rate at which the population is willing to participate in the labour force increases, because the higher wage rate makes employment more attractive. For example, younger people would enter the labour force sooner, many older workers would perhaps not retire as quickly,

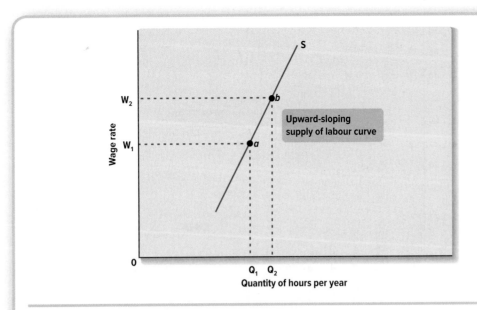

FIGURE 12.2 **The Market Labour Force Supply Curve**

An increase in the wage rate from W_1 to W_2 results in the quantity of labour supplied rising from Q_1 to Q_2: that is, from *a* to *b*. This indicates that the supply-of-labour curve is upward sloping with a relatively steep slope.

and others who were previously not participating in the labour force are more likely to enter it. Second, extra hours supplied might come as a result of present employees working longer hours. To put it another way, as the wage rate increases, more people work, and people work more.

But how would those already in the labour force respond to a higher wage rate? Wouldn't everyone be willing to work more hours through taking on overtime work or a second job? Some would, and some would not. The reason for this is that such decisions involve more than just the maximization of income. For instance, either of your authors could work weekends at McDonald's and increase his income. Why don't we? The answer involves what economists call the *income effect* and the *substitution effect*. It is certainly true that a higher wage will make working additional time more attractive. However, working more hours also means less leisure. As one's income rises, a point is reached where leisure becomes more valuable, and at this point a further increase in the wage rate means that the same level of income can be obtained with less work and more of the valuable leisure time can be enjoyed.

The net effect of these two opposing alternatives is that economists know that the supply curve for labour is upward sloping but relatively inelastic, so that a 10 percent rise in the wage rate (for example) will result in something less than a 10 percent increase in the quantity of labour supplied. This is illustrated in **Figure 12.2**.

Theoretically, if we were to imagine a very high wage rate so that a majority of people valued more leisure over more income, the number of hours people would be willing and able to work would in fact decline. Graphically, the labour force supply curve would start to bend back to the left as it continued to rise. However, we will ignore this possibility.

As **Figure 12.2** shows, an increase in the wage of bakery employees from W_1 to W_2 results in an increase in the quantity of hours that they would be willing to work, as indicated in the movement up on the labour force supply curve, S, from point *a* to point *b*.

Market Equilibrium

Now, to obtain the equilibrium wage rate, we simply bring together the demand-for-labour curve together with the supply-of-labour curve, as we do in **Figure 12.3A**. Here, we see that the equilibrium wage is W_1, and the equilibrium quantity of hours that are bought and sold is Q_1.

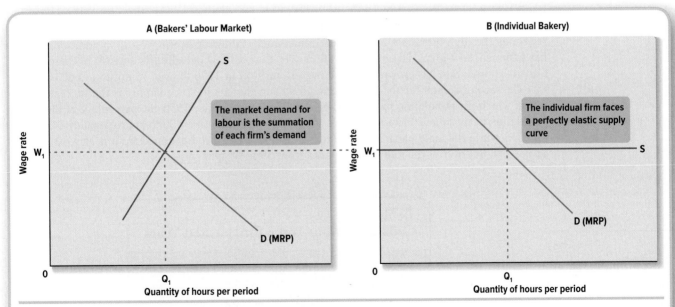

FIGURE 12.3   **The Market Equilibrium Wage Rate**

Figure A shows that given the upward-sloping supply-of-labour curve and the downward-sloping demand-for-labour curve, the equilibrium wage rate is W_1 and the equilibrium quantity is Q_1. For the individual bakery in Figure B, the wage rate is a given of W_1. The quantity of bakery workers it employs will be determined where the wage is equal to its MRP—that is, a quantity of Q_1 hours.

The answer to the question of what determines the wage rate for bakery employees, for example, is the rather conventional one: the supply of and demand for this type of employment. There are, after all, thousands of bakeries across the country having many more thousands of bakery employees, and none of those firms are individually able to determine the wage rate of those employees. But even for occupations that have far fewer practitioners and even fewer employers—think of aerospace engineers, heart surgeons, or musical conductors—the forces of demand and supply still have a huge impact on employment and wage rates in those professions. However, we have uncovered something significant:

> There are both supply and demand elements underlying every wage rate.

Now, if the labour market is competitive, as it is for bakeries, the market-determined wage rate will be the wage rate applicable to each individual bakery. As a result, each bakery is able to hire as many bakery employees as it wishes, up to the point where the wage rate equals the marginal revenue product of labour. This is illustrated graphically in **Figure 12.3B**.

In a competitive labour market, the market supply of and demand for labour determines the market wage rate of W_1. The individual bakery for example faces a perfectly elastic supply curve for labour, S_1, at this market wage rate. This is because a single bakery is very small compared with the whole industry and can obtain as few or as many employees as it wishes at the going wage, and this wage is a "take it or leave it" wage from the bakery's point of view. If it offered a lower wage, nobody would want a job with the firm; conversely, it would never offer a higher wage, since it can obtain as many workers as it wishes at the market wage. The quantity of labour that this bakery hires is determined by the equality of its marginal revenue product for labour and the market wage rate. This quantity, Q_1, is illustrated in **Figure 12.3B** by the intersection of the firm's supply curve (the wage rate) and the demand-for-labour curve, labelled D (MRP).

Changes in the Supply of Labour

Many things affect the overall supply of bakery employees, or, for that matter, the number of employees willing and able to enter any occupation. One of the overriding factors is the size of the labour force in the country. For instance, the size of Canada's labour force has grown considerably over the last 40 years, as can be seen in **Table 12.2**. There are two distinct explanations for this growth. The first is the growth in population. This influence was most significant in the late 1960s and 1970s, reflecting the high birth rate in the years immediately following World War II. In addition, Canada has experienced a great deal of immigration over the past few decades. As a result of these factors, Canada's population has grown from just over 16 million in 1956 to over 36 million in 2016.

The second reason for the very strong growth in the labour force supply is the increase in the rate at which the population participates in the labour force. Since 1950, the percentage of the female population in the labour force supply has steadily grown from under 30 to approximately 61 percent by 2016, while the male participation rate has in the same period declined from nearly 80 to about 71 percent; but overall the rate has increased from 59 to 66 percent.

TABLE 12.2
Canada's Labour Force for Selected Years

1976	10 491 300
1986	13 272 100
1996	14 853 500
2006	17 502 200
2016	19 440 500

Source: Adapted from the Statistics Canada CANSIM database, http://cansim2.statcan.ca, Table 282-0002, retrieved April 5, 2017.

In explaining the cause of the growth in the labour force, we raise the question of exactly how to define the labour force supply. Since we earlier defined the supply as total hours worked rather than the number of individuals working, the average number of hours worked per week also is relevant. It is interesting to note that, although the average hours worked per week has steadily declined during the century, they have, in fact, been increasing in the past few years.

The overall increase in an economy's supply of labour has not fallen evenly across every industry in the economy. Some industries have experienced a larger increase in the supply of labour than others. For example, young people today seem to put a great deal of importance on maximizing their chances for getting a good entry-level job. Thus, more high school graduates are choosing to extend their formal education in colleges, universities, and technical institutes. And the areas they are choosing to focus on tend to be the more "practical" subjects, such as accounting, dental assisting, or computer studies. At the same time, most people want a chance to be creative in their work and to enjoy good working conditions. Thus, the supply of labour for any industry that seems to offer a good prospect for getting started, as well as being interesting, will be high. Examples are the software, medical services, and petroleum industries. Meanwhile, the supply of labour is decreasing for the more traditional industries that are not growing much, such as mining, forestry, and fishing.

If we are looking at what determines the supply of labour to a particular occupation, such as baking, any number of factors, economic and non-economic, come into consideration. We might mention the employee benefits offered (vacation rates, shift work, pension plans), working conditions, and entry requirements. We will look at some of these aspects in a later section when we examine wage differentials.

Changes in the Demand for Labour

We have established the importance of the marginal revenue product of labour in determining the demand for labour. Our discussion so far has assumed that technology and the size of the economy's capital stock remain unchanged. Yet, of course, technology improves and the capital stock grows over time. The effect of this can be seen in the growth of labour productivity, which has the effect of increasing each firm's marginal product and thus graphically shifting its MRP_L curve out to the right.

In addition to an increase in productivity, the demand for any factor is a derived demand. This means that an increase in the demand for an industry's product will cause an increase in its price in the short run and an increase in the number of firms in that industry in the long run. Both will result in an increase in the demand for labour.

Therefore, an increase in the demand for labour in any industry could occur because of increases in labour productivity in that industry or simply because demand for the product is growing.

We can put these trends together in **Figure 12**.4, where we see a shift to the right in the demand for labour curve (D_1 to D_2) because of increases in overall labour productivity or in the demand for the industry's product. In this figure, we also show an increase in the supply of labour: people might be attracted to the industry because they know it is growing and offers the possibility of interesting jobs with attractive working conditions. As shown in **Figure 12**.4, if the demand for labour increases more than the supply does, the equilibrium quantity of labour will rise (from Q_1 to Q_2) and so will the wage rate (from W_1 to W_2). This, for example, could illustrate

Does training in computer science mean better job prospects?
Hero/CORBIS/Glow Images

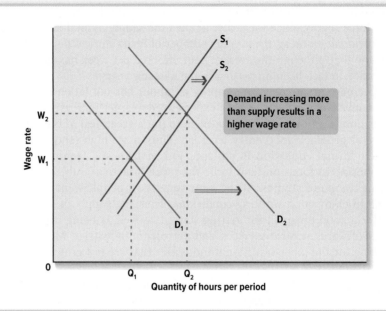

FIGURE 12.4   Increases in the Labour Supply and Demand

Increases in labour productivity and the growth in overall output for this industry cause the demand-for-labour curve to shift to the right, from D_1 to D_2. The supply-of-labour curve also shifts to the right, from S_1 to S_2. Since the demand for labour increased more than the supply, both the equilibrium quantity of labour and the wage rate rise.

what is happening in the computer software industry. Recent graduates trained in information management systems are being offered entry-level jobs at several thousand dollars more per year than students whose major was in the more conventional subjects.

Productivity and the Real Wage

To extend the discussion of the importance of productivity, let us ask this question: What was fictional castaway Robinson Crusoe's real wage? By **real wage**, we mean the purchasing power of any given wage. In contrast, the **nominal wage** is the dollars-and-cents figure received from work. That is to say,

$$\text{Real wage} = \frac{\text{nominal wage}}{\text{price level}} \qquad [12.4]$$

Returning to the question above, Robbie's real wage is whatever he is able to produce for himself. If he produces nothing, his real wage would be nothing. If he produces more this month than the previous month, his real wage has risen.

What is true for Robinson Crusoe, who lived alone on an uninhabited island, is also true for a whole economy. Given the labour force supply, the real wage for Canadians depends on how much is produced by Canadians, and generally speaking, the more Canada produces, the higher Canadians' real wage will be. This inevitable relationship between productivity and the real wage is illustrated in **Figure 12.5**.

What is really being said here is that:

An economy's real output and real income are the same thing.

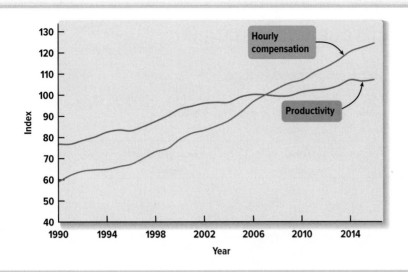

FIGURE 12.5   Trend in Business-Sector Real Hourly Compensation and Productivity, Canada, 1990–2016

Productivity and real hourly compensation have both risen steadily in the last 20 years, but productivity has increasingly lagged behind increases in compensation.

Source: Statistics Canada, Table 383-0008; accessed April 5, 2017.

Thus, an economy's real income (real wage rate) per worker can only increase at about the same rate as its output per worker. In summary:

- Both supply and demand are determinants of wage rates.
- There are distinct long-run trends of growth in both the labour supply and demand.
- The average real wage for labour for the whole economy has increased over time, and this increase is closely related to increases in labour productivity.

 ADDED DIMENSION

Why the Prices of Services Continue to Rise

Many people have observed that the prices of tickets to a concert or the theatre have become almost prohibitive. There is an explanation for this. Live performances require direct contact between those who consume the service and those who provide it. In contrast, the consumer (buyer) of, say, a DVD player has no idea who worked on it or how much labour time went into its production; that is, there is no contact between producer and consumer.

Next, consider the fact that technological change saves labour time in producing the DVD player and often results in a lower price—one that is not achieved at the cost of a reduction in product quality. On the other hand, few such innovations are possible in providing live theatre or musical performances, and therefore it is difficult to increase the productivity of a live performer.

The possible increases in labour productivity in manufacturing that come from technological change increase the wage rates paid throughout that sector. When wages for common labour in manufacturing rise, musicians and actors expect to receive an increase, too. Such increased labour costs must be paid for from increased ticket prices because they cannot come from increased productivity.

This general point, that the service sector faces rising (real) costs of production, can be extended to include most public services workers as well, such as health care professionals, firefighters, teachers, and social service workers.

TEST YOUR UNDERSTANDING

Find answers on the McGraw-Hill online resource.

1. a) Given the data in the following table, and assuming that the output of Sparky the Plug Maker can be sold for $3 per unit, fill in the blanks below.

Hours of Labour	Total Product	Marginal Product	Marginal Revenue Product
0	0	/	/
1	3	_____	_____
2	7	_____	_____
3	13	_____	_____
4	18	_____	_____
5	22	_____	_____
6	25	_____	_____
7	27	_____	_____
8	28	_____	_____

b) If the firm can hire all the labour it wants for $9 per hour, how many hours per week will it hire, and what output will it produce?

2. The labour market for laundry workers is shown below:

Wage Rate	Supply of Labour (billions of hours)	Demand for Labour (billions of hours)
$12	12	16
14	13	15
16	14	14
18	15	13
20	16	12

Data for Busy Bee Laundry are as follows:

Hours of Labour Hired	MRP_L
180	$18
220	16
260	14
300	12
340	10

a) How many hours of labour will Busy Bee hire?

b) If the supply of labour increased by 2 billion at every wage rate, what effect would this have on the quantity of hours that Busy Bee hires?

SECTION SUMMARY

a) The *demand for labour* is a derived demand that is determined by the marginal product of labour, which when converted to money terms becomes

$$MRP_L = \frac{\Delta \text{total revenue}}{\Delta \text{labour inputs}} \text{ or } = MP_L \times P$$

b) The downward-sloping portion of the MRP_L curve is the demand for labour curve, while the *supply of labour curve* is upward sloping, since increases in the wage rate increase the quantity supplied of labour. The *equilibrium wage rate* is determined by the point of intersection of these two curves.

c) In a competitive factor market the individual firm is able to hire all the labour it wishes at the market determined wage rate and will, in fact, hire labour up to the point at which $MRP_L = W$.

d) The supply of labour in any particular labour market increases as a result of

   • increases in population

   • an increase in labour force participation rates

   • changes in the economic and non-economic factors of a particular occupation

e) Increases in demand for labour are the result of

   • an increase in demand for the industry's output

   • an increase in labour productivity

f) the real wage is determined by labour productivity, which depends on technological change and increases in the nation's capital stock.

   • the real wage is measured by

$$\text{Real wage} = \frac{\text{nominal wage}}{\text{price level}}$$

12.2   Imperfect Labour Markets

> **LO2** Explain how monopsonies, trade unions, and trade associations impact the labour market.

In Section 12.1, we investigated competitive labour markets, in which, as expected, the forces of demand and supply held full sway. Now we look at situations in which big firms or trade associations are powerful and see to what extent market forces still operate. Our first look is at monopsonies and how they impact on the labour market.

The Case of Monopsony

A **monopsony** labour market is one in which there is only one buyer. For instance, imagine a firm that was the sole employer of some highly specialized labour. It would need to pay a higher wage to attract additional workers. In other words, the firm would face an upward-sloping supply of labour curve.

As we have seen, a firm operating in a competitive labour market can hire *additional* labour at the going market wage rate. This is not true for the monopsonist. Additional labour can be hired only if a higher wage rate is offered. Furthermore, it will have to pay that higher wage rate not only to additional workers but also to all ones it has already hired. The net result is that a firm operating in a monopsony labour market faces a higher total wage bill as a result of hiring additional labour compared with the firm that operates in a competitive labour market.

Although there are not many examples of monopsonies in Canada, many "company towns" in rural areas of the country are often dominated by single large employers. Since there are few other opportunities in these towns, workers can be in a weak bargaining position and are often paid less than if more competition existed. Let's look at an example.

Sonny runs a pulp mill in the town and hires labour locally. However, since he is the only employer, to attract additional workers he will have to increase the wage not only for new hires but for

TABLE 12.3
Total and Marginal Wage Costs for a Monopsonist

Number of Workers	Hourly Wage	Total Wage Cost (TWC)	Marginal Wage Cost (MWC)
1	$15	$ 15	$15
2	16	32	17
3	17	51	19
4	18	72	21
5	19	95	23
6	20	120	25

the whole labour force. Table 12.3 shows that he can hire a single worker for $15 per hour. However, each additional worker means that he will have to increase the wage by $1 for all the workers. His total wage cost is simply the total cost of hiring each quantity of workers. It is the last column that is significant. The **marginal wage cost** (MWC) shows how much extra it will cost Sonny to hire each additional worker. For instance, to hire a total of 5 workers will cost Sonny $95 at $19 per hour for each. However, if he wants to hire a sixth worker he is going to have to increase the wage to $20, not just for the sixth worker but for all of them, and his wage bill as a result will rise to $120 so that it costs him an extra $25 to hire the sixth worker.

The hourly wage and marginal wage cost, along with Sonny's demand for labour, are illustrated in Figure 12.6. If this were a competitive labour market, the equilibrium wage would be $22 and 8 workers would be hired. However, in order to maximize his profits, the monopsonist would hire workers up to the point at which the extra cost (MWC) is equal to the extra revenue (MRP). This occurs when 6 workers are hired, at which point the MWC and MRP are both $25. In order to hire this quantity of workers, the monopsonist would only have to pay an hourly wage of $20. Clearly monopsony

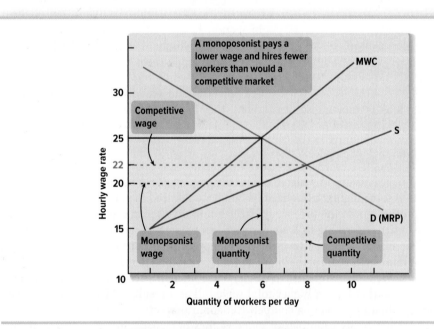

FIGURE 12.6   The Firm's Equilibrium in a Monopsony Market

The monopsonist would hire workers to the point where the MWC equals the MRP. This occurs at the employment of 6 workers where each worker would be paid $20. If this were a competitive labour market, the equilibrium wage would be $22, and 8 workers would be hired.

is looked upon unfavourably, because it leads not only to a drop in employment levels but also to lower wage rates than would be the case in a competitive labour market. The conclusion is:

> The monopsonist hires fewer workers and pays a lower wage than a competitive firm would.

 TEST YOUR UNDERSTANDING

3. Syn Inc. is a monopsonist and has the following demand and supply of labour:

(1) Number of Workers	(2) Hourly Wage	(3) Total Wage Cost	(4) Marginal Wage Cost	(5) Marginal Revenue Product (= Demand)
1	16	_____	_____	28
2	17	_____	_____	27
3	18	_____	_____	26
4	19	_____	_____	25
5	20	_____	_____	24
6	21	_____	_____	23
7	22	_____	_____	22
8	23	_____	_____	21

a) Complete columns 3 and 4.

b) How many workers will Syn Inc. employ, and what will be the wage rate?

We next take a look at another way labour markets are made less competitive, in this case to the benefit of sellers of labour rather than buyers as with the monopsonist.

The Effects of Trade Unions and Professional Associations

Many who earn a living by selling their labour belong, in association with their fellow workers, to a trade union, such as the Canadian Auto Workers' union (now part of Unifor), or to a professional association, such as the Nova Scotia Medical Association. From an economist's point of view, the broad objectives of such groups are to (a) increase the work available to their members, (b) increase the compensation received by their members, and (c) improve the working conditions of their members. If such unions and associations have any influence on how labour markets perform, their existence forces our analysis to go beyond the context of perfectly competitive markets.

As far as increased work and increased compensation are concerned, organizations use three basic approaches to achieve these objectives. **Figure 12.7** looks at the first approach—the attempt to increase the demand for the type of work their members perform.

Figure 12.7 could refer to any type of work, such as that of a medical practitioner, gas line plumber, or a bakery employee. Let us choose the latter for our illustration. D_1 and S are the demand for and supply of labour in a non-unionized environment. This yields a wage of $12 and an equilibrium quantity of 10 000 hours per week.

Now, suppose that bakery employees become unionized and that their union is able to increase the demand for this type of work. The result is that the demand curve shifts out to D_2. This results in the wage rate increasing to $14 and the equilibrium quantity increasing to 12 000 hours. This is obviously to the advantage of the organization and its members.

But how might the organization achieve this increase in demand for its members? One way is for the union to spend its own funds to advertise the employer's product. An ad campaign to encourage people to buy only clothes with a "Union-Made" label would increase the demand for

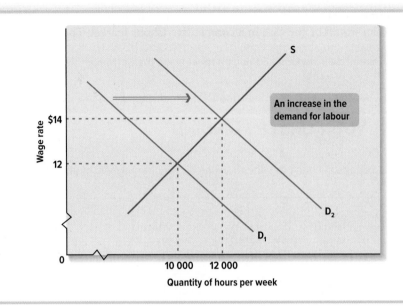

FIGURE 12.7   **The Effects on Wage Compensation of an Increase in Demand for Bakers**

The non-unionized demand and supply for bakers are D₁ and S. Equilibrium occurs at an equilibrium wage of $12 and quantity of 10 000. Effective unionization could result in the demand for labour shifting to the right, as illustrated by D₂. This would increase the wage rate to $14 and the quantity to 12 000.

union-made clothing and thus increase the demand for the union members who make it. Another example would be a "Hire a CPA" campaign paid for by the organization aiming to increase the demand for its members.

Some organizations may not be able to use the above method to increase the demand for their members. However, they may be able to improve pay or employment by restricting the supply of those who are qualified to do the work. **Figure 12.8** illustrates this situation.

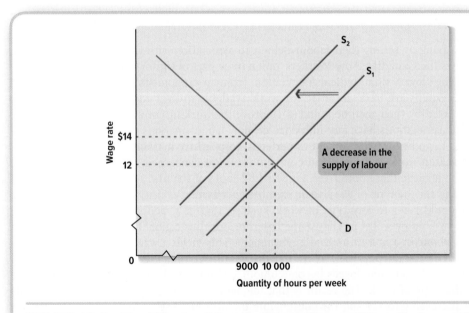

FIGURE 12.8   **The Effects of Supply Restriction on Wage Compensation**

Restricting the supply of labour shifts the supply curve from S₁ to S₂. As a result, the wage rate rises to $14, but equilibrium quantity declines to 9000.

The effect of restricting the supply of labour as shown by the shift from S_1 to S_2 is to cause the wage rate to rise from the non-unionized $12 per hour to $14 per hour. However, in this case the equilibrium quantity declines from the original 10 000 hours per week to only 9000. This approach is not as desirable to the organization and its members as increasing the demand, which raised both the equilibrium wage rate and quantity hired.

How might an organization restrict the supply of labour? One way is for the organization to successfully lobby for laws that restrict those who can perform a certain task; for example, only those certified as brokers can legally sell shares, or only licensed pipefitters can work on gas plumbing. The most effective way for an organization to restrict the supply of labour is to gain control of the certification (or licensing) process itself. Examples are medical associations, which control the licensing of new doctors, or bar associations, which do the same with new lawyers, or university professors, who influence the future supply of their own kind by having a say in how many students successfully complete graduate studies.

Members of the Professional Institute of the Public Service of Canada (PIPSC) union demonstrate against Canadian federal job cuts along Queen Street in Ottawa, November 12, 2012.
Hsandler/Dreamstime.com

We should also point out that any organization that can both increase the demand for its members *and* restrict the supply of them will succeed in raising the wage rate even higher than the $14 used in our example.

Many individuals who sell their labour to an employer do unskilled work that cannot be easily licensed or certified, so the methods discussed above are not open to the organizations that represent them. Is there any other way these organizations might increase the wage rate of those they represent? Yes, and this is the third way unions can improve things for their members. This is the situation that most students probably think of when the word "union" is used. Many (but not all) trade unions are well enough organized to have the bargaining power in negotiating contracts of employment to *simply impose* a wage rate above what would otherwise be market equilibrium. **Figure 12.9** illustrates this case.

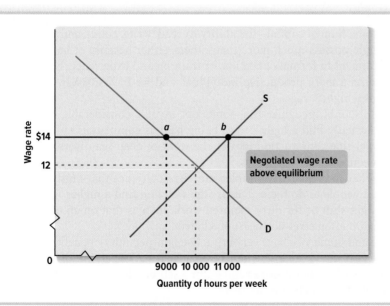

FIGURE 12.9   A Negotiated Wage Rate Above Equilibrium

A union may succeed in obtaining a $14 wage rate in contract negotiations, but the consequence of an imposed wage settlement above equilibrium is that the quantity of hours supplied exceeds the quantity demanded by the horizontal distance *ab*, which, in this case, is 2000 hours per week.

As in the previous figure, **Figure 12.9** illustrates a market equilibrium wage rate of $12 per hour and a quantity of 10 000. If, through bargaining power, the union negotiates a contractual wage rate for bakery employees of $14 per hour, we would have the situation as shown here. This is analogous in many ways to price control by a government, which we examined in Chapter 3. Here, the price floor is being imposed (with agreement from employers) by trade unions. Note that as the result of the higher negotiated wage of $14, the quantity of labour demanded has declined to 9000 hours per week at point *a*, while the quantity supplied has increased to 11 000 at point *b*. The result is that 2000 more hours per week are supplied than are demanded—the distance *ab* in **Figure 12.9**. This distance represents unemployed labour, much of it, unemployed union workers. It is essentially the same phenomenon that occurs when an outsider looks at a job someone else has and wishes he, too, had one like it.

How successful are such attempts to raise the wage rate above what would be market equilibrium? Studies that attempt to measure the effect of trade unions on wage rates seem to agree that union organizations do increase the wage rate. For example, recent studies in the United States indicate a union/non-union wage differential of up to 33 percent. Similar studies in Canada indicate an hourly union/non-union wage differential of about $3. This would result in a 30 percent differential for the hourly wage rate of $10 and 12 percent for the hourly wage rate of $25.

In summary, unions can attempt to raise the wages of their members by

- increasing the demand for their members by advertising the employer's product or their members' skills
- restricting the supply of labour for certain types of jobs by convincing government to establish legal qualifications for the work and then controlling the number of people who would obtain such qualifications
- negotiating a fixed wage rate above equilibrium

Explanations of Wage Differentials

Conceptually, if all people and all jobs were the same, and if we had a competitive labour market with no trade unions or professional associations, we would have only a single equilibrium wage rate. People are not the same, however, and this results in differences in the supply of different kinds of labour. Similarly, all jobs are not the same, and this results in differences in the demand for different types of labour. Further, as we just saw, trade unions and professional associations do alter wage compensation in different occupations. The result is that we have many different wage rates. Let us take a closer look at the wage differentials that exist in our economy.

The accumulation of skills and knowledge in each individual is known as **human capital**. All individuals have some human capital—the ability to read, write, count, and perceive—but it is obvious that some people possess much more than others, either because of natural gift, or because of much greater investment in formal education, or training and experience. Usually, a greater level of human capital means a more productive individual, and we have already established that higher productivity means a higher wage.

In addition, we should recognize that some jobs involve considerable risks that are absent in other jobs, and we usually find a higher wage being paid as compensation for such risks. Examples here would be power-line construction jobs or the work of deep-sea divers, which pay commensurately higher than equivalent low-risk jobs.

It is also true that some jobs have unpleasant characteristics that must be compensated for in order to get enough people to do them. This is why we often find a higher wage rate being paid, for example, for the night shift or for dirty, exposed work, such as that on an oil exploration rig, especially if that rig is 200 kilometres northeast of Aklavik.

On the other hand, some jobs have very attractive non-pecuniary benefits that result in the wage rate being lower than it would otherwise be. These range from lots of time off (for example, for school teachers), to flexible working hours (for example, for a self-employed writer), to the opportunity to be creative (for example, for a landscape architect).

We also need to mention that discrimination in the labour market results in some jobs being difficult to obtain by members of certain groups, such as women or visible minorities. This restricts the supply of labour into these kind of jobs, which raises the wage rate paid in them. In addition, the supply of labour into jobs traditionally held predominantly by women (day-care workers) or visible minorities (janitorial work) and requiring relatively low skills is greater than it might otherwise be, with the result that wage rates are lower.

ADDED DIMENSION

Education and Earning Power

It has long been established by economic research that individuals with more formal education enjoy, on average, higher earning capacity throughout their lives. The following data from the 2006 census illustrate this point. The dollar figures are average incomes for the population over fifteen years of age in Canada.

Level of Formal Education	Median Annual Income
Certificate or diploma below degree level	30 116
Bachelor's degree	52 907
Above bachelor's degree level	69 230

Source: Adapted from "Statistics Canada's Summary Tables, Average Earnings of the Population 15 Years and Over by Highest Level of Schooling, by Provinces and Territory (2006 Census)," www40.statcan.gc.ca/l01/cst01/labor50a-eng.htm, retrieved October 9, 2009.

This is not an exhaustive list of the reasons for wage differentials. There is, for example, an aspect of luck in all this. Some people seem to have just lucked into a job that they really love, and as a result they do the job very well and get better compensation for doing so than others who do the same work—imagine the really happy gardener or hairdresser. But the point is that people are different and jobs are different, so wage rates differ despite the impersonal forces of supply and demand that underlie every wage rate. In summary, wage differentials can exist because

- the level of human capital varies among individuals
- some jobs involve more risks than others
- some jobs have unpleasant characteristics
- some jobs have attractive non-pecuniary benefits
- there is discrimination in labour markets

Table 12.4 indicates the average wage in May 2010 in Canada as a whole for six broad categories of labour.

TABLE 12.4
Hourly Wages by Type of Work

Wage Category	Average Canadian Hourly Wage
Retail sales clerks	$14.48
Chefs and cooks	14.68
Labourers	17.16
Clerical occupations	20.86
Transport and equipment operators	22.97
Occupations in arts and culture	25.04
Construction trades	26.60
Social sciences and government services	31.54
Natural and applied sciences	34.84
Teachers and professors	35.30
Senior management	44.74

Source: Adapted from the Statistics Canada CANSIM database, http://cansim2.statcan.ca, Table 282-0069, retrieved April 6, 2017.

IT'S NEWS TO ME ...

The consulting group Real Research has just released 2018–2024 projections on a variety of broadly defined job categories for Canada as a whole. The five fastest growing and five slowest growing categories are:

Health Care and Social Assistance +22%
Construction +14%
Business Services +13.5%
Education Services +12%
Mining +10%
News Information –2%
Agriculture –6.5%
Manufacturing –7%
Utilities –8.5%
Forestry/Fishing –14%

The report also noted that the average labour payment for all wage and salaried employees will grow 6.5% for the projected period.

On a much more detailed level of 800 specific job occupations, the total employment of 592 of these occupations [is] expected to increase and 208 to decline.

On a final note, it is projected that of the 15 fastest growing occupations, 12 require some level of post-secondary education for entry of new employees.

Source: *Star Power Reporting*, April 2017.

I. Which of the following statements is valid with regard to the projected fastest-growing job categories?

a) They are more service-oriented than resource-oriented categories.
b) They all have double-digit growth rates.
c) They all have growth rates in excess of the projected growth in labour payments.
d) All of the above.

II. The projected patterns of Canada's employment growth indicate which of the following?

a) Canada's traditional reliance on natural resource extraction will continue.
b) Postsecondary education remains important.
c) Manufacturing will remain the key driving category.
d) Resource industries are becoming more important.

TEST YOUR UNDERSTANDING

4. a) Draw supply and demand for labour curves for an entire economy, and label them S_1 and D_1.

b) Indicate the equilibrium wage as W_1 and the equilibrium quantity as Q_1.

c) Increase the demand for labour by drawing in D_2, and restrict the supply of labour by drawing in S_2.

d) Will the new wage rate, W_2, be higher or lower than W_1?

e) Will the new quantity, Q_2, be higher or lower than Q_1?

f) Give two reasons for the increase in the demand for labour, and two for the decrease in the supply of labour referred to in (c).

SECTION SUMMARY

a) A firm operating in a monopsony labour market will find that if it wants to hire more labour, it will have to offer a higher wage rate to new employees, which increases the average wage rate that it must pay. Compared with competitive labour markets, monopsonies hire fewer workers and pay lower wages.

b) Trade unions and professional associations attempt to benefit their members by increasing the demand for their work, raising their nominal wage rates, and improving their working conditions. This is done

- by shifting the demand curve for the members' labour to the right
- by shifting the supply-of-labour curve to the left
- by imposing a negotiated wage rate above the market equilibrium rate

c) Wage rate differentials exist because

- there are variations in the level of human capital between individuals
- some jobs involve more risks than others
- some jobs have unpleasant characteristics
- some jobs have attractive non-pecuniary benefits
- there is discrimination in labour markets

12.3   The Concept of Economic Rent

> **LO3** Explain why factors that are highly inelastic in supply require special analysis.

The original concept of economic rent is rooted in the work of the nineteenth-century classical economist David Ricardo. Ricardo focused on land and assumed that this factor had a single use: agriculture. Since the quantity of land is fixed, he went on to argue that it was perfectly inelastic in supply. Therefore, Ricardo saw the price of land as being purely demand-driven. If land is in high demand, its price will be high, as was the case in Ricardo's England. However, if the demand for land is low, as it was in nineteenth-century North America, its price is very low (in many cases it was free). Whatever the price of land might be, this is the price that the owners of land earn. Ricardo called this **economic rent**.

If we do suppose that the supply of land is perfectly inelastic, as shown in **Figure 12.10**, and demand is relatively high, as with D_1, then the rent will be R_1. A decrease in demand, as illustrated by D_2, will result in the rent decreasing to R_2. Even if the price of land is zero, its supply is the same. Because land has this unique aspect, Ricardo considered the return to land, the economic rent, a surplus and not a cost. What this means is that the rent rate of, say, wheat land on the prairies will increase as a *result* of a higher price of wheat rather than being the *cause* of the higher wheat price. We could also note that, as many shoppers are aware, prices and rents in fashionable downtown areas are appreciably higher than they are out in the suburbs. The reason for the higher prices, the shop owners might claim, is that they have to pay such high rents. Economists, however, would argue the other way around: rents are high because the prices are high as a result of the high demand in these areas.

We know today, however, that land has other uses besides agriculture. The larger the number of alternative uses land might have, the less inelastic the supply of land for any one use. Because the supply curve of any factor is less than perfectly inelastic, we need to distinguish between rent and **transfer earnings** when discussing the return to the factor. Transfer earnings are defined as the payment a factor of production must earn in order to remain in its present use.

Let us now apply the concept of transfer earnings to another factor of production with a very inelastic supply.

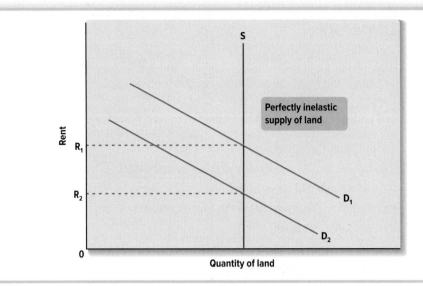

FIGURE 12.10   The Concept of Economic Rent as Applied to Land

If we assume that land has only one use, its supply is perfectly inelastic, as illustrated by S. Given this, the price of land, or the rent it receives, is purely demand-driven. If demand is high, as in D_1, rent is R_1. Low demand, as illustrated by D_2, results in the lower rent of R_2.

Economic Rent and Professional Athletes

We all know that some well-paid professional athletes love the game so much that they would continue to play even if they received less than they are currently earning. The wage rate that would be necessary to ensure they continued to play is their *transfer earnings*. The difference between the transfer-earnings wage and the actual wage received is the *economic rent*. Figure 12.11 will help us understand this concept better.

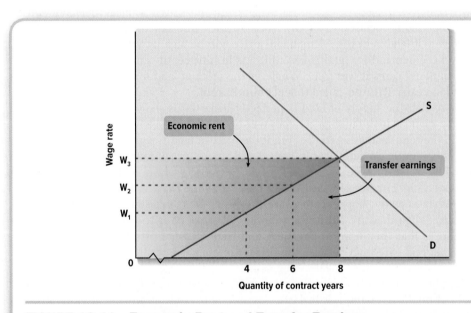

FIGURE 12.11   Economic Rent and Transfer Earnings

At wage rate W_1, our athlete will play for only 4 years. At wage rate W_2, he will play for 6 years. The red-shaded area is the pay necessary to induce him to commit to the full 8 years. Given the wage rate W_3, the entire rectangle is what he actually receives. Therefore, the blue-shaded area is his economic rent.

To fully understand the concept of economic rent, we need to view the supply curve, S, in **Figure 12.11** as showing the minimum price at which a given quantity is willingly supplied. Consider a young athlete struggling in the minor leagues in hopes of making the big time. If the wage rate is W_1, our young athlete will play for a total of four years simply because he loves to play. Yet he knows that most of his contemporaries will not make the big time and that the promise of riches will go unfulfilled. Therefore, he is not willing to play more than four years, because the current wage is not sufficient for him to postpone getting on with his life any longer.

To persuade him to agree to play for a fifth year and a sixth year, a higher wage rate, W_2 for example, would have to be offered. Similarly, he will willingly play for eight years only if the wage offered is again increased, this time to W_3. The red-shaded area under the supply curve therefore represents the transfer earnings necessary to induce our would-be pro to play for the full eight years. On the other hand, if our athlete is paid wage rate W_3 for each of the eight years, his total pay is the entire rectangle. Thus, the blue-shaded area represents his total pay less his transfer earnings, that is, his economic rent. This economic rent is a real bonus for him; it is the pay he receives over and above what he would have been willing to accept in order to continue doing what he is already doing.

To put it another way, transfer earnings (the same as opportunity cost) are what sportspeople (and those in the entertainment business) might earn if they were unable to make it in their chosen profession. For some, this might mean working as a commentator, coach, or agent; for others, it might mean working in a fast-food restaurant. For the big stars of sports and entertainment, their alternative occupation is likely to pay a lot less than they are currently earning. Economic rent, then, is the difference between what they earn and what that alternative job might bring in.

Next, look at **Figure 12.12**, in which the first supply curve, S_1, is elastic and S_2 is inelastic. It should be clear that the more inelastic the supply curve, the greater the economic rent that the particular wage rate, either W_1 or W_2, will generate. Now ask yourself: What is likely to be the elasticity of supply of an exceptionally good athlete who is a star in the major leagues of any professional sport? The answer is, of course, that it is *very* inelastic. This means that the majority of his earnings is an economic rent; the transfer earnings (what he could earn in the next-best alternative occupation) is small.

In addition, the demand for professional athletes, some of whom are very good and some not so good, has increased dramatically in the last several years due to the expansion of the number of teams in all four major sports in North America. Furthermore, these leagues have enjoyed rapidly escalating revenue from television contracts. If you combine this increase in demand with the

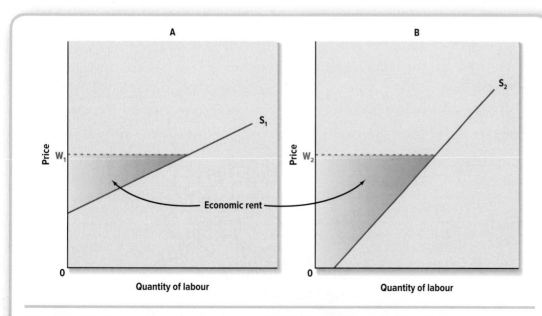

FIGURE 12.12   Economic Rents for Two Different Supply Elasticities

The economic rent that occurs at the same wage rate ($W_1 = W_2$) is greater in the case of the more inelastic supply curve S_2 than with the more elastic S_1.

inelastic supply of the top athletes we have just mentioned, you get a good explanation for the great increases in the wages paid to professional athletes.

What this means is that the high pay many athletes today enjoy is *demand-driven*. To clinch this, let us point out that the world's very best squash players are paid only about $150 000 per year. Although this is a high salary, it is far lower than the salaries received by even average players in the major North American professional sports. Is this because there are so many of the squash players, because they have fewer skills than a football linebacker, or because they do not work as hard as a baseball outfielder? The answer to all these questions is, of course, no.

So why does Clayton Kershaw, a baseball pitcher, get paid perhaps 200 times more than Nick Matthew, one of the world's best squash players? The answer is that the ticket sales and television contract revenue earned by a baseball team are so enormous that the demand for good baseball players is much greater than the demand for good squash players. This demand-side phenomenon explains why Tiger Woods earns tens of millions of dollars, and the concept of economic rent explains the sense, shared by many, that maybe he does not deserve all of it. In addition, Kershaw has a union representing his interests, whereas Matthew does not.

IN A NUTSHELL ...

Different occupations earn different levels of economic rent

As we all know, the very high salaries of athletes in major sports have led team owners to try to impose salary caps (maximums) in one form or another on individual players. The players' unions have, of course, resisted these attempts. What this dispute boils down to is a question of who (the team owner or the athlete) is entitled to what percentage of the economic rent that exists.

ADDED DIMENSION

David Ricardo and Hockey Ticket Prices

The price of a season ticket for any of Canada's NHL teams is out of reach for many Canadian fans, sometimes as high as $6800. Even single tickets are likely to cost over $200. The reason usually given is that, to attract the best players, clubs have no choice but to offer high salaries. Even a journeyman hockey player these days can earn well over $1 million per season, with the stars earning well over $5 million. This reasoning then concludes that the high ticket prices are the result of high wages paid to the players. But is that really the case?

History will help us answer this question. Two centuries ago, British economist David Ricardo pondered the cause of the high price of corn (wheat). France had imposed a blockade on his country in an attempt to starve it into submission and this had caused an escalation of corn prices. British farmers laid the blame at the door of the landowners since farm rents had been increasing every year. As a result, the farmers claimed, they had no choice but to increase prices. Workers complained about the high cost of food and demanded higher wages. Factory owners who were being forced to pay higher wages, in turn, blamed the farmers.

However, Ricardo argued that since the supply of land is fixed (perfectly inelastic), the price of corn is totally demand-determined. The (economic) rent earned by the landowners is a true surplus and in no way related to costs. Put simply, rents were high because farmers could afford to pay them. They could afford to pay because the demand for (domestically produced) corn was high.

Translating into a modern context, then, Ricardo (and most economists) would argue that NHL ticket prices are not high because the salaries of hockey players are high, but because ticket prices are high. And why are ticket prices so high? Because the (insatiable) demand from Canadians for hockey is so high!

TEST YOUR UNDERSTANDING

5. Draw a normal downward-sloping demand curve and a perfectly inelastic supply curve for labour. Label the axes *wages* and *quantity of labour*. Indicate the equilibrium wage as W_1 and quantity as Q_1. What portion of the pay that goes to this labour is economic rent?

SECTION SUMMARY

Economic rent was originally conceived of as the return to land (which, it was assumed, could only be used for agriculture and was perfectly inelastic in supply). The modern view is that it is the return to a factor that is over and above that factor's transfer earnings.

12.4 The Natural Resource Market

LO4 Recognize the relevance of the right rate of exploitation in the natural resource market.

Natural resources are both renewable (trees and wild fish) and non-renewable (minerals). The use of one more unit of a non-renewable resource reduces, forever, the supply with which nature has endowed this planet. For this reason, non-renewable resources are a topic of particular interest to both economists and the public in general. As an example, oil is non-renewable. Does this mean that the supply of the world's oil is perfectly inelastic? In some grand sense, in the very long run, yes. However, we are certain that not all the available oil in the world has been discovered, and so we really do not know the total quantity of that supply.

Furthermore, much of the oil that has been discovered is not for sale at current prices. Therefore, the present supply curve of oil is much more like S$_{\text{SHORT RUN}}$ in **Figure 12.13** and represents not so much the total quantity that exists but the amount currently available for sale.

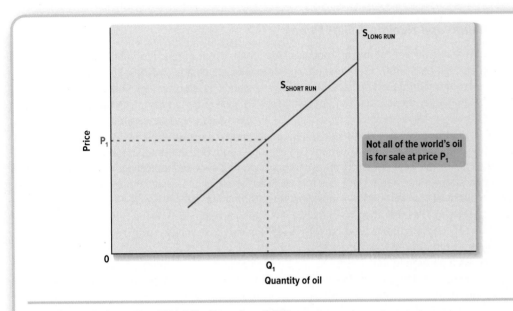

FIGURE 12.13   **The World's Supply of Oil**

Given the facts that not all of the oil in the world has been discovered and that not all the discovered oil is for sale at the present price, say P$_1$, the supply curve for oil is upward sloping, as illustrated by S$_{\text{SHORT RUN}}$. Only in the very long run can we think of the supply curve of oil as being perfectly inelastic, as Illusrtated by the S$_{\text{LONG RUN}}$ curve.

Given that in the very long run, there is only a finite amount of oil available, we need to ask if the price system leads to an overly rapid exploitation of oil. Or is it possible that the future will prove our current rate of use to be too conservative?

This is a highly politicized question, but economists do have something to say about it. Let us try to follow an argument that can get rather complex. The current value of oil to consumers is the amount they are willing to pay in order to obtain one more barrel. Let us assume this figure is $100. Further, let us assume this is also the current market price for oil. An additional barrel extracted and sold now will yield $100 in revenue to the oil producer, which can be held and earn interest that we will assume is 5 percent so that the producer would have a value of $105 per year from now. Alternatively, that producer could leave the barrel of oil in the ground in order to extract and sell it one year from now. Which is better, for the producer: to extract and sell it now and invest the proceeds or extract and sell it one year from now? The answer depends on what the price of the barrel of oil turns out to be in one year. If one year from now its price is $110, the producer should have left it in the ground. If, however, the price turns out to be $102, the producer will realize that it should have been extracted and sold a year ago. Understanding this little conundrum leads us to a very useful conclusion:

> From the producers' point of view, the optimal rate of extraction of oil depends on the rate at which the price of oil is changing and on the interest rate.

To nail this down, again assume that the present price of oil is $100, the rate of interest is 5 percent, and both remain unchanged, so that extracting a barrel of oil today and selling it for $100 would give us approximately (an invested sum of) $128 in five years. If, five years from now, the price of a barrel is also exactly \$128, our rate of extraction is exactly correct. On the other hand, if it turns out to be only \$120, the producers have been extracting oil far too fast. Similarly, if the price turns out to be \$140, the resource owners have been conserving oil too much. Interesting, isn't it?

Let us hasten to say that we are not proposing this idea as the complete solution to the complex question of how quickly we, as a society, should use up non-renewable resources. We do, however, wish to emphasize the point that economists do have some ideas in this area.

Common Property Resources

There is also an interesting question concerning (some) renewable resources that are called **common property resources**. This term means that no one individual or firm (or individual state, for that matter) owns the resource. Wild fish in the ocean are the classic example of a common property resource.

As we saw in the case of non-renewable resources, such as oil, the question here is: What is the correct rate of exploitation of a common property resource? If this question is not addressed and answered by some regulatory body, we can be certain that the resource will be over-extracted and possibly disappear. Consider cod stocks in the Grand Banks, off the coast of Newfoundland. From a social point of view, these stocks should be harvested at a rate that does not exceed their natural rate of reproduction. This will ensure that there are fish to harvest next year, ten years from now, and one hundred years from now.

However, from an individual fisher's point of view, the more fish harvested now, the greater the fisher's income. But isn't a sound conservation policy to that individual's long-term benefit? Yes, but only if all other fishers do not fish intensively until the stocks are all gone—something they are strongly tempted to do. You can see the need for the social regulation of a common property resource. Given the state of the East Coast cod fisheries today, one can conclude that such regulation was not done well in the past.

The idea of overexploiting common property resources was brought home to many in an article by the biologist Garrett Hardin called "The Tragedy of the Commons," which first appeared in the journal *Science* in 1968. Hardin looked at the common pasture land that existed in many European countries in the Middle Ages (and in the United States into the twentieth century). In medieval Europe, peasants were free to graze their animals, often sheep, on the common pasture without fee or payment. It was their traditional right. This was fine as long as such things as wars, poaching, and disease kept the numbers of both humans and sheep in check; but it became a problem when numbers started to rise. Now there was a real risk of too many sheep on not enough pasture. However, each peasant was rational enough to focus on the marginal cost and benefit of adding one more sheep to the common pasture.

The marginal benefit for any one individual was the revenue to be derived from selling one more sheep while the marginal cost came from having slightly thinner sheep, since each additional grazer would reduce the amount of feed for all. Clearly, the extra benefit of grazing one more sheep outweighed the additional cost of each sheep being a little thinner. For each peasant there would be a marginal surplus. However, for the group of peasants this is patently invalid. It is that old fallacy of composition again.

The overproduction of common property resources in general leads to a deadweight loss, as illustrated in **Figure 12.14**.

If there is no restriction and no charge for the use of the land, the marginal private cost is zero (the MPC curve in **Figure 12.14** lies on the horizontal axis) and the equilibrium would be where the marginal private benefit and cost are equal (a quantity of 10). However, there is definitely a social cost involved in the overuse of the land. If we include this external cost, the true cost to society would be reflected in the marginal social cost, and the optimum quantity would be 6. Without some type of restriction, the economy would suffer a deadweight loss—the triangle area in **Figure 12.14**.

The tragedy of the commons is caused by the fact that most people do not take into consideration the impact of their actions on others—they ignore external costs. The problem could, of course, be easily overcome if the government were to regulate the commons and limit the number of sheep, or put a tax or fee on each sheep grazed. Alternatively, they could privatize the grazing land and allow each family to enclose its own parcel of land. This is exactly what happened in Europe during the enclosure movement. But this is impossible in the case of the high seas or the atmosphere, which are quickly becoming depleted or polluted. The tragedy of the commons remains a serious challenge to society and policy makers.

Let us now leave the natural resource market and turn to the capital goods market.

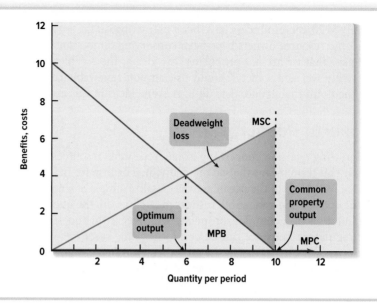

FIGURE 12.14   Common Property Resources and the Deadweight Loss

If external costs are ignored, then given the marginal private costs and demand, a quantity of 10 units of the resource would be used. If external costs are taken into consideration, then the true costs are reflected in the marginal social cost curve and the optimal quantity would be 6 units. Without regulation, there would be overproduction, and the economy would suffer a deadweight loss, as shown.

 TEST YOUR UNDERSTANDING

6. Assume that one year ago the rate of interest was 5 percent and we decided to extract a barrel of oil for $50 and sell it. If the present price of oil is $54, what can be said about last year's decision?

7. The following diagram shows the demand and marginal social costs for a common property resource. Assuming that there was no charge made for the use of this resource:

   a) What quantity would be used?

   b) Shade the area that represents the deadweight loss.

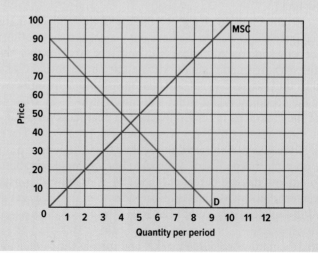

SECTION SUMMARY

a) Two of the interesting questions in the *natural-resource market* are:

- What is the best rate of exploitation of a non-renewable resource such as oil?
- How can we best regulate common property resources, such as wild fish?

b) The *tragedy of the commons* refers to the fact that common property resources tend to be overexploited, which results in a deadweight loss.

12.5 The Capital Goods Market

> **LO5** Explain why the demand for capital goods depends on the productivity of capital goods.

In a sense, the market for capital goods—be they machines used in a factory, a computer system for an office, or a simple carpenter's tool—is very similar to the market for any *product*, as discussed in Chapter 2. This quite conventional demand for and supply of capital goods is illustrated in **Figure 12.15**.

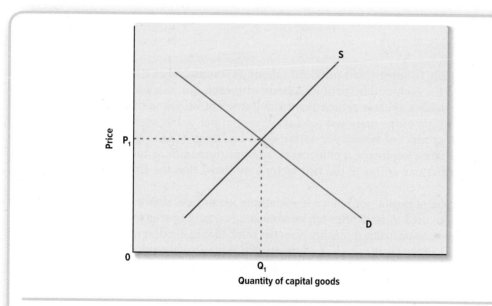

FIGURE 12.15 **The Market for Capital Goods**

The equilibrium price for capital goods occurs at the intersection of the supply and demand curves—that is, at a price of P_1 and a quantity of Q_1.

In the figure, the interaction of the demand for and the supply of capital goods yields an equilibrium price and quantity of P_1 and Q_1. We do not have anything to add about the supply of capital goods other than if the price of an particular good rises the quantity supplied increases.

The demand for capital goods is more interesting. First, we need to point out that the demand for capital goods is, in fact, derived from the marginal revenue product of capital, just as the demand for labour depended on its marginal revenue product. In this case, the MRP of capital is the additional benefit accruing to the firm from the employment of the next unit of capital and is equal to the marginal physical product it produces multiplied by the price of the product. Second, we need to recognize that the purchase of capital goods almost always needs to be financed with borrowed money. Even large firms are not able to lay out millions in cash for a new computer system. Instead, they arrange for a loan to finance the purchase, which is then paid back over time. They must, of course, pay interest on this loan, and it is because of this that the demand for capital goods is (inversely) related to the cost of financing capital purchases, which is the interest rate. In other words, the higher the interest rate, the lower the amount of borrowed funds, and therefore the amount of spending on capital goods. The factors that determine the rate of interest are a matter for discussion in a macroeconomics course.

The demand side of the capital goods market is interesting also because an improvement in technology can certainly affect the demand for such goods. Significant improvements in technology can render existing capital goods obsolete and require that they be replaced by newer versions. This increases the demand and is illustrated graphically by a rightward shift in the demand curve for the new capital goods.

Just as technological change increases the marginal revenue product of labour, it also increases the marginal revenue product of new capital goods that incorporate the new technology, and this can result in (the newer) capital goods being more productive *relative* to labour. Firms will be very tempted to substitute the now more productive capital for labour, which has become relatively less productive and therefore relatively more expensive. In other words, when deciding on amounts of substitutable factors, such as capital and labour, a firm would take into account both productivity and the price of the factors. Thus, if

$$\frac{MP_K}{P_K} > \frac{MP_L}{P_L}$$

it would be profitable to substitute capital for labour. In a sense, what the firm does is compare the value received for each dollar spent on labour with each dollar spent on capital. If a dollar spent on capital yields a greater return than a dollar spent on labour, the firm will invest in more capital. This ratio of the marginal product of capital per dollar spent on capital compared with the marginal product of labour per dollar spent on labour is analogous to the equation we saw in Chapter 5, when exploring a consumer's attempt to maximize total utility. By equating the marginal product per dollar of the two factors, we know that the firm is maximizing total profits.

Such substitution of capital for labour is something we witness almost every day. One of your authors, as a teenager, used to work after school unloading cases of beer from railway cars—one case at a time. Today, one person, using a forklift, does the work that half a dozen kids used to do. As another example, think of the labour saved at a supermarket because of the use of the conveyor belt and the bar-code reader. A third example is the use of computerized test banks in economics courses, which have replaced student graders.

When capital is substituted for labour, it raises questions about whether such automation destroys jobs and is therefore something society needs to be concerned about. Many misconceptions about this issue can be easily cleared up. There is no doubt that automation does indeed eliminate certain types of jobs—the days of young people unloading beer from railway cars are gone. Economists call this the **factor substitution effect** of technological change. But if technological change causing the substitution of capital for labour were the whole story, we would have to wonder how it is that anyone is still working, given the fact that our economy has experienced over 200 years of dramatic changes in technology.

In fact, the substitution effect is not the whole story. Capital substitution increases labour's productivity (the labour that was not replaced by capital) and thus lowers the cost of production. This in turn lowers the price of the final products, which increases both the quantity demanded for those products and thus total output. The increase in total output increases the demand for labour, so the **factor output effect** of technological change *creates* jobs. All of this leads us to the inescapable conclusion that, given that there are more people working in our society today than ever, the output effect of technological change must have been stronger than the substitution effect over the past two centuries or so.

ADDED DIMENSION

The Luddites and the Fear of Machines

Although the twentieth century saw a quantum leap in the number of machines used by society, it generally did not result in mass unemployment. In the short run, however, the replacement of labour by machines can certainly result in loss of specific jobs. In the early days of the Industrial Revolution, these short-term effects devastated the lives of many workers.

Small wonder, then, that working people at the time feared and hated the introduction of machines. A group of them, inspired by a mythical figure called Ned Ludd, swore to fight the invasion of the machines. In the textile manufacturing areas in the north of England, "Luddites" went on a rampage, burning and wrecking factories. These riots, which peaked in 1811 and 1812, were eventually brought to an end by the authorities; a number of Luddites were hanged or deported.

Some argue that we are on the cusp of another phase in the cycle of machines replacing humans in the workplace given the rise of *artificial intelligence* (AI)—a term used in any context wherein a machine mimics cognitive functions such as learning or problem solving. Current applications of AI are understanding human speech, self-driving cars, and intelligent routing in content-delivery networks, and robots with human-like appearance and characteristics are on the horizon.

TEST YOUR UNDERSTANDING

8. Given its current output, Rally Rackets Ltd. is experiencing a marginal product of capital of 60 and a marginal product of labour of 10. If the price of capital is $100 per unit and the price of labour is $25 per unit, how should this firm substitute factors?

SECTION SUMMARY

The demand for *capital goods*, like the demand for all factors, depends on the productivity of capital that is determined by technological change and that lowers the price of capital goods and leads to the substitution of capital for labour so as to maintain the equality

$$\frac{MP_K}{P_K} = \frac{MP_L}{P_L}$$

12.6   The Entrepreneurial Market

LO6   Explain the two views on the ultimate source of profits.

The fourth of our four factors of production is enterprise, or entrepreneurial talent. Few economists have explored the role of entrepreneurial talent in the market economy more than Joseph Schumpeter, who taught at Harvard University in the first half of the twentieth century. Schumpeter saw the entrepreneur as an innovating doer who bridged the gap between a mere idea and a productive application. Eccentric minds invented, and common businesspeople managed, but it was the risk-taking entrepreneur who had the vision and the boldness to take truly new and revolutionary *action* that bridges the gap between invention and routine management. The entrepreneur, in Schumpeter's eyes, is the engine of economic growth and development in a capitalist economy.

GREAT ECONOMISTS: JOSEPH SCHUMPETER

Joseph Schumpeter (1883–1950) was born in Austria-Hungary (the present-day Czech Republic), and for a short time was its Minister of Finance. In 1932 he emigrated to the United States, where he spent most of his academic life teaching at Harvard University. *Capitalism, Socialism and Democracy* (1942) is his best-known work, and is the source of his dynamic, change-oriented, and innovation-based economic analysis.

In that book his roots to the Vienna-based Historical School of economics are clear. Schumpeter argues that capitalism can only be understood as an evolutionary process of dynamic entrepreneurial innovation and not as the static equilibrium-centred system of neoclassical economics. Furthermore, using his concept of "creative destruction," he argues that the revolution of the economic structure from within inevitably and continuously destroys the old and replaces it with the new. Schumpeter recognizes Marx as the source of this concept, despite the fact that, overall, his own work has a distinct anti-Marxian flavour.

Granger Historical Picture Archive/Alamy Stock Photo

From the time of Adam Smith, economists have argued that competition within a capitalist economy would tend to result in (economic) profits being competed down to zero—a process we explored in the context of both the perfectly competitive and the monopolistically competitive market models. What then explained the continued existence of economic profits nearly two centuries after capitalism took root in the Western European and North American economies?

Surely, Schumpeter argued, the source of economic profits was the innovation of the entrepreneur, which was creating unique situations in which profits could be made. In time, a swarm of imitators would enter the field, and such profits would be driven to zero; but in a dynamic and growing economy, another wave of innovation will have already occurred. New profit opportunities would be continuously created.

While entrepreneurs create profits, they are often not the long-term beneficiaries of them. As John Kenneth Galbraith pointed out in *The New Industrial State*, the risk-taking entrepreneur sometimes loses control of his or her growing business to the impersonal forces of what Galbraith calls the technostructure, which is at the heart of the modern transnational corporation. When this happens, more conservative and more bureaucratic managers take over from the risk-taking entrepreneur.

Before we leave this topic, we should point out that there is an alternative explanation for profits: the existence of oligopoly and monopoly influences that inhibit the natural tendency for profits to be competed away. However, this explanation, while valid in many circumstances, just does not have the same ring of truth as Schumpeter's innovative entrepreneur.

SECTION SUMMARY

The two views of *economic profits* are that they are the result of

- entrepreneurial activities, according to Schumpeter
- imperfect competition in the product market

Study Guide

Review

WHAT'S THE BIG IDEA?

The demand for factors of production is a derived demand—derived from the demand for the products these factors produce. If there were no demand for certain products, there would be no demand for the factors. A firm's demand for labour, for instance, is dependent on what that labour is able to produce. And what it can produce is determined by two things: its productivity and the value of the products it can produce. That being the case, the demand for a certain type of labour will increase if there is an increase either in its productivity or in the demand for (and therefore price of) the products.

Now, the productivity of labour is not a constant; it varies with the amount of labour employed. The value of each hour (or day or week) of labour is measured by its productivity (MP) times the price of the product. This is what is meant by marginal revenue product (MRP). As long as the MRP is greater than the wage rate, a firm will continue to employ more labour.

Finally, let us review a few terms. We tend to think of a monopolist as the *sole seller of a product* and a monopsonist as the *sole buyer of labour*. But strictly speaking, a monopolist is the *sole seller of either a product or factor of production* and a monopsonist the *sole buyer of a product or factor of production*. When looking at the labour market, it doesn't matter whether we are looking at a monopolist seller of a product or a monopsonist buyer of labour; the demand for labour is always determined by the marginal revenue product.

NEW GLOSSARY TERMS AND KEY EQUATIONS

common property resources	human capital	monopsony
economic rent	labour force	nominal wage
factor market	labour force supply	product market
factor output effect	marginal revenue product	real wage
factor substitution effect	marginal wage cost	transfer earnings

Equations:

[12.1]   Marginal revenue product (MRP) = marginal product (MP) × price (P)

[12.2]   Marginal revenue product (MRP) = $\dfrac{\Delta \text{ total revenue } (\Delta TR)}{\Delta \text{ labour}}$

[12.3] $MRP_L = W$

[12.4]   Real wage = $\dfrac{\text{nominal wage}}{\text{price level}}$

Comprehensive Problem

(LO 1) Heavenly Bubbles is a small soap company whose main product is hand soap, which sells in a competitive market for $5 per bar. The daily output per worker is shown in Table 12.5. Labour costs $120 per day.

TABLE 12.5

Quantity of Labour	Daily Output	Marginal Product	Total Revenue 1	Marginal Revenue Product 1	Total Revenue 2	Marginal Revenue Product 2
0	0	/	/	/	/	/
1	40	___	___	___	___	___
2	76	___	___	___	___	___
3	108	___	___	___	___	___
4	136	___	___	___	___	___
5	160	___	___	___	___	___
6	180	___	___	___	___	___

Questions

a) Fill in the Marginal Product, Total Revenue 1, and Marginal Revenue Product 1 columns in Table 12.5.
b) How many workers should the firm hire?
c) In Figure 12.16 plot the firm's demand for labour curve (and label it D_1). On the graph indicate the total amount of labour that the firm will hire at a daily wage rate of $120.

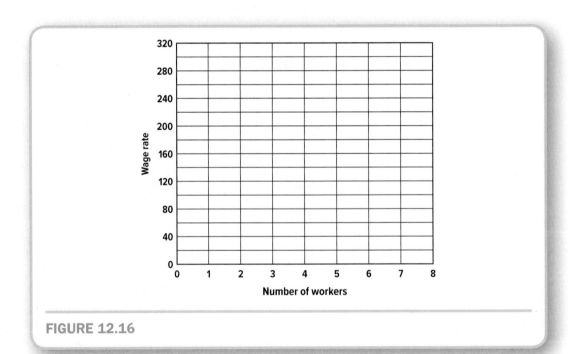

FIGURE 12.16

d) Now assume that the cost of labour increases to $140 per day. How many workers should the firm hire?
e) On the graph in Figure 12.16 indicate the effect of this increase in the cost of labour.

Answers

a) See Table 12.5 (Completed).

TABLE 12.5 (COMPLETED)

Quantity of Labour	Daily Output	Marginal Product	Total Revenue 1	Marginal Revenue Product 1	Total Revenue 2	Marginal Revenue Product 2
0	0	/	/	/	/	/
1	40	40	$200	$200	$ 280	$280
2	76	36	380	180	532	252
3	108	32	540	160	756	224
4	136	28	680	140	952	196
5	160	24	800	120	1120	168
6	180	20	900	100	1260	140

b) 5 workers. (With the cost of labour at $120 per day the firm should employ this number because the marginal revenue product of the fifth worker is also $120.)

c) See **Figure 12.16 (Completed)**.

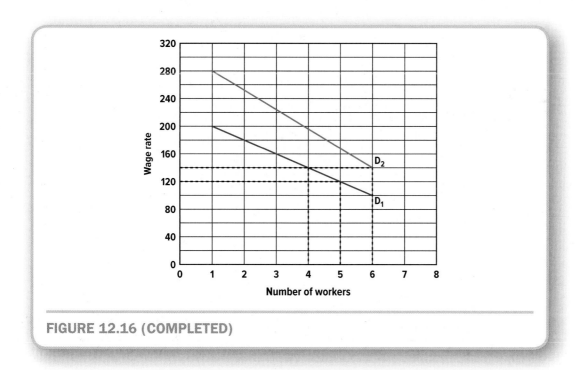

FIGURE 12.16 (COMPLETED)

d) Four workers should be hired. (With the increase in the cost of labour to $140, the firm should reduce the number of to 4 since the marginal revenue product of the fourth worker is also $140.)

e) See **Figure 12.16 (Completed)**.

Questions

f) Suppose the price of each bar of soap rises to $7. Fill in the Total Revenue 2 and Marginal Revenue Product 2 columns in **Table 12.5**.

g) Assuming that the cost of labour remains at the $140 per day, how much labour will the firm now hire?

h) Now draw in the new demand curve for labour, labelled D_2, in **Figure 12.16** and indicate on the graph the number of workers the firm will now hire.

Answers

f) See Table 12.5 (Completed).

g) Six workers should be hired. (With the increase in the price of soap, the firm will hire workers to the point where the wage per worker of $140 is equal to the new marginal revenue product.)

h) See Figure 12.16 (Completed). The increase in the price of soap shifts the demand curve for labour to the right from D_1 to D_2.

Study Problems

Find answers on the McGraw-Hill online resource.

Basic (Problems 1–6)

1. **(LO 1)** Complete Table 12.6, which gives the data for Gimlets Inc.

TABLE 12.6

Quantity of Labour	Total Product	Marginal Product	Price	Total Revenue	Marginal Revenue Product
1	10	_____	$6	_____	_____
2	28	_____	6	_____	_____
3	45	_____	6	_____	_____
4	60	_____	6	_____	_____
5	70	_____	6	_____	_____
6	78	_____	6	_____	_____

2. **(LO 1)** Table 12.7 gives the data for Gumbles Ltd.

TABLE 12.7

Quantity of Labour	1	2	3	4	5	6	7
Marginal Revenue Product (hourly)	$10	$15	$14	$12	$10	$8	$5

How many workers should Gumbles hire at each of the following wage rates?
a) $15 per hour _____
b) $12 per hour _____
c) $9 per hour _____
d) $6 per hour _____

3. **(LO 1)** Suppose that in the country of Gardenia the nominal wage rate is $18 per hour and the price level is 1.2.
a) What is the value of the real wage rate? _____
b) If the nominal wage rate increases by 10 percent, what will be the new value of the real wage rate? _____
c) If instead the price level were to increase by 10 percent, what will be the new value of real wages? _____

4. **(LO 1)** Table 12.8 shows the data for a small company, Willie the Pickle Maker. The marginal product figures are for cases of pickles per day.

TABLE 12.8

(1) Units of Labour	(2) MP_L	(3) MRP_1	(4) MRP_2
1	10	_____	_____
2	9	_____	_____
3	8	_____	_____
4	7	_____	_____
5	5	_____	_____
6	3	_____	_____

a) Fill in column 3 in the table, assuming that the firm sells its products in a competitive market for $24 a case (situation A).
b) Then fill in column 4, assuming that the price of a case of pickles increases to $27 (situation B).
c) If labour costs $216 per day, how many workers will Willie the Pickle Maker hire in each of the two situations? Situation A: _____ Situation B: _____
d) What has happened to the demand curve for labour when comparing these two situations? _____

5. **(LO 1, 2)** The graph in **Figure 12.17A** shows the market demand and supply of security personnel. The graph in **Figure 12.17B** is the MRP of labour (demand for labour) by a single firm that employs security personnel.

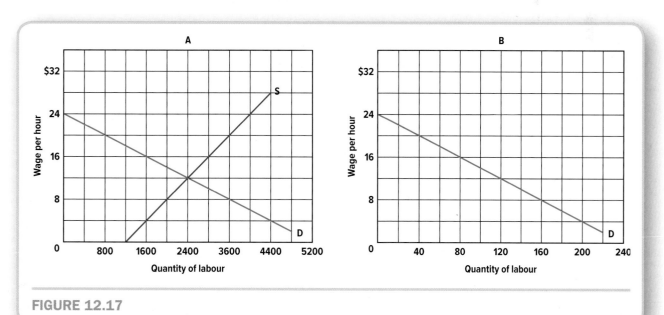

FIGURE 12.17

a) In a perfectly competitive labour market, what will the market wage rate be? How many workers will the single employer hire?
Wage rate: $_____ Quantity of workers hired: _____
b) Suppose that a trade union of security workers is formed and is able to negotiate a wage rate of $16 per hour for its members. What will be the resulting surplus of workers? How many employees will the firm now hire?
Surplus of workers: _____ Quantity of workers hired: _____

6. **(LO 1)** Table 12.9 shows the daily production of simple lawn chairs by Sit Right Inc. The firm is able to hire as many workers as it wishes for $12 per hour and sells the chairs to department stores for $4 each.

TABLE 12.9

Number of Hours Worked	Total Product	Marginal Product	Marginal Revenue Product
1	5	_____	_____
2	12	_____	_____
3	18	_____	_____
4	23	_____	_____
5	26	_____	_____
6	28	_____	_____
7	29	_____	_____
8	29	_____	_____

a) Complete the table.
b) How many workers and hours will the firm employ?
Workers: _____ Hours: _____

Intermediate (Problems 7–9)

7. **(LO 1)** The demand for film animators is illustrated in **Figure 12.18**.

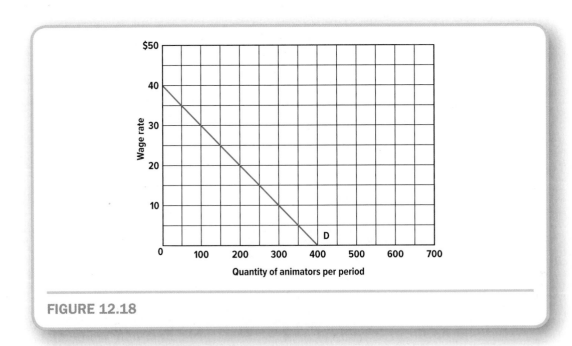

FIGURE 12.18

a) Draw in a supply curve, which is a 45° line from the origin.
b) What are the total earnings per period of the animators as a group? _____
c) How much of the earnings in (b) are transfer earnings, and how much is economic rent?
Transfer earnings: _____ Economic rent: _____
d) If the supply of animators increased, would the total earnings for the group increase or decrease?

8. **(LO 5)** Table 12.10 lists the daily productivity data of capital and labour for the firm Omir in the country of Hanu.

TABLE 12.10

Units	MP_K1	MP_L	MP_L2
1	20	14	_____
2	18	12	_____
3	16	10	_____
4	12	8	_____
5	8	6	_____
6	6	4	_____

a) Assume that both the price of capital and of labour are $1 per unit and the firm can afford to employ only 6 units in total. If the present MP of capital is the column MP_K1, what is the right capital–labour ratio for Omir to use? _____
b) Assume that the price of capital remains at $1 but the price of labour increases to $2. Complete Table 12.10.
c) Assuming that the firm can still afford to employ only 6 units in total, what is now the right capital–labour ratio for Omir to use? _____

9. **(LO 4)** Assume that the current equilibrium price for a barrel of oil is $24, and the interest rate is 5 percent.
a) What does the price of oil need to be in two years to justify extracting it now? _____
b) If oil producers think that the price of a barrel of oil in two years will be more than this figure, should they extract oil this year or not? _____

Advanced (Problems 10–12)

10. **(LO 1)** Table 12.11 shows the supply of labour for Large Ltd., a monopsonist.

TABLE 12.11

Quantity of Daily Labour	Wages Rate	MRP	Total Wage Cost	Marginal Wage Cost
1	$ 60	$160	_____	_____
2	70	170	_____	_____
3	80	160	_____	_____
4	90	150	_____	_____
5	100	140	_____	_____
6	110	120	_____	_____
7	120	90	_____	_____
8	130	50	_____	_____

a) Fill in the blanks in Table 12.11.
b) How many units of labour will be employed, and what will be the daily wage rate?
   Quantity employed: _____ Wage rate: $_____

11. **(LO 3)** The two supply curves in **Figure 12.19** represent the supply of workers in two different occupations.

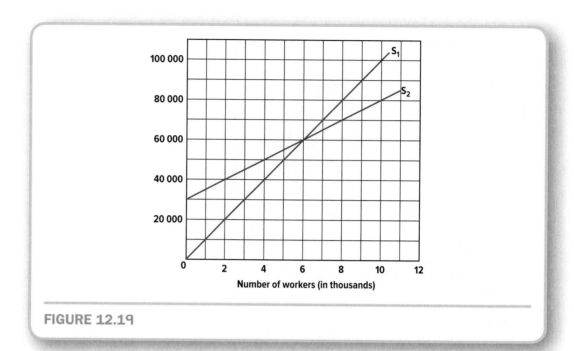

FIGURE 12.19

a) At an annual wage of $60 000 per year, what are the amounts of economic rent and transfer earnings for S_1?
Economic rent: $_____ Transfer earnings: $_____

b) At an annual wage of $60 000 per year, what are the amounts of economic rent and transfer earnings for S_2?
Economic rent: $_____ Transfer earnings: $_____

c) Which of the two curves is more inelastic? _____

12. **(LO 1)** **Figure 12.20** shows the demand for pulp workers in a small town in northern Ontario. Columns 1 and 2 in **Table 12.12** show the supply of labour.

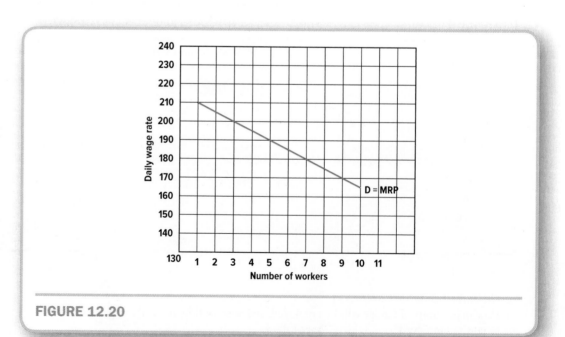

FIGURE 12.20

TABLE 12.12

(1) Number of Workers	(2) Daily Wage	(3) Total Wage Cost	(4) Marginal Wage Cost
1	$150	_____	_____
2	155	_____	_____
3	160	_____	_____
4	165	_____	_____
5	170	_____	_____
6	175	_____	_____
7	180	_____	_____
8	185	_____	_____

a) Draw in the supply curve in **Figure 12.20**.

b) If the labour market were perfectly competitive, what are the equilibrium values of daily wage and number of workers?

Daily wage: $_____ Number of workers: _____

c) Suppose that there was a single monopsonist pulp mill in the town. Fill in columns 3 and 4 in **Table 12.12**.

d) Draw in the marginal wage cost in **Figure 12.20**.

e) What are the equilibrium values of daily wage and number of workers?

Daily wage: $_____ Number of workers: _____

Problems for Further Study

Basic (Problems 1–4)

1. **(LO 1)** What is MRP? How can it be calculated?

2. **(LO 1)** Distinguish between the *real wage* and the *nominal wage*.

3. **(LO 2)** Explain five reasons for wage rate differentials.

4. **(LO 3)** Explain why property rents in downtown areas are higher than in the suburbs.

Intermediate (Problems 5–7)

5. **(LO 2)** Describe three ways in which a union might be able to increase the wage rate received by its members. Make reference to the quantity of members that would be hired in each of the three instances.

6. **(LO 6)** What does Schumpeter see as the key to economic growth? Do you think Schumpeter's idea is likely to become more important in the next twenty years?

7. **(LO 1)** Explain why the wage offered by the monopsonist is lower, and the number of workers employed is less, than in a perfectly competitive labour market.

Advanced (Problems 8–10)

8. **(LO 1)** Use the theory of marginal productivity and the concept of real wage to discuss whether you think Robinson Crusoe's standard of living increased or decreased when Friday came on the scene.

9. **(LO 2)** Discuss the following statement: "The Canadian Medical Association is perhaps the most powerful union in the country."

10. **(LO 4)** Explain the tragedy of the commons and why it leads to a deadweight loss.

CHAPTER 13
International Trade

LEARNING OBJECTIVES

At the end of this chapter, you should be able to:

LO1 Explain the importance of international trade and why nations trade with each other.

LO2 Explain why nations import certain goods, even though they can be made more cheaply at home.

LO3 Explain how the gains from trade are divided between trading partners.

LO4 Describe why some groups win and others lose as a result of freer trade.

LO5 Identify various restrictions to, and some arguments against, free trade.

WHAT'S AHEAD ...

We start this look at international trade by asking why people trade with each other, and in answering that question we discover that all nations trade for exactly the same reason. We explain Ricardo's theory of comparative advantage, which (approximately 200 years ago) helped to sort all this out. We then look at the terms of trade and show how this determines who gets what share of the increased production that results from trade. Finally, we examine some of the reasons nations have restricted trade in the past and what methods they use to do this.

A QUESTION OF RELEVANCE ...

Have you looked at the little tag on your jeans lately? Were they made in Canada? What about your camera? Your fishing rod? Your tennis racket? Your smart phone? Does it concern you that they all might well have been made abroad? It will probably not come as a surprise to you that Canada imports over a third of all its products. Is this good for the country? Surely it would be in Canada's interests to produce its own goods. Or would it? This chapter looks at the question of whether Canada is better or worse off as a result of international trade.

P eople have traded in one form or another since the dawn of time, and most of the great powers in history have also been famous traders: the Phoenicians and the Greeks, medieval Venice and Elizabethan England, and the early American colonies and modern Japan. It seems obvious that great benefits are obtained from trading, but there has always been the underlying suspicion that someone also loses as a result. For many, a great trading nation is one that consistently, and through shrewd practice, always manages to come out on top during trade negotiations. This "beggar thy neighbour" attitude was no great concern for writers immediately preceding Adam Smith, who thought it was part of the natural state of affairs that there are always winners and losers in trade. It was the job of policy makers, they felt, to ensure that their own country was always on the winning side.

It took the mind of Adam Smith to see that whenever two people enter into a voluntary agreement to trade, both parties must gain as a result. If you trade a textbook with a friend in exchange for a ticket to a Maple Leafs hockey game, you obviously want that ticket more than the textbook, and your friend must want the textbook more than the ticket. Trade is to the advantage of both of you, or it would not take place. When we look at international trade, we are simply looking at this single transaction multiplied a billionfold. It is not really nations that trade, but individuals and firms buying from foreign individuals and firms. In many ways, you trade with a friend for the same reason for which you buy products from a Toronto brewery, a Winnipeg car dealer, or a Tokyo fishing rod manufacturer: you hope to gain something as a result, and what you give up in return (usually money) is of less value to you than what you obtain in return.

All of which raises the question of why you personally (or a whole nation, for that matter) would want to buy something rather than make it at home. In other words, why are people not self-sufficient? Why do they not produce everything they personally consume? Well, Adam Smith had an answer for this (as for many things):

> It is the maxim of every prudent master of a family, never to make at home what will cost him more to make than to buy.[1]

There, in essence, is the main argument for trade: Why make something yourself if you can buy it cheaper elsewhere? If it takes Akio three hours to make a certain product, but he can buy it elsewhere from the income he gets from one hour's work in his regular job, why would he bother to make it? In fact, it would pay him to do his own job for three hours; he could afford to buy three units of the product. An additional consideration is the fact that Akio cannot make most of the things he wants— or could make them only after extensive training and with the help of very expensive equipment.

13.1   Specialization and Trade

LO1 Explain the importance of international trade and why nations trade with each other.

Before we start looking at the theory behind international trade, let's look at some data that highlight what can only be called an explosion in international trade over the last thirty years or so.

---

[1]Adam Smith, *The Wealth of Nations* (Edwin Cannan edition, 1877), p. 354.

Current Trends in World Trade

In 1983, the total value of world trade was just over $1800 billion. By 2015, that figure had increased to just under $16 000 billion. Furthermore, for most countries, trade as a percentage of GDP has also risen appreciably. There are a number of reasons behind this. First, there have been significant improvements in transport (think of container ships and ports) and communications technology (think of the Internet) that have both opened up world markets and reduced the cost of moving goods internationally. Second, there has been a movement internationally to reduce, and in some cases remove, trade barriers such as tariffs and quotas between nations. Allied to this, the last thirty years or so have seen the formation or expansion of common trade associations such as the European Union (EU) and the North American Free Trade Agreement (NAFTA). Finally, we should mention the fall of the Soviet Union and the trade-liberalizing policies that followed in China, as well as the fifteen newly independent nations that were previously part of the closed Soviet system.

Figure 13.1 shows just how much international trade has increased since 1970. While world GDP has risen 290 percent over this period, world trade (despite an appreciable downturn due to the 2008–10 recession) has increased a whopping 52 times.

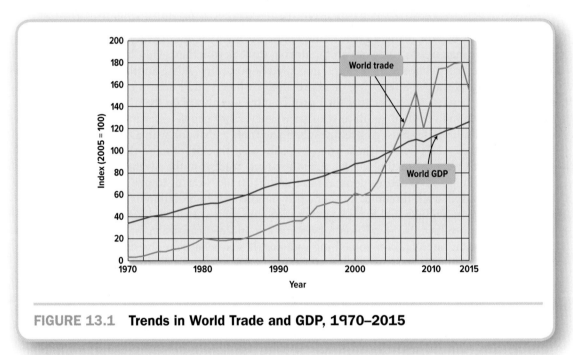

FIGURE 13.1 **Trends in World Trade and GDP, 1970–2015**

Source: World Trade Organization, *Statistical Review 2016*.

While all regions on the planet have experienced big growth in international trade, the leading areas have been Europe and Asia as **Figure 13.2** shows. Note that although the world experienced a big decline due to the 2008–2010 recession, by 2011 international trade had bounced back to continue its upward trend.

It should be noted that a good part of this massive increase in international trade in these three geographical areas has been the result of trade *within* the areas following the introduction of free trade agreements. However, trade *between* these regions is also significant, as **Figure 13.3** shows. (The percentages show the portion of total trade.)

And just who are the leading trading nations these days? Well, perhaps it comes as no great surprise to learn that in the past few years, China has overtaken the United States in the world league, as we can see in **Figure 13.4**. Although down in eleventh place, Canada is still one of the world's great trading nations in terms of the percentage of its GDP traded internationally.

Specialization

Specialization is the cornerstone of trade. We pointed out in Chapter 1 that there are big advantages to be gained from specialization. From an individual point of view, each of us is better suited to doing certain things than doing others. Rather than trying to grow all our own food, make our own clothes,

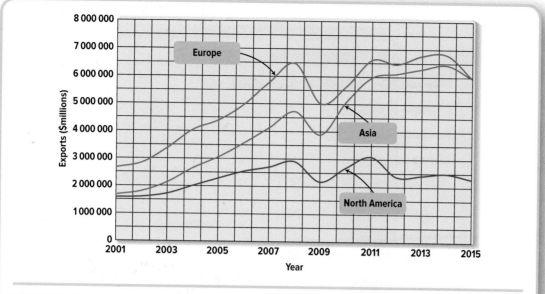

FIGURE 13.2   Trends in International Trade by Major Areas, 2001–2015

Source: World Trade Organization, *Statistical Review 2016*.

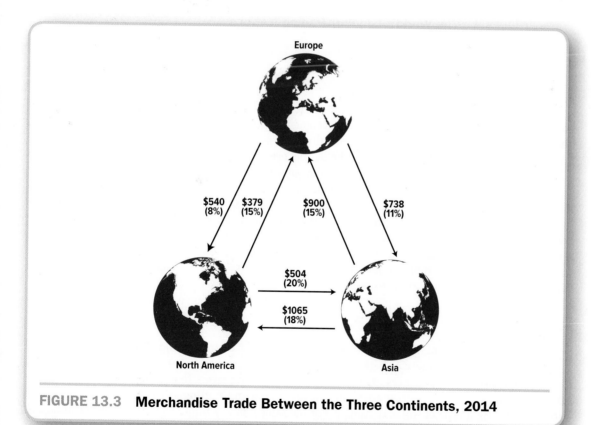

FIGURE 13.3   Merchandise Trade Between the Three Continents, 2014

Source: World Trade Organization, *International Trade Statistics 2015*.

brew our own beer, and so on, it makes more sense to specialize in our chosen occupation and, with the proceeds, obtain things other people can make better and more cheaply. Similarly, firms will be far more productive if they specialize in the production process, that is, make use of the division of labour. As we shall see in this chapter, there are also great benefits to be enjoyed by countries by specializing.

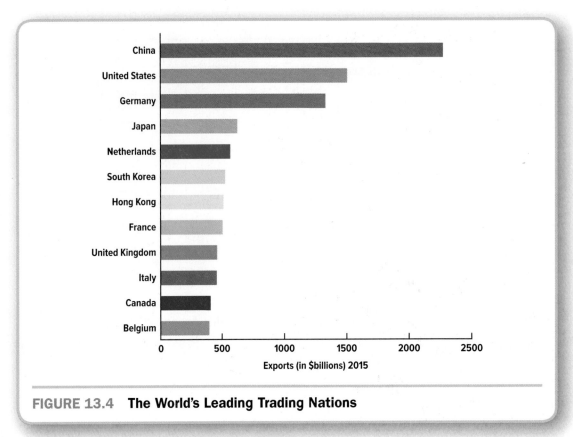

FIGURE 13.4   **The World's Leading Trading Nations**

Source: World Trade Organization, *Statistical Review 2016*.

Specialization and trade go hand in hand, so it follows that more specialization means more trading. Modern nations, firms, and individuals have become increasingly specialized, and with this has come a huge increase in the volume of trade, domestically and internationally. But is there a limit? From a technical point of view, Smith thought not. But he did believe specialization would be limited by the size of the market: the smaller the market, the smaller the output, and therefore the less opportunity or need for extensive specialization. The larger the market, the greater the opportunity for specialization, which would then lower the cost of producing goods. The prime driving force behind the expansion of markets is that it enables firms to produce in higher volumes at a lower cost. All things being equal (including demand), it is the cost of production, and therefore the price of the product, that induces trade. If you can produce a product more cheaply than I, it makes no sense for me to try to produce it myself. And why are you able to produce certain products more cheaply? The answer, presumably, is that you have certain advantages over me. Let us look at some pf these possible advantages.

Factor Endowment

One person has an advantage in production over others if he or she is endowed with certain natural or acquired skills, or has more or better equipment or other resources. Just as there are many reasons some people are better gardeners or truck drivers or hockey players than others, so it is with countries. A country will have a great advantage in producing and trading pineapples, for instance, if it possesses the right type of soil and climate. But the same country might well be at a disadvantage in growing coniferous trees. Another country has an advantage in producing electronic equipment if it has the right capital, the technical expertise, and a well-educated labour force. It might not, however, be able to compete with other countries in raising sheep. Just as with people, countries are well endowed in certain areas and impoverished in others. Japan has a well-educated and motivated work force, possesses great technical expertise, and is highly capitalized, yet it is very poorly provided with arable land and mineral resources.

It is often suggested that countries trade primarily to buy resources they do not naturally possess. Although there is some truth in this, it often obscures the main motivation. Canada, for instance, though not naturally endowed with a warm and sunny climate throughout the year, *could* produce bananas commercially using geodesic domes with artificial light and heating. But the cost would be enormous. It is far cheaper to buy bananas from countries that grow them more easily. Most countries can overcome a resource deficiency by using different methods or other resources, but it does not make sense if this production method results in products more expensive than those obtainable abroad.

In summary, there are four areas of difference between countries that lead to their specialization in certain products. First are the obvious differences in *climate.* Second are major differences in the quantity and quality of *natural resources* a country possesses. Third are the appreciable differences in *human capital* whereby a country might well have a big advantage in traditional skills, n educational attainment, or the motivation or entrepreneurial spirit of its people. Finally, the *role of government* is vital and can have enormous impact in overcoming whatever inherent disadvantages a country might have. It can do this by, for example, providing incentives to certain industries or investing in education and training in particular trades or professions.

An expensive way to grow most produce?
© Fgcanada | Dreamstime.com

 ADDED DIMENSION

Canada, the Great Trader

Canada is certainly one of the world's great trading nations, at least in relative terms. In 2015, for example, it exported $625 billion worth of goods and services and imported $671 billion. Each of these figures represents approximately 30 percent of Canada's GDP. Only a few developed countries, such as Austria and the Netherlands, trade a larger fraction. The United States and Japan, in comparison, trade only about 12 percent of their GDPs (though, of course, in actual dollars, this represents a lot more). The United States is Canada's predominant trading partner, purchasing more than all other countries combined (buying approximately 72 percent of our exports). In fact, Canada sells over twice as much to the United States as it does to all other countries combined and buys approximately 64 percent of all of its imports from that country.

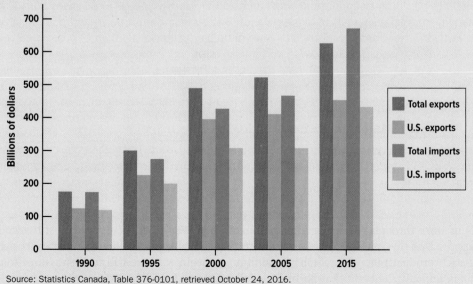

Source: Statistics Canada, Table 376-0101, retrieved October 24, 2016.

Theory of Absolute Advantage

A country will gravitate to producing in those areas where, because of its own factor endowments, it possesses a cost advantage over other producing countries: Canada produces wheat, lumber, and minerals, Chile produces copper and other metal ores, Australia exports mineral fuels, China produces electronic equipment and machines, and so on. **Figure 13.5** shows the distribution of exports for these particular countries. This is what Adam Smith proposed when he put forward his *theory of absolute advantage*. Nations, like firms and individuals, should specialize in producing goods and services for which they have an advantage, and they should trade with other countries for goods and services for which they do not enjoy an advantage.

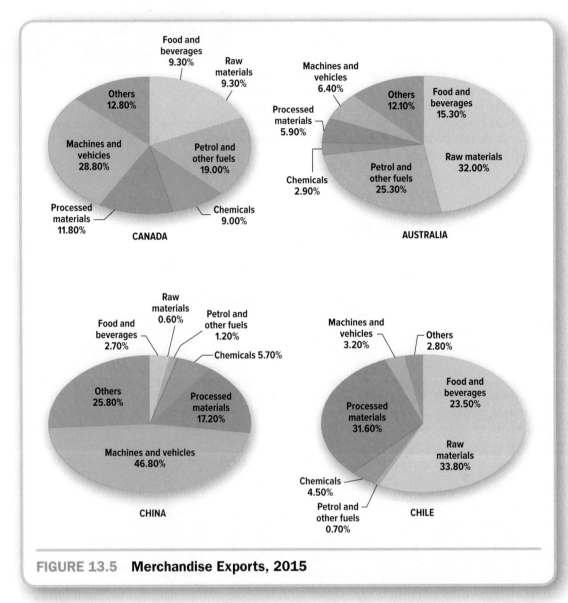

FIGURE 13.5   Merchandise Exports, 2015

Source: Adapted from *Commodity Trade Statistics Database*, United Nations, 2016. The United Nations is the author of the original material.

Let us work through a simple example of this theory. We will concentrate on just two countries and suppose that they produce just two products. We will also assume that the average cost of producing each product remains constant. In addition, to begin with, we will further assume that each country is self-sufficient and that no trade is taking place. **Table 13.1** shows the productivity per worker (average product) of producing wheat and beans in Canada and Mexico. We can see at a glance that Canada produces more wheat than Mexico, whereas Mexico produces more wheat than Canada.

TABLE 13.1
Output per Worker by Country and Industry

	NUMBER OF BUSHELS PER DAY		
	Wheat		Beans
Canada	3	or	2
Mexico	1	or	4

Let us suppose that initially the two countries do not trade with each other and that the working population in each country is 16 million, divided equally between the two industries. Table 13.2 shows what the two countries produce. In this case, half the working population of Canada—8 million workers—is producing wheat. Since each person is capable of producing 3 bushels, the total production is 8 million times 3, or 24 million bushels. The other figures are similarly derived.

TABLE 13.2
Total Outputs Before Trade

	TOTAL NUMBER OF BUSHELS PER DAY (in millions)	
	Wheat	Beans
Canada	24	16
Mexico	8	32
Total	32	48

Now, suppose the two countries decide to enter into a free trade agreement, each country totally specializing in what it does best: Canada producing wheat and Mexico producing beans. With the whole of the working population of 16 million in Canada producing wheat and all 16 million people producing beans in Mexico, the totals can be seen in Table 13.3. With specialization, the two countries combined could produce an additional 16 million bushels of wheat (48 minus the previous 32) and an additional 16 million bushels of beans (64 minus the previous 48). These are referred to as the *gains from trade*. Strictly speaking, the increased total production is really the result of increased specialization. But if a country is going to specialize, it will need to trade in order to obtain those products it is not producing. Specialization, then, implies trade, and it would be impossible to have one without the other.

TABLE 13.3
Total Outputs After Trade

	TOTAL NUMBER OF BUSHELS PER DAY (in millions)	
	Wheat	Beans
Canada	48	0
Mexico	0	64
Total	48	64

TEST YOUR UNDERSTANDING

Find answers on the McGraw-Hill online resource.

1. The following table shows the productivity per worker in the beer and wine industries of Freedonia and Libraland:

	OUTPUT IN HUNDREDS OF LITRES		
	Beer		**Wine**
Freedonia	4	or	1
Libraland	3	or	4

a) Which country should specialize in which product?

b) Suppose that initially the working population of each country is 20 million, with 10 million working in each industry. What is the total output of the two countries?

c) Now suppose that each country decides to specialize in the product in which it has an advantage. What will be the total output of each product, and what are the gains from trade?

SECTION SUMMARY

a) Since 1980, international trade has increased tenfold, and China is now the world's biggest exporter. If trade is voluntary, both parties to the trade must benefit.

b) Differences in factor endowments between nations and the theory of absolute advantage explain why, for example, Canada exports lumber and imports bananas.

c) Differences in trade patterns are the result of

 • differences in climate

 • differences in natural resources

 • differences in human capital

 • government policies

13.2   Theory of Comparative Advantage

LO2 Explain why nations import certain goods, even though they can be made more cheaply at home.

The eminent economist David Ricardo, following in the footsteps of Adam Smith, agreed in principle with Smith, adding a subtle but important refinement to Smith's theory of trade. To see the effect of his modification, let us change our example to that of theoretical trade between the United States and the Philippines, keeping the same two products, wheat and beans. The output per worker in each country is shown in Table 13.4.

TABLE 13.4
Output per Worker by Country and Industry

	NUMBER OF BUSHELS PER DAY		
	Wheat		**Beans**
United States	4	or	4
Philippines	1	or	3

Unlike in our last example of Canada and Mexico, here we see that one country, the United States, can outproduce the other, the Philippines, in *both* products. In fact, you can see from the table that U.S. wheat production is four times that of the Philippines; similarly, the U.S. is one and one-third times as productive as the Philippines in beans. If we were to follow Smith's dictum, presumably the U.S. should produce both products itself. After all, how can it possibly be of any advantage to trade with the Philippines, since it could produce both products more cheaply? The heart of Ricardo's idea is that it is not *absolute advantage* but **comparative advantage** that provides the mutual gains from trade. Let us see exactly what this means, through an example.

Suppose you happen to be absolutely the best lawyer in town. Not only that, but you are also its greatest secretary. Given this, why would you bother to hire a secretary to do your clerical work, since you are faster and, by all measurements, more efficient than anyone you could possibly hire? The answer is that the opportunity cost of doing secretarial work is far greater than that of doing legal work. Your opportunity cost of being a lawyer is the lost salary of not being a secretary. Your opportunity cost of being a secretary is your lost earnings as a lawyer. But because you can earn *comparatively* more as a lawyer than as a secretary, you are well advised to concentrate on that career and hire someone (admittedly less productive than you) to act as your secretary.

 GREAT ECONOMISTS: DAVID RICARDO

Ricardo (1772–1823) was a self-made English businessman who turned to economics and politics at a relatively young age. His *Principles of Political Economy and Taxation* in 1817 made him the acknowledged leader of classical economics and the intellectual heir to Adam Smith. By building a model of the economic world, Ricardo gave the powerful tool of abstraction to economics, and the gift of enabling it to be considered a science.

Granger Historical Picture Archive/ Alamy Stock Photo

Ricardo's idea of comparative advantage directs attention away from comparisons between countries and toward comparisons between products. In Table 13.4, for instance, we might ask: How much does it cost the United States to produce wheat? One might express the cost in dollars and cents. However, knowing that the value of money varies over time and that it is often misleading to translate one currency into another, Ricardo was at pains to express costs in more fundamental terms.

One way would be to use the number of hours it takes to produce something. For instance, if the average worker in the United States can produce four bushels of beans in an average eight-hour day, the cost of one bushel of beans would be 8/4, or 2.0 hours. In contrast, the cost of one bushel of beans in the Philippines would be 8/3, or about 2.66 hours. So beans are more expensive to produce in the Philippines.

However, it is more illuminating to measure costs in terms of *opportunity costs*. This was the method chosen by Ricardo. Recall that the opportunity cost of producing one thing can be measured in terms of another thing that has to be sacrificed in order to get it. As far as the United States and the Philippines are concerned, the cost of producing more wheat is the sacrifice of beans, and the cost of increased bean production is the loss of wheat. Let us work out these costs for each country. The cost of employing a worker in the wheat industry is what that worker could have produced in the bean industry, assuming that the country is fully employed. In other words, for every 4 bushels of wheat an American worker produces, the country sacrifices 4 bushels of beans. In per-unit terms, in the United States 4 bushels of wheat costs 4 bushels of beans, so 1 bushel of wheat costs 1 bushel of beans, and 1 bushel of beans costs 1 bushel of wheat.

In the Philippines the cost of 1 bushel of wheat is 3 bushels of beans, and the cost of 1 bushel of beans is 1/3 bushel of wheat. We summarize these figures in Table 13.5.

TABLE 13.5
Opportunity Costs of Production

	COST OF PRODUCING ONE UNIT	
	Wheat	Beans
United States	1 beans	1 wheat
Philippines	3 beans	1/3 wheat

Now you can understand the significance of comparative costs. If you measure the costs in absolute terms, using hours as we did in our example above, then beans are cheaper to produce in the United States. But in comparative terms, they are very *expensive*. Why is that? Because to produce beans, the United States has to make a big sacrifice in the product in which it is even more productive: wheat. Similarly, although beans, in absolute terms, are very expensive in the Philippines, they are cheap in comparative terms; to produce them the Philippines sacrifices little in wheat production because productivity in the wheat industry is low.

In this example, then, the United States should specialize in producing wheat, since the opportunity cost is only one unit of beans compared with three units of beans in the Philippines. Conversely, the Philippines can produce beans comparatively cheaply, at the cost of 1/3 unit wheat, while in the United States the cost is one unit of wheat. Although the United States has an absolute advantage in both products, it has a comparative advantage only in wheat production and the Philippines has a comparative advantage in bean production.

Let us extract further insights by showing the production possibilities of the two countries on the assumption that the size of the labour force in both the United States and the Philippines is 100 million, and that unit costs are constant. (We are assuming constant unit costs to keep the analysis simple. If you remember from Chapter 1, in reality the law of increasing costs applies, which means that the slope of the production possibilities curve is concave. Assuming constant costs means that the production possibilities curves in this chapter plot as straight lines.)

The respective production possibilities for the United States and the Philippines are shown in Table 13.6. The 400 bushels of wheat, under option A in the United States, is the maximum output of

---

TABLE 13.6
Production Possibilities

UNITED STATES: OUTPUT (millions of bushels per day)						
	A	B	C	D	E	F
Wheat	400	320	240	160	80	0
Beans	0	80	160	240	320	400

PHILIPPINES: OUTPUT (millions of bushels per day)						
	A	B	C	D	E	F
Wheat	100	80	60	40	20	0
Beans	0	60	120	180	240	300

wheat if all of the 100 (million) workers were producing 4 bushels of wheat each. Similarly, if the 100 million American workers produced only beans and no wheat, they would also produce 400 bushels of beans as seen under option F. The figures for B, C, D, and E are derived by calculating the output if 80, 60, 40, and 20 million workers are employed in wheat production, while 20, 40, 60, and 80 million workers are employed in bean production. The figures for the Philippines are similarly obtained.

Suppose that initially the countries do not trade with each other, with the United States producing combination C and the Philippines producing combination B. Before specialization and trade, therefore, their joint totals are as shown in Table 13.7.

TABLE 13.7
Output of Both Countries Before Specialization and Trade

	TOTAL OUTPUT (millions of bushels per day)	
	Wheat	Beans
United States	240	160
Philippines	80	60
Total	320	220

If the two countries now specialize, the United States producing wheat and the Philippines producing beans, their output levels would be as shown in Table 13.8.

TABLE 13.8
Output of Both Countries After Specialization and Trade

	TOTAL OUTPUT (millions of bushels per day)	
	Wheat	Beans
United States	400	0
Philippines	0	300
Total	400	300

You can see by comparing the before and after specialization positions of the two countries that production of both products is now higher. Table 13.9 outlines the gains from trade.

TABLE 13.9
Gains from Specialization and Trade

TOTAL OUTPUT (millions of bushels per day)	
Wheat	Beans
+80	+80

Thus, we can conclude that:

> As long as there are differences in comparative costs between countries, regardless of the differences in absolute costs there is a basis for mutually beneficial trade.

What this example shows is that it is possible for both countries to gain from trade, but several questions remain. Will they? How will the increased production be shared? Will it be shared equally, or will one country receive more than the other? Discussion of the terms of trade will help answer these questions.

TEST YOUR UNDERSTANDING

2. Suppose that the labour force in Freedonia is 10 million. Six million people are producing apples, and the rest are producing pears. Libraland's labour force is 16 million, divided equally between the production of apples and the production of pears. The labour productivity in the two countries is given in the following table:

	OUTPUT PER WORKER (bushels per day)		
	Apples		Pears
Freedonia	5	or	2
Libraland	1	or	3

Make a production possibilities table for Freedonia (A to F) and for Libraland (A to E).

a) Which is Freedonia's present combination (A–F)?

b) Which is Libraland's present combination (A–E)?

3. a) Given the data in question 2, what is the total output of the two countries for both products?

b) If each country were to specialize in the product in which it has a comparative advantage, what will be the total output of the two countries for both products?

c) What will be the gains from trade?

SECTION SUMMARY

a) The theory of comparative advantage explains why one nation is willing to trade with another nation, even though it may be more efficient in producing both (all) the products involved.

b) The trade in any two products between any two nations will result in gains from trade unless the opportunity costs of production happen to be exactly the same in each country.

13.3 Terms of Trade

LO3 Explain how the gains from trade are divided between trading partners.

The expression **terms of trade** refers to the price at which a country sells its exports compared with the price at which it buys its imports. Statistics Canada regularly measures Canada's terms of trade using the following formula:

$$\text{Terms of trade} = \frac{\text{average price of exports}}{\text{average price of imports}} \times 100 \qquad [13.1]$$

If the worldwide demand for Canadian softwood lumber were to increase, for example, it would increase the average price of Canadian exports, with the result that the terms of trade would be said to have moved in Canada's favour. The result would be the same if Canadian prices remained the same but the price of imports dropped. In either case, the sale of our exports would enable us to purchase more imports. Conversely, the terms of trade would shift against Canada if Canadian export prices dropped and/or the price of imported goods rose. This is illustrated in **Figure 13.6**.

Changes in the terms of trade can have a significant effect on Canada's economic performance. This ratio of our exports to import prices directly affects our nominal trade balance and indirectly affects the level of real GDP in Canada. A higher ratio reflects a situation in which most Canadians are better off since our exports would be high—which means more jobs—and the price of imports that Canadians buy would be lower. Canada's terms of trade peaked at a ratio of approximately

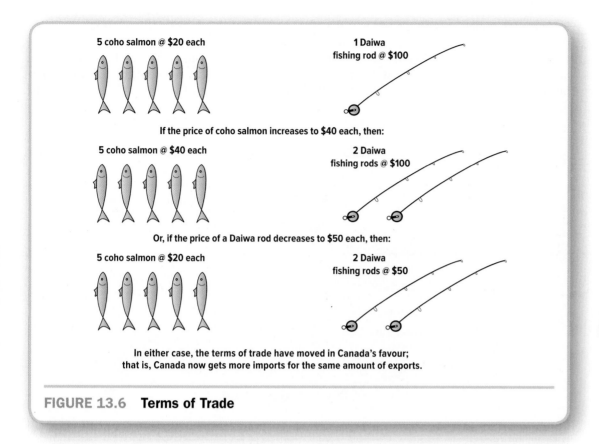

5 coho salmon @ $20 each

1 Daiwa
fishing rod @ $100

If the price of coho salmon increases to $40 each, then:

5 coho salmon @ $40 each

2 Daiwa
fishing rods @ $100

Or, if the price of a Daiwa rod decreases to $50 each, then:

5 coho salmon @ $20 each

2 Daiwa
fishing rods @ $50

**In either case, the terms of trade have moved in Canada's favour;
that is, Canada now gets more imports for the same amount of exports.**

FIGURE 13.6   Terms of Trade

112 in 1973 when world commodity prices were very high, then declined to 82 in 1998. By 2008 the ratio had risen to 104 but has fallen in recent years. It sat at 93 in 2015 as Canada's oil exports continued to drop and the price of oil remained low.

Given our U.S./Philippines example, what would be acceptable prices from the two countries' points of view? Remember that the United States is the wheat producer and exporter. A glance back at Table 13.4 shows that in the United States, 1 bushel of wheat costs 1 bushel of beans. Given this, what price would it be willing to sell its wheat for? Presumably for as high a price as it can get, but certainly not for less than 1 bushel of beans. What about the Philippines? How much would it be willing to pay for wheat? Remember, Table 13.4 tells us that in the Philippines, 1 bushel of wheat costs 3 bushels of beans. Therefore, we can conclude that the Philippines would certainly not pay any higher than this price and would be happy to pay less. As long as the price is above the American minimum and below the Philippines' maximum, both countries would be willing to trade. In other words, feasible terms of trade between the two countries would be anywhere between 1 and 3 units of beans for 1 unit of wheat.

If the price of 1 unit of wheat is less than 1 unit of beans, the U.S. would not sell its wheat, as it is below its costs and less than what sellers can receive at home. Similarly, if the price of 1 wheat was above 3 beans, the Phillippines would refuse to buy wheat, as it could make it domestically at a lower cost.

We could have just as easily expressed things in terms of beans, and a glance back at Table 13.5 shows that feasible terms of trade would be anywhere between 1/3 and 1 bushel of wheat for 1 bushel of beans. In other words, the feasible terms of trade will be between the costs of each product in the two countries. The final terms of trade will depend on the strength of demand in the two countries for these products.

Let us choose one particular rate among the many possible terms of trade and work out the consequences. Suppose, for instance, that the terms end up at 1 bushel of wheat = 2 bushels of beans (or 1 bushel of beans = 1/2 bushel of wheat). Let us now assume, since we need some point to start from, that the Philippines is quite happy consuming the 60 million bushels of beans it was producing before it decided to specialize, as was shown in Table 13.6. However, because of specialization, it is now producing only beans and will therefore have 300 − 60 = 240 million bushels available for export, which it sells to the United States at a rate of one bushel for half a bushel of wheat. It will receive back 120 million bushels of wheat and will finish up with 60 million bushels of beans and 120 million bushels of wheat. Because of trade, it will have gained an additional 40 million bushels of wheat compared with its self-sufficient totals shown in the Before Trade column in Table 13.10.

TABLE 13.10

PHILIPPINES		Before Trade	After Trade
	Beans produced	60	300
	Beans exported	0	−240
Beans consumed		60	60
	Wheat produced	80	0
	Wheat imported	0	+120
Wheat consumed		80	120
	Gain = 40 Wheat		

UNITED STATES		Before Trade	After Trade
	Beans produced	160	0
	Beans imported	0	+240
Beans consumed		160	240
	Wheat produced	240	400
	Wheat exported	0	−120
Wheat consumed		240	280
	Gain = 80 Beans and 40 Wheat		

The United States will also gain. It was the sole producer of wheat, and of the total of 400 million bushels produced, it has sold 120 million bushels to the Philippines in exchange for 240 million bushels of beans. It will end up with 280 million bushels of wheat and 240 million bushels of beans, which is 40 million bushels of wheat and 80 million bushels of beans more than when it was producing both products as shown by comparing the Before Trade and After Trade columns for the United States. In reviewing Table 13.10 recall that we are assuming the Philippines consumes the same 60 million bushels of beans before and after trade.

Terms of Trade and Gains from Trade, Graphically

Let us now look at each country's trading picture separately. Using a graphical approach, Figure 13.7 shows the production possibilities curve for the United States. Before it decided to trade, this was also its consumption possibilities curve, since it could obviously not consume more than it produced. The slope of the curve is 1, which is the cost of 1 bushel of beans (that is, it equals 1 bushel of wheat). The curve to the right is its trading possibilities curve, which shows how much the United States could obtain through a combination of specializing its production and trading. Note that the slope of the trading possibilities curve is equal to 0.5. This is the terms of trade established between the two countries: 1 bushel of wheat for 2 bushels of beans.

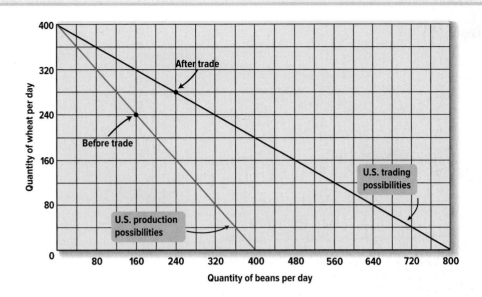

FIGURE 13.7   U.S. Production and Trading Possibilities Curves

The slope of the production possibilities curve shows the cost of producing beans in the United States is 1 bushel of wheat = 1 bushel of beans. The slope of the trading possibilities curve shows the terms of trade: 1 bushel of wheat = 2 bushels of beans. The previous maximum obtainable quantity of beans was 400 million bushels when the United States was self-sufficient. Its new maximum, as a result of trading, is now 800 million bushels.

 ADDED DIMENSION

North American Free Trade Agreement (NAFTA)

In 1993, Canada, the United States, and Mexico formalized the North American Free Trade Agreement (NAFTA) despite considerable political opposition in both Canada and the United States. This agreement was an expansion of the earlier Canada–U.S. Free Trade Agreement of 1988. Unlike the European Union, NAFTA does not create a set of supranational governmental bodies, and it does not create a body of law that supersedes national law.

Since NAFTA, trade has increased dramatically among the three nations. For instance, from 1993 to 2015, total trade between Canada and the United States increased by over 200 percent. In 2015, 78 percent of Canada's merchandised trade was destined for our NAFTA partners.

There is no question that the NAFTA trade agreement had a dramatic impact on trade between the three nations, and many would argue it has benefited all three economies.

You can see from this graph that the United States, at one extreme, could produce the maximum quantity of 400 million bushels of wheat and keep all of it. However, before trade, the maximum amount of beans available was 400 million bushels. Now, if it wished, the U.S. could produce 400 million bushels of wheat, trade *all* of it, and receive in exchange 800 million bushels of beans. (We presume it is able to buy these beans from other countries as well as from the Philippines, given that the latter can only produce 300 million bushels of beans.) More likely, of course, it will opt to have a combination of both products, such as 280 million bushels of wheat and 240 million bushels of beans, as in our numerical example above.

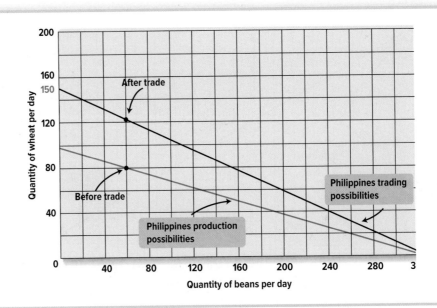

FIGURE 13.8   **Philippines Production and Trading Possibilities Curves**

The Philippines specializes in the production of beans, and its trading possibilities curve lies to the right of the production possibilities curve. In other words, whether it trades or not, the cost of beans remains the same; the cost of wheat, however, is now lower as a result of trade, since the Philippines can now obtain wheat at a cost of 2 bushels of beans per 1 bushel of wheat, whereas producing its own wheat costs 3 bushels of beans per 1 bushel of wheat.

Figure 13.8 shows the situation from the point of view of the Philippines. The inside curve is its production (and therefore its consumption) possibilities curve, representing the maximum of both products that can be produced when the country is self-sufficient. The slope of the curve represents the cost of 1 bushel of beans and is equal to 1/3 bushel of wheat. The outer curve is the trading possibilities curve if the terms of trade are 1 bushel of beans = 1/2 bushel of wheat. You can see that trading allows the Philippines to enjoy increased consumption as well. After specialization, the maximum amount of beans remains unchanged at 300 million bushels. However, the maximum amount of wheat has increased from 100 (if produced in the Philippines) to 150 (by trading all of its 100 million bushels of beans for this quantity of wheat).

The Benefits of Free Trade

Ricardo's theory of comparative advantage, which we have been looking at, is very important because it clearly highlights the major benefits of trade. Free and unrestricted trade gives nations and individuals the opportunity to sell in world markets, and this enables them to specialize production in areas wherein they enjoy a cost advantage over others. The effect will be lower costs of production generally, which translates into *lower prices* for consumers. This in turn will reduce the cost of living and enable people to enjoy a higher standard of living. In addition, free trade increases the levels of output worldwide and means *higher levels of income*, which in turn will lead to improved standards of living.

It all boils down to the fact that specialization increases productivity, so people as a group are better off as the result of lower production costs and higher incomes. But in addition, consumers in countries that do not specialize and do not trade will generally have to make do with a limited choice of domestically produced products that are of lower quality. With global markets, the variety and quality of products are much greater.

IT'S NEWS TO ME ...

The German Federal Constitutional Court today rejected the call for an injunction against its government from finalizing the Canada–European Union trade deal known as CETA.

In response, Germany's Economy Minister, Sigmar Gabriel, said "I am very satisfied with the outcome of the hearing."

Canada's International Trade Minister Chrystia Freeland—who has been actively promoting Canada's interests in several EU countries—has called CETA a gold-plated deal that will give Canada access to a market of 400 million people.

The thrust of the opposition to CETA among some Europeans is that they see it as a blueprint for the Trans-Atlantic Trade and Investment Partnership (TIPP) between the EU and the US which is in an earlier stage of negotiations. They fear that TIIP will undermine the consumer and labour rights of Europeans and weaken environmental protection.

Canada and the EU has committed to signing the deal this year and to seek ratification in their respective parliaments in 2017.

Source: *Star Power Reporting*, October 2016.

I. Which one of the following is most likely false?

    a) CETA will reduce Canada's heavy dependence on the United States as the primary market for her exports.

    b) CETA will achieve more gains from trade for the Canadian economy.

    c) CETA will lower the prices paid by Canadians for many European goods.

    d) CETA will lower Canada's GDP.

II. The opposition to CETA among some Europeans is an example of which one of the following?

    a) the strategic industry argument

    b) the infant industry argument

    c) the cultural identity argument

    d) none of the above

A final benefit of free trade is that it exposes companies to international competition. This means that they cannot sit complacently behind protective barriers but are forced to compete for business with firms around the world. This also tends to discourage the formation of monopolies, since it is much more difficult to be a monopolist in the world market than it is to be a monopolist in the home market.

In summary, free trade has the following advantages:

- lower prices as the result of lower costs of production
- higher incomes
- a greater variety and quality of products
- increased competition

The 1988 Free Trade Agreement with the United States caused a dramatic increase in the volume of trade that Canada has done with that country, as **Figure 13.9** demonstrates.

Some Important Qualifications

These are, indeed, powerful arguments in favour of free trade, but before we leave the topic, let us look at some of the qualifications that must be introduced. First, free trade is never free; transport, insurance, and other freight charges will always need to be added to the cost of production, and that will usually reduce the trading advantage of foreign sellers. (However, in a country as large as Canada, it is often cheaper to transport products to the bordering American states than to transport them from one end of Canada to the other.)

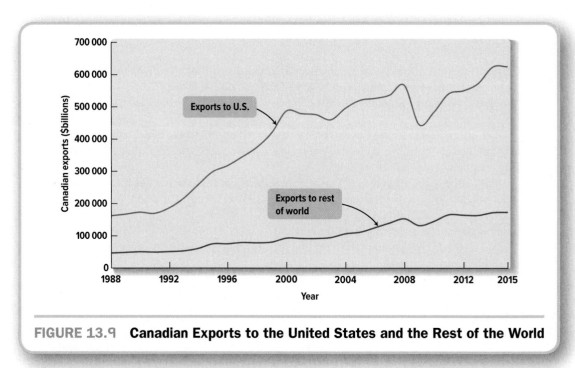

FIGURE 13.9   Canadian Exports to the United States and the Rest of the World

Source: Statistics Canada, Table 376-0101. Accessed January 22, 2014.

In addition, selling in a foreign country is always going to be more difficult (and often more expensive) than selling in the domestic market because of the differences in language, culture, taxation, regulations, and so on.

Besides cost differences, the analysis we have presented so far has assumed constant costs. This leads to the result in our examples that countries should specialize in, perhaps, a single product and produce that product to a maximum. However, as we learned in Chapter 1, if any country tries to concentrate on a single product, its production is subject to the law of increasing costs. This means that one country only enjoys a cost advantage over others *up to a point*. As it tries to push production levels higher, its cost will start to increase so that it no longer enjoys a competitive advantage. This is the reason why few countries specialize entirely and why many countries both produce *and* import the same product. The presence of increasing costs will also lessen the advantages that one country enjoys over another in trade.

 ADDED DIMENSION

Organizations and Treaties of Major Importance for Trade

WTO: The World Trade Organization (WTO), created in 1995 and with 153 member nations, is the only international organization that deals with the rules of trade among nations. Its purpose is to promote free trade and to attempt to resolve trade disputes between member countries.

IMF: The International Monetary Fund (IMF) was created at the Bretton Woods Conference in 1944 in response to the experience of the interwar period (1918–39) when world trade collapsed. Headquartered in Geneva, Switzerland, the IMF has 184 member countries and is dedicated to the promotion of international monetary cooperation, exchange stability, economic growth, and international trade. It makes loans to national governments—at the request of governments themselves—and provides a very sophisticated level of technical assistance.

OECD: The Organisation for Economic Co-operation and Development (OECD), based in Paris, includes thirty developed-nation members and has working relationships with some seventy less-developed countries. The mission of the OECD is to promote policies that achieve sustainable economic growth and development of the world economy, help countries realize sound economic expansion and development, and help world trade grow on a multilateral, nondiscriminatory basis.

EU: The European Union (EU) currently has twenty-eight members (however, the U.K. is negotiating an exit) and grew out of the six-member former European Economic Community, which was established in 1957. The EU, whose capital is in Brussels, is the largest economic/social experiment ever attempted among nations. Over time, the EU has established a common market for goods, services, capital, and labour. Given the size of its population (495 million people) and huge contribution to the world's GDP, its decisions on competition, labour and safety standards, and environmental policies have profound effects on the behaviour of other nations.

G8: This group of eight nations consists of Canada, the United Kingdom, France, Germany, Italy, Japan, the United States, and, recently, Russia. It represents (along with China and Spain) the ten largest economies in the world. The heads of state of these eight countries hold summits in various locations around the globe in which the world's pressing economic, political, and social issues are discussed.

G20: This is an expanded version of the G8. In this case, the ministers of finance and heads of the central banks of the twenty member nations meet to promote financial stability in the world's markets.

NAFTA: The North American Free Trade Agreement (NAFTA) was established with the signing of the 1994 agreement that formed the world's largest free trade area made up of Canada, the United States, and Mexico.

 TEST YOUR UNDERSTANDING

4. The following table shows the average productivity in Freedonia and Libraland:

	OUTPUT PER WORKER (bushels per day)		
	Apples		**Pears**
Freedonia	6	or	3
Libraland	3	or	2

Assuming the two countries wish to trade, would terms of trade of 1 bushel of pears = 2.5 bushels of apples be feasible? What about 1 bushel of pears = 1 bushel of apples? 1 bushel of pears = 1.75 bushels of apples?

5. From the data contained in **Figure 13.7** or **Table 13.6**, how many beans can the United States obtain if it is self-sufficient and producing 240 million bushels of wheat? If, instead, it specializes in wheat production and can trade at terms of 1 bushel of wheat = 2 bushels of beans, how many bushels of beans could it have to accompany its 240 million bushels of wheat? What if the terms were 1 bushel of wheat = 3 bushels of beans?

SECTION SUMMARY

a) How the gains from trade are divided between the trading partners is determined by the terms of trade, calculated as the average price of exports divided by the average price of imports times 100.

b) The major benefits of free trade are

- lower prices
- higher incomes
- a greater variety and quality of products
- increased competition

13.4   The Effect of Free Trade

> **LO4** Describe why some groups win and others lose as a result of freer trade.

Despite the cautions mentioned in the last section, it is still true that there are a number of benefits to be obtained from trade. This leads us to ask: Why does free trade tend to be the exception rather than the rule throughout history? Why does the question of free trade still divide countries and lead to such acrimonious debate? To understand part of the reason, we need to acknowledge that not everyone within a country will benefit from free trade. Let us look at a detailed example.

Suppose that initially we have two self-sufficient countries, France and Germany, each producing wine. The demand and supply conditions in the two countries are different, of course, with both the demand and supply being greater in France than in Germany, as is shown in Table 13.11.

TABLE 13.11
The Market for Wine in France and Germany (millions of litres per month)

FRANCE			GERMANY		
Price ($ per litre)	Quantity Demanded	Quantity Supplied	Price ($ per litre)	Quantity Demanded	Quantity Supplied
3	19	7	3	17	2
4	17	11	4	15	3
5	15	15	5	13	4
6	13	19	6	11	5
7	11	23	7	9	6
8	9	27	8	7	7

The equilibrium price in France is $5 per litre and the equilibrium quantity is 15. In Germany, the equilibrium price and quantity are $8 and 7, respectively. These are shown graphically in Figure 13.10.

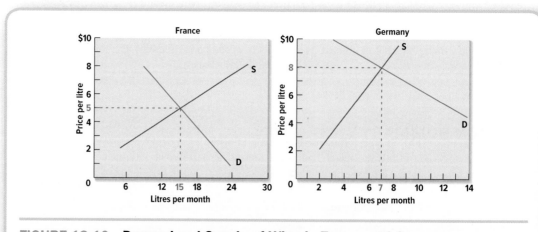

FIGURE 13.10   **Demand and Supply of Wine in France and Germany**

In France the demand and supply of wine are both higher than in Germany. The consequence is a greater quantity of wine traded in France: 15 million litres compared with 7 million in Germany. The price of wine, however, is lower in France than in Germany.

Now suppose that the two countries decide to engage in free trade. To keep things simple, let us assume there are no transport costs. If free trade is now introduced, what will be the price of wine in the two countries? Since we have assumed there are no transport costs, the price in the two countries should be the same. To find this price, all we need do is look at the combined market of France and Germany. In other words, we simply add the demands and supplies of the two countries, as shown in Table 13.12.

TABLE 13.12
Deriving the Total Market Demand and Supply of Wine for France and Germany (in millions of litres per month)

	FRANCE		GERMANY		TOTAL MARKET	
Price ($ per litre)	Demand	Supply	Demand	Supply	Demand	Supply
3	19	7	17	2	36	9
4	17	11	15	3	32	14
5	15	15	13	4	28	19
6	13	19	11	5	24	24
7	11	23	9	6	20	29
8	9	27	7	7	16	34

The total market demand is obtained by adding together the French demand and the German demand at each price. For instance, at $3 per litre, the quantity demanded in France is 19 and in Germany 17, giving a total for the two countries of 36. Similarly, the quantity supplied at $3 is 7 in France and 2 in Germany, giving a total market supply of 9. This is done for all prices. The new market price (let us call it the "world price"), then, will be $6 per litre, and at that price a total of 24 million litres will be produced and sold.

Now let us look at the effect in each market. French winemakers are delighted at the situation, because the world price for wine is higher and their volume of business is higher. They are now producing 19 million litres, up

Bottled wine aging in storage.
Corel

from the 15 million produced before trade, and the price they receive is $6, up from $5. Note also that in France, the quantity produced (19) exceeds the demand from French consumers (13). What happens to the surplus of 6 million litres? It is being exported to Germany. And what is the situation in that country? Well, certainly German consumers are delighted, because the new world price of $6 is lower than the previous domestic price of $8. But we can imagine that the German winemakers are far from happy. The new lower world price has caused a number of producers to cut back production, and presumably some producers are forced out of business and some employees have lost their jobs. Therefore, although the populations of both France and Germany as a whole benefit, not everyone in those countries gains. At the world price of $6, German producers are only producing 5 million litres, down from the previous 7 million and which is below the German demand of 11 million. How is this shortage going to be made up? From the import of French wine. This simply means that the French export of 6 million litres equals the German import of 6 million litres. These points are illustrated graphically in Figure 13.11.

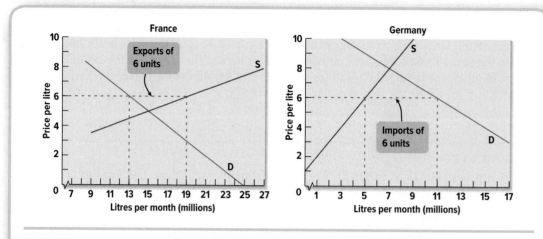

FIGURE 13.11   Demand and Supply of Wine in France and Germany with Free Trade

The new world price of wine is above the previous French price but below the previous German price. The result is a surplus of wine in France of 6 million litres but a shortage in Germany of 6 million litres.

So who loses and who gains as a result of markets being opened up? The answer in our example is that both German wine consumers and French wine producers gain, and French wine consumers and German wine producers lose. Free trade has cost French consumers $1 a litre, and it has cost German winemakers $2 per litre. Previously, German winemakers were selling 7 million litres at $8 per litre, for a total revenue of $56 million. Now, they are selling only 5 million litres for $6 per litre, for a total revenue of $30 million. In total, then, these producers, of whom there may be fewer than 100, have collectively lost $26 million in revenue. It is easy to see why these producers may not be in favour of free trade! In fact, it would pay them to lobby their own parliament and to launch publicity campaigns in an attempt to keep out "cheap" French wines. If they are successful and efforts do not cost more than $26 million, they will be ahead of the game. Table 13.13 illustrates the winners and losers from the introduction of free trade.

TABLE 13.13

Winners	Losers
Domestic (German) consumers who have a greater choice of products at lower prices	**Foreign (French) consumers** who have to pay higher prices
Foreign (French) producers who have a bigger market and can get higher prices	**Domestic (German) producers** who get lower prices as a result of greater competition

This example demonstrates why powerful lobbies and special interest groups have been very vocal throughout history in trying to persuade governments and the public that it is in the country's interests to ban or curtail foreign imports. They will ask their governments to protect them from foreign competition. Such **protectionism** can take many forms, which we will now examine.

ADDED DIMENSION

Trade, Politics, and the Future

We all wonder about what the future holds for humankind. For clues, some of us like to read science fiction books and even more of us are enthralled by futuristic movies such as the *Star Wars* series.

And what do we learn from such fascination?

Well, trade between planets pops up surprisingly often in the *Star Wars* series. Episode I opened with the details of a trade dispute and moved on to the invasion of the peaceful planet of Naboo by the Trade Federation. Yet we also see ample evidence of the idea that the freer the trade between planets the better: the desert Planet Tatooine and the ice planet Hoth would be uninhabited if not for trade, while Coruscant is completely urbanized (one thinks of Dubai here) and other planets have turned their entire surfaces over to agriculture (the young Luke Skywalker harvested atmospheric moisture on a very poor planet).

Operating within the Republic's political system of many planetary members is the Trade Federation with its focus on trade franchises that stunt the possible gains from trade by rent-seeking monopolies. This leads to attempts by some of the heroes in the series to circumvent the legal monopolies, as seen in the smuggling of the narcotic spice (think of the movie *Dune*) by Han Solo in cohort with the gangster Jabba the Hutt.

In short, there is a view of the future as including the familiar pull between the benefits of freer trade and the often uneven distribution of the resulting increased wealth. Furthermore, we see the depiction of the incentive to gain advantages using trade-subverting franchises (at one point Naboo's senator says, "the Republic's bureaucrats are on the payroll of the Trade Federation") which will lead to political challenges that twist and turn in unexpected ways.

Today's world has its counterpart in the 2016 U.S. election's exposing the fact that a vast number of white, working class voters in that country have lost their $35-per-hour manufacturing jobs to free trade and have been left with a sense that the political establishment is strongly pro–free trade and does not represent them anymore. This same sense of disentitlement was also seen in the U.K. referendum being won by the Brexit side, which called for the United Kingdom to leave the European Union.

SECTION SUMMARY

Although the population of a country as a whole gains from free trade, not everyone within that population wins:

- the importing country's producers lose and its consumers gain
- the exporting country's producers gain and its consumers lose

13.5   Trade Restrictions and Protectionism

LO5   Identify various restrictions to, and some arguments against, free trade.

Despite nearly four decades of trade liberalization, there remain many examples of trade restrictions in the world today. We now look at five ways in which this occurs.

The Imposition of Import Quotas

The most obvious way to restrict imports is to ban them entirely or partially, and this can be done with an import **quota**, which is simply a maximum limit placed on each individual foreign exporter. It can also take the form of a requirement that each foreign exporter reduce its exports by a percentage of the previous year's sales.

What will the effect of a quota be? To revisit our wine example, suppose that German winemakers were successful in their efforts to keep out French wines, and the German government imposed a total ban on French wines. At the current price of $6 per litre, there will be an immediate shortage in Germany, whose result will be to push up the price. The rise will continue, encouraging increased German production until the price returns to the pre-free-trade price of $8. In France, the immediate effect of the quota will be a surplus of French wine, which will depress the price of French wine until it, too, is back at the pre-free-trade price of $5 per litre.

Let us move on from our European example and look at trade from the Canadian perspective. Unlike in our example, where the market price was determined by the total demand and supply in just two countries, in reality the prices of wine—and of most products traded internationally—are determined by the world's demand and supply. That is to say, for any one small country, such as Canada, the world price is a given; that country's action will have little impact on the world price. This situation is illustrated in **Figure 13.12**.

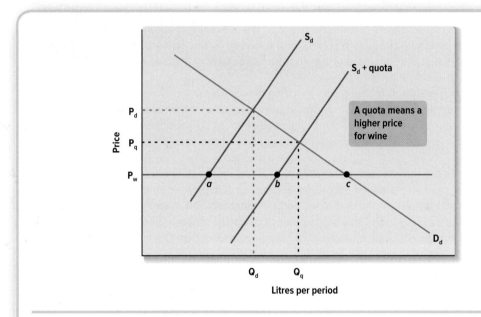

FIGURE 13.12   **The Effects of a Quota**

Initially, the Canadian domestic demand and supply are D_d and S_d, and the world price is P_w. The quantity demanded in Canada at the world price P_w equals c, of which Canadian producers would produce a and foreign producers would export ac to Canada. A quota of ab would raise the price to P_q. As a result, domestic production will increase, and imports would drop to the amount of the quota.

Figure 13.12 shows the domestic demand (D_d) and supply (S_d) of wine in Canada. P_d would be the domestic price and Q_d the domestic production if Canada were totally closed to foreign trade. Suppose that the world price is P_w and that Canada now freely allows imports into the country. This means that if the world price of P_w prevails within Canada, the amount produced by domestic Canadian producers is a, and the amount demanded is c. Since Canadian consumers want to purchase more than Canadian producers are willing to produce, the difference of ac represents the amount of imports.

Now suppose that the Canadian government yields to pressure from Canadian wine producers and imposes a quota of ab on imported wine. In effect, the total supply is equal to the domestic supply plus the amount of the quota. This is represented by the new supply curve, S_d + quota. Since the total available has now been reduced, the price will increase to P_q, and the quantity will fall to Q_q.

From this, it can be seen that the losers will be Canadian consumers (who are paying a higher price for less quantity and variety of wines) and foreign winemakers whose exports are being restricted. The winners will be Canadian winemakers, who are producing more wine and receiving a higher price.

The Imposition of Tariffs

A second way of restricting imports is by the use of a **tariff**, which is a tax on imports. Tariffs are implemented more often than import quotas, because governments can derive considerable revenue from them.

The effects of a tariff are much the same as those of a quota; in both cases the price of the product will increase. With a quota, however, the domestic producers get the whole benefit of the higher price, whereas with a tariff the benefit is shared between the domestic producers and government. An additional benefit of a tariff over a quota is that a quota tends not to discriminate between foreign producers—each and every producer is treated the same way. With a tariff, only the more efficient producers will continue to export, since only they will be able to continue to make a profit. A tariff discriminates against the less efficient producers, and therefore, from an efficiency point of view, it is superior to a quota.

In **Figure 13.13**, suppose, again, that we are describing the Canadian wine market. At the world price of P_w, Canadian producers are supplying a, and Canadian consumers are buying b. The difference, ab, is the amount of imported wine. Suppose that the Canadian government imposes a tariff of t per unit. The price in Canada will rise to P_t. Note that at the higher price, Canadian producers (who do not pay the tariff) will receive the whole price P_t, and will increase production to Q_f. Canadian consumers will reduce consumption to Q_g. In addition, imports will fall to a level represented by the distance $Q_f - Q_g$. The result is very similar to what we saw in the analysis of quotas. Again, it is Canadian consumers and foreign producers who lose out and Canadian producers who gain.

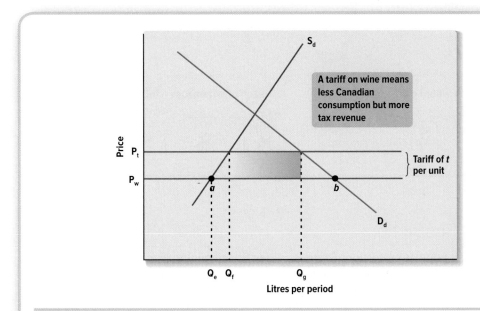

FIGURE 13.13   The Effects of the Imposition of a Tariff

The imposition of a tariff, t, will increase the price of wine in Canada to P_t from P_w. As a result, Canadian production will increase from Q_e to Q_f and imports will drop to $Q_g - Q_f$. The tax revenue to government is equal to t times the quantity of imports, $Q_g - Q_f$, the shaded area.

The other winner in this scenario is the Canadian government, which will receive tax revenue equal to the shaded rectangle in **Figure 13.13**.

IN A NUTSHELL ...

FREE TRADE

Many Winners   **Few Losers**

each of whom gain a little   **each of whom lose a lot**

Other Trade Restrictions

Besides the two most popular protectionist measures—tariffs and quotas—a number of other available methods deserve mention. **Currency-exchange controls** are similar to quotas, but instead of restricting the importation of goods, currency-exchange controls limit the availability of foreign currencies (that is, foreign exchange). The effect is the same because foreigners wish to be paid in their own currencies, and importers unable to get their hands on the appropriate currency will not be able to buy the foreign goods.

The controls might be across-the-board restrictions or restrictions on particular currencies, products, or industries. The effect in all cases will be to increase the domestic price of the products affected, which will be to the benefit of the domestic producer at the expense of the domestic consumer. Another, more subtle but often equally effective way to cut imports is by *bureaucratic regulations*, though not all regulations have that intent. A government might make trade so difficult or time-consuming for the importer that the amount of trade is significantly reduced. For instance, the customs department of a country might tie the importer up with red tape by requiring that all imports be accompanied by ten different forms (all in triplicate) obtainable from ten different government departments. Or the product might have to meet very unrealistic standards of safety, packaging, or hygiene not required for domestically produced items.

A more recent type of trade restriction is known as a **voluntary export restriction** (VER). Rather than imposing tariffs and import quotas, the importing country requests that the exporting country itself voluntarily restrict the amount being exported. In this way, the exporting country is given the power to administer the quotas, which will also prevent the importing country from receiving tariff revenue on the imports. Since the restrictions are voluntary, the exporting country does not have to comply. However, since the importing country has other weapons at its disposal, these restrictions are usually adhered to. One of the first VERs was entered into between the United States and Japan in the early 1980s. At the time, the American economy was suffering a recession, the American auto industry being particularly hard hit. Then–U.S. President Ronald Reagan was able to get the Japanese car manufacturers to limit the number of cars entering the United States to 1.68 million (which was increased in later years). Another example took place in the late 1990s when Canadian exporters of softwood lumber agreed to restrict their exports to the U.S. (under threat of painful tariffs).

In summary, trade can be restricted in five ways:

- import quotas
- tariffs
- currency-exchange controls
- bureaucratic regulations
- voluntary export restrictions

TEST YOUR UNDERSTANDING

6. In **Table 13.12**, if the demand for wine in Germany increased by 9 (million litres) at every price, how much wine would now be produced in Germany and how much would be imported from France?

Protectionism

In this chapter, while we have avoided an outright declaration of support for free trade, we have alluded to the many benefits of trade; and the majority of economists feel that the freer the trade, the better. Nevertheless, even the notable free-trader Adam Smith recognized that some degree of protectionism in ways we have just discussed might be called for at times.

He suggested, for instance, that a country's strategic industries should be offered protection so that, for instance, the country does not become dependent on foreign manufacturers for the production of military hardware and related technology. The problem with this *strategic industry argument*, however, is that most industries would claim to be of strategic importance and therefore deserving of similar protection. The classic example of such thinking occurred in 1845 with the release of an open letter to the French parliament that called on the government to take protective action against unfair competition from the sun. This appeal called for requirements that windows, dormers, skylights, shutters and curtains in all French buildings be permanently closed. The reasoning for this rather exotic appeal was that industries in the lighting industry would have an increase in sales and everyone would be better off.

However, Smith was prescient enough to realize that if a country has had a long history of protectionism, the sudden arrival of free trade is likely to cause dramatic shifts of labour and capital away from industries that can no longer compete to those industries that are growing. This may cause a great deal of suffering in the short term, so Smith felt that a wise government would introduce free trade gradually, to mitigate any suffering. This caveat was of particular importance at the time when Canada, the United States, and Mexico were negotiating the North American Free Trade Agreement. Although many felt that there would be great long-term benefits for all the participating countries, it is equally certain that in the short term a great deal of suffering would be experienced by those industries, firms, and individuals who, through no fault of their own, found themselves unable to compete. This is why tariffs were reduced in stages over a ten-year period.

It should also be mentioned that some economists believe certain infant industries should be given a helping hand by government until they are sufficiently mature to take on foreign competition. This *infant industry argument* is strongest when government feels that undue reliance on the exportation of a few staple products would leave the country in a vulnerable position if a future change in demand or technology were to occur. In order to diversify the economy and develop other industries, many feel that infants should be sheltered from competition. The trouble is, these infant industries often never grow up! In addition, even if there are persuasive arguments in favour of protecting or assisting certain industries, it may be better for government to give this aid in the form of direct subsidies rather than by interfering with normal trading patterns through the imposition of tariffs and quotas.

A third argument against free trade is the *cultural identity argument*. This one is difficult to dismiss solely on economic grounds. Many commentators feel that free trade brings with it mass production and standardization, which may harm the importing country's sense of individuality and cultural identity. As a result, some are totally against free trade, whereas others feel that it should not extend into such areas as communications, health, and education. They firmly believe that a country's radio and television stations, its newspapers and magazines, and its educational institutions and hospitals should not be owned or controlled from abroad. (In some ways, this might also be regarded as a "strategic industry" argument.)

A fourth argument is the belief that the environmental and labour standards of developed nations may be eroded as they try to compete with countries whose standards may be considerably lower and who may have a cost advantage as a result. This could trigger a race to the bottom as standards are lowered in all countries.

Finally, and importantly, it should be stressed that most of this chapter has been about the free trade in *goods and services.* However, the concept of open markets also implies the free movement of both capital and labour. This generally is what is meant by the term *globalization.* And it is this idea of unfettered mobility that has alarmed many who are greatly concerned that their country's resources and its major companies might all become foreign-owned. Further upsetting for many—and one of the major reasons why the majority of Britons voted to leave the European Union (EU)—is the idea of uncontrolled immigration implicit in the idea of labour mobility.

In summary, there are five arguments against free trade:

- the strategic industry argument
- the infant industry argument
- the cultural identity argument
- the lower environmental and labour standards argument
- the argument of lack of control over movements of capital and labour

 TEST YOUR UNDERSTANDING

7. Which industry in Canada do you feel deserves protection because it falls into the category of

a) strategically important?

b) infant industry?

c) culturally important?

d) environmentally important?

 **ADDED DIMENSION**

Free Trade Versus Fair Trade and the Race to the Bottom

Many supporters of free trade in developed countries are nonetheless afraid that entering into a trade agreement with a less-developed country means that they will be competing for jobs with low-wage workers in those countries. The result, they suggest, is that they will either lose their jobs to these other countries or be forced to take lower wages themselves. The idea behind this is that low wages translate to lower prices for goods, which means that production and trade will inevitably shift to low-wage countries. However, there is a logical fallacy to this argument. If low-wage countries had an advantage in trade over high-wage countries, countries like Botswana, Peru, and Cambodia would be the world's great traders. Instead, countries like the United States and others lead the world in trade, despite the fact that they pay some of the highest wages in the world. The reason is that, although they might pay higher wages, they also have much greater productivity rates than other countries, and it is this that largely determines the price of goods. In fact, high-wage countries tend to be high-productivity ones, and low-wage countries low-productivity ones.

However, a recent, and for some alarming, trend is the realization by many multinational corporations that they can get the best of both worlds: the high productivity associated with richer nations and the low wages found in the poorer ones. They are able to do this because proponents of free trade in goods and services have also been successful in advocating the free movement of capital and labour between countries. The result of increased globalization is that multinational corporations now have the freedom to search out those countries with lower wages as well as weaker labour and environmental regulations. In order to attract these multinationals, governments may compete with one another by relaxing standards and eliminating regulations that protect labour, health, and environmental standards. This, it is suggested, will lead to a race to the bottom.

But there is a counterargument: the important thing in trade is the cost per unit of a product and that, as we have suggested, is determined by both the cost of resources and productivity. Now, productivity increases can come from many things, including increased education, a health work force, and improved infrastructure. It is quite possible, then, that freer trade might result in a race to the top through attempts to raise productivity rather than a race to the bottom by reducing costs.

SECTION SUMMARY

a) The two most common forms of trade restrictions are tariffs and quotas, both of which

- increase the domestic price of a product that is imported
- reduce the quantities traded of that product

The other two types of restrictions are

- exchange controls
- voluntary exports restrictions

b) Five arguments against free trade are

- the strategic industry argument
- the infant industry argument
- the cultural identity argument
- the lower environmental and labour standards argument
- the uncontrolled movement of capital and labour argument

Study Guide

Review

WHAT'S THE BIG IDEA?

The idea of a country buying products from abroad which could be just as easily made at home is, to many, one of the more difficult aspects in this chapter. But as the man said, "Just cos we coulda, doesn't mean we shoulda." It's true that even a tiny country like Iceland, for instance, is capable of making cars and computers and growing coniferous trees and wheat. It could even grow pineapples, if it wanted to. But should it? Most definitely not. It is better for that country to concentrate on what it does best—catch fish and mine aluminum and leave it to other countries to produce those other products.

Another principle difficult for many to grasp is that of comparative advantage. Most would agree that if another country can produce a product cheaper than us, perhaps it might be a good idea to buy from them. However, Ricardo would suggest that rather than "How much do beans cost to produce in the U.S. as compared to the cost in, say, the Philippines?" the more important question might be "How much do beans cost to produce in the U.S. as compared to the cost of producing wheat?" It might well be that, in absolute terms, the United States can easily produce beans cheaper than the Philippines; but in fact beans are very expensive to produce in the U.S., because that country is so much better at producing wheat. In other words, producing beans would mean a big sacrifice in producing wheat, whereas producing wheat is a lot cheaper because it does not have to sacrifice many beans.

The other difficult concept is that of the terms of trade. Although it is better to measure costs—as we do throughout this chapter—in terms of units of a product sacrificed, let's use actual dollars in this example. Suppose wheat costs $5 to produce in the United States, whereas the cost is $8 in the Philippines, and suppose the U.S. is the exporter. Now, how much would the U.S. accept for its wheat? Well, certainly as much as possible, but it would accept anything above $5. How about the Philippines? Since it could itself produce wheat for $8, it wouldn't pay more than that; but it would certainly be happy to pay anything less than $8. In other words, anything above $5 but less than $8 would be acceptable to both countries. The terms of trade then would fall somewhere between $5 and $8. (Closer to $5 and the Philippines would be happy; closer to $8 and the U.S. would be.) In other words, the terms of trade range between the cost in the cheaper country to the cost in the more expensive one.

NEW GLOSSARY TERMS AND KEY EQUATION

comparative advantage
currency-exchange controls
protectionism

quota
tariff

terms of trade
voluntary export restriction

Equation:

[13.1]   Terms of trade $= \dfrac{\text{average price of exports}}{\text{average price of imports}} \times 100$

Comprehensive Problem

(LO 2, 3) Suppose that Richland and Prosperity have the output figures shown in Table 13.14. Assume that cost and productivity remain constant.

TABLE 13.14

	AVERAGE PRODUCT PER WORKER		
	Wheat		Wine
Richland	4 bushels	or	2 barrels
Prosperity	2 bushels	or	6 barrels

Questions

a) What is the opportunity cost of producing one bushel of wheat in Richland?
b) What is the opportunity cost of producing one barrel of wine in Richland?
c) What is the opportunity cost of producing one bushel of wheat in Prosperity?
d) What is the opportunity cost of producing one barrel of wine in Prosperity?
e) In what product does Richland have a comparative advantage?
f) In what product does Prosperity have a comparative advantage?

Answers

a) 1 bushel of wheat = ½ barrels of wine. (A worker in Richland can produce either 4 bushels of wheat or 2 barrels of wine. The opportunity cost of 4 wheat is therefore 2 wine. The cost of 1 unit of wheat = 2/4 or ½ wine.)
b) 1 barrel of wine = 2 wheat. (To find the cost of 1 unit of wine, simply take the reciprocal of the wheat cost (that is, invert the number). This gives a cost of 1 wine = 2 wheat.)
c) 1 bushel of wheat = 3 barrels of wine. (In Prosperity, a worker can produce either 2 wheat or 6 wine. The opportunity cost of 2 wheat is therefore 6 wine. The cost of 1 unit of wheat = 3 wine.)
d) 1 barrel of wine = ⅓ (= 0.333) bushels of wheat. (To find the cost of 1 unit of wine take the reciprocal of the wheat cost. This gives a cost of 1 wine = ⅓ wheat.)
e) Richland: wheat. (It can produce wheat cheaper than Prosperity.)
f) Prosperity: wine (It can produce wine cheaper than Richland.)

Questions

Suppose that the labour force in each country is 10 million.
g) Fill in the missing production possibilities data for both countries in Table 13.15.

TABLE 13.15

RICHLAND'S PRODUCTION POSSIBILITIES (millions of units)				
A	B	C	D	E
Wheat	40	30	20	10	0
Wine	——	——	——	——	——

PROSPERITY'S PRODUCTION POSSIBILITIES (millions of units)				
A	B	C	D	E
Wheat	——	——	——	——	——
Wine	0	15	30	45	60

Suppose that both countries are presently producing combination C.

h) Fill in the blanks in Table 13.16.

TABLE 13.16

	TOTAL OUTPUT IN MILLIONS OF UNITS	
	Wheat	Wine
Richland	_____	_____
Prosperity	_____	_____
Total: Both countries	_____	_____

Answers

g) To figure out the production possibilities data for Richland, start at combination E where no wheat is produced. All the labour (10 million) must be employed producing wine, and since each worker can produce 2 barrels of wine, total output = 20 million barrels. Moving to combination D, which represents an additional 10 units of wheat, you know that each unit of wheat costs 1/2 wine. Therefore an additional 10 units of wheat will cost 10 × 1/2 or 5 wine, so that production of wine drops to 15. In general, moving from right to left on the production possibilities table implies that each extra 10 wheat costs 5 wine.

Now do a similar exercise with Prosperity's production possibilities data and note that since 1 wine costs 1/3 wheat, each additional 15 wine costs 15 × 1/3 or 5 wheat.

This gives us the following table:

TABLE 13.15 (COMPLETED)

RICHLAND'S PRODUCTION POSSIBILITIES (millions of units)					
	A	B	C	D	E
Wheat	40	30	20	10	0
Wine	0	5	10	15	20

PROSPERITY'S PRODUCTION POSSIBILITIES (millions of units)					
	A	B	C	D	E
Wheat	20	15	10	5	0
Wine	0	15	30	45	60

---

h) This requires that you copy combinations C from the two production possibilities tables above and total them:

TABLE 13.16 (COMPLETED)

	TOTAL OUTPUT IN MILLIONS OF UNITS	
	Wheat	Wine
Richland	20	10
Prosperity	10	30
Total: Both countries	30	40

Questions

Now suppose that each country specializes in the product in which it has a comparative advantage.
i) Show the results in Table 13.17.

TABLE 13.17

	Wheat	Wine
Richland	_____	_____
Prosperity	_____	_____
Total: Both countries	_____	_____

j) What is the joint gain from trade? Suppose that the two countries establish the terms of trade at 1 wine = 1.5 wheat, and Prosperity decides to export 12 wine to Richland.
k) In Table 13.18, show how the two countries will share the gains from trade.

TABLE 13.18

	GAINS FOR EACH COUNTRY IN MILLIONS OF UNITS	
	Wheat	Wine
Richland	_____	_____
Prosperity	_____	_____
Total: Both countries	_____	_____

Answers

i) Since you've already decided that Richland will specialize in the production of wheat, the production possibilities table above shows the country's maximum wheat production (combination A). Similarly, Prosperity will specialize in wine production and its maximum is shown as combination E in its PP table. This gives us:

TABLE 13.17 (COMPLETED)

	Wheat	Wine
Richland	40	0
Prosperity	0	60
Total: Both countries	40	60

j) 10 wheat and 20 wine. This requires you to simply subtract the pre-trade totals, shown in (h), from these new totals resulting from specialization.
k) As a result of specialization, Prosperity is producing 60 wine. If it trades away 12, it will be left with 48 wine, and in exchange for those 12 wine will receive 12 × 1.5 wheat = 18 wheat. Richland in return will receive these 12 wine and pay 18 wheat. Since it produced 40 wheat, it will be left with 40 – 18 or 22 wheat. The gains for each country, therefore, are (in millions of units):

TABLE 13.18 (COMPLETED)

	GAINS FOR EACH COUNTRY IN MILLIONS OF UNITS	
	Wheat	Wine
Richland	2	2
Prosperity	8	18
Total: Both countries	10	20

Study Problems

Find answers on the McGraw-Hill online resource.

Basic (Problems 1–5)

1. **(LO 3)** If the terms of trade for the country of Onara equals 0.9 and the average price of its imports is 1.4, what is the average price of its exports? _____

2. **(LO 2)** In Onara, the average worker can produce either five bags of pummies or three kilos of clings, whereas in Traf the average worker can produce either four bags of pummies or six kilos of clings. Which country can produce pummies more cheaply and which can produce clings more cheaply? Show the cost in each country.
   Pummies: _____ Cost: _____
   Clings: _____ Cost: _____

3. **(LO 2, 3)** Table 13.19 below shows the maximum output levels for Here and There.

   TABLE 13.19

	Cloth		Computers
Here	100	or	50
There	60	or	120

   a) What is the cost of 1 unit of cloth and a computer in Here?
      1 unit of cloth: _____ 1 computer: _____
   b) What is the cost of 1 unit of cloth and a computer in There?
      1 unit of cloth: _____ 1 computer: _____
   c) In what product does each country have a comparative advantage?
      Here: _____ There: _____
   d) What is the range of feasible terms of trade between the two countries?
      1 unit of cloth: _____ 1 computer: _____

4. **(LO 2)** Table 13.20 below shows the productivity for the countries of Yin and Yang.

   TABLE 13.20

	Machines		Bread
Yin	2	or	10
Yang	3	or	2

   a) If the working populations of Yin and Yang are both 40 million, divided equally between the two industries in each country, show in Table 13.21 how many machines and bread are currently being produced in Yin and Yang.

   TABLE 13.21

	Machines	Bread
Yin	_____	_____
Yang	_____	_____
Total	_____	_____

b) If the two countries decide to specialize, in which product does each country have a comparative advantage?

Yin: _____ Yang: _____

c) If the two countries were to totally specialize, show the totals in the Table 13.22.

TABLE 13.22

	Machines	Bread
Yin	_____	_____
Yang	_____	_____
Total	_____	_____

d) Show the gains from trade in Table 13.23.

TABLE 13.23

Machines	Bread
_____	_____

5. **(LO 2, 3)** Table 13.24 shows the production possibilities for Concordia and Harmonia.

TABLE 13.24

	CONCORDIA'S PRODUCTION				
Product	A	B	C	D	E
Pork	4	3	2	1	0
Beans	0	5	10	15	20
	HARMONIA'S PRODUCTION				
Product	A	B	C	D	E
Pork	8	6	4	2	0
Beans	0	6	12	18	24

a) What are the costs of the two products in each country?

Concordia: 1 unit of pork costs _____

1 unit of beans costs _____

Harmonia: 1 unit of pork costs _____

1 unit of beans costs _____

b) What products should each country specialize in and export?

Concordia: _____

Harmonia: _____

c) If, prior to specialization and trade, Concordia produced combination C and Harmonia produced combination B, what would be the total gains from trade?

Pork: _____

Beans: _____

d) What would be the range of feasible terms of trade between the two countries? _____

Intermediate (Problems 6–10)

6. **(LO 2)** The graph in **Figure 13.14** shows the domestic supply of and demand for mangos in India.

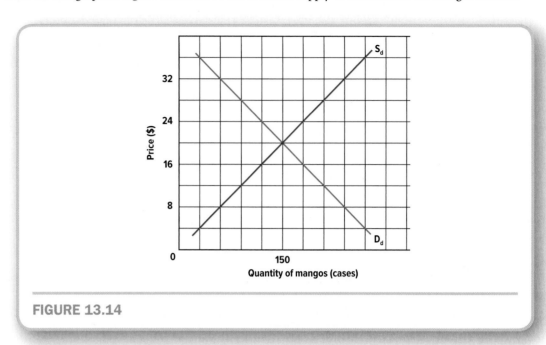

FIGURE 13.14

The world price is $16 a case, and India is open to free trade.
a) Will India export or import mangos? _____
b) What quantity will domestic producers supply? _____
c) What quantity will India export or import? _____
d) If the world price is $28, will India export or import mangos? How much?
(Exports/import): _____ Quantity: _____

7. **(LO 1, 5)** Table 13.25 shows the market for wool in Canada, which is closed to trade.

TABLE 13.25

Price per Tonne ($)	Quantity Demanded Domestically	Quantity Supplied Domestically
1700	145	45
1800	140	60
1900	135	75
2000	130	90
2100	125	105
2200	120	120
2300	115	135
2400	110	150

a) What is the present equilibrium price and domestic production?
Price: _____
Domestic production: _____
b) Suppose that Canada now opens to free trade and the world price of wool is $2000 per tonne. How much wool will Canada produce domestically, and how much will it import?
Domestic production: _____
Imports: _____

c) Assume that the Canadian government, under pressure from the Canadian wool industry, decides to impose an import quota of 20 tonnes. What will be the new price, and how much will the Canadian industry produce?

Price: _____

Domestic production: _____

d) Now suppose that the Canadian government decides to replace the import quota with a tariff. If it wishes to maintain domestic production at the same level as with a quota, what should be the amount of the tariff, and how much revenue will government receive?

Tariff: $ _____

Tariff revenue: $ _____

8. **(LO 4)** Table 13.26 shows the production possibilities for Canada and Japan. Suppose that, prior to specialization and trade, both Canada and Japan are producing combination C.

TABLE 13.26

CANADA'S PRODUCTION POSSIBILITIES					
Product	A	B	C	D	E
DVD players	30	22.5	15	7.5	0
Wheat	0	10	20	30	40
JAPAN'S PRODUCTION POSSIBILITIES					
Product	A	B	C	D	E
DVD players	40	30	20	10	0
Wheat	0	5	10	15	20

a) In **Figure 13.15**, draw the production possibilities curve for each country, and indicate their present output positions.

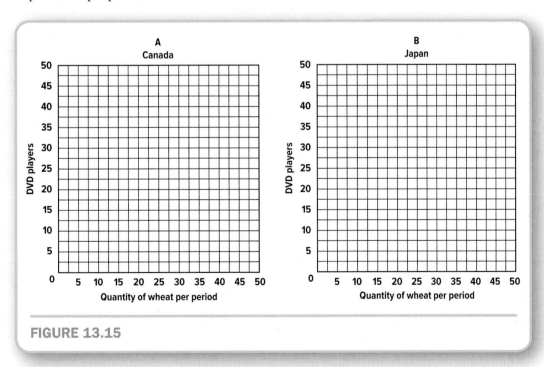

FIGURE 13.15

b) Suppose that the two countries specialize and trade on the basis of 1 DVD player = 1 wheat. Draw the corresponding trading possibilities curves.

c) If Canada still wishes to have 20 wheat, how many more DVDs could it have? _____

d) Show the new combination in Figure 13.15.

e) If Japan still wishes to have 20 DVDs, how much more wheat could it have? _____

f) Show the new combination in Figure 13.15.

9. **(LO 2)** The incomplete Table 13.27 shows the productivity levels of producing beer and sardines in Canada and Mexico.

TABLE 13.27		
	PRODUCTION PER WORKER (average product)	
	Beer	**Sardines**
Canada	6	4
Mexico	3	_____

What should be the Mexican productivity per worker in the sardine industry for no advantage to be gained from trade? _____

10. **(LO 5)** Suppose the Canadian demand for and the Japanese supply of cars to Canada is shown in Table 13.28 (quantities in thousands).

TABLE 13.28			
Price ($)	**Quantity Demanded**	**Quantity Supplied (before tariff)**	**Quantity Supplied (after tariff)**
12 000	180	60	_____
13 000	160	80	_____
14 000	140	100	_____
15 000	120	120	_____
16 000	100	140	_____
17 000	80	160	_____
18 000	60	180	_____
19 000	40	200	_____

a) The present equilibrium price is $_____ and quantity is _____ (thousand).

b) Suppose that the Canadian government imposes a $2000 per car tariff on imported Japanese cars. Show the new supply in the last column above.

c) The new equilibrium price is $_____ and quantity is _____ (thousand).

d) The total revenue received by government will be $_____.

e) Assume, instead, that government imposes an import quota of 100 000 cars. The new equilibrium price is $_____ and quantity is _____ (thousand).

f) Does government now receive any revenue? _____

Advanced (Problems 11–14)

11. **(LO 2, 3, 4)** Latalia has a labour force of 12 million, half in the wool industry and half in rice farming. The labour productivity in the wool industry is 40 kilos per worker per year, and in rice farming it is 100 kilos per worker per year. Latalia has discovered that the international terms of trade are 2 kilos of rice per 1 kilo of wool. It is happy with its current consumption of rice but would like to obtain more wool.

a) Assuming constant per-unit costs, on the graph in Figure 13.16 draw the production and trading possibilities curves for Latalia.

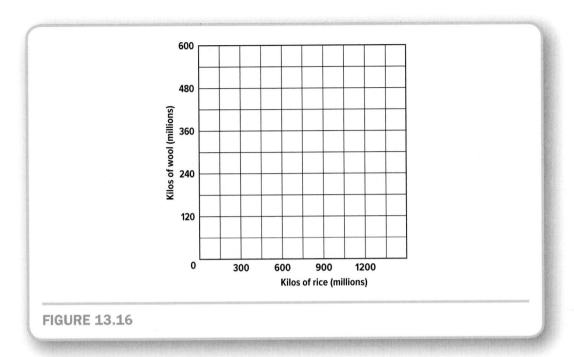

FIGURE 13.16

b) If Latalia were to specialize and trade, what product should it produce? _____
c) What would be Latalia's gain from trade? _____
d) On the graph, indicate the consumption levels before and after trade.

12. **(LO 2, 3)** Suppose three countries have productivity data as shown in Table 13.29.

TABLE 13.29

	PRODUCTIVITY PER WORKER	
	Wheat	Beans
Alpha	1	2
Beta	4	2
Gamma	2	2

a) What is the cost of wheat in each country?
   In Alpha, 1 unit of wheat costs _____.
   In Beta, 1 unit of wheat costs _____.
   In Gamma, 1 unit of wheat costs _____.
b) Which country can produce wheat the most cheaply (comparatively)? _____
c) Which country can produce beans the most cheaply (comparatively)? _____
d) Suppose that the international terms of trade were 1 wheat = 3/4 beans. Which countries would export wheat? _____ Which countries would import wheat? _____
e) Suppose, instead, that the international terms of trade were 1 wheat = 1½ beans. Which countries would export wheat? _____ Which countries would import wheat? _____

13. **(LO 2, 3)** Table 13.30 shows the annual demand and supply of cell phones in Canada (in tens of thousands), where D_C is the domestic demand, D_W is the demand in the rest of the world, S_C is the Canadian supply, and S_W is the quantity supplied by manufacturers in the rest of the world.

TABLE 13.30

Price ($)	D_C	D_W	D_T	S_C	S_W	S_T
25	200	1200	____	20	1200	____
50	180	1100	____	30	1250	____
75	160	1000	____	40	1300	____
100	140	900	____	50	1350	____
125	120	800	____	60	1400	____
150	100	700	____	70	1450	____
175	80	600	____	80	1500	____
200	60	500	____	90	1550	____
225	40	400	____	100	1600	____

a) Complete the total demand (D_T) and total supply (S_T) columns.
b) What are the world price and quantity?
   Price: _____ Quantity: _____
c) If Canada was closed to international trade, what would be the price and quantity in Canada?
   Price: _____ Quantity: _____
d) If Canada were open to international trade, how much would Canada import from the rest of the world? _____
e) If the Canadian government were to impose a quota and limit the amount of imported cell phones to 90 (tens of thousands), what would be the new price and quantity in Canada?
   Price: _____ Quantity: _____

14. **(LO 2, 3)** The average productivity per worker in the kumquat industry in Bolita is 8 kilos; productivity in the daikon industry is 5 kilos. In Neru, the corresponding figures are 6 kilos and 2 kilos.
   a) According to the theory of comparative advantage, Bolita should specialize in and export what product? What product should Nertu specialize in and export?
      Bolita should specialize in _____ and Neru should specialize in _____.
   b) What are the possible terms of trade for daikons between the two countries?
      Between _____ and _____ kumquats per daikon.

Problems for Further Study

Basic (Problems 1–4)

1. **(LO 3)** What is meant by *terms of trade*?

2. **(LO 1)** What is meant by *factor endowment*?

3. **(LO 4)** Who gains and who loses when a country enters into a free trade agreement?

4. **(LO 3)** What are the full names and functions of the following: WTO, EU, NAFTA, OECD?

Intermediate (Problems 5–8)

5. **(LO 1)** How are trade and specialization related?

6. **(LO 3)** List three arguments against free trade.

7. **(LO 1)** Which country, the United States or Canada, exports more as a percentage of its GDP? Why?

8. **(LO 2)** If Japan can produce kumquats cheaper than the Philippines, why would it import them from the Philippines?

Advanced (Problems 9–11)

9. **(LO 2, 5)** If comparative cost is the basis for trade, why are the developing countries (which have very low wage rates) not the world's greatest trading nations?

10. **(LO 1, 2)** Explain the theory of comparative advantage. How does it differ from the theory of absolute advantage?

11. **(LO 1)** What are the four major reasons for differences in trade patterns between countries?

STATISTICAL INFORMATION APPENDIX

World's Highest Unemployment Rates

Rank	Country	Unemployment Rate (%)
1	Namibia	29.7
2	Macedonia	28
3	Bosnia & Herzegovina	27.5
4	West Bank & Gaza	26.9
5	Greece	26.5
6	South Africa	24.9
7	Lesotho	24.4
8	Spain	24.4
9	St. Lucia	22.2
10	Serbia	22.1

Source: *World Bank: World Development Indicators 2016.*

World's Richest Countries

Rank	Country	GNI per capita (in $US)
1	Qatar	$140 720
2	Singapore	81 190
3	Kuwait	79 970
4	Luxembourg	70 750
5	United Arab Republic	70 570
6	Norway	64 590
7	Switzerland	61 930
8	Hong Kong	57 650
9	United States	56 430
10	Saudi Arabia	54 730

Source: *World Bank: World Development Indicators 2016.* Gross national income based on the purchasing power of each country's currency.

World's Poorest Countries

Rank	Country	GNI per Capita (in $US)
1	Central African Republic	$ 600
2	Congo, Democratic Republic of	720
3	Liberia	720
4	Burundi	730
5	Niger	950
6	Guinea	1120
7	Malawi	1140
8	Mozambique	1170
9	Togo	1320
10	Madagascar	1400

Source: *World Bank: World Development Indicators 2016.* Gross national income based on the purchasing power of each country's currency.

World's Highest Inflation Rates

Rank	Country	% Inflation Rate
1	Venezuela	122
2	South Sudan	50
3	Ukraine	49
4	Malawi	21
5	Ghana	17
6	Sudan	17
7	Russian Federation	16
8	Iran	14
9	Belarus	14
10	Myanmar	11

Source: *World Development Indicators 2016.*

World's Highest Life Expectancy

Rank	Country	Age
1	Monaco	89.5
2	Singapore	85.0
3	Japan	85.0
4	Macau	84.5
5	San Marino	83.3
6	Iceland	83.0
7	Hong Kong	82.9
8	Andorra	82.8
9	Switzerland	82.6
10	Israel	82.5
19	**Canada**	**81.9**

Source: *CIA—World Factbook 2016.*

World's Largest Countries by Population

Rank	Country	Millions
1	China	1374
2	India	1269
3	United States	324
4	Indonesia	258
5	Brazil	206
6	Pakistan	202
7	Nigeria	186
8	Bangladesh	156
9	Russia	142
10	Japan	127

Source: *CIA—World Factbook 2016.*

Best Global Brands

Rank	Brand	Brand Value (in $Millions)
1	Apple (U.S.)	178
2	Google (U.S.)	133
3	Coca-Cola (U.S.)	73
4	Microsoft (U.S.)	72.8
5	Toyota (Japan)	54
6	IBM (U.S.)	53
7	Samsung (South Korea)	52
8	Amazon (U.S.)	50
9	Mercedes-Benz (Germany)	44
10	General Electric (U.S.)	43.5

Source: *Interbrand's Best Global Brands 2016.*

World's Most Expensive Cities

Rank	City	Country
1	Zurich	Switzerland
2	Grand Cayman	Cayman Islands
3	New York	U.S.A.
4	Geneva	Switzerland
5	San Francisco	U.S.A.
6	Washington, D.C.	U.S.A.
7	Hong Kong	Hong Kong/China
8	Reykjavik	Iceland
9	Lausanne	Switzerland
10	Oslo	Norway

Source: Expatistan.com, Cost of Living Index, 2016.

World's Cleanest Cities

Rank	City	Country
1	**Calgary**	**Canada**
2	Adelaide	Australia
3	Honolulu	U.S.A.
4	Minneapolis	U.S.A.
5	Kobe	Japan
6	Copenhagen	Denmark
7	Wellington	New Zealand
8	Helsinki	Finland
9	Oslo	Norway
10	Freiburg	Germany

Source: Based on data from http://www.huffingtonpost.ca/cody-battershill/calgary-one-accolade-after-another_b_3620825.html, Mercer Global Financial and HR Consulting. Accessed at Miratel Solutions January, 2017.

World's Most Prosperous Countries

Rank	Country
1	New Zealand
2	Norway
3	Finland
4	Switzerland
5	**Canada**
6	Australia
7	Netherlands
8	Sweden
9	Denmark
10	United Kingdom

Source: Legatum Prosperity Index™ 2016, developed by the Legatum Institute, available at www.prosperity.com.

World's Most Livable Cities

Rank	City	Country
1	Vienna	Austria
2	Zurich	Switzerland
3	Auckland	New Zealand
4	Munich	Germany
5	**Vancouver**	**Canada**
6	Dusseldorf	Germany
7	Frankfurt	Germany
8	Geneva	Switzerland
9	Copenhagen	Denmark
10	Sydney	Australia

Source: Mercer, *Quality of Living Survey 2016.*

World's Most Visited Countries

Rank	Country	Annual Number of Arrivals (in millions per year)
1	France	84.5
2	United States	77.5
3	Spain	68.2
4	China	55.6
5	Italy	50.7
6	Turkey	39.5
7	Germany	35.0
8	United Kingdom	34.4
9	Mexico	32.1
10	Russia	31.3
17	**Canada**	**16.5**

Source: UN World Tourist Organization, 2015.

A

allocative efficiency the production of the combination of products that best satisfies consumers' demands.

average fixed cost total fixed cost divided by the quantity of output.

average product total product (or total output) divided by the quantity of inputs used to produce that total.

average profit the profit per unit produced; that is, the total profit divided by the output.

average revenue the amount of revenue received per unit sold.

average total cost total cost divided by quantity of output.

average variable cost total variable cost divided by total output.

B

barriers to entry obstacles that make it difficult for new participants to enter a market.

break-even output the level of output at which the sales revenue of the firm just covers fixed and variable costs, including normal profit.

break-even price the price at which the firm makes only normal profits, that is, makes zero economic profits.

C

capital the human-made resource that is used to produce other products.

cartel an association of sellers acting in unison.

ceteris paribus other things being equal, or other things remaining the same.

change in demand a change in the quantities demanded at every price, caused by a change in the determinants of demand.

change in supply a change in the quantities supplied at every price, caused by a change in the determinants of supply.

change in the quantity demanded the change in quantity that results from a price change. It is illustrated by a movement along a demand curve.

change in the quantity supplied the change in the amounts that will be produced as a result of a price change. This is shown as a movement along a supply curve.

collusion an agreement among suppliers to set the price of a product or the quantities each will produce.

common property resources resources not owned by an individual or a firm.

comparative advantage the advantage that comes from producing something at a lower opportunity cost than others are able to do.

complementary products products that tend to be purchased jointly and for which demand is, therefore, related.

concentration ratio a measurement of the percentage of an industry's total sales that is controlled by the largest few firms.

constant-cost industry an industry in which the prices of resources and products remain unchanged as the industry expands.

constant returns to scale a concept whereby a firm's output increases by the same percentage as the increase in its inputs.

consumer goods and services products that are used by consumers to satisfy their wants and needs.

consumer surplus the difference between what a customer is willing to pay and the actual price of the product.

cross-elasticity of demand how the quantity demanded of product A responds to a change in the price of product B.

currency-exchange controls government restrictions limiting the amount of foreign currencies that can be obtained.

D

deadweight loss the total surplus lost relative to an efficient market due to market imperfections, taxes, or other factors.

decreasing-cost industry an industry in which the prices of resources and products both fall as the industry expands.

decreasing returns to scale the situation in which a firm's output increases by a smaller percentage than the increase to its inputs.

demand the quantities that consumers are willing and able to buy per period of time at various prices.

demand schedule a table showing the various quantities demanded per period of time at different prices.

depreciation the annual cost of any asset that is expected to be in use for more than one year.

diseconomies of scale bureaucratic inefficiencies in management that result in decreasing returns to scale.

division of labour the dividing of the production process into a series of specialized tasks, each done by a different worker.

dumping the sale of a product abroad for a lower price than is being charged in the domestic market or for a price below the cost of production.

E

economic capacity that output at which average total cost is at a minimum.

economic profit revenue over and above all costs, including normal profits.

economic rent the return to any factor of production above what is required to keep the factor in its present use.

economic surplus the summation of consumer surplus and producer surplus.

economies of scale cost advantages achieved as a result of large-scale operations.

elastic demand quantity demanded that is quite responsive to a change in price (coefficient of elasticity is greater than 1).

elasticity coefficient a number that measures the responsiveness of quantity demanded to a change in price.

elasticity of supply the responsiveness of quantity supplied to a change in price.

enterprise the human resource that innovates and takes risks.

equilibrium price the price at which the quantity demanded equals the quantity supplied such that there is neither a surplus nor a shortage.

equilibrium quantity the quantity that prevails at the equilibrium price.

excess capacity the situation in which a firm's output is below economic capacity.

excise tax a sales tax imposed on a particular product.

explicit cost a cost that is paid to non-owners.

external benefits benefits enjoyed by people other than the producers or consumers of a product.

external costs costs incurred by people other than the producers or consumers of a product.

externalities benefits or costs of a product experienced by people who neither produce nor consume that product.

F

factor market the market for the factors of production.

factor output effect what is said to happen when rising total output leads to an increased demand for labour.

factor substitution effect what is said to happen when one factor replaces another factor as a result of technological change.

factors of production physical or virtual entities that can be used to produce goods and services.

fair-return price a price that guarantees the firm will earn normal profits only— that is, where P = AC.

firm a business organization that hires and organizes factors of production in order to sell goods and services. Also known as a company or business.

first come, first served a service policy in which the requests of customers are attended to in the order in which they arrived.

franchise an arrangement wherein one party (the *franchiser*) grants another (the *franchisee*) the right to use proprietary knowledge, processes, and trademarks that allow it to sell a product under the business's name.

G

game theory a method of analyzing firm behaviour that highlights mutual interdependence among firms.

H

human capital the accumulation of all skills and knowledge acquired by individuals.

I

imperfect competition a market structure in which producers are identifiable and have some control over price.

implicit cost the opportunity cost of using the owners' resources that does not require an actual expenditure of money.

income effect the effect that a price change has on real income and therefore on the quantity demanded of a product.

income elasticity the responsiveness of quantity demanded to a change in income.

increasing-cost industry an industry in which the prices of resources and products both rise as the industry expands.

increasing returns to scale the phenomenon of a firm's output increasing by a greater percentage than the increase in its inputs.

indifference curve a graph plotting that shows the combinations of goods that would give the same satisfaction (or total utility) to an individual (or household).

inelastic demand quantity demanded that is not very responsive to a change in price (coefficient of elasticity is less than 1).

inferior products products for which demands will decrease as a result of an increase in income and increase as a result of a decrease in income.

inputs physical or virtual entities that can be used to produce goods or services.

interest the payment made and the income received for the use of capital.

L

labour human physical and mental effort that can be used to produce goods and services.

labour force the total number of people over the age of 15 who are willing and able to work.

labour force supply the total hours that those in the labour force are willing to work.

laissez-faire the economic doctrine asserting that an economy works best with the minimum amount of government intervention.

land any natural resource that can be used to produce goods and services.

law of diminishing marginal rate of substitution the principle that holds that the more of one good a person has, the less of another good he will be willing to give up to gain an additional unit of the first good.

law of diminishing marginal utility the priniciple that the amount of additional utility decreases as successive units of a product are consumed.

law of diminishing returns the principle that, as more of a variable input is added to a fixed input in the production process, the resulting increase in output will at some point begin to diminish.

law of increasing costs as an economy's production level of any particular item increases, its per-unit cost of production rises.

long run the period during which all inputs are variable.

long-run average cost curve a graphical representation of the per-unit costs of production in the long run.

M

macroeconomics the study of how the major components of an economy interact; it considers unemployment, inflation, interest rate policy, and the spending and taxation policies of government.

marginal the extra or additional unit.

marginal cost the increase in total variable costs (or total costs) as a result of producing one more unit of output.

marginal private benefits the extra benefits the buyer derives from consuming additional quantities of a product.

marginal private costs the extra internal (or private) costs to the producer of increasing production by one additional unit.

marginal product the change in total product as a result of a unit change of input.

marginal rate of substitution the amount of one good a consumer is willing to give up to get one more unit of another good and maintain the same level of satisfaction.

marginal revenue the extra revenue derived from the sale of one more unit.

marginal revenue product the increase in a firm's total revenue that results from the use of one more unit of input.

marginal social benefits the additional benefits to both the consumer (internal benefits) and society (external benefits) of additional quantities of a product.

marginal social costs the additional costs to both the producer (internal costs) and society (external costs) of producing additional units of a product.

marginal utility the amount of additional utility derived from the consumption of an extra unit of a product.

marginal utility per dollar spent the marginal utility from a product that is derived from spending one more dollar on it.

marginal wage cost the extra cost of hiring an additional worker.

market a mechanism that brings buyers and sellers together and assists them in negotiating the exchange of products.

market demand the total demand for a product by all consumers.

market failures the defects in competitive markets that prevent them from achieving an efficient or equitable allocation of resources.

market supply the total supply of a product offered by all producers.

microeconomics the study of the outcomes of decisions by people and firms; it focuses on the supply and demand of goods, the costs of production, and market structures.

minimum efficient scale the smallest-size plant capable of achieving the lowest long-run average cost of production.

minimum wage the lowest rate of pay per hour for workers, as set by government.

monopolistic competition a market in which there are many firms that sell a differentiated product.

monopoly a market in which a single firm (the monopolist) is the sole producer.

monopsony a labour market structure in which there is only one buyer.

mutual interdependence the condition in which a firm's actions depend, in part, on the reactions of rival firms.

N

Nash equilibrium a situation wherein each rival chooses the best actions given the (anticipated) actions of the other(s).

natural monopoly a single producer in a market (usually with large economies of scale) that is able to produce at a lower cost than competing firms could.

nominal wage the wage rate expressed as a dollars-and-cents figure.

non-excludable a feature of certain goods that means that it is impossible (or extremely costly) to prevent nonbuyers from enjoying the benefits.

nonrival goods goods one person's consumption of which does not reduce the amount available for others.

normal products products for which demand will increase as a result of an increase in income and decrease as a result of a decrease in income.

normal profit the minimum profit that must be earned to keep the entrepreneur in that type of business.

normative statement a statement of opinion or belief that cannot be verified.

O

oligopoly a market dominated by a few large firms.

opportunity cost the value of the next-best alternative that is given up as a result of making a particular choice.

optimal purchasing rule in order to maximize utility, consumers should allocate their budgets so that marginal utility per dollar spent on all products is equal.

P

perfect competition a market in which all buyers and sellers are price takers.

perfect price discrimination a situation in which customers are charged the highest price they are willing to pay for each unit of a product bought.

positive statement a statement of fact that can be verified.

price ceiling a government regulation stipulating the maximum price that can be charged for a product.

price controls government regulations to set either a maximum or a minimum price for a product.

price discrimination the selling of an identical product at a different price to different customers for reasons other than differences in the cost of production.

price elasticity of demand a measure of the percentage change of quantity demanded relative to a change in price.

price floor a government regulation stipulating the minimum price that can be charged for a product.

private goods goods or services whose benefits can be denied to nonbuyers and whose consumption by one person reduces the amount available for others.

producer surplus the difference between the amount producers would be willing to accept for each unit of output and the price they receive when the output is sold.

producers' preference an allocation system in which sellers are allowed to determine the method of allocation on the basis of their own preferences.

product differentiation the attempt by a firm to distinguish its product from that of its competitors.

product market the market for consumer goods and services.

production possibilities curve a graphical representation of the various combinations of maximum output that can be produced from the available resources and technology.

production quota an upper limit imposed on the production or sale of a product.

productive efficiency the production of an output at the lowest possible average cost.

profit the income received from the activity of enterprise.

protectionism the economic policy of protecting domestic producers by restricting the importation of foreign products.

public goods goods or services whose benefits are not affected by the number of users and from which no one can be excluded.

public utilities goods or services regarded as essential and therefore usually provided by government.

Q

quasi-public goods private goods that are provided by government because they involve extensive benefits for the general public.

quota a limit imposed on the production or sale of a product.

R

rationing allocating products that are in short supply using ration coupons issued by government, guaranteeing a certain quantity of something per family.

real income income measured in terms of the amount of goods and services that it will buy. It will increase if either actual income increases or prices fall.

real wage the purchasing power of the nominal wage; that is, nominal wage divided by the price level.

rent the payment made and the income received for the use of land.

rent control a government regulation making it illegal to rent out accommodation above a stipulated level.

resources physical or virtual entities that can be used to produce goods and services.

S

scientific method a method of research in which a problem is identified, relevant data are gathered, a hypothesis is formulated from these data, and the hypothesis is empirically tested.

short run any period of time in which at least one input in the production process is fixed (cannot be increased or decreased).

shortage at the prevailing price, the quantity supplied is smaller than the quantity demanded.

shutdown price the price that is just sufficient to cover a firm's variable costs.

socially optimum price the price that produces the best allocation of products (and therefore resources) from society's point of view: P = MC.

subsidy a payment by government to producers to help keep prices low or to encourage increased production.

substitute products any products for which demand varies directly in relation to a change in the price of a similar product.

substitution effect the substitution of one product for another as a result of a change in their relative prices.

sunk cost a cost that is unrecoverable.

supply the quantities that producers are willing and able to sell per period of time at various prices.

supply schedule a table showing the various quantities supplied per period of time at different prices.

surplus at the prevailing price, the quantity demanded is smaller than the quantity supplied.

T

tariff a tax (or duty) levied on imports.

technological improvement changes in production techniques that reduce the costs of production.

technology a method of production; the way in which resources are combined to produce goods and services.

terms of trade the average price of a country's exports compared with the price of its imports.

total cost the sum of both total variable cost and total fixed cost.

total fixed costs costs that do not vary with the level of output.

total product the total output of any productive process.

total revenue the total receipts of a firm from its sales; formally, it is price multiplied by the quantity of the product sold.

total variable cost the total of all costs that vary with the level of output.

transfer earnings a payment that a factor of production must earn in order for it to remain in its present use.

U

unitary elasticity the point at which the percentage change in quantity is exactly equal to the percentage change in price, that is, where the elasticity coefficient is equal to 1.

utility the satisfaction or pleasure derived from the consumption of a product.

V

voluntary export restriction an agreement by an exporting country to restrict the amount of its exports to another country.

W

wages the payment made and the income received for the use of labour.

INDEX

A

absolute advantage, 460–461
abstractions, 41
academic economists, 6
accounting profit, 208
adjustment process, 57, 93
advertising, 245, 377–379
AFC. *See* average fixed costs (AFC)
The Affluent Society (Galbraith), 359
age, 55, 172
agricultural land, urban encroachment on, 210
airlines, 182, 183, 282
Alberta, 95, 103, 324
algebra of demand and supply, 79–82
allocation of resources, 8–10, 13
allocative efficiency, 12, 309–310, 349, 385
Amazon, 250, 254, 349
anti-combines legislation, 362
Appirio, 254
Apple, 250
apps, 223
AR. *See* average revenue (AR)
Aristotle, 176
artificial intelligence (AI), 443
artificial intelligence (AI) companies, 250
at the margin, 162
ATC. *See* average total cost (ATC)
Australia, 321
Austria, 459
Automat, 250
AVC. *See* average variable cost (AVC)
average cost, 241, 347f
average cost curve, 225f
average fixed costs (AFC), 220
average fixed costs (AFC) curve, 221f
average product (AP), 211–216, 217–218
average product (AP) curve, 214f
average profit, 279
average revenue (AR), 271–272, 278,
    340–344, 343f
average total cost (ATC), 219–224
average total cost (ATC) curve, 221f
average variable cost (AVC), 217, 218
average variable cost (AVC) curve, 218f, 221f
Axiom, 254

B

Baldwin, John, 252
barriers to entry, 267, 340
A Beautiful Mind, 392
behaviour economics, 170
Belgium, 315
BMW, 226
Botswana, 483
Brazil, 315
break-even outputs, 274, 279
break-even price, 278–283, 279f
breakfast cereals, 378
Bretton Woods Conference, 472
British Columbia, 103
Brue, S.L., 85, 85n
budget line, 198–200

bulk, 245
bureaucratic regulations, 480–481
buyers, 267
by-products, 245

C

California, 324
Cambodia, 483
Canada, 13, 19, 315, 316
    cap and trade, 324
    child-care costs, 328
    compensation and productivity, 423f
    exports, 472f
    farm marketing boards, 100
    greenhouse gas (GHG) emissions, 321
    highly concentrated Canadian
        industries, 380t
    hourly wages, by type of work, 431t
    income inequality, 314
    international trade, 459
    minimum wage, 103
    NAFTA, 469
    public school breakfast programmes, 11
    rich *vs.* poor, spending differences, 147t
    Temporary Foreign Worker Program, 91
Canada Livestock Feed Board, 100
Canada Pension Plan (CPP), 105
Canadian Dairy Commission, 100
Canadian Economics Association, 311
*Canadian Environmental Protection Act
    (CEPA)*, 322
Canadian Radio- television and
    Telecommunications Commission
    (CRTC), 361
Canadian Transport Commission, 361
Canadian Wheat Board, 100
cap-and-trade system, 324
capital, 8
capital, movement of, 482
capital goods market, 441–443
capital-intensive method of production, 15
capitalism, 19
Capitalism, Socialism and Democracy
    (Schumpeter), 444
carbon taxes, 106, 323–324
cartel, 394–396
cash subsidies, 108
CETA, 471
ceteris paribus, 39
Chamberlin, Edward, 376
change in demand, 52–59, 53f, 53t
    decrease in demand, 57–58, 58f, 58t
    determinants of, 54–55
    increase in demand, 53f, 53t, 56–57, 56t, 57f
    labour demand, 421–422, 422f
    long-run effects, 287–290
    simultaneous changes in demand and supply,
        87–92, 88f, 90f
    vs. change in the quantities demanded, 66f
    wages, effect on, 428f
change in supply, 59–64
    determinants of change in supply, 60–61
    increase in supply, 59t, 60f, 62–63, 62t, 63f

    labour supply, 420–421, 422f
    market adjustment, 92–93, 92f
    simultaneous changes in demand and supply,
        87-92, 88f, 90f
    vs. change in the quantities supplied, 66f
    wages, effect on, 428f
change in the quantity demanded, 40, 41f,
    66f, 67
change in the quantity supplied, 46, 46f, 66f
child-care costs, 328
China, 13, 18, 315
choice, 9
    see also consumer choice
cigarettes, 137, 138f
climate, 459
climate change, 321
Coase, Ronald, 207
cocaine market, 139f
collective behaviour, 85
collective good, 317
collusion, 389–397
collusive oligopoly, 393–397
command economies, 17
Commodities Watch, 268
commodity markets, 266
common property resources,
    439–440, 440f
communism, 17
co-operative economies, 16–17
comparative advantage, 462–466
compensation. *See* wages
competition, 18, 269
Competition Act, 362
competitive economies, 18
competitive industry and firm,
    271–278, 271f
competitive labour market, 415–425
competitive markets. *See* perfect competition
competitive products, 54
complementary products, 54
concentration ratios, 379
Conference Board of Canada, 252, 314
constant-cost industry, 291, 292, 292f
constant returns to scale, 241–243
consumer behaviour, 162
    see also consumer choice
consumer choice
    consumer surplus. *See* consumer surplus
    law of diminishing marginal utility, 162
    objective of the consumer, 164
    optimal purchasing rule, 165–171
    price discrimination, 180–184, 181f
consumer goods and services, 9
consumer surplus, 177–180, 178f
    and elasticities, 179f
    in long-run equilibrium, 310f
    marginal consumer surplus (MCS), 177
    and price discrimination, 181f
    total consumer surplus, 177
Consumers' Research and Protection, 182
consumption, 319
corporate economists, 6
corporation, 206
cost curves, 222–223, 222f
    see also specific cost curves

costs, 206–207
  average cost, 241
  average fixed costs (AFC), 220
  average total cost (ATC), 219–224, 220
  average variable cost (AVC), 217, 218
  of borrowing, 245
  child-care costs, 328
  cutting costs, 224–227
  explicit costs, 207–210
  external costs, 319, 322–325
  implicit costs, 207–210, 210
  law of increasing costs, 21–23
  long run. See long run
  long-run average cost (LRAC), 241
  marginal cost (MC), 216–219, 217, 277f
  marginal private costs, 323, 323f
  marginal social costs, 323, 323f
  marginal wage cost (MWC), 426
  menu costs, 400
  opportunity cost. See opportunity cost
  private costs of production, 319
  in the short run. See short run
  sunk costs, 209, 226
  total cost (TC), 219–224, 220
  total fixed cost (TFC), 219
  total variable cost (TVC), 216
  variable costs, 216–219
  zero marginal costs, 223
CPP. See Canada Pension Plan (CPP)
creative destruction, 444
crime rates, 138–139
cross-elasticity of demand, 147–149
Crown corporations, 206, 363
CRTC, 361
Cuba, 13, 18
cultural identity argument, 482
currency-exchange controls, 480
custom, 18
customary economies, 18
Czech Republic, 315

D

Das Kapital (Marx), 17
day-care centres, 326, 327f
deadweight loss, 355, 439, 440f
decisions in the short run. See short run
decreasing-cost industry, 292, 292f
decreasing returns to scale, 246
demand, 38–44, 40
  see also supply
  algebra of demand and supply, 79–82
  change in demand, 52–59, 87–92
  change in the quantity demanded, 40,
      41f, 66f, 67
  determinants of demand, 89t
  elastic demand, 123, 125t
  individual demand, 38–40
  industry demand, 287–291
  inelastic demand, 123, 125t, 127, 394
  labour demand, 415–418, 421–422, 422f
  law of demand, 39, 42
  and marginal utility, 174–177
  market demand, 42–43, 48, 49t
  price, change in, 169–170, 170f
  price elasticity of demand. See price
      elasticity of demand
demand curve, 40, 80
  individual demand curve, 40f
  kinked demand curve, 399–400, 399f, 400f

  and marginal utility, 175f
  market demand curve, 43f
  slope of, 40–42, 132
  straight-line demand curve, 131, 132
demand schedule, 39, 40, 130t
demand-side view, 65
democracy of the marketplace, 339
Denmark, 315, 316
depreciation, 208
diamond–water paradox, 176
differentiated oligopoly, 265t, 266, 266t
  see also oligopoly
diseconomies of scale, 246–248, 247f
division of labour, 212, 252–253
Douglas Road Elementary School,
      Burnaby, B.C., 11
dumping, 99
Dutch auction, 179
dynamic pricing, 48

E

e-commerce websites, 179
easy entry and exit, 267
economic barriers, 340
economic capacity, 222, 385
economic freedom, 311
economic growth, 3
  causes of, and production possibilities
      curve, 23–27
  economic controversy, 3
  effect of, 24–25f
economic laws, 85
economic profit, 208, 209, 307
economic rent, 433–437, 434f
economic surplus, 310, 355, 355f
economics, 4–7, 6
  abstractions, 41
  controversies, 3–4
  definition, 6
  macroeconomics, 6, 316
  microeconomics, 6–7
  relevance of economics, 2–4
  three fundamental questions of, 14–16
Economics of Imperfect Competition
      (Robinson), 376
economies
  co-operative economies, 16–17
  command economies, 17
  competitive economies, 18
  customary economies, 18
  mixed economies, 18–19
  types of, 16–19
economies of scale, 244–246, 307f, 317, 357
economist, 6
education, and earning power, 431
efficiency, 8–10, 12, 304
  allocative efficiency, 12, 309–310,
      349, 385
  importance of, 12–13
  maximum efficiency, 23–24
  productive efficiency, 12, 20, 309–310, 349
EI. See Employment Insurance (EI)
elastic demand, 123, 125t
elasticity coefficient, 123, 126–127
elasticity measures
  cross-elasticity of demand, 147–149
  elasticity of supply, 141–143, 141f,
      142, 143f
  income elasticity, 145–147, 146f

  price elasticity of demand. See price
      elasticity of demand
  unitary elasticity, 123, 127, 131
elasticity of demand. See price elasticity of demand
elasticity schedule, 130t
employment
  full employment, and production
      possibilities curve, 20
  macro view vs. micro view, 7
  part-time employment, 101
  unemployment, and minimum wage, 101–102
Employment Insurance (EI), 3, 105
enterprise, 8
entrepreneurial market, 443–444
entrepreneurship, 8
environmental standards, 482
equilibrium, 49
  equilibrium price, 49, 144, 308
  equilibrium quantity, 51, 82
  equilibrium wage rate, 419, 419f
European Community, 100
European Union (EU), 473
excess capacity, 225, 226f, 384f
excise taxes, 61, 105, 106–107, 106f, 135, 136f
exclusive rights, 341
expectations of the future, 54, 61
explicit costs, 207–210
external benefits, 319, 325–328
external costs, 319, 322–325
externalities, 319–320

F

factor endowment, 458–459
factor market, 415
factor output effect, 442
factor substitution effect, 442
factors of production, 8
  capital goods market, 441–443
  economic rent, 433–437, 434f
  entrepreneurial market, 443–444
  labour market. See labour markets
  natural resource market, 437–441
fairness, 94
fair-return price, 361f, 362
fair trade, 483
farm marketing boards, 100
farmland, 210
favourite things, 172
Filthy Lucre (Heath), 12
financial economists, 6
firms, 206
  best size, in long run, 248–250
  Coase answer, 207
  cutting costs, 224–227
  excess capacity, 225, 226f
  existence of, 207
  long run vs. short run, 242
  profit maximization, 277, 401–403
  role of the firm, 206–207
  size of, and perfect competition, 306–308
  supply curve, in perfect competition,
      283–286, 284t, 286f
first come, first served, 13
fish market example, 142
for whom (fundamental question), 15
France, 17, 19, 315
franchise, 386–387
Franchise Direct, 386
free, 9

free enterprise, 270
free-market environmentalism, 324
free rider problem, 318
free trade
    see also trade
    benefits of, 470–471
    effect of, 474–477
    vs. fair trade, 483
freedom of entry, 381
fundamental questions of economics,
    14–16
Future Institute, 250

G

G8, 473
G20, 473
gains from trade, 468–470
Galbraith, John Kenneth, 358, 359, 401–403,
    401n, 444
game theory, 391–393
General Mills, 378
The General Theory of the Second Best
    (Lipsey), 311
generalities, 5
German Federal Constitutional Court, 471
Germany, 315, 316
Ghana, 268
Gini coefficient, 314
Gini index, 315
global trade. See trade
globalization, 4, 482
good harvest, 139–140, 140f
government
    and allocation of resources, 13
    blocked entry, and monopolistic
        competition, 387
    economic controversy, 3
    monopolies, regulation of, 359–363
    policy tools, 3
    price setting, 361–362
    taxes and subsidies, 61
        see also subsidy; taxes
governmental economists, 6
greenhouse gas (GHG) emissions, 321
GST (general sales tax), 61, 105
Gu, Wulong, 252

H

Handy, 254
Hardin, Garrett, 439
HBO, 349
Heath, Joseph, 317
high concentration ratios, 379
highest productivity, 215
hockey ticket prices, 437
Hollywood Reporter, 349
how to produce (fundamental question), 15
HST (harmonized sales tax), 61, 105
human capital, 430, 459
hyperspecialization, 254

I

imperfect competition, 376
    monopolistic competition. See
        monopolistic competition

monopolistic competition vs. oligopoly,
    379–380
oligopoly. See oligopoly
    product differentiation, 376–379, 381
imperfect labour markets, 425–433
implicit costs, 207–210, 210
import quotas, 477–479
InBev, 344
income
    and demand, 54
    distribution of. See income distribution
    macro view vs. micro view, 7
    in market economy, 8
    and price elasticity, 123
    real income, 422
income distribution
    and demand, 55
    income inequalities, 313–316
    and marginal utility theory, 172–173
income effect, 42, 201–202
income elastic coefficient, 146
income elastic demand, 146
income elasticity, 145–147, 146f
income inelastic demand, 146
income inequalities, 313–316
income tax, 105
income transfer programs, 314
increasing-cost industry, 291, 292f
increasing returns to scale, 245
indeterminate effect, 89
indifference curve, 197–198
indifference curve analysis, 197–202
individual demand, 38–40
individual demand curve, 40f, 45f
individual supply, 44–46
individual supply curve, 45f
Industrial Revolution, 18
industry, 265
industry demand, 287–291
industry supply, 287–291, 288f
inelastic demand, 123, 125t, 127, 394
infant industry argument, 482
inferior products, 54
innovation, 306
input, 8, 206, 219, 220
Instacart, 254
interest, 8
International Farm Comparison Network, 142
International Monetary Fund (IMF), 472
international trade. See trade
Internet, 48, 291
An Introduction to Positive Economics (Lipsey), 311
invisible hand, 45, 304, 305
iPhone, 398
Ivory Coast, 268

J

Japan, 100, 316, 459
job categories, 432
joint profits, 389

K

Kellogg, 378
Keynes, John Maynard, 5–6, 6n
kinked demand curve, 399–400, 399f, 400f
Krugman, Paul, 315
Kyoto Protocol, 321

L

labour, 8
labour, movement of, 482
labour demand, 415–418, 421–422, 422f
labour force, 418, 420t
labour force supply, 418–419, 420–421, 422f
labour force supply curve, 418f
labour-intensive method of production, 15
labour markets, 101, 101f
    competitive labour market, 415–425
    imperfect labour markets, 425–433
    labour demand, 415–418, 421–422, 422f
    labour force supply, 418–419,
        420–421, 422f
    market equilibrium, 419–420
    monopsony, 425–427, 426f
    productivity and the real wage, 422–423
    professional associations, 427–430
    trade unions, 427–430
    wage differentials, 430–432
labour standards, 482
labour unions, 427–430
laissez-faire, 19, 305, 316
laissez-faire capitalism, 311
land, 8
landowners, 18
largest economic entities, 402
law of demand, 39, 42
law of diminishing marginal productivity, 213
law of diminishing marginal rate of
    substitution, 198
law of diminishing marginal utility, 162–165
    see also marginal utility (MU)
law of diminishing returns, 213
law of increasing costs, 21–23
legal and social foundation, 270
legal barriers, 340
legislative control, 322
less-developed countries, 483
lighthouse, 318
Lipsey, Richard, 311, 317
living wage, 3
long run, 240
    see also long-run average cost (LRAC) curve
    best size of firm, 248–250
    changes in long-run costs, 251–252, 251f
    competitive firm's choices, 279–280
    competitive markets, adjustment of, 305–308
    constant returns to scale, 241–243
    decrease in demand, 289–290, 289f
    diseconomies of scale, 246–248, 247f
    economies of scale, 244–246
    increase in demand, 287–289, 288f
    industry supply, and perfect competition,
        291–293
    market size, 254–255
    monopolistic competition, and long-run
        equilibrium, 381–384, 383f
    small market, 252–255
    vs. short run, 240–241
long-run average cost (LRAC), 241
long-run average cost (LRAC) curve, 241, 249f
    diseconomies of scale, 247f
    economies of scale, 244f
    three possible LRAC curves, 250f
long-run equilibrium, 308f, 310f
long-run supply curve, 142
lottery, 13, 96
low concentration ratios, 379

lower environmental and labour standards argument, 482
LRAC. *See* long-run average cost (LRAC) curve
Luddites, 443
lump-sum profits tax, 360
Luxottica, 344
luxury products, 123, 146

M

machine specialization, 245
macroeconomics, 6, 316
Major League Baseball (MLB), 397
Maluuba, 250
management specialization, 245
Manifesto of the Communist Party (Marx), 17
Manitoba, 103
marginal, 162
marginal approach to profitability, 276–277
marginal consumer surplus (MCS), 177
marginal cost (MC), 216–219, 277f
    and average total cost, 221
    and average variable cost, 221
    monopoly, 347f
    zero marginal costs, 223
marginal cost (MC) curve, 218f, 221f, 225f
marginal pricing, 282
marginal private benefits, 325, 326f
marginal private costs, 323, 323f
marginal product, 211–216, 217
marginal product curve, 214f
marginal product of labour, 213
marginal revenue, 271–272, 277f, 340–344, 343f, 347f
marginal revenue curve, 400f
marginal revenue product (MRP), 415–418
marginal revenue product of labour, 416–417, 416t, 417f
marginal social benefits, 326, 326f
marginal social costs, 323, 323f
marginal utility (MU), 162, 163, 164f
    applications of marginal utility theory, 172–173
    and demand, 174–177
    and demand curve, 175f
    marginal utility per dollar spent, 167, 169, 174
marginal utility per dollar spent, 167, 169, 174
marginal wage cost (MWC), 426
market, 48–49, 265
    adjustment process, 57, 93
    algebra of the market, 79–82
    and allocation of resources, 13
    blindness of, 93–94
    capital goods market, 441–443
    characteristics of the four markets, 265–266, 265t
    competitive markets. *See* perfect competition
    decrease in supply, adjustment to, 92–93, 92f
    entrepreneurial market, 443–444
    how markets differ, 265
    how well markets work, 92–94
    importance of markets, 85–87
    labour markets. *See* labour markets
    modern market, 48
    monopolistic competition. *See* monopolistic competition
    monopoly. *See* monopoly
    natural resource market, 437–441
    oligopoly. *See* oligopoly

perfect competition. *See* perfect competition
    reinventing the market, 48
    shortages, effect of, 50, 50f
    size of market, and long-run, 254–255
    size of market population, and demand, 55
    small market, in long-run, 252–255
    surplus, effect of, 50, 51f
    types of markets, 265–266
market demand, 42–43, 48, 49t
market demand curve, 43f
market economy, 8, 14, 18
market equilibrium, 49–52, 288f, 419–420
market failures, 313–322
market information, 267
market period, 142
market price, 48
market supply, 46–48, 47f, 49t
market supply curve, 47
market system, 267–270
marketing, 245
markets, 18
Marshall, Alfred, 65, 65n, 85, 86, 142, 143f, 162, 170, 172
Marx, Karl, 17, 444
maximum average product, 215
maximum efficiency, 23–24
maximum marginal product, 215
maximum total product, 215
MC. *See* marginal cost (MC)
MCS. *See* marginal consumer surplus (MCS)
Mechanical Turk, 254
Meilleur, Madeleine, 145
menu costs, 400
Menu Foods, 344
merchandise exports, 460f
MES. *See* minimum efficient scale (MES)
Mexico, 469
microeconomics, 6–7
Mill, John Stuart, 16
minimum efficient scale (MES), 249, 250f, 253f
minimum wage, 100–103, 101f, 103
Misbehaving: The Making of Behavioral Economics (Thaler), 170
mixed economies, 18–19
model, 19
modern market, 48
momentary market period, 142
monopolistic competition, 265t, 266, 266t, 376, 381–387
    appraisal of, 384–385
    blocked entry as result of government policy, 387
    characteristics, 381
    franchise phenomenon, 386–387
    long-run equilibrium, 381–384, 383f
    short-run equilibrium, 381–384, 382f
    vs. oligopoly, 379–380
monopoly, 265t, 266t, 339
    allocative inefficiency, 349
    average costs, 347f
    average revenue, 340–344, 343f
    benefits of, 357–359
    disadvantages of, 349–353
    elastic demand, 344
    government price setting, 361–362
    how monopolies came into existence, 339–345
    marginal costs, 347f
    marginal revenue, 340–344, 343f, 347f
    monopolies under the radar, 344
    monopoly sales tax, 360

nationalization, 362–363
    natural monopolies, 357, 357f
    price discrimination, 349–353
    price maker, 340
    profit-maximization output, 345–348
    regulation of, 359–363
    total cost, 346f
    total profits, 346f, 346t
    total revenue, 340–344, 343f, 346f
    vs. perfect competition, 353–356, 354f, 355f
    what monopolies are, 339–345
monopoly sales tax, 360
monopsony, 425–427, 426f
Monsanto, 344
Morgenstern, Oskar, 391
most productive, 215
movement of capital and labour, 482
MRP. *See* marginal revenue product (MRP)
MU. *See* marginal utility (MU)
multinational corporations, 483
mutual interdependence, 388
MWC. *See* marginal wage cost (MWC)

N

NAFTA. *See* North American Free Trade Agreement (NAFTA)
Nash, John, 392
Nash equilibrium, 392
nationalization, 362–363
natural monopolies, 357, 357f
natural resource market, 437–441
natural resources, 459
Nazism, 17
necessities, 146
negotiated wage rate, 429f
Netflix, 349–350
Netherlands, 459
Neumann, John, 391
New Brunswick, 103
The New Industrial State (Galbraith), 359, 401, 444
Newfoundland and Labrador, 103
no free lunch, 27
nominal wage, 422
non-excludable good, 318
noncollusive oligopoly, 398–403
nonprice competition, 388
nonprofit organization, 206
nonrival goods, 318
normal products, 54, 146
normal profit, 209
normative statements, 5
North American Free Trade Agreement (NAFTA), 469, 473, 482
North Korea, 13, 18
Northwest Territories, 103
Norway, 315, 316
Nova Scotia, 103
Nudge (Thaler and Sunstein), 170
Nunavut, 103

O

OECD. *See* Organisation for Economic Co-operation and Development (OECD)
oil prices, 395
oil supply, 438

oligopoly, 266, 266t, 376, 379, 387–389
  appraisal of, 400–401
  characteristics of, 387–388
  collusion, 389–397
  differentiated oligopoly, 265t, 266, 266t
  game theory, 391–393
  kinked demand curve, 399–400, 399f, 400f
  noncollusive oligopoly, 398–403
  price leadership, 398
  and profit maximization, 401–403
  undifferentiated oligopoly, 265t, 266, 266t
  vs. monopolistic competition, 379–380
on-demand economy, 254
Ontario, 95, 102, 103
Ontario Hydro Commission, 361
OPEC. See Organization of Petroleum Exporting
    Countries (OPEC)
opportunity cost, 9
  comparative advantage, 463–464
  example of, 9–10
  and total economic profit, 208
optimal purchasing rule, 165–171
Organisation for Economic Co-operation and
    Development (OECD), 124, 472–473
Organization of Petroleum Exporting Countries
    (OPEC), 124, 394–396
Organization of Petroleum Exporting Countries
    (OPEC) oil embargo, 124
organizational economists, 6
Oser, J., 85, 85n
output, 206, 219, 220
  break-even outputs, 274, 279
  monopolies, 345–348
  perfect competition, 273–274
  real output, 422
overpriced product, 86f
ownership of resources, 15

P

parade of the giants, 314
Paris Agreement, 321
partnership, 206
part-time employment, 101
patents, 341
payoff matrix, 391, 391f, 395f
payroll taxes, 105
pecuniary economies, 245
Penn, Jan, 314
pension plans, 3
perfect competition, 265, 265t, 266, 266t, 267
  allocative efficiency, 309–310
  average revenue, 271–272
  benefits of, 308–312
  break-even price, 278–283, 279f
  competitive industry and firm, 271f
  definition, 269
  examples, 267–269
  external benefits, 319, 325–328
  external costs, 319, 322–325
  externalities, 319–320
  features of, 267
  firm's supply curve, 283–286, 284t, 286f
  industry demand and supply, 287–291
  instability of competitive markets, 316
  Internet, 291
  long-run changes, adjustment to, 305–308
  long-run equilibrium for competitive firm, 306f
  long-run supply, 291–293
  marginal approach to profitability, 276–277

marginal revenue, 271–272
market failures, 313–322
market system, 267–270
  competitive industry and firm, 271–278
  output, 273–274
  plant growth, effect of, 307f
  price, 273–274, 275f
  productive efficiency, 309–310
  profit, 273–274, 275f
  public goods, provision of, 317–319
  quasi-public goods, provision of, 325
  shutdown price, 280–281, 281f
  and size of the firm, 306–308
  subsidy, 325–328
  technological improvement, 306
  total revenue, 271–272
  uncompetition, forces of, 316–317
  vs. monopoly, 353–356, 354f, 355f
perfect price discrimination, 352
perfectly competitive markets, 267–270
perfectly inelastic supply, 144f
perfectly inelastic supply curve, 142
Peru, 483
Phantom of Fine Hall, 392
Philippines, 470, 470f
planned economy, 14
plant growth, 307f
policing, 318
politics, and trade, 477
pollution, 322
pollution tax, 322–324
positive statements, 4–5
Post, 378
preferences, 54, 267
price, 272
  see also price change
  break-even price, 278–283, 279f
  control over, and monopolistic
      competition, 381
  dynamic pricing, 48
  excise taxes, effect of, 106, 106f, 106t
  fair-return price, 361f, 362
  and long-run equilibrium, 308f
  macro view vs. micro view, 7
  marginal pricing, 282
  market price, 48
  as part of supply, 59
  perfect competition, 273–274, 275f
  profitable price, 280f
  related products, 54
  of resources, 60
  services, 423
  and shortages, 50, 50f
  shutdown price, 280–281, 281f
  socially optimum price, 361–362, 361f
  subsidy, effect of, 108, 108f
  substitute products, 61
  and surplus, 50, 51f
  vs. quantity demanded, 39
  vs. quantity supplied, 44–45
price ceilings, 94–98, 95f, 96f
price change
  demand, effect on, 169–170, 170f
  and desire to purchase, 42
  effect of, 126, 126t, 127, 128t
  and price elasticity, 124
  and production, 275f
  and profit, 275f
  and total revenue, 127, 135
price controls, 94–95
price discrimination, 180–184, 181f, 349–353

price elasticity of demand, 122, 126–127, 146f
  alternative calculation method, 129
  applications, 135–140
  and consumer surplus, 179f
  determinants of, 123–124
  elasticity in action, 129
  good harvest, and farmers, 139–140, 140f
  graphing, 130–135, 131f, 132f, 133f
  measurement of, 126–128
  range of elasticities, 133f
  sales taxes, 135–136
  sin taxes, 137–138
  war on drugs, and crime rates, 138–139
price floors, 98–103, 98f
price leadership, 398
price maker, 340
price setting, 361–362
price taker, 340
Prince Edward Island, 103
Principles of Economics (Marshall), 86
Principles of Political Economy and Taxation
    (Ricardo), 463
Principles of Political Economy (Mill), 16
priority spending, 172
prisoners' dilemma, 393
private costs of production, 319
private goods, 318
private property, 270
privatization, 363
producer surplus, 310, 310f
producers, 267
producers' preference, 96
product, 41
  see also specific types of products
product curves, 214f
product development, 377
product differentiation, 376–379, 381
product market, 415
production, 206
  capital-intensive method of production, 15
  how to produce, 15
  labour-intensive method of production, 15
  macro view vs. micro view, 7
  and price change, 275f
  smaller-scale production, 255
  theory of production, 210–216
  what to produce, 14–15
production possibilities, 19–27
  see also production possibilities curve
production possibilities curve, 20, 21f, 22f
  economic growth, causes of, 23–27
  law of increasing costs, 21–23
  shifts in, 23–27
  technological change, effect of, 25f
  underlying assumptions, 20
production quotas, 104–105, 104f
productive efficiency, 12, 20, 309–310, 349
productivity, 12, 217, 422–424
productivity growth, 252
productivity per worker, 211
professional associations, 427–430
professional athletes, 434–437
profit, 8
  accounting profit, 208
  average profit, 279
  different views of, 209
  economic profit, 208, 209, 307
  joint profits, 389
  lump-sum profits tax, 360
  monopoly, 346f, 346t
  normal profit, 209

profit—*Cont.*
    perfect competition, 273–274, 275f
    and price change, 275f
    supernormal profit, 209
    total accounting profit, 208
    total economic profit, 208
    total profit, 273
profit maximization, 277, 345–348, 347,
        401–403
profitability, marginal approach to, 276–277
profitable price, 280f
protectionism, 481–483
public goods, 317–319
public school breakfast programmes, 11
public utilities, 358
purchases, 42

Q

Quaker, 378
quantity demanded, 40
quasi-public goods, 318, 325
Quebec, 103, 324, 328
quota, 477
    import quotas, 477–479
    production quotas, 104–105, 104f

R

rationing, 96–97
Reagan, Ronald, 481
real income, 42
Real Research, 432
real wage, 422–424
related products, 54
relevance of economics, 2–4
rent, 8
rent control, 94–95
research and development, 358
resources, 8
    allocation of resources, 8–10, 13
    availability of, 60–61
    common property resources, 439–440, 440f
    ownership of resources, 15
    price, 60
    scarce resources, 8
revenue curves, 273f
Ricardo, David, 213, 433, 437, 462, 463
road pricing, 3–4
Robinson, Loan, 376
role of government, 459
rounding errors, 129
rush hour, 3–4

S

sales, 42
sales taxes, 106, 135–136
Samsung, 398
Saskatchewan, 103
scalping, 143–145
scarce resources, 8
Schumpeter, Joseph, 358, 443–444
science of choice, 9
scientific method, 5
scissors analogy, 65
sellers' preference, 13, 267
services, 423

short run, 211
    average total cost (ATC), 219–224
    changes in short-run costs,
        251–252, 251f
    competitive firm's choices, 279
    cutting costs, 224–227
    explicit costs, 207–210
    external costs, 322–325
    implicit costs, 207–210, 210
    marginal cost (MC), 216–219, 277f
    monopolistic competition, and short-run
        equilibrium, 381–384, 382f
    theory of production, 210–216
    total cost (TC), 219–224
    variable costs, 216–219
    vs. long run, 240–241
short-run supply curve, 142
shortages, 56
    and decrease in supply, 62
    and price, 50, 50f, 57
shutdown price, 280–281, 281f
Simmons Pet Foods, 344
simultaneous changes in demand and supply,
        87–92, 88f, 90f
sin taxes, 137–138
slope, 80
    demand curve, 40–42, 132
    market supply curve, 47
Slovak Republic, 315, 316
Slovenia, 315, 316
smaller-scale production, 255
small market, 252–255
Smith, Adam, 13, 44, 45, 56, 56n, 176, 212, 252,
        269, 270, 304, 304n, 305, 311, 316, 444,
        455, 481–482
socialism, 19
socially optimum price, 361–362, 361f
sole proprietorship, 206
South Africa, 315
South Korea, 13
specialization, 270, 456–458
Star Wars, 477
state-owned enterprise, 206
Statistics Canada, 252
Stigler, George J., 401, 401n
straight-line demand curve, 131, 132
strategic industry argument, 481
subsidy, 61, 108–110, 108f, 325–328
substitute products, 54, 61, 123–124
substitution effect, 42, 201–202, 419
sunk costs, 209, 226
supernormal profit, 209
suppliers, number of, 61
supply, 44–48, 46
    see also demand
    algebra of demand and supply, 79–82
    change in supply, 59–64, 87–92
    change in the quantity supplied, 46, 46f,
        66f, 67
    determinants of, 89t
    elasticity of supply, 141–143, 141f,
        142, 143f
    excise taxes, effect of, 106–107, 106f, 106t
    individual supply, 44–46
    industry supply, 287–291, 288f
    labour force supply, 418–419, 420–421, 422f
    market supply, 46–48, 47f, 49t
    subsidy, effect of, 108–109, 108f
supply curve, 81
    individual supply curve, 45f
    labour force supply curve, 418f

    long-run supply curve, 142
    market supply curve, 47
    in perfect competition, 283–286,
        284t, 286f
    perfectly inelastic supply curve, 142
    short-run supply curve, 142
supply schedule, 44, 44t
supply-side view, 65
surplus, 58
    consumer surplus. *See* consumer surplus
    economic surplus, 310, 355, 355f
    and price, 50, 51f
    price floors, 99
    producer surplus, 310, 310f
Survey of Labour and Income Dynamics, 102
Sweden, 17, 19, 315, 316

T

tariffs, 479–480, 479f
TaskRabbit, 254
tastes, 54, 162
taxes, 105–110
    carbon taxes, 106, 323–324
    change in, 61
    excise taxes. *See* excise taxes
    GST (general sales tax), 61, 105
    HST (harmonized sales tax), 61, 105
    income tax, 105
    lump-sum profits tax, 360
    macro view *vs.* micro view, 7
    monopoly sales tax, 360
    payroll taxes, 105
    pollution tax, 322–324
    sales taxes, 106, 135–136
    sin taxes, 137–138
TC. *See* total cost (TC)
technical barriers, 340
technical economies of scale, 245, 254
technological change, 25f, 26, 423, 442
technological improvement, 225, 306
technology, 8
    appropriate technology, use of, 15
    and supply, 61
    use of, and production possibilities
        curve, 20
technostructure, 401
Temporary Foreign Worker Program, 91
terms of trade, 466–470
TFC. *See* total fixed cost (TFC)
Thaler, Richard, 170
theory of absolute advantage, 460–462
theory of comparative advantage,
        462–466
theory of production, 210–216
theory of second best, 317
ticket scalping, 143–145
Ticket Speculation Act, 145
total accounting profit, 208
total consumer surplus, 177
total cost (TC), 219–224, 346f
total cost (TC) curve, 222, 223f
total economic profit, 208
total fixed cost (TFC), 219
total fixed cost (TFC) curve,
        222, 223f
total loss, 284
total product, 211–216
total product curve, 214f
total profit, 273

total revenue (TR), 99, 122, 134, 272
  elastic demand and price increase, 127
  inelastic demand and price increase, 127
  loss and gain, 134f
  monopoly, 340–344, 343f, 346f
  perfect competition, 271–272, 275f
  and price change, 127, 128t, 135
  and price elasticity, 130–135, 132f
  and unitary elastic demand, 127
total revenue schedule, 130t
total utility (TU), 163, 164f
total variable cost (TVC), 216
total variable cost (TVC) curve, 222, 223f
totalitarian regimes, 17
TR. *See* total revenue (TR)
trade
  benefits of free trade, 470–471
  benefits of trade, 13–14
  effect of free trade, 474–477
  factor endowment, 458–459
  free trade *vs.* fair trade, 483
  gains from trade, 468–470
  important qualifications, 471–472
  major trade organizations and treaties,
      472–473
  merchandise trade between the three
      continents, 457f
  and politics, 477
  power of trade, 13–14
  protectionism, 481–483
  specialization, 456–458
  terms of trade, 466–470
  theory of absolute advantage, 460–462
  theory of comparative advantage, 462–466
  trade restrictions, 477–481
  trends in world trade, 456, 456f, 457f
  voluntary trade, 13
  world's leading trading nations, 458f
trade-off, 9
trade restrictions, 477–481
trade unions, 427–430
tradition, 18
"The Tragedy of the Commons" (Hardin), 439
Tragically Hip, 145
transfer earnings, 433, 434, 434f

Trudeau, Justin, 323
TU. *See* total utility (TU)
TVC. *See* total variable cost (TVC)

U

Uber, 250, 254, 387
Ukraine, 315, 316
uncompetition, forces of, 316–317
undifferentiated oligopoly, 265t, 266, 266t
    see also oligopoly
unemployment, 101–102
    see also employment
unions, 427–430
unitary elasticity, 123, 127, 131
United Kingdom, 19, 315, 316
United Nations Climate Change
        Conference, 321
United Nations Framework Convention on
        Climate Change (UNFCC), 321
United States, 19, 321
  cap and trade, 324
  income inequality, 315
  international trade, 459
  minimum wage, 102
  NAFTA, 469
  production and trading possibilities
      curve, 469f
  productivity growth, 252
  public school breakfast programmes, 11
  wages in, 483
  wheat belt, 268
University of Twente (Netherlands), 226
urban encroachment, 210
USSR, former, 13, 17
utility, 162
utility maximization, 200–201

V

value in exchange, 176
value in use, 176
Vancouver Sun, 11

variable costs, 216–219
VER. *See* voluntary export restriction (VER)
visible minorities, 430
voluntary export restriction (VER), 481
voluntary trade, 13

W

wages, 8
  change in demand, 428f
  change in supply, 428f
  education, and earning power, 431
  equilibrium wage rate, 419, 419f
  hourly wages, by type of work, 431t
  marginal wage cost (MWC), 426
  minimum wage, 100–103, 101f, 103
  negotiated wage rate, 429f
  nominal wage, 422
  real wage, 422–424
  and supply and demand, 88f
  wage differentials, 430–432
war on drugs, 138–139
wartime, 93
wealth inequalities, 313–316
The Wealth of Nations (Smith), 44, 45, 176
welfare coverage, 3
Western Climate Initiative (WCI), 324
what to produce (fundamental question), 14–15
women, 430
World Trade Organization (WTO), 472
World War II, 95
world's largest economic entities, 402

Y

Yalnizyan, Armine, 315
yield management, 182
Yukon, 103

Z

zero marginal costs, 223